OECD Factbook 2007

ECONOMIC, ENVIRONMENTAL AND SOCIAL STATISTICS

ORGANISATI   **ND DEVELOPMENT**

ORGANISATION FOR ECONOMIC CO-OPERATION AND DEVELOPMENT

The OECD is a unique forum where the governments of 30 democracies work together to address the economic, social and environmental challenges of globalisation. The OECD is also at the forefront of efforts to understand and to help governments respond to new developments and concerns, such as corporate governance, the information economy and the challenges of an ageing population. The Organisation provides a setting where governments can compare policy experiences, seek answers to common problems, identify good practice and work to co-ordinate domestic and international policies.

The OECD member countries are: Australia, Austria, Belgium, Canada, the Czech Republic, Denmark, Finland, France, Germany, Greece, Hungary, Iceland, Ireland, Italy, Japan, Korea, Luxembourg, Mexico, the Netherlands, New Zealand, Norway, Poland, Portugal, the Slovak Republic, Spain, Sweden, Switzerland, Turkey, the United Kingdom and the United States. The Commission of the European Communities takes part in the work of the OECD.

OECD Publishing disseminates widely the results of the Organisation's statistics gathering and research on economic, social and environmental issues, as well as the conventions, guidelines and standards agreed by its members.

This work is published on the responsibility of the Secretary-General of the OECD. The opinions expressed and arguments employed herein do not necessarily reflect the official views of the Organisation or of the governments of its member countries.

Published in French under the title:
Panorama des statistiques de l'OCDE 2007
ÉCONOMIE, ENVIRONNEMENT ET SOCIÉTÉ

OECD Factbook 2007

FOREWORD

In 2006, OECD member countries called on the Organisation to "help its members fully reap the benefits and respond to the challenges of globalisation". The OECD considers that this challenge demonstrates how the political leaders consider globalisation as the most important overarching theme for the future of their societies. It also underlines how both people and policy makers are still looking for the answer to the question: is globalisation good for the overall progress of the society in which I am living?

To answer this question, there are at least three essential elements: good statistical evidence about the overall progress of societies and globalisation-related phenomena, sound analytical tools and the use of a long-term perspective. However, one of the paradoxes of our world today is that people often have too much information. We are bombarded with both relevant and irrelevant information from all sides. What is often missing is an ability to focus on the information that really matters. This can have serious negative consequences for democracy. It can lead to confusion and fragmentation in voting, a withdrawal from political participation, or a reliance on ideology rather than facts or evidence-based knowledge as the basis for public policy choices.

The *OECD Factbook* helps in addressing these issues. It provides, through comparable statistics, a picture of long-term trends of key economic, social and environmental phenomena in member countries and selected non-member economies. It helps the reader put current developments of the country where he/she is living in both an historical perspective and, through international comparisons, in a wider context. In fact, the indicators presented in the *OECD Factbook* underline the impressive results achieved over the last decades in terms of overall improvement of living conditions in almost all countries, but also highlight risks and challenges ahead.

The development of the first *OECD Factbook* published in 2005 was one of the follow-ups to the first OECD World Forum on "Statistics, Knowledge and Policy", held in Palermo (Italy) in November 2004. In June 2007, the second World Forum will take place in Istanbul (Turkey) and will focus on "Measuring and Fostering the Progress of Societies" (see *www.oecd.org/oecdworldforum*). The second World Forum, prepared through "thematic workshops" and "regional events" on almost all continents, will also provide the opportunity to experiment with new tools to promote global dialogue on economic, social and environmental developments.

These new developments confirm the commitment of the OECD to strengthen its role as a key global knowledge builder in order to support quality policy decisions to build a better world.

Angel Gurría
Secretary-General

OECD FACTBOOK 2007 – ISBN 978-92-64-02946-0 – © OECD 2007

PREFACE

The *OECD Factbook* is the most comprehensive horizontal statistical publication published by the Organisation. It is a tool to evaluate the long-term trends of economic, social and environmental variables in OECD countries using solid and comparable statistical data. It draws on the full range of data available within the Organisation, including data from two agencies affiliated to the OECD – the *International Energy Agency (IEA) and the European Conference of Ministers of Transport (ECMT)*.

The *OECD Factbook* is written in non-technical language and aims to:

- provide a wide range of users with a one-stop resource, containing comparative, country-based economic, social and environmental data;

- help users to assess the position and the performance of a single country, looking at a wide range of domains;

- enhance the visibility of the OECD, particularly for non-experts, both in OECD countries and non-OECD economies;

- highlight measurement issues and underline areas where the comparability of statistics across countries is still weak.

To put the development of OECD countries in a more global context, this year's *OECD Factbook* includes more indicators for key non-OECD countries (Brazil, China, India, Russian Federation and South Africa). The special section in this year's volume deals with migration statistics, a fundamental dimension of globalisation to which the Organisation is paying special attention, notably from the statistical point of view.

The tables of the *OECD Factbook 2007* are available on line at *www.sourceoecd.org/factbook*. The online version also contains longer time series and more metadata than the paper version.

The *OECD Factbook* reflects the work of statistical staff throughout the Organisation and was developed in co-operation with the Directorate for Public Affairs and Communications. The Statistics Directorate, which has co-ordinated the project, is grateful for the co-operation of the many staff members involved, but also, of course, for the concerted efforts of statisticians from all OECD countries who have worked, over many years, to develop the wide range of statistics shown here.

Lars Thygesen has co-ordinated the editorial work, co-operating with colleagues from various Directorates in designing the tables, helping to draft many of the texts, checking the quality of data and ensuring the overall coherence of the volume. Jérôme Cukier, Ingrid Herrbach and Katia Sarrazin had overall responsibility for technical work on the manuscript.

Enrico Giovannini
Chief Statistician and
Director of the Statistics Directorate

TABLE OF CONTENTS

OECD FACTBOOK 2007 – ISBN 978-92-64-02946-0 – © OECD 2007

⚛ Science and technology

✿ Environment

◉ Education

→ Public finance

❁ Quality of life

Focus on:
⬒ Migration

READER'S GUIDE

Main features

- Tables or groups of tables are preceded by a short text that explains how the statistics are defined (Definition) and identifies any problems there may be in comparing the performance of one country with another (Comparability). To avoid misunderstandings, the tables must be read in conjunction with the texts that accompany them.

- Tables and graphs are also available as files (see below). In their electronic version, tables may feature longer time series and data for Slovenia are added for many indicators. When appropriate, footnotes may provide additional information.

- While media comment on statistics usually focuses on the short term – what has happened to employment, prices, GDP and so on in the last few months – the *OECD Factbook* takes a longer view; the text and graphs mostly describe developments during the fourteen year period from 1992 to 2005. This long-term perspective provides a good basis for comparing the successes and failures of policies in raising living standards and social conditions in countries.

- Many *Factbook* indicators have been standardised by relating them to each country's gross domestic product (GDP). In cases where GDP needs to be converted to a common currency, *purchasing power parities (PPPs)* have been used rather than exchange rates. When PPPs are used, differences in GDP levels reflect only differences in the volume of goods and services and differences in price levels are eliminated.

Conventions

Unless otherwise specified:

- *OECD total* refers to all the OECD countries listed in a table as a whole.

- *OECD average* refers to the unweighted, arithmetic average of the listed OECD countries.

- For each country, average over periods only take into account the years for which data are available. The *average annual growth rate* of a value over a period is the geometric average of the growth rates of that value across the period (the annual compound growth rate).

- Each table and graph specifies the period covered. The mention, *XXXX or latest year available* (where XXXX is a year) means that data for later years are not taken into account.

Signs, abbreviations and acronyms

..	Missing value, not applicable or not available	ILO	International Labor Organization
		IMF	International Monetary Fund
0	Less than half of the unit precision level of the observation	ITU	International Telecommunications Union
		UN	United Nations
-	Absolute zero	UNCTAD	United Nations Conference on Trade and Development
|	Break in series		
		UNECE	United Nations Economic Commission for Europe
USD	US dollars	UNODC	United Nations Office on Drugs and Crime
		WTO	World Trade Organisation
		UNWTO	World Tourism Organisation

OECD FACTBOOK 2007 – ISBN 978-92-64-02946-0 – © OECD 2007

StatLinks

This book includes OECD's unique *StatLink* service, which enables you to download Excel® versions of tables and graphs. Look for the *StatLinks* at the foot of each one of them. *StatLinks* behave like internet addresses. Simply type the *StatLink* in your Internet browser to obtain the corresponding data in Excel® format.

For more information about OECD's *StatLinks*, please visit: *www.oecd.org/statistics/statlink*.

Accessing OECD publications

- OECD publications cited in the Factbook are available through SourceOECD (*www.sourceoecd.org*), the OECD electronic library.
- All the OECD working papers can be downloaded from SourceOECD.
- All OECD databases mentioned in the book can also be accessed through SourceOECD.
- In addition, print editions of all OECD books can be purchased via the OECD online bookshop (*www.oecdbookshop.org*).

Glossary of Statistical Terms

The online OECD *Glossary of Statistical Terms* (available at *www.oecd.org/statistics/glossary*) is the perfect companion for the *OECD Factbook*. It contains close to 6 000 definitions of terms, acronyms and concepts in an easy to use format. These definitions are primarily drawn from existing international statistical guidelines and recommendations that have been prepared over the last two or three decades by organisations such as the United Nations, ILO, OECD, Eurostat, IMF and national statistical institutes.

POPULATION

TOTAL POPULATION
EVOLUTION OF THE POPULATION
REGIONAL POPULATION

ELDERLY POPULATION
AGEING SOCIETIES
EDERLY POPULATION BY REGION

EVOLUTION OF THE POPULATION

The size and growth of a country's population are both causes and effects of economic and social developments. The natural increase in population (births minus deaths) has slowed in all OECD countries, resulting in a rise in the average age of populations. In several countries, falling rates of natural increase have been partly offset by immigration from outside the OECD area.

Definition

The tables refer to the resident population. For countries such as France, the United Kingdom and the United States which have overseas colonies, protectorates or other territorial possessions, their populations are generally excluded. For full details, see *Sources* below.

Growth rates are the annual changes in the population and are the result of births, deaths and net migration during the year.

The total fertility rate is the total number of children that would be born to each woman if she were to live to the end of her child-bearing years and give birth to children in that period in agreement with the prevailing age-specific fertility rates.

Comparability

For most OECD countries, population data are based on regular, ten-yearly censuses, with estimates for intercensal years being derived from administrative data such as population registers, notified births and deaths and migration records. In several European countries, population estimates are based entirely on administrative records. In general, the population data for OECD countries are reliable, although, for some countries, there are breaks in the series as indicated by vertical lines in the tables.

Note that for some countries the population figures shown here are not those used for calculating GDP and other economic statistics on a "per head" basis. There are several reasons for this, but the differences between the two data sets are normally small.

Long-term trends

In 2004, OECD countries accounted for just over 18% of the world's population of 6.4 billion. China accounted for 20% and India for 17%. Within OECD, the United States accounted for 25% of the OECD total, followed by Japan (11%), Mexico (9%), Germany (7%) and Turkey (6%).

Between 1992 and 2005, the population growth rate for all OECD countries averaged 0.7% per annum. Growth rates much higher than this were recorded for Mexico and Turkey (high birth rate countries) and for Australia, Canada, Luxembourg, Ireland and New Zealand (high net immigration). In the Czech Republic, Hungary and Poland, populations declined from a combination of low birth rates and net emigration. Growth rates were very low, although still positive, in Germany, Italy and the Slovak Republic.

Total fertility rates have declined dramatically over the past few decades, falling on average from 2.7 in 1970 to 1.6 children per woman of childbearing age in 2004. By 2004, the total fertility rate was below its replacement level of 2.1 in all OECD countries except Mexico and Turkey. In all OECD countries, fertility rates have declined for young women and increased at older ages, because women are postponing the age at which they start their families.

Sources

- For member countries: OECD (2006), *Labour Force Statistics 1985-2005: 2006 Edition*, OECD, Paris.
- For Brazil: Instituto Brasileiro de Geografia e Estatistica.
- For China: National Bureau of Statistics.
- For India, Russian Federation, South Africa and the world: UN (2005), *Demographic Yearbook 2002*, United Nations, New York.
- Fertility rates: OECD (2007), *Society at a Glance: OECD Social Indicators – 2006 Edition*, OECD, Paris.

Further information

Analytical publications
- OECD (2006), *OECD Employment Outlook*, OECD, Paris.

Statistical publications
- Maddison, Angus (2003), *The World Economy: Historical Perspectives*, OECD, Paris, also available on CD-ROM, *www.theworldeconomy.org*.
- OECD (2004), *Quarterly Labour Force Statistics*, OECD, Paris.

Methodological publications
- d'Addio, A. C. and M. Mira d'Ercole (2005), *Trends and Determinants of Fertility Rates: The Role of Policies*, OECD Social Employment and Migration Working Papers, No. 27, OECD, Paris.
- OECD (2006), *Labour Force Statistics*, OECD, Paris.

Online databases
- *Employment Statistics.*

Websites
- World Population Prospects: The 2002 Revision Population Database, *http://esa.un.org/unpp*.

OECD FACTBOOK 2007 – ISBN 978-92-64-02946-0 – © OECD 2007

Total population
Thousands

	1992	1993	1994	1995	1996	1997	1998	1999	2000	2001	2002	2003	2004	2005
Australia	17 495	17 667	17 855	18 072	18 311	18 518	18 711	18 926	19 153	19 413	19 641	19 873	20 092	20 329
Austria	7 884	7 993	8 031	8 047	8 059	8 072	8 078	8 092	8 110	8 132	8 084	8 118	8 175	8 233
Belgium	10 045	10 084	10 116	10 137	10 157	10 181	10 203	10 226	10 251	10 287	10 333	10 376	10 410	10 438
Canada	28 367	28 682	28 999	29 302	29 611	29 907	30 157	30 404	30 689	31 021	31 373	31 669	31 974	32 271
Czech Republic	10 318	10 331	10 336	10 331	10 316	10 304	10 294	10 283	10 272	10 224	10 201	10 202	10 207	10 221
Denmark	5 171	5 189	5 206	5 233	5 263	5 285	5 304	5 322	5 340	5 359	5 374	5 387	5 401	5 416
Finland	5 042	5 066	5 088	5 108	5 125	5 140	5 153	5 165	5 176	5 188	5 201	5 213	5 228	5 246
France	57 240	57 467	57 659	57 844	58 026	58 207	58 398	58 661	59 013	59 393	59 778	60 155	60 521	60 873
Germany	80 595	81 179	81 422	81 661	81 895	82 052	82 029		82 024	82 160	82 277	82 456	82 502	82 491	82 466
Greece	10 370	10 466	10 553	10 634	10 709	10 777	10 835	10 883	10 917	10 950	10 988	11 024	11 060	11 099
Hungary	10 369	10 358	10 343	10 329	10 311	10 290	10 267	10 238	10 211	10 188	10 159	10 130	10 107	10 087
Iceland	261	264	266	267	269	271	274	277	281	285	288	289	293	296
Ireland	3 549	3 563	3 583	3 601	3 626	3 664	3 703	3 742	3 790	3 847	3 917	3 979	4 044	4 131
Italy	56 859		56 442	56 623	56 745	56 826	56 941	57 040	57 078	57 189	57 348	57 474	57 478	57 553	58 135
Japan	124 430	124 830	125 180	125 570	125 859	126 157	126 472	126 667	126 926	127 291	127 435	127 619	127 687	127 757
Korea	43 748	44 195	44 642	45 093	45 525	45 954	46 287	46 617	47 008	47 354	47 615	47 849	48 082	48 294
Luxembourg	395	401	407	413	416	421	427	433	436	442	446	450	453	455
Mexico	84 902	86 613		88 402	91 234	92 788	94 305	95 786	97 199	98 658	100 051	101 398	102 708	104 000	105 300
Netherlands	15 184	15 290	15 383	15 459	15 531	15 611	15 707	15 812	15 926	16 046	16 149	16 224	16 281	16 320
New Zealand	3 532	3 572	3 620	3 673	3 732	3 781	3 815	3 835	3 858	3 881	3 939	4 009	4 061	4 099
Norway	4 287	4 312	4 337	4 359	4 381	4 405	4 431	4 462	4 491	4 514	4 538	4 564	4 592	4 623
Poland	38 365	38 459	38 544	38 588	38 618	38 650	38 666	38 654		38 256	38 251	38 232	38 195	38 180	38 161
Portugal	9 833	9 840	9 840	9 847	9 866	9 878		10 129	10 171	10 229	10 305	10 380	10 449	10 509	10 563
Slovak Republic	5 307	5 325	5 347	5 364	5 374	5 383	5 391	5 395	5 401	5 379	5 379	5 379	5 382	5 387
Spain	39 069	39 190	39 296	39 388	39 479	39 583	39 722	39 927	40 264	40 721	41 314	42 005	42 692	43 398
Sweden	8 668	8 719	8 781	8 827	8 841	8 846	8 851	8 858	8 872	8 896	8 925	8 958	8 994	9 030
Switzerland	6 875	6 938	6 994	7 041	7 072	7 089	7 110	7 144	7 184	7 227	7 285	7 339	7 391	7 438
Turkey	58 392	59 515	60 635	61 765	62 909	64 063	65 215	66 350	67 420	68 363	69 304	70 230	71 150	72 064
United Kingdom	57 585	57 714	57 862	58 025	58 164	58 314	58 475	58 684	58 886	59 114	59 322	59 554	59 834	59 989
United States	256 514	259 919	263 126	266 278	269 394	272 647	275 854	279 040	282 194	285 108	287 985	290 850	293 657	296 410
EU 15 total	367 489		368 602	369 849	370 969	371 983	372 972		374 054		375 077	376 559	378 303	380 140	381 871	383 640	385 792
OECD total	1 060 651		1 069 582		1 078 475	1 088 235	1 096 453	1 104 697		1 112 784		1 120 569		1 128 560	1 136 853	1 144 911	1 152 777	1 160 495	1 168 530
Brazil	151 547	153 986	156 431	158 875	161 323	163 780	166 252	168 754	171 280	173 822	176 391	178 985	181 586	184 184
China	1 171 710	1 185 170	1 198 500	1 211 210	1 223 890	1 236 260	1 247 610	1 257 860	1 267 430	1 276 270	1 284 530	1 292 270	1 299 880	1 307 560
India	856 000	872 000	892 000	908 000	928 000	946 000	964 000	983 000	1 001 000	1 019 000	1 037 000	1 055 000	1 073 000	1 091 000
Russian Federation	..	..	148 408	148 376	148 160	147 915	147 671	147 215	146 597	145 976	145 306	144 566	143 821	143 137
South Africa	36 992	37 802	38 631	39 477	40 342	41 227	42 131	43 054	43 686	44 561	45 454	46 430	46 587	46 888
World	5 429 807	5 509 146	5 587 816	5 666 360	5 744 872	5 823 143	5 901 054	5 978 401	6 070 581	6 148 000	6 224 985	6 313 807	6 389 272	..

StatLink http://dx.doi.org/10.1787/175080740766

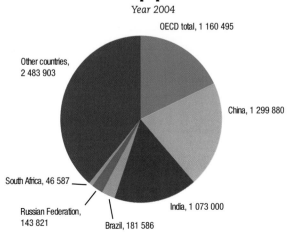

World population
Year 2004

OECD total, 1 160 495
Other countries, 2 483 903
China, 1 299 880
South Africa, 46 587
Russian Federation, 143 821
Brazil, 181 586
India, 1 073 000

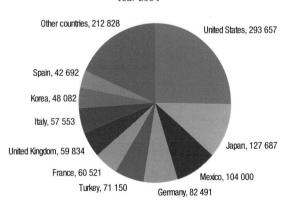

OECD population
Year 2004

Other countries, 212 828
United States, 293 657
Spain, 42 692
Korea, 48 082
Italy, 57 553
United Kingdom, 59 834
France, 60 521
Turkey, 71 150
Japan, 127 687
Mexico, 104 000
Germany, 82 491

StatLink http://dx.doi.org/10.1787/010147648283

Population growth rates
Annual growth in percentage

	1992	1993	1994	1995	1996	1997	1998	1999	2000	2001	2002	2003	2004	2005
Australia	1.22	0.99	1.06	1.22	1.32	1.13	1.04	1.15	1.20	1.36	1.17	1.18	1.10	1.18
Austria	0.78	1.38	0.48	0.20	0.15	0.16	0.07	0.17	0.22	0.27	-0.59	0.42	0.70	0.71
Belgium	0.41	0.39	0.31	0.21	0.20	0.24	0.21	0.23	0.24	0.34	0.45	0.42	0.33	0.27
Canada	1.20	1.11	1.11	1.04	1.05	1.00	0.84	0.82	0.94	1.08	1.13	0.94	0.96	0.93
Czech Republic	0.09	0.13	0.05	-0.05	-0.15	-0.12	-0.10	-0.11	-0.11	-0.47	-0.23	0.01	0.05	0.13
Denmark	0.33	0.33	0.34	0.52	0.57	0.42	0.36	0.33	0.33	0.36	0.28	0.24	0.26	0.28
Finland	0.56	0.48	0.43	0.39	0.33	0.29	0.25	0.23	0.21	0.23	0.25	0.23	0.29	0.34
France	0.46	0.40	0.33	0.32	0.31	0.31	0.33	0.45	0.60	0.64	0.65	0.63	0.61	0.58
Germany	0.76	0.72	0.30	0.29	0.29	0.19	-0.03	..	0.17	0.14	0.22	0.06	-0.01	-0.03
Greece	1.11	0.92	0.84	0.77	0.70	0.63	0.54	0.44	0.32	0.30	0.34	0.33	0.33	0.35
Hungary	-0.04	-0.11	-0.14	-0.14	-0.17	-0.20	-0.22	-0.28	-0.26	-0.23	-0.28	-0.29	-0.23	-0.20
Iceland	1.20	1.03	0.83	0.53	0.56	0.74	1.07	1.24	1.44	1.37	0.88	0.60	1.15	1.12
Ireland	0.71	0.39	0.56	0.50	0.70	1.05	1.06	1.05	1.28	1.50	1.82	1.58	1.63	2.15
Italy	0.17	..	0.32	0.21	0.14	0.20	0.17	0.07	0.19	0.28	0.22	0.01	0.13	1.01
Japan	0.38	0.32	0.28	0.31	0.23	0.24	0.25	0.15	0.20	0.29	0.11	0.14	0.05	0.05
Korea	1.04	1.02	1.01	1.01	0.96	0.94	0.72	0.71	0.84	0.74	0.55	0.49	0.49	0.44
Luxembourg	1.39	1.44	1.42	1.52	0.68	1.30	1.31	1.41	0.88	1.19	1.06	0.85	0.73	0.38
Mexico	..	2.02	..	3.20	1.70	1.63	1.57	1.48	1.50	1.41	1.35	1.29	1.26	1.25
Netherlands	0.76	0.70	0.61	0.49	0.47	0.52	0.62	0.67	0.72	0.75	0.64	0.46	0.35	0.24
New Zealand	1.05	1.15	1.34	1.47	1.60	1.32	0.89	0.53	0.59	0.59	1.51	1.78	1.30	0.93
Norway	0.59	0.58	0.58	0.51	0.51	0.54	0.60	0.69	0.65	0.51	0.53	0.57	0.61	0.68
Poland	0.31	0.25	0.22	0.11	0.08	0.08	0.04	-0.03	..	-0.01	-0.05	-0.10	-0.04	-0.05
Portugal	-0.27	0.07	-	0.07	0.19	0.12	..	0.41	0.58	0.74	0.73	0.67	0.57	0.52
Slovak Republic	0.44	0.34	0.43	0.30	0.19	0.18	0.14	0.08	0.10	-0.40	-	-	0.06	0.10
Spain	0.33	0.31	0.27	0.23	0.23	0.26	0.35	0.52	0.84	1.14	1.46	1.67	1.64	1.65
Sweden	0.59	0.59	0.71	0.52	0.16	0.06	0.06	0.08	0.16	0.27	0.33	0.37	0.40	0.40
Switzerland	1.11	0.91	0.80	0.67	0.44	0.24	0.30	0.48	0.56	0.59	0.80	0.74	0.71	0.64
Turkey	1.96	1.92	1.88	1.86	1.85	1.83	1.80	1.74	1.61	1.40	1.38	1.34	1.31	1.28
United Kingdom	0.25	0.22	0.26	0.28	0.24	0.26	0.28	0.36	0.34	0.39	0.35	0.39	0.47	0.26
United States	1.40	1.33	1.23	1.20	1.17	1.21	1.18	1.16	1.13	1.03	1.01	0.99	0.97	0.94
EU 15 total	0.46	..	0.34	0.30	0.27	0.27	..	..	0.40	0.46	0.49	0.46	0.46	0.56
OECD total	0.93	0.84	0.83	0.91	0.76	0.75	0.73	0.70	0.71	0.73	0.71	0.69	0.67	0.69
Brazil	1.65	1.61	1.59	1.56	1.54	1.52	1.51	1.50	1.50	1.48	1.48	1.47	1.45	1.43
China	1.16	1.15	1.12	1.06	1.06	1.01	0.92	0.82	0.76	0.70	0.65	0.60	0.59	0.59
India	2.03	1.87	2.29	1.79	2.20	1.94	1.90	1.97	1.83	1.80	1.77	1.74	1.71	1.68
Russian Federation	..	..	..	-0.02	-0.15	-0.17	-0.17	-0.31	-0.42	-0.42	-0.46	-0.51	-0.52	-0.48
South Africa	2.19	2.19	2.19	2.19	2.19	2.19	2.19	2.19	1.47	2.00	2.00	2.15	0.34	0.65
World	1.51	1.46	1.43	1.41	1.39	1.36	1.34	1.31	1.54	1.28	1.25	1.43	1.20	..

StatLink http://dx.doi.org/10.1787/215168204412

Population growth rates
Average annual growth in percentage, 1992-2005 or latest available period

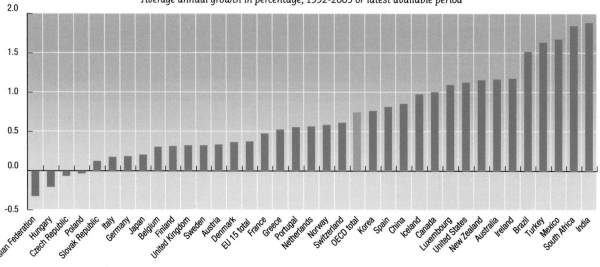

StatLink http://dx.doi.org/10.1787/247140736452

OECD FACTBOOK 2007 – ISBN 978-92-64-02946-0 – © OECD 2007

Total fertility rates
Number of children born to women aged 15 to 49

	1991	1992	1993	1994	1995	1996	1997	1998	1999	2000	2001	2002	2003	2004
Australia	1.88	1.85	1.89	1.87	1.85	1.82	1.80	1.78	1.76	1.76	1.73	1.76	1.75	1.77
Austria	1.49	1.49	1.48	1.44	1.40	1.42	1.37	1.34	1.32	1.34	1.31	1.40	1.38	1.42
Belgium	1.66	1.65	1.61	1.55	1.55	1.55	1.55	1.53	1.61	1.66	1.64	1.62	1.64	1.64
Canada	1.70	1.69	1.66	1.62	1.62	1.62	1.58	1.54	1.51	1.49	1.51	1.50	1.53	1.53
Czech Republic	1.86	1.72	1.67	1.44	1.28	1.18	1.19	1.16	1.13	1.14	1.14	1.17	1.18	1.22
Denmark	1.68	1.76	1.75	1.81	1.80	1.75	1.75	1.72	1.73	1.77	1.74	1.72	1.76	1.78
Finland	1.79	1.85	1.81	1.85	1.81	1.76	1.75	1.70	1.74	1.73	1.73	1.72	1.76	1.80
France	1.77	1.73	1.65	1.66	1.70	1.72	1.71	1.76	1.79	1.88	1.89	1.87	1.88	1.91
Germany	1.33	1.30	1.28	1.24	1.25	1.32	1.37	1.36	1.36	1.38	1.35	1.31	1.34	1.36
Greece	1.38	1.38	1.34	1.35	1.32	1.30	1.31	1.29	1.28	1.27	1.27	1.27	1.28	1.29
Hungary	1.86	1.77	1.69	1.64	1.57	1.46	1.38	1.33	1.29	1.32	1.31	1.30	1.27	1.28
Iceland	2.18	2.21	2.22	2.14	2.08	2.12	2.04	2.04	1.99	2.08	1.95	1.93	1.99	2.04
Ireland	2.08	1.99	1.91	1.85	1.83	1.89	1.92	1.93	1.88	1.89	1.97	1.97	1.96	1.93
Italy	1.31	1.31	1.25	1.21	1.18	1.20	1.22	1.20	1.23	1.23	1.25	1.25	1.26	1.33
Japan	1.53	1.50	1.46	1.50	1.42	1.44	1.44	1.38	1.34	1.36	1.33	1.32	1.29	1.29
Korea	1.74	1.78	1.67	1.67	1.65	1.58	1.54	1.47	1.42	1.47	1.30	1.17	1.19	1.16
Luxembourg	1.60	1.64	1.70	1.72	1.69	1.76	1.71	1.68	1.73	1.76	1.66	1.63	1.63	1.69
Mexico	3.24	3.14	3.03	2.93	2.82	2.73	2.64	2.55	2.48	2.40	2.30	2.30	2.20	2.20
Netherlands	1.61	1.59	1.57	1.57	1.53	1.53	1.56	1.63	1.65	1.72	1.71	1.73	1.75	1.73
New Zealand	2.18	2.10	2.07	2.05	1.99	1.99	1.96	1.89	1.97	1.98	1.97	1.90	1.95	2.01
Norway	1.92	1.88	1.86	1.86	1.87	1.89	1.86	1.81	1.84	1.85	1.78	1.75	1.80	1.83
Poland	2.05	1.93	1.85	1.80	1.61	1.58	1.51	1.44	1.37	1.34	1.29	1.24	1.22	1.23
Portugal	1.57	1.54	1.52	1.44	1.40	1.43	1.46	1.46	1.50	1.55	1.46	1.47	1.44	1.40
Slovak Republic	1.97	1.86	1.75	1.63	1.52	1.47	1.43	1.38	1.33	1.29	1.20	1.18	1.20	1.24
Spain	1.33	1.32	1.27	1.21	1.18	1.17	1.19	1.16	1.20	1.24	1.26	1.26	1.31	1.32
Sweden	2.11	2.09	1.99	1.88	1.73	1.60	1.52	1.50	1.50	1.54	1.57	1.65	1.71	1.75
Switzerland	1.60	1.58	1.51	1.49	1.48	1.50	1.51	1.47	1.48	1.50	1.41	1.39	1.39	1.42
Turkey	3.00	2.93	2.87	2.81	2.75	2.69	2.63	2.56	2.48	2.27	2.25	2.24	2.22	2.21
United Kingdom	1.81	1.79	1.75	1.74	1.70	1.72	1.72	1.71	1.68	1.65	1.63	1.64	1.71	1.76
United States	2.07	2.07	2.05	2.04	2.02	2.04	2.06	2.00	2.01	2.06	2.03	2.01	2.04	2.05
OECD average	1.84	1.81	1.77	1.73	1.69	1.67	1.66	1.63	1.62	1.63	1.60	1.59	1.60	1.62
Brazil	2.69	2.60	2.57	2.54	2.51	2.48	2.45	2.43	2.41	2.39	2.36	2.35	2.33	2.31

StatLink http://dx.doi.org/10.1787/076150234304

Total fertility rates
Number of children born to women aged 15 to 49, 2004

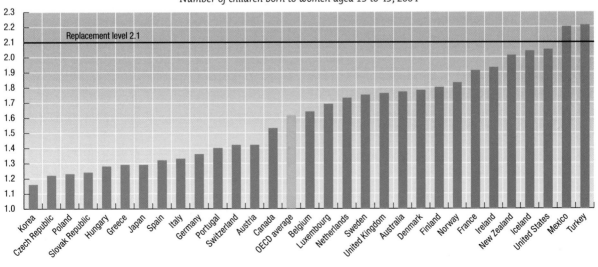

StatLink http://dx.doi.org/10.1787/478338101107

REGIONAL POPULATION

Population is unevenly distributed among regions within countries. Differences in climatic and environmental conditions discourage human settlement in some areas and favour concentration of the population around a few urban centres. This pattern is reinforced by the higher economic opportunities and wider availability of services stemming from urbanisation itself.

Definition

The number of inhabitants of a given region, the total population, can be either the average annual population or the population at a specific date during the year considered. The average population during a calendar year is generally calculated as the arithmetic mean of the population on 1 January of two consecutive years (it is also referred to as the mean population). However, some countries calculate it differently, they use the population based on registers or estimate it on a date close to 1 July (mid-year population).

The geographic concentration index offers a more accurate picture of the spatial distribution of the population, as it takes into account the area of each region.

Overview

The concentration of population is the highest in Australia, Canada, Iceland, the United States and Mexico, where 10% of regions account for no less than 47% of their population. In contrast, the territorial distribution appears more balanced, according to this statistic, in the Slovak Republic, the Czech Republic, Belgium and Denmark.

For the OECD as a whole, regional population density ranges from close to zero in Kitikmeot Region (Canada) to 20 504 persons per km^2 in Paris (France). The variation is particularly large in France, Korea and the United Kingdom. In these countries, there is a sharp contrast between predominantly urban regions which record densities of more than 6 000 inhabitants per km^2 and predominantly rural regions where population densities do not exceed 100 inhabitants per km^2.

In all OECD countries, almost half (46%) of the population lives in predominantly urban regions. In the Netherlands, Belgium, the United Kingdom, Australia, Japan, the United States, Italy, Canada, Korea and Portugal, urban regions account for more that 50% of the national population.

The index of geographic concentration shows that Canada, Australia and Iceland are the countries with the most uneven population distribution; in contrast, geographic concentration is lowest in the Slovak Republic, the Czech Republic, Hungary, Belgium, the Netherlands and Poland.

The geographic concentration index compares the population weight and the geographic weight over all regions in a given country and is constructed to account for both within and between-country differences in the size of all regions. The index lies between 0 (no concentration) and 100 (maximum concentration) in all countries and is suitable for international comparisons of geographic concentration.

Comparability

The main problem with statistical analysis at the sub-national level is the unit of analysis, i.e. the region. The word «region" can mean very different things both within and among countries, with significant differences in area and population.

The smallest OECD region (Melilla, Spain) has an area of 13 square kilometres whereas the largest (Northwest Territories and Nunavut, Canada) has over 3 million square kilometres. Similarly, the population in OECD regions ranges from about 400 inhabitants in Balance ACT (Australia) to more than 47 million in Kanto (Japan).

To address this issue, the OECD has classified regions within each member country. The classification is based on two territorial levels. The higher level (Territorial Level 2) consists of 335 macro regions and the lower level (Territorial Level 3) is composed of more than 1 679 micro regions. Territorial Level 0 indicates the territory of the whole country while Level 1 denotes groups of macro regions. This classification which, for European countries, is largely consistent with the Eurostat classification, facilitates greater comparability of regions at the same territorial level. Indeed, these two levels, which are officially established and relatively stable in all member countries, are used by many as a framework for implementing regional policies.

Source

- OECD (2007), *OECD Regions at a Glance*, OECD, Paris.

Further information

Analytical publications
- OECD (2001), *OECD Territorial Outlook, 2001 Edition*, OECD, Paris.
- OECD (2005), *OECD Territorial Reviews*, OECD, Paris.
- Spiezia, V. (2003), "Measuring Regional Economies", *OECD Statistics Brief*, No. 6, October, OECD, Paris, *www.oecd.org/std/statisticsbrief*.

Statistical publications
- OECD (2005), *Labour Force Statistics 1984-2004 – 2005 Edition*, OECD, Paris.

Online databases
- *OECD Regional Database*.

Share of national population in the 10% of regions with the largest population

Percentage, 2003

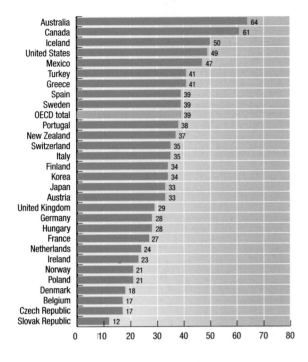

Range of variation in regional population density

(maximum – minimum number of persons per km²)
2003

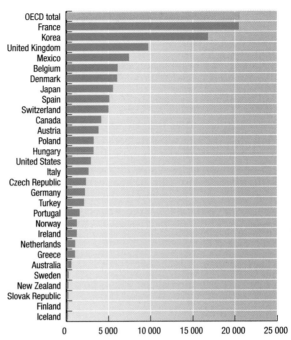

Distribution of the national population into urban, intermediate and rural regions

Percentage, 2003

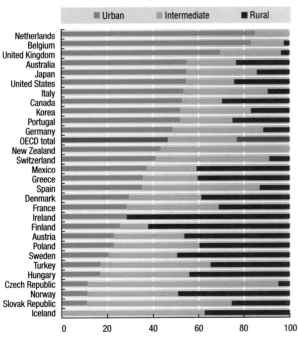

Index of geographic concentration of population

2003

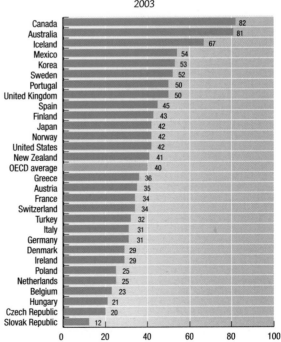

StatLink http://dx.doi.org/10.1787/502542555824

AGEING SOCIETIES

The percentage of the population that is 65 years or older is rising in all OECD countries and is expected to continue doing so. The number of inactive elderly as a ratio of the numbers in the total labour force is also increasing throughout OECD countries. These trends have a number of implications for government and private spending on pensions and health care and, more generally, for economic growth and welfare.

Definition

Population is defined as the resident population, i.e. all persons, regardless of citizenship, who have a permanent place of residence in the country. The labour force is defined according to the ILO Guidelines and consists of those in employment plus persons who are available for work and who are actively seeking employment. Population projections are taken from national sources where these are available, but for some countries they are based on Eurostat and UN projections.

Comparability

Almost all OECD countries now follow the ILO Guidelines for defining the labour force, so there is good comparability between countries.

All population projections require assumptions about future trends in life expectancy, fertility rates and migration. Often, a range of projections is produced using different assumptions about these future trends. The estimates shown here correspond to the median or central variant.

The labour force projections start from the population projections described above but then require additional assumptions about the future labour force participation rates of men and women in different age groups. For the projections shown here, particular care has been taken in modeling future trends in the labour force participation of women and of elderly persons.

Sources

- OECD (2006), *Labour Force Statistics*, OECD, Paris.
- *Eurostat, United Nations, national sources and OECD estimates.*

Further information

Analytical publications

- Burniaux, J.-M., R. Duval and F. Jaumotte (2004), *Coping with Ageing*, OECD Economics Department Working Papers, No. 371, OECD, Paris.
- OECD (2000), *Reforms for an Ageing Society*, OECD, Paris.
- OECD (2001), *Ageing and Income Financial Resources and Retirement in 9 OECD Countries*, OECD, Paris.
- OECD (2001), *Ageing and Transport Mobility Needs and Safety Issues*, OECD, Paris.
- OECD (2003), *Ageing, Housing and Urban Development*, OECD, Paris.
- OECD (2005), *Pensions at a Glance, 2005 Edition*, OECD, Paris.
- OECD (2006), *OECD Employment Outlook*, OECD, Paris.
- OECD (2006), *Ageing and Employment Policies*, series, OECD, Paris.
- Oliveira Martins J., F. Gonand, P. Antolin, C. de la Maisonneuve and K.-Y. Yoo (2005), *The Impact of Ageing on Demand, Factor Markets and Growth*, OECD Economics Department Working Papers, No. 420, OECD, Paris.

Statistical publications

- OECD (2004), *Quarterly Labour Force Statistics*, OECD, Paris.
- OECD (2006), *Main Economic Indicators*, OECD, Paris.

Methodological publications

- OECD (1997), "Sources and Methods – Labour and Wage Statistics", *Main Economic Indicators: April Volume 1997 Issue 4*, OECD, Paris.

Online databases

- *Main Economic Indicators.*
- *Employment Statistics.*

Long-term trends

The youngest populations (low shares of population aged 65 or over) are either in countries with high birth rates such as Mexico, Iceland and Turkey or in countries with high immigration, such as Australia, Canada and New Zealand. All these countries will, however, experience significant ageing over the next 50 years.

The dependency ratio (right panel of the table) is projected to be close to 50% in Belgium, France, Greece, Hungary, Italy and Japan by 2020. This means that, for each elderly inactive person, there will be only two persons in the labour force. The lowest dependency ratios, under 25%, are projected for Iceland, Korea, Mexico and Turkey.

All countries will experience a further sharp increase in the dependency ratio over the period 2020 to 2050.

Population aged 65 and over

	Ratio to the total population							Ratio of inactive elderly to the total labour force						
	2000	2005	2010	2020	2030	2040	2050	2000	2005	2010	2020	2030	2040	2050
Australia	12.4	13.1	14.3	18.3	22.2	24.5	25.7	23.3	23.4	25.2	33.0	41.9	48.1	51.4
Austria	15.4	16.3	17.4	19.3	23.4	26.4	27.4	30.7	32.2	34.0	38.8	50.0	58.2	61.9
Belgium	16.8	17.2	17.5	20.4	24.1	26.1	26.5	38.4	38.8	39.8	48.7	61.3	68.3	70.2
Canada	12.6	13.1	14.1	18.2	23.1	25.0	26.3	23.0	22.5	23.5	30.4	40.2	44.8	48.0
Czech Republic	13.8	14.1	15.4	20.1	22.7	26.5	31.2	26.3	26.9	29.6	40.3	48.7	62.6	79.4
Denmark	14.8	15.1	16.8	20.9	24.1	26.2	25.4	26.3	26.9	30.3	39.8	49.9	57.2	55.3
Finland	14.9	15.9	17.1	22.6	26.0	26.6	27.1	29.1	30.9	33.4	46.2	55.6	57.2	58.6
France	16.1	16.4	16.7	20.3	23.4	25.6	26.2	36.4	36.9	38.4	49.2	59.3	66.5	68.9
Germany	16.4	18.9	20.0	21.9	26.3	29.0	29.6	33.3	36.8	38.8	43.7	56.6	64.2	67.0
Greece	16.6	18.3	18.9	21.3	24.8	29.4	32.5	38.5	40.5	41.3	47.1	57.7	73.4	85.1
Hungary	14.9	15.7	16.7	20.1	21.5	23.9	26.9	35.9	37.0	39.1	47.7	53.9	63.3	74.1
Iceland	11.6	11.7	12.4	15.5	19.2	20.9	21.5	16.2	17.2	17.6	21.8	28.9	32.5	33.6
Ireland	11.2	11.2	11.9	14.9	18.5	22.4	26.3	22.4	21.4	22.0	26.9	33.1	41.6	52.1
Italy	18.3	19.6	20.6	23.3	27.3	32.3	33.7	42.5	45.6	47.5	54.8	68.0	86.2	92.8
Japan	17.4	20.0	23.1	29.2	31.8	36.5	39.6	25.3	30.9	37.8	51.1	58.8	70.3	80.8
Korea	7.2	9.1	11.0	15.6	24.3	32.5	38.2	10.8	12.7	15.4	22.4	36.9	55.7	72.2
Luxembourg	14.1	14.3	14.6	16.6	20.0	22.3	22.1	32.6	32.1	32.1	36.4	46.0	52.6	52.0
Mexico	4.8	5.3	6.1	8.3	11.7	16.7	21.1	8.0	8.9	9.9	12.5	16.8	23.8	31.7
Netherlands	13.6	14.2	15.2	19.1	22.4	23.5	21.8	26.1	26.7	28.1	35.2	43.0	45.6	41.5
New Zealand	11.8	12.1	13.3	17.1	21.9	25.2	26.2	21.9	20.6	21.2	26.5	35.9	43.9	47.2
Norway	15.2	14.7	15.1	18.0	20.6	22.9	23.2	27.2	26.4	26.8	32.6	39.4	45.2	46.4
Poland	12.2	13.2	13.5	18.5	22.7	25.0	29.6	24.9	27.6	28.4	40.5	53.5	63.9	80.6
Portugal	16.2	17.1	17.5	20.1	23.9	28.2	31.6	25.8	26.6	26.6	29.6	35.3	43.6	51.4
Slovak Republic	11.4	11.7	12.8	17.3	21.6	25.0	30.1	23.6	23.5	25.3	35.7	47.8	61.3	80.5
Spain	16.8	16.8	17.4	20.0	25.1	31.6	35.7	38.2	37.2	37.3	42.4	54.5	74.7	90.5
Sweden	17.3	17.3	18.5	21.2	22.8	24.0	23.6	31.9	31.8	33.5	39.5	44.4	47.0	46.4
Switzerland	15.3	15.9	17.2	20.2	24.2	27.0	27.9	25.0	26.4	28.0	33.4	42.1	48.9	51.5
Turkey	5.4	5.9	5.7	7.2	10.1	13.6	17.0	12.4	14.7	14.0	17.2	24.3	33.3	42.8
United Kingdom	15.8	16.0	16.7	19.5	22.5	24.7	25.3	30.8	30.8	31.8	38.2	46.5	52.4	54.7
United States	12.4	12.4	13.0	16.3	19.6	20.4	20.6	21.6	21.1	21.9	28.3	36.4	39.8	41.3
EU 15 total	16.4	17.4	18.1	20.8	24.6	27.8	28.8	34.4	35.8	37.2	43.8	54.4	63.9	68.0
OECD total	13.0	13.8	14.7	17.8	21.3	23.9	25.5	24.8	26.0	27.6	34.0	42.2	49.2	53.8

StatLink http://dx.doi.org/10.1787/684268656317

Ratio of the inactive population aged 65 and over to the labour force

Percentage

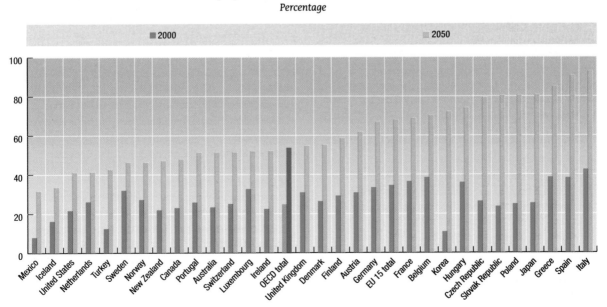

StatLink http://dx.doi.org/10.1787/551858826088

ELDERLY POPULATION BY REGION

In all OECD countries, populations aged 65 years and over have dramatically increased over the last 30 years, both in size and as a percentage of total population. As elderly people tend to be concentrated in few areas within each country, a small number of regions will have to face the social and economic challenges raised by ageing population.

Definition

The elderly population is the number of inhabitants of a given region aged 65 or older. The population can be either the average annual population or the population at a specific date during the year considered. The average population during a calendar year is generally calculated as the arithmetic mean of the population on 1 January of two consecutive years (it is also referred to as the mean population).

The geographic concentration index compares the population weight and the geographic weight over all regions in a given country and is constructed to account for both within and between-country differences in the size of all regions. The index lies between 0 (no concentration) and 100 (maximum concentration) in all countries and is suitable for international comparisons of geographic concentration.

Comparability

As for the other regional statistics, the comparability of elderly population is affected by differences in the definition of the *region* (see Regional population) and the different *geography* of rural and urban communities (see Regional GDP) both within and among countries.

Overview

About 35% of elderly people within the OECD live in only 10% of regions. This percentage is much higher in Australia, Canada and Iceland, where 10% of regions account for more than half of the elderly population of these countries.

Elderly population tends to reside in predominantly urban regions; about 46% of the elderly population in the OECD lives in these types of regions. In the Netherlands, Belgium, the United Kingdom and the United States predominantly urban regions account for at least 54% of the total elderly population. In Norway, the Slovak Republic, the Czech Republic, Turkey, Sweden, Finland, Hungary, Austria, France and Poland, no less than 75% of the elderly population live in *predominantly rural* or *intermediate regions* (see Regional GDP).

According to the geographic concentration index, Canada, Australia and Iceland are the countries with the highest concentration of elderly population. Mexico, Sweden and the United Kingdom have a significantly higher concentration of elderly population than the OECD average (38). In contrast, geographic concentration of elderly people appears much lower in the Slovak Republic, the Czech Republic, Hungary, Belgium, the Netherlands, and Ireland.

Source

• OECD (2007), *OECD Regions at a Glance*, OECD, Paris.

Further information

Analytical publications

• OECD (2001), *OECD Territorial Outlook, 2001 Edition*, OECD, Paris.

• OECD (2006), *OECD Territorial Reviews*, OECD, Paris.

• OECD (2006), *Labour Force Statistics 1985-2005: 2006 Edition*, OECD, Paris.

• Oliveira Martins J., F. Gonand, P. Antolin, C. de la Maisonneuve and K.-Y. Yoo (2005), *The Impact of Ageing on Demand, Factor Markets and Growth*, OECD Economics Department Working Papers, No. 420, OECD, Paris.

• Spiezia, V. (2003), "Measuring Regional Economies", *OECD Statistics Brief*, No. 6, October, OECD, Paris, *www.oecd.org/std/statisticsbrief*.

Statistical publications

• OECD (2006), *Labour Force Statistics 1985-2005: 2006 Edition*, OECD, Paris.

Online databases

• *OECD Regional Database*.

Percentage of elderly population by country

Percentage, 2003 or latest available year

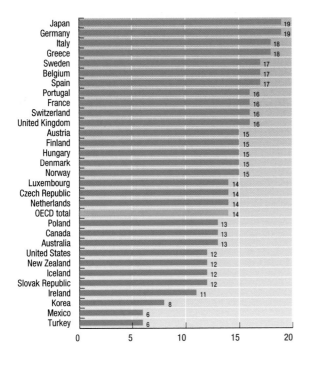

Share of national elderly population in the 10% of regions with the largest elderly population

Percentage, 2003 or latest available year

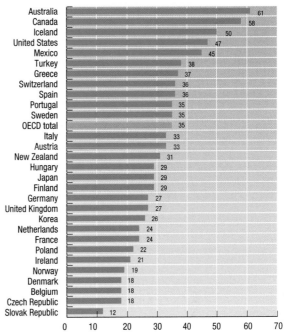

Distribution of elderly population into urban, intermediate and rural regions

Percentage, 2003 or latest available year

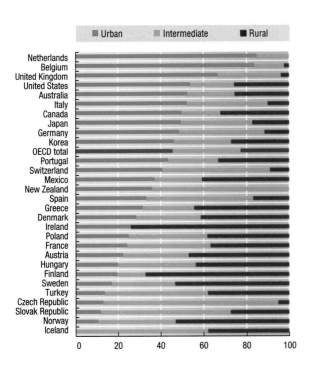

Index of geographic concentration of elderly population

2003 or latest available year

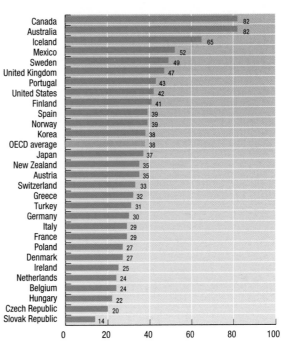

StatLink http://dx.doi.org/10.1787/137826504663

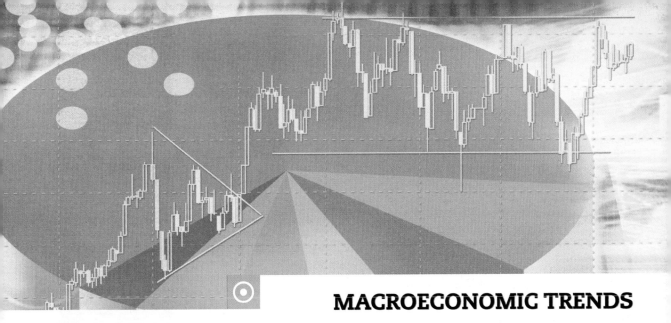

MACROECONOMIC TRENDS

GROSS DOMESTIC PRODUCT (GDP)
SIZE OF GDP
NATIONAL INCOME PER CAPITA
REGIONAL GDP

ECONOMIC GROWTH
EVOLUTION OF GDP
HOUSEHOLD SAVING
INVESTMENT RATES
INFLATION
STEEL PRODUCTION

PRODUCTIVITY
LABOUR PRODUCTIVITY
MULTI-FACTOR PRODUCTIVITY

ECONOMIC STRUCTURE
VALUE ADDED BY ACTIVITY
EVOLUTION OF VALUE ADDED BY ACTIVITY
SMALL AND MEDIUM-SIZED ENTERPRISES

SIZE OF GDP

Gross domestic product (GDP) is the standard measure of the value of the goods and services produced by a country during a period. Per capita GDP is a broad indicator of economic living standards.

Each country calculates GDP in its own currency and, in order to compare countries, these estimates have to be converted into a common currency. Often, the conversion is made using exchange rates, but these give a misleading comparison of the real volumes of goods and services in the GDP. Comparisons of real GDP between countries can best be made using purchasing power parities (PPPs) to convert each country's GDP into a common currency. PPPs are currency converters that equalise the purchasing power of the different currencies. (see also Rates of conversion).

Definition

What does gross domestic product mean?

"Gross" signifies that no deduction has been made for the depreciation of machinery, buildings and other capital products used in production. "Domestic" means that it is production by the residents of the country. As many products are used to produce other products it is necessary to define production in terms of value added.

GDP can be measured in three different ways: as output less intermediate consumption (i.e. value added) plus taxes less subsidies on products (such as VAT); as the income earned from production by summing employee compensation, gross operating surplus of enterprises and government and net taxes on production and imports (VAT, payroll tax, import duties, etc); or as the expenditure on the goods and services produced by summing consumption expenditures, gross fixed capital formation, changes in inventories and exports less imports.

Comparability

Virtually all OECD countries now follow the 1993 System of National Accounts. However, since Luxembourg and, to a lesser extent, Switzerland have a relatively large number of frontier workers, their GDP per capita is overstated compared with other countries. Such workers contribute to the GDP but are excluded from the population figures.

For some countries, the latest year has been estimated by the Secretariat. For several countries, the historical data have also been estimated by the OECD; if countries revise their methodologies but only supply revised data for recent years, the historical data have been estimated by mechanically linking the new and old series.

Source
• OECD (2006), *National Accounts of OECD Countries*, OECD, Paris.

Further information
Analytical publications
• OECD (2003), *The Sources of Economic Growth in OECD Countries*, OECD, Paris.
• OECD (2007), *OECD Economic Outlook: December No. 80 – Volume 2006 Issue 2*, OECD, Paris.

Statistical publications
• Maddison, Angus (2003), *The World Economy: Historical Perspectives*, OECD, Paris, also available on CD-ROM, *www.theworldeconomy.org*.
• OECD (2006), *African Economic Outlook 2005/2006*, OECD, Paris.

Methodological publications
• OECD (2007), *Understanding National Accounts*, OECD, Paris.
• OECD (2000), *OECD Glossaries, System of National Accounts, 1993 – Glossary*, OECD, Paris.
• UN, OECD, IMF, Eurostat (eds.) (1993), *System of National Accounts 1993*, United Nations, Geneva, *http://unstats.un.org/unsd/sna1993*.

Online databases
• *National Accounts.*
• *OECD Economic Outlook Statistics.*

Websites
• OECD Economic Outlook – Sources and Methods, *www.oecd.org/eco/sources-and-methods*.

Long-term trends

In terms of total GDP, the United States is, by far, the largest member country. Japan is the second largest economy followed, at some distance, by the four large EU members – Germany, United Kingdom, France and Italy. The next four largest are Spain, Mexico, Canada and Korea. These rankings have not changed significantly over the period shown.

Per capita GDP for the OECD as a whole was close to 30 000 US dollars per head in 2005. Five OECD countries had per capita GDP in excess of 36 000 US dollars – Luxembourg, Norway, United States, Ireland and Iceland. Half of the 30 OECD members had per capita GDP between 28 000 and 36 000 US dollars, while 10 countries had per capita GDP below 28 000 US dollars. Turkey, Mexico and Poland had the lowest per capita GDP. Note that both GDP and PPPs contain statistical errors, and differences between countries in per capita GDP of 5% or less are not significant.

Note that in the tables, the OECD total excludes the Czech Republic, Hungary, Poland and the Slovak Republic.

OECD FACTBOOK 2007 – ISBN 978-92-64-02946-0 – © OECD 2007

Gross domestic product
Billion US dollars, current prices and PPPs

	1992	1993	1994	1995	1996	1997	1998	1999	2000	2001	2002	2003	2004	2005
Australia	323.4	342.6	366.8	392.8	412.4	437.0	464.3	497.4	524.6	552.4	584.8	624.3	659.5	701.0
Austria	165.2	169.5	177.7	184.8	193.3	197.7	205.0	214.9	230.1	235.2	242.2	257.7	271.7	283.2
Belgium	202.0	204.7	215.7	225.4	230.2	238.6	247.2	253.5	273.2	288.7	303.1	317.3	333.2	345.6
Canada	567.7	594.3	636.0	667.2	690.9	732.2	770.6	825.0	873.1	910.0	938.1	975.6	1 036.4	1 099.1
Czech Republic	116.9	119.7	124.9	135.1	143.5	143.5	143.5	145.9	152.4	161.4	172.7	185.5	198.3	210.9
Denmark	102.5	104.7	112.9	118.7	125.0	131.6	136.5	144.3	153.9	160.2	162.9	166.4	174.7	185.0
Finland	86.1	87.3	92.3	97.9	102.3	112.2	120.7	125.0	135.1	143.6	148.9	145.7	155.9	162.4
France	1 133.1	1 146.4	1 194.4	1 245.6	1 291.8	1 361.3	1 429.4	1 472.7	1 574.8	1 667.3	1 720.5	1 715.4	1 807.8	1 897.8
Germany	1 628.2	1 652.3	1 731.9	1 800.7	1 857.3	1 904.3	1 957.8	2 004.8	2 101.3	2 169.9	2 235.9	2 387.5	2 468.1	2 538.0
Greece	162.6	163.6	170.4	177.6	184.6	195.9	204.9	212.9	228.6	242.5	267.1	287.6	306.3	328.4
Hungary	87.9	89.4	93.9	97.3	100.7	106.0	112.0	117.1	126.0	139.0	150.0	158.3	167.0	176.4
Iceland	5.4	5.6	5.9	6.0	6.5	6.9	7.4	7.7	8.2	8.6	8.7	8.9	9.7	10.7
Ireland	51.2	53.8	58.1	65.0	71.2	82.0	90.2	98.3	109.6	118.8	129.7	138.0	148.3	161.2
Italy	1 100.5	1 115.8	1 163.8	1 221.1	1 262.1	1 299.7	1 363.5	1 392.8	1 474.0	1 528.0	1 570.2	1 570.7	1 614.0	1 644.3
Japan	2 562.9	2 628.3	2 713.2	2 821.1	2 948.7	3 039.6	3 019.4	3 056.3	3 234.2	3 324.8	3 408.0	3 542.5	3 726.9	3 940.5
Korea	431.2	468.2	518.9	578.0	630.2	670.5	631.5	701.4	768.3	817.0	878.6	925.2	996.4	1 067.2
Luxembourg	12.9	13.7	14.6	15.1	15.7	16.1	17.3	20.2	22.3	22.7	24.6	27.4	29.4	32.1
Mexico	589.2	614.5	655.1	627.3	672.1	729.6	774.9	815.6	897.2	918.5	951.2	984.9	1 055.0	1 119.1
Netherlands	297.3	306.1	321.5	338.0	355.3	379.3	398.9	417.2	451.9	488.2	505.2	516.8	546.4	573.0
New Zealand	51.7	55.6	60.2	63.8	66.6	69.9	71.3	76.5	80.2	84.8	89.2	95.4	100.9	106.4
Norway	86.5	90.9	97.7	104.0	114.9	122.4	121.3	133.9	163.0	167.7	166.2	174.6	192.3	218.2
Poland	236.0	250.5	269.3	293.9	318.9	343.9	363.8	381.7	409.1	422.4	442.6	460.5	499.7	530.2
Portugal	126.5	126.7	130.7	139.0	144.5	154.0	164.8	175.9	187.9	196.9	205.7	196.0	202.9	209.8
Slovak Republic	36.5	38.1	41.3	44.6	48.3	50.9	53.5	54.5	58.6	62.8	68.6	73.1	78.9	86.1
Spain	568.7	575.7	601.9	631.1	659.4	690.1	735.9	791.2	849.0	909.4	981.7	1 045.1	1 110.7	1 189.1
Sweden	168.3	168.7	179.0	189.8	196.4	203.2	210.2	224.4	241.2	245.5	253.2	266.0	279.5	290.0
Switzerland	172.8	176.3	182.0	186.4	186.4	197.6	205.6	206.4	219.0	223.1	238.6	247.0	259.0	267.4
Turkey	294.1	325.1	313.8	343.3	375.2	406.3	422.0	403.7	459.7	421.6	453.9	476.6	517.8	555.7
United Kingdom	985.9	1 031.6	1 098.7	1 153.9	1 218.1	1 301.1	1 361.0	1 407.8	1 506.8	1 601.5	1 719.0	1 779.1	1 901.6	1 978.8
United States	6 286.8	6 604.3	7 017.5	7 342.3	7 762.3	8 250.9	8 694.6	9 216.2	9 764.8	10 075.9	10 417.6	10 908.0	11 657.3	12 397.9
EU 15 total	6 790.9	6 920.7	7 263.6	7 603.6	7 907.1	8 267.0	8 643.3	8 956.0	9 539.7	10 018.4	10 470.0	10 816.5	11 350.6	11 818.6
OECD total	18 162.5	18 826.4	19 830.8	20 735.8	21 773.4	22 929.9	23 826.2	24 896.0	26 531.7	27 522.8	28 605.0	29 779.5	31 561.7	33 301.8

StatLink http://dx.doi.org/10.1787/163450108212

Gross domestic product
Billion US dollars, current prices and PPPs, 2005

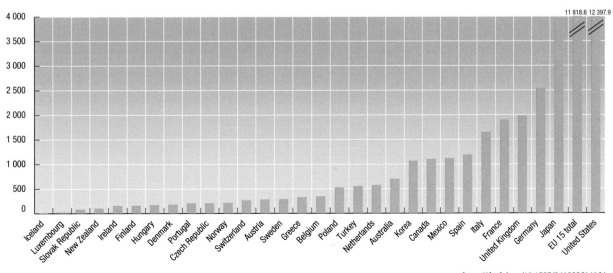

StatLink http://dx.doi.org/10.1787/341288614164

GDP per capita
US dollars, current prices and PPPs

	1992	1993	1994	1995	1996	1997	1998	1999	2000	2001	2002	2003	2004	2005
Australia	18 393	19 293	20 437	21 590	22 390	23 487	24 679	26 128	27 223	28 289	29 609	31 248	32 643	34 240
Austria	21 064	21 443	22 391	23 248	24 282	24 809	25 703	26 889	28 723	29 239	29 963	31 740	33 235	34 393
Belgium	20 108	20 294	21 327	22 235	22 665	23 436	24 227	24 803	26 660	28 078	29 338	30 586	31 985	32 998
Canada	20 013	20 722	21 933	22 771	23 334	24 481	25 554	27 135	28 449	29 336	29 903	30 806	32 413	34 058
Czech Republic	11 335	11 588	12 088	13 074	13 911	13 923	13 935	14 192	14 833	15 788	16 927	18 184	19 426	20 606
Denmark	19 819	20 186	21 680	22 696	23 759	24 895	25 743	27 117	28 823	29 914	30 307	30 869	32 335	34 137
Finland	17 083	17 233	18 143	19 168	19 954	21 819	23 430	24 199	26 098	27 676	28 637	27 951	29 833	30 959
France	19 285	19 430	20 172	20 962	21 665	22 752	23 804	24 408	25 938	27 278	27 961	27 697	29 006	30 266
Germany	20 203	20 353	21 271	22 050	22 679	23 208	23 867	24 422	25 568	26 352	27 108	28 933	29 916	30 777
Greece	15 483	15 500	16 070	16 698	17 236	18 181	18 909	19 564	20 939	22 146	24 307	26 091	27 691	29 578
Hungary	8 509	8 680	9 154	9 417	9 762	10 301	10 909	11 438	12 343	13 644	14 762	15 630	16 519	17 483
Iceland	20 660	21 194	22 235	22 598	24 096	25 424	27 062	27 918	29 028	30 251	30 359	30 739	33 271	36 183
Ireland	14 414	15 062	16 210	18 057	19 637	22 390	24 320	26 217	28 852	30 778	33 032	34 580	36 536	38 850
Italy	19 376	19 633	20 474	21 482	22 196	22 846	23 960	24 471	25 886	26 818	27 471	27 267	27 744	28 094
Japan	20 598	21 055	21 675	22 484	23 448	24 113	23 888	24 135	25 497	26 149	26 742	27 738	29 173	30 842
Korea	9 857	10 594	11 623	12 818	13 843	14 592	13 644	15 047	16 344	17 253	18 453	19 335	20 723	22 098
Luxembourg	32 833	34 505	36 054	36 779	37 759	38 334	40 451	46 799	50 769	51 386	55 071	60 892	64 843	70 245
Mexico	6 832	6 999	7 332	6 957	7 293	7 767	8 089	8 391	9 094	9 180	9 381	9 590	10 145	10 627
Netherlands	19 579	20 017	20 900	21 861	22 882	24 305	25 402	26 393	28 384	30 432	31 288	31 854	33 571	35 120
New Zealand	14 628	15 565	16 631	17 367	17 834	18 474	18 682	19 927	20 773	21 809	22 616	23 789	24 834	25 950
Norway	20 178	21 076	22 522	23 867	26 235	27 797	27 362	30 011	36 293	37 169	36 609	38 253	41 880	47 207
Poland	6 152	6 513	6 987	7 616	8 258	8 898	9 409	9 875	10 693	11 042	11 576	12 058	13 089	13 894
Portugal	12 696	12 708	13 070	13 862	14 370	15 262	16 274	17 294	18 379	19 131	19 841	18 771	19 324	19 889
Slovak Republic	6 880	7 148	7 720	8 312	8 994	9 458	9 918	10 093	10 846	11 618	12 751	13 590	14 651	15 983
Spain	14 516	14 664	15 303	16 023	16 702	17 433	18 527	19 815	21 086	22 333	23 762	24 880	26 018	27 400
Sweden	19 414	19 350	20 384	21 499	22 220	22 975	23 744	25 333	27 185	27 595	28 375	29 690	31 072	32 111
Switzerland	24 882	25 229	25 858	26 320	26 239	27 774	28 823	28 795	30 374	30 626	32 492	33 350	34 740	35 650
Turkey	5 037	5 465	5 181	5 569	5 984	6 502	6 651	6 274	6 814	6 144	6 520	6 739	7 212	7 711
United Kingdom	17 121	17 874	18 988	19 887	20 943	22 312	23 275	23 989	25 588	27 092	28 978	29 873	31 780	32 860
United States	24 470	25 374	26 636	27 542	28 780	30 228	31 485	32 994	34 574	35 308	36 140	37 470	39 660	41 789
EU 15 total	18 390	18 667	19 538	20 400	21 159	22 066	23 020	23 784	25 241	26 390	27 437	28 183	29 398	30 438
OECD total	18 163	18 660	19 496	20 239	21 076	22 045	22 731	23 579	24 886	25 610	26 409	27 275	28 686	30 065

StatLink ⬛⬛ http://dx.doi.org/10.1787/426245553537

GDP per capita
US dollars, current prices and PPPs, 2005

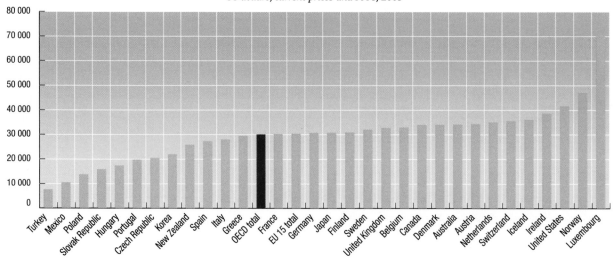

StatLink ⬛⬛ http://dx.doi.org/10.1787/283004217757

OECD FACTBOOK 2007 – ISBN 978-92-64-02946-0 – © OECD 2007

Volume index of GDP per capita
OECD = 100 in 2000, at 2000 price levels and PPPs

	1992	1993	1994	1995	1996	1997	1998	1999	2000	2001	2002	2003	2004	2005
Australia	87.5	90.1	93.2	95.7	98.3	101.6	105.7	108.6	109.4	112.0	114.2	117.5	119.3	121.0
Austria	97.2	96.7	98.9	100.7	103.2	104.9	108.6	111.9	115.4	115.9	116.3	117.1	119.1	120.7
Belgium	91.5	90.3	92.9	94.9	95.9	98.8	100.5	103.4	107.1	107.9	109.0	109.5	111.9	112.7
Canada	91.6	92.7	96.1	97.8	98.3	101.5	104.8	109.7	114.3	115.1	117.2	118.2	120.9	123.3
Czech Republic	50.9	50.8	51.9	55.1	57.4	57.0	56.6	57.4	59.6	61.4	62.7	64.9	67.6	71.5
Denmark	95.6	95.2	100.1	102.7	105.0	107.8	109.8	112.2	115.8	116.2	116.4	116.9	118.8	121.9
Finland	80.0	78.9	81.3	84.2	87.0	92.0	96.6	100.1	104.9	107.4	108.9	110.6	114.1	117.1
France	91.0	89.6	91.1	92.8	93.4	95.2	98.1	100.8	104.2	105.5	105.8	106.3	108.1	108.7
Germany	91.4	90.0	92.2	93.6	94.3	95.8	97.8	99.7	102.7	103.8	103.6	103.4	104.7	105.7
Greece	72.1	70.5	71.6	72.9	74.1	76.3	78.5	80.8	84.1	87.6	90.7	94.8	99.0	102.3
Hungary	38.8	38.7	40.0	40.3	40.9	42.8	45.0	47.0	49.6	51.7	54.1	56.5	59.4	62.1
Iceland	94.6	94.9	97.5	97.1	101.1	105.3	110.3	113.3	116.6	119.2	117.8	120.3	128.0	136.1
Ireland	65.5	66.9	70.5	77.0	82.8	91.6	98.0	107.4	115.9	120.8	125.9	129.2	132.5	136.8
Italy	91.1	90.3	92.2	94.8	95.5	97.2	98.6	100.5	104.0	105.8	105.8	105.1	105.1	104.5
Japan	96.4	96.3	97.1	98.7	101.0	102.2	100.1	99.7	102.5	102.6	102.5	104.1	106.5	109.3
Korea	45.3	47.6	51.1	55.3	58.6	60.7	56.2	61.0	65.7	67.7	72.0	73.9	77.0	79.7
Luxembourg	154.3	158.5	162.2	162.2	162.3	169.7	178.4	190.7	204.0	207.7	213.4	214.5	220.6	227.4
Mexico	32.1	32.1	33.0	30.7	31.5	33.0	34.0	34.8	36.5	36.0	35.8	35.9	36.9	37.5
Netherlands	92.0	91.9	94.0	96.3	99.2	102.9	106.3	110.5	114.1	115.4	114.7	114.6	116.4	117.9
New Zealand	68.8	72.4	75.3	77.2	78.7	78.9	78.5	82.2	83.5	86.2	88.9	90.5	92.6	93.5
Norway	113.5	115.9	121.3	125.9	131.9	137.9	140.7	142.7	145.8	149.1	149.9	150.7	154.5	156.9
Poland	28.2	29.2	30.7	32.8	34.8	37.2	39.0	40.8	43.0	43.5	44.1	45.8	48.3	49.8
Portugal	60.2	58.9	59.3	61.6	63.7	66.1	69.0	71.4	73.9	74.9	74.9	73.5	74.0	73.9
Slovak Republic	32.3	32.8	34.7	36.6	38.8	40.5	42.2	42.8	43.6	45.0	47.0	49.0	51.6	54.7
Spain	68.4	67.5	69.0	70.8	72.4	75.0	78.1	81.3	84.7	86.8	87.9	89.1	90.5	92.2
Sweden	90.1	87.8	90.6	93.7	94.8	96.9	100.4	104.9	109.2	110.1	111.9	113.4	117.6	120.6
Switzerland	113.3	112.3	112.7	112.4	112.6	114.6	117.5	118.5	122.1	122.0	121.4	120.2	122.2	123.8
Turkey	23.8	25.2	23.4	24.7	26.0	28.0	28.5	26.7	27.4	24.9	26.5	27.6	29.6	31.7
United Kingdom	81.8	83.5	86.9	89.2	91.4	93.9	96.8	99.4	102.8	104.8	106.6	109.0	112.1	113.4
United States	113.8	115.4	118.6	120.2	123.2	127.3	131.1	135.5	138.9	138.5	139.4	141.5	145.6	148.9
EU 15 total	85.8	85.2	87.3	89.3	90.6	92.8	95.4	98.0	101.4	103.0	103.6	104.2	105.9	106.9
OECD total	84.7	85.1	87.1	88.6	90.4	93.0	94.7	97.1	100.0	100.4	101.2	102.3	104.8	106.8

StatLink http://dx.doi.org/10.1787/112036854724

Change in relative volume indices of GDP per capita
Absolute differences between the 2005 and 1992 indices

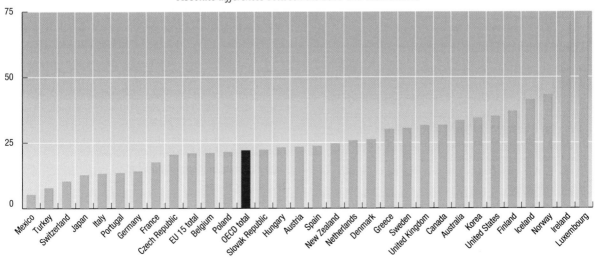

StatLink http://dx.doi.org/10.1787/884622256784

NATIONAL INCOME PER CAPITA

While per capita gross domestic product is the indicator most commonly used to compare income levels two other measures are preferred by many analysts. These are per capita gross national income (GNI) and net national income (NNI).

Definition

GNI is defined as GDP plus net receipts from abroad of wages and salaries and of property income.

Wages and salaries from abroad are those that are earned by residents, that is, by persons who essentially live and consume inside the economic territory but work abroad (this happens in border areas on a regular basis) or for persons that live and work abroad for only short periods (seasonal workers) and whose centre of economic interest thus remains in their home country. Guest-workers and other migrant workers who live abroad for twelve months or more are considered to be resident in the country where they are working. Such persons may send part of their earnings to relatives at home, but these remittances are treated as transfers between resident and non-resident households and do not enter into net receipts from abroad of wages and salaries.

Property income from abroad includes interest, dividends and all or part of the retained earnings of foreign enterprises owned fully or in part by residents. In most countries, net receipts of property income account for most of the difference between GDP and GNI. Note that retained earnings of foreign enterprises owned by residents may not actually return to the residents concerned, and, in some countries, there are restrictions on the repatriation of profits. Receipt of retained earnings is an imputation, and, since there is no actual transaction, it is necessary to impute an outflow of the same amount.

The imputed outflow is treated as a capital transaction (a reinvestment of earnings abroad) and not as an outflow of property income. Countries with large stocks of outward foreign direct investment may be shown as having large receipts of property income from abroad and therefore high GNI even though much of the property income may never actually be returned to the country.

Depreciation, which is deducted from GNI to obtain NNI, is the decline in the market value of fixed capital assets – dwellings, buildings, machinery, transport equipment and physical infrastructure – through wear and tear and obsolescence.

Comparability

Both measures are compiled according to the definitions of the 1993 *System of National Accounts*. There are, however, practical difficulties in the measurement both of international flows of wages and salaries and property income and of depreciation. It is for that reason that GDP per capita is the most widely used indicator of income or welfare, even though it is theoretically inferior to either GNI or NNI.

Source

- OECD (2006), *National Accounts of OECD Countries*, OECD, Paris.

Further information

Analytical publications

- OECD (2003), *The Sources of Economic Growth in OECD Countries*, OECD, Paris.
- OECD (2007), *OECD Economic Outlook: December No. 80 – Volume 2006 Issue 2*, OECD, Paris.

Statistical publications

- Maddison, Angus (2003), *The World Economy: Historical Perspectives*, OECD, Paris, also available on CD-ROM, www.theworldeconomy.org.

Methodological publications

- OECD (2007), *Understanding National Accounts*, OECD, Paris.
- OECD (2000), *OECD Glossaries, System of National Accounts, 1993 – Glossary*, OECD, Paris.
- UN, OECD, IMF, Eurostat (eds.) (1993), *System of National Accounts 1993*, United Nations, Geneva, http://unstats.un.org/unsd/sna1993.

Online databases

- *National Accounts*.
- *OECD Economic Outlook Statistics*.

Websites

- OECD Economic Outlook – Sources and Methods, www.oecd.org/eco/sources-and-methods.

Long-term trends

In the chart, countries are ranked according to GNI, which is usually around 16 or 17% higher than NNI. Note that the country rankings are not much affected by the choice of income measure; countries that would be more than one place lower in the ranking if NNI were used are Japan, and Denmark, and those that would be more than one place higher in the ranking are Greece, Ireland, Sweden and the United Kingdom.

Over the period shown, the growth of per capita GNI mirrors that of per capita GDP, with Ireland, Norway, Korea and Poland at the top end and Germany, Italy and Japan with the lowest rates of growth.

Gross national income per capita

US dollars, current prices and PPPs

	1992	1993	1994	1995	1996	1997	1998	1999	2000	2001	2002	2003	2004	2005
Australia	17 810	18 758	19 677	20 777	21 605	22 751	23 931	25 388	26 483	27 532	28 768	30 373	31 462	32 863
Austria	20 927	21 309	22 223	22 849	24 036	24 440	25 298	26 321	28 171	28 538	29 593	31 455	32 843	34 043
Belgium	20 164	20 550	21 763	22 633	23 137	23 904	24 603	25 289	27 247	28 441	29 709	30 504	31 675	32 901
Canada	19 288	20 005	21 137	21 968	22 544	23 713	24 704	26 217	27 708	28 506	29 154	30 083	31 751	33 495
Czech Republic	11 446	11 575	12 117	13 047	13 719	13 706	13 676	13 857	14 498	15 257	16 156	17 400	18 314	19 692
Denmark	19 372	19 866	21 360	22 453	23 455	24 543	25 452	26 889	28 214	29 492	29 949	30 668	32 232	34 208
Finland	16 435	16 359	17 386	18 534	19 428	21 375	22 808	23 841	25 825	27 488	28 698	28 348	30 361	31 383
France	19 298	19 559	20 235	21 014	21 803	22 885	23 920	24 781	26 279	27 540	28 038	28 660	29 287	30 401
Germany	20 289	20 396	21 169	21 899	22 585	23 024	23 558	24 161	25 313	26 033	26 773	27 394	28 732	29 853
Greece	15 914	15 880	16 470	17 117	17 606	18 572	19 299	19 699	20 988	22 174	24 244	25 867	27 412	29 212
Hungary	..	8 264	8 680	8 788	9 078	9 456	9 989	10 578	11 708	12 926	13 952	14 847	15 548	16 477
Iceland	20 198	20 683	21 551	21 966	23 542	24 845	26 475	27 367	28 220	29 292	30 309	30 251	31 897	34 922
Ireland	13 112	13 762	14 879	16 297	17 828	20 003	21 571	22 578	24 841	25 977	27 366	29 498	31 151	33 199
Italy	19 017	19 301	20 091	21 151	21 915	22 699	23 795	24 364	25 692	26 641	27 256	27 043	27 586	28 002
Japan	20 618	21 082	21 685	22 499	23 703	24 431	24 217	24 446	25 824	26 587	27 190	28 220	29 739	..
Korea	9 841	10 572	11 593	12 774	13 790	14 512	13 422	14 872	16 273	17 222	18 475	19 355	20 771	22 078
Luxembourg	31 196	32 166	32 378	34 059	35 150	36 894	37 212	42 049	44 238	45 645	47 533	49 249	53 299	57 392
Mexico	6 653	6 799	7 114	6 638	6 992	7 525	7 835	8 174	8 874	8 984	9 210	9 414	9 989	..
Netherlands	19 484	20 061	21 082	22 186	23 087	24 629	25 138	26 680	28 997	30 662	31 574	32 216	34 527	35 435
New Zealand	13 720	14 473	15 505	16 251	16 511	17 310	17 783	18 727	19 414	20 568	21 397	22 554	23 205	24 089
Norway	19 732	20 575	22 124	23 557	25 924	27 501	27 136	29 650	35 937	36 907	36 708	38 582	42 062	47 467
Poland	5 868	6 256	6 927	7 507	8 201	8 832	9 345	9 819	10 608	10 970	11 488	11 875	12 511	13 433
Portugal	12 648	12 670	12 976	13 829	14 299	15 058	15 986	16 997	17 906	18 569	19 500	18 346	19 029	19 617
Slovak Republic	..	7 088	7 658	8 349	9 058	9 472	9 926	10 038	10 811	11 627	12 714	13 482	14 708	15 575
Spain	14 371	14 576	15 012	15 923	16 536	17 269	18 338	19 629	20 909	21 973	23 403	24 591	25 672	27 028
Sweden	18 750	18 573	19 880	20 990	21 718	22 468	23 404	25 079	26 948	27 322	28 277	29 965	31 007	32 025
Switzerland	25 597	26 069	26 488	27 190	27 204	29 344	30 628	30 856	32 918	32 334	33 639	36 041	37 638	39 197
Turkey	5 084	5 507	5 207	5 635	6 067	6 628	6 815	6 344	6 869	6 077	6 460	6 682	7 186	7 698
United Kingdom	17 006	17 743	18 996	19 811	20 880	22 329	23 516	23 941	25 609	27 319	29 560	30 483	32 470	33 637
United States	24 185	24 960	26 195	27 296	28 562	30 090	31 615	33 243	35 162	35 775	36 319	37 498	39 590	41 657

StatLink ⟐ http://dx.doi.org/10.1787/846341083632

Gross and net national income per capita

US dollars, current prices and PPPs, 2005 or latest available year

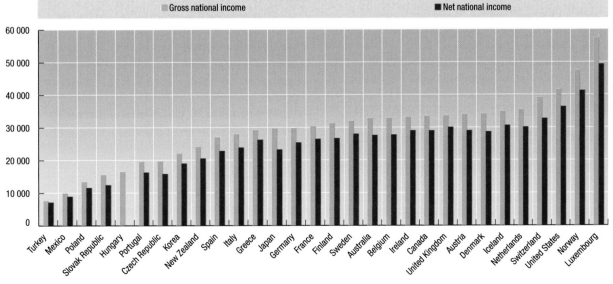

StatLink ⟐ http://dx.doi.org/10.1787/478227715277

REGIONAL GDP

GDP per capita varies significantly among OECD countries, but international disparities in GDP per capita are often smaller than differences among regions within countries. In 2003, GDP per capita in the richest region was twice as large as the poorest one in 80% of OECD countries.

Definition

Regional GDP is measured according to the definitions of the 1993 *System of National Accounts*. GDP per capita is calculated by dividing the GDP of a country or region by the population (number of inhabitants) living there.

The Gini index offers a more precise picture of regional disparities. It looks not only at the regions with the highest and the lowest GDP per capita but also at the differences among all regions. The index ranges between 0 and 1: the higher its value, the larger the regional disparities; a Gini coefficient of 1 would mean that one region has all the GDP. Regional disparities tend to be underestimated when the size of regions is large. This may be the case for Australia, Canada, Mexico and the United States, where GDP figures are only available for Territorial Level 2 regions (see Regional population).

Comparability

As for the other regional statistics, the comparability of regional GDP per capita is affected by differences in the meaning of the word "region" (see Regional population). In addition, different regional type – urban or rural – can affect the comparability of regional GDP per capita. For instance, in the United Kingdom, one might question the relevance of comparing the highly urbanized area of London to the rural region of the Shetland Islands, despite the fact that both regions belong to the same territorial level. To take account of these differences, the OECD has established a regional typology according to which regions have been classified as *predominantly urban*, *predominantly rural* and *intermediate*. This typology, based on the percentage of regional population living in rural or urban communities, enables meaningful comparisons between regions belonging to the same type.

The OECD regional typology is based on two criteria. The first identifies rural communities according to their population density. A community is defined as rural if its population density is below 150 inhabitants per square kilometers (500 inhabitants for Japan because its national population density exceeds 300 inhabitants per square kilometer). The second classifies regions according to the percentage of population living in rural communities. Thus a region is classified as:

- *Predominantly rural*, if more than 50% of its population lives in rural communities.
- *Predominantly urban*, if less than 15% of the population lives in rural communities.
- *Intermediate*, if the percentage of population living in rural communities is between 15 and 50%.

Overview

Differences in GDP per capita among regions of the same country are often substantial. In Turkey, for instance, GDP per capita in the region of Kocaeli is almost 11 times higher than in Agri. In the United Kingdom, GDP per capita in Inner London West is more than nine times higher than in the Isle of Anglesey.

Part of the observed differences in regional GDP per capita may be due to commuting. By working in one area and living in another, commuters tend to increase GDP per capita in the region where they are employed and decrease GDP per capita in the region where they reside. In several urban regions (*e.g.* Inner London – West, District of Columbia, Paris), GDP per capita appears significantly overstated owing to commuting.

More than half (52%) of the population in OECD countries reside in regions with a level of GDP per capita below the national average. In the Slovak Republic, the Czech Republic, Mexico, Belgium, Poland and Denmark no less than 60% of the population lives in regions with low GDP per capita.

Source

- OECD (2007), *OECD Regions at a Glance*, OECD, Paris.

Further information

Analytical publications

- OECD (2001), *OECD Territorial Outlook, 2001 Edition*, OECD, Paris.
- OECD (2003), *Geographic Concentration and Territorial Disparity in OECD Countries*, OECD, Paris.
- OECD (2005), *Local Governance and the Drivers of Growth*, OECD, Paris.
- OECD (2006), *OECD Territorial Reviews – Competitive Cities in the Global Economy*, OECD, Paris.
- Spiezia, V. (2003), "Measuring Regional Economies", *OECD Statistics Brief*, No. 6, October, OECD, Paris, *www.oecd.org/std/statisticsbrief*.

Websites

- OECD Regional Database, *www.oecd.org/gov/territorialindicators*.

OECD FACTBOOK 2007 – ISBN 978-92-64-02946-0 – © OECD 2007

National GDP per capita
US dollars, current prices and PPPs, 2003

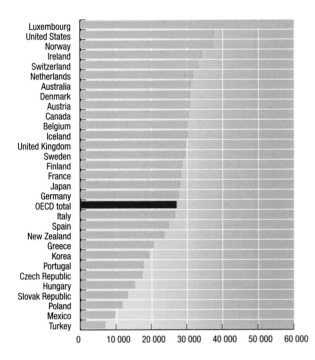

Share of total population living in regions with a GDP per capita below the national average
Percentage, 2003 or latest available year

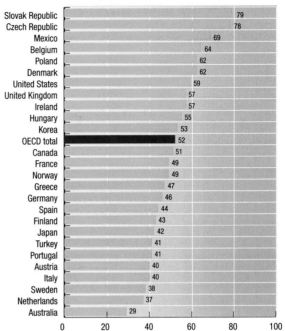

Variation of regional GDP per capita
As a percentage of national GDP per capita, 2003

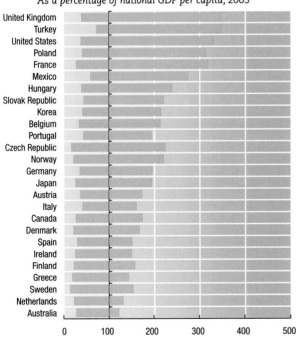

Gini Index of Regional disparities in GDP
2003 or latest available year

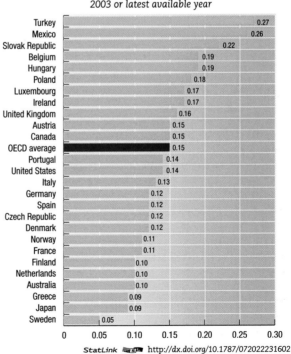

StatLink http://dx.doi.org/10.1787/072022231602

EVOLUTION OF GDP

Gross domestic product (GDP) is the standard measure of the value of production by a country during a period. For the definition refer to Size of GDP. Growth of real GDP, *i.e.* ignoring price changes, is widely used to assess governments' performance in managing their economies.

Definition

In order to calculate the growth rate of GDP free of direct effects of inflation, data at fixed, or constant, prices should be used. Price relativities change over time, and the 1993 *System of National Accounts* recommends that the fixed prices used should be representative of the periods for which the growth rates are calculated, which means that new fixed prices should be introduced frequently, typically every year. The growth rates of GDP between successive periods are linked together to form chain volume indices. All OECD countries derive their "volume" estimates in this way, except for Mexico, Turkey and the Slovak Republic. These three, like many non-OECD countries, only revise their fixed weights every five or ten years. Such practices tend to lead to biased growth rates, usually upward.

The growth rates for OECD total and Euro area are averages of the growth rates of individual countries weighted by the relative size of each country's GDP in US dollars. Conversion to US dollars is done using purchasing power parities so that each country is weighted by the relative

size of its real GDP. Note that OECD total GDP excludes the Czech Republic, Hungary, Poland and the Slovak Republic because growth rates for these countries are not available for the full period.

Comparability

The GDP statistics used for these growth rates have been compiled according to the 1993 *System of National Accounts*, except for Turkey which still uses the 1968 SNA, and GDP estimates at current prices are generally regarded as highly comparable between countries. However, there is more variability in how countries calculate their volume estimates of GDP, particularly in respect of government consumption and some types of capital expenditures.

Long-term trends

Annual growth for OECD total averaged 2.6% from 1992 to 2005. Ireland and Korea substantially outperformed the average with annual growth of over 5%. Growth rates in Ireland were particularly impressive between 1995 and 2000 – the so-called Celtic Tiger period. Korea's growth was badly affected by the financial crisis in Asia; real GDP fell by nearly 7% in 1998 but Korea has since returned to high rates of growth. Luxembourg, Poland and the Slovak Republic all recorded growth of over 4% per year.

At the other end of the scale, four of the largest OECD economies – France, Germany, Italy and Japan – recorded average growth rates of 2% or less over the period.

The Czech Republic, Hungary, Poland and the Slovak Republic all experienced substantial falls in real GDP in the early years of their transition to market-based economies but generally began to achieve positive rates of growth during the second half of the 1990s. Their growth rates are now among the highest of all OECD countries and are expected to remain above the OECD average through 2007.

Sources

- OECD (2006), *National Accounts of OECD Countries*, OECD, Paris, www.sourceOECD.org/nationalaccounts.
- For non-member countries: *national sources*.

Further information

Analytical publications

- OECD (2006), *Development Centre Studies – The Rise of China and India: What's in it for Africa?*, OECD, Paris.
- OECD (2007), *OECD Economic Outlook: December No. 80 – Volume 2006 Issue 2*, OECD, Paris.
- OECD (2007), *Economic Policy Reforms: Going for Growth, 2007 Edition*, OECD, Paris.

Methodological publications

- OECD (2007), *Understanding National Accounts*, OECD, Paris.

Online databases

- *National Accounts*.
- *OECD Economic Outlook Statistics*.

Websites

- OECD Economic Outlook – Sources and Methods, www.oecd.org/eco/sources-and-methods.

Real GDP growth
Annual growth in percentage

	1992	1993	1994	1995	1996	1997	1998	1999	2000	2001	2002	2003	2004	2005
Australia	3.7	4.1	4.5	4.1	3.9	4.5	5.2	4.0	1.9	3.8	3.2	4.1	2.7	2.8
Austria	2.4	0.3	2.7	1.9	2.6	1.8	3.6	3.3	3.4	0.8	0.9	1.1	2.4	2.0
Belgium	1.5	-1.0	3.2	2.4	1.2	3.3	1.9	3.1	3.9	1.0	1.5	0.9	2.6	1.2
Canada	0.9	2.3	4.8	2.8	1.6	4.2	4.1	5.5	5.2	1.8	2.9	1.8	3.3	2.9
Czech Republic	-0.5	0.1	2.2	5.9	4.0	-0.7	-0.8	1.3	3.6	2.5	1.9	3.6	4.2	6.1
Denmark	2.0	-0.1	5.5	3.1	2.8	3.2	2.2	2.6	3.5	0.7	0.5	0.7	1.9	3.0
Finland	-3.7	-0.9	3.6	3.9	3.7	6.1	5.2	3.9	5.0	2.6	1.6	1.8	3.5	2.9
France	1.8	-1.1	2.0	2.2	1.1	2.2	3.5	3.2	4.0	1.9	1.0	1.1	2.3	1.2
Germany	2.2	-0.8	2.7	1.9	1.0	1.8	2.0	2.0	3.2	1.2	0.0	-0.2	1.2	0.9
Greece	0.7	-1.6	2.0	2.1	2.4	3.6	3.4	3.4	4.5	4.5	3.9	4.9	4.7	3.7
Hungary	-3.1	-0.6	2.9	1.5	1.3	4.6	4.9	4.2	5.2	4.1	4.3	4.1	4.9	4.2
Iceland	-3.4	1.3	3.6	0.1	4.8	4.9	5.8	4.0	4.4	3.6	-0.3	2.7	7.7	7.5
Ireland	3.3	2.7	5.8	9.6	8.3	11.7	8.5	10.7	9.4	5.8	6.0	4.3	4.3	5.5
Italy	0.8	-0.9	2.2	2.8	0.7	1.9	1.4	1.9	3.6	1.8	0.3	0.0	1.1	0.0
Japan	1.0	0.2	1.1	1.9	2.6	1.4	-1.8	-0.2	2.9	0.4	0.1	1.8	2.3	2.6
Korea	5.9	6.1	8.5	9.2	7.0	4.7	-6.9	9.5	8.5	3.8	7.0	3.1	4.7	4.0
Luxembourg	1.8	4.2	3.8	1.4	1.5	5.9	6.5	8.4	8.4	2.5	3.8	1.3	3.6	4.0
Mexico	3.6	2.0	4.4	-6.2	5.2	6.8	5.0	3.8	6.6	0.0	0.8	1.4	4.2	3.0
Netherlands	1.5	0.7	2.9	3.0	3.4	4.3	3.9	4.7	3.9	1.9	0.1	0.3	2.0	1.5
New Zealand	1.1	6.4	5.3	4.2	3.5	1.5	0.4	5.3	2.1	3.9	4.7	3.6	3.7	1.9
Norway	3.3	2.7	5.3	4.4	5.3	5.2	2.6	2.1	3.3	2.7	1.1	1.1	3.1	2.3
Poland	2.5	3.7	5.3	7.0	6.2	7.1	5.0	4.5	4.2	1.1	1.4	3.8	5.3	3.2
Portugal	1.1	-2.0	1.0	4.3	3.6	4.2	4.8	3.9	3.9	2.0	0.8	-1.1	1.2	0.4
Slovak Republic	..	1.9	6.2	5.8	6.1	4.6	4.2	1.5	2.0	3.2	4.1	4.2	5.4	6.1
Spain	0.9	-1.0	2.4	2.8	2.4	3.9	4.5	4.7	5.0	3.6	2.7	3.0	3.2	3.5
Sweden	-1.2	-2.0	3.9	3.9	1.3	2.3	3.7	4.5	4.3	1.1	2.0	1.7	4.1	2.9
Switzerland	0.0	-0.2	1.1	0.4	0.5	1.9	2.8	1.3	3.6	1.0	0.3	-0.2	2.3	1.9
Turkey	6.0	8.0	-5.5	7.2	7.0	7.5	3.1	-4.7	7.4	-7.5	7.9	5.8	8.9	7.4
United Kingdom	0.2	2.3	4.3	2.9	2.8	3.0	3.3	3.0	3.8	2.4	2.1	2.7	3.3	1.9
United States	3.3	2.7	4.1	2.5	3.7	4.5	4.2	4.5	3.7	0.8	1.6	2.5	3.9	3.2
Euro area	1.5	-0.8	2.4	2.4	1.5	2.5	2.8	3.0	3.9	1.9	0.9	0.8	2.0	1.4
OECD total	2.2	1.3	3.1	2.5	2.9	3.5	2.6	3.3	4.0	1.2	1.6	2.0	3.2	2.6
Brazil	-0.5	4.9	5.9	4.2	2.7	3.3	0.1	0.8	4.4	1.3	1.9	0.5	4.9	2.3
China	14.2	13.9	13.1	10.9	10.0	9.3	7.8	7.6	8.4	8.3	9.1	10.0	10.1	10.2
India	5.1	5.9	7.3	7.3	7.8	4.8	6.5	6.1	4.4	5.8	3.8	8.5	7.5	8.4
Russian Federation	..	..	..	..	-3.6	1.4	-5.3	6.4	10.0	5.1	4.7	7.3	7.2	6.4
South Africa	-2.2	1.3	3.0	2.8	4.7	2.2	0.5	2.4	4.2	2.7	3.7	3.1	4.8	5.1

StatLink 🔢 http://dx.doi.org/10.1787/843875747717

Real GDP growth
Average annual growth in percentage, 1992-2005

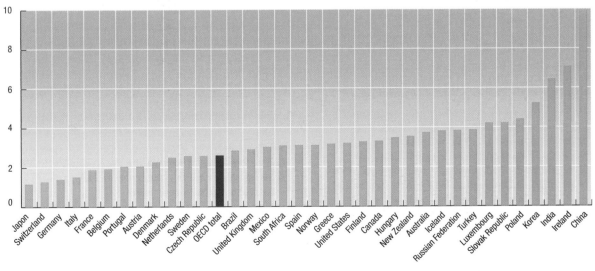

StatLink 🔢 http://dx.doi.org/10.1787/684052144860

HOUSEHOLD SAVING

Household saving is the main domestic source of funds to finance capital investment, which is a major impetus for long-term economic growth.

Definition

In the national accounts, saving is estimated by subtracting household consumption expenditure from household disposable income.

The latter consists essentially of income from employment and from the operation of unincorporated enterprises, plus receipts of interest, dividends and social benefits minus payments of income taxes, interest and social security contributions. Note that enterprise income includes imputed rents paid by owner-occupiers of dwellings.

Household consumption expenditure consists mainly of cash outlays for consumer goods and services but it also includes the imputed expenditures that owner occupiers pay, as occupiers, to themselves as owners of their dwellings.

Comparability

Saving rates may be measured on either a net or a gross basis. Net saving rates are measured after deducting consumption of fixed capital (depreciation) in respect of assets used in enterprises operated by households and in respect of owner-occupied dwellings. Consumption of fixed capital is deducted, as a production cost, from the disposable income of households, so that both saving and disposable income is shown on a net basis. Sometimes, countries have difficulties in estimating consumption of fixed capital for the household sector. The international system of accounts therefore provides for both disposable income and saving to be shown on a gross basis, *i.e.* with both aggregates including consumption of fixed capital. All figures are shown on a net basis.

Because saving is a residual between two large aggregates – disposable income and household consumption expenditure – both of which are subject to estimation errors, estimates of savings are subject to large relative errors and revisions over time.

Source

- OECD (2006), *National Accounts of OECD Countries*, OECD, Paris.

Further information

Analytical publications

- Cotis, J.-P., J. Coppel and L. de Mello (2004), *Is the US Prone to Over-consumption?*, paper presented at The Macroeconomics of Fiscal Policy Federal Reserve Bank of Boston Economic Conference, Cape Cod, 14-16 June, *www.oecd.org/eco/speeches.*

- Harvey, R. (2004), "Comparison of Household Saving Ratios: Euro Area/United States/Japan", *OECD Statistics Brief*, No. 8, June, OECD, Paris, *www.oecd.org/std/statisticsbrief.*

- Kohl, R. and P. O'Brien (1998), *The Macroeconomics of Ageing, Pensions and Savings*, OECD Economics Department Working Papers, No. 200, OECD, Paris.

- de Serres, A. and F. Pelgrin (2003), "The Decline of Private Saving Rates in the 1990s in OECD Countries: How Much Can Be Explained by Non-wealth Determinants?", *OECD Economic Studies*, No. 36, 2003/1, OECD, Paris, *www.oecd.org/oecdeconomicstudies.*

Methodological publications

- OECD (2007), *Understanding National Accounts*, OECD, Paris.

Websites

- OECD Economic Outlook – Sources and Methods, *www.oecd.org/eco/sources-and-methods.*

Long-term trends

Household saving rates are very variable between countries. This is partly due to institutional differences between countries such as the extent to which old-age pensions are funded by government rather than through personal saving and the extent to which governments provide insurance against sickness and unemployment. The age composition of the population is also relevant because the elderly tend to run down financial assets acquired during their working life, so that a country with a high share of retired persons will usually have a low saving rate.

Over the period covered in the table, saving rates have been stable or rising in Austria, France, Italy, Norway and Portugal but have been falling in the other countries. Particularly sharp declines occurred in Australia, Canada, Japan, the United Kingdom and the United States. Negative saving – which means that consumption expenditures by households exceeded their income – was recorded in some countries, in particular in Australia, Denmark, Greece and New Zealand.

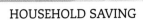
Household net saving rates

As a percentage of disposable household income

	1992	1993	1994	1995	1996	1997	1998	1999	2000	2001	2002	2003	2004	2005
Australia	6.1	6.7	6.1	6.7	6.4	2.9	2.0	1.9	2.4	1.2	-2.3	-3.2	-3.7	..
Austria	..	..	..	11.0	8.6	7.3	8.2	8.8	8.5	7.5	7.7	8.6	9.1	..
Belgium	16.2	17.6	16.6	15.7	13.7	12.6	11.1	11.1	9.7	11.6	11.9	10.4	..	..
Canada	13.3	12.1	9.6	9.4	7.2	5.0	4.9	4.1	4.8	5.3	3.5	2.8	2.7	1.2
Czech Republic	..	..	..	10.0	6.2	6.1	4.1	3.4	3.3	2.2	3.0	2.4	0.2	0.5
Denmark	1.6	2.7	-1.8	1.3	1.0	-1.7	-	-3.6	-2.0	4.1	4.6	4.8	1.1	..
Finland	9.6	7.5	1.1	3.9	0.4	2.0	0.5	2.1	-0.1	0.1	0.6	1.4	2.4	-0.1
France	11.2	12.3	11.5	12.7	11.7	12.7	12.3	12.0	11.8	12.5	13.7	12.5	12.4	11.5
Germany	12.8	12.1	11.5	11.1	10.6	10.2	10.2	9.5	9.3	9.5	10.1	10.4	10.6	10.7
Greece	..	..	..	..	..	..	..	..	-4.1	-5.6	-7.4	-6.3	-5.8	-7.8
Italy	..	..	..	..	..	..	..	9.8	9.0	10.4	10.8	11.0	11.6	..
Japan	..	..	..	..	11.5	11.2	12.1	10.7	8.5	5.2	4.9	4.0	3.2	..
Korea	23.4	21.8	20.6	17.5	17.5	16.1	24.8	17.4	10.7	6.4	2.2	3.9	6.3	4.4
Mexico	..	4.9	3.4	2.4	5.8	10.0	7.5	7.1	10.6	7.7	8.8	..	..	..
Netherlands	..	..	..	15.7	13.9	14.5	13.5	9.9	7.5	10.5	9.4	8.4	8.1	7.1
New Zealand	0.2	-0.6	-3.8	-3.6	-2.6	-4.6	-4.2	-5.3	-3.8	..	..	..	..	..
Norway	5.0	6.1	5.2	4.6	2.2	2.9	5.9	5.6	5.2	4.2	9.0	10.1	..	..
Poland	..	..	..	16.0	11.7	11.6	12.0	10.6	8.4	9.9	6.0	5.3	4.1	2.4
Portugal	..	..	..	..	..	..	..	..	3.6	4.5	4.0	..	..	..
Spain	..	..	..	..	..	..	..	..	5.9	5.7	5.7	6.0	4.6	..
Sweden	..	11.6	10.3	9.1	6.7	4.1	3.1	2.1	3.2	8.6	9.2	9.2	8.7	..
Switzerland	12.1	12.6	12.4	12.9	12.6	11.8	12.0	11.2	13.2	13.0	9.9	9.9	9.1	..
United Kingdom	8.3	7.6	5.9	6.7	5.9	5.8	2.1	0.5	0.5	2.0	0.5	0.7	-0.7	-0.1
United States	7.6	6.1	5.3	5.1	4.2	3.7	4.5	2.5	2.4	1.8	2.5	2.4	1.9	-0.4
Euro area	13.8	13.6	12.8	12.7	12.2	11.4	10.4	9.3	9.0	9.5	9.9	9.7	..	..

StatLink ⩘⩘⩘ http://dx.doi.org/10.1787/270851821748

Household net saving rates

As a percentage of disposable household income

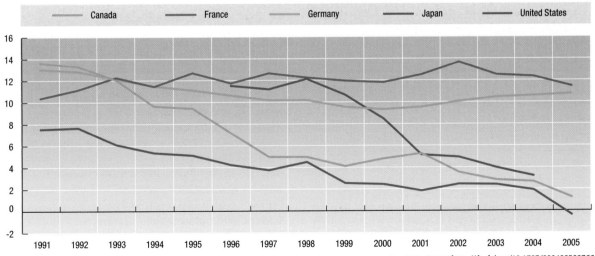

StatLink ⩘⩘⩘ http://dx.doi.org/10.1787/030428502766

INVESTMENT RATES

The share of total GDP that is devoted to investment in fixed assets is an important indicator of future economic growth, although not all types of investment contribute to future growth in the same way. The following tables show the total of gross fixed capital formation (investment or GFCF) as a share of GDP and two of the main components – *dwellings* and *machinery* and *equipment*.

Definition

Gross fixed capital formation (GFCF) is the acquisition, less disposal, of fixed assets, *i.e.* products which are expected to be used in production for several years. *Acquisitions* include both purchases of assets (new or second-hand) and the construction of assets by producers for their own use. *Disposals* include sales of assets for scrap as well as sales of used assets in a working condition to other producers: New Zealand, Mexico and some Central European countries import substantial quantities of used assets.

Fixed assets consist of machinery and equipment; dwellings and other buildings; roads, bridges, airfields and dams; orchards and tree plantations; improvements to land such as fencing, leveling and draining; draught animals and other animals that are kept for the milk and wool that they produce; computer software and databases; entertainment, literary or artistic originals; and expenditures on mineral exploration. What all these things have in common is that they contribute to future production. This may not be obvious in the case of dwellings but, in the national accounts, flats and houses are considered to produce housing services which are consumed by owners or tenants over the life of the building.

In calculating the shares, gross fixed capital formation and GDP are both valued at current market prices.

Comparability

When the *System of National Accounts* was revised in 1993, the scope of GFCF was widened to include mineral exploration, computer software and entertainment, literary and artistic originals. In several countries these three items are only partially covered. In the case of Turkey, which still adheres to the 1968 version of the SNA, they are not included at all

---

Long-term trends

The total investment rate now averages just over 21% for the OECD as a whole but rates are substantially higher than this in Korea, Spain, the Czech Republic and Australia and well below 20% in the United Kingdom, Sweden, Germany and Turkey. For the OECD as a whole, total investment rates are largely unchanged compared to 1992-1994. Particularly sharp falls occurred in Turkey, Germany and Japan, although in Japan, investment rates remain well above the OECD average. Total investment rates are now much higher than at the beginning of the 1990s in Ireland, Iceland and Spain.

Investment in machinery and equipment accounts for more than 30% of GFCF in most OECD countries, but investment rates tend to be higher than this in countries with a significant manufacturing base, such as Japan, Korea, Switzerland and the Czech Republic. Over the period shown, the machinery investment rates have fallen in most countries, with particularly sharp falls in Luxembourg, Korea, Netherlands and Poland, reflecting higher growth of service activities. Rates grew most in Greece and Iceland.

Investment rates in dwellings were particularly high at both the beginning and the end of the period in Norway and Portugal. Ireland, the Slovak Republic and Spain recorded substantial increases over the period, but a number of countries recorded large falls: Turkey, Luxembourg, Sweden, Japan and Korea. In the short term, rates of investment in dwellings are sensitive to the business cycle, but, over the long run, investment rates in dwellings reflect population growth rates either through natural growth or immigration, and rising affluence, as is evident for Ireland and Norway.

Sources
- OECD (2006), *National Accounts of OECD Countries*, OECD, Paris.
- For Brazil, Russian Federation and South Africa: OECD (2006), *Main Economic Indicators*, OECD, Paris.
- For China: National Bureau of Statistics.

Further information
Analytical publications
- OECD (2007), *OECD Economic Outlook: December No. 80 – Volume 2006 Issue 2*, OECD, Paris.

Methodological publications
- Ahmad, N. (2004), "Towards More Harmonised Estimates of Investment in Software", *OECD Economic Studies*, No. 37, 2003/2, OECD, Paris.
- OECD (2000), *OECD Glossaries, System of National Accounts, 1993 – Glossary*, OECD, Paris.
- UN, OECD, IMF, Eurostat (eds.) (1993), *System of National Accounts 1993*, United Nations, Geneva, http://unstats.un.org/unsd/sna1993.

Websites
- OECD Economic Outlook – Sources and Methods, *www.oecd.org/eco/sources-and-methods*.

Gross fixed capital formation
As a percentage of GDP

	1992	1993	1994	1995	1996	1997	1998	1999	2000	2001	2002	2003	2004	2005
Australia	22.2	22.7	23.9	22.9	22.9	24.0	24.2	24.8	22.0	22.9	24.8	25.4	25.8	26.5
Austria	22.9	22.5	22.9	22.1	22.1	22.3	22.4	22.1	22.8	22.1	20.4	21.3	20.9	20.5
Belgium	20.1	19.4	18.9	19.3	19.4	20.0	20.2	20.6	20.8	20.4	19.2	18.8	18.8	19.9
Canada	18.7	18.0	18.8	17.6	17.9	19.8	19.9	19.8	19.2	19.6	19.5	19.6	20.2	20.7
Czech Republic	27.4	27.9	28.2	31.5	32.1	29.9	28.2	27.0	28.0	28.0	27.5	26.7	26.2	24.9
Denmark	17.6	16.9	17.2	18.4	18.6	19.6	20.4	19.8	20.2	19.8	19.6	19.5	19.8	20.7
Finland	19.8	16.4	15.6	16.6	17.1	18.3	19.0	19.0	19.4	19.5	17.9	18.1	18.3	18.8
France	20.1	18.7	18.4	18.1	17.9	17.4	17.9	18.8	19.5	19.5	18.8	18.8	19.2	19.7
Germany	23.6	22.5	22.6	21.9	21.3	21.0	21.1	21.3	21.5	20.0	18.3	17.8	17.4	17.3
Greece	20.9	19.9	18.3	18.3	19.1	19.4	20.8	22.2	23.2	22.8	22.8	24.3	24.4	23.4
Hungary	19.3	18.4	19.6	19.5	20.8	21.6	23.0	23.3	22.9	22.9	22.9	21.9	22.4	22.7
Iceland	18.1	16.3	15.9	15.7	18.9	19.7	23.8	21.4	22.5	21.3	17.7	19.8	23.3	28.4
Ireland	16.7	15.3	16.3	17.4	17.4	19.1	20.5	22.2	23.9	24.3	23.2	23.0	24.6	27.0
Italy	21.1	18.8	18.5	19.1	18.9	18.9	19.3	19.6	20.3	20.3	20.9	20.4	20.6	20.6
Japan	30.8	29.5	28.5	28.0	28.4	27.6	25.9	25.5	25.2	24.7	23.3	22.9	22.9	23.2
Korea	36.9	36.3	36.4	37.3	37.5	35.6	30.3	29.7	31.1	29.5	29.1	29.9	29.5	29.3
Luxembourg	19.7	21.9	20.6	19.9	20.1	21.7	21.8	23.5	20.8	22.6	22.3	21.5	20.6	19.7
Mexico	19.6	18.6	19.4	16.2	17.9	19.5	20.9	21.2	21.4	20.0	19.3	18.9	19.6	19.3
Netherlands	22.2	21.2	20.8	20.8	21.6	21.9	22.2	22.9	21.9	21.1	20.0	19.5	19.1	19.3
New Zealand	17.3	19.0	20.9	22.1	22.0	21.1	20.1	20.9	20.4	20.8	21.3	22.8	23.5	23.9
Norway	19.1	19.8	20.0	19.9	20.3	22.1	25.2	22.0	18.6	18.3	18.1	17.5	18.0	18.7
Poland	16.0	15.1	17.1	17.7	19.8	22.4	24.1	24.4	23.7	20.7	18.7	18.3	18.0	18.1
Portugal	23.4	21.9	21.9	22.5	23.0	25.2	26.5	26.8	27.1	26.5	25.0	22.5	22.2	21.4
Slovak Republic	30.7	29.5	26.2	24.6	31.4	33.6	35.7	29.3	25.7	28.5	27.3	25.0	24.1	26.8
Spain	22.6	20.8	20.7	21.5	21.4	21.8	23.0	24.6	25.8	26.0	26.3	27.2	28.1	29.3
Sweden	18.1	15.5	15.3	15.8	16.0	15.6	16.3	17.1	17.5	17.3	16.5	16.0	16.3	17.2
Switzerland	24.8	23.3	23.6	23.3	22.2	21.7	22.4	22.3	22.8	22.2	21.6	20.7	21.0	21.4
Turkey	23.6	26.5	24.6	23.8	25.1	26.4	24.6	21.9	22.4	18.2	16.6	15.5	17.8	19.6
United Kingdom	16.5	15.7	15.9	16.4	16.5	16.5	17.6	17.2	16.9	16.6	16.5	16.1	16.5	16.8
United States	16.2	16.7	17.2	17.7	18.2	18.6	19.1	19.6	19.9	19.2	17.9	17.9	18.4	19.1
EU15 average	20.3	19.2	18.9	19.2	19.5	20.0	20.7	21.3	21.5	21.2	20.5	20.3	20.5	20.8
OECD average	21.5	20.8	20.8	20.9	21.6	22.1	22.6	22.4	22.3	21.8	21.1	20.9	21.3	21.8
Brazil	16.7	19.1	20.8	20.6	19.3	19.9	19.7	18.9	19.3	19.5	18.3	17.8	19.6	19.9
China	32.2	37.6	36.1	34.7	34.2	33.6	35.0	35.7	36.5	37.3	38.8	42.1	43.8	..
Russian Federation	..	..	..	21.1	20.0	18.3	16.2	14.4	16.9	18.9	17.9	18.4	18.3	18.2
South Africa	15.7	14.7	15.1	15.9	16.3	16.5	17.1	15.5	15.1	15.0	15.0	15.9	16.2	17.0

StatLink 🔗 http://dx.doi.org/10.1787/718601115301

Gross fixed capital formation
As a percentage of GDP

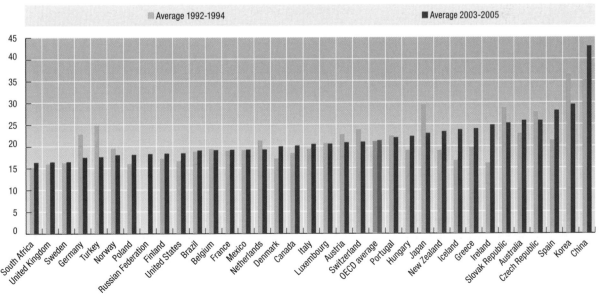

StatLink 🔗 http://dx.doi.org/10.1787/252125572446

Gross fixed capital formation: machinery and equipment

As a percentage of GDP

	1992	1993	1994	1995	1996	1997	1998	1999	2000	2001	2002	2003	2004	2005
Australia	7.5	7.6	8.5	8.3	8.1	8.4	8.1	8.3	7.9	7.7	8.1	7.9	8.1	8.2
Austria	9.0	8.3	8.2	8.0	8.1	8.3	8.4	8.5	9.2	9.1	8.1	8.6	8.2	8.0
Canada	6.0	5.6	5.9	6.1	6.1	7.2	7.6	7.7	7.4	7.0	6.6	6.3	6.3	6.3
Denmark	7.5	7.0	7.4	8.0	7.3	7.8	8.3	7.8	8.1	8.0	7.6	7.4	7.5	8.1
Finland	6.6	5.8	5.7	6.3	6.7	7.1	6.9	6.3	6.1	6.3	5.5	5.5	5.4	5.1
France	5.9	5.5	5.5	5.6	5.6	5.4	5.7	6.1	6.3	6.2	5.6	5.5	5.3	5.4
Germany	9.2	7.7	7.2	7.0	7.0	7.2	7.6	7.9	8.6	7.9	7.1	6.8	6.9	7.1
Greece	..	..	..	4.7	5.5	5.4	5.9	6.7	7.3	6.8	6.7	7.4	7.5	7.5
Hungary	..	..	..	..	..	..	..	..	10.7	9.9	9.2	9.2	9.3	9.1
Iceland	5.7	4.3	4.6	5.0	7.3	7.1	8.8	7.0	8.5	7.0	4.9	4.6	6.0	10.2
Ireland	5.8	6.0	6.3	6.8	7.0	7.0	7.8	8.2	8.0	6.6	6.0	5.3	5.4	6.2
Italy	8.6	7.2	7.6	8.2	8.2	8.4	8.9	9.1	9.5	9.3	9.3	8.6	8.7	8.5
Japan	10.9	9.9	9.3	9.9	10.7	10.7	10.0	10.0	10.1	9.9	9.0	9.0	9.2	..
Korea	13.3	12.4	13.6	14.1	14.1	12.2	8.4	10.3	12.8	11.0	10.4	9.6	9.2	8.9
Luxembourg	7.7	9.9	8.1	7.9	7.5	9.3	8.6	10.5	8.0	8.9	7.2	5.5	5.4	5.3
Mexico	10.0	8.6	8.9	7.6	8.9	10.0	11.1	11.0	10.8	9.7	8.9	8.5	8.7	..
Netherlands	7.7	7.3	7.0	7.3	7.5	7.6	7.4	7.7	6.9	6.3	5.7	5.7	5.5	5.5
New Zealand	8.0	9.1	9.8	9.8	9.4	8.4	8.2	8.2	8.7	9.3	8.7	9.1	8.9	9.0
Norway	4.4	5.5	6.1	6.0	6.3	7.0	8.0	7.4	6.4	5.9	5.8	5.3	5.4	5.3
Poland	..	..	..	7.6	8.7	9.7	10.4	10.2	9.7	8.2	7.3	7.0	7.0	..
Portugal	8.4	7.4	7.6	7.4	7.7	8.6	9.3	9.4	9.5	8.9	7.8	7.1	7.1	6.7
Slovak Republic	..	13.4	12.1	11.4	14.1	16.8	17.8	12.9	11.0	13.5	13.3	12.4	11.4	13.3
Spain	6.5	5.3	5.6	6.0	6.3	6.8	7.5	7.9	8.1	7.6	7.0	6.8	6.8	7.0
Sweden	..	5.8	6.7	7.5	7.7	7.7	8.0	8.6	8.5	7.8	7.2	6.9	6.8	7.4
Switzerland	11.2	10.4	10.2	10.5	10.5	10.5	11.1	11.3	11.6	11.0	10.2	9.6	9.6	9.7
United Kingdom	7.1	6.8	7.2	7.7	8.1	7.8	8.6	8.3	8.0	7.5	6.9	6.2	6.1	5.9
United States	6.0	6.4	6.7	7.1	7.2	7.2	7.3	7.4	7.4	6.6	5.8	5.6	5.6	5.8

StatLink ⬛🔄 http://dx.doi.org/10.1787/756117476466

Gross fixed capital formation in machinery and equipment

As a percentage of GDP

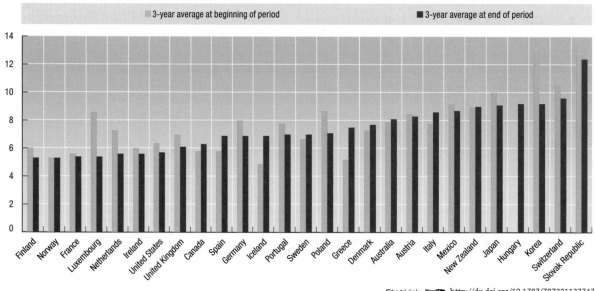

StatLink ⬛🔄 http://dx.doi.org/10.1787/787321137747

OECD FACTBOOK 2007 – ISBN 978-92-64-02946-0 – © OECD 2007

Gross fixed capital formation: housing
As a percentage of GDP

	1992	1993	1994	1995	1996	1997	1998	1999	2000	2001	2002	2003	2004	2005
Australia	6.3	6.7	6.8	5.7	5.5	6.1	6.3	7.1	5.9	6.7	7.6	8.0	7.6	7.1
Austria	5.6	5.8	6.1	6.6	6.6	6.5	6.1	5.8	5.3	4.9	4.6	4.4	4.4	4.3
Canada	5.8	5.5	5.5	4.5	4.8	5.0	4.7	4.6	4.5	5.0	5.7	6.0	6.5	6.5
Denmark	3.1	3.0	3.2	3.5	3.6	3.9	3.9	4.0	4.2	3.9	3.8	4.2	4.6	4.9
Finland	4.8	4.0	3.9	3.7	3.7	4.4	4.7	5.2	5.3	4.7	4.5	4.9	5.2	5.6
France	4.3	4.3	4.4	4.3	4.2	4.1	4.1	4.2	4.1	4.1	4.1	4.2	4.4	4.6
Germany	6.7	7.1	7.8	7.7	7.6	7.4	7.2	7.2	6.8	6.3	5.8	5.7	5.5	5.2
Greece	12.2	11.1	9.5	9.4	9.0	9.2	9.8	10.0	9.1	9.0	9.7	10.3	9.7	9.1
Hungary	..	..	..	..	..	..	..	..	3.5	4.4	4.8	5.0	5.3	4.5
Iceland	7.1	6.6	6.4	6.1	6.7	6.9	7.1	7.5	7.8	7.4	7.8	8.4	9.2	9.9
Ireland	4.7	4.1	5.0	5.3	6.0	6.7	7.2	8.0	8.4	8.7	8.8	10.6	12.3	13.9
Italy	4.8	4.7	4.5	4.3	4.1	3.9	3.7	3.7	3.8	3.8	3.8	3.9	4.0	4.3
Japan	5.1	5.2	5.5	5.2	5.7	5.0	4.3	4.3	4.3	4.0	3.9	3.8	3.8	..
Korea	7.9	8.1	7.3	7.3	7.0	6.5	6.0	5.1	4.3	4.7	5.0	5.5	5.7	5.9
Luxembourg	4.8	4.3	3.5	3.3	2.9	2.9	3.0	2.6	2.4	2.8	2.3	2.6	2.5	2.4
Mexico	4.6	5.0	5.1	4.8	4.6	4.6	4.6	4.7	4.8	4.7	4.7	4.6	4.7	..
Netherlands	5.3	5.4	5.6	5.6	5.7	5.8	5.8	5.9	5.9	6.1	5.8	5.7	6.1	6.3
New Zealand	4.2	4.7	5.5	5.6	5.8	5.9	5.0	5.7	4.8	4.6	5.6	6.6	6.9	6.7
Norway	13.8	13.7	13.3	13.5	13.5	14.4	16.5	14.3	11.8	12.0	12.0	12.0	12.4	13.1
Poland	..	..	..	2.2	2.2	2.4	2.6	2.8	3.0	2.8	2.8	2.7	2.9	..
Portugal	12.3	11.9	11.7	12.3	12.4	13.6	13.8	13.6	13.8	14.0	13.4	11.9	11.6	11.2
Slovak Republic	..	..	..	1.2	1.4	1.8	3.0	3.8	4.4	3.5	3.3	3.1	3.0	3.0
Spain	4.3	4.2	4.2	4.4	4.8	4.7	5.0	5.5	6.1	6.5	7.1	7.8	8.4	8.9
Sweden	5.2	3.3	2.0	1.5	1.6	1.4	1.4	1.5	1.8	2.0	2.1	2.2	2.5	2.8
Switzerland	4.8	4.9	5.7	5.6	4.9	4.5	4.5	4.3	4.2	4.1	3.9	4.4	4.8	5.1
Turkey	7.8	8.6	9.5	8.4	7.8	7.6	7.0	6.6	5.3	5.2	3.8	3.2	3.5	4.9
United Kingdom	3.1	3.1	3.1	3.1	2.9	2.9	2.9	2.8	2.9	3.0	3.3	3.5	3.8	4.0
United States	3.8	4.0	4.3	4.1	4.3	4.2	4.5	4.6	4.6	4.7	4.9	5.3	5.8	6.2

StatLink http://dx.doi.org/10.1787/418265773755

Gross fixed capital formation in housing
As a percentage of GDP

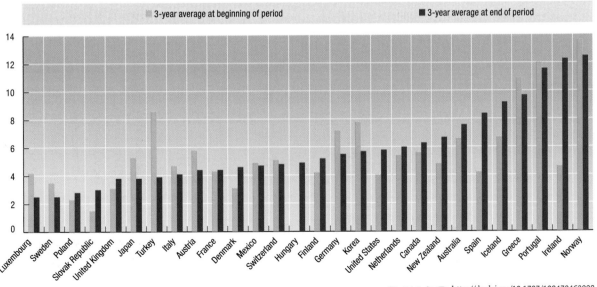

■ 3-year average at beginning of period   ■ 3-year average at end of period

StatLink http://dx.doi.org/10.1787/108470463028

INFLATION

There are several ways in which inflation can be measured. The most common is by reference to a *consumer price index* (CPI) which measures the changes in prices of a basket of goods and services purchased by a representative set of households. The CPI is a narrow measure of inflation and does not measure changes in the prices of other goods and services, such as those used for intermediate consumption or the prices of capital products. A much broader indicator of inflation is provided by the GDP deflator, and this is the inflation measure shown here.

Definition

The GDP deflator is an implicit, not an explicit deflator. It is derived by dividing the GDP measured in current prices by GDP measured in constant prices. It is therefore a weighted average of the price indices of:

- goods and services consumed by households;
- expenditure by government on goods, services and salaries;
- fixed capital assets;
- changes in inventories;
- exports of goods and services;
- imports of goods and services (minus).

While the CPI measures the price changes of goods and services consumed by households, the GDP deflator measures the price changes of the goods and services produced by a country. Hence, the treatment of exports and imports merits special attention. The GDP deflator will go up, indicating more inflation, if the prices of exports rise; although higher inflation is usually thought of as a bad thing, it may actually be beneficial to a country if the prices of its exports rise, since it is non-residents who pay the higher prices. At the same time, an increase in the price of imports is subtracted from the GDP deflator, although an increase in import prices may still give rise to inflation when the higher-priced imports are incorporated into domestically produced goods.

Comparability

The comparability of the inflation rates shown here depends on the methods used to calculate in volume terms the expenditure components of GDP. Most countries use similar methods for consumer goods and imports and exports, but there are clear differences in the methods used to derive volume estimates for government consumption.

Some countries calculate their volume estimates of government consumption by deflating their current price estimates using representative input price indexes, while others weight together output indicators for services provided by hospitals, schools, etc.

Long-term trends

Taking the period 1992-2005 as a whole, inflation in the OECD area fell to a record low of 1.2% in 1999. It then gradually increased and, between 2001 and 2005, it remained stable at 2.2%. Since 1996, member countries of the Euro area have generally averaged lower inflation than other EU countries.

The graph shows that inflation rates averaged over the period were mostly well below 5% per year for all countries except Greece, Mexico and Turkey and the four new OECD countries from Central Europe. All seven high-inflation countries have, however, drastically reduced inflation rates over the period with particularly sharp falls in Poland, the Czech Republic and Turkey. At the other extreme, Japan, Switzerland, Germany, Austria and France, recorded inflation rates well below the OECD average.

Several countries, including Finland, France, Germany, Norway and Switzerland, recorded deflation for one or more years, but Japan is the only country where the long-term average was negative. The volatile inflation rates for Norway partly reflect fluctuations in export prices for petroleum.

Source

- OECD (2005), *National Accounts of OECD Countries*, OECD, Paris.

Further information
Analytical publications

- OECD (2007), *OECD Economic Outlook: December No. 80 – Volume 2006 Issue 2*, OECD, Paris.

Websites

- Inflation Measures: Too High-Too Low – Internationally Comparable? Documents for the meeting held at the OECD, 21-22 June 2005, *www.oecd.org/std/price-indices*.
- OECD Purchasing Power Parities, *www.oecd.org/std/ppp*.

GDP deflator
Annual growth in percentage

	1992	1993	1994	1995	1996	1997	1998	1999	2000	2001	2002	2003	2004	2005
Australia	1.4	0.9	1.2	2.3	1.3	1.3	0.1	2.1	4.8	2.9	3.0	3.3	3.9	4.8
Austria	3.6	2.7	2.7	1.9	1.0	-	0.3	0.6	1.8	1.8	1.4	1.3	1.7	1.9
Belgium	3.4	4.0	2.1	1.2	0.6	1.2	1.8	0.7	1.7	1.8	1.8	1.7	2.3	2.2
Canada	1.3	1.4	1.1	2.3	1.6	1.2	-0.4	1.7	4.1	1.1	1.1	3.4	3.0	3.2
Czech Republic	12.4	21.0	13.4	10.2	10.3	8.4	11.1	2.8	1.5	4.9	2.8	0.9	3.5	0.7
Denmark	1.7	0.7	1.5	1.3	2.0	2.0	1.2	1.7	3.0	2.5	2.3	1.9	2.2	2.8
Finland	0.7	2.0	1.4	4.8	-0.2	2.2	3.4	0.9	2.6	3.0	1.3	-0.4	0.6	0.6
France	2.1	1.9	1.5	1.2	1.7	1.1	0.9	-0.1	1.4	2.0	2.4	1.9	1.7	1.9
Germany	5.0	3.7	2.4	1.9	0.5	0.3	0.6	0.4	-0.7	1.2	1.4	1.0	0.9	0.6
Greece	14.8	14.4	11.2	9.8	7.4	6.8	5.2	3.0	3.4	2.7	3.7	3.6	3.3	3.4
Hungary	21.5	21.3	19.5	26.7	21.2	18.5	12.6	8.4	9.9	8.4	7.9	5.7	4.3	2.0
Iceland	3.5	1.8	2.6	3.0	2.5	2.9	5.0	3.2	3.6	8.6	5.6	0.5	2.4	2.9
Ireland	2.8	5.2	1.7	3.0	2.2	3.6	6.5	4.0	5.5	5.5	5.0	2.5	1.8	3.5
Italy	4.4	3.9	3.6	5.0	5.2	2.5	2.6	1.3	2.0	3.0	3.4	3.1	2.9	2.1
Japan	1.6	0.5	0.1	-0.5	-0.7	0.5	-0.1	-1.3	-1.7	-1.2	-1.6	-1.6	-1.2	-1.3
Korea	7.6	6.3	7.8	7.4	5.1	4.6	5.8	-0.1	0.7	3.5	2.8	2.7	2.7	-0.4
Luxembourg	3.7	6.0	3.5	2.3	3.0	-1.9	-0.4	5.3	2.0	0.1	2.7	4.9	1.7	4.7
Mexico	14.4	9.5	8.3	37.9	30.7	17.7	15.4	15.1	12.1	5.8	7.0	8.5	7.4	5.4
Netherlands	2.3	1.9	2.3	2.0	1.3	2.6	1.9	1.8	4.1	5.1	3.8	2.2	0.7	1.7
New Zealand	2.1	1.6	1.8	2.0	1.3	2.2	1.4	0.7	3.5	3.4	0.2	2.7	3.1	3.0
Norway	-0.6	2.3	-0.1	2.9	4.1	2.9	-0.7	6.6	15.9	1.1	-1.6	2.6	5.6	8.4
Poland	38.6	30.6	37.2	28.0	17.9	13.9	11.1	6.1	7.3	3.5	2.2	0.4	4.0	2.8
Portugal	11.4	7.4	7.3	3.4	2.6	3.8	3.7	3.3	3.0	3.7	3.9	2.7	3.1	2.6
Slovak Republic	..	15.4	13.4	9.9	5.4	5.8	4.6	6.3	8.3	5.0	4.6	4.7	6.0	2.3
Spain	6.7	4.5	3.9	4.9	3.5	2.4	2.5	2.6	3.5	4.2	4.3	4.1	4.0	4.1
Sweden	1.0	3.0	2.7	3.6	1.0	1.7	0.6	0.9	1.4	2.1	1.6	2.0	0.2	1.2
Switzerland	2.2	2.4	1.5	0.8	-0.1	-0.1	-0.3	0.7	0.8	0.6	1.6	1.2	0.6	-0.1
Turkey	63.7	67.8	106.5	87.2	77.8	81.5	75.7	55.6	49.9	54.8	44.1	22.5	9.9	5.4
United Kingdom	4.0	2.7	1.6	2.7	3.5	2.9	2.7	2.2	1.3	2.2	3.1	3.1	2.6	2.2
United States	2.3	2.3	2.1	2.0	1.9	1.7	1.1	1.4	2.2	2.4	1.8	2.1	2.8	3.0
Euro area	4.4	3.6	2.8	2.7	2.0	1.5	1.6	0.9	1.4	2.4	2.6	2.1	1.9	1.9
EU 15 total	4.1	3.3	2.5	2.7	2.2	1.7	1.7	1.2	1.4	2.4	2.6	2.3	2.0	1.9
OECD total	2.7	2.1	1.8	2.1	1.7	1.7	1.4	1.2	1.8	2.2	2.1	2.2	2.3	2.2
Brazil	..	..	..	..	..	..	..	..	8.4	7.4	10.2	15.0	8.2	7.2

StatLink http://dx.doi.org/10.1787/120883822882

GDP deflator
Average annual growth in percentage, 1992-2005

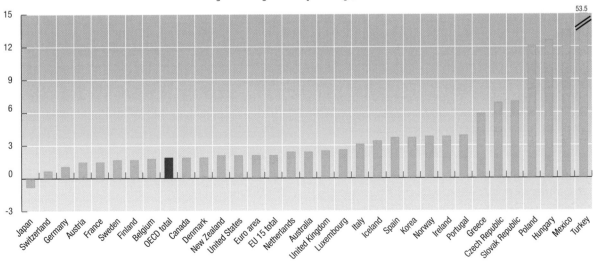

StatLink http://dx.doi.org/10.1787/462255827344

STEEL PRODUCTION

Steel is a core commodity in industrial societies. The OECD regularly monitors capacity, production, consumption, trade and employment in steel for its member countries as well as for all other major steel producing countries and areas.

The table omits production by minor steel producing countries (those with less than 2 million tonnes of production per year).

Definition

Steel production is here measured in tonnes of *steel mill product equivalents*. This is measured by crude steel production converted to ingot equivalent and then divided by a conversion factor (in most cases equal to 1.3) to account for losses between steel mill production and ingot production.

Comparability

The methodology and data sources are kept under continuous review by the OECD to ensure a high degree of comparability. However, the conversion from crude steel production to steel mill product equivalents uses standard conversion factors which, depending on the product mix, may not be accurate for all countries and at all periods. Small differences between countries may not be significant.

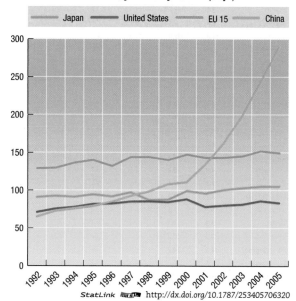

Steel production in selected countries
Million tonnes, product equivalent (Mtpe)

StatLink http://dx.doi.org/10.1787/253405706320

Long-term trends

Over the period shown, world steel production has grown at an average pace of 3.5% per year, more than two and a half times the rate of growth achieved by the OECD countries. Experience within the OECD has been mixed with falling production in the United Kingdom and Luxembourg, and strong growth in Korea, Mexico, Turkey and, from a low base, in Austria and Finland.

Among the non-OECD countries, steel production in China has been growing at an average of slightly more than 12% per year, more than 6% in India and over 3% in Brazil. In the Russian Federation, growth since 1993 has averaged only around 1% per annum, though production levels have been recovering well in the latter half of the period.

By the end of the period, China had extended its position as the world's largest steel producer. Its production in 2005 of 290 million tonnes was almost three times that of the second largest producing country, Japan. The next largest producers were the United States, Russian Federation, and Korea.

Source

• OECD (2006), *Iron and Steel Industry in 2004: 2006 Edition*, OECD, Paris.

Further information
Statistical publications

• OECD (2005), *Developments in Steelmaking Capacity of Non-OECD Economies, 2003 Edition*, OECD, Paris.

OECD FACTBOOK 2007 – ISBN 978-92-64-02946-0 – © OECD 2007

Steel production
Million tonnes, product equivalent (Mtpe)

	1992	1993	1994	1995	1996	1997	1998	1999	2000	2001	2002	2003	2004	2005
Australia	6.1	7.0	7.6	7.6	7.6	8.0	8.1	7.4	6.4	6.4	6.8	6.9	6.7	7.0
Austria	3.6	3.7	4.0	4.5	4.0	4.7	4.7	4.7	5.1	5.3	5.6	5.6	5.9	6.4
Belgium	9.3	9.1	10.2	10.4	9.7	9.7	10.3	9.9	10.5	9.7	10.2	10.0	10.6	10.6
Canada	11.8	12.3	11.9	12.4	12.6	13.3	13.6	13.9	14.2	13.1	13.7	13.7	14.0	14.2
Czech Republic	5.3	5.1	5.4	5.5	5.2	5.4	5.3	4.6	5.4	5.5	5.7	5.9	6.1	5.1
Finland	2.9	3.0	3.2	3.0	3.1	3.5	3.7	3.7	3.8	3.7	3.7	4.5	4.5	4.4
France	16.1	15.4	16.2	16.2	15.8	17.7	18.1	18.1	18.8	17.3	18.2	17.8	18.7	17.5
Germany	35.5	33.7	36.7	37.7	35.7	40.4	39.6	37.8	41.7	40.3	40.5	40.3	41.7	41.0
Italy	22.3	23.1	23.5	25.0	21.5	23.2	23.1	22.2	24.1	23.9	23.4	24.1	25.6	26.5
Japan	91.2	92.7	91.5	94.6	92.0	97.4	87.2	87.8	99.3	96.0	100.6	103.1	105.2	105.2
Korea	26.1	30.8	31.5	34.3	36.3	39.7	37.3	38.4	40.3	41.0	42.4	43.3	44.5	44.7
Luxembourg	2.5	2.7	2.5	2.2	2.1	2.3	2.2	2.3	2.3	2.5	2.5	2.4	2.4	2.5
Mexico	6.9	7.5	8.4	10.0	11.0	11.9	11.9	13.0	13.1	11.1	12.0	13.0	14.3	14.3
Netherlands	4.9	5.4	5.5	5.8	5.7	6.0	5.7	5.5	5.1	5.4	5.5	5.9	6.0	6.3
Poland	7.3	7.4	8.3	9.1	8.2	9.2	8.0	7.3	8.5	7.1	6.9	7.5	8.7	7.6
Slovak Republic	3.2	3.2	3.2	3.3	3.1	3.3	2.9	3.1	3.2	3.4	3.7	4.0	3.9	4.0
Spain	11.0	11.6	12.1	12.4	10.9	12.3	13.3	13.4	14.3	14.9	14.8	14.8	15.9	16.0
Sweden	3.9	4.1	4.5	4.5	4.4	4.6	4.6	4.6	4.7	5.0	5.2	5.2	5.4	5.2
Turkey	9.1	10.2	11.2	11.7	12.2	13.0	12.7	12.9	12.9	13.5	14.9	16.5	18.5	18.8
United Kingdom	14.3	14.7	15.3	15.6	16.0	16.5	15.5	14.6	13.6	12.2	10.5	12.0	12.4	11.9
United States	71.1	75.6	77.8	81.7	82.3	85.0	85.3	84.3	88.1	78.1	79.9	81.2	85.8	83.2
EU 15 total	128.5	129.1	135.9	139.6	131.5	143.5	143.6	139.7	147.0	142.7	142.9	144.8	143.6	149.0
OECD total	370.2	384.7	396.5	413.5	405.5	433.3	419.7	416.0	442.3	421.8	433.6	444.0	463.5	456.8
Brazil	20.3	21.3	21.8	21.4	21.8	22.7	22.6	22.2	24.8	23.8	26.5	27.8	29.4	29.5
China	65.5	73.0	76.2	79.3	85.1	92.7	98.8	108.3	111.1	134.3	162.8	198.5	243.5	290.0
India	14.3	15.0	15.9	18.2	19.9	20.4	19.7	20.4	22.6	22.9	24.1	26.6	27.3	32.3
Russian Federation	48.8	42.5	35.8	38.1	36.7	36.4	33.2	38.9	44.8	49.4	50.4	51.9	55.7	56.0
World	609.7	621.6	622.7	648.3	649.9	694.7	678.5	689.6	742.7	752.3	802.1	859.9	938.5	999.0

StatLink http://dx.doi.org/10.1787/307317253065

World steel production
Million tonnes, product equivalent (Mtpe)

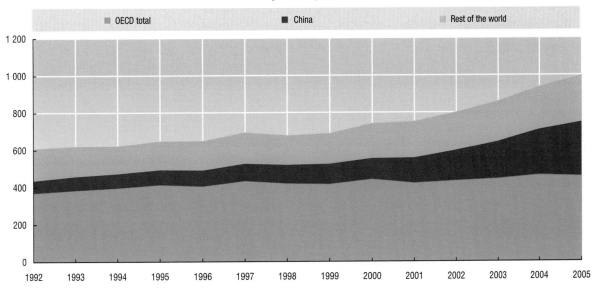

StatLink http://dx.doi.org/10.1787/412884154630

LABOUR PRODUCTIVITY

Productivity growth can be measured by relating changes in output to changes in one or more inputs to production. The most common productivity measure is labour productivity, which links changes in output to changes in labor input. It is a key economic indicator and is closely associated with standards of living.

Definition

GDP estimates are based on the 1993 *System of National Accounts*. Estimates of the hours actually worked reflect regular work hours of full-time and part-time workers, paid and unpaid overtime, hours worked in additional jobs and time not worked because of public holidays, annual paid leave, time spent on illness and maternity leave, strikes and labour disputes, bad weather, economic conditions and other reasons.

Comparability

National statisticians and the OECD work to ensure that the data on hours actually worked are as comparable as possible, but they are based on a range of different sources of varying reliability. In most countries, the data are taken from household labour force surveys, while the rest use establishment surveys, administrative sources or a combination of sources. One problem is that for several EU countries, the estimates are made by the OECD using results from the *Spring European Labor Force Survey*. The results reflect a single observation in the year, and the survey data have to be supplemented by information

from other sources for hours not worked due to public holidays and annual paid leave. Annual working hours reported for the remaining countries are provided by national statistical offices and are estimated using the best available sources. In general, the data are best used for comparisons of trends over time rather than for inter-country comparisons of level of productivity.

Although the GDP estimates are based on common definitions, the methods used by most countries to estimate value added in government services assume that labor productivity growth is zero. This means that countries with large government sectors or with government sectors that were growing during the period considered will, by assumption, have lower growth in GDP per hour worked than other countries.

Note that in the charts, EU15 excludes Austria and OECD excludes Austria, the Czech Republic, Hungary, Poland, the Slovak Republic and Turkey.

Sources

- *OECD Productivity Database, www.oecd.org/statistics/productivity.*
- OECD (2006), *National Accounts of OECD Countries*, OECD, Paris.

Further information

Analytical publications

- Ahmad, N., F. Lequiller, P. Marianna, D. Pilat, P. Schreyer and A. Wölfl (2003), *Comparing Labour Productivity Growth in the OECD Area: The Role of Measurement*, OECD Science, Technology and Industry Working Papers, No. 2003/14, OECD, Paris.

Methodological publications

- OECD (2001), "The Measurement of Productivity: What Do the Numbers Mean?", *Measuring Productivity – OECD Manual Measurement of Aggregate and Industry-level Productivity Growth*, OECD, Paris, Chapter 3, pp. 29-61.
- OECD (2006), "Clocking In (and Out): Several Facets of Working Time", *OECD Employment Outlook*, Chapter 1, see also Annex I.A1, OECD, Paris.
- Pilat, D. and P. Schreyer (2004), "The OECD Productivity Database – An Overview", *International Productivity Monitor*, No. 8, Spring, CSLS, Ottawa, pp. 59-65.
- Schreyer, P. and D. Pilat (2001), "Measuring Productivity", *OECD Economic Studies*, OECD, Paris.
- Van Ark, B. (2004), "The Measurement of Productivity: What Do the Numbers Mean?", *Fostering Productivity – Patterns, Determinants and Policy Implications*, G. Gelauff, L. Klomp, S. Raes and T. Roelandt (eds.), Elsevier, Amsterdam; Boston, Chapter 3, pp. 29-61.

Websites

- OECD Compendium of Productivity Indicators, *www.oecd.org/statistics/productivity.*

Long-term trends

Over the full period since 1992, Italy, Mexico and Spain have recorded the lowest growth rates in GDP per hour worked, while Ireland, Korea, and the four new OECD countries from Central Europe have been among the leaders. Australia, Canada, France, Germany, Japan, United Kingdom and the United States all had growth rates near to the OECD average.

The graph focuses on performance in the latest five years; it clearly shows that the Czech Republic, the Slovak Republic, Hungary and Korea had the fastest labor productivity growth over the period 2000-2005. In Italy, Mexico and Portugal, GDP per hour worked has actually declined and average annual growth in Italy, Mexico, the Netherlands, Portugal, Spain and Switzerland has been below 1%. Among the larger OECD countries, the United Kingdom, France, Japan and the United States all had growth rates near to the OECD average, while in Canada and Germany, GDP per hour worked grew at lower rates.

The estimates shown here are not adjusted for differences in the business cycle; cyclically adjusted estimates might show a somewhat different pattern.

GDP per hour worked
Annual growth in percentage

	1992	1993	1994	1995	1996	1997	1998	1999	2000	2001	2002	2003	2004	2005
Australia	3.4	2.5	0.0	0.8	4.5	3.4	3.4	2.5	-1.2	3.9	1.9	2.2	0.4	0.0
Austria	..	..	..	..	1.2	0.7	2.5	3.2	2.7	0.3	0.9	0.5	1.9	1.2
Belgium	1.4	2.3	3.7	1.0	0.9	1.6	1.0	2.4	1.9	-0.5	1.6	1.4	3.3	-0.5
Canada	2.0	1.0	1.9	1.4	0.2	4.1	1.8	2.5	2.9	1.0	1.5	0.3	0.4	2.1
Czech Republic	..	..	2.1	4.0	4.4	-1.0	0.8	4.8	4.1	6.7	0.9	4.9	3.8	6.8
Denmark	1.8	1.4	6.2	1.7	2.1	0.8	-0.4	0.8	2.1	-0.6	0.9	2.2	2.6	1.4
Finland	3.2	5.1	3.8	2.1	2.3	2.9	3.6	1.1	3.6	2.0	1.0	2.1	2.8	2.1
France	2.3	1.0	2.3	2.8	0.4	2.1	2.6	1.6	3.7	0.9	3.1	1.4	0.6	1.4
Germany	2.5	1.6	2.9	2.5	2.3	2.5	1.2	1.4	2.6	1.8	1.5	1.2	0.7	1.3
Greece	-2.1	-3.3	1.6	1.6	3.9	5.7	-0.6	1.2	3.9	5.0	3.6	3.3	4.9	2.7
Hungary	..	5.9	-1.9	4.6	2.0	3.1	3.4	0.0	4.1	6.1	3.3	3.5	5.8	4.2
Iceland	-4.3	3.3	3.4	-4.0	3.2	5.9	2.7	-2.4	1.4	4.1	2.3	3.2	8.2	3.0
Ireland	4.8	2.2	2.4	4.5	4.3	8.0	3.9	5.4	4.5	3.6	4.9	3.6	1.6	1.1
Italy	2.3	2.7	3.8	3.2	-0.2	2.2	-0.4	1.1	2.8	0.1	-0.2	-0.1	1.1	0.4
Japan	1.5	3.0	1.3	2.5	1.7	2.2	0.6	2.9	2.9	1.8	2.3	1.9	2.7	2.9
Korea	4.6	4.1	5.6	5.7	5.0	5.0	2.9	7.0	3.3	2.3	5.7	4.5	4.4	4.3
Luxembourg	0.1	2.5	2.3	-2.1	0.2	2.9	2.5	3.3	2.9	-1.9	1.3	1.5	4.2	1.0
Mexico	0.1	-1.6	-0.3	-9.0	-1.1	-0.7	4.0	0.3	7.0	1.4	-2.8	2.1	0.6	0.4
Netherlands	1.8	2.4	3.0	2.1	-2.2	1.6	2.1	3.5	0.3	-0.1	1.8	-0.4	2.7	0.7
New Zealand	0.4	1.3	1.3	0.1	0.7	1.7	0.8	2.8	0.9	2.1	1.7	1.5	-0.4	0.1
Norway	2.9	2.3	4.0	3.4	3.6	2.6	0.2	1.5	3.6	3.8	2.2	2.8	1.1	1.5
Poland	..	..	..	..	..	..	..	..	..	3.9	4.1	4.7	4.0	3.2
Portugal	4.4	0.4	1.8	1.8	4.6	4.3	2.2	1.3	4.2	-0.1	0.1	0.8	-0.7	0.9
Slovak Republic	..	..	..	4.1	5.8	6.1	6.5	3.6	3.7	3.3	7.5	5.2	3.4	4.4
Spain	2.8	2.3	2.9	0.8	1.0	0.3	-0.2	0.1	0.1	0.7	0.6	0.8	0.7	0.9
Sweden	2.2	2.3	2.3	2.0	1.7	3.3	2.2	1.8	3.2	0.5	3.3	3.1	2.8	2.1
Switzerland	0.9	0.8	0.5	1.7	2.2	2.6	0.9	-0.8	2.8	1.7	0.9	-0.7	0.0	2.8
United Kingdom	4.7	3.7	2.7	1.4	1.8	1.4	2.5	2.3	3.5	1.2	2.3	2.7	2.4	0.6
United States	3.2	0.3	1.0	0.1	2.4	1.6	2.0	2.5	2.3	2.0	2.9	3.0	2.7	1.8
EU 15 total	2.8	2.0	2.9	2.2	1.2	2.1	1.3	1.5	2.7	0.9	1.5	1.3	1.4	1.0
OECD total	2.4	1.4	1.7	1.1	1.5	1.9	2.2	2.2	2.7	1.6	1.8	2.2	2.0	1.7

StatLink http://dx.doi.org/10.1787/605448634334

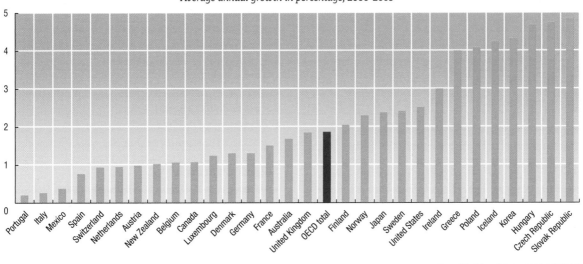

GDP per hour worked
Average annual growth in percentage, 2000-2005

StatLink http://dx.doi.org/10.1787/500470770341

MULTI-FACTOR PRODUCTIVITY

Growth accounting typically involves breaking down the growth of gross domestic product (GDP) into three components – the contribution of labour, the contribution of capital, and multi-factor productivity (MFP).

MFP is the change in GDP that cannot be explained by changes in the quantities of capital and labour that are made available to generate the GDP. MFP is sometimes described as disembodied technological progress, because it is the increase in GDP that is not embodied in either labour or capital. MFP comes from more efficient management of the processes of production through better ways of using labour and capital, through better ways of combining them, or through reducing the amount of intermediate goods and services needed to produce a given amount of output. Growth in MFP is a significant factor in explaining the long-term growth of real GDP.

Definition

The growth accounting framework, as applied here, decomposes annual growth in GDP into growth in labour and capital inputs and multi-factor productivity growth. The rate of growth of GDP is a weighted average of the rates of growth of capital and labour inputs. The weights attached to each input are the output elasticities for each factor of production. Since output elasticities cannot be directly observed, the factor shares of labour and capital are often used as weights. The rate of multi-factor productivity growth is the part of GDP growth which is not explained by the measured contribution of the factor inputs.

Comparability

The growth accounts for OECD countries are based on the OECD Productivity Database where the main problems of consistency of data sources and comparability across countries are addressed.

Output is measured as real GDP, compiled according to the 1993 System of National Accounts, although there may be some differences in how countries convert current price GDP to real GDP. Labour input is measured as total hours actually worked, and capital input is measured as the flow of capital services, based on an identical method for all countries.

Since MFP is obtained as a residual – i.e. that part of GDP growth that is left over when the growth of labour and capital inputs have been deducted – MFP necessarily contains any errors that may have been made in measuring GDP and labour and capital inputs. This is a particularly important issue as regards the measurement of capital inputs in the form of computers, software and communications equipment. To correct for differences in methods between countries, the OECD uses a standard method for these types of capital goods.

It must also be emphasised that the data used here relate to the total economy and therefore include the government sector. Measuring output and productivity for the government sector is difficult and statistical practices as well as the size of the government sector may vary between countries. This should be kept in mind when interpreting the present series.

Source
- OECD Productivity Database, www.oecd.org/statistics/ productivity.

Further information
Analytical publications
- OECD (2004), Understanding Economic Growth A Macro-level, Industry-level, and Firm-level Perspective, OECD, Paris.
- OECD (2003), The Sources of Economic Growth in OECD Countries, OECD, Paris.
- OECD (2005), OECD Science, Technology and Industry Scoreboard, OECD, Paris.

Methodological publications
- OECD (2001), Measuring Productivity – OECD Manual Measurement of Aggregate and Industry-level Productivity Growth, OECD, Paris.
- Schreyer, P., P.-E. Bignon and J. Dupont (2003), OECD Capital Services Estimates, OECD Statistics Working Papers, No. 2003/6, OECD, Paris.

Websites
- OECD Compendium of Productivity Indicators, www.oecd.org/statistics/productivity.

Long-term trends

Multi-factor productivity growth was one of the factors that helped strengthen growth in Greece, Japan, New Zealand, Sweden and the United States between the periods 1995-2000 and 2000-2005. In other countries, including Australia, Belgium, Canada, Finland, Germany, Ireland, the Netherlands and the United Kingdom, MFP growth slowed down from 1995-2000 to 2000-2005. Multi-factor productivity growth was positive during the period 1995-2000 and negative in the period 2000-2005 in Austria, Denmark, Italy and Portugal.

Multi-factor productivity

Annual growth in percentage

	1992	1993	1994	1995	1996	1997	1998	1999	2000	2001	2002	2003	2004	2005
Australia	3.5	1.1	0.7	1.3	3.6	2.3	2.7	1.0	-0.5	2.3	0.7	2.0	-0.4	..
Austria	..	..	..	..	0.9	0.4	2.0	2.5	2.0	-0.4	0.2	-	..	..
Belgium	0.6	1.0	3.0	0.8	0.4	1.3	0.4	1.8	1.4	-0.9	1.1	0.9	..	..
Canada	0.8	0.5	1.7	0.9	-0.3	3.0	1.1	1.8	2.1	-	0.9	-0.2	0.1	1.3
Denmark	1.2	0.4	5.2	1.0	1.3	0.2	-1.1	-0.1	1.1	-1.5	-0.4	0.7	..	..
Finland	0.7	3.2	3.8	2.3	2.7	3.2	3.5	1.5	3.7	2.0	1.0	2.0	..	..
France	1.4	-0.2	1.6	2.0	-0.1	1.5	1.9	1.0	2.8	0.2	1.9	0.8	0.4	0.8
Germany	1.5	0.3	2.2	1.7	1.3	1.7	0.7	0.8	1.9	0.9	0.6	0.5	0.6	0.9
Greece	-2.1	-3.5	1.1	1.1	2.7	4.3	-0.7	0.5	2.7	3.7	2.4	2.2	..	..
Ireland	4.2	2.0	2.5	4.6	4.1	7.6	3.4	4.7	3.7	2.9	4.0	2.7	..	..
Italy	1.2	1.5	3.0	2.5	-0.7	1.4	-0.8	0.3	1.9	-0.6	-1.0	-0.9	..	..
Japan	0.2	1.1	0.4	1.4	0.8	1.0	-0.9	1.2	2.1	0.7	1.3	1.5	2.3	..
Netherlands	1.0	1.4	2.4	1.7	-1.5	1.4	1.6	2.8	0.2	-0.4	0.9	-0.6	..	..
New Zealand	-0.1	2.7	0.6	-0.5	-	1.0	0.1	2.5	1.1	0.6	1.3	..	..	..
Portugal	..	..	..	..	3.5	3.3	1.4	0.5	3.0	-0.7	-0.5	-0.1	..	..
Spain	1.1	0.7	1.8	0.3	0.2	-0.1	-0.5	-0.4	-0.4	-0.1	-0.2	0.1	0.1	..
Sweden	0.7	0.5	2.0	1.5	0.7	2.2	1.4	1.2	2.3	-0.1	2.6	2.6	..	..
United Kingdom	2.5	2.5	2.3	0.9	1.1	0.9	1.4	1.4	2.6	0.6	1.4	1.9	..	..
United States	2.5	0.1	0.8	-0.3	1.7	1.0	1.1	1.5	1.3	0.8	2.1	2.3	2.4	1.5

StatLink http://dx.doi.org/10.1787/684571114544

Multi-factor productivity

Average annual growth in percentage, 1995-2000 and 2000-2005 (or closest comparable periods)

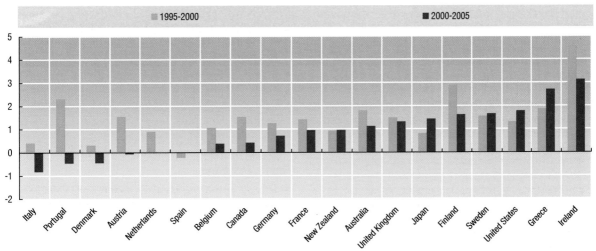

StatLink http://dx.doi.org/10.1787/713605483818

VALUE ADDED BY ACTIVITY

The contributions of primary, secondary and tertiary activities to total value added have changed sharply over recent decades. Agriculture, fishing and forestry are now relatively small in almost all OECD countries. The share of manufacturing has also fallen in most countries while services now account for well over 60% of total gross value added in most OECD countries.

Definition

Gross value added is defined as output minus intermediate consumption and equals the sum of employee compensation, gross operating surplus and taxes less subsidies on production and imports, except for next taxes on products. The shares of each sector are calculated by dividing the value added in each sector by total value added. Total gross value added is less than GDP because it excludes value-added tax (VAT) and similar product taxes.

Industry consists of mining and quarrying, manufacturing, and production and distribution of electricity, gas and water; trade consists of retail and wholesale trade and repair services; real estate covers rents for dwellings including the imputed rents of owner-occupiers; government includes public administration, law and order and defence.

Comparability

All OECD member countries except for Turkey follow the international 1993 *System of National Accounts*, so there is good comparability between countries as regards the definitions of value added and the coverage of the six sectors. However, the decline of industry and the rise of service activities are overstated to some extent because of the move in the last decade towards outsourcing by industrial enterprises of service activities that were previously carried out internally. For example, if cleaning and security services were earlier provided by employees of a manufacturing enterprise, their salaries would have formed part of value added by industry, but if these services are now purchased from specialised producers, the salaries of the employees will form part of the value added of "other business services". There will appear to have been a decline in the share of industry and a rise in the share of services although there may have been no change in the quantity of cleaning and security services actually produced.

Long-term trends

The share of agriculture has been declining throughout the period in almost all countries and, towards the end of the period, makes a significant contribution only in Iceland (fishing), New Zealand and Turkey. Shares in industry have also been falling throughout the period. Manufacturing is the most important activity within industry except in Norway, where oil and gas production are more important.

All service activities account for around 70% of total gross value added for the OECD countries as a whole, with very high shares in Denmark, France, Greece, Luxembourg and the United Kingdom and rather low shares in the Czech Republic, Korea, Norway and Turkey. It should be noted, however, that, in most countries, the largest part of service value added is goods-related and consists of trade, transport and business services purchased by industry. A high share of service value added does not necessarily mean that a country has become a service economy; the production, transport and distribution of goods remain the predominant activities in most OECD countries in terms of employment and value added.

Source

- OECD (2006), *National Accounts of OECD Countries*, OECD, Paris.

Further information

Analytical publications

- Lal, K. (2003), *Measurement of Output, Value Added, GDP in Canada and the United States*, OECD Statistics Working Papers, No. 2003/4, OECD, Paris.
- OECD (1996), *Services: Measuring Real Annual Value Added*, OECD, Paris.
- OECD (2002), *Measuring the Non-Observed Economy: A Handbook*, OECD, Paris.

Methodological publications

- OECD (2007), *Understanding National Accounts*, OECD, Paris.

Online databases

- *STAN: OECD Structural Analysis Statistics – online database.*

Websites

- OECD National Accounts Archive, *www.oecd.org/std/ national-accounts/papers*.
- OECD National Accounts, *www.oecd.org/std/national-accounts*.

Value added in agriculture and industry

As percentage of total value added

	Agriculture, hunting, forestry and fishing							Industry, including energy						
	1990	1995	2000	2002	2003	2004	2005	1990	1995	2000	2002	2003	2004	2005
Australia	3.6	3.8	4.0	3.3	3.5	3.3	3.1	23.4	22.4	20.7	20.1	19.3	19.8	21.0
Austria	4.0	2.7	2.1	2.0	1.9	1.9	1.6	24.9	22.5	23.0	22.6	22.3	22.1	22.1
Belgium	2.1	1.5	1.4	1.2	1.1	1.0	1.0	26.0	23.2	22.0	20.7	19.9	19.9	19.2
Czech Republic	8.7	5.0	3.9	3.3	3.1	3.3	2.9	34.9	31.7	31.6	30.5	29.5	30.9	31.6
Denmark	4.0	3.5	2.6	2.2	2.0	1.9	1.5	20.5	20.4	21.3	20.4	19.6	18.5	18.9
Finland	6.3	4.3	3.5	3.3	3.2	3.1	2.9	25.0	28.4	28.2	27.3	26.7	26.1	25.4
France	3.8	3.4	2.8	2.7	2.5	2.5	2.2	20.1	18.7	17.7	16.6	15.9	15.7	15.1
Germany	1.5	1.3	1.3	1.1	1.1	1.2	1.0	31.3	25.4	25.1	24.6	24.4	24.7	25.4
Greece	7.9	7.7	5.7	5.4	5.1	4.4	4.0	16.8	14.3	13.0	13.2	12.5	11.7	12.1
Hungary	..	8.5	5.4	4.7	4.3	4.8	4.3	..	25.8	27.3	24.6	25.1	25.4	25.3
Iceland	11.2	11.0	8.6	9.0	7.5	6.7	..	20.5	20.3	17.2	17.4	16.7	16.4	..
Ireland	8.9	7.0	3.4	2.6	2.5	2.5	2.1	29.6	32.6	35.0	34.2	30.1	28.0	26.1
Italy	3.5	3.3	2.8	2.6	2.5	2.5	2.3	25.9	25.0	23.4	22.4	21.4	21.4	20.8
Japan	2.5	1.9	1.7	1.6	1.6	1.6	..	28.9	25.2	24.0	22.5	22.7	22.8	..
Korea	8.9	6.3	4.9	4.1	3.8	3.8	3.3	30.2	30.3	32.4	29.9	29.4	31.3	31.1
Luxembourg	1.5	1.0	0.7	0.6	0.6	0.5	0.4	22.3	15.3	12.6	11.7	11.2	10.9	10.4
Mexico	7.8	5.2	4.0	3.8	3.8	3.8	..	24.2	22.6	22.6	21.1	20.3	20.6	..
Netherlands	4.3	3.5	2.6	2.3	2.3	2.2	2.2	23.5	21.9	19.3	18.4	18.3	18.5	18.7
New Zealand	6.7	7.2	8.6	7.0	..	..	..	22.7	21.8	20.1	19.3	..	..	..
Norway	3.4	3.0	2.1	1.7	1.5	1.5	1.6	29.3	29.6	37.7	32.8	33.0	34.8	37.9
Poland	..	8.0	5.0	4.5	4.4	5.1	4.8	..	28.4	24.0	22.4	23.7	25.4	24.8
Portugal	9.0	5.7	3.8	3.3	3.4	3.3	2.8	22.6	22.0	20.0	19.2	18.7	18.5	18.3
Slovak Republic	..	5.9	4.5	5.1	4.5	4.5	4.3	..	32.7	29.2	26.6	29.0	29.0	28.9
Spain	5.5	4.5	4.4	4.0	4.0	3.8	3.3	24.4	21.9	20.9	19.5	18.9	18.3	17.7
Sweden	3.3	2.7	1.9	1.8	1.8	1.8	1.2	23.8	25.9	24.6	23.1	22.7	23.1	23.4
Switzerland	2.8	2.0	1.5	1.3	1.2	1.3	1.2	23.2	23.3	21.5	21.4	20.9	20.9	21.0
Turkey	17.6	15.7	14.2	11.7	11.9	11.5	10.5	25.8	26.4	23.5	25.5	25.1	25.3	25.9
United Kingdom	1.8	1.8	1.0	0.9	1.0	0.9	0.9	27.3	25.7	21.9	19.0	17.7	17.0	17.4
United States	2.1	1.6	1.2	1.0	1.2	1.3	..	23.5	22.2	19.4	17.5	17.3	17.0	..

StatLink http://dx.doi.org/10.1787/427805243352

Value added in industry

As a percentage of total value added, 2005 or latest available year

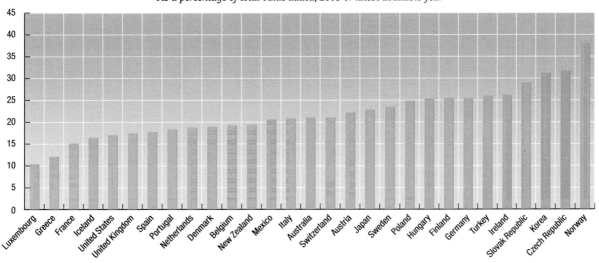

StatLink http://dx.doi.org/10.1787/323641537474

VALUE ADDED BY ACTIVITY

Value added in construction and in transport, trade, hotels and restaurants
As percentage of total value added

	Construction							Transport, trade, hotels and restaurants						
	1990	1995	2000	2002	2003	2004	2005	1990	1995	2000	2002	2003	2004	2005
Australia	6.8	6.0	5.4	6.3	6.8	6.9	7.0	22.8	23.5	22.1	22.3	22.3	22.0	21.0
Austria	6.9	7.8	7.9	7.5	7.8	7.6	7.6	25.7	24.2	24.4	24.9	24.9	24.7	24.4
Belgium	5.4	5.1	5.0	4.8	4.8	4.9	4.8	22.5	21.9	21.1	22.0	22.8	22.9	23.1
Czech Republic	8.2	6.6	6.5	6.2	6.4	6.5	6.6	16.8	24.4	25.8	26.8	26.7	25.3	24.7
Denmark	5.1	4.7	5.5	5.1	5.2	5.5	5.6	21.9	22.3	21.8	21.8	22.0	22.2	22.5
Finland	8.3	4.4	5.5	5.2	5.3	5.4	5.9	21.8	20.8	21.5	22.6	22.9	22.9	22.5
France	6.5	5.9	5.2	5.3	5.3	5.6	5.8	20.0	19.3	18.9	19.5	19.7	19.4	19.3
Germany	6.1	6.8	5.2	4.6	4.4	4.1	3.9	17.4	18.0	18.2	18.0	17.7	17.9	18.1
Greece	8.3	7.0	8.2	8.4	9.1	8.7	7.3	26.4	27.7	30.0	29.9	29.9	31.7	32.1
Hungary	..	4.5	5.1	5.2	4.8	4.9	4.8	..	21.9	20.7	21.4	21.0	20.7	20.1
Iceland	9.6	7.9	8.4	7.2	8.1	8.3	..	22.4	23.1	22.0	20.5	20.5	20.2	..
Ireland	5.4	5.3	7.5	7.9	8.4	8.9	10.0	20.5	17.3	17.8	17.0	17.9	17.9	17.2
Italy	6.2	5.3	5.0	5.4	5.6	5.9	6.0	23.5	24.2	23.9	23.9	23.4	23.1	23.2
Japan	9.6	8.0	7.1	6.5	6.5	6.2	..	19.6	21.8	20.2	19.9	19.6	19.7	..
Korea	11.3	11.6	8.4	8.6	9.6	9.3	9.2	20.2	18.2	18.2	18.3	17.8	17.1	17.1
Luxembourg	7.1	6.5	5.7	6.7	6.5	6.3	5.8	23.6	21.3	21.8	22.5	21.8	22.3	21.8
Mexico	3.9	3.9	5.1	5.0	5.2	5.4	..	33.4	29.4	32.2	30.3	30.3	30.9	..
Netherlands	6.0	5.4	5.6	5.7	5.5	5.5	5.5	21.8	21.7	23.1	23.2	22.6	22.3	21.6
New Zealand	4.1	4.1	4.3	4.6	..	..	..	24.5	24.6	22.1	23.1	..	..	..
Norway	4.6	4.5	4.1	4.5	4.4	4.4	4.4	23.3	22.2	18.7	19.7	19.0	18.3	17.2
Poland	..	6.7	7.7	6.3	5.9	5.6	5.8	..	25.7	27.3	28.5	27.7	27.2	27.3
Portugal	5.7	6.3	7.6	7.6	6.7	6.5	6.3	24.9	24.3	24.1	24.5	24.5	24.5	24.6
Slovak Republic	..	5.1	7.1	7.2	6.1	6.3	6.8	..	24.6	25.1	24.3	25.1	25.1	26.1
Spain	8.6	7.5	8.3	9.4	10.0	10.7	11.6	25.1	26.9	26.1	26.1	25.8	25.7	25.5
Sweden	6.7	4.4	4.0	4.4	4.3	4.5	4.8	20.1	19.9	19.7	19.5	19.5	19.4	19.7
Switzerland	8.1	6.6	5.3	5.4	5.5	5.4	5.5	23.6	22.3	21.2	21.6	21.7	21.8	21.6
Turkey	6.4	5.5	5.2	4.1	3.6	3.6	4.5	31.2	33.2	34.4	35.5	35.4	35.7	35.9
United Kingdom	6.7	5.0	5.3	5.7	5.8	5.9	5.8	21.6	21.4	22.8	22.2	22.1	21.9	21.6
United States	4.6	4.2	4.7	4.9	4.9	5.0	..	21.9	22.2	19.7	19.5	19.3	19.3	..

StatLink ⬛🔗 http://dx.doi.org/10.1787/054322562783

Value added in transport, trade, hotels and restaurants
As a percentage of total value added, 2005 or latest available year

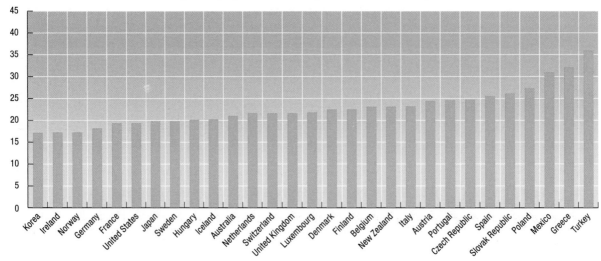

StatLink ⬛🔗 http://dx.doi.org/10.1787/041555100574

OECD FACTBOOK 2007 – ISBN 978-92-64-02946-0 – © OECD 2007

Value added in business services and in government and personal services

As percentage of total value added

	Banks, insurance, real estate and other business services							Government, health, education and other and personal services						
	1990	1995	2000	2002	2003	2004	2005	1990	1995	2000	2002	2003	2004	2005
Australia	25.2	25.9	29.3	29.2	29.2	29.0	28.7	18.3	18.5	18.5	18.8	18.9	18.9	19.2
Austria	17.7	19.9	21.7	22.2	22.3	23.0	23.4	20.8	22.8	20.9	20.8	20.8	20.6	20.8
Belgium	22.6	25.6	27.8	28.1	27.7	27.8	28.1	21.5	22.7	22.6	23.3	23.6	23.6	23.7
Czech Republic	16.9	16.8	16.2	16.1	16.7	16.6	17.1	13.4	15.5	16.0	17.0	17.6	17.5	17.0
Denmark	21.5	22.2	22.3	23.2	23.6	24.0	24.0	27.0	26.9	26.4	27.3	27.6	27.8	27.5
Finland	16.2	18.8	20.5	20.4	20.0	20.6	21.0	22.3	23.2	20.8	21.2	22.0	22.0	22.4
France	27.2	28.2	30.7	30.7	31.1	31.4	32.0	22.7	25.1	24.7	25.2	25.5	25.5	25.6
Germany	23.0	26.4	27.5	28.6	29.2	29.2	29.2	20.8	22.2	22.8	23.1	23.1	22.7	22.4
Greece	16.9	20.6	20.9	19.4	19.5	18.9	19.4	20.6	21.7	22.2	23.7	23.8	24.7	25.0
Hungary	..	18.8	20.0	21.2	20.9	20.8	22.0	..	21.2	21.5	23.0	24.0	23.3	23.5
Iceland	16.6	16.1	20.0	21.4	22.1	23.3	..	19.9	21.6	23.8	24.6	25.1	25.2	..
Ireland	16.3	17.3	20.5	21.3	23.4	23.9	25.2	19.2	20.3	15.8	17.0	17.6	18.8	19.5
Italy	20.1	22.4	24.7	25.6	26.5	26.6	26.9	20.7	19.8	20.1	20.2	20.5	20.5	20.8
Japan	20.3	22.7	25.0	26.4	26.5	26.3	..	19.3	20.5	22.1	23.1	23.2	23.3	..
Korea	14.9	18.3	20.1	21.9	21.6	20.6	20.9	14.4	15.3	16.1	17.3	17.8	17.8	18.3
Luxembourg	28.5	39.2	43.8	41.7	43.0	42.1	44.2	17.3	16.7	15.4	16.8	17.0	17.8	17.4
Mexico	13.1	17.4	12.0	13.2	13.0	12.8	..	17.6	21.5	24.1	26.6	27.3	26.5	..
Netherlands	20.8	24.2	27.3	26.6	26.6	26.9	27.4	23.5	23.2	22.1	23.8	24.5	24.7	24.6
New Zealand	25.4	25.8	27.1	28.1	..	..	..	16.6	16.5	17.7	17.9	..	..	..
Norway	18.3	18.2	17.5	19.0	19.4	19.0	18.3	21.1	22.5	19.9	22.3	22.6	21.9	20.7
Poland	..	12.6	18.1	18.3	18.1	17.5	17.7	..	18.6	18.0	19.9	20.2	19.3	19.6
Portugal	20.3	19.9	20.6	20.5	20.9	20.7	20.8	18.2	21.7	24.0	25.0	25.8	26.6	27.2
Slovak Republic	..	17.5	17.1	19.4	18.0	19.4	18.6	..	14.3	17.0	17.4	17.4	15.7	15.3
Spain	17.2	17.9	19.5	20.5	20.6	20.7	21.1	19.1	21.3	20.8	20.5	20.7	20.8	20.9
Sweden	19.6	22.0	24.0	24.0	23.7	23.6	23.4	26.7	25.0	25.8	27.3	27.9	27.6	27.4
Switzerland	18.3	19.9	25.2	24.2	24.2	24.1	24.5	23.9	26.1	25.2	26.1	26.5	26.5	26.2
Turkey	6.6	7.4	8.5	8.9	9.2	9.5	9.2	12.4	11.9	14.2	14.3	14.9	14.4	14.2
United Kingdom	21.9	24.5	27.5	30.0	30.9	31.5	31.7	20.6	21.5	21.5	22.2	22.5	22.7	22.6
United States	24.8	26.3	31.6	32.1	32.2	32.4	..	23.2	23.4	23.2	24.9	25.2	24.9	..

StatLink http://dx.doi.org/10.1787/886238075566

Value added in banks, insurance, real estate and other business services

As a percentage of total value added, 2005 or latest available year

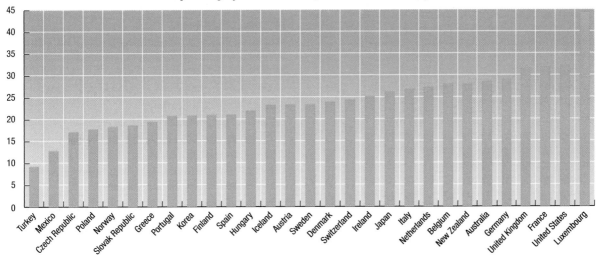

StatLink http://dx.doi.org/584231132887

EVOLUTION OF VALUE ADDED BY ACTIVITY

While total GDP has been growing in all OECD countries in most years since 1990, that growth is not evenly spread over all the different kinds of economic activities. Some economic activities have grown faster than others and some have tended to decline in importance. A convenient way to show how the patterns of growth are changing is to divide the economy into primary, secondary and tertiary sectors – agriculture, industry and services, respectively.

Definition

Gross value added is defined as output minus intermediate consumption and equals employee compensation, net operating surplus and depreciation of capital assets. The growth rates shown here refer to volume estimates of gross value added.

Industry consists of mining and quarrying; manufacturing; production and distribution of electricity, gas and water; and construction. Services consists of retail and wholesale trade; transport and communications; real estate, finance, insurance and business services; education, health and other personal services; public administration; and defence.

Comparability

All OECD member countries except for Turkey follow the international *System of National Accounts*, so there is good comparability between countries as regards the definitions and coverage. However, the decline of industry and the rise of service activities are overstated to some extent because of the move in the last decade towards outsourcing of service activities that were previously carried out internally within industrial enterprises. For example, if cleaning and security services were earlier provided by employees of a manufacturing enterprise, their salaries would have formed part of value added by industry but if these services are now purchased from specialized producers, the salaries of the employees will form part of the value added of the service sector. No change in the quantity of cleaning and security services produced may have occurred.

Long-term trends

For OECD countries as a whole, agriculture has been growing by about 1% per year since 1992, industry by 2.6% per year and services by 3% per year.

Annual growth in agriculture is generally very uneven, with changes from year to year of 10% or more being quite common. Growth in industry is somewhat smoother in most countries, while year-to-year growth in services tends to be very smooth in all countries, one reason being that services include government services.

The graphs show growth rates averaged over the three latest years for which data are available. Over this recent period, agriculture declined in nine countries – most pronounced in Portugal, Luxembourg, Spain, France, Finland and Greece. Industry grew in most countries, although there were declines in Portugal, Italy, the Netherlands and Denmark. The service sector, however, grew in all countries with particularly sharp increases in Turkey, Greece, New Zealand and Iceland.

Source
- OECD (2006), *National Accounts of OECD Countries*, OECD, Paris.

Further information
Analytical publications
- OECD (2007), *OECD Economic Outlook: December No. 80 – Volume 2006 Issue 2*, OECD, Paris.

Statistical publications
- Maddison, Angus (2003), *The World Economy: Historical Perspectives*, OECD, Paris, also available on CD-ROM, *www.theworldeconomy.org*.
- OECD (2006), *Quaterly National Accounts*, OECD, Paris.

Methodological publications
- OECD (2007), *Understanding National Accounts*, OECD, Paris.
- OECD (2000), *OECD Glossaries, System of National Accounts, 1993 – Glossary*, OECD, Paris.
- UN, OECD, IMF, Eurostat (eds.) (1993), *System of National Accounts 1993*, United Nations, Geneva.

Online databases
- STAN: OECD Structural Analysis Statistics – online database.

Websites
- OECD National Accounts, *www.oecd.org/std/national-accounts*.

Real value added in agriculture, forestry and fishing

Annual growth in percentage

	1992	1993	1994	1995	1996	1997	1998	1999	2000	2001	2002	2003	2004	2005
Australia	6.4	3.4	-16.9	23.2	7.5	-0.5	10.2	5.2	4.0	3.2	-23.5	31.4	-0.7	3.7
Austria	-0.8	-1.0	5.6	-1.1	-0.1	3.7	6.4	3.7	-3.0	0.3	-3.1	-1.8	6.0	-2.7
Belgium	16.4	6.2	-6.8	2.2	-0.3	2.8	3.5	6.3	0.9	-11.9	13.6	-16.4	10.8	7.8
Czech Republic	-21.0	51.7	-17.3	-4.9	-3.1	-13.4	6.1	5.3	4.1	-2.8	3.4	3.8	7.1	3.0
Denmark	2.1	23.5	3.7	5.2	2.2	2.1	2.4	-3.5	8.3	3.8	-3.7	0.4	-0.6	2.3
Finland	-5.2	5.0	-2.2	-3.8	-2.9	8.9	-9.0	-1.3	8.7	1.9	2.0	-7.0	1.6	0.7
France	10.0	-4.7	1.5	3.6	5.1	1.7	1.7	3.7	-1.4	-2.8	5.0	-15.3	21.1	-11.2
Germany	-3.2	-1.6	-9.4	5.2	4.0	3.4	-6.0	12.7	-0.4	3.8	-7.0	-4.8	21.0	-4.0
Greece	-2.9	-1.4	5.9	-4.0	-3.3	0.4	2.3	3.5	-3.7	-2.8	-5.0	-6.6	4.5	-2.5
Hungary	-16.5	-7.9	-0.4	2.7	4.2	-0.2	-1.4	0.9	-7.4	16.5	-9.8	-0.7	54.4	-2.4
Iceland	-	5.8	-4.8	-0.7	3.8	-0.6	-3.8	-2.9	-2.0	1.5	2.6	-3.1	3.8	..
Italy	2.8	-0.6	1.3	1.5	1.5	2.8	2.4	6.0	-2.3	-2.5	-3.1	-4.9	13.5	-2.3
Japan	2.7	-9.1	2.4	-6.0	2.4	-2.9	-0.1	-1.3	9.8	-2.4	6.0	-5.8	-2.2	..
Korea	9.3	-6.0	0.4	5.3	2.3	4.6	-6.4	5.9	1.2	1.1	-3.5	-5.3	9.2	-0.1
Luxembourg	37.6	2.9	-5.8	9.4	-3.2	-16.3	15.2	14.4	-13.0	-14.3	6.0	-12.0	-5.7	8.3
Mexico	-1.0	3.1	0.2	1.8	3.8	0.2	3.0	1.5	0.4	5.9	-0.9	3.8	3.2	..
Netherlands	3.1	2.7	3.8	2.0	-2.4	7.4	-5.6	5.8	2.1	-4.5	-1.5	4.1	6.0	1.1
New Zealand	-12.0	16.9	0.6	7.4	7.7	0.7	-4.2	4.4	2.5	1.6	-0.6	0.9	-0.4	..
Norway	-5.0	14.6	2.8	6.5	-0.8	-1.4	2.3	-0.7	-1.7	-3.7	7.9	0.7	2.4	1.2
Poland	..	6.0	-14.9	10.2	1.7	0.2	3.6	-0.5	-4.1	6.6	1.0	2.7	6.0	-0.6
Portugal	3.7	2.3	-2.1	-1.1	4.8	-8.1	-3.2	4.6	-4.2	-3.2	2.4	-3.1	0.8	-7.9
Slovak Republic	..	..	8.1	-3.6	-2.4	10.0	5.4	0.3	1.9	12.6	16.7	0.7	-0.1	8.1
Spain	1.0	2.8	-4.7	-6.1	20.6	7.1	3.1	-1.0	2.4	-2.0	0.4	-0.7	1.9	-10.0
Sweden	-1.8	1.1	-3.4	0.1	-0.8	1.6	-5.4	2.1	2.4	4.4	2.8	-0.1	7.7	-6.4
Switzerland	-	-5.3	-6.3	2.1	-2.1	-5.3	2.3	-4.2	7.2	-8.0	-0.7	-8.5	10.1	-2.1
Turkey	4.3	-1.3	-0.7	2.0	4.4	-2.3	8.4	-5.0	3.9	-6.5	6.9	-2.5	2.0	5.6
United Kingdom	4.2	-8.1	-1.2	-1.3	-3.3	3.4	2.2	3.3	-0.8	-9.4	12.3	-2.1	-1.0	2.3
United States	8.4	-3.0	6.0	-10.0	5.8	10.3	4.7	11.7	12.7	-7.5	-2.9	10.3	-1.7	..

StatLink 🔢 http://dx.doi.org/10.1787/777584321017

Real value added in agriculture, forestry and fishing

Annual growth in percentage averaged over the latest three years available

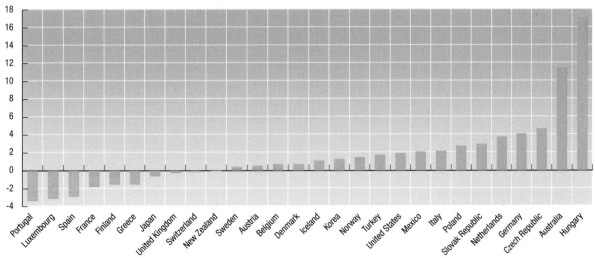

StatLink 🔢 http://dx.doi.org/10.1787/313340544800

EVOLUTION OF VALUE ADDED BY ACTIVITY

Real value added in industry
Annual growth in percentage

	1992	1993	1994	1995	1996	1997	1998	1999	2000	2001	2002	2003	2004	2005
Australia	2.6	4.2	3.7	2.7	1.8	4.6	3.1	3.0	-0.6	3.4	5.3	1.4	1.6	1.6
Austria	0.6	-0.4	4.0	3.1	2.3	2.8	3.9	4.3	5.0	1.3	1.0	1.3	2.4	2.1
Belgium	-0.9	-3.9	3.4	3.4	1.2	6.3	0.1	0.9	5.2	-0.1	-0.2	-0.6	2.9	-0.1
Czech Republic	6.8	-11.7	4.0	10.2	10.8	-5.0	-5.1	2.2	7.1	-1.8	2.8	-0.5	8.3	13.7
Denmark	1.4	-5.0	8.1	5.5	-0.5	5.2	1.9	2.9	3.3	-1.6	-1.9	-1.7	-	0.9
Finland	-2.4	0.8	6.7	2.8	5.4	8.9	8.2	5.5	9.6	3.6	3.0	2.6	4.2	3.7
France	1.2	-5.9	2.9	3.4	-1.0	-0.3	3.9	2.8	5.0	2.4	0.1	1.2	1.9	1.7
Germany	-0.4	-6.2	3.2	-1.0	-2.4	2.4	0.5	0.8	4.5	-0.1	-1.8	-0.2	2.2	2.0
Greece	-1.5	-2.2	-0.3	0.2	2.1	-0.9	7.6	2.3	5.5	9.5	2.0	6.5	-2.9	-1.9
Hungary	-5.2	1.4	5.7	5.7	1.3	10.8	7.5	6.7	8.2	1.2	3.6	4.1	3.9	3.9
Iceland	-4.1	-1.6	1.0	-0.6	6.8	6.5	3.4	4.2	7.6	2.6	-3.9	4.5	8.0	..
Italy	-0.3	-3.2	4.2	3.8	-0.6	0.7	0.2	0.3	2.5	0.7	-0.2	-1.3	1.6	-1.7
Japan	-1.9	-2.6	-2.3	0.7	3.2	1.5	-5.0	-0.1	2.9	-4.3	-2.1	3.3	2.9	..
Korea	2.6	6.6	9.5	9.8	7.2	4.5	-8.2	12.2	11.7	3.1	6.4	6.1	8.8	5.7
Luxembourg	0.4	4.9	3.7	2.2	-0.4	5.1	5.0	7.0	6.0	-0.1	5.0	1.2	3.9	-0.7
Mexico	4.4	0.3	4.8	-7.8	10.1	9.3	6.3	4.7	6.1	-3.5	-0.1	-0.2	4.2	..
Netherlands	-1.0	-1.4	3.9	2.0	1.6	0.1	2.2	3.6	4.9	1.2	-	-2.3	1.6	-0.6
New Zealand	1.7	7.0	6.2	2.8	3.5	0.2	-3.6	5.6	0.7	1.5	7.8	2.6	3.0	..
Norway	5.8	0.9	8.4	6.1	4.8	5.2	-1.6	-1.3	3.1	1.0	0.1	-0.1	2.2	0.5
Poland	..	4.9	7.8	9.2	6.4	10.4	4.8	3.0	4.6	-2.4	-2.4	5.5	9.7	4.4
Portugal	-1.7	-2.8	3.5	6.1	6.8	6.7	4.1	0.7	3.8	2.1	-1.5	-3.3	0.4	-1.8
Slovak Republic	..	..	8.2	5.0	16.3	-5.8	-2.1	-3.4	0.8	2.8	5.5	15.2	4.1	6.9
Spain	-2.1	-4.4	1.6	4.2	1.6	4.7	5.3	5.9	4.7	4.8	1.8	2.5	2.1	2.3
Sweden	-4.3	-1.4	9.5	10.0	1.9	4.8	5.6	7.2	7.0	-0.6	3.8	1.9	9.6	4.1
Switzerland	0.1	-1.0	3.3	-0.2	-1.9	1.0	1.7	0.1	0.8	2.7	0.8	-0.3	1.0	2.5
Turkey	6.0	8.1	-5.0	8.7	6.9	9.5	1.8	-6.2	5.8	-7.2	7.1	5.5	8.8	8.2
United Kingdom	-0.7	1.4	5.1	1.5	1.7	1.7	1.1	1.1	1.6	-0.6	-0.7	0.9	1.6	-0.9
United States	0.8	3.1	6.7	5.2	2.8	4.1	4.1	4.8	4.0	-4.1	0.8	1.6	4.3	..

StatLink ⋯ http://dx.doi.org/10.1787/338652536206

Real value added in industry
Annual growth in percentage averaged over the latest three years available

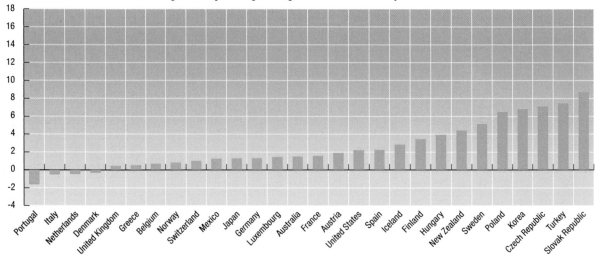

StatLink ⋯ http://dx.doi.org/10.1787/337260400701

OECD FACTBOOK 2007 – ISBN 978-92-64-02946-0 – © OECD 2007

EVOLUTION OF VALUE ADDED BY ACTIVITY

Real value added in services
Annual growth in percentage

	1992	1993	1994	1995	1996	1997	1998	1999	2000	2001	2002	2003	2004	2005
Australia	3.8	3.6	5.7	3.9	4.7	4.2	5.8	4.4	3.5	3.8	3.6	3.9	3.2	3.5
Austria	4.0	0.9	2.1	2.0	2.2	1.4	3.8	2.3	3.5	0.7	0.7	1.3	2.5	2.3
Belgium	1.8	-0.4	2.7	2.9	0.6	1.9	2.5	3.4	3.3	2.5	1.8	2.0	1.4	1.8
Czech Republic	-3.5	8.5	3.3	2.5	-0.7	1.5	2.1	0.3	1.5	5.7	2.4	5.0	1.4	3.1
Denmark	1.8	1.5	3.6	2.2	3.4	2.3	1.9	3.0	4.6	1.5	1.3	1.4	1.8	3.2
Finland	-4.0	-1.7	2.6	4.6	3.6	4.5	4.2	3.5	3.3	2.5	0.4	0.5	3.3	2.6
France	1.6	0.9	1.2	0.4	1.5	1.9	2.8	2.9	3.7	1.7	1.1	1.5	2.1	1.4
Germany	4.0	1.9	2.2	3.7	3.1	1.6	2.9	2.2	3.4	2.1	1.3	-	1.1	0.8
Greece	2.5	0.8	0.8	3.9	2.4	5.0	3.0	1.9	4.9	3.1	5.1	5.3	5.9	5.2
Hungary	-2.6	1.5	4.5	-3.3	2.4	2.5	3.8	3.2	4.0	4.2	5.3	4.1	2.7	5.0
Iceland	-1.0	0.4	3.7	2.7	5.7	5.1	9.6	7.6	6.9	4.3	0.7	4.2	7.4	..
Italy	1.1	0.7	1.3	2.2	1.2	2.1	1.7	2.2	4.3	2.4	1.0	0.3	0.8	0.8
Japan	3.1	2.5	2.6	3.2	3.0	2.3	0.8	0.9	0.6	2.1	1.7	1.1	1.4	..
Korea	7.1	6.8	7.7	8.1	6.2	5.1	-3.9	6.6	6.1	4.8	7.8	1.6	1.9	3.0
Luxembourg	4.4	5.6	5.0	2.5	2.0	5.4	6.4	8.2	8.1	4.2	3.5	1.0	3.1	4.9
Mexico	3.9	2.8	4.9	-6.4	3.0	6.6	4.7	3.6	7.3	1.2	1.6	2.1	4.4	..
Netherlands	1.8	1.6	1.7	3.3	3.8	5.6	4.7	4.8	3.7	2.3	0.3	1.3	2.1	2.3
New Zealand	2.5	4.9	5.1	4.5	3.3	2.5	2.4	5.0	2.9	5.2	4.2	4.0	4.5	..
Norway	3.4	2.5	3.9	3.4	5.2	5.8	4.2	4.3	3.3	4.1	0.8	1.6	3.4	3.5
Poland	..	0.6	4.7	4.5	5.6	5.1	5.0	5.4	4.2	2.6	3.0	2.8	3.1	2.9
Portugal	3.5	-0.1	-2.4	3.1	2.1	3.9	4.3	4.4	4.4	2.9	1.6	0.4	1.6	0.9
Slovak Republic	..	..	-1.6	6.3	1.5	12.5	5.7	1.3	2.8	5.5	1.0	-1.7	4.0	3.0
Spain	1.0	-0.5	2.0	2.6	1.4	2.9	3.8	4.3	5.1	3.6	3.0	2.9	3.6	4.4
Sweden	-1.7	0.2	1.8	2.4	1.4	1.4	3.0	3.4	3.9	1.4	1.2	1.7	2.5	2.6
Switzerland	0.3	-0.3	-0.3	0.5	1.8	2.4	4.1	0.8	4.8	0.2	0.4	-0.4	1.6	2.5
Turkey	5.6	8.4	-3.7	7.1	6.5	7.9	3.1	-3.0	7.2	-6.2	6.7	6.1	8.5	6.4
United Kingdom	0.4	2.9	4.6	3.4	3.8	4.1	4.8	3.9	5.0	3.6	2.6	3.7	4.4	3.3
United States	2.3	1.8	2.5	2.8	4.0	5.0	5.3	4.4	3.5	2.6	1.5	2.9	4.4	..

StatLink http://dx.doi.org/10.1787/121808307121

Real value added in services
Annual growth in percentage averaged over the latest three years available

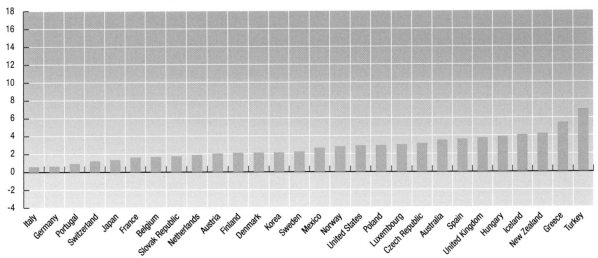

StatLink http://dx.doi.org/10.1787/688722080005

SMALL AND MEDIUM-SIZED ENTERPRISES

Statistics showing the distribution of enterprises by size class are important in illustrating the potential contribution of small enterprises to economic growth. Of particular relevance in the context of the tables presented below is that small firms are often the most dynamic and innovative, reflecting the fact that many of them are recent start-ups. Note, however, that because they are not longitudinal, the data do not show the contribution that small enterprises make to economic and employment growth over time as they move from the start-up phase to some optimal size. Many studies have used longitudinal datasets to establish their important contribution in this context.

Definition

An *enterprise* is a legal entity possessing the right to conduct business on its own; for example to enter into contracts, own property, incur liabilities for debts, and establish bank accounts. It may consist of one or more local units or establishments corresponding to production units situated in a geographically separate place and in which one or more persons work for the enterprise to which they belong.

The *number of employees* includes all persons, workers and employees, covered by a contractual arrangement and working in the enterprise and who receive compensation for their work, whether full-time or part-time. In particular, the following are considered as employees: salaried managers, students who have a formal commitment whereby they contribute to the unit's process of production in return for remuneration and/or education services, employees engaged under a contract specifically designed to encourage the recruitment of unemployed persons. This category includes persons on sick leave, paid leave or vacation. It excludes working proprietors, active business partners, unpaid family workers and home-workers, irrespective of whether or not they are on the payroll.

Comparability

All countries present information using the *enterprise* as the statistical unit except Japan, Korea and Mexico, which use *establishments*. This may create some incomparability but, because most enterprises are also establishments, this is not expected to be significant. An area where considerable differences can and do arise, however, concerns the coverage of data on enterprises/establishments. In many countries, this information is based on business registers, economic censuses or surveys that may have a size-class cut off. Indeed, all countries have thresholds of one sort or another, depending, often, on the tax legislation and permissible business burdens in place across countries. For Ireland, only enterprises with 3 or more persons engaged are reflected, while the data for Korea do not include establishments with fewer than 4 persons engaged. Enterprises that operate purely in the underground economy will naturally be very difficult, if not impossible, to capture, and these are most likely to be small. However, despite these differences, it is possible to make sensible comparisons across countries.

Employment data for Australia and Switzerland refer to the *total employment* rather than the *number of employees*.

Data for New Zealand, Norway, Sweden and the United States are for 2002, while data for Belgium, Poland, Switzerland and Turkey are for 2001 and data for Australia (Employment) are for 2000.

Finally, data in the "Less than 10" and "Less than 20" size classes for Mexico and New Zealand include statistical units with no persons engaged.

Overview

The contribution and importance of small enterprises across economies varies considerably. Generally, however, the larger the economy, the lower the proportion of small enterprises. This partly reflects the greater scope for growth in larger markets, where there is a greater pool of workers and larger demand, but it also partly reflects a statistical phenomenon. For example, when an enterprise opens a new establishment in the same economy within which it is registered, the enterprise will grow and move from being a small to a large enterprise. However, if it opens a new establishment in another country, this will be recorded as the creation of an enterprise in that country.

In most economies, the percentage of businesses with less than 10 persons employed is over 70%. The reverse is true where the number of employees is concerned, where businesses with more than 20 employees contribute around 70% or more.

Source

- OECD (2005), *OECD SME and Entrepreneurship Outlook – 2005 Edition*, OECD, Paris.

Further information

Analytical publications

- Birch, D. (1979), *The Job Generation Process*, MIT Program on Neighborhood and Regional Change, Cambridge.
- OECD (2005), *Local Economic and Employment Development Entrepreneurship A Catalyst for Urban Regeneration*, OECD, Paris.
- OECD (2006), *The SME Financing Gap (Vol. I): Theory and Evidence*, OECD, Paris.

Statistical publications

- OECD (2006), *Structural and Demographic Business Statistics: 1996-2003, 2006 Edition*, OECD, Paris.

Employment and number of enterprises in manufacturing

Breakdown by size-class of enterprise, 2003 or latest available year

Number of employees	As percentage of total employment in manufacturing							As a percentage of total number of enterprises in manufacturing						
	Less than 20	20 or more	Less than 10	10-19	20-49	50-249	250 or more	Less than 20	20 or more	Less than 10	10-19	20-49	50-249	250 or more
Australia	22.1	77.9	14.1	8.0	12.5	..	..	..	..	..	..	..	..	..
Austria	15.5	84.5	7.8	7.7	11.4	27.9	45.3	85.2	14.8	72.5	12.7	8.0	5.3	1.5
Belgium	13.3	86.7	7.0	6.3	12.9	25.1	48.7	87.8	12.2	79.4	8.4	7.1	4.1	1.0
Czech Republic	12.0	88.0	5.5	6.6	11.0	28.5	48.5	94.3	5.7	90.2	4.1	3.0	2.1	0.6
Denmark	12.9	87.1	6.0	6.9	12.3	26.9	47.9	83.3	16.7	71.7	11.6	9.3	6.0	1.4
Finland	12.7	87.3	..	..	10.0	23.2	54.2	90.1	9.9	..	..	5.2	3.7	1.0
France	16.7	83.3	10.2	6.6	12.7	22.6	48.0	90.0	10.0	82.8	7.2	6.0	3.2	0.8
Germany	13.1	86.9	5.2	7.9	7.7	23.8	55.4	81.5	18.5	60.2	21.3	8.4	8.0	2.1
Hungary	17.1	82.9	10.4	6.7	11.3	25.3	46.3	92.1	7.9	86.2	5.8	4.3	2.8	0.8
Iceland	..	..	..	..	..	..	..	86.4	13.6	75.7	10.6	8.0	5.1	0.6
Ireland	10.3	89.7	4.1	6.2	13.5	32.2	44.0	61.3	38.7	39.5	21.8	20.5	14.7	3.5
Italy	30.7	69.3	14.6	16.0	18.0	24.8	26.6	92.9	7.1	82.6	10.3	4.8	2.0	0.3
Japan	23.6	76.4	12.6	11.0	17.3	30.0	29.1	84.6	15.4	71.6	13.0	9.5	5.1	0.8
Korea	25.3	74.7	11.4	14.0	20.8	..	..	75.9	24.1	50.3	25.6	16.3	..	..
Luxembourg	..	..	..	..	..	..	..	78.1	21.9	65.9	12.2	10.7	8.3	2.9
Mexico	21.6	78.4	17.6	4.0	6.5	19.2	52.7	94.1	5.9	90.5	3.6	2.7	2.3	0.9
Netherlands	18.2	81.8	10.1	8.1	14.6	29.8	37.5	85.4	14.6	74.5	10.9	8.1	5.3	1.1
New Zealand	22.0	78.0	12.0	10.0	14.5	..	..	90.4	9.6	81.4	9.0	5.9	..	..
Norway	16.1	83.9	8.4	7.7	14.0	28.4	41.5	78.1	21.9	62.7	15.3	12.6	7.8	1.6
Poland	23.3	76.7	19.4	3.8	8.9	27.9	39.9	92.9	7.1	89.7	3.2	3.4	3.0	0.8
Portugal	30.1	69.9	18.7	11.4	17.9	30.3	21.6	89.4	10.6	79.8	9.6	6.6	3.5	0.4
Slovak Republic	8.7	91.3	4.4	4.4	5.3	25.6	60.4	71.3	28.7	50.6	20.7	9.3	14.4	5.0
Spain	27.7	72.3	14.8	12.9	20.3	24.5	27.5	89.1	10.9	78.0	11.1	7.6	2.8	0.5
Sweden	13.6	86.4	7.7	5.8	9.8	21.3	55.3	91.8	8.2	85.8	6.0	4.5	2.9	0.8
Switzerland	22.7	77.3	14.9	7.8	13.0	29.2	35.1	87.8	12.2	79.1	8.7	6.7	4.5	0.9
United Kingdom	16.3	83.7	9.2	7.0	11.8	26.1	45.8	84.7	15.3	72.9	11.8	8.5	5.5	1.3
United States	8.7	91.3	4.2	4.5	..	..	..	73.2	26.8	58.2	15.0	..	..	..

StatLink http://dx.doi.org/10.1787/070342673513

Enterprises with less than 20 employees

As a percentage of total number of employees or total number of enterprises, 2003 or latest available year

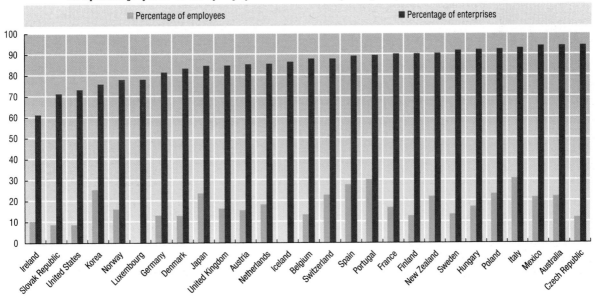

StatLink http://dx.doi.org/10.1787/680187234436

ECONOMIC GLOBALISATION

TRADE
SHARE OF TRADE IN GDP
TRADE IN GOODS
TRADE IN SERVICES
TRADING PARTNERS
BALANCE OF PAYMENTS

FOREIGN DIRECT INVESTMENT (FDI)
FDI FLOWS AND STOCKS
ACTIVITIES OF MULTINATIONALS

SHARE OF TRADE IN GDP

International trade in goods and services is a principal channel of economic integration. A convenient way to measure the importance of international trade is to calculate the share of trade in GDP.

International trade tends to be more important for countries that are small (in terms of geographic size or population) and surrounded by neighbouring countries with open trade regimes than for large, relatively self-sufficient countries or those that are geographically isolated and thus penalised by high transport costs. Other factors also play a role and help explain differences in trade-to-GDP ratios across countries, such as history, culture, trade policy, the structure of the economy (especially the weight of non-tradable services in GDP), re-exports and the presence of multinational firms, which leads to much intra-firm trade.

Definition

The rates shown in this table correspond to the average of imports and exports (of both goods and services) at current prices as a percentage of GDP. The data are taken from national accounts statistics compiled according to the 1993 *System of National Accounts*. Goods consist of merchandise imports and exports. Services cover transport, insurance, travel, banking and insurance, other business services, cultural and recreational services and government services.

Comparability

The ratios shown in this table are compiled using common standards and definitions and are highly comparable.

The trade-to-GDP ratio is often called the "trade openness ratio". However, the term openness may be somewhat misleading. In fact, a low ratio for a country does not necessarily imply high tariff or non-tariff obstacles to foreign trade, but may be due to the factors mentioned above, especially size and geographic remoteness from potential trading partners.

Please note that the trade-to-GDP ratio shown by WTO, IMF and OECD trade indicators refers to the *sum of the imports and exports* and not to the *average*, as is the case here.

Source

- OECD (2006), *National Accounts of OECD Countries*, OECD, Paris.

Further information

Statistical publications

- OECD (2006), *Main Economic Indicators*, OECD, Paris.
- OECD (2006), *International Trade by Commodity Statistics*, OECD, Paris.
- OECD (2006), *Monthly Statistics of International Trade*, OECD, Paris.
- OECD (2006), *Statistics in International Trade in Services*, OECD, Paris.

Methodological publications

- Lindner, A., *et al.* (2001), "Trade in Goods and Services: Statistical Trends and Measurement Challenges", *OECD Statistics Brief*, No. 1, October, OECD, Paris, *www.oecd.org/std/statisticsbrief*.
- UN, EC, IMF, OECD, UNCTAD and the WTO (2002), *Manual on Statistics of International Trade in Services*, United Nations, New York.

Websites

- OECD International Trade Statistics, *www.oecd.org/std/its*.

Long-term trends

In 2005, the unweighted average of the trade-to-GDP ratios for all OECD countries was 45% and 51% for the EU15. For the reasons noted above, there were large differences in these ratios across countries. The ratios exceeded 50% for small countries – Austria, Belgium, the Czech Republic, Hungary, Ireland, Luxembourg, the Netherlands and the Slovak Republic – but were under 15% for the two largest OECD countries – Japan and the United States.

Between 1992 and 2005, trade-to-GDP ratios for the OECD as a whole increased by 13 percentage points, and the EU15 increased by 14 points. Substantial increases in trade-to-GDP ratios were recorded for Luxembourg, Hungary and Belgium.

OECD FACTBOOK 2007 – ISBN 978-92-64-02946-0 – © OECD 2007

Trade in goods and services

As a percentage of GDP

	1992	1993	1994	1995	1996	1997	1998	1999	2000	2001	2002	2003	2004	2005
Australia	17.8	18.3	19.1	19.4	19.3	20.3	19.9	20.9	22.5	21.1	20.4	18.8	20.0	21.0
Austria	34.9	32.8	34.0	35.2	36.3	39.6	41.0	41.8	44.7	46.6	46.4	46.7	49.5	51.9
Belgium	64.9	61.5	63.8	65.6	67.7	71.8	72.5	73.2	83.2	83.0	80.2	78.8	81.8	86.0
Canada	27.3	30.2	33.4	35.7	36.4	38.5	40.4	41.4	42.7	40.7	39.4	36.2	36.2	36.0
Czech Republic	51.3	51.4	48.9	52.9	51.8	54.7	54.8	56.0	64.9	66.6	61.3	62.9	71.3	70.8
Denmark	34.7	34.0	35.1	35.6	35.5	37.0	37.2	38.2	43.6	44.0	44.4	42.0	42.8	46.2
Finland	25.4	29.4	31.9	32.6	33.4	34.7	34.0	33.7	38.4	36.1	35.0	34.4	36.0	39.0
France	21.5	20.6	21.4	22.2	22.4	24.2	24.9	25.1	28.1	27.5	26.3	25.1	25.6	26.6
Germany	24.3	22.3	23.0	23.7	24.4	26.8	28.0	29.0	33.2	33.8	33.4	33.7	35.7	38.1
Greece	19.6	18.7	18.3	18.8	19.0	20.6	21.2	23.5	27.2	26.0	23.3	22.7	22.7	22.0
Hungary	30.5	29.5	31.1	43.1	46.6	52.8	60.5	63.4	73.9	71.7	63.9	62.7	65.1	67.1
Iceland	30.3	31.2	33.2	33.7	36.0	36.0	37.1	36.2	37.5	39.7	37.2	36.3	37.5	38.3
Ireland	56.6	60.2	65.3	70.3	71.2	72.8	80.8	82.0	91.6	92.3	85.1	75.7	76.6	74.9
Italy	18.3	19.8	21.1	23.8	22.4	23.3	23.6	23.5	26.6	26.4	25.2	24.3	25.0	26.3
Japan	8.8	8.1	8.1	8.5	9.6	10.4	10.0	9.5	10.3	10.3	10.7	11.2	12.4	13.6
Korea	27.2	26.3	27.0	29.4	29.6	32.7	39.7	35.7	39.2	36.7	34.6	36.8	41.9	41.2
Luxembourg	92.2	91.7	93.9	95.8	101.0	112.2	119.3	124.6	139.5	137.8	129.4	123.7	137.9	148.6
Mexico	17.8	17.2	19.2	29.1	31.1	30.4	31.8	31.6	32.0	28.7	27.8	28.6	30.6	30.7
Netherlands	52.7	51.6	53.9	56.5	57.0	60.5	60.2	60.9	67.3	64.4	60.9	59.9	62.9	66.1
New Zealand	30.1	29.1	29.7	28.6	27.8	27.9	29.2	30.9	34.7	33.9	31.5	29.0	29.5	29.1
Norway	34.5	34.8	35.1	34.9	36.3	37.3	36.8	35.7	38.0	37.2	34.3	33.7	35.6	36.7
Poland	21.0	20.5	20.6	22.1	23.0	25.4	28.4	27.1	30.3	28.9	30.4	34.6	38.6	37.2
Portugal	29.9	28.8	30.3	31.8	31.7	32.6	33.5	33.0	35.2	33.9	32.1	31.4	32.4	32.9
Slovak Republic	68.8	58.1	56.3	56.3	58.1	60.6	64.4	63.0	71.5	76.7	74.5	77.4	76.5	79.8
Spain	18.0	18.5	20.8	22.4	23.4	25.9	26.8	27.6	30.6	29.8	28.4	27.5	28.0	28.2
Sweden	26.7	30.4	33.4	36.0	34.8	37.9	39.3	39.4	43.0	42.6	40.6	40.2	42.2	44.9
Switzerland	33.5	33.0	32.9	32.9	33.7	37.1	37.8	38.9	42.8	43.0	40.5	40.0	42.3	44.5
Turkey	15.9	16.5	20.9	22.1	24.7	27.5	26.1	25.0	27.8	32.5	30.0	29.0	31.8	30.7
United Kingdom	24.2	26.0	26.9	28.6	29.6	28.7	27.4	27.3	29.1	28.7	27.8	27.0	26.9	28.3
United States	10.4	10.4	10.9	11.7	11.8	12.2	11.9	12.2	13.2	12.1	11.7	11.8	12.7	13.4
EU15 average	36.3	36.4	38.2	39.9	40.7	43.2	44.6	45.5	50.8	50.2	47.9	46.2	48.4	50.7
OECD average	32.3	32.0	33.3	35.3	36.2	38.4	40.0	40.3	44.8	44.4	42.2	41.4	43.6	45.0

StatLink 🔐 http://dx.doi.org/10.1787/360170770017

Trade to GDP ratios

Difference between 2005 and 1992 ratios in percentage points

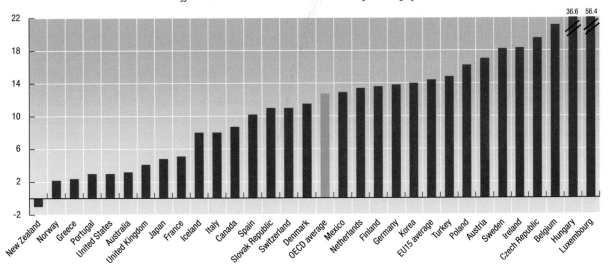

StatLink 🔐 http://dx.doi.org/10.1787/884508608807

TRADE IN GOODS

Since its creation, the OECD has sought to promote international trade, considering it an effective way of enhancing economic growth and raising living standards. Member countries benefit from increased trade as do OECD's trade partners in the rest of the world.

Definition

According to United Nations guidelines, international merchandise trade statistics record all goods which add to or subtract from the stock of material resources of a country by entering (imports) or leaving (exports) its economic territory. Goods simply being transported through a country or goods temporarily admitted or withdrawn (except for goods for inward or outward processing) are not included in the international merchandise trade statistics.

Comparability

All OECD countries use the United Nations guidelines so far as their data sources allow. There are some, generally minor, differences across countries in the coverage of certain types of transactions such as postal trade, imports and exports of military equipment under defence agreements, sea products traded by domestic vessels on the high seas and goods entering or leaving bonded customs areas.

Exports are usually valued *free on board* (f.o.b.), with the exception of the United States which values exports *free alongside ship* (f.a.s.), which is lower than f.o.b. by the cost of loading the goods on board. Imports are valued by most countries at *cost, insurance and freight* (c.i.f.) *i.e.* the cost of the goods plus the costs of insurance and freight to bring the goods to the borders of the importing country. The following countries, however, report their imports at f.o.b. values: Australia, Canada, the Czech Republic, Mexico and the Slovak Republic. The trade balances shown in the table are, therefore, not strictly comparable because imports are not valued in the same way by all countries.

The introduction by the European Union of the single market in 1993 resulted in some loss of accuracy for intra-EU trade because customs documents were no longer available to record all imports and exports. Note that while the OECD data mostly follow the UN recommendations, trade statistics reported by Eurostat follow the Community definitions. As a result, OECD trade statistics for European Union countries are not strictly comparable with those reported by Eurostat.

OECD total includes Hungary and Poland from 1992, the Czech Republic from 1993, Korea from 1994 and the Slovak Republic from 1997.

Sources

- UN Commodity Trade Statistics Database.
- OECD (2006), *International Trade by Commodity Statistics*, OECD, Paris.

Further information

Analytical publications

- OECD (2005), *Trade and Structural Adjustment: Embracing Globalisation*, OECD, Paris.
- OECD (2006), *Trade Based Money Laundering*, OECD, Paris.
- OECD (2006), *The Development Dimension – Aid for Trade: Making it Effective*, OECD, Paris.

Statistical publications

- OECD (2006), *Monthly Statistics of International Trade*, OECD, Paris.

Methodological publications

- Lindner, A., *et al.* (2001), "Trade in Goods and Services: Statistical Trends and Measurement Challenges", *OECD Statistics Brief*, No. 1, October, OECD, Paris, *www.oecd.org/std/statisticsbrief*.
- United Nations (1998), *International Merchandise Trade Statistics: Compilers Manual*, United Nations, New York, *http://unstats.un.org/unsd/trade/methodology.htm*.
- OECD (2007), *International Trade by Commodity Statistics – Definitions*, OECD, Paris.

Online databases

- ITCS International Trade by Commodity Statistics.
- Monthly International Trade.

Websites

- OECD International Trade Indicators, *www.oecd.org/statistics/trade*.

Long-term trends

Over the ten-year period from 1995 to 2004, relative import growth (*i.e.* growth in a single country divided by growth for all OECD countries) was low in Japan and Switzerland while relative import growth in some new member countries – Hungary, the Czech Republic and Poland – was particularly high. Concerning BRIC countries, China and India showed high relative import growth while growth for Brazil and the Russian Federation was rather low.

Over the same period, relative growth rates of exports of goods were again high for Hungary, the Czech Republic, Poland, and Turkey. Japan, the United States, Italy and the United Kingdom were among the countries with below average growth rates.

China had higher growth in imports as well as exports than any country in this comparison.

The United States' negative trade balance has been large throughout the period and growing in most years. The United Kingdom, Spain and Turkey also recorded high negative trade balances for goods, while Germany and Japan both had large trade surpluses. The Russian Federation and China had significant trade surpluses, too.

Trade balance: exports of goods minus imports of goods
Billion US dollars

	1992	1993	1994	1995	1996	1997	1998	1999	2000	2001	2002	2003	2004	2005
Australia	1.9	0.1	-2.7	-4.4	-1.2	1.0	-5.0	-9.5	-4.0	2.4	-4.5	-14.6	-17.3	-13.2
Austria	-9.7	-8.7	-10.2	-8.5	-10.1	-6.9	-6.2	-6.2	-5.2	-4.4	-0.1	-2.3	-0.3	-2.2
Belgium	..	11.4	13.3	15.4	11.4	12.3	14.4	14.3	13.5	11.6	17.7	20.7	21.0	14.0
Belgium-Luxembourg	-2.3	..	..	..	..	..	..	..	..	..	..	..	..	..
Canada	5.3	5.9	7.7	16.5	19.2	18.1	13.3	23.2	37.6	39.4	30.2	31.8	43.4	45.7
Czech Republic	..	0.2	-0.9	-3.9	-5.8	-4.4	-2.2	-2.0	-3.2	-3.1	-2.2	-2.5	-0.9	1.7
Denmark	5.7	6.5	5.8	4.7	5.7	3.7	1.7	4.7	5.2	5.8	6.4	8.4	7.9	8.3
Finland	2.8	5.5	6.4	10.9	9.7	10.0	10.8	10.2	11.7	10.7	11.0	10.9	10.7	6.8
France	-6.8	6.2	5.0	10.6	6.2	16.8	14.7	9.5	-8.5	-4.4	1.1	-4.5	-20.5	-41.6
Germany	22.0	37.4	45.6	59.6	68.3	67.1	72.3	69.3	54.8	85.7	125.6	146.8	193.6	200.4
Greece	-15.3	-14.0	-11.7	-15.0	-15.7	-15.8	-19.4	-18.8	-18.8	-17.9	-21.8	-31.2	-37.6	-37.4
Hungary	-0.4	-3.6	-4.2	-2.6	-3.1	-2.1	-2.7	-3.0	-4.0	-3.2	-3.3	-4.7	-4.8	-3.5
Iceland	-0.2	-	0.1	-	-0.1	-0.2	-0.6	-0.5	-0.7	-0.3	-	-0.4	-0.8	-1.9
Ireland	6.1	7.2	8.2	11.5	12.4	14.4	19.9	24.0	25.6	26.4	36.0	38.7	42.0	39.7
Italy	-10.2	22.2	22.1	27.2	43.9	29.9	26.5	14.7	1.8	8.1	7.7	2.0	-1.9	-12.7
Japan	106.9	120.6	121.6	107.1	61.8	82.2	107.5	107.2	99.6	54.0	79.1	88.5	110.5	79.1
Korea	..	..	-6.5	-10.4	-19.6	-8.5	39.0	23.9	11.8	9.3	10.4	15.0	29.4	23.2
Luxembourg	..	..	..	..	..	..	..	-2.8	-2.8	-2.9	-2.9	-3.7	-4.6	-4.9
Mexico	-16.0	-13.6	-18.7	6.8	6.2	0.5	-8.0	-5.7	-5.8	-7.6	-5.7	-5.6	-8.8	-7.6
Netherlands	5.5	17.2	15.3	19.6	16.5	15.5	10.9	2.7	5.4	5.6	11.9	18.3	32.8	36.9
New Zealand	0.2	0.6	-0.1	-0.7	-0.6	-0.8	-0.6	-2.4	-1.2	-	-1.2	-2.0	-2.8	-4.5
Norway	9.1	7.9	7.3	9.0	14.0	12.8	2.9	11.3	25.5	26.0	24.7	29.0	33.8	48.3
Poland	-2.7	-4.7	-4.4	-6.1	-12.7	-16.5	-18.8	-18.5	-17.3	-14.2	-14.1	-14.4	-14.4	-12.2
Portugal	-12.0	-8.8	-9.1	-10.2	-10.6	-11.1	-12.8	-15.3	-15.6	-15.4	-14.2	-15.3	-19.2	-23.1
Slovak Republic	..	..	..	..	..	-2.1	-2.4	-1.1	-0.9	-2.1	-2.2	-0.7	-1.5	-2.4
Spain	-34.9	-18.7	-19.0	-23.0	-21.0	-18.2	-25.8	-36.4	-39.5	-38.8	-40.0	-53.4	-76.5	-96.8
Sweden	6.0	7.5	9.4	15.8	18.9	18.3	16.4	16.3	14.2	12.8	15.9	18.2	22.8	18.9
Switzerland	-	2.5	2.4	1.5	1.5	0.2	-1.2	0.4	-2.0	-2.1	4.2	4.2	6.8	4.7
Turkey	-8.2	-14.1	-5.2	-14.1	-20.4	-22.3	-19.0	-14.1	-26.7	-10.1	-15.5	-22.1	-34.4	-43.3
United Kingdom	-35.3	-28.0	-31.3	-25.9	-28.7	-26.3	-46.9	-53.2	-56.6	-65.4	-78.8	-85.8	-113.1	-131.4
United States	-106.2	-138.4	-176.7	-187.9	-194.8	-210.5	-263.9	-366.4	-477.7	-449.1	-509.1	-581.4	-707.4	-828.0
EU 15 total	-78.7	42.8	49.7	92.7	106.8	109.8	76.4	33.0	-14.7	17.4	75.5	67.9	57.0	-25.2
OECD total	-88.9	6.2	-30.4	3.7	-48.7	-43.0	-85.1	-224.0	-383.7	-343.0	-333.8	-411.9	-512.2	-739.1
Brazil	13.6	11.4	7.9	-7.6	-9.6	-12.6	-10.1	-4.1	-4.0	-0.6	10.3	21.9	29.3	39.2
China	4.4	-12.2	5.4	16.7	12.2	40.4	44.3	29.2	24.1	22.5	30.4	25.5	32.1	102.0
India	-3.5	-0.8	-1.9	-4.4	-5.0	-3.9	-4.7	-8.9	-1.9	-3.4	-4.8	-7.7	-18.2	-35.5
Russian Federation	..	..	..	..	27.6	19.7	28.1	42.6	69.2	58.8	60.5	76.3	106.1	142.7
South Africa	..	..	..	..	..	..	..	..	3.4	3.7	-3.2	-3.1	-7.5	-8.4

StatLink ᵐˢˡ http://dx.doi.org/10.1787/756420834703

Trade balance: exports of goods minus imports of goods
Billion US dollars, 2005

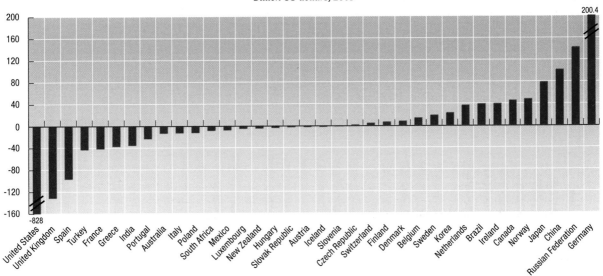

StatLink ᵐˢˡ http://dx.doi.org/10.1787/058421166542

Imports of goods
Billion US dollars

	1992	1993	1994	1995	1996	1997	1998	1999	2000	2001	2002	2003	2004	2005
Australia	40.7	42.4	49.9	57.4	61.4	61.8	60.8	65.5	67.8	60.9	69.5	84.8	103.8	118.9
Austria	54.1	50.4	55.2	66.3	67.1	63.6	67.1	68.7	67.4	69.0	71.4	91.5	111.2	120.0
Belgium	..	114.8	127.6	152.3	159.4	158.3	164.9	164.6	171.7	178.7	198.1	234.8	285.5	320.1
Belgium-Luxembourg	125.0	..	..	..	..	..	..	..	..	..	..	..	..	..
Canada	122.6	131.7	148.4	164.5	171.0	197.1	201.3	215.6	240.0	221.6	222.4	240.2	273.4	314.4
Czech Republic	..	12.7	14.9	20.8	27.4	27.2	30.5	28.8	32.2	36.5	40.7	51.2	68.1	76.5
Denmark	35.7	31.0	36.5	45.6	45.0	44.5	46.2	44.3	44.4	44.3	49.3	56.2	66.9	75.0
Finland	20.7	18.0	23.3	29.5	30.9	31.0	32.4	31.6	34.1	32.2	33.6	41.6	50.1	58.5
France	238.9	210.1	228.3	273.5	277.7	266.6	285.8	292.8	304.0	304.2	303.8	362.4	434.4	476.0
Germany	408.2	342.6	381.7	464.3	444.4	445.3	471.6	473.5	495.4	486.3	490.1	601.8	718.2	777.4
Greece	25.2	22.8	20.9	25.9	27.0	27.0	30.3	29.5	29.8	28.2	32.5	44.9	52.8	54.9
Hungary	11.1	12.5	14.9	15.5	16.2	21.2	25.7	28.0	32.1	33.7	37.6	47.7	60.2	66.7
Iceland	1.7	1.4	1.5	1.8	2.0	2.0	2.5	2.5	2.6	2.3	2.3	2.8	3.6	5.0
Ireland	22.5	21.8	25.9	32.3	35.8	39.2	44.4	46.5	50.7	51.1	52.3	54.2	62.3	70.3
Italy	188.7	157.6	167.9	204.0	208.2	208.1	215.6	220.3	237.3	236.1	246.6	297.4	351.1	380.6
Japan	233.5	241.7	276.1	336.1	349.2	338.8	280.6	309.9	379.7	348.6	337.6	383.5	455.2	515.9
Korea	..	..	103.1	137.9	144.1	144.6	93.3	119.8	160.5	141.1	152.1	178.8	224.5	261.2
Luxembourg	..	..	..	..	..	..	..	10.6	10.6	11.2	11.5	13.6	16.8	17.6
Mexico	61.9	65.3	79.3	72.5	89.5	109.8	125.3	142.0	171.1	165.1	165.7	170.5	196.8	221.8
Netherlands	134.5	129.8	130.5	157.7	162.5	158.3	156.8	167.9	174.7	169.9	163.4	209.0	257.7	283.2
New Zealand	9.2	9.3	11.9	13.9	14.7	14.5	12.5	14.3	13.9	13.3	15.0	18.6	23.2	26.2
Norway	26.1	24.0	27.4	33.0	35.6	35.8	37.5	34.2	34.4	33.0	34.9	41.2	48.5	55.5
Poland	15.9	18.8	21.6	28.9	37.1	42.3	47.0	45.9	48.9	50.2	55.1	68.0	88.2	101.5
Portugal	30.6	24.2	27.1	33.6	35.2	35.1	37.0	39.8	39.9	39.5	40.0	47.1	54.9	61.2
Slovak Republic	..	..	..	..	..	11.7	13.1	11.1	12.7	14.7	16.6	22.6	29.1	34.4
Spain	99.7	79.7	91.0	116.5	123.6	124.4	137.2	147.9	152.9	155.0	165.9	209.7	259.3	289.6
Sweden	50.0	46.7	52.0	61.6	64.0	63.2	68.6	68.5	73.1	63.5	67.1	84.2	100.5	111.4
Switzerland	65.7	62.0	67.9	80.2	78.2	75.9	80.1	79.9	82.5	84.2	83.7	96.4	110.0	121.2
Turkey	22.9	29.4	23.3	35.7	43.6	48.6	45.9	40.7	54.5	41.4	51.3	69.3	97.5	116.8
United Kingdom	222.5	209.4	234.0	268.2	287.6	307.5	320.3	323.8	339.4	338.0	359.4	393.5	461.3	515.8
United States	553.5	603.2	689.0	770.8	817.6	898.0	944.4	1 059.2	1 258.1	1 180.1	1 202.3	1 305.1	1 525.3	1 732.3
EU 15 total	1 656.4	1 458.8	1 601.7	1 931.3	1 968.4	1 972.0	2 078.1	2 130.3	2 225.6	2 207.1	2 285.0	2 741.8	3 282.8	3 611.4
OECD total	2 821.2	2 713.3	3 130.9	3 700.2	3 856.2	4 001.4	4 078.5	4 327.7	4 816.4	4 633.7	4 771.8	5 522.7	6 590.3	7 380.0
Brazil	22.3	27.3	35.5	53.7	56.7	65.1	60.8	51.7	58.9	58.5	49.7	50.8	65.3	76.4
China	80.6	104.0	115.6	132.1	138.8	142.4	139.5	165.7	225.1	243.6	295.2	412.8	561.2	660.0
India	24.2	23.1	28.2	36.1	38.4	38.7	37.9	45.8	47.1	47.7	57.3	70.8	98.0	138.9
Russian Federation	..	..	..	..	61.1	67.6	43.7	30.3	33.9	41.9	46.2	57.3	75.6	98.6
South Africa	..	..	..	..	..	..	..	..	26.8	24.2	26.2	34.5	47.7	55.0

StatLink ▦▤▄ http://dx.doi.org/10.1787/317587241172

Relative growth of imports of goods
Growth over the period 1996-2005, OECD total = 1

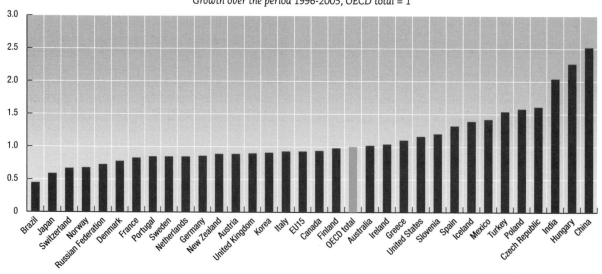

StatLink ▦▤▄ http://dx.doi.org/10.1787/254155305243

OECD FACTBOOK 2007 – ISBN 978-92-64-02946-0 – © OECD 2007

Exports of goods
Billion US dollars

	1992	1993	1994	1995	1996	1997	1998	1999	2000	2001	2002	2003	2004	2005
Australia	42.6	42.5	47.3	53.0	60.2	62.8	55.8	56.0	63.8	63.3	65.0	70.2	86.4	105.8
Austria	44.4	41.6	45.0	57.8	57.1	56.7	60.9	62.4	62.3	64.7	71.3	89.2	110.8	117.7
Belgium	..	126.1	140.9	167.7	170.8	170.7	179.3	178.9	185.2	190.3	215.8	255.5	306.5	334.1
Belgium-Luxembourg	122.7	..	..	..	..	..	..	..	..	..	..	..	..	..
Canada	127.9	137.6	156.1	181.0	190.2	215.1	214.6	238.9	277.6	261.1	252.6	272.1	316.9	360.1
Czech Republic	..	12.9	14.0	16.8	21.7	22.7	28.3	26.8	29.1	33.4	38.5	48.7	67.2	78.2
Denmark	41.4	37.5	42.3	50.3	50.7	48.2	47.9	49.0	49.6	50.1	55.7	64.6	74.8	83.3
Finland	23.5	23.5	29.8	40.4	40.6	41.0	43.2	41.8	45.8	42.8	44.7	52.5	60.8	65.2
France	232.1	216.2	233.3	284.1	283.9	283.4	300.5	302.3	295.6	299.8	304.9	357.9	413.9	434.4
Germany	430.2	380.0	427.3	523.9	512.7	512.4	543.8	542.8	550.2	572.0	615.6	748.5	911.8	977.8
Greece	9.8	8.8	9.2	11.0	11.3	11.2	10.9	10.7	11.0	10.3	10.8	13.7	15.2	17.5
Hungary	10.7	8.9	10.7	12.9	13.1	19.1	23.0	25.0	28.1	30.5	34.3	43.0	55.5	63.2
Iceland	1.5	1.5	1.6	1.8	1.9	1.9	1.9	2.0	1.9	2.0	2.2	2.4	2.8	3.1
Ireland	28.5	29.0	34.1	43.8	48.2	53.6	64.2	70.5	76.3	77.4	88.3	92.9	104.3	110.0
Italy	178.5	179.8	190.0	231.3	252.1	238.0	242.1	235.1	239.1	244.2	254.3	299.4	349.1	367.9
Japan	340.5	362.3	397.7	443.3	410.9	421.0	388.1	417.1	479.2	402.6	416.7	472.0	565.7	594.9
Korea	..	..	96.6	127.5	124.5	136.2	132.3	143.7	172.3	150.4	162.5	193.8	253.8	284.4
Luxembourg	..	..	..	..	..	..	..	7.8	7.9	8.3	8.6	10.0	12.2	12.7
Mexico	45.9	51.7	60.6	79.3	95.7	110.2	117.3	136.3	165.3	157.5	160.0	164.9	188.0	214.2
Netherlands	139.9	147.0	145.8	177.4	179.0	173.8	167.6	170.5	180.1	175.5	175.3	227.3	290.5	320.1
New Zealand	9.4	9.9	11.8	13.3	14.2	13.7	11.9	11.9	12.7	13.3	13.8	16.5	20.3	21.7
Norway	35.1	31.9	34.8	42.0	49.6	48.5	40.4	45.5	59.9	59.0	59.6	70.3	82.2	103.8
Poland	13.2	14.1	17.2	22.9	24.4	25.7	28.2	27.4	31.6	36.1	41.0	53.5	73.8	89.4
Portugal	18.6	15.4	18.0	23.4	24.6	24.0	24.2	24.5	24.4	24.1	25.8	31.8	35.7	38.1
Slovak Republic	..	..	..	..	..	9.6	10.7	10.1	11.8	12.6	14.5	22.0	27.6	32.0
Spain	64.8	61.1	71.9	93.5	102.6	106.2	111.4	111.5	113.3	116.1	125.9	156.3	182.7	192.8
Sweden	56.0	54.1	61.3	77.4	82.9	81.5	85.0	84.8	87.4	76.3	82.9	102.4	123.2	130.3
Switzerland	65.7	64.5	70.3	81.6	79.7	76.2	78.9	80.3	80.5	82.1	87.9	100.7	116.8	125.9
Turkey	14.7	15.3	18.1	21.6	23.2	26.2	27.0	26.6	27.8	31.3	35.8	47.3	63.1	73.5
United Kingdom	187.1	181.4	202.7	242.2	258.9	281.2	273.4	270.7	282.9	272.6	280.6	307.7	348.2	384.4
United States	447.3	464.8	512.3	583.0	622.8	687.5	680.4	692.8	780.3	731.0	693.2	723.7	817.9	904.3
EU 15 total	1 577.7	1 501.6	1 651.4	2 024.0	2 075.2	2 081.8	2 154.5	2 163.4	2 210.9	2 224.5	2 360.5	2 809.8	3 339.8	3 586.3
OECD total	2 732.3	2 719.5	3 100.5	3 703.9	3 807.5	3 958.4	3 993.4	4 103.7	4 432.7	4 290.7	4 438.0	5 110.9	6 078.0	6 640.9
Brazil	36.0	38.7	43.4	46.1	47.2	52.5	50.7	47.7	54.9	57.9	60.0	72.8	94.6	115.7
China	84.9	91.7	121.0	148.8	151.0	182.8	183.8	194.9	249.2	266.1	325.6	438.2	593.3	762.0
India	20.7	22.2	26.3	31.7	33.5	34.8	33.2	36.9	45.2	44.3	52.5	63.0	79.8	103.4
Russian Federation	..	..	..	..	88.7	87.4	71.8	72.9	103.1	100.7	106.7	133.7	181.6	241.2
South Africa	..	..	..	..	..	..	..	..	30.2	27.9	23.0	31.5	40.3	46.7

StatLink http://dx.doi.org/10.1787/441184221752

Relative growth of exports of goods
Growth over the period 1996-2005, OECD total = 1

StatLink http://dx.doi.org/10.1787/102105153218

TRADE IN SERVICES

International trade in services is growing in importance both among OECD countries and with the rest of the world. Traditional services – transport, insurance on merchandise trade, and travel – account for about half of total international trade in services, but trade in newer types of services, particularly those that can be conducted via the Internet, is growing rapidly.

Definition

International trade in services is defined according to the 5th edition of the *IMF Balance of Payments Manual* (BPM5). Services include transport (both freight and passengers), travel (mainly expenditure on goods and services by tourists and business travellers), communications services (postal, telephone, satellite, etc.), construction services, insurance and financial services, computer and information services, royalties and license fees, other business services (merchanting, operational leasing, technical and professional services, etc.), cultural and recreational services (rents for films, fees for actors and other performers, but excluding purchases of films, recorded music, books, etc.) and government services not included in the list above.

Comparability

BPM5 was issued in 1993 and countries began to implement it in the next two or three years. Prior to that, services were defined according to BPM4. All OECD countries now report international trade in services broadly according to the BPM5 framework, and BPM4 is of interest principally for some historic series that have not been revised. The main difference between them is that BPM5 makes a clear distinction between transactions in services and payments of income. In the 4th edition, labour and non-financial property incomes were included with services. Countries have tried to preserve continuity by revising earlier figures in line with BPM5 but this has not always been possible.

Sources

- OECD (2006), *Main Economic Indicators*, OECD, Paris.
- OECD (2006), *OECD Statistics on International Trade in Services: Volume I: Detailed Tables by Service Category – 1995-2004*, OECD, Paris.

Further information

Analytical publications

- OECD (2004), *Export Credit Financing Systems in OECD Member and non-Member Countries*, OECD, Paris.
- OECD (2004), *Promoting Trade in Services: Experience of the Baltic States*, OECD, Paris.
- OECD (2005), *Trade and Structural Adjustment: Embracing Globalisation*, OECD, Paris.
- OECD (2006), *OECD Trade Policy Studies – Liberalisation and Universal Access to Basic Services: Telecommunications, Water and Sanitation, Financial Services, and Electricity*, OECD, Paris.
- OECD (2007), *Infrastructure to 2030 (Vol. 2): Mapping Policy for Electricity, Water and Transport*, OECD, Paris.

Statistical publications

- OECD (2002), *Measuring Globalisation: The Role of Multinationals in OECD Economies, Volume II: Services 2001 Edition*, OECD, Paris.
- OECD (2006), *International Trade by Commodity Statistics*, OECD, Paris.
- OECD (2006), *Statistics in International Trade in Services*, OECD, Paris.

Methodological publications

- IMF (1993), *Balance of Payments Manual*, 5th edition, IMF, Washington, DC.

Websites

- OECD International Trade in Services, *www.oecd.org/std/ trade-services*.

Long-term trends

Between 1997 and 2005, growth of service imports was highest in Ireland and was also well above average in Greece and Iceland. Imports of services grew relatively slowly in Japan.

In the same period, the growth rate of service exports for Ireland was again well above the average and relatively high growth was also recorded for India, Luxembourg and Greece. Rather low relative growth occurred in Turkey, France, and Mexico.

Averaged over the last three years, trade in services was relatively balanced for most countries but large surpluses were recorded for United States, United Kingdom, Euro Area and Spain and substantial deficits occurred in Germany and Japan.

The fastest growing services in OECD exports are now insurance and computer and information services, and for imports insurance and government services not included elsewhere (*n.i.e.*). Construction services has been the slowest growing export category.

Services trade balance: exports of services minus imports of services

Billion US dollars

	1992	1993	1994	1995	1996	1997	1998	1999	2000	2001	2002	2003	2004	2005
Australia	-2.6	-1.5	-1.3	-0.9	0.2	0.2	-0.9	0.1	0.9	0.7	1.2	1.8	0.5	0.5
Austria	9.4	7.5	7.4	4.6	4.6	1.0	2.4	1.8	1.6	1.8	0.6	1.9	2.4	5.9
Belgium	..	..	..	-0.1	0.2	1.3	0.8	1.4	2.1	1.8	1.8	1.7	3.6	4.5
Canada	-10.0	-10.5	-8.5	-7.4	-6.7	-6.4	-4.3	-4.5	-3.9	-5.0	-4.6	-8.5	-9.8	-11.3
Czech Republic	..	1.0	0.5	1.8	1.9	1.8	1.9	1.2	1.4	1.5	0.7	0.5	0.5	0.8
Denmark	2.3	1.6	0.5	0.7	1.3	0.1	-0.3	2.0	2.4	3.4	2.0	3.5	3.3	4.7
Finland	-2.9	-2.2	-1.8	-2.2	-1.7	-1.6	-1.1	-1.1	-0.7	1.1	2.4	1.5	2.9	1.8
France	..	..	..	14.3	15.1	16.7	17.4	18.6	19.8	17.8	17.1	15.8	10.9	10.0
Germany	-36.1	-38.3	-46.1	-53.4	-51.7	-48.1	-51.6	-57.9	-55.0	-54.1	-42.8	-50.5	-53.4	-50.3
Greece	..	..	..	..	..	7.2	7.0	7.6	8.2	7.9	9.7	13.0	19.2	19.5
Hungary	0.8	0.2	0.2	0.6	1.5	1.7	1.7	1.3	0.8	1.1	-	-1.2	-0.3	0.9
Iceland	-	-	-	-	-	-	-	-0.1	-0.1	-	-	-0.1	-0.2	-0.5
Ireland	-3.0	-3.0	-4.1	-6.3	-7.7	-9.0	-9.9	-10.8	-12.8	-11.9	-13.0	-12.5	-12.7	-12.5
Italy	0.8	3.3	5.2	6.3	7.2	7.8	4.9	1.2	1.1	-	-2.9	-2.7	1.5	-0.4
Japan	-44.0	-43.0	-47.9	-57.3	-62.3	-54.1	-49.3	-54.0	-47.6	-43.7	-42.0	-35.5	-39.0	-27.9
Korea	-2.9	-2.1	-1.8	-3.0	-6.2	-3.2	1.0	-0.7	-2.8	-3.9	-8.2	-7.4	-8.0	-13.7
Luxembourg	..	..	..	3.2	3.5	4.0	4.2	5.4	6.8	6.4	8.0	10.0	12.6	15.8
Mexico	-2.3	-2.1	-2.0	0.7	0.4	-0.7	-0.9	-1.8	-2.3	-3.6	-4.0	-4.6	-4.6	-4.7
Netherlands	-0.1	-0.1	0.2	1.1	2.0	3.3	2.5	2.6	-2.1	-2.5	-1.0	-0.7	4.3	6.8
New Zealand	-0.9	-0.6	-0.3	-0.2	-0.2	-0.6	-0.7	-0.2	-0.1	0.1	0.6	0.9	0.7	0.1
Norway	..	..	0.2	0.5	1.4	1.4	0.7	1.0	1.9	2.5	1.8	1.8	2.5	-0.3
Poland	..	..	2.8	3.5	3.4	3.2	4.2	1.4	1.4	0.8	0.8	0.5	1.0	1.9
Portugal	..	..	..	..	1.4	1.5	1.9	2.0	2.0	2.6	3.1	4.0	5.2	5.1
Slovak Republic	..	0.3	0.8	0.7	0.2	0.2	0.2	0.2	0.4	0.5	0.5	0.2	0.3	0.3
Spain	12.4	11.7	14.8	17.4	19.0	18.2	19.7	20.5	19.4	20.6	21.1	26.2	26.9	28.2
Sweden	-2.3	0.1	0.2	-0.4	-0.9	-1.3	-1.6	-1.3	-1.5	-0.6	-0.8	2.0	5.8	7.9
Switzerland	11.4	12.1	12.0	13.4	13.1	13.7	14.3	15.3	16.2	13.9	14.9	18.4	21.2	23.7
Turkey	5.8	6.7	7.1	9.6	6.7	10.9	13.5	7.5	11.4	9.1	7.9	10.5	12.8	14.0
United Kingdom	9.3	10.1	9.9	14.1	17.4	23.1	24.3	22.1	20.8	20.8	24.9	31.3	47.5	42.6
United States	57.7	62.1	67.3	77.8	86.9	90.2	82.1	82.7	74.9	64.4	61.2	52.4	54.1	66.0
Euro area	..	..	..	..	..	..	..	-7.9	-5.8	-0.2	16.9	24.9	37.9	44.0
OECD total	..	..	..	..	..	82.1	84.3	63.6	63.6	53.1	62.0	76.4	114.3	140.4
Brazil	-3.3	-5.6	-5.3	-7.5	-8.1	-9.3	-9.0	-7.0	-7.2	-7.8	-5.0	-4.9	-4.7	-8.1
China	-0.2	-0.8	0.3	-6.1	-2.0	-3.4	-2.8	-5.3	-5.6	-5.9	-6.8	-8.6	-9.7	-9.4
India	-1.8	-1.4	-2.2	-3.5	-3.9	-3.3	-2.8	-2.8	-2.5	-2.8	-1.6	-2.4	..	..
Russian Federation	..	..	-7.0	-9.6	-5.4	-5.9	-4.1	-4.3	-6.7	-9.1	-9.9	-10.9	-13.4	-14.8
South Africa	-1.0	-1.4	-1.3	-1.4	-0.7	-0.6	-0.3	-0.5	-0.8	-0.6	-0.7	-0.3	-1.3	-1.6

StatLink ⬚⬚⬚ http://dx.doi.org/10.1787/506173866783

Services trade balance: exports of services minus imports of services

Billion US dollars, average 2003-2005

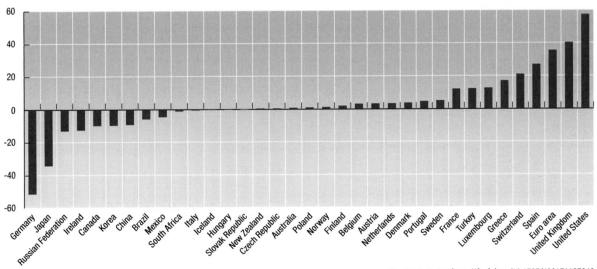

StatLink ⬚⬚⬚ http://dx.doi.org/10.1787/430171127240

Imports of services
Billion US dollars

	1992	1993	1994	1995	1996	1997	1998	1999	2000	2001	2002	2003	2004	2005
Australia	13.8	13.4	15.4	17.4	18.9	19.2	18.0	18.8	18.9	17.3	18.3	21.8	27.9	30.4
Austria	17.9	19.2	20.6	24.6	25.4	26.7	27.1	29.5	29.8		31.5	34.8	41.1	46.8	45.9
Belgium	..	..	..	29.7	29.0	27.8	30.0		31.2	32.3		33.6	35.9	42.9	49.1	51.3
Canada	30.8	32.4	32.5	33.5	35.9	38.0	38.1	40.6	44.1	43.8	45.0	52.1	58.9	64.9
Czech Republic	..	3.7	4.7	4.9	6.3	5.4	5.7	5.9	5.4	5.6	6.4	7.3	9.2	10.0
Denmark	10.9	10.6	11.8	13.2	13.9	14.2	15.6	18.4	22.1	23.5	25.1	27.9	33.3	37.8
Finland	7.5	6.6	7.3	9.6	8.8	8.2	7.8		7.6	8.4		8.1	8.1	10.0	12.3	15.2
France	..	..	..	64.5	66.8	64.2	67.5		63.1	60.8		62.4	68.7	82.9	98.5	106.0
Germany	104.1	102.0	111.6	133.4	135.3	130.7	135.6		141.9	138.2		142.7	145.1	173.1	196.1	204.8
Greece	..	..	..	..	..	4.1	4.5		9.7	11.5		11.6	9.6	11.2	14.0	14.7
Hungary	2.6	2.6	3.0	3.6	3.5	4.1	4.2		4.4	4.8	5.6	6.9	9.2	10.6	11.9
Iceland	0.6	0.6	0.6	0.6	0.7	0.8	1.0	1.0	1.2	1.1	1.1	1.5	1.8	2.5
Ireland	7.1	6.7	8.4	11.3	13.4	15.2		23.9		27.7	32.8		37.5	42.8	54.5	65.4	69.9
Italy	53.2	45.6	45.7	51.1	53.4	54.2	59.1		57.7	55.6		57.8	63.0	74.3	83.3	90.6
Japan	93.0	96.2	106.2	122.8	130.0	123.4	111.7	114.9	116.8	108.2	107.8	108.8	133.7	134.0
Korea	13.6	15.1	18.6	25.8	29.6	29.5	24.5	27.2	33.4	32.9	36.6	40.4	49.9	58.8
Luxembourg	..	..	..	7.5	8.5	8.7	9.9		11.5	13.2		13.3	12.3	15.4	20.9	24.8
Mexico	11.5	11.5	12.3	9.0	10.2	11.8	12.4	13.5	16.0	16.2	16.7	17.1	18.6	20.8
Netherlands	38.3	38.0	41.1	44.8	45.3	45.8	47.2		49.5	51.4		53.8	57.0	63.9	69.5	73.3
New Zealand	3.6	3.5	4.0	4.7	4.9	4.8	4.4	4.5	4.5	4.3	4.8	5.7	7.2	8.2
Norway	..	..	12.0	13.1	13.4	14.3	14.8	14.9	15.5	15.1	16.7	19.2	23.0	29.6
Poland	..	..	3.9	7.1	6.3	5.7	6.6	7.0	9.0	9.0	9.2	10.6	12.5	14.3
Portugal	..	..	..	..	6.5	6.2	6.9		7.3	7.1		6.8	7.2	8.3	9.7	10.0
Slovak Republic	..	1.7	1.6	1.8	2.0	2.1	2.3	1.8	1.8	2.0	2.3	3.0	3.4	4.1
Spain	21.3	18.9	18.9	22.9	25.5	25.6	28.6		32.0	33.2		35.2	38.8	48.0	59.2	65.5
Sweden	18.3	12.7	14.0	16.8	18.4	19.7	21.4	23.0	24.2	23.6	24.0	28.7	33.1	35.3
Switzerland	10.4	10.1	11.2	13.2	13.8	12.2	13.2	14.1	13.7	14.6	15.4	16.9	21.9	23.3
Turkey	3.8	4.2	4.0	5.3		6.7	8.8	10.2	9.3	9.0	6.9	6.9	8.5	11.3	11.9
United Kingdom	54.5	52.4	60.0	65.7	73.0	78.6	88.3	97.0	99.8	100.3	110.1	127.3	150.0	160.4
United States	119.6	123.8	133.1	141.4	152.6	165.9	180.7	199.2	223.7	221.8	231.1	250.3	290.3	314.6
Euro area	..	..	..	..	..	..	..	278.8	280.9	288.8	300.2	353.7	415.6	452.4
OECD total	..	..	..	..	..	976.3		1 021.2		1 084.2	1 138.7		1 146.4	1 209.0	1 382.9	1 619.8	1 743.9
Brazil	7.4	9.6	10.3	13.6	12.7	15.3	16.7	14.2	16.7	17.1	14.5	15.4	17.3	24.2
China	9.4	12.0	16.3	25.2	22.6	28.0	26.7	31.6	36.0	39.3	46.5	55.3	72.1	83.8
India	6.7	6.5	8.2	10.3	11.2	12.4	14.5	17.3	19.2	20.1	21.0	25.8	..	..
Russian Federation	..	..	15.4	20.2	18.7	20.0	16.5	13.4	16.2	20.6	23.5	27.1	33.7	39.4
South Africa	4.4	4.7	5.1	6.0	5.7	6.0	5.7	5.8	5.8	5.2	5.4	8.1	10.3	11.9

StatLink 🔗 http://dx.doi.org/10.1787/125028012358

Relative growth in imports of services
Growth over the period 1997-2005, OECD total = 1

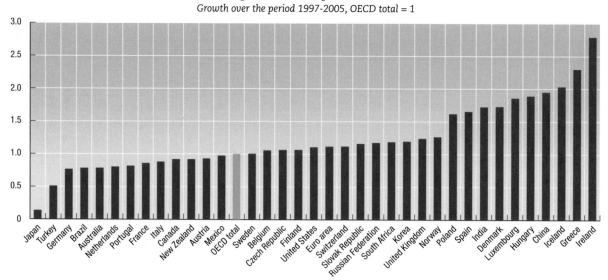

StatLink 🔗 http://dx.doi.org/10.1787/453658633404

OECD FACTBOOK 2007 – ISBN 978-92-64-02946-0 – © OECD 2007

Exports of services
Billion US dollars

	1992	1993	1994	1995	1996	1997	1998	1999	2000	2001	2002	2003	2004	2005
Australia	11.2	11.9	14.2	16.5	19.1	19.3	17.2	18.9	19.9	18.1	19.6	23.6	28.5	31.0
Austria	27.2	26.7	28.0	29.2	30.0	27.7	29.5	31.3	31.4	33.3	35.3	43.0	49.1	51.8
Belgium	..	..	..	29.6	29.3	29.1	30.8	32.6	34.3	35.4	37.7	44.6	52.7	55.7
Canada	20.8	21.9	24.0	26.1	29.2	31.6	33.9	36.1	40.2	38.8	40.4	43.7	49.1	53.6
Czech Republic	..	4.7	5.2	6.7	8.2	7.2	7.6	7.1	6.9	7.1	7.1	7.8	9.7	10.8
Denmark	13.2	12.2	12.3	13.9	15.1	14.3	15.3	20.4	24.5	26.9	27.1	31.4	36.6	42.5
Finland	4.6	4.4	5.5	7.4	7.1	6.7	6.7	6.5	7.7	9.2	10.4	11.5	15.2	17.0
France	..	..	..	78.9	81.9	80.9	84.8	81.7	80.6	80.2	85.8	98.7	109.4	116.0
Germany	68.1	63.7	65.5	79.9	83.6	82.6	84.0	84.0	83.2	88.6	102.3	122.7	142.7	154.5
Greece	..	..	..	..	..	11.2	11.5	17.4	19.6	19.5	19.2	24.2	33.2	34.3
Hungary	3.4	2.8	3.1	4.3	5.0	5.7	5.9	5.6	5.6	6.6	6.9	8.0	10.4	12.8
Iceland	0.6	0.6	0.6	0.7	0.8	0.8	1.0	0.9	1.0	1.1	1.1	1.4	1.6	2.0
Ireland	4.0	3.8	4.3	5.0	5.7	6.2	14.1	16.9	20.0	25.6	29.8	42.0	52.7	57.3
Italy	54.0	48.9	50.9	57.5	60.6	62.0	64.0	58.9	56.7	57.9	60.1	71.6	84.7	90.1
Japan	49.0	53.2	58.3	65.5	67.7	69.3	62.4	60.9	69.2	64.5	65.7	73.3	94.7	106.1
Korea	10.7	12.9	16.8	22.8	23.4	26.3	25.6	26.5	30.5	29.1	28.4	33.0	41.9	45.1
Luxembourg	..	..	..	10.7	12.0	12.7	14.2	16.9	20.0	19.8	20.3	25.4	33.6	40.7
Mexico	9.2	9.4	10.3	9.7	10.6	11.1	11.5	11.7	13.7	12.7	12.7	12.5	14.0	16.1
Netherlands	38.2	37.9	41.4	45.9	47.2	49.0	49.7	52.1	49.3	51.3	56.0	63.2	73.7	80.1
New Zealand	2.6	2.9	3.7	4.5	4.7	4.2	3.8	4.3	4.4	4.4	5.3	6.6	7.9	8.3
Norway	..	..	12.2	13.7	14.8	15.7	15.5	15.9	17.4	17.6	18.6	21.0	25.5	29.3
Poland	..	..	6.7	10.7	9.7	8.9	10.8	8.4	10.4	9.8	10.0	11.2	13.5	16.2
Portugal	..	..	..	..	7.9	7.7	8.8	9.3	9.0	9.4	10.3	12.3	14.9	15.1
Slovak Republic	..	2.0	2.3	2.5	2.2	2.3	2.4	2.1	2.2	2.5	2.8	3.3	3.7	4.4
Spain	33.7	30.6	33.6	40.3	44.5	43.9	48.4	52.5	52.6	55.8	59.9	74.2	86.2	93.7
Sweden	15.9	12.8	14.2	16.4	17.5	18.4	19.7	21.7	22.7	23.0	23.3	30.7	38.9	43.2
Switzerland	21.8	22.2	23.2	26.6	26.9	26.0	27.5	29.4	29.9	28.5	30.3	35.3	43.1	47.0
Turkey	9.6	10.9	11.1	14.9	13.4	19.7	23.7	16.8	20.4	16.0	14.8	19.0	24.0	25.9
United Kingdom	63.8	62.4	69.8	79.8	90.5	101.7	112.6	119.1	120.6	121.1	135.0	158.5	197.6	203.0
United States	177.3	185.9	200.4	219.2	239.5	256.1	262.8	281.9	298.6	286.2	292.3	302.7	344.4	380.6
Euro area	..	..	..	..	..	..	..	270.9	275.1	288.6	317.2	378.6	453.6	496.4
OECD total	..	..	..	..	..	1 058.4	1 105.6	1 147.8	1 202.2	1 199.5	1 271.0	1 459.3	1 734.1	1 884.2
Brazil	4.1	4.0	4.9	6.1	4.7	6.0	7.6	7.2	9.5	9.3	9.6	10.4	12.6	16.1
China	9.2	11.2	16.6	19.1	20.6	24.6	23.9	26.2	30.4	33.3	39.7	46.7	62.4	74.4
India	4.9	5.1	6.0	6.8	7.2	9.1	11.7	14.5	16.7	17.3	19.5	23.4	..	..
Russian Federation	..	..	8.4	10.6	13.3	14.1	12.4	9.1	9.6	11.4	13.6	16.2	20.3	24.6
South Africa	3.4	3.3	3.7	4.6	5.1	5.4	5.4	5.2	5.0	4.6	4.7	7.8	9.0	10.2

StatLink http://dx.doi.org/10.1787/132503403475

Relative growth in exports of services
Growth over the period 1997-2005, OECD total = 1

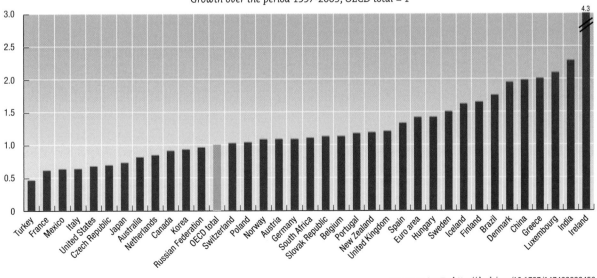

StatLink http://dx.doi.org/10.1787/147423020453

TRADING PARTNERS

The pattern of OECD merchandise trade – where imports come from and where exports go to – has undergone significant shifts over the last decade. These are in response to changes in the distribution of global income and to globalisation – in particular, the outsourcing of manufacturing from OECD countries to the rest of the world.

These tables refer to total OECD imports and exports and show merchandise trade both within the OECD area and with countries in the rest of the world.

Definition

NAFTA is the North American Free Trade Area and consists of Canada, Mexico and the United States. OECD Asia and Oceania includes Australia and New Zealand as well as Japan and Korea. Non-OECD America covers the Caribbean, South America and Central America, except Mexico. Middle East covers the Gulf Arabian Countries, Iran, Israel, Jordan, Lebanon, the Occupied Palestinian Territory and the Syrian Arab Republic.

The definitions of merchandise imports and exports are explained under "Trade in goods".

Comparability

OECD countries follow common definitions and procedures in compiling their merchandise trade statistics which are comparable and of good quality. The removal of customs frontiers following the creation of a common market in Europe required EU countries to adopt a system of recording trade flows through sample surveys of exporters and importers. This led to some fall in the reliability of merchandise trade statistics for trade between the EU countries. Statistics on trade between EU countries and non-EU countries, however, were not affected.

Source

- OECD (2006), *International Trade by Commodity Statistics*, OECD, Paris.

Further information

Analytical publications

- OECD, IOM and the World Bank (eds.) (2004), *Trade and Migration: Building Bridges for Global Labour Mobility*, OECD, Paris.
- OECD (2004), *Agriculture, Trade and the Environment: The Dairy Sector*, OECD, Paris.
- OECD (2004), *The Impact of Regulations on Agro-Food Trade: The Technical Barriers to Trade (TBT) and Sanitary and Phytosanitary Measures (SPS) Agreements*, OECD, Paris.
- OECD (2004), *Trade and Competitiveness in Argentina, Brazil and Chile Not as Easy as A-B-C*, OECD, Paris.
- OECD (2004), *Internationalisation and Trade in Higher Education: Opportunities and Challenges*, OECD, Paris.
- OECD (2005), *OECD Trade Policy Studies – Environmental Requirements and Market Access*, OECD, Paris.
- OECD (2005), *Trade and Structural Adjustment: Embracing Globalisation*, OECD, Paris.
- OECD (2006), *Trade Based Money Laundering*, OECD, Paris.
- OECD (2006), *The Development Dimension – Aid for Trade: Making it Effective*, OECD, Paris.

Statistical publications

- OECD (2006), *Monthly Statistics of International Trade*, OECD, Paris.
- OECD (2006), *Statistics in International Trade in Services*, OECD, Paris.

Methodological publications

- United Nations (1998), *International Merchandise Trade Statistics: Compilers Manual*, United Nations, New York.

Online databases

- *ITCS International Trade by Commodity Statistics.*
- *Monthly International Trade.*

Websites

- OECD International Trade Statistics, *www.oecd.org/std/its.*
- OECD International Trade Indicators, *www.oecd.org/statistics/trade.*

Long-term trends

Since 1988, there has been a steady decline in the share of OECD imports and exports among OECD member countries. In 1988, imports from OECD countries accounted for 80% of total OECD imports but by 2005 this had fallen to 67%. For exports the fall in intra-OECD trade was less marked – down from 81% in 1988 to 75% in 2005.

Outside the OECD area, the trade shares with Africa have fallen, they have risen with non-OECD America and the Middle East. Non-OECD Asia covers Central Asia, China, the Indian Sub-continent and South East. OECD imports from these countries have risen from 7% to 17% over the period and exports to them from 7.5% to 12%. A large change occurred in trade between OECD and China. In 1988 China supplied a little over 1% of total OECD imports but by 2005 this had risen to more than 9%. China's importance as a destination for OECD countries has increased less sharply, rising from 1% in 1988 to 4% in 2005.

Partner countries and regions of OECD merchandise trade
As a percentage of total OECD merchandise trade

	1988	1993	1994	1995	1996	1997	1998	1999	2000	2001	2002	2003	2004	2005
OECD	**80.4**	**76.3**	**76.1**	**76.1**	**75.7**	**75.6**	**77.4**	**77.7**	**75.9**	**75.9**	**75.6**	**74.2**	**73.6**	**70.5**
G7	**52.3**	**50.5**	**50.4**	**49.7**	**49.0**	**49.1**	**50.1**	**50.4**	**49.2**	**48.8**	**47.8**	**45.0**	**44.9**	**42.3**
NAFTA	16.3	19.7	20.2	19.0	19.7	21.2	21.7	22.7	23.8	23.1	22.2	18.1	18.9	18.6
Canada	1.3	4.7	4.8	4.5	4.6	4.8	4.9	5.1	5.3	5.1	4.8	4.5	4.2	4.3
Mexico	0.3	1.9	2.0	1.8	2.0	2.3	2.5	2.7	3.2	3.1	3.0	2.7	2.5	2.5
United States	14.7	13.0	13.5	12.7	13.1	14.0	14.3	14.9	15.4	14.8	14.3	10.8	12.1	11.8
OECD Asia Oceania	6.5	8.6	9.1	8.9	8.4	8.1	7.4	7.7	8.0	7.3	7.1	6.9	6.8	6.6
Japan	3.6	5.6	6.0	5.7	5.3	5.1	4.7	4.9	4.9	4.5	4.2	4.0	3.8	3.7
Korea	1.5	1.7	1.8	2.0	1.9	1.7	1.9	1.9	1.9	1.7	1.7	1.8	1.8	1.8
OECD Europe	57.8	48.1	46.7	48.1	47.5	46.4	48.3	47.2	44.1	45.5	46.1	49.4	47.9	44.9
Switzerland	2.6	2.1	1.9	2.0	1.9	1.8	1.9	1.8	1.6	1.7	1.6	1.7	1.6	1.1
EU15	52.8	43.2	42.1	43.2	42.4	41.1	42.8	42.0	39.0	40.1	40.5	43.2	41.7	39.2
Austria	1.7	1.4	1.4	1.3	1.3	1.3	1.4	1.3	1.2	1.3	1.3	1.4	1.4	1.3
Belgium-Luxembourg	4.7	3.6	3.5	3.6	3.4	3.2	3.3	3.1	2.9	3.1	3.2	3.4	3.4	2.1
France	8.0	6.6	6.3	6.3	6.1	5.9	6.2	6.1	5.5	5.7	5.7	6.0	5.8	5.5
Germany	12.7	10.7	10.2	10.6	10.3	9.6	10.1	9.8	9.0	9.3	9.4	10.1	10.0	9.6
Italy	5.5	4.2	4.1	4.3	4.2	4.0	4.2	4.0	3.7	3.8	3.9	4.2	4.0	2.6
Netherlands	5.1	4.0	3.9	4.1	4.0	4.0	4.0	3.9	3.7	3.7	3.7	3.9	3.8	3.7
Spain	2.1	2.1	2.1	2.3	2.3	2.3	2.5	2.6	2.4	2.4	2.6	2.8	2.8	2.7
Sweden	2.2	1.5	1.5	1.6	1.6	1.5	1.6	1.6	1.5	1.4	1.4	1.5	1.5	1.4
United Kingdom	6.6	5.7	5.5	5.5	5.6	5.7	5.8	5.7	5.4	5.5	5.4	5.4	5.1	4.8
Non-OECD	17.6	22.1	22.4	22.5	22.9	23.4	21.6	21.3	23.1	23.1	23.4	24.8	25.7	27.4
Africa	3.3	2.7	2.4	2.3	2.4	2.3	2.2	2.1	2.2	2.3	2.2	2.3	2.4	3.0
South Africa	0.8	0.5	0.4	0.5	0.5	0.5	0.5	0.4	0.4	0.5	0.4	0.5	0.5	0.5
America	2.1	3.0	3.1	3.1	3.1	3.3	3.2	3.0	3.0	3.0	2.8	2.6	2.8	3.1
South America	1.6	2.2	2.3	2.3	2.3	2.4	2.3	2.0	2.1	2.1	1.9	1.8	2.0	2.2
Brazil	0.7	0.8	0.8	0.9	0.9	0.9	0.9	0.8	0.8	0.9	0.8	0.8	0.8	0.8
Asia	7.2	11.3	12.1	12.4	12.4	12.6	11.5	11.8	12.8	12.5	13.0	13.8	14.2	14.6
China	1.3	2.4	2.7	2.8	2.9	3.1	3.2	3.4	3.9	4.2	4.9	5.8	6.3	6.9
India	0.5	0.5	0.6	0.6	0.6	0.6	0.6	0.5	0.5	0.5	0.6	0.6	0.7	0.8
Chinese Taipei	1.4	2.0	1.9	1.9	1.8	1.8	1.8	1.8	2.0	1.7	1.6	1.5	1.6	1.1
Europe	2.2	1.9	2.0	2.1	2.2	2.3	2.2	1.9	2.2	2.4	2.5	2.9	3.1	3.6
Russian Federation	0.2	1.0	1.0	1.0	1.1	1.1	1.0	0.8	1.0	1.1	1.1	1.3	1.5	1.7
Middle East	2.6	3.0	2.7	2.5	2.6	2.8	2.4	2.4	2.9	2.9	2.7	2.9	3.0	3.4

StatLink ᴍᴇᴵ᠌ http://dx.doi.org/10.1787/443643730656

Partner countries and regions of OECD merchandise trade
As a percentage of total OECD merchandise trade

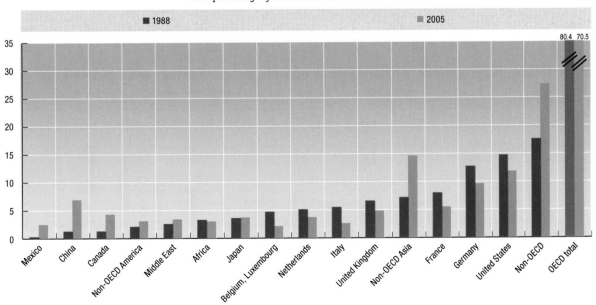

StatLink ᴍᴇᴵ᠌ http://dx.doi.org/10.1787/741363833631

Partner countries and regions of OECD merchandise imports

As a percentage of total OECD merchandise imports

	1988	1993	1994	1995	1996	1997	1998	1999	2000	2001	2002	2003	2004	2005
OECD	**80.2**	**76.1**	**75.9**	**76.3**	**75.6**	**75.4**	**76.8**	**75.9**	**73.1**	**73.3**	**72.9**	**71.3**	**70.4**	**66.6**
G7	**52.5**	**51.4**	**51.3**	**50.8**	**50.2**	**50.0**	**50.5**	**49.8**	**47.5**	**47.0**	**45.9**	**43.1**	**42.7**	**39.6**
NAFTA	14.7	18.7	19.4	18.9	19.7	20.8	20.7	21.1	21.7	21.1	19.9	16.1	16.5	16.0
Canada	1.3	5.1	5.1	5.0	5.0	5.1	5.2	5.4	5.6	5.5	5.2	4.8	4.6	4.6
Mexico	0.4	1.8	1.9	2.0	2.2	2.5	2.6	2.9	3.3	3.3	3.3	3.0	2.7	2.7
United States	13.0	11.9	12.3	11.9	12.4	13.1	12.9	12.8	12.8	12.2	11.5	8.3	9.2	8.7
OECD Asia Oceania	7.8	10.4	10.8	10.2	9.2	9.2	9.0	9.3	9.4	8.5	8.2	7.9	7.9	7.6
Japan	4.7	7.6	7.9	7.2	6.4	6.4	6.2	6.4	6.3	5.6	5.4	5.1	4.9	4.7
Korea	1.6	1.6	1.6	1.7	1.6	1.6	1.6	1.9	2.0	1.8	1.8	1.8	1.9	1.8
OECD Europe	58.0	46.9	45.8	47.3	46.7	45.5	47.1	45.6	42.0	43.6	44.5	47.6	46.0	42.7
Switzerland	2.3	2.0	1.9	1.9	1.8	1.7	1.7	1.6	1.4	1.5	1.5	1.5	1.5	1.0
EU15	53.3	42.3	41.3	42.5	41.8	40.6	42.1	40.6	37.1	38.3	39.0	41.4	39.9	37.2
Austria	1.5	1.3	1.3	1.2	1.1	1.1	1.2	1.2	1.0	1.1	1.2	1.3	1.2	1.2
Belgium-Luxembourg	4.6	3.4	3.3	3.4	3.2	3.0	3.0	2.9	2.6	2.8	2.9	3.1	3.1	1.9
France	7.6	6.3	6.1	6.1	5.9	5.8	6.1	5.8	5.1	5.3	5.3	5.6	5.3	4.8
Germany	14.6	10.8	10.4	10.9	10.6	10.0	10.5	10.2	9.2	9.6	10.0	10.8	10.7	10.2
Italy	5.6	4.5	4.5	4.6	4.6	4.3	4.5	4.2	3.7	3.8	3.9	4.1	3.9	2.6
Netherlands	5.3	3.9	3.8	4.0	3.9	3.9	4.0	3.7	3.5	3.5	3.5	3.8	3.8	3.7
Spain	1.8	1.8	1.9	2.0	2.1	2.1	2.2	2.1	1.9	2.0	2.1	2.3	2.2	2.1
Sweden	2.3	1.6	1.7	1.7	1.7	1.7	1.7	1.6	1.5	1.4	1.4	1.5	1.5	1.4
United Kingdom	5.6	5.2	5.0	5.1	5.2	5.2	5.2	5.1	4.9	4.8	4.6	4.5	4.1	4.0
Non-OECD	18.0	22.6	22.8	22.6	23.3	23.9	22.4	23.2	26.0	25.7	25.9	27.6	28.9	31.5
Africa	3.6	2.8	2.5	2.4	2.6	2.5	2.2	2.1	2.4	2.5	2.3	2.6	2.7	3.5
South Africa	1.0	0.5	0.4	0.5	0.5	0.5	0.5	0.5	0.5	0.5	0.5	0.5	0.5	0.5
America	2.5	3.0	3.1	2.9	3.0	3.0	2.8	2.8	3.0	2.9	3.0	2.9	3.2	3.4
South America	2.1	2.3	2.4	2.3	2.3	2.3	2.1	2.1	2.2	2.2	2.2	2.2	2.5	2.7
Brazil	1.0	0.9	1.0	0.9	0.8	0.8	0.8	0.8	0.8	0.9	0.9	0.9	1.0	1.0
Asia	6.9	11.8	12.3	12.4	12.8	13.2	13.2	13.7	14.6	14.5	15.2	16.0	16.6	17.2
China	1.3	3.2	3.6	3.7	4.0	4.4	4.5	4.9	5.5	5.9	6.8	7.7	8.5	9.4
India	0.4	0.6	0.6	0.6	0.6	0.6	0.6	0.6	0.6	0.6	0.7	0.7	0.7	0.7
Chinese Taipei	1.5	2.1	2.0	1.9	1.9	1.9	1.9	1.9	2.1	1.8	1.7	1.6	1.6	1.0
Europe	2.2	1.9	2.0	2.1	2.1	2.1	2.0	2.0	2.4	2.4	2.5	2.8	3.1	3.8
Russian Federation	0.2	1.1	1.2	1.2	1.2	1.2	1.1	1.1	1.4	1.4	1.4	1.6	1.8	2.1
Middle East	2.7	3.0	2.7	2.6	2.7	2.9	2.2	2.5	3.5	3.3	2.9	3.2	3.3	3.9

StatLink ▄▄▄█▄ http://dx.doi.org/10.1787/103588371604

Partner countries and regions of OECD merchandise imports

As a percentage of total OECD merchandise imports

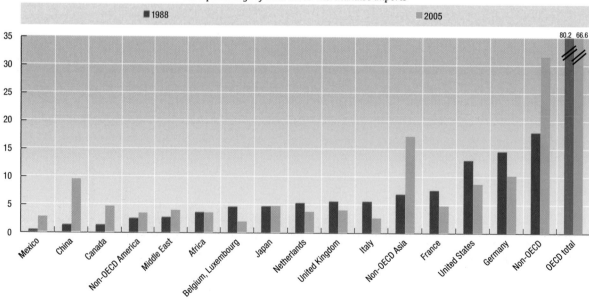

StatLink ▄▄▄█▄ http://dx.doi.org/10.1787/871442307376

OECD FACTBOOK 2007 – ISBN 978-92-64-02946-0 – © OECD 2007

Partner countries and regions of OECD merchandise exports

As a percentage of total OECD merchandise exports

	1988	1993	1994	1995	1996	1997	1998	1999	2000	2001	2002	2003	2004	2005
OECD	**80.5**	**76.6**	**76.3**	**75.9**	**75.7**	**75.8**	**77.9**	**79.6**	**79.0**	**78.8**	**78.5**	**77.4**	**77.1**	**74.8**
G7	**52.2**	**49.7**	**49.5**	**48.6**	**47.9**	**48.2**	**49.7**	**51.1**	**51.0**	**50.8**	**49.9**	**47.1**	**47.4**	**45.2**
NAFTA	17.9	20.6	21.1	19.2	19.7	21.6	22.6	24.5	26.1	25.2	24.6	20.2	21.4	21.5
Canada	1.3	4.4	4.5	4.1	4.2	4.5	4.6	4.8	4.8	4.6	4.5	4.2	3.9	4.0
Mexico	0.3	2.0	2.1	1.6	1.8	2.2	2.4	2.6	3.0	2.9	2.7	2.5	2.3	2.4
United States	16.3	14.1	14.6	13.5	13.7	14.8	15.6	17.1	18.3	17.6	17.4	13.5	15.2	15.2
OECD Asia Oceania	5.3	6.7	7.5	7.6	7.6	7.0	5.7	6.1	6.5	6.0	5.9	5.9	5.6	5.5
Japan	2.5	3.6	4.1	4.1	4.1	3.8	3.2	3.3	3.4	3.2	2.9	2.8	2.6	2.6
Korea	1.4	1.8	2.0	2.2	2.2	1.9	1.2	1.6	1.8	1.6	1.7	1.7	1.7	1.7
OECD Europe	57.5	49.3	47.7	49.0	48.4	47.2	49.6	49.0	46.4	47.6	47.9	51.4	50.1	47.4
Switzerland	2.9	2.2	2.0	2.0	2.0	1.8	2.0	1.9	1.7	1.8	1.8	1.8	1.7	1.2
EU15	52.4	44.1	43.0	43.9	42.9	41.6	43.7	43.4	41.0	42.1	42.1	45.1	43.7	41.4
Austria	1.8	1.6	1.5	1.5	1.5	1.4	1.5	1.5	1.4	1.4	1.4	1.6	1.6	1.5
Belgium-Luxembourg	4.7	3.9	3.8	3.8	3.6	3.4	3.5	3.4	3.2	3.4	3.5	3.8	3.8	2.3
France	8.4	6.8	6.6	6.6	6.2	5.9	6.3	6.3	6.0	6.2	6.1	6.5	6.3	6.2
Germany	10.7	10.5	10.0	10.3	9.9	9.3	9.7	9.4	8.8	9.0	8.8	9.5	9.2	9.0
Italy	5.4	3.9	3.8	4.0	3.8	3.7	3.9	3.9	3.7	3.8	3.9	4.3	4.1	2.6
Netherlands	4.9	4.1	4.1	4.2	4.1	4.1	4.1	4.1	3.9	3.8	3.8	4.0	3.8	3.8
Spain	2.4	2.3	2.3	2.5	2.5	2.5	2.8	3.0	2.8	2.9	3.0	3.4	3.4	3.4
Sweden	2.1	1.3	1.3	1.5	1.5	1.4	1.4	1.4	1.4	1.3	1.3	1.5	1.4	1.4
United Kingdom	7.6	6.3	6.0	5.9	6.0	6.2	6.4	6.3	6.1	6.3	6.3	6.3	6.0	5.7
Non-OECD	17.2	21.5	22.0	22.5	22.4	23.0	20.8	19.3	20.1	20.4	20.6	21.7	22.1	22.9
Africa	3.1	2.5	2.3	2.2	2.2	2.1	2.3	2.0	1.9	2.0	2.0	2.1	2.1	2.5
South Africa	0.6	0.4	0.4	0.5	0.5	0.4	0.5	0.4	0.4	0.4	0.4	0.4	0.5	0.5
America	1.7	3.0	3.2	3.3	3.3	3.7	3.7	3.1	3.0	3.1	2.7	2.3	2.5	2.6
South America	1.1	2.0	2.1	2.3	2.3	2.6	2.6	2.0	1.9	2.0	1.6	1.3	1.4	1.6
Brazil	0.3	0.6	0.7	0.9	0.9	1.0	1.0	0.8	0.8	0.9	0.7	0.6	0.6	0.7
Asia	7.5	10.8	11.8	12.4	12.0	12.0	9.8	9.9	10.9	10.3	10.7	11.5	11.7	11.7
China	1.2	1.7	1.8	1.8	1.8	1.8	1.8	1.9	2.2	2.4	2.9	3.6	3.9	4.1
India	0.6	0.5	0.5	0.6	0.6	0.5	0.5	0.5	0.5	0.5	0.5	0.6	0.7	0.8
Chinese Taipei	1.4	1.9	1.9	1.9	1.7	1.8	1.7	1.7	2.0	1.5	1.5	1.5	1.6	1.2
Europe	2.2	1.9	1.9	2.1	2.3	2.5	2.4	1.9	1.9	2.4	2.6	3.0	3.1	3.4
Russian Federation	0.2	0.9	0.8	0.8	0.9	1.1	0.9	0.5	0.6	0.8	0.8	1.0	1.1	1.3
Middle East	2.6	3.0	2.6	2.4	2.5	2.6	2.6	2.3	2.2	2.4	2.5	2.6	2.6	2.8

StatLink 🔗 http://dx.doi.org/10.1787/168143245750

Partner countries and regions of OECD merchandise exports

As a percentage of total OECD merchandise exports

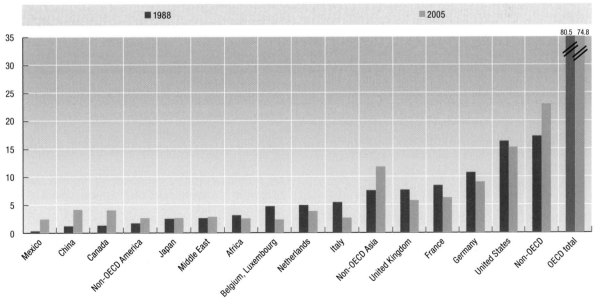

StatLink 🔗 http://dx.doi.org/10.1787/807547430664

BALANCE OF PAYMENTS

The current account balance is the difference between current receipts from abroad and current payments to abroad. When the current account of the balance of payments is positive, the country can use the surplus to repay foreign debts or to lend to the rest of the world. When the current account balance is negative, the deficit will be financed by borrowing from abroad or by liquidating foreign assets acquired in earlier periods.

Definition

The current account balance is the difference between a country's current transactions with the rest of the world and its current payments to the rest of the world. Current transactions consist of exports and imports of goods; exports and imports of services such as tourism, international freight and passenger transport, insurance and financial services; income consisting of wages and salaries, dividends, interest and other property income; and transfers.

Note that property income includes retained earnings of foreign-owned subsidiaries. All earnings of foreign-owned subsidiaries are treated as if they were remitted abroad and the part which is actually retained in the country where the subsidiary is located is then shown as a re-investment flow in the capital account.

Comparability

The data in this table are taken from balance of payments statistics compiled according to the International Monetary Fund (IMF) *Balance of Payments Manual* (BPM5). The IMF closely monitors balance of payments statistics reported by its member countries through regular meetings of balance of payments compilers. As a result, there is relatively good comparability across countries.

Because all earnings of foreign-owned subsidiaries are treated as though they are remitted even though a large part may in practice be retained by the subsidiaries in the countries where they are located, the existence of foreign-owned subsidiaries in an economy will tend to reduce its current account balance.

Long-term trends

Current account balances as a percentage of GDP have been negative throughout the period since 1992 in Australia, Mexico, New Zealand, the United States and the United Kingdom; this is partly due to the way in which earnings of foreign owned-subsidiaries are treated. Countries which have recorded current account surpluses throughout the period include Japan, Luxembourg, the Netherlands, Norway and Switzerland.

Since 1992, current account balances have generally moved from deficit to surplus in Canada, Finland, Korea and Sweden.

The chart shows current account balances averaged over the last three years. Deficits averaged 5% or more of GDP in Iceland, Hungary, Portugal, New Zealand, Greece, the United States, Australia and Spain. Surpluses in excess of 5% were recorded by Finland, Sweden, the Netherlands, Luxembourg, Switzerland, Norway and the Russian Federation.

Sources

- For member countries and South Africa: OECD (2006), *Main Economic Indicators*, OECD, Paris.
- For Brazil, China, India and Russian Federation: National sources.

Further information

Analytical publications

- OECD (2004), *Export Credit Financing Systems in OECD Member and Non-member Countries*, OECD, Paris.

Methodological publications

- IMF (1993), *Balance of Payments Manual*, 5th edition, IMF, Washington, DC.
- UN, EC, IMF, OECD, UNCTAD and the WTO (2002), *Manual on Statistics of International Trade in Services*, United Nations, New York.

Online databases

- *Main Economic Indicators*.
- *OECD Economic Outlook Statistics*.

Websites

- OECD Economic Outlook – Sources and Methods, *www.oecd.org/eco/sources-and-methods*.

Current account balance of payments
As a percentage of GDP

	1992	1993	1994	1995	1996	1997	1998	1999	2000	2001	2002	2003	2004	2005
Australia	-3.5	-3.1	-4.8	-5.0	-3.6	-2.8	-4.7	-5.1	-3.6	-2.0	-3.7	-5.2	-5.9	-5.5
Austria	-0.4	-0.8	-1.6	-2.6	-2.3	-3.1	-2.4	-3.2	-2.5		-1.9	0.3	-0.2	0.2	1.1
Belgium	..	..	..	5.4	5.0	5.5	5.2		5.1	4.0		3.4	4.6	4.1	3.5	2.5
Canada	-3.6	-3.9	-2.3	-0.8	0.5	-1.3	-1.2	0.3	2.7	2.3	1.7	1.2	2.1	2.3
Czech Republic	..	1.2	-1.8	-2.5	-6.6	-6.2	-2.0	-2.4	-4.8	-5.3	-5.5	-6.3	-6.0	-2.1
Denmark	2.1	2.8	1.5	0.7	1.4	0.4	-0.9	1.9	1.6	2.6	2.9	3.4	2.3	2.9
Finland	-4.6	-1.3	1.1	4.1	4.0	5.6	5.6		6.2	8.7		9.6	10.2	6.5	7.8	4.9
France	..	..	..	0.7	1.3	2.6	2.6		2.9	1.4		1.6	1.0	0.4	-0.3	-1.6
Germany	-1.1	-0.9	-1.4	-1.2	-0.6	-0.5	-0.7		-1.3	-1.7		-	2.0	1.9	3.7	4.0
Greece	..	..	..	..	..	-3.4	-2.4	-3.3	-6.8	-6.3	-5.9	-5.8	-5.1	-6.3
Hungary	0.8	-8.7	-9.2	-3.3	-3.8	-4.3	-7.0	-7.6	-8.4	-6.0	-6.9	-7.9	-8.4	-6.8
Iceland	-2.4	0.7	1.9	0.7	-1.8	-1.7	-6.7	-6.8	-10.2	-4.4	1.6	-4.8	-9.9	-16.2
Ireland	1.1	3.5	2.8	2.6	2.8	2.3		0.8		0.2	-0.4		-0.7	-0.9	-	-0.6	-2.7
Italy	-2.3	0.8	1.2	2.2	3.1	2.8	1.9		0.7	-0.5		-0.1	-0.8	-1.3	-0.9	-1.6
Japan	3.0	3.1	2.7	2.1	1.4		2.3	3.1	2.6	2.6	2.1	2.9	3.2	3.8	3.6
Korea	-1.2	0.2	-1.0	-1.7	-4.1	-1.6	11.7	5.5	2.4	1.7	1.0	2.0	4.1	1.9
Luxembourg	..	..	..	12.1	11.2	10.4	9.2		8.4	13.2		8.8	11.7	7.5	11.8	11.8
Mexico	-6.7	-5.8	-7.0	-0.6	-0.8	-1.9	-3.8	-2.9	-3.2	-2.8	-2.2	-1.4	-1.0	-0.7
Netherlands	2.0	4.1	4.9	6.1	5.1	6.5	3.2		3.8	1.9		2.4	2.5	5.5	8.5	7.7
New Zealand	-4.1	-3.7	-3.8	-5.0	-5.7	-6.3	-3.9	-6.2	-5.2	-2.7	-3.9	-4.3	-6.6	-8.9
Norway	..	..	3.0	3.5	6.9	6.3	-	5.3	15.0	15.4	12.8	13.0	13.6	16.6
Poland	..	..	0.9	0.6	-2.1	-3.7	-4.0	-7.4	-5.8	-2.8	-2.5	-1.9	-4.2	-1.7
Portugal	..	..	..	..	-4.3	-6.0	-7.1		-8.6	-10.4		-9.8	-7.9	-5.9	-7.3	-9.2
Slovak Republic	..	-4.4	4.8	2.6	-9.2	-8.4	-8.8	-4.8	-3.4	-8.3	-7.9	-0.8	-3.4	-8.6
Spain	-3.5	-1.1	-1.2	-0.3	-0.2	-0.1	-1.2		-2.9	-4.0		-3.9	-3.3	-3.5	-5.3	-7.4
Sweden	-2.8	-1.3	1.1	3.4	3.5	4.1	3.9	4.2	3.9	3.9	4.1	7.4	6.8	7.1
Switzerland	5.9	7.8	6.4	6.6	7.1	9.4	9.4	11.1	12.5	8.0	8.4	13.4	13.5	14.8
Turkey	-0.6	-3.6	2.0	-1.4	-1.3	-1.4	1.0	-0.7	-4.9	2.3	-0.8	-3.4	-5.1	-6.4
United Kingdom	-2.1	-1.8	-1.0	-1.2	-0.9	-0.1	-0.4	-2.4	-2.6	-2.2	-1.6	-1.3	-1.6	-2.2
United States	-0.8	-1.3	-1.7	-1.5	-1.6	-1.7	-2.5	-3.3	-4.3	-3.9	-4.5	-4.8	-5.7	-6.4
Brazil	1.6	-	-0.2	-2.6	-3.0	-3.8	-4.3	-4.7	-4.0	-4.6	-1.7	0.8	1.9	1.8
China	1.3	-1.9	1.4	0.2	0.8	3.9	3.1	1.9	1.7	1.3	2.4	2.8	3.6	7.2
India	-1.9	-0.5	-1.1	-1.8	-1.3	-1.5	-1.0	-1.1	-0.6	0.8	1.4	2.5	-0.9	-1.5
Russian Federation	..	..	..	2.3	2.8	-	0.1	12.6	18.0	11.1	8.4	8.2	9.9	10.9
South Africa	1.5	2.1	-	-1.6	-1.2	-1.5	-1.6	-0.5	-0.1	0.1	0.6	-1.4	-3.5	-4.2

StatLink ᵐˢ⁵ http://dx.doi.org/10.1787/563160435415

Current account balance of payments
As a percentage of GDP, average 2003-2005

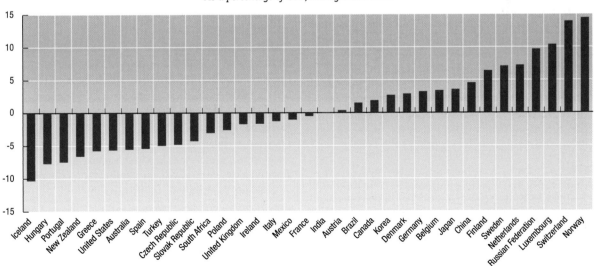

StatLink ᵐˢ⁵ http://dx.doi.org/10.1787/384786485451

FDI FLOWS AND STOCKS

Foreign direct investment (FDI) is a key element in the rapidly evolving process of international economic integration. FDI creates direct, stable and long-lasting links between economies. FDI encourages the transfer of technology and know-how between countries, and it allows the host economy to promote its products more widely in international markets. Finally, FDI is an additional source of funding for capital investment.

Definition

Foreign direct investment (FDI) is defined as investment by a resident entity in one economy with the objective of obtaining a lasting interest in an enterprise resident in another economy. The *lasting interest* means the existence of a long-term relationship between the direct investor and the enterprise and a significant degree of influence by the direct investor on the management of the direct investment enterprise. Absolute control by the foreign investor is not required, and ownership of 10% of the voting power is the criterion used.

Inward stocks are the direct investments held by non-residents; *outward stocks* are the investments held in other economies.

The stock tables also show the distribution of stocks according to industry (mainly manufacturing) and services.

Comparability

International standards call for FDI stocks to be valued at market prices but most OECD countries report their FDI stocks using book values as recorded in the balance sheets of direct investors. Book values may be very different from market values and the rules for establishing book values also vary between countries.

Despite improvements in recent years, there are also methodological differences between countries as regards the inward and outward flow of FDI. For more details, see the joint IMF/OECD analysis of how countries apply the international standards (see the methodological publications below).

Totals for OECD and EU are only for the countries for which data are available. Data for 2004 and 2005 are provisional.

Source

- OECD (2005), *International Direct Investment Statistics Yearbook*, OECD, Paris.

Further information

Analytical publications

- OECD (2005), *International Investment Perspectives*, OECD, Paris.
- OECD (2006), *Reviews of Foreign Direct Investment*, OECD, Paris.
- OECD (2006), *Policy Framework for Investment: A Review of Good Practices*, OECD, Paris.

Statistical publications

- OECD (2002), *Measuring Globalisation: The Role of Multinationals in OECD Economies*, OECD, Paris.
- OECD (2005), *Measuring Globalisation: OECD Economic Globalisation Indicators*, OECD, Paris.

Methodological publications

- IMF, OECD (1999), *Report on the Survey of Implementation of Methodological Standards for Direct Investment*.
- OECD (1996), *OECD Benchmark Definition of Foreign Direct Investment*, Third edition, OECD, Paris.
- OECD (2001), *Non-Tariff Measures in the ICT Sector: A Survey*, OECD, Paris.
- OECD (2005), *Measuring Globalisation: OECD Handbook on Economic Globalisation Indicators*, OECD, Paris.

Websites

- OECD International Investment, *www.oecd.org/daf/ investment*.

Long-term trends

Both inflows and outflows of FDI worldwide dropped drastically in 2001 following the spectacular investment boom of the late 1990s. FDI into the OECD area continued to decline until 2004 when inflows picked up timidly by 6% and outflows by 27%. The global environment for FDI improved in 2005 while at the same time corporate profitability was generally strong. Direct investment into OECD picked up in 2005 when inflows reached $622 bn. The United States and the United Kingdom were the main destinations for FDI in the OECD. Investment flows to EU countries also increased notably by 75% while half of the increase accounts for FDI flows into the United Kingdom, which tripled in 2005. Investments into China, amongst the foremost destinations of FDI, further progressed. FDI outflows from the OECD dropped slightly by 8% reaching $716 bn in 2005. This drop in 2005 was to a large extent influenced by the one-off decline in US inflows due to temporary effects of the changes in tax legislation. Nevertheless, OECD area continued to be net outward investor at around $95 bn in 2005, less than in 2004 but quite high by historical standards.

Outward and inward FDI stocks
Millions of US dollars

	Outward direct investment stocks							Inward direct investment stocks						
	1990	1995	2000	2001	2002	2003	2004	1990	1999	2000	2001	2002	2003	2004
Australia	30 495	53 009	85 385	109 688	108 849	150 733	197 632	73 615	104 074	111 138	111 827	141 549	199 880	267 420
Austria	4 747	11 832	24 820	28 511	42 483	55 961	67 833	10 972	19 721	30 431	34 328	43 507	53 844	61 703
Canada	84 813	132 322	237 647	250 691	275 711	318 718	375 055	112 850	123 182	212 723	213 755	225 902	282 211	316 494
Czech Republic	..	498	738	1 136	1 473	2 284	3 759	..	7 350	21 647	27 093	38 672	45 286	57 246
Denmark	..	27 602	73 074	78 236	86 697	102 587	118 702	..	23 801	73 573	75 383	82 743	100 236	108 094
Finland	11 227	17 666	52 109	52 224	63 921	76 050	82 556	5 132	8 465	24 272	24 070	34 006	50 257	55 662
France	110 121	231 113	445 087	508 842	586 307	724 445	829 310	84 931	191 433	259 773	295 308	385 187	527 625	619 579
Germany	130 760	248 634	486 750	551 083	602 691	727 201	754 619	74 067	104 367	462 529	416 826	529 323	655 587	675 629
Greece	..	..	5 852	7 020	9 001	12 337	13 791	..	..	14 113	13 941	15 560	22 454	28 482
Hungary	..	265	1 279	1 554	2 166	3 509	6 031	569	11 304	22 856	27 378	36 213	48 345	62 726
Iceland	75	240	663	840	1 255	1 733	4 025	147	149	491	676	797	1 190	1 998
Ireland	..	..	27 925	40 819	54 025	64 457	..	..	..	127 088	134 051	178 566	217 164	..
Italy	60 195	117 278	180 274	182 373	194 488	238 888	280 481	60 009	65 347	121 169	113 434	130 814	180 891	220 720
Japan	201 440	258 612	278 441	300 116	304 237	335 500	370 544	9 850	33 508	50 322	50 319	78 140	89 729	96 984
Korea	..	..	..	19 967	20 735	24 986	..	..	..	53 208	62 658	66 070	..	..
Luxembourg	..	4 695	7 927	8 810	16 007	17 386	..	..	18 503	23 492	26 347	34 970	41 750	..
Mexico	..	..	..	12 077	12 869	16 587	22 219	22 424	41 130	97 170	140 376	158 651	172 834	191 509
Netherlands	106 896	194 016	305 459	332 151	396 514	531 151	595 361	68 729	116 051	243 730	282 879	349 955	457 984	501 072
New Zealand	..	9 293	6 065	8 808	9 162	11 458	12 510	..	25 728	28 070	23 641	30 520	39 390	51 950
Norway	10 889	25 439	46 302	55 403	72 487	82 788	..	12 404	19 836	30 261	32 590	42 649	48 967	..
Poland	..	735	1 018	1 156	1 457	2 147	3 221	109	7 843	34 227	41 247	48 320	57 851	85 509
Portugal	..	3 834	19 552	22 086	21 147	35 883	48 336	..	18 973	32 043	36 023	44 635	62 200	70 566
Slovak Republic	..	185	379	507	486	633	692	..	1 297	4 679	5 730	8 531	11 284	14 504
Spain	..	42 000	167 718	191 649	233 937	292 464	371 154	..	110 291	156 347	177 252	257 095	339 652	395 189
Sweden	50 720	72 188	123 234	123 268	146 510	183 769	204 085	12 636	31 089	93 972	91 584	119 315	157 029	197 983
Switzerland	66 087	141 587	229 756	249 265	288 949	338 408	396 442	34 245	57 064	86 810	88 766	124 812	161 989	195 929
Turkey	..	..	3 668	4 581	5 847	6 138	7 060	..	..	19 209	19 677	18 791	33 533	32 489
United Kingdom	229 307	330 432	897 845	869 700	994 136	1 187 045	1 268 532	203 905	199 772	438 631	506 686	523 319	606 157	707 924
United States	616 655	989 810	1 531 607	1 693 131	1 860 418	2 062 551	2 399 224	505 346	680 066	1 421 017	1 518 473	1 517 403	1 585 898	1 727 062
OECD total	1 714 426	2 928 362	5 240 573	5 705 694	6 413 964	7 607 798	8 433 171	1 291 940	2 020 343	4 241 784	4 582 865	5 262 604	6 317 286	6 744 423
of which:														
Manufacturing	39%	39%	25%	24%	22%	22%	..	39%	33%	26%	25%	24%	23%	..
Services	49%	52%	61%	62%	62%	65%	..	49%	52%	59%	60%	61%	63%	..
Brazil	..	..	..	49 689	54 423	54 892	69 196	..	..	..	121 948	100 847	132 799	161 259
China	..	..	..	..	..	..	52 704	..	..	..	..	..	..	536 954
India	..	..	2 616	4 006	5 825	7 079	9 568	..	..	20 326	25 419	31 221	39 104	44 511
Russian Federation	..	2 420	20 141	44 219	62 349	90 873	107 291	..	345	32 204	52 919	70 884	96 729	122 295
South Africa	15 010	23 301	32 325	17 580	21 980	27 185	38 483	9 210	15 014	43 451	30 569	29 611	45 715	63 071

StatLink ⟐⟐ http://dx.doi.org/10.1787/562017054722

FDI stocks
As a percentage of GDP, 2004 or latest available year

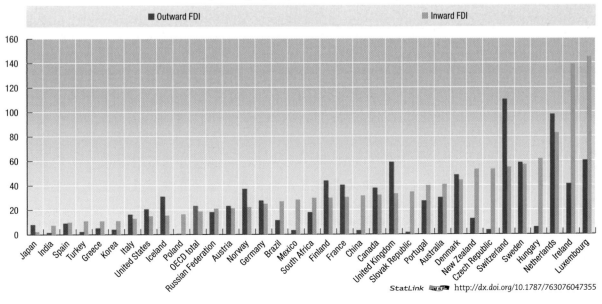

StatLink ⟐⟐ http://dx.doi.org/10.1787/763076047355

Inflows of foreign direct investment
Millions of US dollars

	1992	1993	1994	1995	1996	1997	1998	1999	2000	2001	2002	2003	2004	2005
Australia	5 720	4 282	5 025	11 963	6 111	7 633	6 003	3 268	13 950	8 297	17 674	9 675	42 036	-36 810
Austria	1 433	1 137	2 103	1 904	4 429	2 656	4 534	2 975	8 842	5 921	357	7 151	3 687	8 905
Belgium	..	..	..	..	..	..	..	..	..	..	15 641	32 127	42 064	23 710
Canada	4 722	4 730	8 204	9 255	9 633	11 522	22 803	24 747	66 796	27 670	22 146	7 619	1 533	33 824
Czech Republic	..	653	868	2 562	1 428	1 301	3 716	6 326	4 980	5 645	8 483	2 109	4 975	10 988
Denmark	1 015	1 669	4 898	4 180	768	2 799	7 726	14 657	31 306	11 525	6 633	2 597	-10 721	5 020
Finland	406	864	1 578	1 063	1 109	2 116	12 141	4 610	8 836	3 732	7 927	3 322	3 539	4 558
France	17 849	16 443	15 574	23 679	21 960	23 171	30 984	46 546	43 258	50 485	49 079	42 538	31 388	63 540
Germany	-2 089	368	7 134	12 025	6 573	12 243	24 597	56 077	198 313	26 419	53 571	29 228	-15 123	32 643
Greece	1 589	1 244	1 166	1 198	1 196	1 089	72	561	1 108	1 589	50	1 276	2 103	606
Hungary	1 477	2 446	1 144	5 102	3 300	4 171	3 337	3 313	2 763	3 936	2 994	2 137	4 657	6 700
Iceland	-13	..	-2	9	83	148	148	67	170	173	91	328	654	2 329
Ireland	1 458	1 068	856	1 442	2 616	2 710	8 856	18 211	25 784	9 653	29 350	22 803	11 165	-22 759
Italy	3 211	3 751	2 236	4 816	3 535	4 962	4 280	6 911	13 377	14 873	14 558	16 430	16 824	19 498
Japan	2 755	210	888	41	228	3 225	3 193	12 744	8 318	6 245	9 240	6 324	7 819	2 778
Korea	728	588	809	1 776	2 325	2 844	5 412	9 333	9 283	3 528	2 392	3 526	9 246	4 339
Luxembourg	..	..	..	..	..	..	..	..	..	..	115 175	90 318	77 260	43 729
Mexico	4 393	4 389	15 069	9 679	10 087	14 165	12 409	13 631	17 588	27 151	18 275	14 184	18 674	18 055
Netherlands	6 169	6 443	7 158	12 307	16 660	11 137	36 925	41 206	63 866	51 937	25 060	21 760	442	43 604
New Zealand	1 089	2 212	2 616	2 850	3 922	1 917	1 826	940	1 344	4 591	-275	2 049	4 371	2 834
Norway	810	1 461	2 778	2 408	3 168	3 946	4 354	7 062	6 908	2 009	679	3 803	2 547	14 464
Poland	678	1 715	1 875	3 659	4 498	4 908	6 365	7 270	9 343	5 714	4 131	4 870	12 355	7 724
Portugal	1 904	1 516	1 255	660	1 344	2 362	3 005	1 157	6 637	6 232	1 801	8 601	2 368	3 112
Slovak Republic	..	179	273	241	396	231	707	429	2 383	1 584	4 127	594	1 107	1 907
Spain	13 351	9 572	9 276	6 285	6 821	6 388	11 798	18 744	39 582	28 347	39 249	25 950	24 775	22 973
Sweden	41	3 845	6 350	14 447	5 437	10 967	19 843	60 929	23 245	11 900	11 734	1 285	-1 852	13 692
Switzerland	411	-83	3 368	2 224	3 078	6 642	8 942	11 714	19 266	8 859	6 284	16 505	750	5 781
Turkey	844	636	608	885	722	805	940	783	982	3 352	1 137	1 752	2 837	9 686
United Kingdom	15 475	14 821	9 255	19 968	24 441	33 245	74 349	87 973	118 824	52 650	24 052	16 846	56 253	164 499
United States	19 823	51 362	46 121	57 776	86 502	105 603	179 045	289 444	321 274	167 021	80 841	67 091	133 162	109 754
EU 15 total	72 768	73 209	77 150	114 868	110 812	132 354	269 256	503 070	803 966	359 981	394 237	322 233	244 171	427 329
OECD total	116 207	147 990	166 793	225 299	246 294	301 415	528 455	894 142	1 289 314	635 756	572 455	464 799	490 895	621 682
Brazil	2 061	1 292	3 072	4 859	11 200	19 650	31 913	28 576	32 779	22 457	16 590	10 144	18 166	15 193
China	11 156	27 515	33 787	35 849	40 180	44 237	43 751	38 753	38 399	44 241	49 308	47 077	54 937	79 127
India	277	550	973	2 144	2 426	3 577	2 635	2 169	3 584	5 472	5 626	4 585	..	..
Russian Federation	..	..	690	2 065	2 579	4 865	2 761	3 309	2 714	2 748	3 461	7 958	15 444	14 183
South Africa	3	11	374	1 248	816	3 811	550	1 503	969	7 270	735	783	701	6 257

StatLink ⬛ http://dx.doi.org/10.1787/586781321878

Inflows of foreign direct investment
Millions of US dollars, average 2003-2005

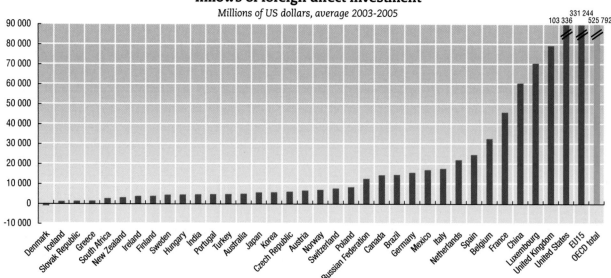

StatLink ⬛ http://dx.doi.org/10.1787/358778347642

OECD FACTBOOK 2007 – ISBN 978-92-64-02946-0 – © OECD 2007

Outflows of foreign direct investment

Millions of US dollars

	1992	1993	1994	1995	1996	1997	1998	1999	2000	2001	2002	2003	2004	2005
Australia	5 267	1 947	2 817	3 282	7 088	6 428	3 345	-421	3 158	11 962	8 035	15 526	17 488	-39 787
Austria	1 697	1 190	1 257	1 131	1 935	1 988	2 745	3 301	5 741	3 138	5 812	7 143	7 392	9 382
Belgium	..	..	..	..	..	..	..	..	..	..	12 705	36 933	33 545	22 946
Canada	3 589	5 700	9 294	11 462	13 094	23 059	34 349	17 250	44 678	36 037	26 761	21 526	43 248	34 084
Czech Republic	..	90	120	37	153	25	127	90	43	165	206	207	1 014	856
Denmark	2 236	1 261	3 955	3 063	2 519	4 207	4 477	16 434	23 093	13 376	5 695	1 124	-10 371	8 072
Finland	-752	1 407	4 298	1 497	3 597	5 292	18 642	6 616	24 035	8 372	7 629	-2 282	-1 076	2 703
France	30 407	19 736	24 372	15 758	30 419	35 581	48 613	126 859	177 482	86 783	50 486	53 197	57 044	115 607
Germany	18 595	17 196	18 858	39 052	50 806	41 794	88 837	108 692	56 567	39 691	18 964	6 180	1 884	45 606
Greece	..	..	..	..	..	..	-276	552	2 137	616	655	413	1 030	1 450
Hungary	..	11	48	59	-4	462	278	250	620	368	278	1 644	1 122	1 346
Iceland	6	14	24	25	63	56	74	123	393	342	320	373	2 553	6 693
Ireland	214	218	436	820	728	1 014	3 902	6 109	4 630	4 066	11 035	5 555	15 813	12 931
Italy	5 949	7 231	5 109	5 731	6 465	12 245	16 078	6 722	12 318	21 476	17 138	9 079	19 273	41 536
Japan	17 302	13 915	18 116	22 628	23 418	25 992	24 154	22 748	31 538	38 349	32 280	28 798	30 962	45 830
Korea	1 162	1 340	2 461	3 552	4 670	4 449	4 740	4 198	4 999	2 420	2 617	3 426	4 658	4 312
Luxembourg	..	..	..	..	..	..	..	..	..	..	125 824	99 852	81 711	52 368
Mexico	..	..	..	..	..	..	..	..	..	4 404	891	1 254	4 432	6 171
Netherlands	12 697	10 063	17 554	20 176	32 098	24 522	36 475	57 611	75 649	50 602	32 046	44 223	17 292	119 382
New Zealand	391	-1 389	2 008	1 783	-1 240	-1 566	401	1 073	609	408	-1 134	195	1 074	-318
Norway	394	933	2 172	2 856	5 892	5 015	3 201	5 504	7 614	-1 323	4 201	2 140	3 526	3 414
Poland	13	18	29	42	53	45	316	31	16	-90	230	300	778	1 455
Portugal	684	107	283	685	728	2 092	4 029	3 191	8 134	6 263	-150	8 035	7 963	1 146
Slovak Republic	..	13	18	43	63	95	147	-377	29	65	11	13	152	146
Spain	2 171	3 174	4 111	4 158	5 590	12 547	18 938	44 384	58 224	33 113	32 744	27 555	60 567	38 748
Sweden	409	1 358	6 701	11 214	5 025	12 648	24 379	21 929	40 667	6 375	10 630	21 260	11 947	26 029
Switzerland	6 049	8 765	10 798	12 214	16 151	17 748	18 769	33 264	44 698	18 326	8 212	15 443	26 851	42 754
Turkey	65	14	49	113	110	251	367	645	870	497	175	499	859	1 048
United Kingdom	17 741	26 063	32 206	43 560	34 056	61 620	122 861	201 437	233 488	58 885	50 347	66 439	94 929	101 080
United States	48 266	83 950	80 167	98 750	91 885	104 803	142 644	224 934	159 212	142 349	154 460	140 579	244 128	9 072
EU 15 total	103 005	92 854	120 345	158 573	181 777	223 433	418 807	736 162	940 528	433 381	381 561	384 706	398 942	598 986
OECD total	185 509	208 176	248 465	315 419	343 174	410 296	651 719	1 045 473	1 239 005	687 660	619 104	616 629	781 787	716 062
Brazil	137	491	1 037	1 384	-467	1 042	2 721	1 690	2 282	-2 258	2 482	249	9 471	2 517
China	4 000	4 400	2 000	2 000	2 114	2 563	2 634	1 775	916	6 884	2 518	-152	1 805	11 306
India	..	..	83	117	239	113	48	79	510	1 398	1 678	1 324	..	..
Russian Federation	..	..	281	605	922	3 185	1 270	2 208	3 177	2 533	3 533	9 727	13 782	12 393
South Africa	1 939	292	1 261	2 494	1 048	2 324	1 634	1 584	277	-3 515	-402	553	1 305	68

StatLink ᵐˢᴸ http://dx.doi.org/10.1787/246772351771

Outflows of foreign direct investment

Millions of US dollars, average 2003-2005

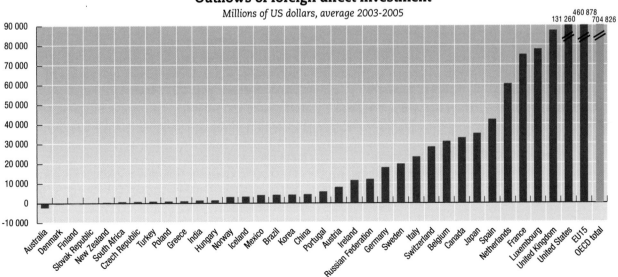

ACTIVITIES OF MULTINATIONALS

Firms in OECD countries increasingly adopt global strategies and establish overseas sales, marketing, production and research units to cope with new competitive pressures. Indicators on the activity of affiliates under foreign control are thus an important complement to information on FDI when analysing the weight and economic contribution of such firms in host countries.

While data on the manufacturing sector have been available since the beginning of the 1980s, the OECD did not start collecting data on the activity of affiliates under foreign control in services until the second half of the 1990s, and data are not yet available for all OECD countries.

Definition

An affiliate under foreign control is defined as one in which a single foreign investor holds more than 50% of the shares with voting rights. The notion of control allows all of a company's activities to be attributed to the controlling investor. This means that variables such as a company's turnover, staff or exports are all attributed to the controlling investor and the country from which he or she comes. Control may be direct or indirect.

Comparability

Fewer countries are able to supply estimates of employment in service affiliates than in manufacturing affiliates because collection of employment data on services began later. For employment in manufacturing, there are breaks in the series for the Czech Republic (1999/2000), France (2001/2002), Germany (2001/2002) and for the United States (1996/1997) because of changes to the data collection methods. For employment in services, the main problem in comparability is that financial institutions are excluded by Belgium, Germany, Ireland, Netherlands, Portugal, Spain, Sweden, the United Kingdom and the United States.

Long-term trends

The shares of foreign affiliates in manufacturing employment show considerable variation across OECD countries ranging from under 10% in Switzerland, Turkey and Portugal to 30% or more in Sweden, Belgium, the Czech Republic, Hungary, Luxembourg and Ireland. Employment in service sector foreign affiliates is lower in all countries although as noted above, comparability is affected in several countries by the exclusion of employment in banking and insurance services.

In the period from 1997 to 2004, employment in foreign-controlled manufacturing affiliates grew or remained stable in all countries for which data are available except Spain and Ireland, where the rate slightly fell and in Austria, Portugal and the United States where the shares have remained fairly stable. Particularly sharp increases were recorded by the Czech Republic, Belgium, Finland, Norway, Poland and Sweden.

Source

• OECD (2005), *OECD Science, Technology and Industry Scoreboard*, OECD, Paris.

Further information

Analytical publications

• OECD (2005), *Measuring Globalisation: OECD Economic Globalisation Indicators*, OECD, Paris.

Statistical publications

• OECD (2002), *Measuring Globalisation: The Role of Multinationals in OECD Economies*, OECD, Paris.

Methodological publications

• OECD (2005), *Measuring Globalisation: OECD Handbook on Economic Globalisation Indicators*, OECD, Paris.

Online databases

• *Measuring Globalisation Statistics.*

Websites

• OECD Measuring Globalisation, *www.oecd.org/sti/measuring-globalisation.*

• OECD Science, Technology and Industry, *www.oecd.org/sti.*

Employment in affiliates under foreign control
As percentage of total employment

	Share of employment in manufacturing							Share of employment in services						
	1998	1999	2000	2001	2002	2003	2004	1998	1999	2000	2001	2002	2003	2004
Australia	..	..	22.7	..	..	..	..	..	..	10.5	..	..	..	..
Austria	18.6	..	19.6	18.0	..	..	..	8.7	..	..	9.7	..	..	..
Belgium	..	..	..	..	32.3	34.5	32.8	..	..	..	..	17.2	16.2	15.3
Czech Republic	13.2	16.2 |	25.3	28.9	27.2	32.6	37.2	9.7	..	14.2	..	..	21.1	22.7
Denmark	..	10.2 |	15.1	14.1	14.4	..	..	..	6.1	..	..	..	..	..
Finland	13.8	15.9	15.9	17.2	17.4	..	..	8.9	9.0	11.1	11.9	..	..	..
France	27.8	28.5 |	30.1	30.8 |	26.4	26.8	26.2	6.2	6.1	6.1	5.6	5.2	..	..
Germany	6.0	6.2	6.0	5.8 |	14.8	15.5	15.4	..	..	3.2	2.9 |	7.2	6.1	..
Hungary	45.0	46.5	44.5	45.2	43.6	42.4	..	14.6	..	15.2	15.1	14.8	15.9	..
Ireland	47.5	49.1	48.1	49.2	48.4	46.7	..	..	..	..	..	22.3	..	..
Italy	..	..	..	10.8	10.9	..	..	..	..	..	5.1	5.4	..	..
Luxembourg	46.3	41.4	45.9	..	..	..	..	16.3	..	..	..	..	..	..
Netherlands	21.9	18.9	18.3	21.0	25.7	..	..	..	..	8.7	9.1	12.1	..	..
Norway	17.4	19.9	21.4	23.1	22.2	22.3	..	..	..	..	..	..	..	..
Poland	14.8	18.6	20.9	21.9	24.1	25.4	28.1	7.4	..	..	13.4	15.3	15.3	17.1
Portugal	8.8	8.9	10.1	9.5	8.9	..	..	3.5	3.9	4.0	4.7	..	..	..
Spain	..	16.5	16.8	16.4	15.9	15.4	15.6	..	..	..	..	8.7	10.0	9.5
Sweden	21.1	24.1	29.1	32.7	34.8	33.2	32.4	11.8	14.0	14.5	..	..	..	..
Switzerland	..	..	5.3	5.4	5.8	6.6	7.8	..	..	..	..	..	..	..
Turkey	5.5	5.4	5.7	7.0	..	..	..	..	..	..	..	..	..	..
United Kingdom	17.0	17.7	19.6	24.0	24.6	26.1	26.6	..	..	..	..	..	11.6	12.0
United States	11.1	11.2	11.5	11.1	11.3	11.4	..	..	..	..	..	3.8	..	..

StatLink 🔗 http://dx.doi.org/10.1787/741787541436

Employment in manufacturing and services in affiliates under foreign control
As a percentage of total employment, 2004 or latest available year

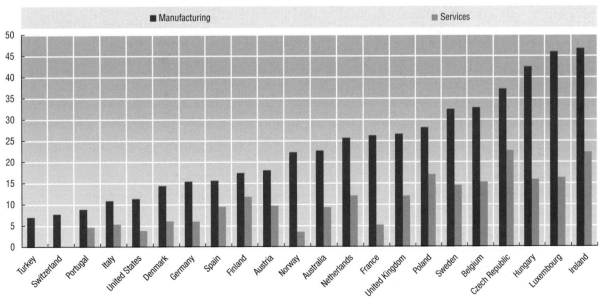

StatLink 🔗 http://dx.doi.org/10.1787/686245338253

```
                500,000 •   +
             65,679,200 •   −
             43,628,500 •   −
             36,286,400 •   +
         34,432,741,064 •   ◊

         34,432,741,064 •   ✳

            220,061,246 •   +
                242,765 •   +
             54,975,316 •   −
          3,458,295,462 •   +
          9,423,290,000 •   −
            627,646,320 •   −
            242,347,296 •   +
                312,759 •   +
          6,184,652,108 •   +
          6,184,652,108 •   ◊
```

PRICES

PRICES AND INTEREST RATES
CONSUMER PRICE INDICES (CPI)
PRODUCER PRICE INDICES (PPI)
LONG-TERM INTEREST RATES

PURCHASING POWER AND EXCHANGE RATES
RATES OF CONVERSION
EFFECTIVE EXCHANGE RATES

CONSUMER PRICE INDICES (CPI)

Consumer price indices have a long history in official statistics. They measure the erosion of living standards through price inflation and are probably the best known economic statistics among the media and general public.

Definition

Consumer price indices measure the change in the prices of a basket of goods and services that are typically purchased by specific groups of households. For the indices in these tables, the groups of households have been broadly defined and cover virtually all households except for "institutional" households – prisons and military barracks for example – and, in some countries, households in the highest income group.

The index for food covers food and non-alcoholic beverages but excludes purchases in restaurants. The index for energy is intended to cover all forms of energy, including fuels for motor vehicles, heating and other household uses.

Comparability

There are a number of differences in the ways that these indices are calculated. The most important ones concern the treatment of dwelling costs, adjustments for changes in the quality of goods and services, the frequency with which the basket weights are updated and the index formulae used. In addition, there are practical difficulties in measuring consumer prices in countries experiencing very high inflation – such as Hungary, Mexico and Turkey during the period considered here.

Long-term trends

For most OECD countries, consumer price indices have grown only moderately since 1992, with inflation lower in the latter part of the period compared with the years up to 1995. Over the period as a whole, inflation has been exceptionally low in Japan, averaging less than 1% per year but quite substantial in Greece, Mexico, Turkey and the four recent member countries in Central Europe – Czech Republic, Hungary, Poland and Slovak Republic.

As regards the five non-member economies shown, CPIs have risen sharply since 1992 in Brazil, India, Russian Federation and South Africa. In China, however, prices rose sharply up to 1996, but since then have either fallen or increased only moderately.

Food and energy are shown separately because they are important items in the consumer price indices of all countries and because their price movements tend to be more volatile than other goods and services. Food prices have risen over the period by less than total consumer prices, and increases have been moderate in most of the European Union countries. However, substantial increases occurred in 2001 and, except in Europe, between 1996 and 1998. Energy prices have been rather volatile; for example they rose over 10% in 2000 and 2005 but actually fell in 1998 and 2002. Over the period as whole, energy prices have risen faster that the total consumer price indices.

Source
• OECD (2006), *Main Economic Indicators*, OECD, Paris.

Further information
Analytical publications
• Brook, A.M. et al. (2004), *Oil Price Developments: Drivers, Economic Consequences and Policy Responses*, OECD Economics Department Working Papers, No. 412, OECD, Paris.
• OECD (2007), *OECD Economic Outlook: December No. 80 – Volume 2006 Issue 2*, OECD, Paris.

Methodological publications
• OECD (1999), *Main Economic Indicators: July Volume 1999 Issue 7*, OECD, Paris.
• OECD (2002), "Comparative Methodological Analysis: Consumer and Producer Price Indices", *Main Economic Indicators, Volume 2002, Supplement 2*, OECD, Paris.
• ILO, IMF, OECD, Eurostat, World Bank (2004), *Consumer Price Index Manual: Theory and Practice*, ILO, Geneva.

Websites
• OECD Main Economic Indicators, *www.oecd.org/std/mei*.

CONSUMER PRICE INDICES (CPI)

CPI: all items
Year 2000 = 100

	1992	1993	1994	1995	1996	1997	1998	1999	2000	2001	2002	2003	2004	2005
Australia	83.8	85.3	86.9	90.9	93.3	93.5	94.3	95.7	100.0	104.4	107.5	110.5	113.1	116.1
Austria	85.5	88.6	91.2	93.3	95.0	96.3	97.2	97.7	100.0	102.7	104.5	105.9	108.1	110.6
Belgium	86.3	88.7	90.8	92.1	94.0	95.5	96.4	97.5	100.0	102.5	104.2	105.8	108.0	111.0
Canada	88.1	89.7	89.8	91.8	93.2	94.7	95.7	97.3	100.0	102.5	104.8	107.7	109.7	112.2
Czech Republic	49.8	60.1	66.2	72.2	78.5	85.2	94.3	96.2	100.0	104.7	106.6	106.8	109.8	111.8
Denmark	84.6	85.7	87.4	89.2	91.1	93.1	94.8	97.2	100.0	102.4	104.8	107.0	108.3	110.2
Finland	89.2	91.2	92.2	92.9	93.5	94.6	95.9	97.0	100.0	102.6	104.2	105.1	105.3	106.0
France	89.1	91.0	92.5	94.2	96.0	97.2	97.8	98.3	100.0	101.6	103.6	105.8	108.0	109.9
Germany	86.1	89.9	92.3	93.9	95.3	97.1	98.0	98.6	100.0	102.0	103.4	104.5	106.2	109.3
Greece	57.1	65.4	72.5	79.0	85.4	90.2	94.5	96.9	100.0	103.4	107.1	110.9	114.1	118.2
Hungary	26.6	32.6	38.7	49.7	61.3	72.5	82.8	91.1	100.0	109.1	114.9	120.2	128.3	132.9
Iceland	81.0	84.3	85.6	87.0	89.0	90.6	92.1	95.1	100.0	106.4	111.9	114.2	117.8	122.5
Ireland	82.8	84.0	85.9	88.1	89.6	91.0	93.2	94.7	100.0	104.9	109.7	113.6	116.0	118.9
Italy	77.4	81.0	84.2	88.7	92.2	94.1	95.9	97.5	100.0	102.8	105.3	108.1	110.5	112.7
Japan	96.7	98.0	98.6	98.5	98.6	100.4	101.1	100.7	100.0	99.2	98.4	98.1	98.1	97.8
Korea	70.8	74.2	78.8	82.3	86.4	90.2	97.0	97.8	100.0	104.1	106.9	110.7	114.7	117.8
Luxembourg	85.9	89.0	91.0	92.7	93.8	95.1	96.0	96.9	100.0	102.7	104.8	106.9	109.3	112.0
Mexico	26.3	28.9	30.9	41.7	56.0	67.6	78.3	91.3	100.0	106.4	111.7	116.8	122.3	127.2
Netherlands	83.7	85.8	88.2	89.9	91.7	93.7	95.6	97.7	100.0	104.2	107.6	109.9	111.2	113.1
New Zealand	87.1	88.2	89.7	93.1	95.2	96.3	96.5	97.5	100.0	102.6	105.4	107.2	109.7	113.0
Norway	84.0	85.9	87.1	89.2	90.4	92.7	94.8	97.0	100.0	103.0	104.3	106.9	107.4	109.1
Poland	23.7	32.5	43.2	55.3	66.2	76.1	84.9	91.0	100.0	105.4	107.4	108.2	111.8	114.3
Portugal	74.8	79.8	84.1	87.6	90.3	92.4	95.0	97.2	100.0	104.4	108.1	111.6	114.2	116.9
Slovak Republic	43.9	54.1	61.4	67.4	71.3	75.7	80.7	89.3	100.0	107.3	110.7	120.2	129.2	132.7
Spain	76.7	80.2	84.0	87.9	91.0	92.8	94.5	96.7	100.0	103.6	106.8	110.0	113.4	117.2
Sweden	89.2	93.4	95.4	97.7	98.3	98.9	98.7	99.1	100.0	102.4	104.6	106.6	107.0	107.5
Switzerland	90.9	93.9	94.7	96.4	97.2	97.7	97.7	98.5	100.0	101.0	101.6	102.3	103.1	104.3
Turkey	1.0	1.6	3.3	6.3	11.4	21.2	39.2	64.6	100.0	154.4	223.8	280.4	310.1	341.6
United Kingdom	81.3	82.6	84.7	87.6	89.7	92.5	95.7	97.2	100.0	101.8	103.5	106.5	109.7	112.8
United States	81.5	83.9	86.1	88.5	91.1	93.2	94.7	96.7	100.0	102.8	104.5	106.8	109.7	113.4
EU 15 total	82.2	85.3	87.9	90.6	92.9	94.9	96.5	97.7	100.0	102.4	104.6	106.9	109.2	111.7
OECD total	70.7	73.7	77.0	81.4	85.7	89.6	93.1	96.2	100.0	103.5	106.1	108.7	111.3	114.2
Brazil	0.1	1.9	42.0	69.7	80.7	86.3	89.1	93.4	100.0	106.8	115.9	132.9	141.7	151.4
China	54.9	62.9	78.1	91.5	99.1	101.8	101.0	99.6	100.0	100.7	100.0	101.1	105.1	107.0
India	53.8	57.2	63.0	69.5	75.7	81.1	91.9	96.1	100.0	103.8	108.2	112.4	116.6	121.5
Russian Federation	0.2	1.7	6.9	20.6	30.4	34.9	44.6	82.8	100.0	121.5	140.7	159.9	177.3	199.8
South Africa	55.8	61.2	66.6	72.4	77.8	84.4	90.3	94.9	100.0	105.7	115.4	122.1	123.8	128.1

StatLink ᠁ http://dx.doi.org/10.1787/567821686052

CPI: all items
Average annual growth in percentage, 1992-2005 or latest available period

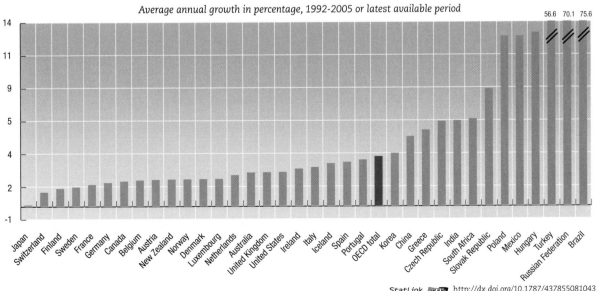

StatLink ᠁ http://dx.doi.org/10.1787/437855081043

CONSUMER PRICE INDICES (CPI)

CPI: food
Year 2000 = 100

	1992	1993	1994	1995	1996	1997	1998	1999	2000	2001	2002	2003	2004	2005
Australia	80.2	82.1	84.0	88.1	90.7	93.2	96.0	99.4	100.0	106.2	110.2	114.3	116.6	118.9
Austria	94.7	96.8	98.2	96.5	96.6	98.1	100.0	99.4	100.0	103.6	105.1	106.9	109.0	110.4
Belgium	91.4	90.9	92.7	93.9	95.2	97.3	99.2	99.1	100.0	104.6	107.0	109.2	110.5	112.5
Canada	89.9	91.6	91.6	94.0	95.1	96.5	97.9	99.0	100.0	104.9	107.5	109.0	111.0	113.6
Czech Republic	..	..	79.6	89.0	96.1	100.3	104.7	98.9	100.0	105.0	103.0	100.7	104.2	103.9
Denmark	85.3	85.0	87.5	90.2	91.7	94.9	96.9	97.5	100.0	103.9	106.1	107.7	106.6	107.3
Finland	107.0	106.3	106.5	98.1	96.7	97.1	99.0	98.9	100.0	104.4	107.4	108.1	108.9	109.5
France	91.4	91.2	92.0	93.1	94.1	95.8	97.4	97.8	100.0	105.5	108.4	110.9	111.4	111.6
Germany	95.9	96.4	98.0	99.0	99.6	101.0	102.0	100.7	100.0	104.5	105.3	105.2	104.8	105.2
Greece	61.0	67.1	76.0	82.4	88.2	91.8	95.9	98.1	100.0	105.1	110.7	116.2	116.9	117.6
Hungary	27.1	35.0	43.3	56.6	66.4	78.0	89.0	91.6	100.0	113.7	118.6	120.3	127.1	129.2
Iceland	82.5	84.5	82.6	84.9	87.6	90.5	93.0	96.0	100.0	106.9	111.4	108.5	109.6	106.8
Ireland	82.6	82.4	85.1	87.6	89.1	90.4	94.1	97.0	100.0	106.5	110.2	111.8	111.5	110.7
Italy	82.9	84.6	87.7	93.0	96.7	96.6	97.6	98.5	100.0	104.1	107.9	111.3	113.7	113.7
Japan	99.8	100.7	101.5	99.8	99.7	101.4	103.2	102.4	100.0	99.4	98.3	98.1	99.2	97.9
Korea	68.6	70.5	78.2	80.2	82.5	86.0	94.7	99.1	100.0	105.0	110.0	115.1	124.3	128.1
Luxembourg	89.0	88.8	90.3	92.5	93.3	94.3	96.8	98.0	100.0	104.8	108.9	111.0	113.0	114.8
Mexico	27.1	28.6	29.9	41.7	59.3	70.7	82.0	94.9	100.0	105.1	109.1	115.1	123.5	130.2
Netherlands	93.0	92.7	94.5	94.8	94.8	96.4	98.6	99.7	100.0	107.0	110.5	111.7	107.8	106.5
New Zealand	90.0	91.1	90.4	91.4	92.6	94.7	98.1	99.0	100.0	106.8	109.9	109.3	109.7	111.0
Norway	85.0	84.2	85.4	86.7	88.1	91.1	95.4	98.1	100.0	98.1	96.4	99.7	101.5	103.1
Poland	..	..	..	63.3	74.5	83.7	89.6	91.2	100.0	104.6	104.0	102.7	108.8	111.2
Portugal	84.2	85.0	88.1	90.5	92.3	92.6	95.9	97.9	100.0	106.5	108.6	111.4	112.6	112.0
Slovak Republic	50.0	60.3	70.6	79.4	82.7	87.4	92.5	95.0	100.0	106.1	107.6	111.3	116.6	115.0
Spain	..	84.3	88.8	93.2	96.3	95.6	96.7	98.0	100.0	105.9	111.2	115.7	120.2	124.0
Sweden	100.4	101.1	102.9	104.3	97.1	97.4	98.5	100.0	100.0	102.9	106.2	106.6	106.1	105.4
Switzerland	96.7	96.5	97.0	97.6	97.1	97.8	98.6	98.5	100.0	102.2	104.6	105.9	106.6	105.9
Turkey	1.1	1.8	3.9	7.6	13.1	25.1	46.2	68.2	100.0	149.1	223.0	282.8	304.3	320.6
United Kingdom	89.5	91.1	92.0	95.5	98.6	98.7	100.0	100.3	100.0	103.3	104.1	105.4	106.0	107.3
United States	81.5	83.4	85.8	88.6	91.9	94.2	96.0	97.8	100.0	103.3	104.6	106.9	110.9	113.0
EU 15 total	89.0	90.2	92.4	94.9	96.7	97.6	99.0	99.2	100.0	104.6	107.0	108.8	109.7	110.4
OECD total	73.0	75.3	78.6	83.2	87.8	91.5	95.4	97.8	100.0	104.4	107.2	109.6	112.6	114.2
China	..	..	83.8	103.0	110.8	110.7	107.2	102.7	100.0	100.0	99.4	102.8	113.1	116.4
Russian Federation	0.2	1.8	7.0	21.4	30.0	33.9	43.1	84.9	100.0	121.3	136.2	151.4	167.2	190.2
South Africa	54.3	58.0	66.0	71.7	76.1	83.3	88.4	92.7	100.0	105.4	122.1	131.9	134.9	137.9

StatLink ⬛ http://dx.doi.org/10.1787/485854833577

CPI: food
Average annual growth in percentage, 1992-2005 or latest available period

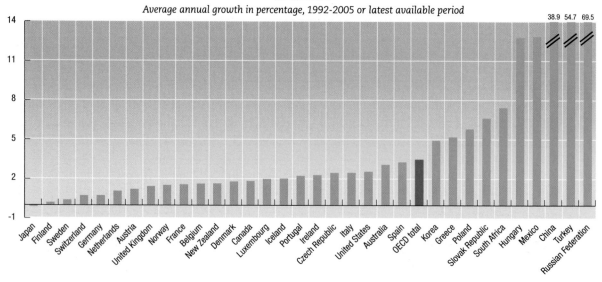

StatLink ⬛ http://dx.doi.org/10.1787/726426810050

OECD FACTBOOK 2007 – ISBN 978-92-64-02946-0 – © OECD 2007

CPI: energy
Year 2000 = 100

	1992	1993	1994	1995	1996	1997	1998	1999	2000	2001	2002	2003	2004	2005
Australia	80.3	81.5	81.7	84.2	85.8	87.3	84.3	85.8	100.0	102.5	103.3	108.6	115.5	126.9
Austria	81.3	80.7	81.9	84.9	90.3	93.0	90.0	90.3	100.0	100.5	98.1	99.1	105.4	115.1
Belgium	78.6	81.4	82.1	81.5	86.1	88.8	85.7	87.4	100.0	100.6	97.4	97.3	103.7	115.7
Canada	78.1	79.0	79.5	80.5	82.9	84.9	81.4	86.1	100.0	103.2	101.2	109.2	116.5	127.8
Czech Republic	..	..	..	..	58.6	67.3	83.6	88.8	100.0	106.1	108.5	109.5	113.3	120.6
Denmark	74.4	73.8	73.8	75.2	80.1	82.6	83.7	89.2	100.0	101.5	103.7	104.6	107.0	115.0
Finland	76.4	85.0	83.2	77.3	85.2	86.7	85.6	88.8	100.0	98.2	97.3	102.0	105.9	113.1
France	81.2	82.8	83.9	85.5	89.6	91.4	88.8	89.2	100.0	98.4	96.9	99.2	103.9	114.2
Germany	80.7	81.7	84.5	83.8	84.6	87.0	84.2	87.7	100.0	105.7	106.0	110.2	114.7	126.5
Greece	73.5	81.5	84.5	88.3	95.6	91.8	88.8	85.4	100.0	98.3	98.1	102.0	107.9	123.2
Hungary	22.7	26.8	29.9	41.4	53.5	67.3	77.4	86.8	100.0	105.5	108.7	115.6	128.6	137.9
Iceland	..	80.6	80.9	81.4	85.0	88.9	86.9	89.4	100.0	104.1	101.9	103.9	111.7	118.6
Ireland	79.7	80.0	80.5	80.9	84.0	86.9	86.4	88.0	100.0	97.4	100.7	104.8	113.6	128.0
Italy	87.1	90.9	94.5	99.0	88.6	90.2	89.0	89.6	100.0	101.8	99.0	102.2	104.4	113.4
Japan	106.6	106.7	104.9	102.8	100.1	102.9	98.4	96.9	100.0	100.5	98.1	98.2	99.8	103.5
Korea	50.8	53.7	53.7	54.7	60.2	70.5	90.9	91.3	100.0	107.0	103.6	107.4	113.2	119.6
Luxembourg	77.9	81.5	79.2	78.1	82.6	85.7	81.3	83.5	100.0	98.4	94.4	96.6	105.5	121.5
Mexico	20.7	23.3	26.0	37.2	50.5	62.4	71.9	84.9	100.0	108.6	117.4	128.4	138.4	146.9
Netherlands	74.4	71.1	73.8	74.2	79.0	85.2	85.1	87.1	100.0	107.0	109.5	114.5	120.8	135.2
New Zealand	81.9	83.3	83.1	84.9	87.1	89.0	87.4	88.4	100.0	99.1	100.5	104.6	115.1	127.1
Norway	76.2	79.2	79.2	83.7	86.7	91.1	87.5	89.7	100.0	108.4	105.9	126.8	123.4	126.3
Poland	..	..	..	50.5	60.1	70.5	81.2	88.1	100.0	107.0	112.2	116.9	122.1	128.5
Portugal	81.7	86.2	88.8	89.8	91.8	95.5	96.1	94.3	100.0	105.1	106.2	111.3	117.3	128.9
Slovak Republic	..	..	..	43.2	45.7	47.3	49.0	69.9	100.0	113.9	127.7	153.0	174.9	188.6
Spain	72.6	78.1	80.9	83.7	86.8	88.9	85.5	88.2	100.0	99.0	98.2	99.6	104.4	114.4
Sweden	71.6	81.3	81.7	83.1	88.5	92.9	92.9	92.7	100.0	107.1	108.6	121.8	125.5	132.2
Switzerland	75.8	80.2	79.3	81.5	84.8	87.5	82.4	85.0	100.0	98.7	93.8	95.0	99.4	109.7
Turkey	..	..	3.3	5.9	12.2	22.3	36.6	64.0	100.0	192.2	279.9	337.1	361.1	417.4
United Kingdom	76.5	78.5	82.0	84.8	86.9	89.5	89.8	93.5	100.0	97.4	97.0	99.8	106.1	117.7
United States	82.7	83.6	84.0	84.5	88.4	89.5	82.6	85.6	100.0	103.8	97.6	109.5	121.5	142.1
EU 15 total	79.2	81.7	84.2	85.9	86.9	89.2	87.5	89.5	100.0	101.3	100.6	103.8	108.6	119.5
OECD total	68.0	70.4	72.9	76.1	80.6	84.7	83.5	87.3	100.0	104.5	103.3	110.9	118.8	133.0

StatLink http://dx.doi.org/10.1787/352480223117

CPI: energy
Average annual growth in percentage, 1992-2005 or latest available period

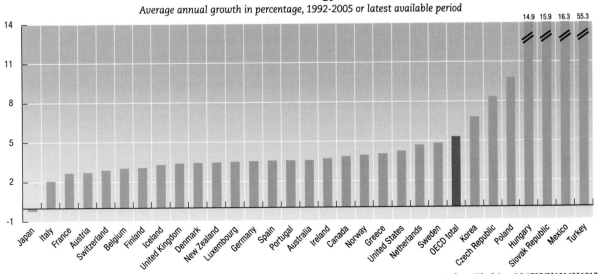

StatLink http://dx.doi.org/10.1787/821014551817

PRODUCER PRICE INDICES (PPI)

A variety of tools are used to measure price changes taking place in an economy. These include consumer price indices (CPI), price indices relating to specific goods and/or services, GDP deflators and producer price indices (PPI). Whereas CPIs are designed to measure changes over time in average retail prices of a fixed basket of goods and services taken as representing the consumption habits of households, the purpose of PPIs is to provide measures of average movements of prices received by the producers of commodities.

Producer price indices measure changes in prices at an early stage in the production process. Because of this, they are often seen as advance indicators of price changes throughout the economy, including changes in the prices of consumer goods and services.

Definition

Producer prices are defined as "ex-factory prices" and exclude any taxes, transport and trade margins that the purchaser may have to pay. Manufacturing covers the production of semi-processed goods and other intermediate goods as well as final products such as consumer goods and capital equipment.

Comparability

The price indices shown here are intended to be producer price indices for manufacturing. In practice many countries do not calculate such indices for the manufacturing sector alone. The indices for Austria, Greece, Italy, Luxembourg, Mexico, Spain, Switzerland and Turkey all have broader coverage, usually including (in addition to manufacturing) mining, electricity, gas and water and, in some countries, agriculture.

An additional problem is that Austria and Turkey calculate wholesale price indices rather than producer price indices. Wholesale prices include taxes and transport and trade margins in addition to the ex-factory cost of the goods.

There are also differences between countries in the ways in which they adjust prices for quality changes, in the frequency with which the weights are updated, and in the price index formulae used.

Long-term trends

Compared with consumer prices, producer prices have risen more slowly throughout the period. More than half of OECD countries recorded average annual increases of under 2% and in two countries – Japan and Switzerland – producer prices were actually lower at the end of the period than in 1992. All countries recorded unusually sharp rises in 1995, 2000 and 2005 due to sharp movements in world commodity prices, but for most of the period annual increases have been modest in the EU15 countries, in Australia, Canada, Japan, Korea, New Zealand and the United States. However PPIs rose sharply in both Mexico and Turkey, and the four new OECD member countries from central Europe also experienced above averaged increases in their PPIs; rises were particularly large in Hungary and Poland and more moderate in the Czech Republic and Slovak Republic.

Source

• OECD (2006), *Main Economic Indicators*, OECD, Paris.

Further information

Analytical publications

• Brook, A.M. et al. (2004), *Oil Price Developments: Drivers, Economic Consequences and Policy Responses*, OECD Economics Department Working Papers, No. 412, OECD, Paris.

• OECD (2007), *OECD Economic Outlook: December No. 80 – Volume 2006 Issue 2*, OECD, Paris.

Methodological publications

• IMF, ILO, OECD, Eurostat, UN, World Bank (2004), *Producer Price Index Manual: Theory and Practice*, IMF, Washington, DC.

• OECD (2002), "Comparative Methodological Analysis: Consumer and Producer Price Indices", *Main Economic Indicators*, Volume 2002, Supplement 2, OECD, Paris.

Websites

• OECD Main Economic Indicators, *www.oecd.org/std/mei*.

PPI: manufacturing
Year 2000 = 100

	1992	1993	1994	1995	1996	1997	1998	1999	2000	2001	2002	2003	2004	2005
Australia	84.7	86.4	87.0	90.2	91.0	92.1	92.7	93.3	100.0	103.1	103.3	103.8	107.9	114.3
Austria	96.5	96.1	97.4	97.7	97.7	98.1	97.6	96.7	100.0	101.5	101.1	102.8	107.8	110.1
Belgium	87.9	86.5	88.0	90.0	90.7	92.4	91.0	91.1	100.0		99.5	99.2	98.8	102.9	105.6
Canada	78.6	81.5	86.4	92.8	93.2	93.9	94.2	95.9	100.0	101.0	101.0	99.7	102.8	104.3
Czech Republic	65.8	72.0	75.9	82.3	86.3	90.4	94.6	94.6	100.0	102.7	101.3	101.0	107.0	109.2
Denmark	91.0	90.4	90.7	93.5	94.8	96.3	95.7	96.0	100.0	102.9	103.9	104.0	105.1	108.2
Finland	88.0	91.0	92.4	94.1	92.3	93.3	91.7	91.2	100.0	98.9	96.6	95.5	95.3	98.0
France	99.9	97.6	98.9	103.9	101.1	100.5	99.6	98.0	100.0	101.2	101.0	101.3	102.5	104.3
Germany	94.0	94.0	94.7	96.7	96.8	97.4	97.2	97.0	100.0	101.3	101.5	102.1	103.9	106.8
Greece	..	..	..	80.0	85.3	87.9	90.4	92.3	100.0	102.9	104.8	106.3	110.2	116.2
Hungary	..	..	..	53.0	64.5	77.3	85.4	89.3	100.0	104.3	101.7	103.2	105.9	110.9
Ireland	83.5	87.3	88.3	89.6	89.2	89.5	91.9	93.6	100.0	101.7	100.5	92.4	90.2	90.1
Italy	78.8	81.8	84.9	91.5	93.2	94.4	94.6	94.3	100.0	101.9	102.1	103.7	106.5	110.8
Japan	108.2	106.5	104.6	103.8	102.1	102.7	101.3	99.9	100.0	97.7	95.6	94.8	95.9	97.8
Korea	77.2	78.4	79.6	83.5	85.3	88.2	101.0	97.7	100.0	97.9	96.4	98.1	105.5	108.8
Luxembourg	98.8	97.1	97.3	100.7	96.5	98.1	99.8	95.0	100.0	99.8	99.0	100.4	109.3	118.0
Mexico	27.6	29.5	31.3	44.3	59.6	69.1	78.6	90.9	100.0	103.3	107.8	115.9	126.7	132.0
Netherlands	87.2	85.6	86.2	88.1	89.4	92.1	89.9	90.1	100.0	101.0	99.8	100.5	104.7	111.2
New Zealand	90.0	93.0	93.7	93.8	93.0	91.7	92.5	93.4	100.0	104.8	105.1	103.8	105.8	109.7
Norway	81.8	81.6	83.3	84.9	86.1	86.8	87.6	90.6	100.0	100.6	97.5	99.2	105.5	112.5
Poland	..	..	..	69.1	76.6	83.1	88.4	92.9	100.0	99.9	99.9	102.3	109.1	108.8
Portugal	73.1	74.5	76.9	80.8	85.5	88.1	83.9	86.9	100.0	102.7	103.1	103.5	106.5	110.3
Slovak Republic	..	..	..	78.2	81.9	86.0	88.6	91.6	100.0	105.9	106.7	109.4	113.2	115.6
Spain	81.3	83.2	86.8	92.3	93.9	94.8	94.2	94.8	100.0	101.7	102.4	103.9	107.4	112.7
Sweden	81.1	85.6	89.5	98.3	96.1	96.9	96.4	95.9	100.0	101.5	100.9	99.8	100.7	104.5
Switzerland	104.0	104.5	104.0	103.9	102.0	101.3	100.1	99.1	100.0	100.5	100.0	100.0	101.2	102.0
Turkey	1.3	2.0	4.2	7.8	13.8	25.1	43.1	66.0	100.0	161.6	242.6	304.6	338.4	366.3
United Kingdom	85.5	88.8	91.1	94.8	97.2	98.1	98.1	98.5	100.0	99.7	99.8	101.3	103.8	106.7
United States	87.9	89.2	90.4	93.1	95.2	95.5	94.5	96.1	100.0	100.8	100.1	102.7	107.1	113.0
EU 15 total	88.2	89.2	91.1	95.1	95.7	96.5	96.0	95.8	100.0	101.1	101.1	101.8	104.2	107.4
OECD total	77.8	79.4	81.9	86.7	89.7	92.2	93.6	95.3	100.0	101.5	102.0	103.9	107.5	111.8
Brazil	0.1	1.6	38.4	61.0	64.9	70.1	72.6	84.7	100.0	112.6	131.4	167.6	185.1	195.4
China	..	..	..	..	104.3	104.0	99.7	97.3	100.0	98.7	96.5	98.8	104.7	109.9
India	..	..	..	78.7	82.2	85.9	90.9	94.1	100.0	105.2	107.8	113.5	121.0	126.7
Russian Federation	0.1	1.6	6.8	23.1	34.9	40.1	42.9	68.3	100.0	118.2	130.5	151.9	187.4	225.9
South Africa	56.6	61.2	66.8	73.4	79.3	85.0	88.3	92.9	100.0	107.1	121.4	127.0	129.5	134.3

StatLink ⬛️🖳 http://dx.doi.org/10.1787/036154510166

PPI: manufacturing
Average annual growth in percentage, 1992-2005 or latest available period

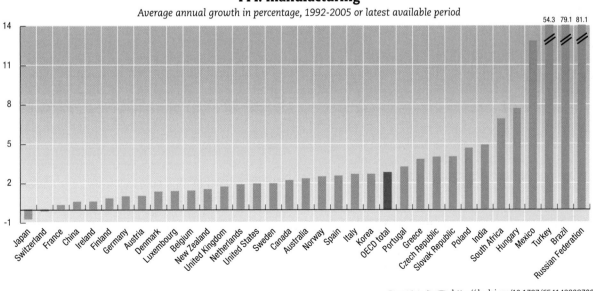

StatLink ⬛️🖳 http://dx.doi.org/10.1787/654143838722

LONG-TERM INTEREST RATES

Long-term interest rates are one of the determinants of business investment. Low interest rates encourage investment in new equipment and high interest rates discourage it. Investment is, in turn, a major source of economic growth.

Definition

These interest rates refer to government bonds with a residual maturity of about ten years. They are not the interest rates at which the loans were issued, but the interest rates implied by the prices at which the bonds are traded on financial markets. For example if a bond was initially bought for 100 with an interest rate of 9%, but the bond is now trading at 90, the interest rate has risen to 10% ([9/90] x 100).

Comparability

The monthly rates shown are where possible averages of daily rates.

They are in all cases interest rates on bonds whose capital repayment is guaranteed by governments.

Long-term trends

Interest rates are determined by three factors:
– the price that lenders charge for postponing consumption, the risk that the borrower may not repay the capital and the fall in the real value of the capital that the lender expects to occur because of inflation during the lifetime of the loan. The interest rates shown here refer to government borrowing and the risk factor is very low. To an important extent the interest rates in this table are driven by the expected rates of inflation.

From 1992 long-term interest rates fell for a few years but edged upwards again in 1994/1995. Since then they have been falling steadily in most member countries. For the 20 member countries in the table for which data are available for the full period from 1992 to 2005, long-term interest rates averaged 9.2% in 1992 but only 3.7% by 2005. For many countries the long-term interest rates recorded in 2005 were historically low.

The most striking feature of the table is the reduction in the variance of interest rates among countries. The convergence of long-term interest rates is mostly explained by the increasing integration of financial markets – one aspect of globalisation – and was particularly pronounced among members of the euro area. Japan and Switzerland are exceptions; their interest rates have remained low but are not converging to the OECD average.

Evolution of long-term interest rates
Percentage

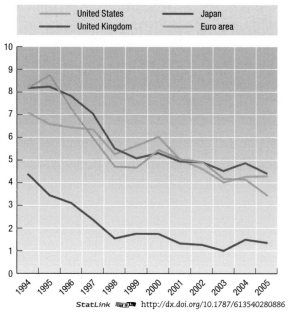

StatLink http://dx.doi.org/10.1787/613540280886

Source

• OECD (2006), *Main Economic Indicators*, OECD, Paris.

Further information

Analytical publications

• OECD (2006), *Financial Market Trends*, series, OECD, Paris.

• OECD (2007), *OECD Economic Outlook: December No. 80 – Volume 2006 Issue 2*, OECD, Paris.

Methodological publications

• OECD (1998), *Main Economic Indicators – Sources and Methods: Interest Rates and Share Price Indices*, OECD, Paris.

Long-term interest rates
Percentage

	1992	1993	1994	1995	1996	1997	1998	1999	2000	2001	2002	2003	2004	2005
Australia	9.20	7.38	8.89	9.21	8.21	6.95	5.49	6.01	6.31	5.62	5.84	5.37	5.59	5.34
Austria	8.14	6.71	7.03	7.13	6.32	5.68	4.71	4.68	5.56	5.08	4.97	4.15	4.15	3.39
Belgium	8.66	7.22	7.70	7.38	6.30	5.59	4.70	4.71	5.57	5.06	4.89	4.15	4.06	3.37
Canada	8.06	7.24	8.36	8.16	7.24	6.14	5.28	5.54	5.93	5.48	5.30	4.80	4.58	4.07
Czech Republic	..	..	..	..	..	..	..	..	..	6.31	4.88	4.12	4.75	3.51
Denmark	8.99	7.30	7.83	8.27	7.19	6.26	5.04	4.92	5.66	5.09	5.06	4.31	4.30	3.40
Finland	11.97	8.83	9.04	8.79	7.08	5.96	4.79	4.72	5.48	5.04	4.98	4.14	4.11	3.35
France	8.59	6.78	7.22	7.54	6.31	5.58	4.64	4.61	5.39	4.94	4.86	4.13	4.10	3.41
Germany	7.85	6.52	6.88	6.86	6.23	5.66	4.58	4.50	5.27	4.80	4.78	4.07	4.04	3.35
Greece	..	..	..	..	..	..	8.48	6.31	6.11	5.30	5.12	4.27	4.26	3.59
Iceland	..	..	6.98	9.65	9.24	8.71	7.66	8.47	11.20	10.36	7.96	6.65	7.49	9.05
Ireland	9.32	7.58	8.04	8.23	7.25	6.26	4.75	4.77	5.48	5.02	4.99	4.13	4.06	3.32
Italy	13.27	11.19	10.52	12.21	9.40	6.86	4.88	4.73	5.58	5.19	5.03	4.30	4.26	3.56
Japan	5.33	4.32	4.36	3.44	3.10	2.37	1.54	1.75	1.74	1.32	1.26	1.00	1.49	1.35
Korea	15.08	12.07	12.29	12.40	10.89	11.70	12.80	8.72	8.50	6.66	6.47	4.93	4.45	4.66
Luxembourg	..	..	7.15	7.23	6.30	5.60	4.73	4.67	5.52	4.86	4.68	3.32	2.84	2.41
Netherlands	8.10	6.36	6.86	6.90	6.15	5.58	4.63	4.63	5.41	4.96	4.89	4.12	4.10	3.37
New Zealand	8.40	6.93	7.63	7.78	7.89	7.19	6.29	6.41	6.85	6.39	6.53	5.87	6.07	5.88
Norway	9.61	6.88	7.43	7.43	6.77	5.89	5.40	5.50	6.22	6.24	6.38	5.05	4.37	3.75
Portugal	..	..	10.48	11.47	8.56	6.36	4.88	4.78	5.60	5.16	5.01	4.18	4.14	3.44
Spain	11.70	10.21	10.00	11.27	8.74	6.40	4.83	4.73	5.53	5.12	4.96	4.13	4.10	3.39
Sweden	10.02	8.54	9.50	10.24	8.03	6.61	4.99	4.98	5.37	5.11	5.30	4.64	4.43	3.38
Switzerland	6.40	4.55	4.96	4.52	4.00	3.36	3.04	3.04	3.93	3.38	3.20	2.66	2.74	2.10
United Kingdom	9.06	7.47	8.17	8.24	7.82	7.05	5.52	5.08	5.31	4.94	4.91	4.52	4.87	4.41
United States	7.01	5.87	7.08	6.58	6.44	6.35	5.26	5.64	6.03	5.02	4.61	4.02	4.27	4.29
Euro area	..	..	8.18	8.73	7.23	5.96	4.70	4.66	5.44	5.03	4.92	4.16	4.14	3.44
Russian Federation	..	..	..	..	..	..	..	87.38	35.16	19.38	15.82	8.90	7.79	7.76
South Africa	15.44	13.97	14.83	16.11	15.48	14.70	15.12	14.90	13.79	11.41	11.50	9.62	9.53	8.07

StatLink http://dx.doi.org/10.1787/347204845347

Long-term interest rates
Percentage, 2005

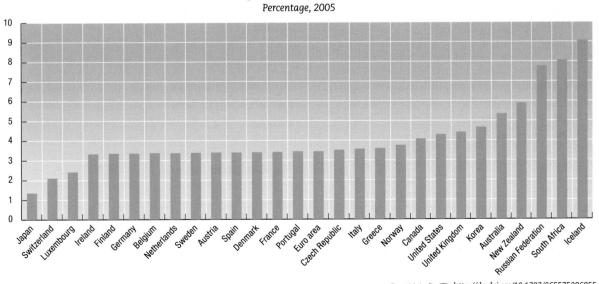

StatLink http://dx.doi.org/10.1787/365575226855

RATES OF CONVERSION

To compare a single country's real GDP over a period of years, it is necessary to remove any movements that are due to price changes. In the same way, in order to compare the real GDPs of a group of countries at a single point in time, it is necessary to remove any differences in their GDPs that are due to differences in their price levels. Price indices are used to remove the effects of price changes in a single country over time; purchasing power parities (PPP) are used to remove the effects of the different levels of prices within a group of countries at a single point in time.

Definition

PPPs are currency converters that equalise price levels between countries. The PPPs shown here have been calculated by comparing the prices in OECD countries of a common basket of about 2 500 goods and services. Countries are not required to price all the items in the common basket because some of the items may be hard to find in certain countries, but the common basket has been drawn up in such a way that each country can find prices for a wide range of the goods and services that are representative of their markets.

The goods and services to be priced cover all those that enter into final expenditure – household consumption, government services, capital formation and net exports. Prices for the different items are weighted by their shares in total final expenditures to obtain the GDP PPPs shown here.

Comparability

The PPPs shown here have been calculated jointly by the OECD and Eurostat using standard procedures. In consultation with their member countries, OECD and Eurostat keep their methodology under review and improvements are made regularly.

Long-term trends

Over the period 1992-2005, movements of PPPs and exchange rates were rarely similar and even when they moved in the same direction they were not of the same magnitude – see for example Ireland and Portugal in the graph on the opposite page.

Exchange rates are sometimes used to convert the GDPs of different currencies to a common currency. However, comparisons of GDP based on exchange rates do not reflect the real volumes of goods and services in the GDPs of the countries being compared. For many of the low income countries, the differences between GDP converted using exchange rates and real GDP converted using PPPs are considerable. The differences are illustrated in the second graph.

For Slovak Republic, for example, the difference between PPP-converted GDP and exchange rate-converted is over eighty per cent. In general, the use of exchange rates understates the real GDP of low-income countries and overstates the real GDP of high-income countries.

The price level indices in the third table are the PPPs divided by exchange rates, with the OECD set to 100. In general, there is a positive correlation between income levels and price levels; Denmark, Iceland, Norway and Switzerland, four high-income countries, had the highest price levels in 2005 while the Czech Republic, Hungary, Poland, the Slovak Republic and Turkey, five four poorer OECD countries, had price levels around fifty to sixty per cent of the OECD average.

Source

• OECD (2005), *Purchasing Power Parities and Real Expenditures – 2002 Benchmark Year, 2004 Edition*, OECD, Paris.

Further information

Analytical publications

• Schreyer, P. and F. Koechlin (2002), "Purchasing Power Parities – Measurement and Uses", *OECD Statistics Brief*, No. 3, March, OECD, Paris, *www.oecd.org/std/statisticsbrief*.

Statistical publications

• OECD (2006), *National Accounts of OECD Countries*, OECD, Paris.

• OECD (2006), *Main Economic Indicators*, OECD, Paris.

Websites

• OECD Purchasing Power Parities, *www.oecd.org/std/ppp*.

• Joint World Bank-OECD Seminar on Puchasing Power Parities, 2001, *www.oecd.org/std/ppp/seminar2001*.

Purchasing power parities
National currency units per US dollar

	1992	1993	1994	1995	1996	1997	1998	1999	2000	2001	2002	2003	2004	2005
Australia	1.35	1.34	1.33	1.32	1.32	1.32	1.31	1.30	1.31	1.33	1.34	1.35	1.36	1.38
Austria	0.941	0.946	0.951	0.950	0.941	0.937	0.938	0.931	0.914	0.918	0.912	0.878	0.868	0.866
Belgium	0.914	0.929	0.929	0.922	0.919	0.927	0.929	0.940	0.922	0.897	0.883	0.865	0.865	0.863
Canada	1.23	1.22	1.21	1.21	1.21	1.21	1.19	1.19	1.23	1.22	1.23	1.24	1.25	1.25
Czech Republic	7.7	9.1	10.1	10.9	11.7	12.6	13.9	14.3	14.4	14.6	14.3	13.9	14.0	14.1
Denmark	8.85	8.70	8.66	8.59	8.55	8.56	8.52	8.41	8.41	8.33	8.43	8.47	8.40	8.40
Finland	0.964	0.961	0.954	0.980	0.971	0.960	0.970	0.982	0.979	0.974	0.967	1.002	0.974	0.969
France	0.977	0.973	0.967	0.959	0.950	0.932	0.927	0.928	0.915	0.898	0.900	0.930	0.918	0.901
Germany	1.011	1.026	1.028	1.027	1.010	1.006	1.004	1.004	0.982	0.974	0.959	0.905	0.894	0.883
Greece	0.442	0.494	0.538	0.579	0.612	0.638	0.664	0.681	0.685	0.693	0.678	0.684	0.695	0.695
Hungary	34	41	48	59	70	83	93	100	107	110	115	120	124	125
Iceland	74.5	74.1	74.5	75.2	75.3	76.4	79.0	81.1	83.2	88.7	92.2	93.4	94.0	94.6
Ireland	0.79	0.81	0.81	0.82	0.83	0.83	0.87	0.92	0.95	0.98	1.00	1.01	1.00	1.00
Italy	0.732	0.744	0.754	0.776	0.795	0.807	0.800	0.809	0.808	0.817	0.825	0.850	0.861	0.862
Japan	186	183	179	175	170	169	167	162	155	149	144	138	133	128
Korea	597	621	656	690	712	732	767	755	753	761	779	783	782	756
Luxembourg	0.95	0.99	1.00	1.00	1.01	1.02	1.01	0.98	0.99	0.99	0.98	0.93	0.92	0.92
Mexico	1.91	2.04	2.17	2.93	3.76	4.35	4.96	5.63	6.12	6.33	6.58	7.00	7.31	7.48
Netherlands	0.905	0.902	0.903	0.903	0.900	0.902	0.909	0.926	0.925	0.917	0.921	0.923	0.897	0.882
New Zealand	1.47	1.47	1.46	1.46	1.47	1.45	1.45	1.43	1.45	1.47	1.47	1.46	1.47	1.46
Norway	9.14	9.14	8.94	9.01	8.93	9.08	9.34	9.21	9.01	9.10	9.14	9.03	8.93	8.73
Poland	0.53	0.68	0.91	1.15	1.32	1.50	1.65	1.75	1.82	1.84	1.83	1.83	1.85	1.85
Portugal	0.548	0.575	0.604	0.612	0.626	0.636	0.646	0.649	0.651	0.657	0.658	0.702	0.707	0.704
Slovak Republic	9.7	11.0	12.2	13.1	13.6	14.2	14.8	15.6	16.1	16.3	16.2	16.6	17.2	17.1
Spain	0.663	0.677	0.689	0.709	0.719	0.730	0.733	0.733	0.742	0.749	0.743	0.749	0.756	0.762
Sweden	9.16	9.23	9.28	9.42	9.31	9.37	9.46	9.34	9.19	9.32	9.36	9.25	9.18	9.21
Switzerland	2.03	2.03	2.02	2.00	2.01	1.93	1.90	1.93	1.90	1.89	1.80	1.76	1.73	1.70
Turkey	0.004	0.006	0.012	0.023	0.039	0.071	0.124	0.192	0.271	0.423	0.612	0.755	0.832	0.877
United Kingdom	0.621	0.623	0.620	0.624	0.628	0.624	0.633	0.644	0.633	0.623	0.610	0.624	0.619	0.619
United States	1.00	1.00	1.00	1.00	1.00	1.00	1.00	1.00	1.00	1.00	1.00	1.00	1.00	1.00

StatLink http://dx.doi.org/10.1787/552625318718

Changes in exchange rates and purchasing power parities
Average annual growth in percentage, 1992-2005

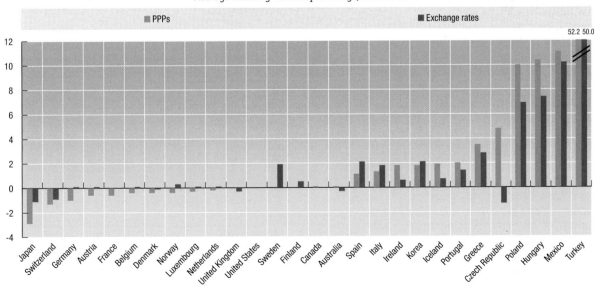

StatLink http://dx.doi.org/10.1787/082287486381

RATES OF CONVERSION

Exchange rates
National currency units per US dollar

	1992	1993	1994	1995	1996	1997	1998	1999	2000	2001	2002	2003	2004	2005
Australia	1.362	1.473	1.369	1.350	1.277	1.348	1.592	1.550	1.727	1.935	1.841	1.542	1.359	1.313
Austria	0.799	0.845	0.830	0.733	0.769	0.886	0.899	0.939	1.085	1.117	1.061	0.885	0.805	0.805
Belgium	0.797	0.856	0.830	0.731	0.768	0.886	0.900	0.939	1.085	1.117	1.061	0.885	0.805	0.805
Canada	1.209	1.290	1.366	1.373	1.364	1.385	1.484	1.486	1.485	1.548	1.570	1.400	1.301	1.212
Czech Republic	28.26	29.15	28.79	26.54	27.15	31.70	32.28	34.59	38.64	38.02	32.73	28.13	25.69	23.95
Denmark	6.038	6.482	6.360	5.604	5.798	6.604	6.699	6.980	8.088	8.321	7.884	6.577	5.988	5.996
Finland	0.755	0.962	0.878	0.735	0.772	0.872	0.899	0.939	1.085	1.117	1.061	0.885	0.805	0.805
France	0.807	0.863	0.846	0.761	0.780	0.890	0.899	0.939	1.085	1.117	1.061	0.885	0.805	0.805
Germany	0.799	0.845	0.830	0.733	0.769	0.887	0.900	0.939	1.085	1.117	1.061	0.885	0.805	0.805
Greece	0.559	0.672	0.711	0.680	0.706	0.801	0.867	0.897	1.069	1.117	1.061	0.885	0.805	0.805
Hungary	78.99	91.91	105.12	125.72	152.61	186.63	214.26	237.06	282.29	286.49	257.45	224.30	202.61	199.53
Iceland	57.62	67.64	69.99	64.77	66.69	70.97	71.17	72.43	78.84	97.67	91.59	76.69	70.19	62.88
Ireland	0.746	0.868	0.850	0.793	0.794	0.839	0.893	0.939	1.085	1.117	1.061	0.885	0.805	0.805
Italy	0.636	0.812	0.833	0.841	0.797	0.879	0.897	0.939	1.085	1.117	1.061	0.885	0.805	0.805
Japan	126.67	111.18	102.23	94.07	108.82	121.00	130.89	113.89	107.83	121.48	125.25	115.94	108.15	110.10
Korea	780.01	802.44	804.27	771.40	804.42	950.51	1 400.48	1 186.71	1 130.64	1 290.41	1 251.05	1 190.96	1 145.20	1 024.23
Luxembourg	0.797	0.856	0.830	0.731	0.768	0.886	0.900	0.939	1.085	1.117	1.061	0.885	0.805	0.805
Mexico	3.095	3.115	3.389	6.421	7.601	7.924	9.153	9.553	9.453	9.344	9.661	10.790	11.281	10.890
Netherlands	0.798	0.843	0.826	0.729	0.765	0.885	0.901	0.939	1.085	1.117	1.061	0.885	0.805	0.805
New Zealand	1.860	1.851	1.687	1.524	1.454	1.513	1.869	1.892	2.205	2.382	2.163	1.724	1.509	1.421
Norway	6.215	7.094	7.057	6.337	6.457	7.072	7.545	7.797	8.797	8.993	7.986	7.078	6.739	6.441
Poland	1.363	1.814	2.273	2.425	2.696	3.277	3.492	3.964	4.346	4.097	4.082	3.888	3.651	3.234
Portugal	0.672	0.801	0.828	0.748	0.769	0.874	0.899	0.939	1.085	1.117	1.061	0.885	0.805	0.805
Slovak Republic	..	30.77	32.04	29.74	30.65	33.62	35.23	41.36	46.23	48.35	45.30	36.76	32.23	31.04
Spain	0.615	0.765	0.805	0.749	0.761	0.880	0.898	0.939	1.085	1.117	1.061	0.885	0.805	0.805
Sweden	5.823	7.785	7.716	7.134	6.707	7.635	7.947	8.262	9.161	10.338	9.721	8.078	7.346	7.472
Switzerland	1.406	1.477	1.367	1.182	1.236	1.450	1.450	1.503	1.688	1.687	1.557	1.345	1.243	1.248
Turkey	0.007	0.011	0.030	0.046	0.081	0.152	0.261	0.419	0.624	1.228	1.512	1.503	1.426	1.340
United Kingdom	0.570	0.666	0.653	0.634	0.641	0.611	0.604	0.618	0.661	0.694	0.667	0.612	0.546	0.550
United States	1.000	1.000	1.000	1.000	1.000	1.000	1.000	1.000	1.000	1.000	1.000	1.000	1.000	1.000
Euro area	0.773	0.854	0.843	0.765	0.788	0.882	0.894	0.939	1.085	1.117	1.061	0.885	0.805	0.805
Brazil	0.0016	0.0322	0.6393	0.9177	1.0051	1.0780	1.1605	1.8147	1.8301	2.3577	2.9208	3.0771	2.9251	2.4344
China	5.515	5.762	8.619	8.351	8.314	8.290	8.279	8.278	8.279	8.277	8.277	8.277	8.277	8.194
India	25.92	30.49	31.37	32.43	35.43	36.31	41.26	43.06	44.94	47.19	48.61	46.58	45.32	44.10
Russian Federation	..	1.0007	2.3915	4.6260	5.1675	5.8375	9.7051	24.6199	28.1292	29.1685	31.3485	30.6920	28.8137	28.2844
South Africa	2.852	3.268	3.551	3.627	4.299	4.608	5.528	6.110	6.940	8.609	10.541	7.565	6.460	6.359

StatLink http://dx.doi.org/10.1787/765051022466

Percentage differences in GDP when converted to US dollars using exchange rates and PPPs
PPP-based GDP minus exchange rate-based GDP as per cent of exchange rate-based GDP, 2005

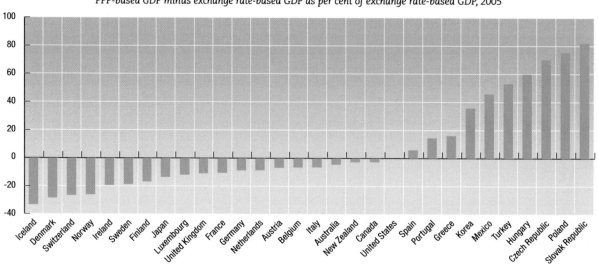

StatLink http://dx.doi.org/10.1787/388537451176

OECD FACTBOOK 2007 – ISBN 978-92-64-02946-0 – © OECD 2007

Indices of price levels
OECD = 100

	1992	1993	1994	1995	1996	1997	1998	1999	2000	2001	2002	2003	2004	2005
Australia	91	86	90	86	95	97	84	85	81	77	80	90	98	103
Austria	108	105	106	114	113	104	107	100	90	91	95	102	106	106
Belgium	105	102	104	111	110	103	105	101	90	89	92	100	105	105
Canada	93	89	82	78	82	86	82	81	88	88	87	91	94	101
Czech Republic	25	29	32	36	40	39	44	42	40	43	48	51	53	58
Denmark	134	126	126	135	136	128	130	122	111	111	118	132	137	137
Finland	117	94	100	118	116	109	110	106	96	97	101	116	118	118
France	111	106	106	111	112	103	105	100	90	89	94	108	112	110
Germany	116	114	115	124	121	112	114	108	96	97	100	105	109	108
Greece	72	69	70	75	80	79	78	77	68	69	71	79	84	85
Hungary	40	42	42	42	42	44	44	43	40	43	49	55	60	61
Iceland	118	103	98	102	104	106	113	113	112	101	111	125	131	148
Ireland	97	88	88	91	96	98	100	99	93	98	104	117	121	122
Italy	105	86	84	81	92	91	91	87	79	81	86	98	105	105
Japan	134	154	162	164	144	138	130	144	153	137	127	122	120	114
Korea	70	73	75	79	82	76	56	64	71	66	69	67	67	72
Luxembourg	109	108	111	121	121	113	115	106	97	99	102	108	112	112
Mexico	56	62	59	40	46	54	55	60	69	75	75	66	63	67
Netherlands	104	100	101	109	108	101	103	100	91	91	96	107	109	108
New Zealand	72	75	80	85	93	95	79	77	70	69	75	87	95	101
Norway	135	121	117	126	127	127	126	120	109	113	127	131	130	133
Poland	36	35	37	42	45	45	48	45	45	50	49	48	49	56
Portugal	75	67	67	72	75	72	73	70	64	65	69	81	86	86
Slovak Republic	..	34	35	39	41	42	43	38	37	37	40	46	52	54
Spain	99	83	79	83	87	82	83	79	73	75	77	87	92	93
Sweden	144	111	111	117	128	121	121	115	107	100	107	117	122	121
Switzerland	132	129	137	149	150	131	134	130	120	125	128	134	136	134
Turkey	50	52	38	44	45	46	48	46	46	38	45	52	57	64
United Kingdom	100	88	88	87	90	101	107	106	102	100	101	105	111	110
United States	92	94	92	88	92	99	102	101	106	111	111	103	98	98
EU 15 total	107	98	98	102	105	101	103	99	90	90	94	102	107	107
OECD total	100	100	100	100	100	100	100	100	100	100	100	100	100	100

StatLink http://dx.doi.org/10.1787/523610286136

Comparative price levels
OECD = 100, year 2005

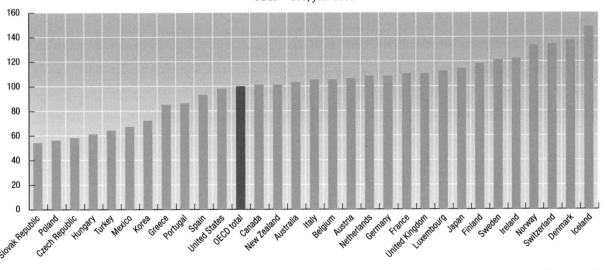

StatLink http://dx.doi.org/10.1787/717131147885

EFFECTIVE EXCHANGE RATES

A broad interpretation of international competitiveness would involve comparison of the success of different countries in raising productivity, fostering innovation and improving living standards. The two competitiveness indicators shown here have a narrower objective – namely to measure changes in a country's price competitiveness in international markets based on changes in that country's exchange rate and price level (either consumer goods prices or unit labour costs in manufacturing) relative to those of its competitors. In addition, we present indices of nominal effective exchange rates. This indicator reflects only variations in market exchange rates, which is just one of the factors that enter the calculation of the two competitiveness indicators mentioned above.

Definition

The nominal effective exchange rate indices are calculated by comparing, for each country, the change in its own exchange rate against the US dollar to a weighted average of changes in its competitors' exchange rates (also against the US dollar), using the weighting matrix for the current year (based on the importance of bilateral trade).

The other two indicators, relative consumer price indices and relative unit labour costs in manufacturing, can be described as indices of real effective exchange rates. Unlike nominal effective exchange rates, they take into account not only changes in market exchange rates, but also variations in relative price levels (using, respectively, consumer prices and unit labour costs in manufacturing), and therefore can be used as indicators of competitiveness. The change in a country's index of relative consumer prices between two years is obtained by comparing the change in the country's consumer price index (converted into US dollars at market exchange rates) to a weighted average of changes in its competitors' consumer price indices (also expressed in US dollars), using the weighting matrix for the current year (based on the importance of bilateral trade). Changes in the index of relative unit labour costs in manufacturing are calculated in the same way.

Comparability

All three indices shown here are constructed using a common procedure.

Long-term trends

A rise in the indices represents a deterioration in that country's competitiveness. Note that the indices only show changes in the international competitiveness of each country over time and that differences between countries in the levels of the indices have no significance.

All three indices are rather variable from year to year, so that it is difficult to detect long-term movements. Between 2000 and 2005, Japan, Sweden and the United States have generally improved their international competitiveness as judged by both relative consumer price indices and unit labour costs in manufacturing, while the competitive positions of Australia, Canada, Hungary and New Zealand have generally deteriorated. For both groups of countries, these changes reflected in large part movements in these countries' nominal effective exchange rates. By contrast, in the case of the United States, the improvement in competitiveness in terms of unit labour costs since 2000 has been significantly larger than the change in their nominal effective exchange rate, and therefore must have been due to favourable developments in unit labour costs in manufacturing, which in turn reflected trends in productivity and wage costs.

Source
• OECD (2007), *OECD Economic Outlook: December No. 80 – Volume 2006 Issue 2*, OECD, Paris.

Further information
Statistical publications
• OECD (2006), *Main Economic Indicators*, OECD, Paris.
Methodological publications
• Durand, M., C. Madaschi and F. Terribile (1998), *Trends in OECD Countries' International Competitiveness*, OECD Economics Department Working Papers, No. 195, OECD, Paris.

• Durand, M., J. Simon and C. Webb (1992), *OECD's Indicators of International Trade and Competitiveness*, OECD Economics Department Working Papers, No. 120, OECD, Paris.
Online databases
• *OECD Economic Outlook Statistics*.
Websites
• OECD Economic Outlook – Sources and Methods, *www.oecd.org/eco/sources-and-methods*.

Nominal effective exchange rates
Year 2000 = 100

	1992	1993	1994	1995	1996	1997	1998	1999	2000	2001	2002	2003	2004	2005
Australia	104.8	99.5	107.2	103.9	113.9	115.4	107.4	107.6	100.0	93.7	97.2	108.6	117.2	120.1
Austria	92.5	95.6	97.8	102.5	101.5	99.6	101.6	102.3	100.0	100.4	101.0	104.4	105.5	104.7
Belgium	95.8	97.9	102.2	107.9	106.2	102.0	104.4	104.1	100.0	101.2	103.0	108.3	110.2	109.7
Canada	112.9	107.7	102.8	102.0	103.9	104.3	99.4	99.1	100.0	97.0	95.5	105.5	112.0	119.8
Czech Republic	..	94.7	98.1	98.8	100.4	97.4	99.1	98.7	100.0	105.0	117.0	116.7	117.0	124.4
Denmark	93.8	98.2	100.5	105.7	104.7	102.3	104.9	104.2	100.0	101.8	103.3	108.1	109.5	108.7
Finland	88.3	79.5	90.1	103.6	101.1	98.9	101.7	104.7	100.0	102.1	104.3	110.3	112.4	111.7
France	93.6	97.4	100.4	104.5	104.9	102.1	104.5	103.8	100.0	100.9	102.5	107.4	109.0	108.5
Germany	89.0	93.9	98.5	106.0	104.5	100.9	104.6	104.5	100.0	101.2	103.1	109.4	111.6	110.4
Greece	129.3	120.5	115.1	113.8	111.9	109.9	106.6	107.0	100.0	101.0	102.8	107.8	109.5	108.5
Hungary	..	214.4	192.8	153.0	130.3	120.7	109.3	105.4	100.0	101.9	108.9	108.3	110.4	111.2
Iceland	103.1	97.1	92.9	93.3	92.8	94.8	97.4	99.0	100.0	85.2	87.9	92.1	93.2	103.6
Ireland	113.1	107.4	109.2	111.2	114.1	113.9	110.5	107.3	100.0	101.2	103.6	112.6	115.1	114.9
Italy	115.2	99.2	99.1	91.3	100.5	101.8	104.0	103.8	100.0	101.3	103.2	108.3	110.1	109.3
Japan	60.1	74.4	86.4	92.5	80.6	77.1	80.0	91.9	100.0	92.3	88.4	91.4	95.3	92.4
Korea	119.6	117.8	119.1	119.5	121.4	112.4	81.3	93.3	100.0	92.4	95.4	94.8	94.8	105.7
Luxembourg	98.6	99.2	102.0	105.4	104.2	102.0	103.0	102.8	100.0	100.4	101.5	105.0	106.2	105.7
Mexico	259.3	272.4	263.8	138.6	117.7	115.5	102.6	97.9	100.0	102.8	99.7	87.1	81.9	84.3
Netherlands	92.7	97.2	101.8	108.8	107.3	102.1	105.7	105.4	100.0	101.4	103.7	110.8	113.4	112.8
New Zealand	97.4	102.0	109.4	116.9	124.3	127.3	114.3	110.3	100.0	98.7	106.8	121.6	129.7	135.8
Norway	101.1	100.0	100.8	104.5	104.6	105.6	102.4	102.2	100.0	103.3	112.1	109.7	106.0	110.3
Poland	..	170.5	139.2	122.7	114.4	106.3	104.0	97.0	100.0	110.2	105.4	94.8	92.7	103.8
Portugal	106.3	102.5	101.7	104.9	104.5	103.1	103.0	102.4	100.0	100.9	102.0	104.7	105.4	105.0
Slovak Republic	..	98.2	97.1	100.4	101.3	106.0	105.9	98.3	100.0	97.6	98.0	103.5	108.0	110.2
Spain	124.2	111.0	105.7	106.0	107.1	102.8	104.0	103.1	100.0	101.1	102.5	106.3	107.5	107.0
Sweden	112.4	92.5	93.6	94.0	103.5	100.2	99.9	99.7	100.0	91.9	94.1	99.5	101.3	98.7
Switzerland	82.9	86.8	95.6	104.0	102.7	96.9	101.0	101.8	100.0	104.0	109.3	111.1	111.5	110.7
Turkey	6 053.0	4 239.0	1 719.1	990.8	581.1	345.5	207.8	137.2	100.0	56.3	41.8	36.8	35.8	37.8
United Kingdom	82.8	76.6	79.0	76.4	78.1	91.1	97.0	97.4	100.0	99.0	100.2	96.3	100.8	99.3
United States	68.3	72.7	76.9	78.5	82.9	88.8	98.0	97.6	100.0	105.3	105.8	99.6	95.1	92.7
Euro area	95.2	94.2	100.8	109.5	111.7	104.6	110.8	109.9	100.0	102.5	106.4	119.4	123.8	122.0

StatLink ᴍˢ˥ http://dx.doi.org/10.1787/267765578278

Nominal effective exchange rates
Year 1992 = 100

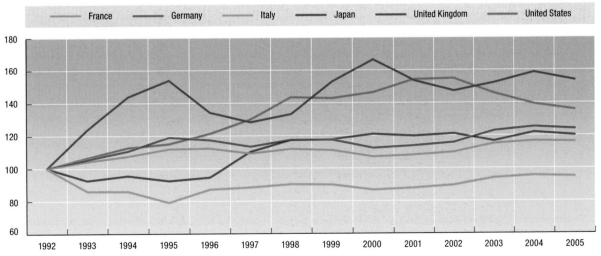

StatLink ᴍˢ˥ http://dx.doi.org/10.1787/160826502311

Relative consumer price indices
Year 2000 = 100

	1992	1993	1994	1995	1996	1997	1998	1999	2000	2001	2002	2003	2004	2005
Australia	110.5	102.1	107.1	105.3	115.3	114.1	104.3	104.9	100.0	96.1	101.4	114.7	124.0	127.7
Austria	105.3	106.5	106.7	109.7	107.2	103.5	103.8	102.7	100.0	100.2	100.5	103.2	104.0	103.3
Belgium	107.9	107.8	109.5	113.1	110.4	104.9	105.7	104.2	100.0	100.8	102.0	106.6	108.2	108.2
Canada	127.5	118.8	109.1	106.8	106.9	106.2	100.2	99.4	100.0	96.9	96.0	106.7	112.5	119.3
Czech Republic	..	77.3	81.1	83.9	89.3	90.9	99.5	98.1	100.0	106.7	118.5	115.8	116.5	123.3
Denmark	101.7	102.6	102.2	105.9	104.3	101.6	103.7	103.8	100.0	101.5	103.3	108.1	108.7	107.4
Finland	122.8	102.7	106.6	114.4	107.7	103.6	104.8	104.6	100.0	101.3	102.4	106.6	106.3	103.5
France	108.4	109.5	109.4	111.6	110.9	106.4	107.1	104.8	100.0	99.7	101.0	105.7	107.2	105.9
Germany	109.6	113.4	114.0	118.3	113.6	108.0	109.1	106.5	100.0	99.9	100.6	105.3	106.5	104.8
Greece	99.7	100.4	101.2	104.4	107.3	108.0	106.5	106.9	100.0	100.9	103.6	109.6	111.8	112.1
Hungary	..	95.9	93.6	88.9	89.8	95.3	95.9	98.7	100.0	108.2	119.1	121.6	129.5	131.9
Iceland	104.7	98.6	92.3	90.9	90.3	91.7	93.9	96.5	100.0	88.7	94.8	99.3	101.8	115.4
Ireland	118.8	110.1	109.8	110.8	112.6	111.2	107.8	104.3	100.0	103.6	109.1	119.9	122.4	122.1
Italy	122.5	103.4	100.5	93.3	103.3	103.7	105.1	104.1	100.0	101.2	103.2	108.7	110.2	108.9
Japan	83.0	96.3	104.0	105.7	88.4	83.5	84.3	94.6	100.0	89.5	83.9	85.0	86.2	81.2
Korea	110.2	107.0	108.3	109.5	113.5	107.0	81.5	92.9	100.0	94.6	99.6	101.1	102.7	115.5
Luxembourg	104.8	104.8	106.0	108.6	106.0	102.8	103.0	102.2	100.0	100.6	101.9	105.5	106.8	106.4
Mexico	93.3	99.7	95.3	64.5	72.1	83.4	84.2	92.1	100.0	106.5	106.7	95.3	91.5	95.0
Netherlands	108.1	108.5	108.6	112.7	109.6	103.7	106.5	105.8	100.0	102.9	106.6	113.9	115.4	113.7
New Zealand	104.0	106.4	112.1	120.1	127.4	129.7	115.9	110.3	100.0	98.9	108.1	122.9	131.4	138.8
Norway	108.0	104.0	101.3	103.7	102.4	103.6	100.9	101.4	100.0	103.8	111.9	109.9	104.8	109.0
Poland	..	73.5	74.3	79.3	85.1	88.0	93.4	90.8	100.0	112.8	107.7	95.4	94.4	105.3
Portugal	104.0	100.9	99.3	102.8	102.7	101.4	102.1	102.2	100.0	102.5	104.7	108.4	109.2	108.3
Slovak Republic	..	85.2	84.3	86.2	86.0	90.9	91.9	90.7	100.0	101.2	102.5	115.5	126.4	129.3
Spain	121.0	107.8	103.0	104.5	106.1	101.5	102.3	102.1	100.0	102.0	104.4	109.1	111.1	111.8
Sweden	130.0	106.8	105.3	104.4	112.4	106.7	103.6	101.6	100.0	91.6	93.9	99.2	99.2	95.0
Switzerland	102.1	104.0	108.7	115.2	111.0	102.5	104.2	103.0	100.0	102.1	105.8	106.0	104.9	102.8
Turkey	84.1	90.2	66.3	71.8	72.6	77.5	85.1	89.5	100.0	81.5	88.6	96.1	100.9	114.1
United Kingdom	88.2	78.6	78.9	76.0	77.3	90.6	97.3	97.2	100.0	98.0	98.5	95.5	100.7	99.7
United States	83.8	85.0	85.2	83.9	86.5	91.0	98.2	96.9	100.0	105.7	105.8	99.6	95.4	93.9
Euro area	128.9	121.2	120.7	124.9	123.7	112.8	115.4	111.4	100.0	101.7	105.4	117.7	121.4	119.0

StatLink http://dx.doi.org/10.1787/267817858588

Relative consumer price indices
Year 1992 = 100

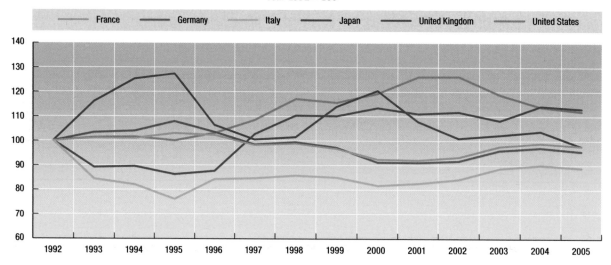

StatLink http://dx.doi.org/10.1787/333602857637

OECD FACTBOOK 2007 – ISBN 978-92-64-02946-0 – © OECD 2007

Relative unit labour costs in manufacturing
Year 2000 = 100

	1992	1993	1994	1995	1996	1997	1998	1999	2000	2001	2002	2003	2004	2005
Australia	133.1	117.2	118.6	114.6	119.0	120.0	106.9	105.3	100.0	92.8	98.8	112.1	125.6	134.7
Austria	145.7	147.5	136.2	134.9	138.5	125.5	111.4	108.5	100.0	96.9	96.9	99.8	92.6	91.8
Belgium	107.9	107.0	107.6	110.9	106.8	99.6	101.9	105.1	100.0	102.9	103.3	107.8	108.9	110.3
Canada	120.1	108.6	101.1	101.9	108.6	107.5	103.2	101.7	100.0	100.2	101.9	115.8	122.0	129.9
Czech Republic	..	81.9	88.0	82.9	88.6	88.2	96.6	99.1	100.0	103.9	118.3	116.1	117.2	124.2
Denmark	95.0	99.7	95.1	99.3	103.5	98.5	103.0	103.3	100.0	101.8	104.7	109.8	116.6	117.5
Finland	127.6	97.4	103.1	118.8	112.3	106.5	108.9	110.1	100.0	104.5	104.0	109.5	113.3	113.5
France	124.7	126.6	124.6	122.9	122.4	113.7	108.7	105.7	100.0	98.2	99.0	107.5	110.0	110.2
Germany	99.8	102.6	103.9	113.4	109.9	103.3	106.1	104.9	100.0	98.9	100.0	104.1	104.1	98.4
Greece	94.8	88.7	92.7	100.7	103.9	107.3	102.1	104.1	100.0	100.5	103.5	108.7	116.2	119.2
Hungary	..	135.5	131.1	108.2	98.6	103.0	99.3	104.9	100.0	109.5	124.8	125.1	131.1	129.1
Iceland	80.5	73.5	72.2	72.5	72.1	76.2	82.5	91.7	100.0	87.2	92.9	97.6	100.3	116.5
Ireland	202.0	186.3	176.8	158.1	154.5	131.6	127.1	116.5	100.0	99.3	94.4	102.6	110.0	109.5
Italy	113.5	104.1	99.3	86.2	96.6	98.4	103.1	105.3	100.0	101.4	108.2	117.0	120.8	123.9
Japan	76.5	90.6	94.8	100.9	85.5	80.4	85.9	97.0	100.0	91.9	84.4	83.2	82.4	78.3
Korea	115.6	114.3	119.1	130.8	140.7	126.2	87.8	93.6	100.0	92.7	97.8	95.6	98.9	107.1
Luxembourg	115.2	114.0	112.4	113.6	109.0	105.6	105.3	101.4	100.0	102.8	102.2	99.9	98.2	91.2
Mexico	123.5	134.3	130.9	80.3	82.2	90.2	88.8	92.2	100.0	106.5	109.9	99.1	98.0	103.5
Netherlands	110.1	109.5	105.8	109.6	105.5	104.0	107.3	106.6	100.0	102.5	107.2	116.2	118.5	116.7
New Zealand	73.6	79.7	93.4	104.1	115.9	119.1	104.2	106.0	100.0	100.7	117.2	138.2	155.6	161.7
Norway	77.2	75.6	79.6	84.2	84.0	90.9	94.4	97.4	100.0	102.6	116.5	116.8	114.5	117.9
Poland	..	84.1	89.6	97.6	100.4	100.9	105.9	99.5	100.0	104.3	93.8	76.7	69.6	78.3
Portugal	101.3	92.2	95.8	100.8	92.4	94.1	95.7	98.7	100.0	103.0	105.7	109.1	111.8	111.0
Slovak Republic	..	67.3	78.5	83.6	92.3	100.4	103.1	99.3	100.0	97.4	98.0	104.7	113.6	118.5
Spain	103.8	94.6	91.7	92.5	97.0	96.4	98.7	99.2	100.0	102.8	105.9	109.4	112.2	112.5
Sweden	157.0	112.2	105.7	105.1	118.0	111.2	106.5	101.3	100.0	96.3	93.3	96.2	91.7	88.9
Switzerland	86.7	86.3	94.8	103.5	99.8	95.4	98.0	100.0	100.0	105.7	112.7	114.3	114.2	113.0
Turkey	113.6	109.7	71.7	61.9	60.8	67.1	73.7	87.2	100.0	73.4	72.2	71.3	79.3	87.8
United Kingdom	74.9	66.2	67.8	67.4	69.1	83.9	94.6	96.8	100.0	96.9	100.9	96.6	101.1	101.4
United States	90.1	88.1	87.5	84.6	84.8	89.4	95.0	95.4	100.0	102.4	99.1	92.4	85.7	82.5
Euro area	125.4	121.2	117.9	121.8	122.5	110.1	112.4	111.6	100.0	100.7	105.9	120.7	125.4	122.8

StatLink http://dx.doi.org/10.1787/182628230873

Relative unit labour costs in manufacturing
Year 1992 = 100

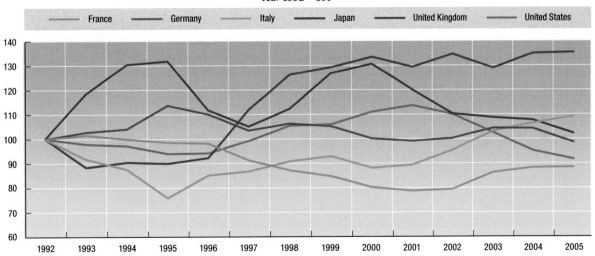

StatLink http://dx.doi.org/10.1787/588746271412

ENERGY

PRIMARY ENERGY SUPPLY

An analysis of energy problems requires a comprehensive presentation of basic supply and demand data for all fuels in a manner which will allow the easy comparison of the contribution each fuel makes to the economy and their interrelationships through the conversion of one fuel into another. This type of presentation is suitable for the study of energy substitution, energy conservation and forecasting.

Definition

The table refers to total primary energy supply (TPES). TPES equals production plus imports minus exports minus international marine bunkers plus or minus stock changes. The IEA energy balance methodology is based on the calorific content of the energy commodities and a common unit of account. The unit of account adopted by the IEA is the tonne of oil equivalent (toe) which is defined as 10^7 kilocalories (41.868 gigajoules). This quantity of energy is, within a few per cent, equal to the net heat content of 1 tonne of crude oil. The difference between the "net" and the "gross" calorific value for each fuel is the latent heat of vaporisation of the water produced during combustion of the fuel. For coal and oil, net calorific value is about 5% less than gross, for most forms of natural and manufactured gas the difference is 9-10%, while for

electricity there is no difference as the concept has no meaning in this case. The IEA balances are calculated using the physical energy content method to calculate the primary energy equivalent. The forecasts provided in the table refer to the Reference Scenario of the *World Energy Outlook*. The Reference Scenario projects supply and demand if present policies were to continue. The *World Energy Outlook* also presents an Alternative Policy Scenario which analyses how the global energy market could evolve if countries were to adopt all of the policies they are currently considering related to energy security and energy-related CO_2 emissions.

Comparability

While every effort is made to ensure the accuracy of the data, quality is not homogeneous for all countries/ regions. In some countries data are based on secondary sources, and where incomplete or unavailable, the IEA has made estimates. In general, data are likely to be more accurate for production and trade than for international marine bunkers or stock changes. Moreover, statistics for combustible renewables and waste are less accurate than traditional commercial energy data in most countries.

Long-term trends

Over the 33-year period of 1971 to 2004, the world's total primary energy supply increased by 102%, reaching 11 223 Mtoe (million tonnes of oil equivalent). This equates to a compound growth rate of 2.1% per annum. By comparison, world population grew by 1.6% and gross domestic product by 3.4% per annum over the same period.

Energy supply growth was fairly constant over the period, except in 1974-1975 and in the early 1980s as a consequence of the first two oil shocks, and in the early 1990s following the dissolution of the Soviet Union.

Although the OECD is still the largest energy user, its share of total primary energy supply declined significantly from 61% in 1971 to 49% in 2004. Strong economic development in Asia led to a large increase in the share of Asia (including China) in world energy supply, from 13% in 1971 to 26% in 2004. By contrast, the combined share of the former USSR and non-OECD Europe decreased significantly in the late 1980s.

Sources
- IEA (2006), *Energy Balances of OECD Countries*, IEA, Paris.
- IEA (2006), *Energy Balances of Non-OECD Countries*, IEA, Paris.
- IEA (2006), *World Energy Outlook 2006*, IEA, Paris.

Further information
Analytical publications
- IEA (2006), *Energy Policies of IEA Countries*, series, IEA, Paris.
- IEA (2006), *Energy Technology Perspectives: Scenarios and Strategies to 2050*, IEA, Paris.

Online databases
- *World Energy Statistics and Balances*.

Websites
- International Energy Agency, *www.iea.org*.

Total primary energy supply
Million tonnes of oil equivalent (Mtoe)

	1971	1990	1995	1996	1997	1998	1999	2000	2001	2002	2003	2004	2005	2030
Australia	52.2	87.6	94.4	100.9	103.4	106.3	108.6	110.5	108.3	111.9	112.9	115.8	120.2	..
Austria	19.0	25.0	27.1	28.8	28.8	29.2	29.2	29.0	30.7	31.1	33.0	33.2	34.6	..
Belgium	39.9	49.1	52.3	56.3	56.9	58.2	58.4	58.9	58.6	56.6	59.2	57.7	58.2	..
Canada	141.8	209.4	231.3	236.4	240.3	239.5	246.8	250.2	246.0	250.0	262.6	269.1	266.8	..
Czech Republic	45.6	49.0	41.1	42.3	42.5	41.1	38.4	40.4	41.4	42.0	44.2	45.5	44.9	..
Denmark	19.2	17.9	20.0	22.6	21.0	20.7	19.9	19.3	19.9	19.6	20.7	20.1	19.5	..
Finland	18.4	29.2	29.6	31.9	33.1	33.5	33.4	33.0	33.8	35.5	37.7	38.1	34.8	..
France	162.2	227.3	240.8	254.3	246.8	254.9	255.1	257.6	266.4	266.1	271.1	275.2	274.8	..
Germany	307.9	356.2	342.4	353.9	351.2	349.2	341.7	343.6	353.5	345.3	347.1	348.0	346.8	..
Greece	9.2	22.2	23.5	24.2	25.1	26.4	26.6	27.8	28.7	29.0	29.9	30.5	31.0	..
Hungary	19.1	28.6	25.7	26.2	25.8	25.4	25.4	25.0	25.4	25.8	26.3	26.4	27.7	..
Iceland	1.0	2.2	2.3	2.5	2.5	2.7	3.1	3.2	3.4	3.4	3.4	3.5	3.6	..
Ireland	7.1	10.4	11.0	11.8	12.5	13.3	13.9	14.3	15.2	15.4	15.1	15.2	15.9	..
Italy	114.5	148.0	160.7	160.3	162.6	167.3	170.4	172.7	173.6	173.5	181.3	184.5	187.5	..
Japan	269.6	446.0	502.5	517.2	522.6	516.6	525.4	528.9	520.8	521.7	516.1	533.2	532.2	606.0
Korea	17.0	92.7	147.7	163.1	176.4	162.2	178.5	190.9	193.8	201.9	206.3	213.1	221.5	..
Luxembourg	4.1	3.6	3.4	3.5	3.4	3.3	3.5	3.7	3.8	4.0	4.3	4.8	4.8	..
Mexico	43.5	124.3	132.7	136.7	141.4	147.8	149.7	150.4	152.2	155.6	160.0	165.5	173.3	..
Netherlands	51.3	66.7	72.5	75.6	74.2	74.5	73.7	75.8	78.0	78.7	80.9	82.2	82.3	..
New Zealand	7.2	13.8	15.8	16.7	17.2	16.9	17.7	17.3	17.4	17.7	17.3	17.6	17.5	..
Norway	13.6	21.5	23.9	23.2	24.6	25.5	26.8	25.8	26.5	25.1	27.2	27.7	30.0	..
Poland	86.3	99.9	99.7	103.6	102.5	95.8	93.1	89.4	90.0	89.1	91.4	91.7	89.4	..
Portugal	6.5	17.8	20.7	20.5	21.6	23.3	25.1	25.3	25.4	26.5	25.8	26.6	27.3	..
Slovak Republic	14.2	21.3	17.8	18.1	18.1	17.6	17.7	17.7	18.6	18.7	18.6	18.3	18.5	..
Spain	43.1	91.1	102.8	101.4	107.9	113.3	118.8	124.7	127.8	131.6	136.1	142.2	145.6	..
Sweden	36.5	47.6	50.9	52.1	50.8	51.7	51.3	48.7	51.7	52.7	51.7	53.9	51.1	..
Switzerland	17.1	25.0	25.0	25.5	26.1	26.4	26.4	26.2	27.7	26.8	26.9	27.1	27.1	..
Turkey	19.5	53.0	61.9	67.3	71.0	72.2	71.0	77.0	71.0	75.2	78.8	81.9	86.4	..
United Kingdom	211.0	212.2	223.4	233.1	227.1	230.3	231.6	232.9	234.6	228.5	232.3	233.7	230.8	..
United States	1 593.2	1 927.6	2 088.5	2 140.5	2 163.8	2 182.2	2 241.1	2 304.2	2 258.6	2 288.5	2 280.9	2 325.9	2 319.2	2 929.0
EU 25 total	..	..	1 592.4	1 649.3	1 640.1	1 657.2	1 653.4	1 665.3	1 704.1	1 697.3	1 735.7	1 757.3	..	1 973.0
OECD total	3 390.8	4 525.8	4 891.2	5 050.3	5 101.0	5 127.1	5 222.0	5 324.5	5 302.7	5 347.4	5 398.9	5 507.9	5 523.3	6 860.0
Brazil	69.6	134.0	154.9	163.2	171.5	177.3	182.5	185.7	186.9	191.4	193.7	204.9	..	349.0
China	391.7	866.5	1 051.7	1 091.1	1 092.6	1 094.8	1 099.3	1 122.6	1 120.4	1 212.8	1 381.3	1 609.4	..	3 395.0
India	182.0	361.6	436.5	451.4	467.9	475.8	499.3	512.0	519.8	533.7	548.7	572.9	..	1 104.0
Russian Federation	..	..	628.4	616.6	595.1	581.4	603.0	614.0	621.3	617.8	639.7	641.5	..	854.0
South Africa	45.3	91.2	104.1	105.8	108.2	109.4	109.4	112.9	116.2	113.8	121.8	131.1	..	..
World	5 567.1	8 737.6	9 267.0	9 525.6	9 620.5	9 685.1	9 873.2	10 089.2	10 146.4	10 368.3	10 718.4	11 223.3	..	17 095.0

StatLink http://dx.doi.org/10.1787/636108411483

Total primary energy supply by region
Million tonnes of oil equivalent (Mtoe)

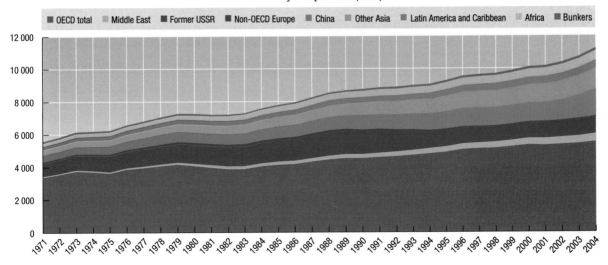

Legend: ■ OECD total ■ Middle East ■ Former USSR ■ Non-OECD Europe ■ China ■ Other Asia ■ Latin America and Caribbean ■ Africa ■ Bunkers

StatLink http://dx.doi.org/10.1787/422224686665

ENERGY SUPPLY AND ECONOMIC GROWTH

It is not an easy task to monitor the overall trend in energy efficiency of a country, since there are numerous elements to consider such as climate change, outsourcing of goods produced by energy-intensive industries, etc. A common way to measure progress in energy intensity is to look at the changes in the ratio of energy use to GDP. Indeed, some experts look at energy intensity to derive trends of energy efficiency, but such an analysis has many limitations.

Definition

The table shows total primary energy supply (TPES) per thousand US dollars of GDP. The ratios are calculated by dividing each country's annual TPES by each country's annual GDP expressed in constant 2000 prices and converted to US dollars using purchasing power parities (PPPs) for the year 2000.

TPES consists of primary energy production adjusted for net trade and stock changes. Production of secondary energy (*e.g.* oil/coal products, electricity from fossil fuels, etc.) is not included since the "energy equivalent" of the primary fuels used to create the secondary products or electric power has already been counted. TPES is expressed in tonnes of oil equivalent (see the IEA sources below for details on how TPES is calculated).

Long-term trends

Sharp improvements in the efficiency of key end uses, shifts to electricity, and some changes in manufacturing output and consumer behaviour have occurred in many OECD countries since 1971. As a consequence, energy supply per unit of GDP fell significantly, particularly in the 1979-1990 period.

Contributing to the trend were higher fuel prices, long-term technological progress, government energy efficiency programmes and regulations. Overall growth in per capita GDP, combined with higher living standards and slow population growth, produced steadily rising demand after 1985.

The ratio of energy supply to GDP (TPES/GDP) fell less than the ratio of energy consumption to GDP (TFC/GDP), because of increased use of electricity. The main reason for this is that losses in electricity generating outweighed intensity improvements achieved in end uses such as household appliances.

Among OECD countries, the ratio of energy consumption to GDP varies considerably. Apart from energy prices, winter weather is a key element in these variations, as are raw materials processing techniques, the distance goods must be shipped, the size of dwellings, use of private rather than public transport and other lifestyle factors.

Comparability

Care should be taken when comparing energy intensities between countries and over time. Different national circumstances such as density of population, country size, average temperatures and economic structure will affect the ratios. A decrease in the TPES/GDP ratio may be partly attributable to a restructuring of the economy by transferring energy-intensive industries such as iron and steel out of the country – i.e. by purchasing energy-intensive products from abroad. The harmful effects of such outsourcing may actually increase the damage to the environment if the producers abroad use less energy efficient techniques.

Total primary energy supply per unit of GDP

Tonnes of oil equivalent (toe) per thousand 2000 US dollar of GDP calculated using PPPs, 2004

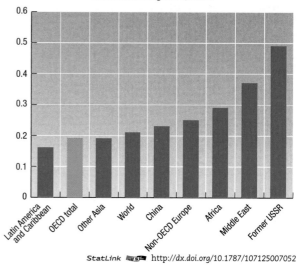

StatLink ☰☐☜☐ http://dx.doi.org/10.1787/107125007052

Sources

- IEA (2006), *Energy Balances of OECD Countries*, IEA, Paris.
- IEA (2006), *Energy Balances of Non-OECD Countries*, IEA, Paris.

Further information

Analytical publications

- IEA (2006), *Energy Policies of IEA Countries*, series, IEA, Paris.
- IEA (2006), *World Energy Outlook 2006*, IEA, Paris.

Online databases

- World Energy Statistics and Balances.

Websites

- International Energy Agency, *www.iea.org*.

OECD FACTBOOK 2007 – ISBN 978-92-64-02946-0 – © OECD 2007

ENERGY SUPPLY AND ECONOMIC GROWTH

Total primary energy supply per unit of GDP

Tonnes of oil equivalent (toe) per thousand 2000 US dollars of GDP calculated using PPPs

	1971	1990	1995	1996	1997	1998	1999	2000	2001	2002	2003	2004	2005
Australia	0.25	0.24	0.22	0.22	0.22	0.22	0.21	0.21	0.20	0.20	0.19	0.19	0.20
Austria	0.18	0.14	0.14	0.14	0.14	0.14	0.13	0.13	0.13	0.13	0.14	0.14	0.14
Belgium	0.30	0.22	0.22	0.23	0.23	0.23	0.22	0.22	0.21	0.20	0.21	0.20	0.20
Canada	0.41	0.33	0.33	0.33	0.32	0.31	0.30	0.29	0.28	0.28	0.29	0.28	0.27
Czech Republic	0.45	0.34	0.30	0.29	0.30	0.29	0.27	0.27	0.27	0.27	0.28	0.27	0.25
Denmark	0.22	0.15	0.15	0.16	0.15	0.14	0.13	0.13	0.13	0.13	0.13	0.13	0.12
Finland	0.31	0.26	0.28	0.29	0.28	0.27	0.25	0.25	0.25	0.26	0.27	0.26	0.23
France	0.22	0.18	0.18	0.18	0.18	0.17	0.17	0.16	0.17	0.16	0.17	0.16	0.16
Germany	0.29	0.21	0.18	0.18	0.18	0.18	0.17	0.16	0.17	0.16	0.16	0.16	0.16
Greece	0.10	0.16	0.16	0.16	0.16	0.16	0.16	0.16	0.15	0.15	0.15	0.14	0.14
Hungary	0.28	0.25	0.25	0.25	0.24	0.23	0.22	0.20	0.20	0.19	0.19	0.18	0.18
Iceland	0.35	0.35	0.37	0.38	0.36	0.37	0.40	0.40	0.41	0.41	0.40	0.39	0.38
Ireland	0.28	0.19	0.16	0.16	0.15	0.15	0.14	0.13	0.13	0.13	0.12	0.11	0.11
Italy	0.16	0.12	0.12	0.12	0.12	0.12	0.12	0.12	0.12	0.12	0.12	0.12	0.13
Japan	0.20	0.16	0.16	0.16	0.16	0.16	0.16	0.16	0.16	0.16	0.15	0.16	0.15
Korea	0.17	0.22	0.24	0.25	0.25	0.25	0.25	0.25	0.24	0.24	0.23	0.23	0.23
Luxembourg	0.67	0.28	0.22	0.22	0.20	0.18	0.18	0.17	0.18	0.18	0.19	0.20	0.19
Mexico	0.15	0.20	0.19	0.19	0.18	0.18	0.18	0.17	0.17	0.17	0.17	0.17	0.18
Netherlands	0.24	0.20	0.19	0.19	0.18	0.18	0.17	0.17	0.17	0.17	0.18	0.18	0.17
New Zealand	0.16	0.23	0.22	0.23	0.23	0.23	0.23	0.22	0.21	0.20	0.19	0.19	0.18
Norway	0.23	0.19	0.18	0.16	0.16	0.17	0.17	0.16	0.16	0.15	0.16	0.16	0.17
Poland	0.41	0.36	0.32	0.32	0.29	0.26	0.24	0.23	0.22	0.22	0.22	0.21	0.20
Portugal	0.10	0.13	0.14	0.14	0.14	0.14	0.15	0.14	0.14	0.15	0.14	0.15	0.15
Slovak Republic	0.39	0.40	0.37	0.35	0.34	0.31	0.31	0.31	0.31	0.30	0.28	0.26	0.25
Spain	0.12	0.14	0.15	0.14	0.15	0.15	0.15	0.15	0.15	0.15	0.15	0.15	0.15
Sweden	0.27	0.24	0.25	0.25	0.24	0.23	0.22	0.20	0.21	0.21	0.21	0.21	0.19
Switzerland	0.12	0.13	0.13	0.13	0.13	0.13	0.13	0.12	0.13	0.12	0.12	0.12	0.12
Turkey	0.14	0.16	0.16	0.17	0.16	0.16	0.17	0.17	0.17	0.16	0.16	0.16	0.15
United Kingdom	0.28	0.18	0.17	0.18	0.17	0.16	0.16	0.16	0.15	0.15	0.14	0.14	0.14
United States	0.41	0.27	0.26	0.26	0.25	0.24	0.24	0.24	0.23	0.23	0.22	0.22	0.21
EU 25 total	..	..	0.18	0.18	0.18	0.17	0.17	0.16	0.16	0.16	0.16	0.16	..
OECD total	0.30	0.22	0.21	0.21	0.21	0.20	0.20	0.20	0.19	0.19	0.19	0.19	0.18
Brazil	0.17	0.14	0.14	0.14	0.14	0.15	0.15	0.15	0.14	0.15	0.15	0.15	..
China	0.90	0.48	0.32	0.30	0.28	0.26	0.24	0.23	0.21	0.21	0.22	0.23	..
India	0.30	0.25	0.24	0.23	0.23	0.22	0.21	0.21	0.20	0.20	0.19	0.18	..
Russian Federation	..	..	0.67	0.68	0.64	0.64	0.63	0.59	0.58	0.54	0.52	0.49	..
South Africa	0.20	0.26	0.30	0.29	0.29	0.29	0.28	0.27	0.27	0.26	0.26	0.28	..
World	0.31	0.26	0.24	0.24	0.23	0.23	0.22	0.22	0.21	0.21	0.21	0.21	..

StatLink ⎙ http://dx.doi.org/10.1787/346531608526

Total primary energy supply per unit of GDP

Tonnes of oil equivalent (toe) per thousand 2000 US dollars of GDP calculated using PPPs, 2005

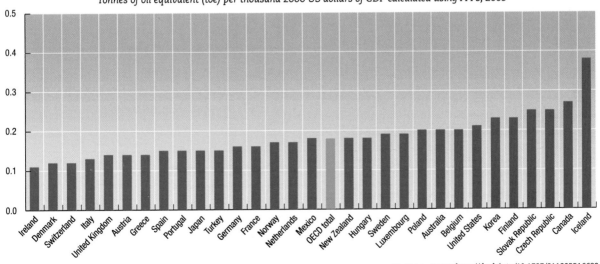

StatLink ⎙ http://dx.doi.org/10.1787/811885516682

ENERGY SUPPLY PER CAPITA

Total primary energy supply per capita is a common, albeit an imperfect measure of energy efficiency in a country. For instance, neither the impact of climate on energy use (heating, cooling) nor the size of the country and the density of the population are properly taken into account when comparing countries. Energy analysts usually prefer to compare energy use per unit of output or per unit of GDP. However, the ratio has been presented here since its use is widespread.

Definition

The table refers to total primary energy supply (TPES) per head of population. The ratio is expressed in tonnes of oil equivalent (toe) per person. TPES consists of primary energy production adjusted for net trade and stock changes. Production of secondary energy (e.g. oil/coal products, electricity from fossil fuels, etc.) is not included since the "energy equivalent" of the primary fuels used to create the secondary products or electric power has already been counted. TPES is expressed in tonnes of oil equivalent (see the IEA sources below for details on how TPES is calculated). The forecasts provided in the table refer to the Reference Scenario of the *World Energy Outlook*.

Comparability

Care should be taken when comparing energy supply per capita between countries and over time. Different national circumstances such as density of population, country size, temperatures, economic structure and domestic energy resources affect the ratios.

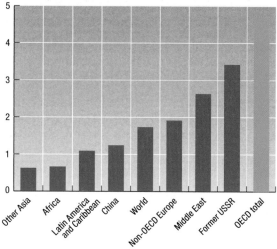

Total primary energy supply per capita

Tonnes of oil equivalent (toe) per capita, 2004

StatLink http://dx.doi.org/10.1787/814282523787

Long-term trends

The level of energy supply on a per capita basis varied significantly across OECD countries. The countries with the highest ratios were those countries with the smallest populations. In 2005, the energy supply per capita for Iceland was 12.4 toe/capita and for Luxembourg was 10.7 toe/capita. The high ratio for Iceland is explained partly by the climate but also be the availability of cheap – and non-polluting – thermal energy from hot springs. In the case of Luxembourg, the high ratio is partly due to low sales taxes on petroleum products; motorists and other consumers from neighbouring countries – Belgium, France and Germany – buy their supplies in Luxembourg.

The United States and Canada are also large consumers of energy per capita, with ratios of 7.8 and 8.3 toe/capita in 2005. On the other end of the scale, the countries with the lowest TPES/capita were Turkey (1.2 toe/capita) and Mexico (1.6 toe/capita).

Between 1971 and 2005, there are striking differences in the trends of the OECD countries. Compared to 1971, TPES/capita in 2005 was eight times higher in Korea and more than doubled in Greece, Iceland, Portugal, Spain and Turkey. On the other hand, the ratio decreased in four OECD countries over this period: Luxembourg (-11%), Poland (-11%), Denmark (-7%) and the Czech Republic (-5%).

In general, the TPES/capita of non-OECD countries is lower than that of the OECD countries. In 2004, the ratio for China (1.2 toe/capita) was twice as much as in 1971. South Africa (2.9 toe/capita), Brazil (1.1 toe/capita) and India (0.5 toe/capita) grew slightly more slowly.

Sources
- IEA (2006), *Energy Balances of OECD Countries*, IEA, Paris.
- IEA (2006), *Energy Balances of Non-OECD Countries*, IEA, Paris.
- IEA (2006), *World Energy Outlook 2006*, IEA, Paris.

Further information
Analytical publications
- IEA (2006), *Energy Policies of IEA Countries*, series, IEA, Paris.

Online databases
- *World Energy Statistics and Balances.*

Websites
- International Energy Agency, *www.iea.org*.

OECD FACTBOOK 2007 – ISBN 978-92-64-02946-0 – © OECD 2007

Total primary energy supply per capita
Tonnes of oil equivalent (toe) per capita

	1971	1990	1995	1996	1997	1998	1999	2000	2001	2002	2003	2004	2005	2030
Australia	3.96	5.10	5.19	5.48	5.56	5.65	5.70	5.73	5.55	5.66	5.65	5.73	5.90	..
Austria	2.53	3.26	3.41	3.62	3.61	3.66	3.65	3.62	3.82	3.85	4.07	4.06	4.24	..
Belgium	4.14	4.93	5.16	5.54	5.59	5.70	5.71	5.75	5.70	5.48	5.71	5.54	5.58	..
Canada	6.46	7.56	7.89	7.98	8.04	7.94	8.12	8.15	7.93	7.97	8.29	8.42	8.30	..
Czech Republic	4.64	4.73	3.98	4.10	4.13	3.99	3.74	3.93	4.05	4.11	4.34	4.46	4.40	..
Denmark	3.88	3.48	3.82	4.29	3.97	3.91	3.74	3.62	3.71	3.64	3.84	3.72	3.60	..
Finland	4.00	5.85	5.80	6.22	6.43	6.49	6.46	6.37	6.52	6.83	7.23	7.29	6.65	..
France	3.10	3.91	4.05	4.27	4.13	4.25	4.23	4.25	4.36	4.33	4.39	4.43	4.42	..
Germany	3.93	4.49	4.19	4.32	4.28	4.26	4.16	4.18	4.29	4.19	4.21	4.22	4.21	..
Greece	1.02	2.15	2.21	2.26	2.33	2.44	2.45	2.55	2.62	2.64	2.71	2.76	2.80	..
Hungary	1.84	2.76	2.48	2.54	2.51	2.47	2.48	2.45	2.50	2.54	2.60	2.61	2.75	..
Iceland	4.79	8.52	8.72	9.23	9.34	9.85	11.15	11.55	11.80	11.79	11.72	11.94	12.36	..
Ireland	2.37	2.97	3.06	3.25	3.42	3.57	3.70	3.76	3.94	3.92	3.78	3.75	3.89	..
Italy	2.12	2.61	2.81	2.79	2.83	2.91	2.96	2.99	3.00	2.99	3.12	3.17	3.22	..
Japan	2.57	3.61	4.00	4.11	4.14	4.08	4.15	4.17	4.09	4.09	4.04	4.18	4.17	4.96
Korea	0.52	2.16	3.27	3.58	3.84	3.51	3.83	4.06	4.09	4.24	4.31	4.43	4.59	..
Luxembourg	12.03	9.35	8.23	8.28	8.09	7.78	8.06	8.39	8.68	9.06	9.47	10.51	10.67	..
Mexico	0.87	1.53	1.47	1.48	1.51	1.54	1.54	1.52	1.52	1.54	1.56	1.59	1.65	..
Netherlands	3.89	4.47	4.69	4.87	4.76	4.74	4.66	4.76	4.86	4.87	4.99	5.05	5.03	..
New Zealand	2.51	4.04	4.27	4.43	4.51	4.40	4.60	4.48	4.46	4.46	4.28	4.32	4.21	..
Norway	3.49	5.07	5.48	5.30	5.58	5.76	6.02	5.74	5.86	5.53	5.95	6.03	6.50	..
Poland	2.63	2.62	2.58	2.68	2.65	2.48	2.41	2.34	2.35	2.33	2.39	2.40	2.34	..
Portugal	0.75	1.78	2.06	2.04	2.14	2.30	2.46	2.47	2.47	2.55	2.47	2.52	2.59	..
Slovak Republic	3.12	4.02	3.32	3.37	3.37	3.26	3.27	3.28	3.44	3.48	3.46	3.41	3.43	..
Spain	1.26	2.33	2.61	2.57	2.73	2.85	2.98	3.10	3.14	3.19	3.24	3.33	3.37	..
Sweden	4.51	5.56	5.77	5.89	5.74	5.85	5.79	5.49	5.81	5.91	5.77	6.00	5.66	..
Switzerland	2.69	3.68	3.53	3.58	3.66	3.70	3.68	3.63	3.80	3.65	3.63	3.63	3.62	..
Turkey	0.53	0.94	1.00	1.07	1.11	1.12	1.08	1.14	1.04	1.08	1.11	1.14	1.19	..
United Kingdom	3.77	3.71	3.85	4.01	3.89	3.94	3.95	3.96	3.97	3.85	3.90	3.91	3.84	..
United States	7.67	7.71	7.83	7.94	7.93	7.90	8.02	8.16	7.92	7.94	7.84	7.91	7.82	8.16
EU 25 total	..	..	3.55	3.67	3.64	3.67	3.66	3.67	3.67	3.75	3.72	3.79	3.82	4.24
OECD total	3.84	4.34	4.49	4.60	4.61	4.60	4.65	4.71	4.65	4.66	4.67	4.73	4.72	5.31
Brazil	0.71	0.90	0.96	1.00	1.03	1.05	1.07	1.07	1.06	1.07	1.07	1.11	..	1.48
China	0.47	0.76	0.87	0.90	0.89	0.88	0.88	0.89	0.88	0.95	1.07	1.24	..	2.36
India	0.33	0.43	0.47	0.48	0.49	0.48	0.50	0.50	0.50	0.51	0.52	0.53	..	0.77
Russian Federation	..	..	4.24	4.17	4.04	3.96	4.12	4.20	4.26	4.25	4.42	4.46	..	6.81
South Africa	2.01	2.59	2.66	2.65	2.64	2.61	2.55	2.57	2.59	2.51	2.66	2.88	..	..
World	1.45	1.64	1.62	1.64	1.63	1.62	1.63	1.64	1.63	1.65	1.68	1.74	..	2.10

StatLink ᴍᴤ▇ http://dx.doi.org/10.1787/685543775775

Total primary energy supply per capita
Tonnes of oil equivalent (toe) per capita, 2005

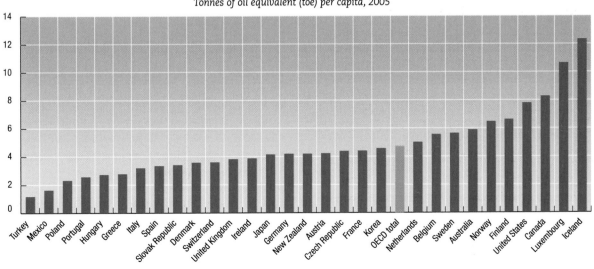

StatLink ᴍᴤ▇ http://dx.doi.org/10.1787/363123317518

ELECTRICITY GENERATION

The amount of electricity generated by a country and the breakdown of the production by fuel is a reflection of its natural resources, imported energy, national policies on security of energy supply, population, electrification rate and the development and growth of the economy in general.

Definition

The table refers to electricity generation from fossil fuels, nuclear, hydro (excluding pumped storage), geothermal, solar, biomass, etc. It includes electricity produced in electricity-only plants and in combined heat and power plants. Both main activity producer and autoproducer plants have been included, where data are available. Main activity producers generate electricity for sale to third parties as their primary activity. Autoproducer undertakings generate electricity wholly or partly for their own use as an activity which supports their primary activity. Both types of plants may be privately or publicly owned. The forecasts provided in the table refer to the Reference Scenario of the *World Energy Outlook*.

Comparability

Some countries, both OECD and non-OECD, have trouble reporting electricity generation from autoproducer plants. It is also difficult to obtain information on electricity generated by combustible renewables and waste in some non-OECD countries. For example, electricity generated from waste biomass in sugar refining remains largely unreported.

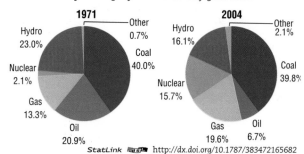

World electricity generation by fuel
As a percentage of world electricity generation

StatLink ⫘⫘⫘ http://dx.doi.org/10.1787/383472165682

Long-term trends

World electricity generation rose at an average annual rate of 3.7% from 1971 to 2004, greater than the 2.1% growth in total primary energy supply. This increase was largely due to more electrical appliances, development of electrical heating in several developed countries and rural electrification programmes in developing countries.

The share of electricity production from fossil fuels has gradually fallen, from just under 75% in 1971 to 66% in 2004. This decrease was due to a progressive move away from oil, which fell from 20.9% to 6.7%.

Oil for power generation has been displaced in particular by dramatic growth in nuclear electricity generation, which rose from 2.1% in 1971 to 15.7% in 2004. The share of coal remained stable, at 40% while that of natural gas increased from 13.3% to 19.6%. The share of hydro-electricity decreased from 23.0% to 16.1%. Due to large programmes to develop wind and solar energy in several OECD countries, the share of new and renewable energies, such as solar, wind, geothermal, biomass and waste increased. However, these energy forms remain limited: in 2004, they accounted for only 2.1% of total electricity production.

Sources

- IEA (2006), *Energy Balances of OECD Countries*, IEA, Paris.
- IEA (2006), *Energy Balances of Non-OECD Countries*, IEA, Paris.
- IEA (2006), *World Energy Outlook 2006*, IEA, Paris.

Further information

Analytical publications

- IEA (2005), *Projected Costs of Generating Electricity*, IEA, Paris.
- IEA (2005), *Russian Electricity Reform: Emerging Challenges and Opportunities*, IEA, Paris.
- IEA (2005), *Saving Electricity in a Hurry: Dealing with Temporary Shortfalls on Electricity Suppliers*, IEA, Paris.
- IEA (2006), *China's Power Sector Reforms*, IEA, Paris.
- IEA (2006), *Energy Efficiency Policy Profiles Light's labour's lost: Policies for Energy-Efficient Lighting*, IEA, Paris.

Statistical publications

- IEA (2006), *Electricity Information: 2006 Edition*, IEA, Paris.

Online databases

- *World Energy Statistics and Balances*.

Websites

- International Energy Agency, *www.iea.org*.

OECD FACTBOOK 2007 – ISBN 978-92-64-02946-0 – © OECD 2007

Electricity generation
Terawatt hours (TWh)

	1971	1990	1995	1996	1997	1998	1999	2000	2001	2002	2003	2004	2005	2030
Australia	53.1	154.4	173.0	177.3	182.8	195.6	203.0	207.4	216.5	226.1	227.9	239.3	248.2	..
Austria	28.2	49.3	55.2	53.6	55.7	55.9	59.3	60.2	60.7	60.4	57.7	61.6	63.1	..
Belgium	33.2	70.3	73.5	75.1	77.9	82.1	83.4	82.8	78.6	80.9	83.6	84.4	84.9	..
Canada	221.8	481.9	559.9	572.8	573.5	561.5	578.8	605.5	589.7	601.0	589.9	598.4	628.3	..
Czech Republic	36.4	62.3	60.6	63.8	64.2	64.6	64.2	72.9	74.2	76.0	82.8	83.8	81.9	..
Denmark	18.6	26.0	36.7	53.6	44.3	41.1	38.9	36.1	37.7	39.3	46.2	40.5	36.8	..
Finland	21.7	54.4	63.2	69.4	69.2	70.2	69.5	70.0	74.5	74.9	84.2	85.8	70.5	..
France	155.9	417.2	491.1	509.3	501.1	507.3	521.4	536.4	544.6	553.9	561.8	567.1	570.6	..
Germany	327.3	547.7	532.8	550.7	548.0	552.4	550.3	567.1	581.8	566.9	595.7	610.0	612.1	..
Greece	11.6	34.8	41.3	42.4	43.3	46.2	49.4	53.4	53.1	54.0	57.9	58.8	59.2	..
Hungary	15.0	28.4	34.0	35.1	35.4	37.2	37.8	35.2	36.4	36.2	34.2	33.7	35.7	..
Iceland	1.6	4.5	5.0	5.1	5.6	6.3	7.2	7.7	8.0	8.4	8.5	8.6	8.7	..
Ireland	6.3	14.2	17.6	18.9	19.7	20.9	21.8	23.7	24.6	24.8	24.9	25.2	25.7	..
Italy	123.9	213.2	237.4	239.4	246.5	253.7	259.3	270.0	271.9	277.5	283.4	293.1	293.6	..
Japan	382.9	838.2	962.3	984.1	1 008.7	1 014.6	1 032.5	1 053.2	1 035.2	1 054.7	1 041.6	1 071.0	1 049.1	1 280.0
Korea	10.5	105.4	181.1	202.6	222.4	216.4	235.9	263.7	281.4	330.4	344.9	366.6	391.2	..
Luxembourg	1.3	0.6	0.5	0.4	0.4	0.4	0.4	0.4	0.5	2.8	2.8	3.4	3.3	..
Mexico	31.0	124.1	157.5	168.2	180.9	181.2	189.9	203.7	209.2	214.6	217.9	224.1	233.7	..
Netherlands	44.9	71.9	81.0	85.2	86.6	91.2	86.9	89.7	93.8	96.1	96.8	100.8	100.2	..
New Zealand	15.5	32.2	35.2	36.1	35.5	35.7	37.6	38.6	38.8	40.4	40.4	41.8	42.0	..
Norway	63.5	121.6	122.1	104.4	110.8	116.1	122.3	139.6	119.2	130.3	106.8	110.1	137.3	..
Poland	69.5	134.4	137.0	141.2	140.9	140.8	140.0	143.2	143.7	142.5	150.0	152.6	155.4	..
Portugal	7.9	28.4	33.2	34.4	34.1	38.9	42.9	43.4	46.2	45.7	46.5	44.8	46.2	..
Slovak Republic	10.9	25.5	26.4	25.5	25.1	25.7	28.1	30.8	31.9	32.2	31.0	30.5	30.7	..
Spain	61.6	151.2	165.6	173.4	189.2	193.4	205.9	222.2	233.2	241.6	257.9	277.1	291.5	..
Sweden	66.5	146.0	148.3	140.6	149.2	158.8	154.8	145.2	161.6	146.7	135.4	151.7	159.0	..
Switzerland	31.2	54.9	62.2	55.9	61.8	62.0	68.5	66.0	70.8	65.2	65.1	63.6	57.8	..
Turkey	9.8	57.5	86.3	94.9	103.3	111.0	116.4	124.9	122.7	129.4	140.6	150.7	162.0	..
United Kingdom	255.8	317.8	332.5	349.3	349.2	361.1	365.3	374.6	382.5	384.7	395.9	393.2	396.6	..
United States	1 703.4	3 202.8	3 558.4	3 651.2	3 672.2	3 804.5	3 873.5	4 025.7	3 838.6	4 026.1	4 054.4	4 147.7	4 258.3	5 913.0
EU 25 total	..	..	2 610.7	2 707.6	2 725.6	2 791.7	2 823.1	2 899.8	2 978.6	2 987.3	3 081.5	3 153.8	..	4 303.0
OECD total	3 820.7	7 570.8	8 470.6	8 713.9	8 837.3	9 046.8	9 244.9	9 593.0	9 461.5	9 763.6	9 866.2	10 119.8	10 333.6	14 468.0
Brazil	51.6	222.8	275.6	291.3	308.1	321.9	334.8	349.2	327.9	345.7	364.9	387.5	..	731.0
China	138.4	621.2	1 007.7	1 080.0	1 134.5	1 166.2	1 239.3	1 355.6	1 471.7	1 640.5	1 907.4	2 199.6	..	7 624.0
India	66.4	289.4	417.6	436.7	465.8	496.9	537.4	562.2	580.9	598.4	635.2	667.8	..	2 314.0
Russian Federation	..	..	859.0	846.2	833.2	826.2	845.4	876.5	889.3	889.3	914.3	929.9	..	1 324.0
South Africa	54.7	165.4	186.6	199.5	207.7	203.0	200.4	207.8	208.2	215.7	232.3	242.2	..	..
World	5 244.8	11 814.5	13 219.1	13 645.9	13 944.8	14 286.7	14 688.7	15 354.0	15 447.0	16 071.7	16 674.6	17 449.8	..	33 750.0

StatLink 🖳 http://dx.doi.org/10.1787/642626372620

World electricity generation by fuel
Terawatt hours (TWh)

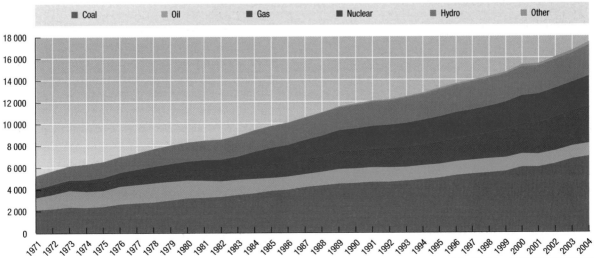

■ Coal   ■ Oil   ■ Gas   ■ Nuclear   ■ Hydro   ■ Other

StatLink 🖳 http://dx.doi.org/10.1787/730002804273

RENEWABLE ENERGY

More and more governments are recognising the importance of promoting sustainable development and combating climate change when setting out their energy policies. As energy use has increased, greenhouse gas emissions have spiraled up and their concentration in the atmosphere has increased. One way to reduce emissions is to replace energy from fossil fuels by energy from renewables.

Definition

The table refers to the contribution of renewables to total primary energy supply (TPES) in OECD countries. Renewables include the primary energy equivalent of hydro (excluding pumped storage), geothermal, solar, wind, tide and wave. It also includes solid biomass, liquid biomass, biogas, industrial waste and municipal waste. Biomass is defined as any plant matter used directly as fuel or converted into fuels (e.g. charcoal) or electricity and/or heat. Included here are wood, vegetal waste (including wood waste and crops used for energy production), ethanol, animal materials/wastes and sulphite lyes. Municipal waste comprises wastes produced by the residential, commercial and public service sectors that are collected by local authorities for disposal in a central location for the production of heat and/or power. The forecasts provided in the table refer to the Reference Scenario of the World Energy Outlook.

Long-term trends

In OECD countries, total renewables supply grew by 2.2% per annum between 1971 and 2005 as compared to 1.5% per annum for total primary energy supply. Annual growth for hydro (1.1%) was lower than for other renewables such as geothermal (6.0%) and combustible renewables and waste (2.5%). Due to a very low base in 1971, solar and wind experienced the most rapid growth in OECD member countries, especially where government policies have stimulated expansion of these energy sources.

For total OECD, the contribution of renewables to energy supply increased from 4.7% in 1971 to 6.1% in 2005. The contribution of renewables varied greatly by country. On the high end, renewables represented 74% in Iceland and 44% in Norway. On the low end, renewables contributed only 1% to 2% of supply for Ireland, Korea, Luxembourg and the United Kingdom.

In general, the contribution of renewables to the energy supply in non-OECD countries is higher than in OECD countries. In 2004, renewables contributed 40% to the supply of Brazil, 39% in India, 16% in China, 10% in South Africa and 3% in the Russian Federation.

Comparability

Biomass and waste data are often based on small sample surveys or other incomplete information. Thus, the data give only a broad impression of developments and are not strictly comparable between countries. In some cases, complete categories of vegetal fuel are omitted due to lack of information.

Sources

- IEA (2006), *Energy Balances of OECD Countries*, IEA, Paris.
- IEA (2006), *Energy Balances of Non-OECD Countries*, IEA, Paris.
- IEA (2006), *World Energy Outlook 2006*, IEA, Paris.

Further information

Analytical publications

- IEA (2004), *Renewable Energy: Market and Policy Trends in IEA Countries*, IEA, Paris.
- IEA (2005), *Projected Costs of Generating Electricity*, IEA, Paris.
- IEA (2006), *Energy Technology Perspectives: Scenarios and Strategies to 2050*, IEA, Paris.
- IEA (2006), *Renewable Energy RD&D Priorities: Insights from IEA Technology Programme*, IEA, Paris.

Statistical publications

- IEA (2006), *Renewables Information: 2006 Edition*, IEA, Paris.

Online databases

- IEA Global Renewable Energy Policies and Measures Database, http://renewables.iea.org.
- *World Energy Statistics and Balances.*

Websites

- IEA OPEN Energy Technology Bulletin, www.iea.org/impagr/cip/index.htm.
- International Energy Agency, www.iea.org.

Contribution of renewables to energy supply

As a percentage of total primary energy supply

	1971	1990	1995	1996	1997	1998	1999	2000	2001	2002	2003	2004	2005	2030
Australia	8.7	6.0	6.1	6.3	6.4	6.0	6.0	5.9	6.1	6.1	5.8	5.6	5.3	..
Austria	10.9	20.7	22.4	21.0	21.7	21.1	23.3	23.2	22.5	22.0	20.1	21.3	22.1	..
Belgium	-	1.5	1.6	1.4	1.4	1.4	1.5	1.5	1.7	1.7	2.0	2.3	3.5	..
Canada	15.2	16.1	16.7	17.1	16.7	16.3	16.7	16.9	16.1	16.7	15.5	15.4	16.4	..
Czech Republic	0.2	0.2	1.5	1.5	1.7	1.7	2.4	2.0	2.1	2.5	2.9	3.6	3.6	..
Denmark	1.7	6.7	7.7	7.3	8.4	8.8	9.7	10.9	11.3	12.3	13.0	14.6	15.7	..
Finland	26.9	18.8	20.7	19.8	20.9	22.2	22.2	24.3	23.0	22.6	21.7	23.7	23.4	..
France	8.4	7.0	7.4	7.1	6.9	6.8	7.1	6.7	6.9	6.2	6.3	6.3	6.1	..
Germany	1.2	1.8	2.2	2.2	2.5	2.8	2.8	3.1	3.4	3.8	3.9	4.3	5.3	..
Greece	7.4	5.0	5.6	5.8	5.5	5.2	5.6	5.3	4.7	4.9	5.3	5.2	5.2	..
Hungary	2.9	1.7	2.5	1.9	2.0	1.9	1.9	2.1	2.0	3.5	3.5	3.7	4.8	..
Iceland	42.4	64.5	67.0	64.9	66.4	67.0	70.9	71.3	72.9	72.4	72.6	71.7	73.8	..
Ireland	0.6	1.6	1.5	1.5	1.6	2.0	1.9	1.7	1.7	1.9	1.9	2.1	2.3	..
Italy	5.1	4.5	4.9	5.3	5.4	5.5	5.9	6.0	6.2	5.9	6.0	7.8	7.7	..
Japan	2.7	3.5	3.3	3.2	3.4	3.4	3.3	3.2	3.2	3.3	3.5	3.4	3.0	6.3
Korea	0.6	0.6	0.7	0.8	0.9	1.2	1.2	1.3	1.4	1.0	1.1	1.0	1.0	..
Luxembourg	-	0.8	1.5	1.2	1.5	1.5	1.4	1.4	1.6	1.2	1.4	1.5	1.4	..
Mexico	16.6	11.1	11.4	11.3	10.6	10.3	10.5	10.6	10.1	9.6	9.6	9.8	9.9	..
Netherlands	-	1.4	1.6	1.8	2.1	2.2	2.3	2.4	2.4	2.6	2.6	2.9	3.5	..
New Zealand	30.8	34.7	32.7	30.2	28.6	30.9	31.0	28.5	26.2	28.4	28.2	29.9	29.2	..
Norway	39.9	53.3	48.5	43.4	43.5	43.9	44.6	51.6	44.2	50.1	38.5	38.8	43.5	..
Poland	1.6	2.4	4.8	4.2	4.3	4.5	4.5	4.7	5.0	5.2	5.1	5.2	5.6	..
Portugal	18.8	18.5	16.1	18.5	17.4	16.0	13.4	15.2	16.1	13.8	16.8	14.7	13.2	..
Slovak Republic	2.4	1.5	4.0	3.9	3.9	4.0	4.4	4.6	4.4	4.2	3.7	4.2	4.7	..
Spain	6.4	6.9	5.6	7.1	6.4	6.2	5.3	5.7	6.5	5.4	6.9	6.3	6.0	..
Sweden	20.2	24.7	25.7	23.2	27.1	27.6	27.6	31.9	29.1	26.4	25.9	26.5	27.9	..
Switzerland	14.9	14.2	17.0	14.8	16.1	16.0	18.0	17.4	18.1	16.7	17.1	17.5	17.5	..
Turkey	31.1	18.2	17.4	16.7	15.8	15.9	15.1	13.1	13.2	13.4	12.7	13.2	11.8	..
United Kingdom	0.1	0.5	0.9	0.8	0.9	1.0	1.0	1.1	1.1	1.3	1.4	1.6	1.8	..
United States	3.7	5.2	5.3	5.4	5.2	5.1	4.9	4.8	4.3	4.3	4.5	4.5	4.5	8.2
EU 25 total	..	..	5.3	5.3	5.5	5.6	5.7	5.9	6.0	5.9	6.1	6.5	..	13.2
OECD total	4.7	5.9	6.2	6.2	6.1	6.1	6.1	6.1	5.8	5.9	5.9	6.1	6.1	10.2
Brazil	56.5	44.3	40.7	39.0	37.9	37.8	37.9	37.2	35.6	37.2	39.6	40.0	..	40.7
China	40.0	24.4	21.2	20.5	20.6	20.8	21.0	20.8	21.4	20.0	17.6	15.6	..	10.3
India	67.7	50.3	44.7	43.5	42.6	42.6	41.1	40.7	40.7	40.1	39.7	38.8	..	25.5
Russian Federation	..	..	3.8	3.3	3.4	3.3	3.5	3.4	3.5	3.4	3.1	3.5	..	3.6
South Africa	10.4	11.5	11.0	11.1	11.1	11.1	11.3	11.3	11.2	11.7	11.0	10.2	..	..
World	13.9	13.4	13.8	13.6	13.7	13.8	13.8	13.7	13.6	13.6	13.5	13.3	..	13.7

StatLink ᵐˢ┛ http://dx.doi.org/10.1787/633182527251

OECD renewable energy supply

Million tonnes of oil equivalent (Mtoe)

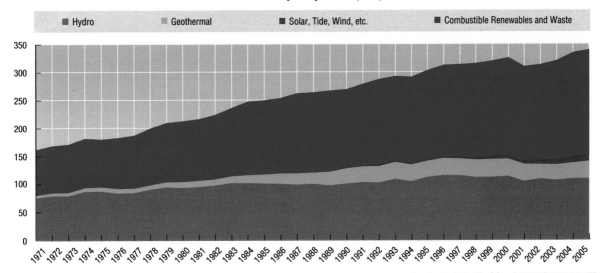

StatLink ᵐˢ┛ http://dx.doi.org/10.1787/780621121478

ENERGY PRODUCTION

Energy production is a function of the natural resources of a country and the economic incentives to exploit those resources. Countries will also take into consideration energy security and environmental protection when making decisions on how much and what type of energy to produce.

Definition

Production refers to the quantities of fuels extracted from the ground after the removal of inert matter or impurities (*e.g.* sulphur from natural gas). For non-combusted energy such as nuclear, hydro and solar, the primary energy equivalent is calculated using the physical energy content method.

Comparability

In general, data on energy production are of high quality. In some instances, information has been based on secondary sources or estimated by the IEA.

Total energy production by product
As a percentage of total energy production

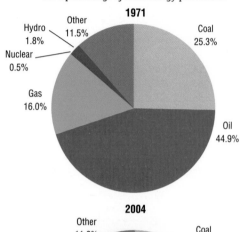

1971

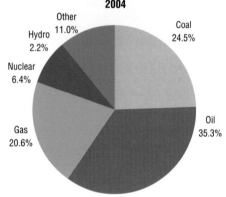

2004

StatLink ⛐⛐ http://dx.doi.org/10.1787/462333046844

Long-term trends

World energy production increased by 97% between 1971 and 2004, reaching 11 213 million tonnes of oil equivalent (Mtoe). The OECD, with a 34% share of the global production, was the main energy producing region in 2004. The United States accounted for 15% of world energy production, China for 14%, the Middle East region for 13% and the Russian Federation for 10%. Since 1971, the shares of the OECD, Middle East and Former USSR decreased, while Latin America and non-OECD Europe remained stable. On the other hand, energy production in China (as well as the rest of Asia) increased dramatically since 1971.

The energy mix has changed significantly between 1971 and 2004. Nuclear energy, which experienced an annual average growth of 10% since 1971, increased its share of production from 0.5% to 6.4%. Renewable energy also experienced a high growth rate over the last 33 years, but its share was very low in 1971, making this growth less meaningful. The share of natural gas in total production increased from 16.0% in 1971 to 20.6% in 2004, causing the share of oil to fall from 44.9% to 35.3%. The share of coal production remained at around 25%.

Sources
- IEA (2006), *Energy Balances of OECD Countries*, IEA, Paris.
- IEA (2006), *Energy Balances of Non-OECD Countries*, IEA, Paris.

Further information
Analytical publications
- NEA (2006), *Forty Years of Uranium Resources, Production and Demand in Perspective: The Red Book Retrospective*, NEA, Paris.
- IEA (2005), *Resources to Reserves: Oil and Gas Technologies for the Energy Markets of the Future*, IEA, Paris.
- IEA (2006), *Energy Policies of IEA Countries*, series, IEA, Paris.

Online databases
- *World Energy Statistics and Balances.*

Websites
- International Energy Agency, *www.iea.org.*

OECD FACTBOOK 2007 – ISBN 978-92-64-02946-0 – © OECD 2007

Total production of energy
Million tonnes of oil equivalent (Mtoe)

	1971	1990	1995	1996	1997	1998	1999	2000	2001	2002	2003	2004	2005
Australia	53.9	157.5	186.9	189.8	201.1	216.5	213.6	233.6	249.2	254.5	253.8	261.8	271.2
Austria	7.4	8.1	8.7	8.6	8.8	8.9	9.7	9.7	9.7	9.8	9.7	9.9	10.1
Belgium	6.8	13.1	11.8	12.2	13.3	13.0	13.7	13.5	13.1	13.3	13.5	13.5	14.1
Canada	155.7	273.7	348.7	358.2	364.9	365.5	366.0	372.4	376.9	383.9	385.8	397.5	400.7
Czech Republic	40.0	40.1	31.8	32.5	32.8	30.8	28.0	29.9	30.5	30.7	33.0	34.2	32.5
Denmark	0.3	10.0	15.6	17.7	20.2	20.4	23.8	27.7	27.1	28.5	28.4	31.0	31.2
Finland	5.0	12.1	13.2	13.6	15.0	13.6	15.4	15.1	15.2	16.1	16.1	15.9	16.2
France	47.7	111.9	128.0	131.9	128.9	126.0	127.9	131.3	132.9	134.7	136.2	137.4	136.8
Germany	175.2	186.2	145.0	143.3	143.6	136.0	137.2	135.3	134.7	134.5	134.6	136.0	136.1
Greece	2.1	9.2	9.3	9.1	9.6	9.8	9.5	10.0	10.0	10.2	9.9	10.3	10.4
Hungary	11.9	14.3	13.4	13.1	12.8	12.0	11.6	11.3	10.9	11.2	10.4	10.2	10.6
Iceland	0.4	1.4	1.6	1.6	1.7	1.8	2.2	2.3	2.5	2.5	2.5	2.5	2.7
Ireland	1.4	3.5	4.1	3.6	2.9	2.5	2.5	2.2	1.8	1.6	1.9	1.9	1.6
Italy	19.6	25.3	29.4	30.3	30.4	30.3	29.2	28.2	26.9	27.5	27.6	30.1	30.0
Japan	35.8	76.8	100.4	103.6	108.1	111.0	106.4	107.4	106.2	98.7	85.5	96.8	97.5
Korea	6.4	21.9	21.0	22.7	24.1	27.7	31.3	33.4	34.2	34.9	37.9	38.0	42.5
Luxembourg	-	-	0.1	-	0.1	0.1	-	0.1	0.1	0.1	0.1	0.1	0.1
Mexico	43.4	194.8	202.3	213.3	223.2	228.5	223.0	226.1	230.3	230.0	242.5	253.9	252.9
Netherlands	37.4	60.5	66.2	74.0	65.8	63.0	59.0	57.2	61.0	60.5	58.5	67.9	62.7
New Zealand	3.4	12.0	13.0	14.0	14.8	13.9	14.5	14.3	14.1	14.5	13.1	13.0	12.4
Norway	6.0	120.3	186.5	209.6	215.1	208.0	211.7	229.0	226.4	235.2	235.6	238.6	233.3
Poland	99.3	99.4	99.3	98.8	100.0	87.6	83.9	79.6	80.3	80.2	79.9	78.8	76.9
Portugal	1.4	3.4	3.3	3.8	3.8	3.7	3.4	3.9	4.1	3.6	4.3	3.9	3.6
Slovak Republic	2.7	5.3	5.0	5.0	5.0	5.0	5.5	6.3	6.7	6.8	6.6	6.5	6.7
Spain	10.5	34.6	31.5	32.7	31.7	32.3	30.7	31.7	33.5	31.8	33.0	32.5	30.1
Sweden	7.4	29.8	31.9	32.1	32.5	34.1	33.8	31.1	34.5	32.4	31.6	35.1	33.5
Switzerland	2.9	9.7	10.8	10.3	10.8	11.0	11.5	11.5	12.0	11.6	11.8	11.8	10.9
Turkey	13.8	25.8	26.5	27.1	28.0	29.1	27.5	25.9	24.4	24.1	23.6	24.1	26.6
United Kingdom	109.8	208.0	257.5	268.9	268.3	271.9	281.6	272.4	262.0	258.0	246.4	225.2	204.5
United States	1 435.8	1 650.5	1 662.2	1 686.7	1 684.9	1 698.1	1 679.6	1 676.3	1 698.5	1 666.0	1 632.7	1 641.0	1 614.9
EU 25 total	..	..	916.5	943.5	937.5	913.5	917.6	907.3	906.9	904.8	895.9	895.1	..
OECD total	2 343.1	3 419.1	3 665.2	3 768.2	3 801.7	3 811.9	3 793.8	3 828.5	3 869.3	3 847.2	3 806.3	3 859.5	3 812.9
Brazil	49.2	98.1	105.6	111.6	118.6	127.0	136.0	143.8	147.7	162.0	171.7	176.3	..
China	394.2	889.3	1 070.3	1 101.7	1 100.7	1 093.8	1 074.2	1 089.8	1 121.8	1 202.3	1 352.7	1 536.8	..
India	166.5	333.4	384.4	391.3	402.8	402.6	408.5	417.0	426.3	436.5	450.6	466.9	..
Russian Federation	..	..	953.9	947.3	921.6	928.4	950.6	966.5	996.1	1 034.5	1 106.9	1 158.5	..
South Africa	37.8	114.5	133.7	133.9	142.0	143.5	144.1	144.7	144.4	143.1	152.9	156.0	..
World	5 679.5	8 801.7	9 293.3	9 537.5	9 674.9	9 801.6	9 797.1	10 048.0	10 188.5	10 294.7	10 680.9	11 213.4	..

StatLink http://dx.doi.org/10.1787/053818088200

Total energy production by region
Million tonnes of oil equivalent (Mtoe)

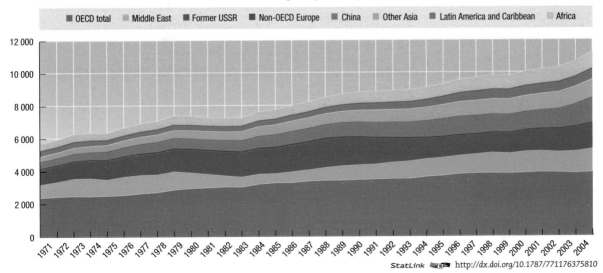

StatLink http://dx.doi.org/10.1787/771176375810

OIL PRODUCTION

The Middle East and North Africa are exceptionally well-endowed with energy resources, holding 61% of the world's proven oil reserves. Current oil production is relatively low in comparison to these reserves and further development of them will be critical to meeting global energy needs in the coming decades.

Definition

Crude oil production refers to the quantities of oil extracted from the ground after the removal of inert matter or impurities. It includes crude oil, natural gas liquids (NGLs) and additives. Crude oil is a mineral oil consisting of a mixture of hydrocarbons of natural origin, being yellow to black in colour, of variable density and viscosity. NGLs are the liquid or liquefied hydrocarbons produced in the manufacture, purification and stabilisation of natural gas. Additives are non-hydrocarbon substances added to or blended with a product to modify its properties, for example, to improve its combustion characteristics (e.g. MTBE and tetraethyl lead).

Refinery production refers to the output of secondary oil products from an oil refinery.

Comparability

In general, data on oil production are of high quality. In some instances, information has been based on secondary sources or estimated by the IEA.

Share of refinery production by product

As a percentage of refinery production

1971

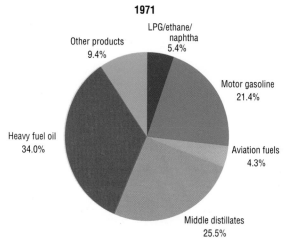

2004

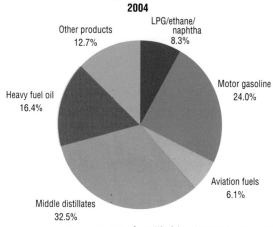

StatLink 🔗 http://dx.doi.org/10.1787/106532718285

Long-term trends

World crude oil production increased by 58% over the 34-year period from 1971 to 2005. In 2005, the production reached 3 923 million tonnes or about 82 million barrels per day. Growth was not constant over the period as production declined in the aftermath of two oil shocks.

In 2005, the Middle East region's share of supply was 31% of the world total. However, both production and share varied significantly over the period, with the Middle East representing 32% in 1971 falling to less than 19% in 1985. Increased production in the 1980s and 1990s put the OECD on par with the Middle East during that period, but in 2004, the share of oil production by the OECD had fallen to 24%.

Refinery production of secondary oil products changed significantly between 1971 and 2004. The share of heavy fuel oil in the refinery mix fell from 34% in 1971 to 16% in 2004 whereas the share of middle distillates increased from 25% to 33%.

Sources
- IEA (2006), *Energy Balances of OECD Countries*, IEA, Paris.
- IEA (2006), *Energy Balances of Non-OECD Countries*, IEA, Paris.

Further information

Analytical publications
- IEA (2005), *Resources to Reserves: Oil and Gas Technologies for the Energy Markets of the Future*, IEA, Paris.
- IEA (2005), *Saving Oil in a Hurry*, IEA, Paris.
- IEA (2006), *Energy Policies of IEA Countries*, series, IEA, Paris.

Online databases
- World Energy Statistics and Balances.

Websites
- International Energy Agency, *www.iea.org*.

OECD FACTBOOK 2007 – ISBN 978-92-64-02946-0 – © OECD 2007

Production of crude oil
Million tonnes

	1971	1990	1995	1996	1997	1998	1999	2000	2001	2002	2003	2004	2005
Australia	14.3	27.5	26.9	26.4	26.7	29.4	23.7	32.1	33.1	31.3	29.1	29.1	26.0
Austria	2.6	1.2	1.1	1.1	1.0	1.1	1.1	1.1	1.0	1.0	1.0	1.1	0.9
Belgium	-	-	-	-	-	-	-	-	-	-	-	-	-
Canada	70.6	91.6	110.3	113.5	119.0	124.7	119.9	124.8	126.6	132.9	140.4	145.8	143.4
Czech Republic	-	0.2	0.2	0.2	0.4	0.4	0.4	0.4	0.4	0.4	0.5	0.6	0.6
Denmark	-	6.0	9.2	10.1	11.2	11.4	14.5	17.8	16.9	18.1	18.1	19.3	18.5
Finland	-	-	-	-	0.1	0.1	0.1	0.1	0.1	0.1	0.1	0.1	0.1
France	2.5	3.5	3.0	2.7	2.3	2.1	2.0	1.9	1.6	1.5	1.4	1.4	1.2
Germany	7.6	5.3	3.9	3.7	3.7	3.8	3.8	4.3	4.3	4.6	4.8	4.9	4.8
Greece	-	0.8	0.5	0.5	0.5	0.3	-	0.3	0.2	0.2	0.1	0.1	0.1
Hungary	2.0	2.3	2.3	2.1	2.0	1.8	1.8	1.7	1.6	1.6	1.6	1.6	1.4
Iceland	-	-	-	-	-	-	-	-	-	-	-	-	-
Ireland	-	-	-	-	-	-	-	-	-	-	-	-	-
Italy	1.3	4.7	5.5	5.7	6.1	5.8	5.2	4.8	4.2	5.8	5.9	5.7	6.4
Japan	0.8	0.5	0.7	0.7	0.7	0.6	0.6	0.6	0.6	0.6	0.6	0.7	0.7
Korea	-	-	-	-	0.5	0.4	0.5	0.7	0.6	0.5	0.5	0.4	0.5
Luxembourg	-	-	-	-	-	-	-	-	-	-	-	-	-
Mexico	25.4	151.1	153.6	160.4	169.0	171.9	166.9	169.3	175.5	178.3	189.3	191.4	187.6
Netherlands	1.7	4.0	3.5	3.1	2.9	2.7	2.5	2.4	2.3	3.1	3.1	2.9	2.3
New Zealand	-	1.9	1.7	2.2	2.9	2.3	2.1	1.9	1.8	1.6	1.3	1.1	1.0
Norway	0.3	82.1	138.5	156.8	156.5	149.8	149.4	161.0	162.5	157.7	153.6	151.8	138.8
Poland	0.4	0.2	0.4	0.4	0.4	0.4	0.5	0.7	0.8	0.8	0.8	0.9	0.9
Portugal	-	-	-	-	-	-	-	-	-	-	-	-	-
Slovak Republic	0.2	0.1	0.1	0.1	0.1	0.1	0.1	0.1	0.1	0.1	0.1	-	-
Spain	0.1	1.1	0.8	0.5	0.4	0.5	0.3	0.2	0.3	0.3	0.3	0.3	0.2
Sweden	-	-	-	-	-	-	-	-	-	-	-	-	-
Switzerland	-	-	-	-	-	-	-	-	-	-	-	-	-
Turkey	3.5	3.7	3.5	3.5	3.5	3.2	2.9	2.8	2.5	2.4	2.4	2.3	2.3
United Kingdom	0.2	91.6	130.5	130.1	128.4	132.5	137.2	126.4	116.8	116.1	106.2	95.5	84.6
United States	527.7	413.3	383.3	382.5	380.9	369.8	354.2	353.0	349.9	348.1	338.4	325.9	306.6
EU 25 total	..	..	160.9	160.4	159.5	163.3	169.7	162.3	151.0	154.2	144.3	134.7	122.3
OECD total	661.1	892.7	979.1	1 006.2	1 018.8	1 015.2	989.4	1 008.0	1 003.6	1 007.1	999.6	982.7	928.9
Brazil	8.4	32.4	35.7	40.3	43.8	50.6	57.2	64.3	67.4	75.6	77.9	77.5	86.3
China	39.4	138.3	150.0	157.3	160.7	161.2	160.2	163.2	164.2	167.2	169.8	176.2	183.3
India	7.3	34.6	38.4	36.2	37.4	36.5	36.4	36.4	36.2	37.4	37.7	38.3	36.9
Russian Federation	..	..	305.1	299.5	303.9	301.4	303.2	321.7	345.8	377.2	418.6	456.3	469.9
South Africa	-	-	0.4	0.4	0.4	0.3	0.3	0.3	0.3	0.2	0.1	0.2	0.2
World	2 487.1	3 151.7	3 294.4	3 384.0	3 479.3	3 553.8	3 480.8	3 605.3	3 611.1	3 591.5	3 707.8	3 870.8	3 923.3

StatLink ⬛🖳 http://dx.doi.org/10.1787/042052468410

Production of crude oil by region
Million tonnes

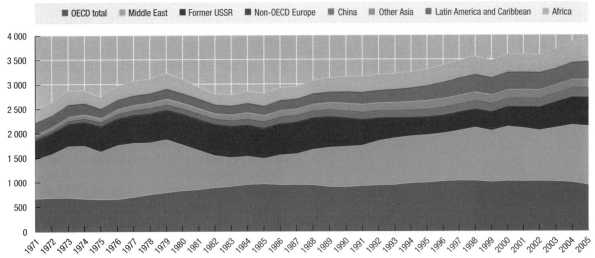

- ■ OECD total
- ■ Middle East
- ■ Former USSR
- ■ Non-OECD Europe
- ■ China
- ■ Other Asia
- ■ Latin America and Caribbean
- ■ Africa

StatLink ⬛🖳 http://dx.doi.org/10.1787/040447222352

OIL PRICES

The price of crude oil, from which petroleum products such as gasoline are derived, is influenced by a number of factors beyond the traditional movements of supply and demand, notably geopolitics. Some of the lowest cost reserves are located in sensitive areas of the world. There is not one price for crude oil but many. World crude oil prices are established in relation to three market traded benchmarks (West Texas Intermediate [WTI], Brent, Dubai), and are quoted at premiums or discounts to these prices.

Definition

Crude oil import prices come from the Crude Oil Import Register. Information is collected according to type of crude and average prices are obtained by dividing value by volume as recorded by customs administrations for each tariff position. Values are recorded at the time of import and include cost, insurance and freight (CIF) but exclude import duties.

The nominal crude oil spot price from 1985 to 2005 is for Dubai and from 1970 to 1984 for Arabian Light. The real price was calculated using the deflator for GDP at market prices and was rebased with base year 1970 = 100.

Comparability

Average crude oil import prices are affected by the quality of the crude oil that is imported into a country. High quality crude oils such as UK Forties, Norwegian Oseberg and Venezuelan Light will be more expensive than lower quality crude oils such as Canadian Heavy and Venezuelan Extra Heavy. For a given country, the mix of crude oils imported each month will affect the average monthly price.

Long-term trends

The 1973 Arab oil embargo had a major price impact as Arabian Light prices surged from USD 1.84/barrel in 1972 to USD 10.77 in 1974.

The first spike after 1973 came in 1981, in the wake of the Iranian revolution, when prices rose to a high of nearly USD 40. Prices declined gradually after this crisis. They dropped considerably in 1986 when Saudi Arabia increased its oil production substantially.

The first Gulf crisis in 1990 brought a new peak. In 1997, crude oil prices started to decline due to the impact of the Asian financial crisis.

Prices started to increase again in 1999 with OPEC target reductions and tightening stocks. A dip occurred in 2001 and 2002, but the expectation of war in Iraq raised prices to over USD 30 in the first quarter of 2003. Prices remained high in the latter part of 2003 and in 2004. Crude oil prices increased dramatically in late August 2005 after Hurricane Katrina hit the eastern coast of the US Gulf of Mexico. Prices remained high in 2006 with Dubai hitting USD 72.29/barrel in the middle of July and WTI climbing to USD 76.95/barrel at the beginning of August.

After the 1986 oil price decrease, the real price of crude oil (adjusted for inflation) has remained relatively stable until the sharp increase in crude oil prices in August 2005.

Sources

- IEA (2006), *Energy Prices and Taxes*, IEA, Paris.
- IEA (2006), *World Energy Outlook 2006: Middle East and North Africa Insights*, IEA, Paris.

Further information

Analytical publications

- IEA (2006), *China's Power Sector Reforms: Where to next?*, IEA, Paris.
- IEA (2006), *Energy Policies of IEA Countries*, series, IEA, Paris.
- IEA (2006), *Natural Gas Market Review 2006: Towards a Global Gas Market*, IEA, Paris.
- IEA (2006), *Optimising Russian Natural Gas: Reform and Climate Policy*, IEA, Paris.

Online databases

- *Energy Prices and Taxes*.

Websites

- IEA Oil Market Report: *www.omrpublic.iea.org*.
- International Energy Agency, *www.iea.org*.

OECD FACTBOOK 2007 – ISBN 978-92-64-02946-0 – © OECD 2007

Crude oil import prices
US dollars per barrel, average unit value, CIF

	1976	1990	1995	1996	1997	1998	1999	2000	2001	2002	2003	2004	2005
Australia	..	24.21	18.53	21.81	21.78	14.60	18.38	30.79	26.61	25.80	31.24	40.93	56.71
Austria	12.85	24.58	18.78	22.06	21.31	14.34	17.54	29.39	25.32	24.64	29.59	38.21	53.15
Belgium	12.64	21.11	16.94	20.53	18.65	11.97	17.33	27.87	24.20	24.35	27.72	35.35	50.06
Canada	..	24.15	17.76	21.26	20.59	13.15	17.85	29.10	24.87	24.97	29.53	38.13	52.37
Czech Republic	..	..	15.60	..	..	..	..	26.59	23.74	23.37	28.13	34.82	51.28
Denmark	12.98	23.18	17.49	21.25	20.15	13.49	17.71	29.66	24.82	24.88	29.68	38.78	54.40
Finland	..	..	17.83	21.69	19.44	12.80	18.31	28.13	23.49	24.51	27.72	36.09	51.12
France	..	..	17.14	20.82	18.99	12.43	17.45	28.18	24.13	24.63	28.87	37.61	52.74
Germany	13.27	23.17	17.07	20.68	19.01	12.48	17.51	28.09	24.15	24.40	28.44	36.65	52.30
Greece	12.13	22.42	16.54	20.08	18.45	11.66	16.64	26.95	23.22	24.08	27.17	34.53	50.33
Hungary	..	..	16.08	19.32	16.74	10.77	16.05	26.22	..	..	..	..	..
Ireland	..	25.55	17.65	21.19	19.99	13.55	17.14	29.88	25.31	25.52	29.66	39.24	55.24
Italy	12.41	23.23	16.90	20.53	18.88	12.21	17.10	27.77	23.87	24.34	28.58	36.60	51.33
Japan	12.59	22.64	18.02	20.55	20.55	13.68	17.38	28.72	25.01	24.96	29.26	36.59	51.57
Korea	..	..	17.32	20.11	20.34	13.72	16.91	28.22	24.87	24.12	28.80	36.15	50.19
Netherlands	13.06	21.83	16.92	20.39	18.37	11.98	16.97	27.59	23.48	23.99	27.67	35.02	50.00
New Zealand	..	21.97	18.73	21.86	21.65	14.63	18.16	29.95	26.14	25.89	31.00	41.71	56.07
Norway	..	18.46	16.41	21.62	16.71	12.23	17.46	28.91	23.43	24.46	30.41	39.20	53.08
Portugal	12.14	22.75	17.22	20.35	18.95	12.21	17.38	28.20	24.02	24.27	28.72	37.89	51.94
Spain	12.54	21.88	16.96	20.45	18.34	11.80	16.99	27.16	23.32	23.95	28.13	36.03	50.54
Sweden	13.22	23.02	17.23	20.86	18.90	12.61	17.68	28.13	24.03	23.86	28.60	36.47	51.78
Switzerland	13.87	24.23	17.69	21.71	20.50	13.38	18.35	29.53	25.04	25.34	30.26	38.73	55.81
Turkey	..	23.11	16.78	20.25	18.79	11.99	16.07	26.61	22.98	23.57	27.05	34.90	50.65
United Kingdom	12.57	22.92	17.29	21.08	19.32	12.64	18.01	28.45	24.45	24.58	29.13	37.75	53.79
United States	13.48	21.07	16.74	20.16	18.34	12.02	17.06	27.54	22.07	23.52	27.66	35.86	48.82

StatLink http://dx.doi.org/10.1787/437433814516

Crude oil spot prices
US dollars per barrel

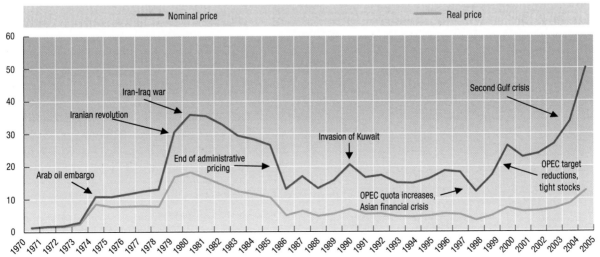

StatLink http://dx.doi.org/10.1787/427671144466

LABOUR MARKET

EMPLOYMENT
EMPLOYMENT RATES BY GENDER
EMPLOYMENT RATES BY AGE GROUP
PART-TIME EMPLOYMENT
SELF-EMPLOYMENT
HOURS WORKED

UNEMPLOYMENT
UNEMPLOYMENT RATES
LONG-TERM UNEMPLOYMENT
REGIONAL UNEMPLOYMENT

EMPLOYMENT RATES BY GENDER

Employment rates show the percentage of persons of working age who are in employment. In the short term, these rates are sensitive to the economic cycle, but in the longer term they are significantly affected by government policies with regard to higher education and income support and by policies that facilitate employment of women.

Employment rates for men and women differ both between countries and over time in individual countries. Employment rates are here shown for total employment and for men and women separately.

Definition

Employment rates are calculated as the ratio of the employed to the working age population. To calculate this employment rate, the population of working age is divided into two groups: those who are employed and those who are not. Employment is generally measured through household labour force surveys and, according to the ILO Guidelines, employed persons are defined as those aged 15 or over who report that they have worked in gainful employment for at least one hour in the previous week. Those not in employment consist of persons who are out of work but seeking employment, students and all others who have excluded themselves from the labour force for one reason or another, such as incapacity or the need to look after young children or elderly relatives.

Working age is generally defined as persons in the 15 to 64 age bracket although in some countries working age is defined as 16 to 64.

Comparability

All OECD countries use the ILO Guidelines for measuring employment, but the operational definitions used in national labour force surveys vary slightly in Iceland and Turkey. Employment levels are also likely to be affected by changes in the survey design and/or the survey conduct, but employment rates are likely to be fairly consistent over time.

For the denominators – the population in each age group – the data are taken from labour force surveys.

Long-term trends

Over the period shown in the tables, total employment rates (men and women) have fallen in 10 countries and risen in 21. Particularly large falls were recorded in Turkey, Poland, Czech Republic, Sweden and Slovak Republic and particularly large increases occurred in Ireland, Spain and the New Zealand.

Growth in employment rates was very different for men and women. Employment rates for men decreased in 18 countries during the period with an annual fall of more than 0.5% in Poland, Turkey and Germany. For women, on the other hand, employment rates grew in 25 countries with increases of 1.5% per year or more recorded for Spain, Ireland, Greece, Netherlands, Italy and Belgium.

Clearly, these differences in the growth of employment rates are leading to convergence in the rates for women and men although differences remain large in many countries.

Source

- OECD (2006), *OECD Employment Outlook*, OECD, Paris.

Further information

Analytical publications

- Durand, M., J. Simon and C. Webb (1992), *OECD's Indicators of International Trade and Competitiveness*, OECD Economics Department Working Papers, No. 120, OECD, Paris.
- Jeaumotte, F. (2003), *Female Labour Force Participation*, OECD Economics Department Working Papers, No. 376, OECD, Paris.
- OECD (2002-2004), *Babies and Bosses – Reconciling Work and Family Life*, series, OECD, Paris.

Statistical publications

- OECD (2004), *Quarterly Labour Force Statistics*, OECD, Paris.
- OECD (2006), *Labour Force Statistics*, OECD, Paris.

Online databases

- *Employment Statistics.*

Websites

- OECD Labour Statistics Database, *www.oecd.org/statistics/labour*.
- Putting More Women to Work: A Colloquium on Employment, Child Care and Taxes, *www.oecd.org/employment/colloquium/women*.

Employment rates: total

Share of persons of working age (15 to 64 years) in employment

	1992	1993	1994	1995	1996	1997	1998	1999	2000	2001	2002	2003	2004	2005
Australia	64.9	64.7	66.0	67.7	67.6	67.4	67.9	68.4	69.3	69.0	69.4	70.0	70.3	71.6
Austria	..	..	68.3	68.6	67.7	67.7	67.7	68.2	68.2	68.0	68.5	68.7	67.8	68.6
Belgium	56.5	56.0	55.7	56.3	56.3	57.0	57.3	58.9	60.9	59.7	59.7	59.3	60.5	61.0
Canada	66.8	66.5	67.0	67.5	67.3	68.0	68.9	70.0	70.9	70.8	71.4	72.2	72.5	72.5
Czech Republic	..	69.0	69.2	69.4	69.3	68.7	67.5	65.9	65.2	65.3	65.7	64.9	64.2	64.8
Denmark	74.5	72.4	72.4	73.9	74.0	75.4	75.3	76.5	76.4	75.9	76.4	75.1	76.0	75.5
Finland	64.7	60.6	59.9	61.1	61.9	62.8	64.1	66.1	67.0	67.7	67.7	67.4	67.2	68.0
France	59.7	59.1	58.4	59.1	59.2	58.9	59.4	59.8	61.1	62.0	62.2	62.5	62.4	62.3
Germany	66.2	65.1	64.5	64.6	64.3	63.8	64.7	65.2	65.6	65.8	65.3	64.6	65.0	65.5
Greece	53.6	53.5	54.1	54.5	54.9	54.8	55.6	55.4	55.9	55.6	57.7	58.9	59.6	60.3
Hungary	58.0	54.5	53.5	52.9	52.7	52.7	53.8	55.7	56.0	56.2	56.2	57.0	56.8	56.9
Iceland	79.2	78.2	78.5	80.5	80.4	80.0	82.2	84.2	84.6	84.6	82.8	84.1	82.8	84.4
Ireland	50.7	50.9	51.9	54.1	55.0	56.3	59.6	62.5	64.5	65.0	65.0	65.0	65.5	67.1
Italy	52.3	52.5	51.5	51.2	51.4	51.6	52.2	52.9	53.9	54.9	55.6	56.2	57.4	57.5
Japan	69.6	69.5	69.3	69.2	69.5	70.0	69.5	68.9	68.9	68.8	68.2	68.4	68.7	69.3
Korea	61.9	61.8	62.8	63.5	63.7	63.7	59.2	59.6	61.5	62.1	63.3	63.0	63.6	63.7
Luxembourg	61.5	60.9	60.2	58.5	59.1	59.9	60.2	61.6	62.7	63.0	63.6	62.7	62.6	63.6
Mexico	58.7	59.3	58.7	58.2	59.1	61.0	61.3	61.2	60.9	60.1	60.1	59.6	60.8	59.6
Netherlands	63.8	63.8	63.9	65.1	66.2	68.1	69.8	71.3	72.3	72.5	72.4	71.8	71.2	71.1
New Zealand	65.4	66.1	68.0	70.1	71.1	70.6	69.6	70.1	70.7	71.8	72.4	72.5	73.5	74.6
Norway	71.6	71.3	72.2	73.5	75.3	77.0	78.3	78.0	77.9	77.5	77.1	75.8	75.6	75.2
Poland	59.9	58.9	58.3	58.1	58.4	58.8	58.9	57.5	55.0	53.5	51.7	51.4	51.9	53.0
Portugal	66.5	64.9	64.0	63.2	63.6	64.7	66.8	67.4	68.3	68.6	68.1	67.1	67.8	67.5
Slovak Republic	..	..	59.8	60.2	61.9	61.1	60.5	58.1	56.8	56.9	56.9	57.7	57.0	57.7
Spain	50.5	48.0	47.4	48.3	49.3	50.7	52.4	55.0	57.4	58.8	59.5	60.7	62.0	64.3
Sweden	77.2	72.6	71.5	72.2	71.6	70.7	71.5	72.9	74.2	75.2	74.9	74.3	73.5	73.9
Switzerland	77.6	77.0	75.6	76.4	77.0	76.9	78.0	78.4	78.4	79.2	78.9	77.9	77.4	77.2
Turkey	53.7	50.0	52.4	52.4	52.5	51.3	51.4	50.8	48.9	47.8	46.7	45.5	46.1	45.9
United Kingdom	69.0	68.2	68.7	69.2	69.7	70.6	71.0	71.5	72.2	72.5	72.3	72.6	72.7	72.6
United States	70.8	71.2	72.0	72.5	72.9	73.5	73.8	73.9	74.1	73.1	71.9	71.2	71.2	71.5
EU 15 total	61.1	60.2	59.9	60.3	60.5	60.8	61.7	62.5	63.5	64.1	64.2	64.3	64.8	65.2
OECD total	64.3	63.9	64.0	64.3	64.6	65.0	65.2	65.4	65.7	65.5	65.1	64.9	65.2	65.5
Brazil	67.1	67.2	..	67.7	65.1	65.3	64.4	64.6	..	64.3	65.4	65.0	66.4	67.0

StatLink 🔗 http://dx.doi.org/10.1787/172580205657

Employment rates: total

Average annual growth in percentage, 1992-2005 or latest available period

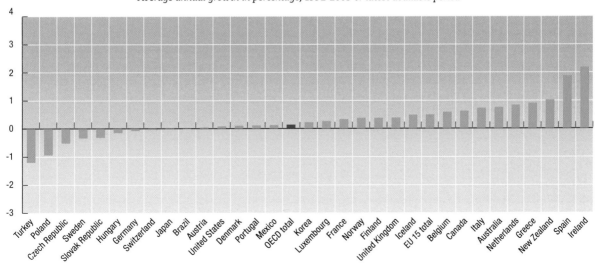

StatLink 🔗 http://dx.doi.org/10.1787/013607334122

Employment rates: men

Share of men of working age (15 to 64 years) in employment

	1992	1993	1994	1995	1996	1997	1998	1999	2000	2001	2002	2003	2004	2005
Australia	74.2	73.8	75.0	76.4	76.3	75.8	76.2	76.6	77.1	76.4	76.8	77.1	77.6	78.5
Austria	..	..	77.5	78.1	77.0	76.8	76.6	77.0	76.8	76.2	75.9	76.0	74.9	75.4
Belgium	68.4	67.0	66.5	66.9	66.8	67.1	67.0	67.5	69.8	68.5	68.1	67.1	67.9	67.7
Canada	72.6	72.4	73.0	73.4	73.2	73.8	74.3	75.4	76.2	75.7	75.9	76.4	76.7	76.7
Czech Republic	..	77.6	77.5	77.9	78.1	77.4	76.3	74.3	73.6	73.6	74.2	73.4	72.4	73.3
Denmark	78.5	75.9	77.6	80.7	80.5	81.3	80.2	81.2	80.7	80.2	80.2	79.7	79.9	80.1
Finland	65.6	61.5	61.1	63.1	64.2	65.2	66.8	68.4	69.4	70.0	69.2	69.0	68.8	69.4
France	68.6	67.2	66.1	66.7	66.8	66.3	66.6	66.8	68.1	69.0	68.6	68.6	68.1	67.8
Germany	76.4	74.9	74.0	73.7	72.8	72.1	72.9	72.8	72.9	72.8	71.7	70.4	70.8	71.4
Greece	72.3	71.7	72.2	72.2	72.6	71.9	71.6	70.9	71.3	70.9	72.5	73.5	74.0	74.5
Hungary	64.0	60.0	59.6	60.2	60.2	60.3	60.6	62.6	62.7	63.0	62.9	63.4	63.1	63.1
Iceland	84.3	82.3	82.4	84.0	84.3	84.2	86.0	88.2	88.2	88.0	85.7	86.8	86.2	87.4
Ireland	64.2	63.5	64.8	66.7	66.6	67.8	71.0	73.5	75.6	76.0	74.7	74.5	75.2	76.2
Italy	68.3	69.3	67.8	67.0	66.9	66.8	67.1	67.6	68.2	68.7	69.2	69.7	69.7	69.7
Japan	82.2	82.3	81.9	81.9	82.1	82.4	81.7	81.0	80.9	80.5	79.9	79.8	80.0	80.4
Korea	75.5	75.2	76.3	76.8	76.7	76.2	71.3	71.3	73.1	73.5	74.9	75.0	75.2	75.0
Luxembourg	76.3	76.6	74.9	74.3	74.4	74.3	74.6	74.4	75.0	74.9	75.5	73.3	73.1	73.4
Mexico	84.2	84.3	82.9	81.0	82.7	84.3	84.7	84.6	84.0	83.4	82.6	82.0	82.5	80.2
Netherlands	76.3	75.2	74.9	76.0	76.9	78.4	79.9	80.8	81.3	81.1	80.6	79.3	78.1	77.4
New Zealand	73.5	74.4	76.2	78.6	79.0	78.6	77.3	77.4	78.2	79.1	79.8	79.4	80.8	81.5
Norway	76.4	75.8	76.8	78.1	80.0	81.7	82.8	82.1	81.7	81.0	80.2	78.7	78.4	78.3
Poland	66.9	65.9	64.9	64.7	65.2	66.1	65.8	63.6	61.2	59.2	57.0	56.7	57.4	59.0
Portugal	77.3	74.9	73.5	72.1	72.0	72.5	75.6	75.6	76.3	76.5	75.7	73.9	74.1	73.4
Slovak Republic	..	..	67.2	67.6	69.2	68.4	67.8	64.3	62.2	62.1	62.5	63.4	63.2	64.6
Spain	68.5	64.4	63.3	64.0	64.7	66.1	68.3	70.8	72.7	73.8	73.9	74.5	74.9	76.4
Sweden	78.2	73.1	72.2	73.5	73.2	72.4	73.6	74.8	76.2	76.9	76.4	75.7	75.0	75.9
Switzerland	88.6	88.0	86.3	87.3	86.8	85.9	87.2	87.1	87.3	87.6	86.2	85.1	84.5	83.9
Turkey	75.5	74.2	74.6	74.6	74.9	74.8	74.3	72.7	71.7	69.3	66.9	65.9	67.9	68.2
United Kingdom	76.2	74.8	75.3	76.1	76.3	77.4	78.0	78.3	78.9	79.1	78.6	78.9	78.9	78.6
United States	78.3	78.7	79.0	79.5	79.7	80.1	80.5	80.5	80.6	79.4	78.0	76.9	77.2	77.6
EU 15 total	72.5	71.1	70.5	70.7	70.6	70.8	71.6	72.1	72.9	73.2	72.9	72.6	72.6	72.9
OECD total	76.1	75.6	75.4	75.5	75.7	76.0	76.1	76.1	76.3	75.8	75.1	74.6	74.9	75.0
Brazil	83.8	83.7	..	83.1	80.8	80.7	79.5	78.8	..	78.2	78.7	77.9	79.3	79.4

StatLink ᵐⁱˢᵖ http://dx.doi.org/10.1787/755168731713

Employment rates: men

Average annual growth in percentage, 1992-2005 or latest available period

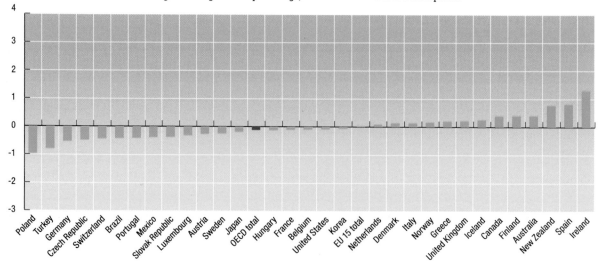

StatLink ᵐⁱˢᵖ http://dx.doi.org/10.1787/061104606286

OECD FACTBOOK 2007 – ISBN 978-92-64-02946-0 – © OECD 2007

Employment rates: women

Share of women of working age (15 to 64 years) in employment

	1992	1993	1994	1995	1996	1997	1998	1999	2000	2001	2002	2003	2004	2005
Australia	55.6	55.5	56.9	59.0	58.9	58.9	59.6	60.0	61.4	61.7	62.1	62.9	63.1	64.7
Austria	..	..	58.8	58.9	58.2	58.4	58.5	59.3	59.4	59.8	61.0	61.5	60.7	62.0
Belgium	44.6	44.9	44.8	45.4	45.6	46.7	47.5	50.2	51.9	50.7	51.1	51.4	53.0	54.1
Canada	61.0	60.5	61.1	61.6	61.5	62.1	63.5	64.6	65.6	65.9	67.0	67.9	68.4	68.3
Czech Republic	..	60.4	61.0	61.0	60.6	59.9	58.7	57.4	56.9	57.0	57.1	56.3	56.0	56.3
Denmark	70.4	68.7	67.1	67.0	67.4	69.4	70.3	71.6	72.1	71.4	72.6	70.5	72.0	70.8
Finland	63.8	59.7	58.7	59.0	59.5	60.4	61.3	63.6	64.5	65.4	66.1	65.7	65.5	66.5
France	50.8	51.1	50.8	51.6	51.8	51.7	52.4	53.0	54.3	55.2	55.8	56.4	56.7	56.9
Germany	55.7	55.1	54.7	55.3	55.5	55.3	56.3	57.4	58.1	58.7	58.8	58.7	59.2	59.6
Greece	36.2	36.4	37.1	38.0	38.5	39.1	40.3	40.7	41.3	41.2	43.1	44.5	45.5	46.2
Hungary	52.3	49.3	47.8	45.9	45.5	45.5	47.3	49.0	49.6	49.8	49.8	50.9	50.7	51.0
Iceland	74.0	74.0	74.6	76.8	76.5	75.6	78.3	80.2	81.0	81.1	79.8	81.2	79.4	81.2
Ireland	37.1	38.2	38.9	41.5	43.3	44.7	48.2	51.3	53.3	54.0	55.2	55.4	55.8	58.0
Italy	36.5	35.8	35.4	35.4	36.0	36.4	37.3	38.3	39.6	41.1	42.0	42.7	45.2	45.3
Japan	56.9	56.6	56.5	56.4	56.8	57.6	57.2	56.7	56.7	57.0	56.5	56.8	57.4	58.1
Korea	48.7	48.8	49.8	50.5	51.1	51.6	47.3	48.1	50.0	50.9	52.0	51.1	52.2	52.5
Luxembourg	46.2	44.8	44.9	42.2	43.6	45.4	45.6	48.5	50.0	50.8	51.5	52.0	51.9	53.7
Mexico	35.1	36.0	36.2	37.0	37.4	39.9	40.1	39.8	40.1	39.4	39.9	39.4	41.3	41.5
Netherlands	51.0	52.0	52.6	53.9	55.2	57.6	59.4	61.6	63.0	63.7	64.0	64.2	64.3	64.8
New Zealand	57.5	58.0	59.9	61.7	63.4	62.8	62.1	63.0	63.5	64.8	65.3	65.7	66.5	68.0
Norway	66.7	66.6	67.5	68.8	70.4	72.2	73.6	73.8	74.0	73.8	73.9	72.7	72.7	72.0
Poland	53.1	52.1	51.9	51.8	51.8	51.8	52.2	51.6	48.9	47.8	46.4	46.2	46.4	47.0
Portugal	56.1	55.3	55.0	54.8	55.6	57.2	58.3	59.5	60.5	61.0	60.8	60.6	61.7	61.7
Slovak Republic	..	..	52.6	53.0	54.6	54.0	53.5	52.1	51.5	51.8	51.4	52.2	50.9	50.9
Spain	32.5	31.5	31.5	32.5	33.8	35.2	36.5	39.1	42.0	43.8	44.9	46.8	49.0	51.9
Sweden	76.2	72.1	70.7	70.9	69.9	68.9	69.4	70.9	72.2	73.5	73.4	72.8	71.8	71.8
Switzerland	66.6	66.1	64.9	65.6	67.1	67.8	68.8	69.6	69.4	70.7	71.5	70.7	70.3	70.4
Turkey	31.9	25.8	30.4	30.2	30.3	28.0	28.5	28.9	26.2	26.3	26.6	25.2	24.3	23.7
United Kingdom	61.9	61.8	62.1	62.5	63.3	64.0	64.2	65.0	65.6	66.0	66.3	66.4	66.6	66.8
United States	63.5	64.0	65.2	65.8	66.3	67.1	67.4	67.6	67.8	67.1	66.1	65.7	65.4	65.6
EU 15 total	49.7	49.3	49.4	49.9	50.4	50.9	51.8	53.0	54.2	55.0	55.6	56.0	56.9	57.5
OECD total	52.7	52.4	52.9	53.3	53.7	54.2	54.5	54.9	55.3	55.4	55.3	55.3	55.7	56.1
Brazil	51.4	51.6	..	53.1	50.3	50.7	50.1	51.3	..	51.3	52.9	52.9	54.3	55.3

StatLink http://dx.doi.org/10.1787/481458146017

Employment rates: women

Average annual growth in percentage, 1992-2005 or latest available period

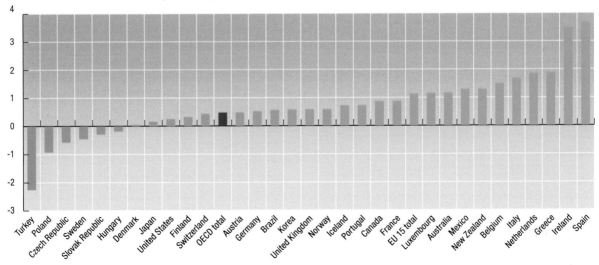

StatLink http://dx.doi.org/10.1787/810647071688

EMPLOYMENT RATES BY AGE GROUP

The employment rates in this chapter show the percentage of persons of working age who are in employment, broken down into three age groups. The youngest age group contains persons who are just entering the labour market, the second group those in their prime working lives, and the third group those who are approaching retirement.

Employment rates in these different age groups are significantly affected by government policies with regard to higher education, pensions and retirement age.

Definition

To calculate the employment rate for a given age group, the total population in that age group is divided between those in employment and those who are not. The numbers in employment are then expressed as a percentage of the total numbers in that age group.

Employment is generally measured through household labour force surveys and, according to the ILO Guidelines, employed persons are defined as those aged 15 or over who report that they have worked in gainful employment for at least one hour in the previous week. Those not in employment consist of persons who are out of work but seeking employment, students and all others who have excluded themselves from the labour force for one reason or another, such as incapacity or the need to look after young children or elderly relatives.

Comparability

All OECD countries use the ILO Guidelines for measuring employment, but the operational definitions used in national labour force surveys vary slightly in Iceland and Turkey. Employment levels are also likely to be affected by changes in the survey design and/or the survey conduct, but employment rates are likely to be fairly consistent over time.

For the denominators – the population in each age group – the data are taken from labour force surveys.

Long-term trends

In general, employment rates for those in the prime age group – 25 to 54 – are very similar between countries with ratios for most countries over 70% in 2005. Rates are most variable between countries for those in the youngest age group where, in 2005, they ranged from under 25% in Poland and Luxembourg to over 60% in the Netherlands, Denmark, Australia and Iceland. Employment rates for the oldest age group also vary considerably between countries, with more than 60% of this age group in employment in 2004 in Iceland, New Zealand, Sweden, Norway, Switzerland, Japan and the United States but less than 30% employed in Poland.

Over the period 1992-2005, employment rates for the youngest age group have been falling for the OECD as a whole. This partly reflects government policies to encourage young people to increase their educational qualifications, but the falls have been particularly marked in countries where total employment rates have been falling, such as the Czech Republic, Poland and Turkey; when the labour market is tight, young people have particular difficulties in finding employment. For those in the prime working age group – 25 to 54 – employment rates have remained stable for the OECD as a whole, but there were significant falls in the employment rates for Turkey, Poland and Czech Republic and large gains in Ireland, Spain and the Netherlands. Persons in the top age group have fared particularly well overall, with the largest increases in employment rates for New Zealand, the Netherlands, Hungary, Belgium, Slovak republic and Czech Republic.

Source
- OECD (2006), *OECD Employment Outlook*, OECD, Paris.

Further information
Analytical publications
- Burniaux, J.-M., R. Duval and F. Jaumotte (2004), *Coping with Ageing*, OECD Economics Department Working Papers, No. 371, OECD, Paris.
- OECD (2000), *From Initial Education to Working Life: Making Transitions Work*, OECD, Paris.
- OECD (2006), *Ageing and Employment Policies*, OECD, Paris.

Statistical publications
- OECD (2004), *Quarterly Labour Force Statistics*, OECD, Paris.
- OECD (2006), *Labour Force Statistics*, OECD, Paris.

Websites
- OECD Labour Statistics Database, *www.oecd.org/statistics/labour*.
- OECD Ageing and Employment Policies, *www.oecd.org/els/employment/olderworkers*.
- NERO Meeting on Labour Market Issues, Paris, 25 June 2004, *www.oecd.org/eco/nero*.
- Youth Employment Summit, *www.yesweb.org*.

Employment rates for age group 15-24

Persons in employment as a percentage of population in that age group

	1992	1993	1994	1995	1996	1997	1998	1999	2000	2001	2002	2003	2004	2005
Australia	56.1	56.0	58.6	60.8	60.5	58.9	59.9	61.0	62.1	61.2	61.1	61.8	62.4	63.6
Austria	..	..	59.5	57.3	55.7	54.8	54.1	54.0	53.1	52.0	52.1	51.5	51.9	53.1
Belgium	31.4	28.1	27.5	26.6	26.1	25.2	26.0	25.5	30.3	28.5	28.5	27.1	28.1	26.6
Canada	54.8	53.4	53.8	53.8	52.7	51.5	52.5	54.5	56.3	56.3	57.5	58.3	58.0	57.8
Czech Republic	..	46.9	47.5	46.6	45.8	44.2	43.0	40.1	38.3	36.1	33.7	31.4	28.5	27.3
Denmark	63.1	60.3	62.1	65.9	66.0	68.2	66.4	66.0	67.1	61.7	64.0	59.4	61.3	62.0
Finland	35.3	30.1	27.9	29.0	29.8	33.3	34.9	38.8	39.8	40.3	39.4	38.5	38.1	39.2
France	26.7	24.2	22.0	21.8	21.3	19.9	20.8	20.7	23.2	24.3	24.1	27.0	26.4	26.0
Germany	55.2	52.7	51.4	49.1	47.0	45.8	46.7	47.1	47.2	47.0	44.8	42.4	41.9	42.6
Greece	28.4	27.5	26.7	26.5	25.4	24.5	28.1	26.8	26.9	26.0	26.8	26.2	27.4	25.3
Hungary	35.4	31.5	30.8	31.3	30.4	31.3	35.3	35.7	32.5	30.7	28.5	26.7	23.6	21.8
Iceland	54.5	52.4	51.7	54.9	54.8	55.7	61.6	65.1	68.2	66.8	59.4	68.1	66.3	71.6
Ireland	35.9	34.4	33.5	37.3	36.4	38.3	43.0	46.4	48.2	47.0	45.3	45.8	44.8	46.3
Italy	27.8	30.0	28.3	27.3	26.9	27.0	27.2	27.3	27.8	27.4	26.7	26.0	27.2	25.5
Japan	44.6	44.8	45.0	44.7	45.0	45.3	44.6	42.9	42.7	42.0	41.0	40.3	40.0	40.9
Korea	34.6	33.6	34.5	34.6	33.7	32.2	27.1	27.6	29.4	30.1	31.5	30.8	31.2	29.9
Luxembourg	49.3	45.7	42.8	38.2	36.9	34.7	33.1	31.7	31.8	32.3	32.3	26.4	23.4	25.0
Mexico	50.5	51.6	50.3	48.6	48.9	49.7	50.9	50.5	49.6	47.7	46.0	44.7	45.2	43.7
Netherlands	56.9	55.5	55.4	56.3	58.3	61.1	62.4	66.0	67.0	66.8	66.7	64.9	63.2	61.9
New Zealand	53.7	53.9	56.5	59.4	59.5	58.2	55.7	54.6	54.6	55.8	56.6	56.3	56.8	56.9
Norway	48.9	47.8	48.4	49.2	52.3	55.1	57.9	57.8	58.1	56.5	56.9	55.3	54.4	52.9
Poland	32.3	29.5	28.0	27.3	27.9	28.8	28.6	24.3	24.5	22.1	20.0	19.6	20.0	20.9
Portugal	48.0	43.1	40.5	37.6	37.1	39.2	42.8	42.6	42.0	42.7	41.9	38.4	36.9	36.1
Slovak Republic	..	..	34.4	34.8	36.8	36.4	35.0	31.0	29.0	27.9	27.2	27.6	26.5	25.6
Spain	34.8	29.5	28.3	28.6	28.3	29.4	31.0	34.4	36.3	37.1	36.6	36.8	38.4	41.9
Sweden	52.1	42.4	41.3	42.5	40.3	39.7	41.6	43.8	46.1	47.8	46.5	45.1	42.8	42.5
Switzerland	65.0	64.6	60.3	60.1	63.3	62.9	63.2	64.8	65.1	63.9	65.4	63.5	62.0	59.9
Turkey	44.3	39.5	43.0	41.0	42.0	40.3	39.5	39.7	37.0	35.3	33.0	30.5	31.6	31.2
United Kingdom	61.4	58.8	58.8	59.0	60.2	60.8	60.8	60.8	61.5	61.0	60.9	59.7	60.1	58.1
United States	56.7	57.2	58.1	58.3	57.6	58.0	59.0	59.0	59.7	57.7	55.7	53.9	53.9	53.9
EU 15 total	41.9	39.8	39.0	38.3	37.8	37.8	38.8	39.5	40.7	40.8	40.2	39.6	39.9	39.8
OECD total	46.6	45.7	45.7	45.2	45.0	45.0	45.4	45.5	45.7	44.8	43.7	42.7	43.0	42.9
Brazil	59.2	58.7	..	57.7	54.7	54.0	52.1	51.7	..	50.8	51.7	50.8	52.4	52.7

StatLink 🔗 http://dx.doi.org/10.1787/043526443286

Employment rates for age group 15-24

Persons in employment as a percentage of population in that age group, 2005

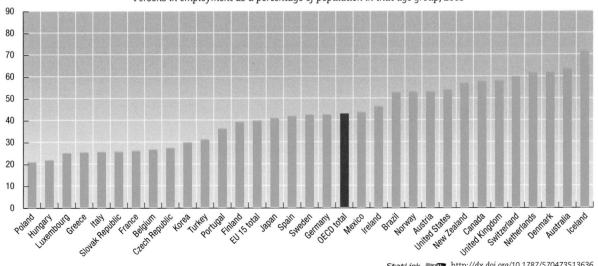

StatLink 🔗 http://dx.doi.org/10.1787/570473513636

Employment rates for age group 25-54

Persons in employment as a percentage of population in that age group

	1992	1993	1994	1995	1996	1997	1998	1999	2000	2001	2002	2003	2004	2005
Australia	73.3	72.9	73.6	75.2	74.9	74.9	75.3	75.5	76.3	76.3	76.7	77.2	77.4	78.8
Austria	..	..	79.5	80.4	80.1	80.6	80.7	81.6	82.2	82.4	83.2	83.7	82.6	82.6
Belgium	73.6	73.6	73.1	73.8	73.9	74.6	74.4	76.4	77.9	76.6	76.6	76.1	77.3	78.3
Canada	75.0	74.9	75.5	76.2	76.2	77.3	78.3	79.2	79.9	79.8	80.3	80.8	81.3	81.3
Czech Republic	..	86.3	86.3	86.3	85.8	85.0	83.7	81.9	81.6	82.1	82.5	81.7	81.4	82.0
Denmark	83.1	80.8	80.5	81.7	82.2	82.8	83.4	84.4	84.3	84.5	84.7	83.5	84.0	83.9
Finland	79.3	75.0	74.9	76.1	76.8	77.5	79.0	80.4	80.9	81.5	81.6	81.1	81.0	81.7
France	77.4	77.0	76.3	77.0	76.9	76.4	76.8	77.0	78.3	79.3	79.4	79.1	79.3	79.6
Germany	77.7	76.8	76.2	76.8	76.8	76.7	78.0	78.7	79.3	79.3	78.8	78.2	78.1	77.4
Greece	67.6	67.8	68.6	68.8	69.5	69.7	69.9	70.0	70.2	70.4	71.9	73.1	73.7	74.3
Hungary	75.7	72.5	71.7	70.7	70.4	70.2	70.3	72.3	73.0	73.1	73.0	73.7	73.6	73.7
Iceland	88.0	87.0	87.5	89.1	89.3	88.2	88.9	90.9	90.6	90.7	90.0	89.2	88.0	88.2
Ireland	60.1	60.9	62.7	64.7	66.3	67.4	70.6	73.2	75.3	76.4	76.6	76.0	76.7	78.0
Italy	68.3	66.7	65.8	65.5	65.7	65.8	66.3	67.1	68.0	69.2	70.1	70.8	72.1	72.2
Japan	80.2	79.8	79.5	79.3	79.6	79.9	79.2	78.7	78.6	78.6	78.0	78.3	78.6	79.0
Korea	73.1	73.0	73.6	74.2	74.7	74.8	70.2	70.3	72.2	72.6	73.4	73.1	73.4	73.4
Luxembourg	74.1	73.3	73.5	71.9	73.2	74.4	74.7	76.7	78.2	78.7	79.1	78.8	79.3	80.6
Mexico	64.7	65.1	65.0	65.1	66.2	68.5	68.4	67.9	68.3	67.8	68.4	68.1	69.6	68.7
Netherlands	73.3	73.8	73.7	75.0	75.8	77.5	79.3	80.4	81.2	81.6	81.2	81.1	80.6	80.9
New Zealand	74.7	74.9	76.2	77.6	78.4	77.8	76.8	77.6	78.6	79.3	79.6	79.8	80.8	82.0
Norway	81.2	80.7	81.3	82.4	83.7	85.0	85.8	85.5	85.3	85.1	84.4	82.9	83.1	83.2
Poland	74.8	74.4	73.8	74.2	74.6	74.7	75.0	73.7	70.9	69.3	67.5	67.6	68.3	69.5
Portugal	79.6	79.5	78.7	78.7	78.7	79.3	80.1	80.6	81.8	82.2	81.5	81.0	81.1	80.8
Slovak Republic	..	..	78.4	78.7	80.3	79.3	78.5	76.1	74.7	74.8	75.1	76.0	74.7	75.3
Spain	60.5	58.7	58.4	59.5	60.6	62.0	63.6	66.1	68.4	69.5	70.1	71.3	72.7	74.4
Sweden	86.8	83.2	81.9	82.6	81.8	80.7	81.3	82.5	83.8	84.6	84.2	83.5	82.9	83.9
Switzerland	84.6	83.8	83.2	84.2	83.6	83.4	85.0	85.1	85.4	86.0	86.0	84.8	84.7	85.1
Turkey	61.0	58.0	59.8	60.5	60.1	59.0	59.2	58.2	56.7	55.5	54.6	54.0	54.1	54.1
United Kingdom	76.6	76.3	76.5	77.1	77.4	78.3	79.0	79.6	80.2	80.5	80.3	80.7	80.7	81.1
United States	78.3	78.5	79.2	79.7	80.2	80.9	81.1	81.4	81.5	80.5	79.3	78.8	79.0	79.3
EU 15 total	73.9	72.9	72.7	73.2	73.4	73.7	74.6	75.5	76.4	77.0	77.0	77.1	77.5	77.7
OECD total	74.8	74.4	74.5	74.9	75.2	75.6	75.7	75.8	76.1	75.9	75.5	75.3	75.6	75.8
Brazil	73.4	73.9	..	75.0	72.8	73.3	72.8	73.2	..	73.1	74.2	74.0	75.4	75.9

StatLink http://dx.doi.org/10.1787/818163733726

Employment rates for age group 25-54

Persons in employment as a percentage of population in that age group, 2005

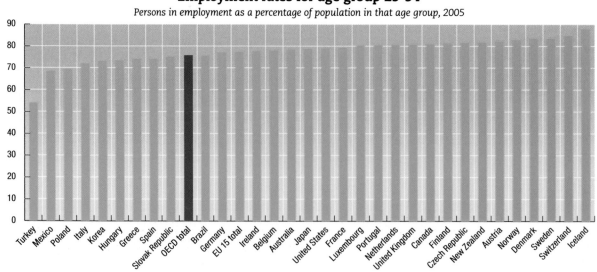

StatLink http://dx.doi.org/10.1787/818671451808

OECD FACTBOOK 2007 – ISBN 978-92-64-02946-0 – © OECD 2007

Employment rates for age group 55-64

Persons in employment as a percentage of population in that age group

	1992	1993	1994	1995	1996	1997	1998	1999	2000	2001	2002	2003	2004	2005
Australia	39.3	38.9	40.5	41.7	42.4	42.7	43.9	44.3	46.2	46.7	48.7	50.5	52.0	53.7
Austria	..	..	28.4	30.4	29.2	28.6	29.0	29.6	28.1	28.2	29.1	30.1	28.8	31.8
Belgium	22.4	21.9	22.4	23.3	21.8	22.0	22.5	24.7	25.0	25.2	25.8	28.1	30.1	32.1
Canada	43.7	43.0	43.6	43.2	43.5	44.4	45.2	46.8	48.1	48.2	50.1	53.0	53.9	54.8
Czech Republic	..	31.3	32.3	34.8	37.3	38.3	37.1	37.5	36.3	37.1	40.8	42.3	42.6	44.6
Denmark	52.3	51.3	50.2	49.3	47.5	51.4	50.4	54.2	54.6	56.5	57.3	60.7	61.8	59.8
Finland	37.3	34.8	33.5	34.4	35.6	35.7	36.2	39.2	42.3	45.9	47.8	49.9	51.0	52.6
France	33.9	33.9	33.4	33.5	33.5	33.6	33.0	34.2	34.3	36.5	39.3	40.3	40.6	40.7
Germany	35.9	35.9	35.9	37.4	38.0	38.3	38.4	37.8	37.6	37.9	38.6	39.0	41.8	45.5
Greece	39.4	38.8	39.5	40.5	40.7	40.7	39.1	38.4	39.0	38.0	38.9	41.0	39.4	41.6
Hungary	22.9	19.1	17.0	17.1	17.4	17.3	16.6	19.4	21.9	23.5	25.6	29.0	31.1	33.0
Iceland	83.0	83.2	84.7	85.1	83.8	83.7	86.7	85.9	84.2	85.6	87.2	83.3	82.0	84.8
Ireland	38.3	38.9	39.5	39.4	40.3	40.2	41.6	43.8	45.2	46.6	48.0	49.3	49.5	51.7
Italy	31.4	30.4	29.4	28.4	28.7	28.0	27.9	27.6	27.7	28.0	28.9	30.3	30.5	31.4
Japan	64.6	64.5	63.7	63.7	63.6	64.2	63.8	63.4	62.8	62.0	61.6	62.1	63.0	63.9
Korea	62.2	61.5	62.9	63.6	63.2	63.8	58.7	58.2	57.8	58.3	59.5	57.8	58.5	58.7
Luxembourg	24.7	26.1	23.2	24.0	22.6	23.7	25.0	26.3	27.2	24.8	27.9	30.0	30.0	31.7
Mexico	53.9	53.8	52.4	50.4	52.1	54.8	53.6	55.0	52.8	52.1	53.1	53.8	55.0	52.5
Netherlands	28.7	28.2	29.0	29.4	30.5	31.7	33.4	35.1	37.6	39.2	42.7	42.8	44.2	44.9
New Zealand	41.6	44.5	47.3	50.4	53.9	54.5	55.7	56.9	57.2	60.7	63.4	64.3	67.2	69.7
Norway	60.9	60.7	61.6	63.1	64.6	66.0	67.2	67.3	67.1	67.4	68.4	68.6	68.0	67.6
Poland	35.4	35.1	34.4	33.8	33.0	33.6	32.3	32.5	28.4	29.0	27.9	28.6	28.0	29.1
Portugal	47.2	44.9	45.9	44.6	46.2	47.1	49.7	50.4	50.8	50.0	50.9	51.1	50.3	50.5
Slovak Republic	..	..	21.3	21.7	22.8	21.4	22.8	22.3	21.3	22.3	22.9	24.6	26.8	30.4
Spain	36.1	34.5	32.7	32.4	33.2	34.1	35.1	35.1	37.0	39.2	39.7	40.8	41.3	43.1
Sweden	66.9	63.4	61.9	62.0	63.4	62.7	63.1	64.0	65.1	67.0	68.4	69.0	69.5	69.6
Switzerland	63.6	63.1	61.1	61.7	63.3	63.9	64.4	64.6	63.3	67.3	64.6	65.7	65.1	65.0
Turkey	42.4	37.7	40.8	41.7	41.6	40.5	41.1	39.3	36.4	35.9	35.3	32.7	33.1	30.8
United Kingdom	47.8	46.6	47.4	47.5	47.8	48.5	48.3	49.4	50.4	52.1	53.1	55.4	56.2	56.8
United States	53.4	53.8	54.4	55.1	55.9	57.2	57.7	57.7	57.8	58.6	59.5	59.9	59.9	60.8
EU 15 total	37.3	36.5	36.1	36.4	36.8	37.1	37.3	37.7	38.3	39.3	40.7	41.9	42.9	44.5
OECD total	46.9	46.3	46.1	46.4	46.9	47.7	47.7	48.0	47.9	48.5	49.4	50.3	51.0	52.0
Brazil	53.6	52.6	..	53.3	50.7	51.1	51.0	52.2	..	51.2	52.7	52.1	52.5	54.0

StatLink http://dx.doi.org/10.1787/486177018244

Employment rates for age group 55-64

Persons in employment as a percentage of population in that age group, 2005

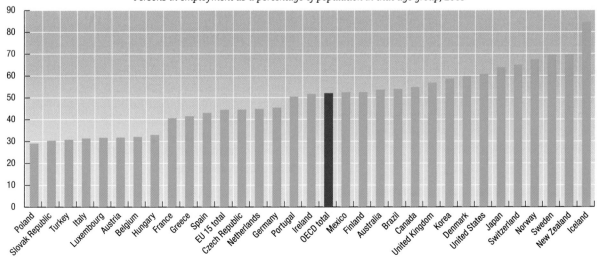

StatLink http://dx.doi.org/10.1787/882532848817

PART-TIME EMPLOYMENT

Part-time work accounted for a substantial share of overall employment growth in many OECD countries between 1992 and 2005. Part-time work has been an important factor behind employment growth of groups that are often under-represented in the labour force, such as women, youths and, to a lesser extent, older workers.

Recent surveys in a large number of OECD countries show that most people who work part-time do so from choice. This suggests that countries with little part-time employment could foster increased employment by policies that promote the availability of part-time positions. This would particularly benefit women with young children.

Definition

Part-time employment refers to persons who usually work less than 30 hours per week in their main job. Both employees and the self-employed may be part-time workers.

Employment is generally measured through household labour force surveys and, according to the ILO Guidelines, employed persons are defined as those aged 15 or over who report that they have worked in gainful employment for at least one hour in the previous week. The rates shown here refer to the numbers of persons who usually work less than 30 hours per week as a percentage of the total number of those in employment.

Comparability

All OECD countries use the ILO Guidelines for measuring employment, but the operational definitions used in national labour force surveys vary slightly in Iceland and Turkey. Employment levels are also likely to be affected by changes in the survey design and/or the survey conduct, but employment rates are likely to be fairly consistent over time. Information on the number of hours worked is collected in household labour force surveys and the rates shown here are considered to be of good comparability.

Long-term trends

For the OECD as a whole, part-time employment increased by more than one-third between 1992 and 2005. Part-time employment rates grew considerably in Austria, Germany, Ireland, Italy, Korea, Luxembourg and Spain but they also fell in several countries including Greece, Iceland, Mexico, United States and, particularly, Turkey.

The chart shows great variation between countries in part-time employment in 2005. Switzerland, Japan, Australia and Netherlands, over 25% of all those in employment were working part-time while the incidence of part-time employment were under 10% in the Slovak Republic, Hungary, Czech Republic, Turkey, Greece, Korea and Portugal. The average incidence of part-time employment for the OECD as a whole was a little over 16% in 2005 and was two percentage points higher in the EU15 countries.

Source

- OECD (2006), *OECD Employment Outlook*, OECD, Paris.

Further information

Analytical publications

- OECD (1999), *Implementing the OECD Jobs Strategy: Assessing Performance and Policy*, OECD, Paris.
- OECD (2002-2004), *Babies and Bosses – Reconciling Work and Family Life*, series, OECD, Paris.
- OECD (2003), *The Sources of Economic Growth in OECD Countries*, OECD, Paris.

Statistical publications

- OECD (2006), *Labour Force Statistics*, OECD, Paris.

Websites

- OECD Productivity Database, *www.oecd.org/statistics/ productivity*.
- OECD Labour Statistics Database, *www.oecd.org/statistics/ labour*.

Incidence of part-time employment

As a percentage of total employment

	1992	1993	1994	1995	1996	1997	1998	1999	2000	2001	2002	2003	2004	2005
Australia	24.9	24.3	24.4	25.0	25.2	26.0	25.9	26.1	26.2	27.2	27.5	27.9	27.1	27.3
Austria	..	..	..	11.1	10.9	10.8	11.5	12.3	12.2	12.4	13.6	13.6	15.5	16.2
Belgium	14.3	14.7	14.6	14.6	14.8	15.0	15.6	19.9	19.0	17.0	17.2	17.7	18.3	18.1
Canada	18.6	19.2	18.9	18.8	19.1	19.1	18.8	18.4	18.1	18.1	18.8	18.9	18.5	18.3
Czech Republic	..	3.6	3.6	3.4	3.4	3.4	3.3	3.4	3.2	3.2	2.9	3.2	3.1	3.3
Denmark	18.9	19.0	17.3	16.9	16.6	17.2	17.1	15.3	16.1	14.7	16.2	15.8	17.5	18.0
Finland	8.1	8.9	8.9	8.7	8.5	9.3	9.7	9.9	10.4	10.5	11.0	11.3	11.3	11.2
France	12.6	13.2	13.8	14.2	14.0	14.8	14.7	14.6	14.2	13.8	13.7	12.9	13.3	13.6
Germany	12.3	12.8	13.5	14.2	14.9	15.8	16.6	17.1	17.6	18.3	18.8	19.6	20.1	21.8
Greece	7.2	7.1	7.8	7.8	8.0	8.3	9.1	8.0	5.5	4.9	5.6	5.6	6.0	6.1
Hungary	..	..	..	2.8	2.7	2.9	2.9	3.2	2.9	2.5	2.6	3.2	3.3	3.2
Iceland	22.1	22.4	22.6	22.5	20.9	22.4	23.2	21.2	20.4	20.4	20.1	..	..	..
Ireland	11.3	13.1	13.5	14.3	14.2	15.0	17.6	17.9	18.1	17.9	18.1	18.8	18.7	18.6
Italy	10.0	10.0	10.0	10.5	10.5	11.3	11.2	11.8	12.2	12.2	11.9	12.0	14.9	14.7
Japan	20.4	21.1	21.4	20.1	21.8	23.3	23.6	24.1	22.6	24.9	25.1	26.0	25.5	25.8
Korea	4.8	4.5	4.5	4.3	4.3	5.0	6.7	7.7	7.0	7.3	7.6	7.7	8.4	9.0
Luxembourg	9.5	9.8	10.7	11.3	10.4	11.0	12.6	12.1	12.4	13.3	12.6	13.3	13.3	14.0
Mexico	..	..	..	16.6	14.9	15.5	15.0	13.7	13.5	13.7	13.5	13.4	15.1	..
Netherlands	27.3	27.9	28.9	29.4	29.3	29.1	30.0	30.4	32.1	33.0	33.9	34.6	35.0	35.7
New Zealand	21.1	20.8	21.0	20.9	21.9	22.3	22.7	23.0	22.2	22.4	22.6	22.3	22.0	21.7
Norway	22.1	22.0	21.5	21.4	21.6	21.0	20.8	20.7	20.2	20.1	20.6	21.0	21.1	20.8
Poland	..	..	..	..	..	11.9	11.8	14.0	12.8	11.6	11.7	11.5	12.0	11.7
Portugal	8.8	8.8	9.5	8.6	9.2	10.2	10.0	9.4	9.4	9.2	9.7	10.0	9.6	9.8
Slovak Republic	..	..	2.7	2.3	2.1	2.0	2.0	1.8	1.9	1.9	1.6	2.3	2.7	2.6
Spain	5.3	6.0	6.4	7.0	7.5	7.9	7.7	7.8	7.7	7.8	7.7	8.0	8.5	11.4
Sweden	15.0	15.4	15.8	15.1	14.8	14.2	13.5	14.5	14.0	13.9	13.8	14.1	14.4	13.5
Switzerland	22.7	23.2	23.2	22.9	23.7	24.0	24.2	24.8	24.4	24.8	24.8	25.1	24.9	25.1
Turkey	11.9	9.1	9.1	6.5	5.5	6.3	6.1	7.9	9.4	6.2	6.6	6.0	6.7	5.8
United Kingdom	21.5	22.1	22.4	22.3	22.9	22.9	23.0	22.9	23.0	22.7	23.4	23.8	24.1	23.6
United States	14.7	14.7	14.2	14.0	13.9	13.5	13.4	13.3	12.6	12.8	13.1	13.2	13.2	12.8
EU 15 total	13.6	14.1	14.6	14.8	15.1	15.6	15.9	16.1	16.2	16.2	16.4	16.6	17.4	18.0
OECD total	15.1	15.1	15.1	14.8	14.9	15.2	15.3	15.5	15.2	15.4	15.6	15.8	16.1	16.3
Brazil	15.0	16.3	..	16.2	15.3	15.9	16.3	16.9	..	16.0	17.0	17.1	17.3	17.9

StatLink ᴍⁱˢⁱ http://dx.doi.org/10.1787/584007524323

Incidence of part-time employment

As a percentage of total employment, 2005 or latest available year

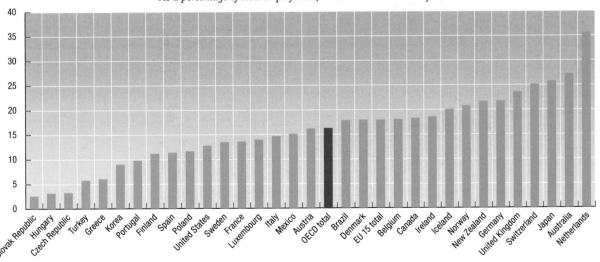

StatLink ᴍⁱˢⁱ http://dx.doi.org/10.1787/716343220302

SELF-EMPLOYMENT

Self-employment may be seen either as a survival strategy for those who cannot find any other means of earning an income or as evidence of entrepreneurial spirit and a desire to be one's own boss. The self-employment rates shown in this section reflect these various motives.

Definition

Employment is generally measured through household labour force surveys and, according to the ILO Guidelines, employed persons are defined as those aged 15 or over who report that they have worked in gainful employment for at least one hour in the previous week.

Self-employed persons include employers, own-account workers, members of producers' co-operatives, and unpaid family workers. The last of these are unpaid in the sense that they do not have a formal contract to receive a fixed amount of income at regular intervals, but they share in the income generated by the enterprise; unpaid family workers are particularly important in farming and retail trade. Note that all persons who work in corporate enterprises, including company directors, are considered to be employees.

The rates shown here are the percentages of the self-employed in total civilian employment i.e., total employment less military employees.

Comparability

All OECD countries use the ILO Guidelines for measuring employment, but the operational definitions used in national labour force surveys vary slightly in Iceland and Turkey. Employment levels are also likely to be affected by changes in the survey design and/or the survey conduct, but employment rates are likely to be fairly consistent over time.

Note that the composition of the self-employed with regard to the four categories listed above varies considerably among countries. In particular, countries with relatively large numbers of small farms, Brazil, Mexico and Turkey, for example, will have relatively large numbers of unpaid family workers.

Long-term trends

In 2005, the total self-employment rates (men and women together) ranged from under 8% in Luxembourg, Norway and the United States to well over 30% in Korea, Brazil, Mexico, Greece and Turkey. In general, self-employment rates are highest in countries with low per capita income although Italy, with a self-employment rate of 27%, is a striking exception. Ireland and Spain are also countries with both high per capita incomes and high self-employment rates.

Over the period shown in the table, self-employment rates have been falling in most countries although there have been small increases in Sweden and Germany and much larger increases in the Czech Republic and the Slovak Republic.

The levels and changes in total self-employment rates conceal significant differences between men and women. In more than half of the countries, over 15% of all men in employment were self-employed; the corresponding figure for women was under 10% (figures for 2005).

Growth rates have also differed. Self-employment rates for men rose in nine countries – by small amounts in Switzerland, Italy, Belgium, Portugal and Sweden and by significant amounts in Germany, the Slovak Republic and the Czech Republic. For women, self-employment grew only in five countries – marginally in Canada and New Zealand and by larger amounts in the Slovak Republic and the Czech Republic.

Source

• OECD (2006), *Labour Force Statistics*, OECD, Paris.

Further information

Analytical publications

• OECD (2000), "The Partial Renaissance of the Self-Employed", *OECD Employment Outlook*, Chapter 5, OECD, Paris, pp. 155-199.
• OECD (2005), *OECD SME and Entrepreneurship Outlook – 2005 Edition*, OECD, Paris.
• OECD (2006), *OECD Employment Outlook*, OECD, Paris.

Statistical publications

• OECD (2004), *Quarterly Labour Force Statistics*, OECD, Paris.

Online databases

• *Employment Statistics*.

Websites

• OECD Directorate for Employment, Labour and Social Affairs, *www.oecd.org/els*.
• OECD Entrepreneurship at Local Level, *www.oecd.org/tds/ leed/entrepreneurship*.

Self-employment rates: total
As a percentage of total civilian employment

	1992	1993	1994	1995	1996	1997	1998	1999	2000	2001	2002	2003	2004	2005
Australia	16.1	16.5	15.9	15.4	15.1	15.1	14.6	14.5	14.1	13.8	13.9	13.5	13.2	13.0
Austria	13.4	13.1	13.8	14.4	14.0	13.6	13.7	13.4	13.1	13.2	13.1	12.8	12.8	13.3
Belgium	18.4	18.9	18.9	18.8	18.8	18.6	18.2	17.8	..	..	..	..	..	..
Canada	10.1	10.7	10.7	10.6	11.1	11.4	11.7	11.3	10.6	9.9	9.8	9.8	9.5	9.4
Czech Republic	..	9.4	10.6	12.0	12.3	12.4	13.8	14.5	15.2	15.2	16.1	17.3	16.9	16.1
Denmark	10.8	10.8	10.0	9.6	9.5	9.1	9.4	9.1	8.7	8.9	9.0	8.8	8.7	8.7
Finland	15.7	16.0	16.3	15.6	15.3	14.9	14.3	14.0	13.7	13.0	12.9	12.9	12.8	12.7
France	12.2	11.7	11.3	10.8	10.4	10.1	9.8	9.5	9.2	8.9	8.8	8.8	8.9	9.0
Germany	10.1	10.4	10.6	10.7	10.8	10.9	11.0	10.8	11.0	11.1	11.2	11.4	12.1	12.4
Greece	47.4	46.7	46.7	46.1	45.7	45.2	43.6	42.1	42.0	39.9	39.3	39.0	36.6	36.4
Hungary	20.4	18.1	17.8	18.0	18.1	17.4	16.1	15.7	15.2	14.5	13.9	13.5	14.3	13.8
Iceland	19.3	18.0	18.4	19.6	18.2	17.7	17.9	17.7	18.0	16.8	16.6	14.0	14.1	14.3
Ireland	23.9	23.4	22.7	22.2	20.9	20.8	20.3	19.2	18.9	18.1	17.8	17.5	18.0	17.4
Italy	28.6	28.9	29.0	29.3	29.3	29.1	29.1	28.6	28.5	28.2	27.7	27.5	28.4	27.0
Japan	20.2	19.1	18.7	18.3	17.7	17.6	17.4	17.2	16.7	15.9	15.5	15.2	15.0	14.7
Korea	37.3	37.9	37.1	36.8	36.7	36.8	38.3	37.6	36.8	36.7	36.0	34.9	34.0	33.6
Luxembourg	8.5	8.3	8.4	8.4	8.3	8.2	8.0	7.7	7.4	7.0	6.9	6.8	6.7	..
Mexico	43.9	43.8	43.7	40.9	40.4	39.9	38.8	37.9	36.4	36.8	37.2	37.1	37.0	35.7
Netherlands	11.1	11.6	12.3	12.4	12.5	12.6	11.8	11.3	12.0	11.5	11.6	..	..	..
New Zealand	21.2	21.2	21.1	21.0	21.0	20.1	20.4	21.2	20.8	19.9	19.4	19.4	19.2	18.5
Norway	10.3	10.2	9.8	9.4	8.7	8.2	8.3	7.8	7.4	7.2	7.1	7.3	7.4	7.5
Poland	30.2	31.2	30.9	29.7	29.5	28.3	27.2	26.9	27.4	28.0	28.1	27.3	26.7	25.8
Portugal	25.7	26.3	27.7	27.9	28.6	28.9	28.3	27.2	26.5	27.0	26.7	26.8	26.0	25.2
Slovak Republic	..	..	6.3	6.5	6.4	6.3	6.8	7.7	8.0	8.4	8.6	9.8	12.0	12.7
Spain	25.7	26.0	25.9	25.2	24.7	23.6	22.8	21.3	20.2	19.8	19.0	18.3	18.1	18.3
Sweden	9.8	10.8	11.1	11.2	11.0	10.8	10.6	10.6	10.3	10.0	9.8	9.6	9.9	9.8
Switzerland	11.8	12.7	12.7	12.7	13.4	13.8	14.0	14.0	13.2	12.9	12.5	11.9	11.4	11.2
Turkey	60.3	57.8	59.1	58.5	57.2	55.4	55.4	55.0	51.4	52.8	50.2	49.4	49.2	45.8
United Kingdom	15.7	15.6	15.7	15.6	14.9	14.5	13.7	13.2	12.8	12.8	12.7	13.2	13.6	13.5
United States	8.7	8.8	8.8	8.5	8.4	8.2	7.9	7.7	7.4	7.4	7.2	7.6	7.6	7.5
EU 15 total	17.2	17.2	17.3	17.2	17.0	16.8	16.5	16.0	15.7	15.6	15.5	15.5	15.8	15.7
OECD total	19.9	19.7	19.8	19.4	19.2	19.0	18.7	18.3	17.7	17.6	17.4	17.3	17.4	16.9
Brazil	38.2	37.9	..	38.6	37.0	37.8	37.7	38.5	..	35.6	35.7	35.6	34.9	34.9

StatLink http://dx.doi.org/10.1787/260074785513

Self-employment rates: total
As a percentage of total civilian employment, 2005 or latest available year

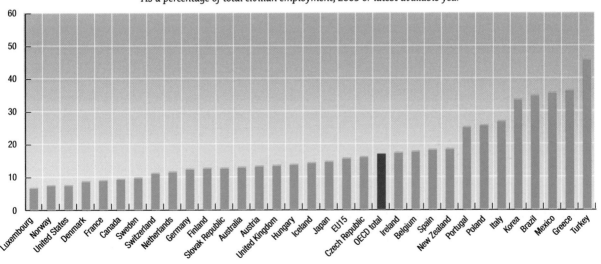

StatLink http://dx.doi.org/10.1787/658248633085

Self-employment rates: men
As a percentage of total male civilian employment

	1992	1993	1994	1995	1996	1997	1998	1999	2000	2001	2002	2003	2004	2005
Australia	18.5	19.0	18.3	17.9	17.6	17.4	17.1	17.1	16.7	16.6	16.7	16.3	16.0	15.6
Austria	..	..	..	..	14.1	14.0	14.1	13.9	13.9	14.1	14.2	14.0	14.8	15.3
Belgium	18.9	19.4	19.6	19.7	19.9	19.9	19.6	19.4	..	..	..	..	..	..
Canada	11.6	12.1	12.0	11.8	12.2	12.5	12.9	12.5	11.7	11.2	10.8	11.0	10.8	10.5
Czech Republic	..	12.0	13.7	15.1	15.7	15.9	17.3	18.4	19.1	19.1	20.3	21.7	21.5	20.4
Denmark	..	..	..	12.4	12.4	..	12.4	12.2	11.6	12.4	12.5	11.9	11.9	11.6
Finland	20.5	21.0	21.1	20.2	19.7	19.0	18.2	18.1	17.8	16.8	16.7	16.7	16.7	16.7
France	14.0	13.7	13.3	12.9	12.6	12.3	11.8	11.5	11.1	10.8	10.5	10.7	10.7	10.9
Germany	11.5	11.9	12.3	12.5	12.7	13.0	13.1	13.2	13.4	13.4	13.6	14.0	14.9	14.9
Greece	48.2	47.7	47.6	47.4	46.9	46.8	44.9	43.8	43.7	42.1	41.4	41.0	39.4	39.1
Hungary	23.9	21.9	21.9	22.1	22.6	21.5	19.9	19.5	19.2	18.1	17.3	17.1	17.9	17.3
Iceland	25.6	24.2	25.6	27.3	23.9	23.2	23.9	23.7	24.0	23.0	23.6	19.3	19.3	20.2
Ireland	31.5	30.9	30.3	29.9	28.1	28.1	27.4	26.1	25.8	25.2	25.2	24.7	25.4	24.8
Italy	31.3	31.4	31.6	32.3	32.5	32.4	32.5	32.1	32.3	32.2	31.7	31.5	32.4	31.2
Japan	17.4	16.6	16.4	16.2	15.9	15.9	15.7	15.8	15.5	15.0	14.9	14.7	14.7	14.6
Korea	34.9	35.4	34.7	34.3	34.4	34.7	36.3	36.1	35.7	36.0	35.7	35.3	34.4	34.0
Mexico	45.9	45.1	44.2	41.4	41.0	39.8	38.9	38.1	36.8	37.2	37.3	37.1	36.7	35.8
Netherlands	..	..	..	13.7	13.8	14.0	13.3	12.7	13.4	13.0	13.5	..	..	..
New Zealand	26.3	26.3	25.8	25.5	25.9	24.9	25.5	26.4	25.9	24.9	24.5	24.6	24.0	23.0
Norway	13.7	13.3	12.8	12.2	11.4	10.9	11.0	10.3	9.4	9.4	9.7	10.1	10.3	10.2
Poland	31.2	32.2	32.4	31.4	31.1	30.0	29.1	29.2	29.5	29.9	30.4	29.8	28.9	27.9
Portugal	26.8	27.4	29.0	29.9	30.3	30.0	29.5	28.4	27.8	28.5	28.3	28.4	27.9	26.8
Slovak Republic	..	..	8.6	8.7	8.7	8.4	9.1	10.4	10.8	11.4	11.9	13.0	16.0	17.2
Spain	26.2	26.9	27.0	26.3	26.2	25.4	24.4	23.3	22.3	21.9	21.4	20.7	20.5	20.8
Sweden	14.3	15.5	15.7	15.7	15.6	15.3	14.8	14.8	14.5	14.1	14.0	13.9	14.3	14.0
Switzerland	11.4	12.4	12.5	13.3	14.0	14.1	14.6	14.6	13.8	13.6	13.0	12.4	11.9	11.7
Turkey	53.3	52.8	52.7	52.1	50.5	49.8	49.8	48.9	46.5	47.5	45.1	44.5	45.0	42.2
United Kingdom	20.4	20.3	20.6	20.6	19.6	19.1	18.0	17.7	16.7	17.0	17.0	17.6	18.3	18.2
United States	10.6	10.9	10.3	9.9	9.8	9.5	9.2	8.9	8.6	8.5	8.4	8.8	8.9	8.8
EU 15 total	19.8	19.8	19.8	19.4	19.3	18.9	18.9	18.6	18.3	18.2	18.0	18.2	18.5	18.3
OECD total	21.6	21.6	21.4	20.9	20.8	20.5	20.3	20.0	19.5	19.4	19.3	19.3	19.5	19.0
Brazil	37.9	37.7	..	38.8	38.2	39.0	39.2	40.0	..	37.4	37.2	37.4	36.7	36.2

StatLink http://dx.doi.org/10.1787/852231456437

Self-employment rates: men
As a percentage of total male civilian employment, 2005 or latest available year

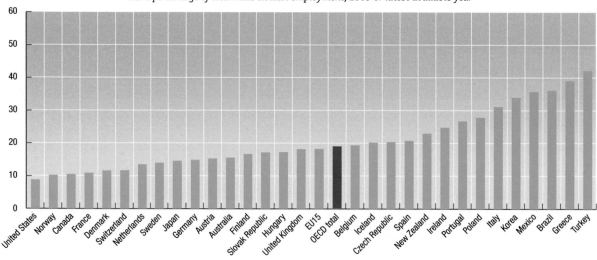

StatLink http://dx.doi.org/10.1787/548318126523

OECD FACTBOOK 2007 – ISBN 978-92-64-02946-0 – © OECD 2007

Self-employment rates: women
As a percentage of total female civilian employment

	1992	1993	1994	1995	1996	1997	1998	1999	2000	2001	2002	2003	2004	2005
Australia	12.8	13.1	12.6	12.1	11.9	12.2	11.4	11.1	10.7	10.3	10.5	10.1	9.9	9.8
Austria	..	..	..	..	13.8	13.2	13.1	12.6	12.2	12.1	11.8	11.3	10.3	10.9
Belgium	17.7	18.1	17.7	17.6	17.4	16.9	16.2	15.7	..	..	..	..	..	..
Canada	8.3	9.0	9.2	9.1	9.7	10.2	10.4	9.9	9.2	8.4	8.5	8.4	8.0	8.1
Czech Republic	..	6.2	6.8	8.0	7.9	8.0	9.1	9.6	10.2	10.2	10.7	11.5	10.9	10.4
Denmark	..	..	..	6.3	6.1	..	5.8	5.6	5.5	4.9	5.2	5.3	5.2	5.3
Finland	10.7	10.8	11.1	10.5	10.5	10.2	10.0	9.5	9.2	8.9	8.8	8.8	8.6	8.5
France	9.8	9.2	8.8	8.3	7.9	7.5	7.3	7.1	6.9	6.7	6.8	6.7	6.8	6.9
Germany	8.1	8.2	8.3	8.3	8.1	8.1	8.2	7.8	7.9	8.3	8.2	8.4	8.8	9.4
Greece	45.9	44.9	45.2	43.8	43.7	42.4	41.3	39.3	38.9	36.1	35.7	35.6	32.1	32.0
Hungary	16.4	13.7	13.0	13.0	12.7	12.4	11.6	11.1	10.5	10.2	10.0	9.2	10.1	9.9
Iceland	11.8	10.7	10.4	10.6	11.6	11.4	11.1	10.8	11.0	9.8	8.7	8.1	8.3	7.5
Ireland	10.4	10.8	10.0	9.7	9.5	9.5	9.6	9.1	9.0	8.0	7.5	7.7	7.8	7.4
Italy	23.6	24.3	24.2	23.8	23.6	23.2	23.0	22.6	22.0	21.6	21.2	21.1	22.2	20.6
Japan	24.4	22.8	22.0	21.5	20.5	20.0	19.8	19.4	18.4	17.3	16.3	15.8	15.4	15.0
Korea	41.0	41.7	40.7	40.4	40.1	39.8	41.4	39.7	38.4	37.6	36.5	34.4	33.4	32.9
Mexico	39.3	41.0	42.6	39.8	39.1	40.1	38.6	37.6	35.7	36.0	37.1	37.2	37.6	35.5
Netherlands	..	..	..	10.7	10.6	10.7	9.8	9.4	10.2	9.5	9.1	..	..	..
New Zealand	14.9	14.8	15.3	15.4	15.0	14.1	14.3	15.0	14.7	14.0	13.3	13.2	13.6	13.4
Norway	6.5	6.6	5.8	6.1	5.7	5.1	5.3	5.0	4.8	4.7	4.2	4.3	4.3	4.5
Poland	29.0	29.9	29.3	27.7	27.5	26.3	25.0	24.1	24.8	25.7	25.4	24.3	24.1	23.1
Portugal	24.2	25.0	26.0	25.5	26.5	27.5	26.8	25.8	24.9	25.1	24.9	24.9	23.7	23.4
Slovak Republic	..	..	3.4	3.8	3.5	3.8	4.0	4.5	4.6	4.9	4.7	5.9	7.1	7.1
Spain	24.7	24.4	23.6	23.3	22.0	20.3	19.7	17.8	16.7	16.2	15.1	14.5	14.3	14.5
Sweden	5.1	5.8	6.3	6.4	6.0	5.9	6.0	6.1	5.7	5.6	5.3	5.1	5.2	5.3
Switzerland	12.4	13.1	13.0	11.9	12.6	13.6	13.2	13.2	12.3	12.0	11.7	11.4	10.7	10.7
Turkey	76.7	72.3	74.6	74.0	73.6	70.0	69.9	70.0	64.7	66.8	63.0	61.9	60.7	56.2
United Kingdom	10.1	10.0	9.8	9.6	9.3	9.1	8.7	8.0	8.3	7.8	7.8	8.2	8.3	8.2
United States	6.4	6.4	7.1	6.9	6.9	6.7	6.4	6.2	6.1	6.1	5.9	6.1	6.1	5.9
EU 15 total	12.4	12.3	12.1	12.1	11.9	11.5	11.5	11.1	10.9	10.8	10.6	10.7	10.9	10.8
OECD total	17.2	16.7	17.2	16.9	16.7	16.4	16.1	15.7	15.0	14.8	14.6	14.4	14.4	13.9
Brazil	38.6	38.1	..	38.4	35.3	36.1	35.5	36.3	..	33.0	33.5	33.1	32.5	33.1

StatLink http://dx.doi.org/10.1787/578658875860

Self-employment rates: women
As a percentage of total female civilian employment, 2005 or latest available year

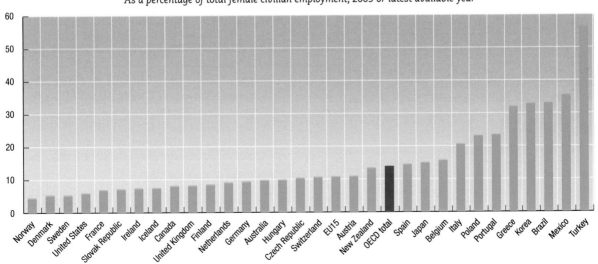

StatLink http://dx.doi.org/10.1787/506725488687

HOURS WORKED

Governments of some OECD countries have pursued policies to make it easier for parents to reconcile work and family, and some of these policies also tend to reduce working time. Examples include the extension of annual paid leave, maternity/parental leave and workers' options for working part-time schedules or, albeit less frequently, the reduction of the full-time workweek.

Definition

For this table, the total numbers of hours worked over the year are divided by the average numbers of people in employment.

Employment is generally measured through household labour force surveys and, according to the ILO Guidelines, employed persons are defined as those aged 15 years or over who report that they have worked in gainful employment for at least one hour in the previous week.

Long-term trends

In the large majority of OECD countries, hours worked have fallen over the period from 1992 to 2005. However, this decline was not particularly large in most countries, as compared to the decline in earlier decades and some of the decline in average hours between these two years may reflect transitory business cycle effects, since labour markets generally were more buoyant in 1992 (near the end of a long expansion in many OECD countries) than in 2005.

The average hours worked per year per employed person fell from 1 784 in 1992 to 1 719 in 2005; this is equivalent to a reduction in hours worked of more than one 40-hour workweek. The table shows that working hours fell in a majority of countries; hours increased in only Denmark, Hungary (more markedly), Mexico, New Zealand and Sweden. Reductions in hours worked were most marked in France, Ireland, Japan and Korea. With the exception of France, these were all countries that had rather high numbers of hours worked at the beginning of the period.

Although one should exercise caution when comparing across countries, it is clear from the table and chart that actual hours worked in the Czech Republic, Greece, Hungary, Korea and Poland are above the average for OECD countries as a whole and that actual hours worked are relatively low in Belgium, France, Germany, the Netherlands and Norway.

Estimates of the hours actually worked are based on household labour force surveys in most countries, while the rest use establishment surveys, administrative sources or a combination of sources. They reflect regular work hours of full-time and part-time workers, over-time (paid and unpaid), hours worked in additional jobs and time not worked because of public holidays, annual paid leave, time spent on illness and maternity leave, strikes and labour disputes, bad weather, economic conditions and several other minor reasons.

Comparability

National statisticians and the OECD secretariat work to ensure that these data are as comparable as possible, but they are based on a range of different sources of varying reliability. For example, for several EU countries, the estimates are made by the OECD using results from the Spring European Labour Force Survey. The results reflect a single observation in the year and the survey data have to be supplemented by information from other sources for hours not worked due to public holidays and annual paid leave. Annual working hours reported for the remaining countries are provided by national statistical offices and are estimated using the best available sources. The data are intended for comparisons of trends over time and are not fully suitable for inter-country comparisons because of differences in their sources and other uncertainties about their international comparability.

Data cover dependent and self-employed as well as full-time and part-time employment.

Source
• OECD (2006), *OECD Employment Outlook*, OECD, Paris.

Further information
Analytical publications
• Durand, M., J. Martin and A. Saint-Martin (2004), "The 35-hour week: Portrait of a French exception", *OECD Observer, No. 244, September 2004*, OECD, Paris.
• Evans, J., D. Lippoldt and P. Marianna (2001), *Trends in Working Hours in OECD Countries*, OECD Labour Market and Social Policy Occasional Papers, No. 45, OECD, Paris.

Methodological publications
• OECD (2004), "Clocking In (and Out): Several Facets of Working Time", *OECD Employment Outlook* , Chapter 1, see also Annex I.A1, OECD, Paris.

Websites
• OECD Labour Statistics Database, *www.oecd.org/statistics/labour*.

Average hours actually worked

Hours per year per person in employment

	1992	1993	1994	1995	1996	1997	1998	1999	2000	2001	2002	2003	2004	2005
Australia	1 779	1 774	1 785	1 793	1 792	1 784	1 778	1 763	1 783	1 756	1 734	1 737	1 735	1 730
Austria	..	..	..	1 646	1 664	1 668	1 664	1 638	1 632	1 630	1 632	1 642	1 650	1 656
Belgium	1 594	1 552	1 551	1 549	1 547	1 566	1 555	1 545	1 545	1 547	1 548	1 542	1 522	1 534
Canada	1 759	1 763	1 780	1 775	1 784	1 765	1 765	1 769	1 766	1 760	1 743	1 733	1 751	1 737
Czech Republic	..	2 064	2 043	2 064	2 066	2 067	2 075	2 088	2 092	2 000	1 980	1 972	1 986	2 002
Denmark	1 532	1 531	1 494	1 499	1 495	1 512	1 528	1 539	1 554	1 562	1 556	1 554	1 540	1 551
Finland	1 755	1 756	1 777	1 776	1 775	1 771	1 761	1 765	1 750	1 734	1 727	1 720	1 724	1 714
France	1 696	1 683	1 676	1 651	1 656	1 650	1 638	1 631	1 592	1 579	1 537	1 532	1 555	1 546
Germany	1 566	1 550	1 547	1 534	1 518	1 509	1 503	1 492	1 473	1 458	1 445	1 439	1 441	1 437
Greece	2 105	2 125	2 092	2 082	2 058	2 026	2 023	2 067	2 080	2 086	2 087	2 087	2 060	2 053
Hungary	1 899	1 899	2 032	2 039	2 034	2 060	2 052	2 067	2 061	2 019	2 026	1 997	1 996	1 994
Iceland	1 859	1 828	1 813	1 832	1 860	1 839	1 817	1 873	1 885	1 847	1 812	1 807	1 810	1 794
Ireland	1 843	1 823	1 824	1 823	1 826	1 783	1 713	1 692	1 688	1 679	1 666	1 646	1 642	1 638
Italy	1 910	1 894	1 893	1 889	1 896	1 884	1 899	1 894	1 871	1 866	1 844	1 820	1 813	1 801
Japan	1 965	1 905	1 898	1 884	1 892	1 864	1 842	1 810	1 821	1 809	1 798	1 801	1 789	1 775
Korea	2 650	2 667	2 651	2 658	2 648	2 592	2 496	2 502	2 520	2 506	2 465	2 434	2 394	2 354
Mexico	1 822	1 821	1 842	1 863	1 900	1 930	1 879	1 923	1 888	1 864	1 888	1 857	1 848	1 909
Netherlands	1 402	1 373	1 362	1 344	1 389	1 382	1 370	1 350	1 368	1 368	1 338	1 354	1 357	1 367
New Zealand	1 800	1 854	1 849	1 842	1 833	1 821	1 825	1 838	1 830	1 817	1 817	1 813	1 826	1 809
Norway	1 437	1 434	1 432	1 414	1 407	1 402	1 400	1 398	1 380	1 362	1 345	1 338	1 363	1 360
Poland	..	..	..	..	..	..	..	..	1 988	1 974	1 979	1 984	1 983	1 994
Portugal	1 768	1 756	1 744	1 799	1 753	1 723	1 720	1 732	1 691	1 696	1 697	1 678	1 694	1 685
Slovak Republic	..	..	1 854	1 879	1 840	1 834	1 798	1 809	1 811	1 799	1 746	1 673	1 737	1 739
Spain	1 825	1 816	1 816	1 815	1 811	1 813	1 834	1 817	1 815	1 817	1 798	1 800	1 799	1 769
Sweden	1 565	1 582	1 621	1 626	1 635	1 639	1 638	1 647	1 625	1 603	1 580	1 563	1 585	1 587
Switzerland	1 707	1 704	1 725	1 702	1 674	1 662	1 669	1 690	1 685	1 646	1 629	1 639	1 669	1 659
United Kingdom	1 729	1 723	1 737	1 739	1 738	1 737	1 731	1 719	1 708	1 711	1 692	1 683	1 669	1 672
United States	1 826	1 835	1 842	1 849	1 840	1 850	1 852	1 853	1 841	1 819	1 814	1 806	1 808	1 804

StatLink http://dx.doi.org/10.1787/330835656764

Average hours actually worked

Hours per year per person in employment, 2005 or latest available year

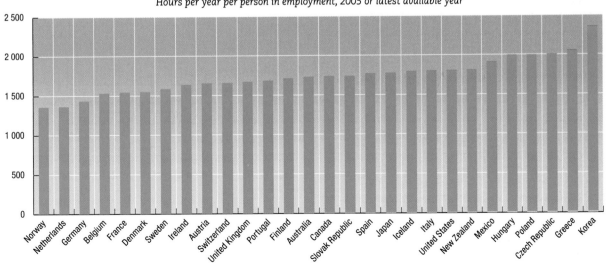

StatLink http://dx.doi.org/10.1787/075816831582

UNEMPLOYMENT RATES

Most OECD countries publish unemployment rates that are based on the numbers of persons who are registered as unemployed at government labour offices. Because they are available soon after the end of the month or quarter to which they refer, the numbers of registered unemployed are treated as the "headline" unemployment figures by many countries. However, the rules for registering at labour offices vary from country to country, so that unemployment statistics based on this source are not comparable between countries. The unemployment rates shown here use ILO Guidelines that provide common definitions of unemployment and of the labour force.

Definition

Unemployed persons are defined as those who report that they are without work, that they are available for work and that they have taken active steps to find work in the last four weeks. The ILO Guidelines specify what actions count as active steps to find work and these include answering vacancy notices, visiting factories, construction sites and other places of work, and placing advertisements in the press as well as registering with labour offices.

The unemployment rate is defined as the number of unemployed persons as a percentage of the civilian labour force, where the latter consists of the unemployed plus those in civilian employment, which are defined as persons who have worked for one hour or more in the last week.

When unemployment is high, some persons become discouraged and stop looking for work. They are then excluded from the labour force so that the unemployment rate may fall, or stop rising, even though there has been no underlying improvement in the labour market.

Comparability

All OECD countries use the ILO Guidelines for measuring unemployment, but the operational definitions used in national labour force surveys vary slightly in Iceland, Mexico and Turkey. Unemployment levels are also likely to be affected by changes in the survey design and/or the survey conduct, but unemployment rates are likely to be fairly consistent over time.

Long-term trends

In almost all countries, unemployment rates rose in the early part of the 1990s but have been falling since then. Falls have been particularly marked in Australia, Finland, Denmark and Canada.

There is no obvious pattern in the differences in unemployment rates for men and women. Unemployment rates for women are usually higher than for men, but in several countries unemployment rates for women are lower – Canada, Hungary, Korea, Sweden and the United Kingdom, for example. This is also true in Japan for the recent years. Part of the reason may be that women are more easily discouraged than men and so withdraw in larger numbers from the labour force when unemployment rises.

The charts shows unemployment rates averaged over the last decade. As regards total unemployment rates, countries can be divided into three groups: a low unemployment group with rates below 5% (Luxembourg to Japan); a middle group with unemployment rates between 5% and 8.5% (United States to Germany); and a high unemployment group with average rates of 10% and above (Italy to the Slovak Republic).

Source
- OECD (2006), *Main Economic Indicators*, OECD, Paris.

Further information
Analytical publications
- OECD (2006), *Society at a Glance: OECD Social Indicators – 2006 Edition*, OECD, Paris.

Statistical publications
- OECD (2004), *Quarterly Labour Force Statistics*, OECD, Paris.
- OECD (2006), *OECD Employment Outlook*, OECD, Paris.

Online databases
- *Employment Statistics*.

Websites
- OECD Labour Statistics Database, *www.oecd.org/statistics/labour*.
- OECD Employment Policy, *www.oecd.org/els/employment*.

Unemployment rates: total
As a percentage of civilian labour force

	1992	1993	1994	1995	1996	1997	1998	1999	2000	2001	2002	2003	2004	2005
Australia	10.5	10.6	9.5	8.2	8.2	8.3	7.7	6.9	6.3	6.8	6.4	6.1	5.5	5.1
Austria	..	4.0	3.8	3.9	4.3	4.4	4.5	3.9	3.6	3.6	4.2	4.3	4.9	5.2
Belgium	7.1	8.6	9.8	9.7	9.5	9.2	9.3	8.5	6.9	6.6	7.5	8.2	8.4	8.4
Canada	11.2	11.4	10.4	9.5	9.6	9.1	8.3	7.6	6.8	7.2	7.7	7.6	7.2	6.8
Czech Republic	..	4.4	4.3	4.1	3.9	4.8	6.4	8.6	8.7	8.0	7.3	7.8	8.3	7.9
Denmark	8.6	9.6	7.7	6.8	6.3	5.2	4.9	5.1	4.3	4.5	4.6	5.4	5.5	4.8
Finland	11.7	16.4	16.9	15.2	14.6	12.7	11.3	10.2	9.7	9.1	9.1	9.0	8.9	8.4
France	9.9	11.1	11.7	11.1	11.6	11.5	11.1	10.5	9.1	8.4	8.9	9.5	9.6	9.9
Germany	6.4	7.7	8.3	8.0	8.5	9.2	8.8	7.9	7.2	7.4	8.2	9.1	9.5	9.4
Greece	7.8	8.6	8.9	9.1	9.7	9.6	11.1	12.0	11.3	10.8	10.3	9.7	10.5	9.8
Hungary	9.9	12.1	11.0	10.4	9.6	9.0	8.4	6.9	6.4	5.7	5.8	5.9	6.1	7.2
Ireland	15.4	15.6	14.3	12.3	11.7	9.9	7.5	5.7	4.3	4.0	4.5	4.7	4.5	4.4
Italy	8.8	9.8	10.6	11.2	11.2	11.2	11.3	11.0	10.1	9.1	8.6	8.4	8.0	7.7
Japan	2.2	2.5	2.9	3.1	3.4	3.4	4.1	4.7	4.7	5.0	5.4	5.3	4.7	4.4
Korea	2.5	2.9	2.5	2.1	2.0	2.6	7.0	6.6	4.4	4.0	3.3	3.6	3.7	3.7
Luxembourg	2.1	2.6	3.2	2.9	2.9	2.7	2.7	2.4	2.3	2.1	2.8	3.7	5.1	4.5
Netherlands	5.3	6.2	6.8	6.6	6.0	4.9	3.8	3.2	2.8	2.2	2.8	3.7	4.6	4.7
New Zealand	10.4	9.5	8.1	6.3	6.1	6.6	7.4	6.8	6.0	5.3	5.2	4.6	3.9	3.7
Norway	6.5	6.6	6.0	5.4	4.8	4.0	3.2	3.2	3.4	3.6	3.9	4.5	4.4	4.6
Poland	..	14.0	14.4	13.3	12.3	10.9	10.2	13.4	16.1	18.2	19.9	19.6	19.0	17.7
Portugal	4.3	5.6	6.9	7.3	7.3	6.8	5.1	4.5	4.0	4.0	5.0	6.2	6.7	7.6
Slovak Republic	..	..	13.7	13.1	11.3	11.9	12.6	16.3	18.8	19.3	18.7	17.6	18.2	16.3
Spain	14.7	18.3	19.5	18.4	17.8	16.7	15.0	12.5	11.1	10.4	11.1	11.1	10.6	9.2
Sweden	5.6	9.0	9.4	8.8	9.6	9.9	8.2	6.7	5.6	4.9	4.9	5.6	6.4	..
Switzerland	3.0	3.9	3.9	3.5	3.9	4.2	3.6	3.0	2.7	2.6	3.2	4.2	4.4	4.5
United Kingdom	9.7	10.2	9.3	8.5	7.9	6.8	6.1	5.9	5.4	5.0	5.1	4.9	4.7	4.8
United States	7.5	6.9	6.1	5.6	5.4	4.9	4.5	4.2	4.0	4.7	5.8	6.0	5.5	5.1
EU 15 total	9.1	10.1	10.4	10.1	10.1	9.9	9.3	8.5	7.6	7.2	7.6	8.0	8.1	7.9
OECD total	7.4	7.8	7.7	7.3	7.2	6.9	6.8	6.6	6.2	6.4	6.9	7.1	6.9	6.6

StatLink ᔓᔑ http://dx.doi.org/10.1787/716703343438

Unemployment rates: total
As a percentage of civilian labour force, average 1995-2005 or latest available period

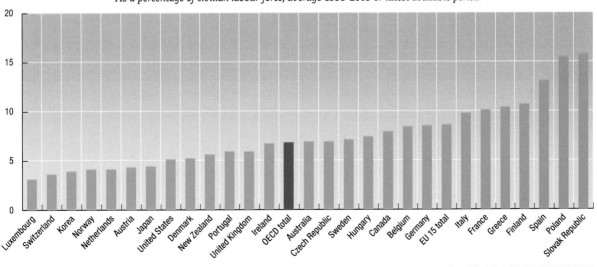

StatLink ᔓᔑ http://dx.doi.org/10.1787/173873044425

Unemployment rates: men
As a percentage of male civilian labour force

	1992	1993	1994	1995	1996	1997	1998	1999	2000	2001	2002	2003	2004	2005
Australia	11.2	11.4	9.9	8.7	8.5	8.6	8.1	7.2	6.5	7.1	6.6	5.9	5.5	5.0
Austria	..	3.1	3.0	3.1	3.6	3.6	3.8	3.3	3.1	3.2	4.0	4.0	4.5	4.9
Belgium	5.1	6.7	7.7	7.6	7.4	7.3	7.6	7.2	5.6	5.9	6.6	7.7	7.5	7.6
Canada	12.0	11.9	10.9	9.8	9.9	9.3	8.5	7.8	6.9	7.5	8.1	7.9	7.5	7.0
Czech Republic	..	3.5	3.7	3.5	3.4	4.0	5.0	7.3	7.3	6.7	6.0	6.2	7.1	6.5
Denmark	8.0	9.3	7.1	5.7	5.3	4.5	3.9	4.5	4.0	4.1	4.3	4.8	5.1	4.4
Finland	13.6	18.1	18.7	15.3	14.5	12.3	10.8	9.7	9.0	8.6	9.1	9.1	8.8	8.2
France	8.0	9.6	10.1	9.4	10.0	10.1	9.5	9.0	7.6	7.0	7.9	8.6	8.7	9.0
Germany	4.4	5.3	5.9	5.8	6.6	7.3	7.0	6.4	6.0	6.3	7.2	8.2	8.7	8.8
Greece	4.9	5.7	6.0	6.2	6.0	6.2	7.3	7.9	7.5	7.3	6.8	6.2	6.6	6.1
Hungary	11.0	13.5	12.3	11.8	10.2	9.7	9.0	7.5	7.0	6.3	6.2	6.1	6.1	7.0
Ireland	15.1	15.4	14.2	12.2	11.5	9.9	7.7	5.7	4.3	4.1	4.7	5.0	4.9	4.6
Italy	6.4	7.4	8.2	8.6	8.7	8.7	8.8	8.5	7.8	7.1	6.7	6.5	6.4	6.1
Japan	2.1	2.4	2.8	3.1	3.3	3.4	4.2	4.8	4.9	5.2	5.5	5.5	4.9	4.6
Korea	2.8	3.3	2.8	2.3	2.4	2.8	7.8	7.4	5.0	4.5	3.7	3.8	3.9	4.0
Luxembourg	1.7	2.2	2.6	2.0	2.2	2.0	1.9	1.8	1.8	1.7	2.1	3.0	3.7	3.5
Netherlands	4.1	5.4	6.0	5.5	4.7	3.7	3.0	2.3	2.3	1.8	2.5	3.5	4.3	4.4
New Zealand	11.0	10.1	8.5	6.2	6.1	6.6	7.5	7.0	6.1	5.3	5.0	4.3	3.5	3.4
Norway	7.2	7.3	6.6	5.7	4.7	3.9	3.1	3.4	3.6	3.7	4.1	4.9	4.8	4.8
Poland	..	12.7	13.1	12.1	11.0	9.1	8.5	11.8	14.4	16.9	19.1	19.0	18.2	16.6
Portugal	3.6	4.8	6.1	6.5	6.4	6.1	4.1	4.0	3.2	3.2	4.1	5.4	5.9	6.6
Slovak Republic	..	..	13.3	12.6	10.2	11.1	12.2	16.3	18.9	19.8	18.6	17.4	17.4	15.5
Spain	11.6	15.4	16.2	14.8	14.3	13.1	11.2	9.0	7.9	7.5	8.1	8.2	8.0	7.0
Sweden	6.7	10.6	10.8	9.7	10.2	10.3	8.3	6.6	5.9	5.2	5.3	6.0	6.6	..
Switzerland	2.4	3.3	3.4	3.0	3.6	4.3	3.2	2.6	2.2	2.0	3.0	3.9	4.0	3.9
United Kingdom	11.5	12.1	11.0	9.9	9.2	7.6	6.8	6.5	5.8	5.5	5.6	5.5	5.0	5.1
United States	7.9	7.2	6.2	5.6	5.4	4.9	4.4	4.1	3.9	4.8	5.9	6.3	5.6	5.1
EU 15 total	7.4	8.8	9.2	8.7	8.8	8.4	7.8	7.1	6.4	6.1	6.6	7.0	7.1	7.0
OECD total	..	..	7.2	6.7	6.6	6.3	6.3	6.1	5.7	6.0	6.6	6.8	6.6	6.2

StatLink ᴍᴤ http://dx.doi.org/10.1787/427421482475

Unemployment rates: men
As a percentage of male civilian labour force, average 1995-2005 or latest available period

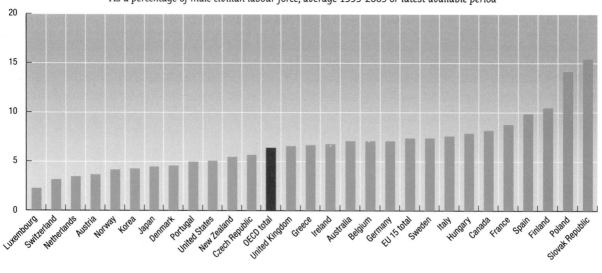

StatLink ᴍᴤ http://dx.doi.org/10.1787/635031340604

OECD FACTBOOK 2007 – ISBN 978-92-64-02946-0 – © OECD 2007

Unemployment rates: women
As a percentage of female civilian labour force

	1992	1993	1994	1995	1996	1997	1998	1999	2000	2001	2002	2003	2004	2005
Australia	9.5	9.8	9.0	7.9	7.9	8.1	7.5	6.8	6.2	6.6	6.2	6.2	5.7	5.3
Austria	..	5.1	5.0	5.0	5.3	5.4	5.4	4.7	4.3	4.2	4.5	4.7	5.3	5.5
Belgium	10.0	11.5	12.7	12.7	12.5	11.9	11.6	10.2	8.5	7.5	8.7	8.9	9.5	9.5
Canada	10.2	10.7	9.8	9.1	9.3	8.9	8.0	7.3	6.7	6.9	7.1	7.2	6.9	6.5
Czech Republic	..	5.4	5.2	4.8	4.7	5.9		8.0	10.3	10.4	9.7	9.0	9.9	9.9	9.8
Denmark	9.2	9.8	8.5	8.1	7.5	6.2	6.0	5.8	4.8	5.0	5.0	6.1	6.0	5.3
Finland	9.5	14.5	14.9	15.0	14.7	13.2	11.9	10.7	10.5	9.6	9.1	8.9	9.0	8.6
France	12.2	13.0	13.6	13.2	13.4	13.3	12.9	12.2	10.9	10.0	10.0	10.5	10.5	10.9
Germany	8.9	10.9	11.4	10.9	11.0	11.6	11.1	9.9	8.7	8.9	9.4	10.1	10.5	10.3
Greece	12.9	13.6	13.7	13.8	15.4	14.8	17.1	18.1	17.2	16.2	15.6	15.0	16.2	15.3
Hungary	8.7	10.4		9.4	8.7		8.8	8.1	7.7	6.3	5.6	5.0	5.4	5.6	6.1	7.4
Ireland	16.0	16.0	14.6	12.5	11.8	9.9	7.3	5.6	4.2	3.8	4.1	4.3	4.1	4.0
Italy	12.9	13.9	14.6	15.3	15.2	15.3	15.4	14.8	13.6	12.2	11.5	11.3	10.5	10.1
Japan	2.2	2.6	3.0	3.2	3.4	3.4	4.0	4.5	4.5	4.7	5.1	4.9	4.4	4.2
Korea	2.1	2.3	2.0	1.7	1.6	2.3	5.7	5.3		3.6	3.3	2.7	3.3	3.4	3.4
Luxembourg	2.8	3.3	4.1	4.3	4.2	3.9	4.0	3.3	3.1	2.7	3.8	4.7	7.0	5.9
Netherlands	7.2	7.4	7.9	8.1	7.7	6.6	5.0	4.4	3.6	2.8	3.1	3.9	4.8	5.1
New Zealand	9.5	8.8	7.6	6.3	6.1	6.6	7.4	6.5	5.8	5.3	5.3	5.0	4.4	4.0
Norway	5.7	5.7	5.3	5.1	4.8	4.2	3.3	3.1	3.2	3.4	3.6	4.0	4.0	4.4
Poland	..	15.6	16.0	14.7	13.9		13.0	12.2	15.3	18.1	19.8	20.9	20.4	19.9	19.1
Portugal	5.2	6.7	7.9	8.2	8.2	7.6		6.3	5.2	4.9	5.0	6.0	7.2	7.6	8.6
Slovak Republic	..	..	14.1	13.8	12.7	12.8	13.1		16.4	18.6	18.7	18.7	17.8	19.2	17.2
Spain	20.5	23.5	25.4	24.6	23.7	22.6	21.1	18.1	16.0	14.8	15.7	15.3	14.4	12.2
Sweden	4.4	7.3	7.8	7.9	9.0	9.5	8.0	6.8	5.3	4.5	4.6	5.2	6.1	..
Switzerland	3.7	4.7	4.5	4.1	4.2	4.1	4.0	3.5	3.2	3.4	3.4	4.5	4.9	5.1
United Kingdom	7.5	7.8	7.2	6.8	6.3	5.8	5.3	5.1	4.8	4.4	4.5	4.3	4.2	4.3
United States	7.0	6.6		6.0	5.6	5.4	5.0	4.6	4.3		4.1	4.7	5.6	5.7	5.4	5.1
EU 15 total	10.4	11.8	12.2	12.0	11.9	11.8	11.2	10.3	9.2	8.7	8.9	9.2	9.2	9.0
OECD total	..	..	8.3	8.0		7.9		7.7		7.6		7.3		6.8	6.9	7.4	7.5	7.3	7.1

StatLink http://dx.doi.org/10.1787/170588788754

Unemployment rates: women
As a percentage of female civilian labour force, average 1995-2005 or latest available period

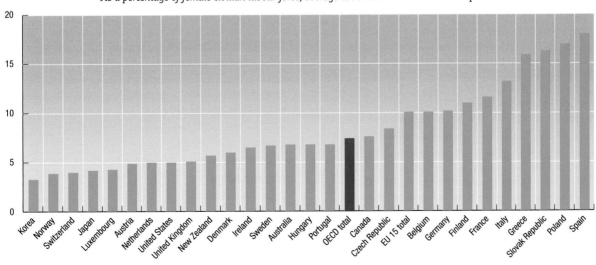

StatLink http://dx.doi.org/10.1787/626405585145

LONG-TERM UNEMPLOYMENT

Long-term unemployment is here measured as those who have been unemployed for 12 months or more as a percentage of the total number of persons unemployed. Clearly, long-term unemployment is of particular concern to policy makers. Quite apart from the mental stress caused to the unemployed and their families, high rates of long-term unemployment indicate that labour markets are operating inefficiently and, in countries which pay generous unemployment benefits, the existence of long-term unemployment is a significant burden on government finances.

Definition

Long-term unemployment is conventionally defined either as those unemployed for 6 months or more or, as here, those unemployed for 12 months or more.

Unemployment is defined in most OECD countries according to the ILO Guidelines. Unemployment is usually measured by household labour force surveys and the unemployed are defined as those persons who report that they have worked in gainful employment for less than one hour in the previous week, who are available for work and who have taken actions to seek employment in the previous four weeks. The ILO Guidelines specify the kinds of actions that count as seeking work.

Comparability

All OECD countries use the ILO Guidelines for measuring unemployment, but the operational definitions used in national labour force surveys vary slightly in Iceland and Turkey. Unemployment levels are also likely to be affected by changes in the survey design and/or the survey conduct, but unemployment rates are likely to be fairly consistent over time.

In comparing rates of long-term unemployment, it is important to bear in mind differences in institutional arrangements between countries. Rates of long-term unemployment will generally be higher in countries where unemployment benefits are relatively generous and are available for long periods of unemployment. In countries where the benefits are low and of limited duration, unemployed persons will more quickly lower their salary expectations or consider taking jobs that are in other ways less attractive than those which they formerly held.

Long-term trends

In 2005, rates of long-term unemployment varied from 10% or less in Canada, Korea, Mexico, New Zealand and Norway to 50% or more in the Czech Republic, Germany, Greece, Italy, Poland and the Slovak Republic. Lower rates of long-term unemployment are generally found in countries that have enjoyed relatively high rates of economic growth in recent years. There appears to be a two-way causal relationship here – on the one hand, jobs are easier to find in a fast growing economy and, on the other, economies may grow faster by making unemployment an unattractive proposition.

Over the period shown in the table, long-term unemployment rates have been relatively stable for the OECD as a whole, but there have been some sharp rises in several countries and equally sharp falls in others. Rates of long-term unemployment have more than doubled in the Czech Republic, Hungary, and Japan. On the other hand, since 1992, the share of long-term unemployed has more than halved in Korea, Norway and New Zealand.

Source
- OECD (2006), *Labour Force Statistics*, OECD, Paris.

Further information

Analytical publications
- OECD (2002), "The Ins and Outs of Long-term Unemployment", *OECD Employment Outlook*, Chapter 4, OECD, Paris, pp. 187-243.
- OECD (2006), *OECD Employment Outlook*, OECD, Paris.

Statistical publications
- OECD (2004), *Quarterly Labour Force Statistics*, OECD, Paris.

Online databases
- *Employment Statistics.*

Websites
- OECD Labour Statistics Database, *www.oecd.org/statistics/labour.*
- OECD Employment Outlook, *www.oecd.org/els/employmentoutlook.*

Long-term unemployment

Persons unemployed for 12 months or more as a percentage of total unemployed

	1992	1993	1994	1995	1996	1997	1998	1999	2000	2001	2002	2003	2004	2005
Australia	33.4	36.7	36.1	32.0	28.5	31.2	29.7	28.3	25.5	22.0	22.3	21.3	20.5	17.7
Austria	..	..	18.4	29.1	24.9	27.5	30.3	29.2	25.8	23.3	19.2	24.5	27.6	25.3
Belgium	59.1	53.0	58.3	62.4	61.3	60.5	61.7	60.5	56.3	51.7	49.6	46.3	49.6	51.6
Canada	13.5	16.5	17.9	16.8	16.8	16.1	13.8	11.7	11.2	9.5	9.6	10.0	9.5	9.6
Czech Republic	..	18.5	22.3	31.2	31.3	30.5	31.2	37.1	48.8	52.7	50.7	49.9	51.8	53.6
Denmark	27.0	25.2	32.1	27.9	26.5	27.2	26.9	20.5	20.0	22.2	19.7	19.9	22.6	25.9
Finland	..	30.6	..	37.6	34.5	29.8	27.5	29.6	29.0	26.2	24.4	24.7	23.4	24.9
France	36.2	34.2	38.5	42.5	39.6	41.4	44.2	40.4	42.6	37.6	33.8	42.9	41.6	42.5
Germany	33.5	40.3	44.3	48.7	47.8	50.1	52.6	51.7	51.5	50.4	47.9	50.0	51.8	54.0
Greece	49.6	50.9	50.5	51.4	56.7	55.7	54.9	55.3	56.4	52.8	52.7	56.3	54.8	53.7
Hungary	20.4	33.5	41.3	50.6	54.4	51.3	49.8	49.5	49.0	46.6	44.8	42.2	45.1	46.1
Iceland	6.8	12.2	15.1	16.8	19.8	16.3	16.1	11.7	11.8	12.5	11.1	8.1	11.2	..
Ireland	58.8	59.1	64.3	61.6	59.5	57.0	..	55.3	..	33.1	29.4	35.5	34.3	34.3
Italy	58.2	57.7	61.5	63.6	65.6	66.3	59.6	61.4	61.3	63.4	59.2	58.2	49.7	52.2
Japan	15.9	15.6	17.5	18.1	19.3	21.8	20.3	22.4	25.5	26.6	30.8	33.5	33.7	33.3
Korea	3.8	2.6	5.4	4.4	3.8	2.6	1.5	3.8	2.3	2.3	2.5	0.6	1.1	0.8
Luxembourg	14.3	31.6	29.6	23.2	27.6	34.6	31.3	32.3	22.4	28.4	27.4	24.9	20.8	26.3
Mexico	..	..	..	1.3	2.2	1.4	0.8	1.7	1.1	1.1	0.9	1.0	1.1	2.4
Netherlands	43.9	52.4	49.4	46.8	50.0	49.1	47.9	43.5	..	..	26.7	29.2	32.5	40.1
New Zealand	31.7	33.3	32.7	25.7	20.8	19.3	19.3	20.9	19.3	16.7	14.5	13.5	11.7	9.4
Norway	23.5	27.2	28.8	24.2	14.2	12.4	8.3	7.1	5.3	5.5	6.4	6.4	9.2	9.5
Poland	34.7	39.1	40.4	40.0	39.0	38.0	37.4	34.8	37.9	43.1	48.4	49.7	47.9	52.2
Portugal	30.9	43.5	43.4	50.9	53.1	55.6	44.7	41.2	42.9	38.1	35.5	32.8	43.2	48.6
Slovak Republic	..	..	42.6	54.1	52.6	51.6	51.3	47.7	54.6	53.7	59.8	61.1	60.6	68.1
Spain	47.4	50.1	56.2	57.1	55.9	55.7	54.3	51.2	47.6	44.0	40.2	39.8	37.7	32.6
Sweden	13.5	15.8	25.7	27.8	30.1	33.4	33.5	30.1	26.4	22.3	21.0	17.8	18.9	..
Switzerland	20.0	20.3	29.0	33.6	25.6	28.2	34.9	39.6	29.0	29.9	21.8	26.3	33.5	38.8
Turkey	44.2	46.8	45.9	36.4	44.3	41.6	40.3	28.2	21.1	21.3	29.4	24.4	39.2	39.6
United Kingdom	35.4	42.5	45.4	43.6	39.8	38.6	32.7	29.6	28.0	27.8	22.9	22.8	21.4	22.4
United States	11.1	11.5	12.2	9.7	9.5	8.7	8.0	6.8	6.0	6.1	8.5	11.8	12.7	11.8
EU 15 total	41.7	44.1	48.4	50.3	49.4	50.2	49.2	47.5	46.9	45.3	41.5	43.4	42.4	43.8
OECD total	28.8	32.0	35.5	34.2	34.4	35.1	33.2	31.8	31.5	29.6	29.6	30.9	31.9	32.8

StatLink http://dx.doi.org/10.1787/465837743540

Long-term unemployment

Persons unemployed for 12 months or more as a percentage of total unemployed, 2005 or latest available year

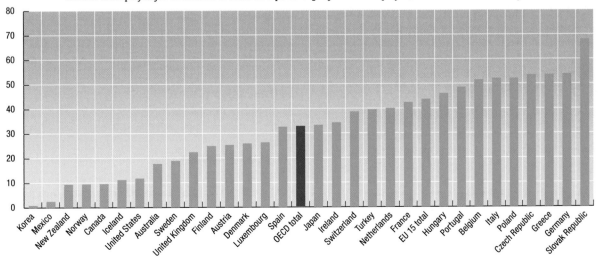

StatLink http://dx.doi.org/10.1787/037445021326

REGIONAL UNEMPLOYMENT

Unemployment rates vary significantly among OECD countries but large international differences hide even larger differences among regions. In 2003, regional differences in unemployment rates were above 10 percentage points in more than one third of OECD countries.

Definition

Unemployed persons are defined as those who report that they are without work, that they are available for work and that they have taken active steps to find work in the last four weeks. The ILO Guidelines specify what actions count as active steps to find work and these include answering vacancy notices, visiting factories, construction sites and other places of work, and placing advertisements in the press as well as registering with labour offices.

The unemployment rate is defined as the number of unemployed persons as a percentage of the labour force, where the latter consists of unemployed and employed persons.

When unemployment is high, some persons become discouraged and stop looking for work. They are then excluded from the labour force so that the unemployment rate may fall, or stop rising, even though there has been no underlying improvement in the labour market.

The Gini index offers a more precise picture of regional disparities. It looks not only at the regions with the highest and the lowest GDP per capita but also at the differences among all regions. The index ranges between 0 and 1: the higher its value, the larger the regional disparities. Regional disparities tend to be underestimated when the size of regions is large.

Comparability

As for the other regional statistics, the comparability of unemployment rates is affected by differences in the meaning of the word region (see Regional population) and the different geography of rural and urban communities (see Regional GDP), both within and among countries.

Overview

In 2003, Italy was the country with the largest disparity in unemployment rates with a Gini index equal to 0.43. According to this index, regional disparities were also large in Iceland, Canada, Belgium, Germany and Spain. In most other countries, regional disparities were close to the OECD average (0.18). Only in the Netherlands Japan and Ireland did unemployment rates reflect a more even regional pattern.

The percentages of the labour force located in regions where unemployment rates are above the national average reveal the share of the national workforce that is affected by regional disparities in unemployment rates. In 2003, 49% of the OECD labour force was based in regions with unemployment rates above the national rate.

Significant international differences in unemployment rates hide even larger differences among regions. In Italy, Poland, Germany and Spain differences in regional unemployment rates were greater than 20 percentage points. In Canada, the Slovak Republic, Finland, Turkey, Belgium and the Czech Republic these differences were smaller but still large (above 10 percentage points). Only in Mexico, the Netherlands, Korea, and Ireland, did unemployment rates reflect a more even regional pattern.

Source

• OECD (2007), OECD *Regions at a Glance*, OECD, Paris.

Further information

Analytical publications

• OECD (2001), OECD *Territorial Outlook, 2001 Edition*, OECD, Paris.

• OECD (2003), *Geographic Concentration and Territorial Disparity in OECD Countries*, OECD, Paris.

• OECD (2005), *Local Governance and the Drivers of Growth*, OECD, Paris.

• Spiezia, V. (2003), *OECD Statistics Brief*, OECD, Paris.

Websites

• OECD Regional Database, *www.oecd.org/gov/ territorialindicators*.

Unemployment rate
As a percentage of the labour force, 2003 or latest available year

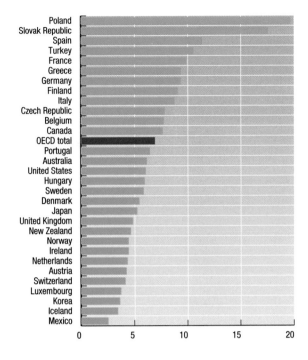

Percentage of the labour force living in regions with an unemployment rate above the national average
2003 or latest available year

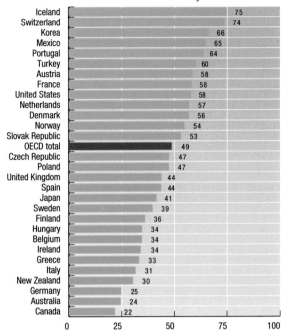

Variation of regional unemployment rates
Minimum and maximum regional rates, as a percentage of national rates, 2003 or latest available year

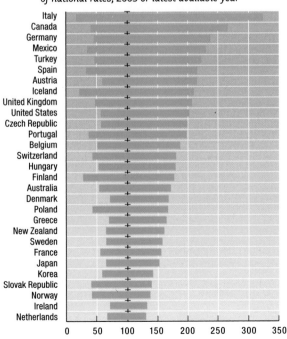

Gini Index of Regional disparities in unemployment rates
2003 or latest available year

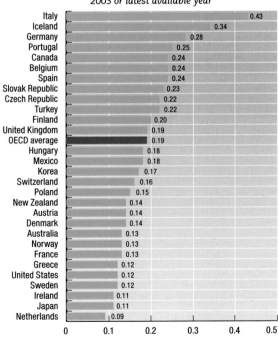

StatLink http://dx.doi.org/10.1787/853355202711

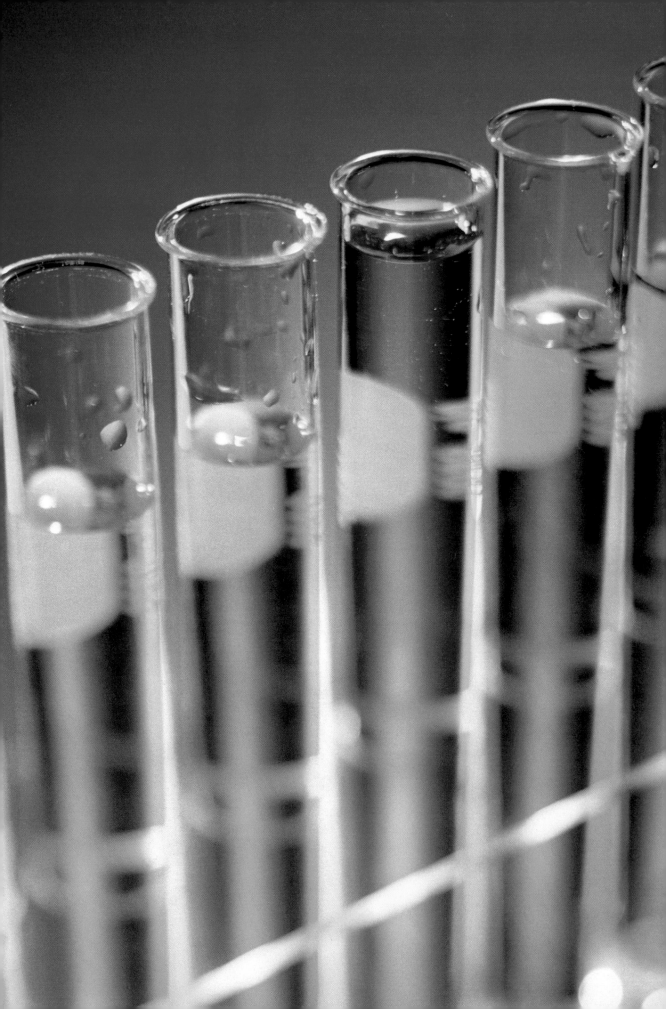

SCIENCE AND TECHNOLOGY

RESEARCH AND DEVELOPMENT (R&D)
EXPENDITURE ON R&D
RESEARCHERS
PATENTS

ICT
SIZE OF THE ICT SECTOR
INVESTMENT IN ICT
COMPUTER AND INTERNET ACCESS BY HOUSEHOLDS

COMMUNICATIONS
EXPORTS OF INFORMATION AND COMMUNICATIONS EQUIPMENT
TELEPHONE ACCESS

EXPENDITURE ON R&D

Expenditure on research and development (R&D) is a key indicator of government and private sector efforts to obtain competitive advantage in science and technology. In 2004, research and development amounted to 2.3% of GDP for the OECD as a whole.

Definition

Research and development (R&D) comprise creative work undertaken on a systematic basis in order to increase the stock of knowledge, including knowledge of man, culture and society, and the use of this stock of knowledge to devise new applications. R&D is a term covering three activities: basic research, applied research, and experimental development. *Basic research* is experimental or theoretical work undertaken primarily to acquire new knowledge of the underlying foundation of phenomena and observable facts, without any particular application or use in view. *Applied research* is also original investigation undertaken in order to acquire new knowledge. It is, however, directed primarily towards a specific practical aim or objective. *Experimental development* is systematic work, drawing on existing knowledge gained from research and/or practical experience, that is directed to producing new materials, products or devices, to installing new processes, systems and services, or to improving substantially those already produced or installed.

The main aggregate used for international comparisons is gross domestic expenditure on R&D (GERD). This consists of the total expenditure (current and capital) on R&D by all resident companies, research institutes, university and government laboratories, etc. It excludes R&D expenditures financed by domestic firms but performed abroad.

Comparability

The R&D data shown here have been compiled according to the guidelines of the *Frascati Manual*. It should, however, be noted that over the period shown, several countries have improved the coverage of their surveys of R&D activities in the services sector (Japan, Netherlands, Norway and United States) and in higher education (Finland, Greece, Japan, Netherlands, Spain and the United States). Other countries, including especially Italy, Japan and Sweden, have worked to improve the international comparability of their data. Some of the changes shown in the table reflect these methodological improvements as well as the underlying changes in R&D expenditures.

For Korea, social sciences and humanities are excluded from the R&D data. For the United States, capital expenditure is not covered.

Data for Brazil and India are not completely according to *Frascati Manual* guidelines, and were compiled from national sources. Data for Brazil, India and South Africa are underestimated, as are the data for China before 2000.

Long-term trends

Since 2000, R&D expenditure relative to GDP (R&D intensity) has increased in Japan, and it has decreased slightly in the United States.

In 2003 and 2004, Sweden, Finland, and Japan were the only three OECD countries in which the R&D-to-GDP ratio exceeded 3%, well above the OECD average of 2.3%. Since the mid-1990s, R&D expenditure (in real terms) has been growing the fastest in Iceland and Turkey, both with average annual growth rates above 10%.

R&D expenditure for China has been growing even faster than GDP, resulting in a rapidly increasing R&D intensity, growing from 0.9% in 2000 to 1.3% in 2005.

Source
• OECD (2006), *Main Science and Technology Indicators*, OECD, Paris.

Further information
Analytical publications
• OECD (2005), *OECD Science, Technology and Industry Scoreboard*, OECD, Paris.
• OECD (2006), *OECD Science, Technology and Industry Outlook 2006*, OECD, Paris.

Statistical publications
• OECD (2006), *OECD Science, Technology and R&D Statistics on CD-ROM*, OECD, Paris.

Methodological publications
• OECD (2003), *Frascati Manual 2002: Proposed Standard Practice for Surveys on Research and Experimental Development*, OECD, Paris.

Online databases
• STAN: *OECD Structural Analysis Statistics – online database*, ANBERD: R&D Expenditure in Industry.

Websites
• OECD Science, Technology and Industry, *www.oecd.org/sti*.

Gross domestic expenditure on R&D
As a percentage of GDP

	1992	1993	1994	1995	1996	1997	1998	1999	2000	2001	2002	2003	2004	2005
Australia	1.48	..	1.53	..	1.61	..	1.47	..	1.51	..	1.64	..	..	..
Austria	1.42	1.44	1.51	1.54	1.59	1.69	1.77	1.88	1.91	2.03	2.12	2.20	2.24	2.35
Belgium	..	1.66	1.65	1.67	1.77	1.83	1.86	1.94	1.97	2.08	1.94	1.89	1.90	..
Canada	1.64	1.70	1.76	1.72	1.68	1.68	1.79	1.82	1.94	2.13	2.06	2.00	1.99	1.96
Czech Republic	1.62	1.14	1.03	0.95	0.98	1.09	1.17	1.16	1.23	1.22	1.22	1.26	1.27	..
Denmark	1.64	1.72	..	1.82	1.84	1.92	2.04	2.18	..	2.39	2.51	2.56	2.48	..
Finland	2.11	2.14	2.26	2.26	2.52	2.69	2.86	3.21	3.38	3.38	3.43	3.48	3.51	..
France	2.33	2.37	2.32	2.29	2.27	2.19	2.14	2.16	2.15	2.20	2.23	2.18	2.16	..
Germany	2.35	2.28	2.18	2.19	2.19	2.24	2.27	2.40	2.45	2.46	2.49	2.52	2.49	..
Greece	..	0.47	..	0.49	..	0.51	..	0.67	..	0.65	..	0.62	..	..
Hungary	1.04	0.96	0.88	0.73	0.65	0.72	0.68	0.68	0.79	0.94	1.01	0.94	0.89	..
Iceland	1.35	1.35	1.40	1.56	..	1.87	2.05	2.36	2.73	3.04	3.08	2.92	..	..
Ireland	1.02	1.16	1.25	1.26	1.30	1.27	1.23	1.18	1.13	1.10	1.10	1.16	1.20	..
Italy	1.15	1.10	1.02	0.97	0.99	1.03	1.05	1.02	1.05	1.09	1.13	1.11	..	..
Japan	2.71	2.63	2.58	2.69	2.78	2.84	2.95	2.96	2.99	3.07	3.12	3.15	3.13	..
Korea	1.94	2.12	2.32	2.37	2.42	2.48	2.34	2.25	2.39	2.59	2.53	2.63	2.85	..
Luxembourg	..	..	..	..	..	..	..	..	1.71	..	..	1.78	1.75	..
Mexico	..	0.22	0.29	0.31	0.31	0.34	0.38	0.43	0.37	0.39	0.44	0.43	..	..
Netherlands	1.83	1.85	1.89	1.91	1.93	1.96	1.86	1.94	1.82	1.80	1.72	1.76	1.78	..
New Zealand	1.00	1.01	..	0.95	..	1.09	..	0.99	..	1.13	..	1.14	..	..
Norway	..	1.72	..	1.70	..	1.64	..	1.65	..	1.60	1.67	1.73	1.61	..
Poland	0.78	0.78	0.71	0.65	0.67	0.67	0.68	0.70	0.66	0.64	0.58	0.56	0.58	..
Portugal	0.61	0.61	0.59	0.57	0.60	0.62	0.69	0.75	0.80	0.85	0.80	0.78	..	..
Slovak Republic	1.78	1.38	0.90	0.93	0.92	1.09	0.79	0.66	0.65	0.64	0.58	0.58	0.53	..
Spain	0.86	0.86	0.79	0.79	0.81	0.80	0.87	0.86	0.91	0.92	0.99	1.05	1.07	..
Sweden	..	3.15	..	3.32	..	3.51	..	3.62	..	4.25	..	3.95	..	..
Switzerland	2.59	..	..	..	2.67	..	..	..	2.57	..	..	..	2.94	..
Turkey	0.49	0.44	0.36	0.38	0.45	0.49	0.50	0.63	0.64	0.72	0.66	..	..	..
United Kingdom	2.03	2.06	2.01	1.95	1.88	1.81	1.80	1.87	1.86	1.87	1.89	1.88	..	..
United States	2.64	2.52	2.42	2.51	2.55	2.58	2.62	2.66	2.74	2.76	2.65	2.68	2.68	..
EU 15 total	1.83	1.83	1.78	1.77	1.77	1.77	1.78	1.84	1.86	1.89	1.90	1.90	..	..
OECD total	2.16	2.11	2.06	2.07	2.10	2.12	2.15	2.19	2.23	2.27	2.24	2.25	2.26	..
Brazil	..	..	..	..	..	..	..	..	1.01	1.05	1.00	0.97	0.91	..
China	0.74	0.70	0.64	0.57	0.57	0.64	0.65	0.76	0.90	0.95	1.07	1.13	1.23	1.34
India	..	0.71	0.65	0.63	0.65	0.70	0.72	0.74	0.77	0.75	0.73	0.71	0.69	..
Russian Federation	0.74	0.77	0.84	0.85	0.97	1.04	0.95	1.00	1.05	1.18	1.25	1.28	1.16	..
South Africa	..	0.61	..	..	..	0.60	..	..	..	0.73	..	0.80	0.87	..

StatLink http://dx.doi.org/10.1787/127085150828

Gross domestic expenditure on R&D
As a percentage of GDP, 2005 or latest available year

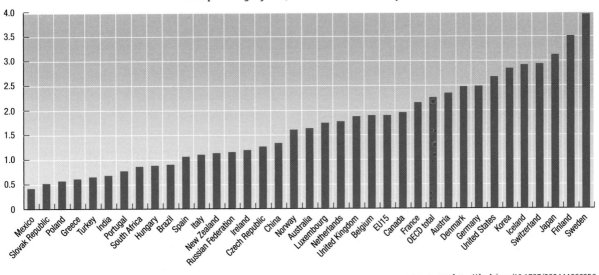

StatLink http://dx.doi.org/10.1787/083444666356

RESEARCHERS

Researchers are the central element of the research and development system. In 2002, approximately 3.6 million persons in the OECD area were employed in research and development and approximately two-thirds of these were engaged in the business sector.

Definition

Researchers are defined as professionals engaged in the conception and creation of new knowledge, products, processes, methods and systems as well as those who are directly involved in the management of projects. They include researchers working in both civil and military research in government, universities, research institutes as well as in the business sector.

Comparability

The number of researchers is expressed in full-time equivalent (FTE) on R&D (i.e. a person working half-time on R&D is counted as 0.5 person-year) and includes staff engaged in R&D during the course of one year. The data have been compiled on the basis of the methodology of the *Frascati Manual*, but comparability over time is affected to some extent by improvements in the coverage of national R&D surveys and efforts by countries to improve the international comparability of their data.

For the United States, the total researchers figure for 2000-2002 is an OECD estimate, and data since 1985 exclude military personnel.

Data for Brazil and India are not completely according to *Frascati Manual* guidelines, and were compiled from national sources. Data for Brazil and South Africa are underestimated, as are the data for China before 2000.

Long-term trends

In 2002, there were about 6.9 researchers per thousand employees in the OECD area, compared with 5.8 per thousand in 1992. The number of researchers has steadily increased over the last two decades. Among the major OECD regions, Japan has the highest number of researchers relative to total employment, followed by the United States and the European Union.

Finland, Japan, New Zealand and Sweden have the highest number of research workers per thousand persons employed. Rates are also high in the United States, Denmark and Norway. Research workers per thousand employees are low in Mexico, Turkey, Italy and the Czech Republic.

Among the major non-member countries, growth has been steady in China, although, at 1.2 in 2004, it still remains well below the OECD average. The rate for the Russian Federation has been falling since 1994, but was still above 7 researchers per thousand employed in 2004.

Source
● OECD (2006), *Main Science and Technology Indicators*, OECD, Paris.

Further information
Analytical publications
● OECD (2005), *OECD Science, Technology and Industry Scoreboard*, OECD, Paris.

Statistical publications
● OECD (2006), *OECD Science, Technology and R&D Statistics on CD-ROM*, OECD, Paris.

Methodological publications
● OECD (2003), *Frascati Manual 2002: Proposed Standard Practice for Surveys on Research and Experimental Development*, OECD, Paris.

Websites
● OECD Measuring Science and Technology, *www.oecd.org/sti/measuring-scitech*.
● OECD Science, Technology and Industry, *www.oecd.org/sti*.
● OECD Science, Technology and Industry Scoreboard, *www.sourceoecd.org/scoreboard*.

Researchers
Per thousand employed, full-time equivalent

	1991	1992	1993	1994	1995	1996	1997	1998	1999	2000	2001	2002	2003	2004
Australia	..	6.8	..	7.0	..	7.3	..	7.3	..	7.3	..	7.8	..	..
Austria	..	..	3.3	..	..	..	..	4.7	..	..	5.8	..	..	..
Belgium	4.7	..	5.5	5.9	6.0	6.5	6.7	7.0	7.4	7.5	7.8	7.4	7.5	7.7
Canada	5.1	5.5	5.7	6.4	6.4	6.6	6.6	6.6	6.7	7.2	7.5	7.2	..	..
Czech Republic	..	..	..	..	2.3	2.5	2.4	2.5	2.8	2.9	3.1	3.1	3.3	3.4
Denmark	4.6	5.0	5.3	..	6.1	6.3	6.5	..	6.9	..	7.0	9.2	9.1	9.5
Finland	6.0	..	7.4	..	8.2	..	12.3	13.9	14.5	15.1	15.8	16.4	17.7	17.3
France	5.7	6.2	6.5	6.6	6.7	6.8	6.8	6.7	6.8	7.1	7.2	7.5	7.8	..
Germany	6.3	..	..	..	6.2	6.1	6.3	6.3	6.6	6.6	6.7	6.8	7.0	..
Greece	1.7	..	2.2	..	2.5	..	2.9	..	3.7	..	3.7	..	3.9	..
Hungary	3.2	3.0	3.1	3.1	2.9	2.9	3.1	3.2	3.3	3.8	3.8	3.9	3.9	3.8
Ireland	4.4	4.8	4.1	4.3	4.5	4.8	5.0	5.1	4.9	5.0	5.1	5.3	5.5	5.8
Italy	3.3	3.3	3.4	3.5	3.5	3.5	3.0	2.9	2.9	2.9	2.9	3.0	2.9	..
Japan	7.5	7.7	7.9	8.1	8.3	9.2	9.2	9.7	9.9	9.7	10.2	9.9	10.4	10.4
Korea	..	..	..	..	4.9	4.8	4.8	4.7	4.9	5.1	6.3	6.4	6.8	6.9
Luxembourg	..	..	..	..	..	..	..	..	..	6.2	..	..	6.6	7.1
Mexico	..	..	0.4	0.5	0.6	0.6	0.6	0.5	0.6	..	..	..	0.8	..
Netherlands	..	..	4.6	4.9	4.9	4.9	5.1	5.1	5.1	5.2	5.5	4.6	4.5	..
New Zealand	4.0	5.1	5.3	..	4.7	..	6.2	..	6.2	..	9.1	..	10.2	..
Norway	6.6	..	7.2	..	7.5	..	7.9	..	8.0	..	8.7	..	9.2	..
Poland	..	..	..	3.0	3.2	3.3	3.4	3.4	3.6	3.5	3.7	3.8	4.5	4.6
Portugal	1.9	2.1	2.2	2.3	2.6	2.8	3.0	3.1	3.3	3.4	3.5	3.8	4.0	..
Slovak Republic	..	..	..	4.9	4.6	4.6	4.7	4.8	4.5	4.9	4.7	4.5	4.7	5.2
Spain	2.9	3.0	3.2	3.6	3.5	3.7	3.8	4.0	3.9	4.7	4.7	4.8	5.2	5.5
Sweden	5.9	..	7.2	..	8.2	..	9.2	..	9.6	..	10.6	..	11.0	..
Switzerland	..	4.4	..	..	..	5.6	..	..	..	6.4	..	..	..	6.1
Turkey	0.6	0.7	0.7	0.7	0.8	0.9	0.9	0.9	0.9	1.1	1.1	1.1	..	..
United Kingdom	4.6	4.7	4.8	4.9	5.3	5.2	5.1	5.5	..	..	..	..	..	..
United States	8.1	..	8.2	..	8.1	..	8.8	..	9.3	9.3	9.5	9.6	..	..
EU 15 total	4.7	4.8	5.0	..	5.2	5.3	5.3	5.5	5.6	5.7	5.9	6.0	6.1	..
OECD total	5.7	5.8	5.9	6.0	5.9	6.1	6.2	6.4	6.5	6.6	6.8	6.9	..	..
Brazil	..	..	..	..	..	..	..	..	..	0.8	0.9	0.9	1.0	1.0
China	0.7	0.7	0.7	0.8	0.8	0.8	0.8	0.7	0.7	1.0	1.0	1.1	1.2	1.2
Russian Federation	..	..	..	9.1	9.2	8.5	8.2	7.7	7.8	7.8	7.8	7.5	7.4	7.1
South Africa	..	..	..	..	..	..	..	..	..	..	1.2	..	1.3	1.6

StatLink http://dx.doi.org/10.1787/027265544466

Researchers
Per thousand employed, full-time equivalent, 2004 or latest available year

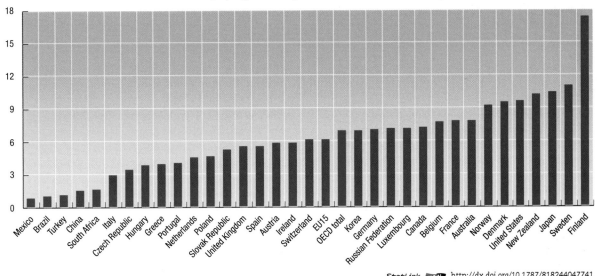

StatLink http://dx.doi.org/10.1787/818244047741

PATENTS

Patent-based indicators provide a measure of the output of a country's R&D, i.e. its inventions. The methodology used for counting patents can influence the results. Simple counts of patents filed at a national patent office are affected by various kinds of limitations, such as weak international comparability (home advantage for patent applications) and highly heterogeneous patent values. The OECD has developed *triadic patent families*, which are designed to capture all important inventions only and to be internationally comparable.

Definition

A patent family is defined as a set of patents taken in various countries (i.e. patent offices) to protect the same invention. Triadic patent families are a set of patents taken at all three of these major patent offices – the European Patent Office (EPO), the Japan Patent Office (JPO) and the United States Patent and Trademark Office (USPTO).

Triadic patent family counts are attributed to the country of residence of the inventor and to the date when the patent was first registered.

Comparability

The concept of triadic patent families has been developed in order to improve the international comparability and quality of patent-based indicators. Indeed, only patents applied

in the same set of countries are included in the family: home advantage and influence of geographical location are therefore eliminated. Furthermore, patents included in the family are typically of higher value: patentees only take on the additional costs and delays of extending protection to other countries if they deem it worthwhile.

Share of countries in triadic patent families
Percentage, year 2003

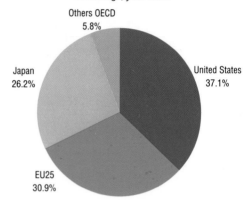

Source: OECD, Patent database, November 2006.

StatLink ᴍᴤ▥ http://dx.doi.org/10.1787/345362402082

Long-term trends

The beginning of the 21st century was marked by a slowdown, with patent families increasing by 1% to 2% a year, following a steady growth of 6% a year on average until 2000. About 53 000 triadic patent families were filed in 2003.

The United States accounts for 37.1% of the OECD total in 2003, followed by the European Union (30.9%) and Japan (26.2%). Since the mid 1990s, the United States' share of patent families increased, whereas the relative proportion of patent families originating from Europe and Japan has tended to decrease.

The ratio of triadic patent families to population identifies Finland, Switzerland, Japan, Sweden and Germany as the five most innovative countries in 2003. Finland had the highest propensity to patent, with 122 patent families per million population and Switzerland had 121. Most countries have seen their patent intensity increase over the last decade, and the largest increase occurred in Korea. By size, China has less then 0.1 patent families per million population.

The numbers of triadic patent families are still insignificant for the five non-member countries shown in the table, although the numbers are growing quite rapidly in China and, to a lesser extent, in India.

Source

• OECD (2005), *OECD Science, Technology and Industry Scoreboard*, OECD, Paris.

Further information

Analytical publications

• Johnson, D. (2002), *The OECD Technology Concordance (OTC): Patents by Industry of Manufacture and Sector of Use*, OECD Science, Technology and Industry Working Papers, No. 2002/5, OECD, Paris.

• Lichtenberg, F. and S. Virabhak (2002), *Using Patents Data to Map Technical Change in Health-Related Areas*, OECD Science, Technology and Industry Working Papers, No. 2002/16, OECD, Paris.

• OECD (2006), *OECD Reviews of Innovation Policy – Switzerland*, OECD, Paris.

Methodological publications

• Dernis, H. and M. Khan (2004), *Triadic Patent Families Methodology*, OECD Science, Technology and Industry Working Papers, No. 2004/2, OECD, Paris.

Online databases

• *OECD Patent Database.*

Websites

• OECD Intellectual Property Rights, *www.oecd.org/sti/ipr.*

• OECD Work on Patents, *www.oecd.org/sti/ipr-statistics.*

Number of triadic patent families

	1991	1992	1993	1994	1995	1996	1997	1998	1999	2000	2001	2002	2003
Australia	154	180	193	227	219	216	252	296	337	360	369	388	431
Austria	172	145	171	209	213	210	247	265	275	294	302	269	276
Belgium	235	290	329	342	367	342	408	418	422	430	449	447	454
Canada	275	270	285	353	380	436	543	532	595	643	661	685	710
Czech Republic	10	7	8	4	3	11	11	14	12	11	13	12	15
Denmark	102	131	155	177	180	215	208	217	229	239	222	215	200
Finland	157	224	242	344	307	347	424	449	494	538	580	606	634
France	1 774	1 630	1 692	1 864	1 877	2 085	2 105	2 274	2 303	2 372	2 368	2 352	2 356
Germany	3 655	3 851	4 005	4 351	4 727	5 323	5 463	5 901	6 389	7 144	7 275	7 244	7 111
Greece	4	6	2	4	1	13	9	8	11	6	5	7	9
Hungary	22	18	22	19	25	23	32	17	34	34	24	22	23
Iceland	3	-	1	3	4	7	4	5	6	8	6	7	8
Ireland	27	24	18	31	27	26	35	32	55	56	60	61	59
Italy	663	572	626	618	600	676	708	792	794	822	847	839	844
Japan	8 861	8 152	8 435	8 206	9 370	10 307	10 625	10 999	12 064	12 954	12 684	12 928	13 564
Korea	92	121	161	213	324	323	412	470	524	579	598	694	747
Luxembourg	9	9	14	7	13	14	14	18	18	17	22	21	19
Mexico	6	6	6	5	13	10	13	13	12	15	16	16	16
Netherlands	557	613	592	662	709	791	784	842	876	883	901	937	1 019
New Zealand	18	26	12	21	20	31	39	44	42	50	49	55	53
Norway	55	71	70	83	86	73	89	89	92	102	104	108	113
Poland	9	5	11	4	5	9	9	4	8	10	8	11	11
Portugal	4	4	3	1	3	3	6	4	5	7	7	5	6
Slovak Republic	-	2	2	1	2	1	3	2	3	4	2	1	2
Spain	69	64	71	83	87	85	98	111	115	122	122	112	115
Sweden	388	515	502	622	671	773	827	910	960	948	881	818	809
Switzerland	715	706	702	707	723	768	764	815	891	921	919	892	895
Turkey	-	-	2	2	2	2	3	7	4	5	6	7	7
United Kingdom	1 244	1 299	1 368	1 465	1 493	1 594	1 542	1 645	1 985	2 088	2 074	2 014	2 024
United States	10 183	10 554	10 362	10 920	11 990	12 842	14 431	14 868	16 296	17 554	18 064	18 954	19 222
EU 15 total	9 059	9 376	9 791	10 781	11 274	12 499	12 878	13 886	14 930	15 968	16 114	15 946	15 936
EU 25 total	9 106	9 419	9 841	10 815	11 318	12 549	12 941	13 942	14 998	16 044	16 168	16 001	15 990
OECD total	29 463	29 492	30 063	31 550	34 439	37 557	40 107	42 061	45 850	49 217	49 636	50 726	51 754
Brazil	6	13	20	12	13	15	27	26	25	27	32	32	35
China	13	16	15	16	19	21	40	41	72	87	128	144	177
India	8	6	8	6	12	17	26	27	29	58	71	78	87
Russian Federation	36	42	28	47	51	46	51	70	61	65	61	58	56
South Africa	18	31	33	20	24	27	33	33	33	37	38	37	38
World	29 781	29 829	30 412	31 909	34 845	38 072	40 735	42 775	46 674	50 164	50 642	51 738	52 855

StatLink ⟡ http://dx.doi.org/10.1787/554407112085

Number of triadic patent families
Per million population, 2003

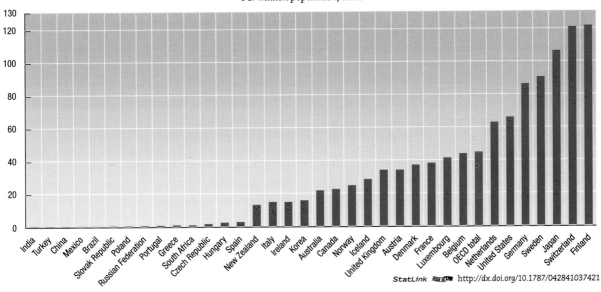

StatLink ⟡ http://dx.doi.org/10.1787/042841037421

SIZE OF THE ICT SECTOR

Information and communication technologies (ICT) have been at the heart of economic changes for more than a decade. ICT-producing sectors play an important role, notably by contributing to rapid technological progress and productivity growth.

Definition

In 1998, the OECD countries reached agreement on an industry-based definition of the ICT sector based on Revision 3 of the International Standard Industrial Classification (ISIC Rev. 3). The principles underlying the definition are the following.

For manufacturing industries, the products of a candidate industry must be intended to fulfill the function of information processing and communication including transmission and display, must use electronic processing to detect, measure and/or record physical phenomena or control a physical process.

For services industries, the products of a candidate industry must be intended to enable the function of information processing and communication by electronic means.

Comparability

The existence of a widely accepted definition of the ICT sector is the first step towards making comparisons across time and countries possible. However, the definition is not as yet consistently applied and data provided by member countries have been combined with different data sources to estimate ICT aggregates compatible with national accounts totals. For this reason, statistics presented here may differ from figures contained in national reports and in previous OECD publications.

Source

- OECD (2005), *OECD Science, Technology and Industry Scoreboard*, OECD, Paris.

Further information

Analytical publications

- OECD (2003), *ICT and Economic Growth: Evidence from OECD countries, industries and firms*, OECD, Paris.
- OECD (2004), *Understanding Economic Growth – A Macro-level, Industry-level, and Firm-level Perspective*, OECD, Paris.
- OECD (2007), *Guide to Measuring the Information Society*, OECD, Paris.
- OECD (2005), *OECD Communications Outlook*, OECD, Paris.
- OECD (2006), *OECD e-Government Studies*, OECD, Paris.
- OECD (2006), *OECD Reviews of Risk Management Policies – Norway: Information Security*, OECD, Paris.
- OECD (2006), *OECD Information Technology Outlook 2006*, OECD, Paris.

Online databases

- *Telecommunications Database*.

Websites

- OECD Telecommunications and Internet Policy, *www.oecd.org/sti/telecom*.
- OECD Science, Technology and Industry, *www.oecd.org/sti*.

Long-term trends

The ICT sector grew strongly in OECD countries over the 1990s. For the 1995-2003 period the share of ICT services has grown most in the Ireland, Finland, Hungary and Sweden. In 2003, Finland's ICT manufacturing sector's share of manufacturing value added represented 22% of total manufacturing value added. In 2003, the ICT manufacturing sector represented between 1.2% and 22.2% of total manufacturing value added in OECD countries. The average share for the 25 OECD countries for which data are available was about 6.5%.

The Telecommunication services sector is largest, as a percentage of business services value added, in Hungary, Portugal, Australia and Finland. It is smallest in Greece, Korea and the Netherlands.

Share of ICT in value added

Year 2003

	Share of ICT manufacturing in total manufacturing value added		Share of ICT services in total business services value added		
	ICT manufacturing	Percentage point change 1995-2003	Telecomminucation services	Other ICT services	Percentage point change 1995-2003
Australia	3.3	..	4.9	4.4	..
Austria	6.6	-0.7	3.1	6.6	0.9
Belgium	3.4	-0.6	3.3	6.5	1.5
Canada	4.4	-1.9	4.2	4.7	1.5
Czech Republic	4.3	1.3	4.6	1.9	0.2
Denmark	4.9	0.5	2.9	6.9	0.1
Finland	22.2	13.4	4.7	6.5	3.3
France	5.4	-1.3	2.9	6.6	1.0
Germany	5.2	0.3	3.7	4.0	1.6
Greece	1.2	0.2	0.4	6.0	0.5
Hungary	7.8	3.0	6.8	4.1	3.3
Ireland	9.7	-7.1	2.7	10.7	6.9
Italy	4.0	-0.2	2.7	5.2	1.1
Japan	12.5	-0.3	3.2	2.2	1.0
Korea	20.2	4.2	0.5	8.0	1.8
Mexico	5.9	0.7	3.2	1.1	0.3
Netherlands	6.0	-1.2	2.1	8.8	1.5
New Zealand	1.5	..	..	..	..
Norway	4.6	0.3	3.4	6.2	1.7
Portugal	4.1	4.1	5.8	4.3	0.4
Slovak Republic	3.2	-0.1	4.3	1.7	0.5
Spain	2.4	-1.3	4.5	3.7	1.0
Sweden	4.2	-3.5	3.5	7.8	2.9
United Kingdom	6.7	-1.6	4.0	7.9	1.6
United States	8.1	-1.1	4.2	6.9	1.4
OECD total	6.5	0.3	3.6	5.5	1.6

StatLink http://dx.doi.org/10.1787/446085222557

Share of ICT in value added

Share of ICT manufacturing and ICT services value added, 2003

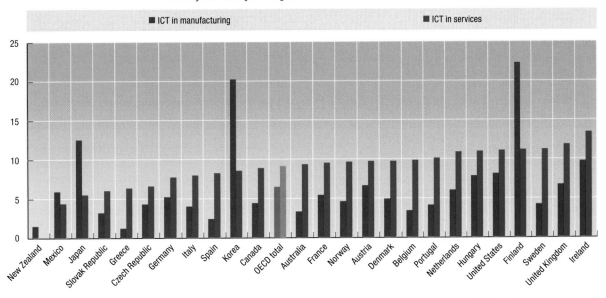

StatLink http://dx.doi.org/10.1787/451711870771

INVESTMENT IN ICT

Investment in physical capital is important for growth. It is a way to expand and renew the capital stock and enable new technologies to enter the production process. Information and communication technology (ICT) has been the most dynamic component of investment in recent years.

Definition

Investment is defined in accordance with the 1993 *System of National Accounts*. It covers the acquisition of equipment and computer software that is used in production for more than one year. ICT has three components: information technology equipment (computers and related hardware), communications equipment and software. Software includes acquisition of pre-packaged software, customised software and software developed in house.

The investment shares shown in the table and graph are percentages of each country's gross fixed capital formation, excluding residential construction.

Comparability

Correct measurement of ICT investment in both nominal and volume terms is crucial for estimating the contribution of ICT to economic growth and performance. Data availability and measurement of ICT investment based on national accounts vary considerably across OECD countries, especially as regards the measurement of investment in software, the methods of deflation, the breakdown by institutional sector and the length of time series.

Expenditure on software has only recently been treated as investment in the national accounts, and methodologies still vary across countries. The United States is among the few countries that produces estimates of expenditure on the three separate software components; other countries usually provide estimates for some software components only. To tackle the specific problems relating to software in the national accounts, a joint OECD-EU task force on the measurement of software in the national accounts has developed recommendations concerning the capitalisation of software.

Note that ICT components that are incorporated in other products, such as motor vehicles or machine tools, are included in the value of those other products and are excluded from ICT investment as defined here.

Source
• OECD Productivity Database.

Further information
Analytical publications
• OECD (2003), *ICT and Economic Growth: Evidence from OECD countries, industries and firms*, OECD, Paris.
• OECD (2005), *OECD Communications Outlook*, OECD, Paris.
• OECD (2005), *OECD Science, Technology and Industry Scoreboard*, OECD, Paris.
• OECD (2006), *OECD Information Technology Outlook 2006*, OECD, Paris.

Statistical publications
• OECD (2006), *National Accounts of OECD Countries*, OECD, Paris.
• OECD (2007), *STAN Industry Structural Analysis Database on CD-Rom*, OECD, Paris.

Methodological publications
• Ahmad, N. (2003), *Measuring Investment in Software*, OECD Science, Technology and Industry Working Papers, No. 2003/6, OECD, Paris.
• Lequillier, F. et al. (2003), *Report of the OECD Task Force on Software Measurement in the National Accounts*, OECD Statistics Working Papers, No. 2003/1, OECD, Paris.
• Schreyer, P., P.-E. Bignon and J. Dupont (2003), *OECD Capital Services Estimates*, OECD Statistics Working Papers, No. 2003/6, OECD, Paris.

Online databases
• *STAN: OECD Structural Analysis Statistics – online database.*
Websites
• OECD Productivity Database, *www.oecd.org/statistics/ productivity.*

Long-term trends

ICT shares in total non-residential investment doubled, and in some cases, almost quadrupled between 1980 and 2005. In 2003/2005, ICT shares were particularly high in Sweden, Finland, Australia, the United Kingdom and the United States.

Software has been the fastest growing component of ICT investment. In many countries, its share in non-residential investment multiplied several times between 1980 and 2003. Software's share in total investment is highest in Denmark, Finland, France, Sweden and the United States.

Shares of ICT investment in non-residential fixed capital formation

As a percentage of total non-residential fixed capital formation, total economy

	1992	1993	1994	1995	1996	1997	1998	1999	2000	2001	2002	2003	2004	2005
Australia	18.3	18.4	18.7	19.1	19.8	21.0	20.9	22.5	26.0	24.7	23.9	22.9	21.6	..
Austria	11.0	11.8	13.0	12.4	11.8	11.9	13.8	14.3	13.7	15.1	14.0	13.2	..	..
Belgium	18.8	15.9	16.9	18.0	18.4	19.4	21.5	21.7	24.2	23.3	20.3	19.9	..	..
Canada	16.1	16.9	16.4	16.8	18.0	17.5	18.8	19.9	20.6	20.2	19.2	18.6	18.2	17.0
Denmark	17.6	19.3	17.5	19.1	19.1	19.6	19.1	20.2	19.5	18.8	19.4	19.6	..	..
Finland	18.5	22.9	25.7	25.8	20.2	25.1	25.2	26.4	26.3	25.9	27.6	26.6	..	..
France	10.5	10.9	11.7	12.5	13.8	15.8	17.0	18.2	17.7	18.8	17.8	17.3	16.4	16.4
Germany	13.1	13.2	13.0	13.3	14.1	14.5	15.3	16.6	17.5	17.8	17.0	15.4	14.9	15.3
Greece	9.3	13.2	11.7	10.0	10.9	11.0	12.4	11.7	12.8	14.3	11.5	10.8	..	..
Ireland	5.7	5.8	6.7	9.6	8.7	8.2	9.6	10.9	14.2	11.4	9.6	8.1	..	..
Italy	14.2	14.3	15.1	14.8	15.1	16.3	15.9	15.4	16.1	16.9	15.7	15.8	..	..
Japan	9.1	9.3	9.3	10.5	12.7	12.9	13.8	15.1	15.9	15.8	14.5	15.6	15.9	..
Korea	..	..	..	12.2	12.7	13.5	15.2	18.1	20.8	20.0	18.8	16.4	15.5	..
Netherlands	13.0	13.7	13.5	13.1	14.0	15.5	17.1	17.6	17.7	17.7	16.8	17.8	..	..
New Zealand	17.7	15.8	16.0	14.9	15.3	16.2	18.9	18.1	21.0	19.5	19.6	..	..	..
Norway	8.4	8.4	9.3	9.9	9.8	10.0	9.6	10.9	11.8	12.5	12.6	..	..	..
Portugal	10.6	10.7	11.4	12.2	12.2	12.0	13.0	13.4	12.4	13.1	11.9	13.6	..	..
Spain	11.6	12.6	12.9	12.5	14.6	14.5	14.7	14.9	14.7	13.5	12.4	11.3	11.6	..
Sweden	19.4	24.6	23.8	23.5	22.7	24.2	26.3	27.9	30.5	27.8	25.5	26.6	..	..
United Kingdom	15.6	17.2	19.1	21.7	22.7	21.3	24.3	23.7	25.0	23.4	22.0	21.8	..	..
United States	24.0	23.8	23.8	24.7	25.6	27.1	27.6	29.8	31.7	30.4	29.4	29.1	28.8	27.8

StatLink ⬛🖷 http://dx.doi.org/10.1787/766812683616

Shares of ICT investment in non-residential fixed capital formation

As a percentage of total non-residential fixed capital formation, total economy, 2005 or latest available year

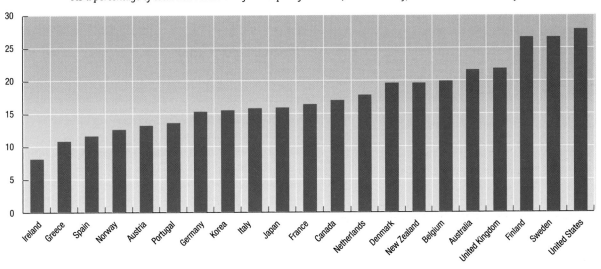

StatLink ⬛🖷 http://dx.doi.org/10.1787/830011422675

COMPUTER AND INTERNET ACCESS BY HOUSEHOLDS

Computers are increasingly present in homes in OECD countries, both in countries that already have high penetration rates and in those where adoption has lagged.

Definition

The table shows the number of households that reported having at least one personal computer in working order in their household. The second part of the table shows the percentage of households who reported that they had access to the Internet. In almost all cases this access is via a personal computer either using a dial-up, ADSL or cable broadband access.

Comparability

Over a very short period, national statistical offices have made great progress in providing indicators of the use of information and communication technology. From an international perspective, the major drawback of official statistics on ICT use is that they remain based on different standards and measure rapidly changing behaviour at different points in time. Most countries use existing surveys, such as labour force, time use, household expenditure or general social surveys. Others rely on special surveys.

Another issue for international comparability is the choice between households and individuals as the survey unit. Household surveys generally provide information on both the household and the individuals in the household. Person-based data typically provide information on the number of individuals with access to a technology, those using the technology, the location at which they use it and the purpose of use.

Statistics on ICT use by households may run into problems of international comparability because of structural differences in the composition of households. On the other hand, statistics on individuals may use different age groups, and age is an important determinant of ICT use. Household- and person-based measures yield different figures in terms of levels and growth rates. Such differences complicate international comparisons and make benchmarking exercises based on a single indicator of Internet access or use misleading, since country rankings change according to the indicator used.

The OECD has addressed issues of international comparability by developing a model survey on ICT use in households/by individuals. The model survey is designed to be flexible; it uses modules addressing different topics so that additional components can be added as technologies reflecting usage practices and policy interests change. The ICT access and use by households and individuals model survey is available on the OECD website.

Long-term trends

Penetration rates are highest in Iceland, Denmark, Japan, Sweden, Korea, the Netherlands, Luxembourg, Norway and the United Kingdom where 70 % or more of households had access to a home computer by 2005. On the other hand, shares in Turkey, Mexico, the Czech Republic and Greece were below 40%. Between 2001 and 2005, the percentages of households with access to a home computer increased particularly sharply in Japan, the United Kingdom and Germany.

The picture with regard to Internet access is similar. In Korea, Iceland, the Netherlands, Denmark, Switzerland and Sweden, more than 70% of households had Internet access by 2005. In Turkey, Mexico and the Czech Republic, on the other hand, only about one-fifth or less had Internet access by 2005.

Data on Internet access by household composition – with or without dependent children – are available for most OECD countries. In general, they show that households with children were more likely to have Internet access at home in 2004.

Sources

- OECD, ICT Database and Eurostat, *Community Survey on ICT Usage in Households and by Individuals*, September 2006
- OECD Key ICT Indicators, *www.oecd.org/sti/ictindicators*.

Further information

Analytical publications

- OECD (2004), *Access Pricing in Telecommunications*, OECD, Paris.
- OECD (2005), *OECD Science, Technology and Industry Scoreboard*, OECD, Paris.
- OECD (2006), *OECD Information Technology Outlook 2006*, OECD, Paris.

Statistical publications

- OECD (2003), *OECD Telecommunications Database*, CD-ROM, OECD, Paris.

Websites

- OECD Telecommunications and Internet Policy, *www.oecd.org/sti/telecom*.
- OECD Science, Technology and Industry, *www.oecd.org/sti*.

Households with access to home computers and the Internet

	Percentage of households with access to a home computer					Percentage of households with access to the Internet				
	2001	2002	2003	2004	2005	2001	2002	2003	2004	2005
Australia	58.0	61.0	66.0	67.0	..	42.0	46.0	53.0	56.0	..
Austria	..	49.2	50.8	58.6	63.1	..	33.5	37.4	44.6	46.7
Belgium	..	..	..	..	..	..	..	..	..	50.2
Canada	59.9	63.9	66.6	68.7	..	49.9	54.3	56.9	59.8	..
Czech Republic	..	27.8	23.8	..	30.0	..	..	14.8	19.4	19.1
Denmark	69.6	72.2	78.5	79.3	83.8	59.0	55.6	64.2	69.4	74.9
Finland	52.9	54.5	57.4	57.0	64.0	39.5	44.3	47.4	50.9	54.1
France	32.4	36.6	45.7	49.8	..	18.1	23.0	31.0	33.6	..
Germany	53.0	61.0	65.2	68.7	69.9	36.0	46.1	54.1	60.0	61.6
Greece	..	25.3	28.7	29.0	32.6	..	12.2	16.3	16.5	21.7
Hungary	..	..	..	31.9	42.3	..	..	..	14.2	22.1
Iceland	..	..	..	85.7	89.3	..	..	..	80.6	84.4
Ireland	..	..	42.2	46.3	54.9	..	..	35.6	39.7	47.2
Italy	..	39.9	47.7	47.4	45.7	..	33.7	32.1	34.1	38.6
Japan	58.0	71.7	78.2	77.5	80.5	..	48.8	53.6	55.8	57.0
Korea	76.9	78.6	77.9	77.8	78.9	63.2	70.2	68.8	86.0	92.7
Luxembourg	..	52.6	58.0	67.3	74.5	..	39.9	45.4	58.6	64.6
Mexico	11.6	15.2	..	18.0	18.4	6.1	7.4	..	8.7	9.0
Netherlands	..	69.0	70.8	..	77.9	..	58.0	60.5	..	78.3
New Zealand	47.0	..	..	..	..	37.4	..	..	..	..
Norway	..	..	71.2	71.5	74.2	..	..	60.5	60.1	64.0
Poland	..	..	..	36.1	40.1	..	..	..	26.0	30.4
Portugal	39.0	26.8	38.3	41.3	42.5	18.0	15.1	21.7	26.2	31.5
Slovak Republic	..	..	..	39.0	46.7	..	..	..	23.0	23.0
Spain	..	..	47.1	52.1	54.6	..	17.4	27.5	33.6	35.5
Sweden	69.2	..	..	..	79.7	53.3	..	..	..	72.5
Switzerland	62.2	65.4	68.9	70.6	..	54.7	61.9	66.4	69.8	73.5
Turkey	..	..	..	10.2	..	..	..	..	7.0	..
United Kingdom	49.0	57.9	63.2	65.3	70.0	40.0	49.7	55.1	55.9	60.2
United States	56.2	..	61.8	..	..	50.3	..	54.6	..	..

StatLink http://dx.doi.org/10.1787/657277848147

Households with access to a home computer
Percentage of all households, 2005 or latest available year

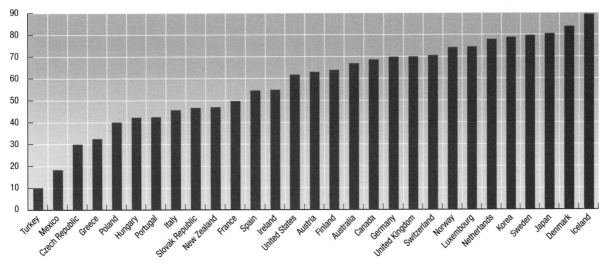

StatLink http://dx.doi.org/10.1787/415703732862

EXPORTS OF INFORMATION AND COMMUNICATIONS EQUIPMENT

Exports of ICT goods accounted for much of the growth in trade over the past decade. In all OECD countries, they grew more rapidly than total manufacturing exports. This is especially the case for high-technology exports.

Definition

The OECD has developed a commodity-based definition of the ICT sector based on the CPC (Central Product Classification) and the Harmonised System (HS). The definition of ICT goods includes the following broad categories: telecommunications equipment; computer and related equipment; electronic components; audio and video equipment; and other ICT goods.

Comparability

The data for this table are taken from the statistics on international trade. These are compiled according to internationally agreed standards and are generally considered to be of good comparability. Note, however, that the data for Australia, Austria, Belgium, China, the Czech Republic, Finland and Portugal in the graph refer to 2004 and not 2005.

Exports of ICT equipment
Billions of US dollars

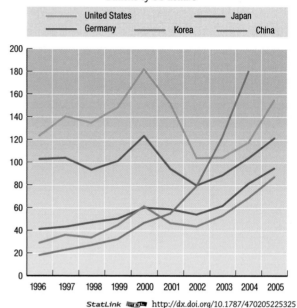

StatLink http://dx.doi.org/10.1787/470205225325

Sources

• ITCS *International Trade by Commodity Statistics.*

Further information

Analytical publications

• OECD (2006), *OECD Information Technology Outlook 2006*, OECD, Paris.

Methodological publications

• OECD (2003), *A proposed classification of ICT goods*, OECD, Paris, *www.oecd.org/dataoecd/5/61/22343094.pdf.*

Websites

• OECD Key ICT indicators, *www.oecd.org/sti/ictindicators.*

OECD FACTBOOK 2007 – ISBN 978-92-64-02946-0 – © OECD 2007

Exports of ICT equipment
Million US dollars

	1996	1997	1998	1999	2000	2001	2002	2003	2004	2005
Australia	2 098	2 133	1 733	1 754	1 976	1 900	1 663	1 928	2 093	..
Austria	3 025	3 493	3 797	4 192	5 045	5 237	5 223	6 072	7 297	..
Belgium	8 463	8 344	9 373	9 547	11 456	12 209	10 083	11 951	12 821	..
Canada	12 080	14 913	14 573	15 730	22 636	15 011	10 713	10 670	12 671	16 615
Czech Republic	885	962	1 513	1 339	2 128	3 201	4 663	5 837	8 923	..
Denmark	3 548	3 805	3 961	4 016	4 306	4 138	5 264	5 020	5 684	7 042
Finland	5 935	6 920	8 656	9 353	11 630	9 414	9 707	10 888	11 128	..
France	25 892	28 156	32 249	32 768	35 715	31 534	24 992	25 151	28 746	33 187
Germany	41 631	43 701	47 466	50 793	60 373	59 104	54 523	62 070	81 589	94 994
Greece	160	219	257	306	480	381	390	447	571	527
Hungary	663	3 294	4 761	5 943	7 776	7 510	8 874	11 877	16 840	16 537
Iceland	2	3	4	5	12	9	13	17	18	25
Ireland	13 271	16 224	18 638	23 523	26 352	30 794	21 804	19 382	19 270	24 931
Italy	13 046	11 697	11 890	11 781	12 790	12 829	9 900	10 909	12 389	15 030
Japan	103 213	104 229	93 612	101 359	123 542	94 518	79 852	88 959	104 011	121 474
Korea	29 171	36 248	33 906	45 061	61 525	46 793	43 875	53 360	69 019	87 163
Luxembourg	..	..	..	1 110	1 118	1 517	1 285	1 092	1 220	1 390
Mexico	16 410	20 412	24 776	30 432	38 312	38 055	35 626	35 136	40 360	43 870
Netherlands	25 022	27 981	31 591	35 395	41 218	35 768	30 923	39 124	49 324	64 748
New Zealand	232	232	299	178	184	168	188	363	462	494
Norway	1 301	1 432	1 513	1 502	1 430	1 526	1 302	1 487	1 650	1 858
Poland	648	917	1 296	1 272	1 424	1 771	2 136	2 557	3 169	4 123
Portugal	1 369	1 383	1 465	1 781	1 893	2 065	1 483	1 878	2 150	..
Slovak Republic	..	310	386	409	461	573	608	1 001	1 747	3 200
Spain	4 969	5 115	5 793	6 055	6 137	6 161	5 592	6 940	7 474	8 280
Sweden	11 164	12 513	13 224	15 098	16 657	9 353	10 131	11 221	14 521	15 818
Switzerland	4 141	3 919	4 090	4 337	4 652	4 298	3 463	3 965	4 462	5 554
Turkey	504	647	1 045	924	1 115	1 188	1 708	2 117	3 086	3 395
United Kingdom	41 844	43 340	47 693	49 226	55 870	53 396	44 349	39 962	39 558	59 755
United States	123 802	140 814	135 108	148 465	182 262	152 150	104 239	104 573	117 791	154 917
OECD total	370 687	402 541	419 563	613 655	740 475	642 570	534 571	575 954	680 044	..
Brazil	..	1 176	1 190	1 479	2 571	..	2 413	2 322	..	4 021
China	18 584	23 194	27 419	32 663	46 996	55 305	79 377	123 303	180 422	..
India	659	545	317	444	714	880	939	1 262	..	..
Russian Federation	..	917	609	755	..	..	..	..	..	1 157
South Africa	..	..	..	..	..	545	493	615	761	798

StatLink ᴪ http://dx.doi.org/10.1787/887456303683

Exports of ICT equipment
Million US dollars, 2005 or latest available year

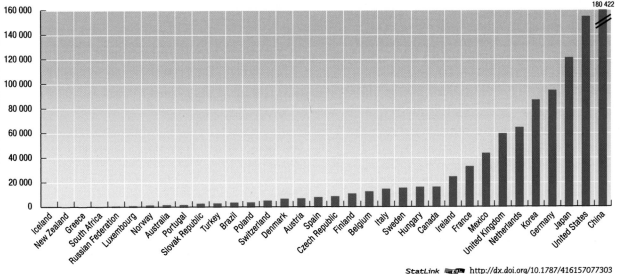

StatLink ᴪ http://dx.doi.org/10.1787/416157077303

TELEPHONE ACCESS

The number of telephone connections – more precisely the number of fixed and mobile telecommunications access paths – has increased dramatically in OECD countries. This is associated both with growing use of the Internet and, particularly in recent years, with the growing popularity of cellular mobile telephones.

Long-term trends

Access to communications networks continues to expand in all OECD countries. At the end of 2004, the total number of fixed and mobile telecommunications paths had increased to more than 1.3 billion. This represented a modest 0.6% increase over 2003 and an average increase of more than 11% in each year since 1998.

Growth was not occurring across all access paths. The number of cellular mobile communication subscribers continues to climb. An additional 93 million mobile subscribers were added in 2004. By way of contrast, some segments of the fixed connection market have begun to decrease. The number of fixed access lines decreased in both 2003 and 2004 and will most likely continue to do so over the coming years.

By 2004, all but four OECD countries – Mexico, New Zealand, Turkey and Poland – had more than one telecommunications access path per inhabitant and eleven countries reported more than one and a half per inhabitant – Denmark, Finland, Germany, Greece, Iceland, Italy, Luxembourg, the Netherlands, Norway, Sweden, Switzerland and the United Kingdom.

Among the five non-OECD countries shown here, growth has been spectacular in China, which had less than one access path per 100 inhabitants in 1991 but almost 50 in 2004. The Russian Federation has now the highest number of paths per 100 inhabitants among these countries. For four of the five non-members, access paths per inhabitant are between 50 and 78, with India as the exception. Although there has been steady growth over the period, there were still only about 8 access paths per 100 inhabitants of India in 2004.

A growing trend toward liberalisation, and the consequent use of prepaid cards in competitive markets, has helped drive the growth of mobile communications in both OECD and non-OECD countries. In 2004 the total number of cellular mobile users in non-member countries overtook the total for the OECD area.

Definition

For the OECD member countries, *access paths* are the total of fixed lines (standard analogue access lines and ISDN channels) plus the number of mobile telephone subscribers. For Brazil, China, India, Russian Federation and South Africa, *access paths* are the sum of main telephone lines in operation, ISDN channels and cellular mobile telephone subscribers.

Comparability

For OECD countries, the data are collected according to agreed definitions and are highly comparable. The data shown for the five large non-OECD countries are reported by the International Telecommunications Union (ITU). The definition used by the ITU is slightly narrower than that used by the OECD, although data reported for the two sets of countries can be regarded as broadly comparable.

Mobile cellular subscribers
OECD and non-OECD share in the world total, 1996-2004

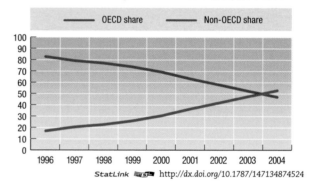

StatLink http://dx.doi.org/10.1787/147134874524

Sources
- OECD (2005), *OECD Communications Outlook*, OECD, Paris.
- ITU (2005), *World Telecommunications Indicators Database*.

Further information
Analytical publications
- Caspary, G. and D. O'Connor (2003), *Providing Low-cost Information Technology Access to Rural Communities in Developing Countries: What Works? What Pays?*, OECD Development Centre Working Papers, No. 229, OECD, Paris.
- OECD (2006), *OECD Information Technology Outlook 2006*, OECD, Paris.

Websites
- OECD Telecommunications and Internet Policy, *www.oecd.org/sti/telecom*.

OECD FACTBOOK 2007 – ISBN 978-92-64-02946-0 – © OECD 2007

Telephone access

Telecommunication access paths per 100 inhabitants

	1991	1992	1993	1994	1995	1996	1997	1998	1999	2000	2001	2002	2003
Australia	49.5	51.4	53.7	57.3	62.7	74.4	78.7	82.9	91.0	101.6	117.0	125.5	132.9
Austria	44.2	46.2	47.6	49.3	52.0	55.0	61.4	75.5	102.2	125.5	130.4	131.3	135.3
Belgium	41.5	43.1	44.3	46.3	48.8	52.7	60.7	66.8	82.6	107.5	125.0	128.0	131.9
Canada	59.2	60.9	63.0	66.0	68.8	72.5	77.7	83.7	89.7	97.8	105.0	106.7	108.1
Czech Republic	16.6	17.7	19.1	21.1	23.7	29.3	36.8	45.8	56.4	81.2	108.4	124.7	135.9
Denmark	60.7	62.2	66.0	70.0	77.8	88.0	89.4	101.1	117.0	134.0	145.5	152.6	156.1
Finland	60.4	61.4	63.7	68.0	75.9	86.0	100.6	117.0	127.6	139.8	147.6	152.9	154.2
France	52.0	54.0	54.2	56.3	59.7	58.4	64.2	75.1	90.3	105.0	116.3	118.2	122.1
Germany	43.0	45.9	49.4	54.1	56.0	61.0	65.0	73.6	87.2	119.7	131.7	136.7	144.3
Greece	..	..	45.2	48.4	51.1	54.8	59.2	70.3	88.3	109.0	129.1	142.0	150.8
Hungary	11.0	12.7	15.2	18.8	24.1	30.7	37.7	44.5	52.0	67.3	85.5	103.9	114.0
Iceland	57.5	59.5	61.0	64.0	67.2	75.8	85.0	103.0	129.9	145.4	149.8	157.3	163.2
Ireland	30.6	32.6	34.3	36.8	40.1	46.3	54.9	69.5	89.0	100.5	120.0	128.2	134.2
Italy	41.6	43.1	44.5	46.9	44.7	55.8	66.5	82.2	100.4	122.0	139.0	142.9	147.6
Japan	46.7	48.0	49.3	..	..	72.4	82.7	91.0	100.6	111.3	116.8	119.9	122.8
Korea	34.0	36.3	38.8	41.7	45.6	50.8	60.5	75.3	108.9	115.1	118.8	126.4	128.7
Luxembourg	49.5	52.5	55.3	58.5	62.9	71.4	78.9	85.9	110.4	142.8	176.5	185.6	216.3
Mexico	7.4	8.3	9.1	..	..	10.7	11.7	13.9	19.2	26.8	35.6	43.3	48.2
Netherlands	48.4	49.8	51.3	53.2	56.0	61.5	72.7	70.8	103.8	132.9	133.9	134.9	143.0
New Zealand	45.8	47.3	47.8	52.6	56.2	58.3	64.8	78.8	85.7	101.6	107.0	109.2	75.5
Norway	56.9	59.4	62.7	68.9	79.1	87.9	100.2	113.0	130.9	148.8	153.1	157.4	160.0
Poland	..	10.3	11.5	13.1	15.0	17.5	21.5	27.0	35.0	46.7	58.7	68.6	78.5
Portugal	27.4	31.0	33.8	36.6	39.5	44.4	54.5	71.0	87.5	107.4	120.1	124.3	137.0
Slovak Republic	..	..	16.8	18.9	21.1	23.7	29.6	37.2	43.2	56.1	70.1	82.8	95.0
Spain	34.4	35.8	37.2	38.6	37.0	47.2	52.3	60.0	81.7	106.1	119.7	137.3	140.9
Sweden	75.7	76.2	77.5	83.9	91.3	97.5	106.0	118.0	131.6	147.4	156.2	162.7	170.1
Switzerland	62.6	64.1	65.7	68.3	71.9	71.9	80.6	91.6	113.3	137.0	146.3	151.5	155.5
Turkey	14.4	16.3	20.6	22.5	19.9	24.1	27.8	32.3	40.2	49.6	54.5	61.0	66.5
United Kingdom	46.6	47.9	51.2	56.0	50.9	64.2	68.9	79.0	98.8	119.4	135.6	141.4	144.6
United States	58.3	60.2	62.2	66.5	71.6	77.7	72.2	78.4	84.9	106.9	110.4	116.3	116.8
OECD average	43.6	44.1	45.1	49.4	44.7	54.7	60.8	68.6	80.6	97.8	106.3	112.3	116.0
Brazil	6.9	7.3	7.6	8.4	9.3	11.2	13.5	16.5	23.8	31.9	37.5	41.2	47.2
China	0.7	1.0	1.5	2.4	3.6	5.0	6.7	8.9	12.0	17.8	24.9	32.9	41.4
India	0.7	0.8	0.9	1.1	1.3	1.6	2.0	2.3	2.8	3.6	4.4	5.2	6.4
Russian Federation	15.0	15.4	15.9	16.3	17.0	17.7	19.5	20.4	21.9	24.0	28.1	36.5	49.9
South Africa	9.5	9.4	9.6	10.7	11.5	13.0	15.9	20.3	25.4	31.3	35.1	41.0	47.6

StatLink 🔗 http://dx.doi.org/10.1787/003814771482

Telephone access

Number of telecommunication access paths per 100 inhabitants, 2004

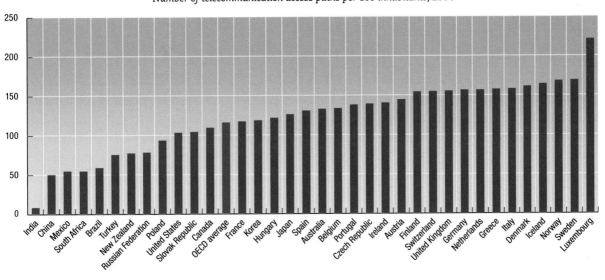

StatLink 🔗 http://dx.doi.org/10.1787/477153844632

ENVIRONMENT

WATER AND NATURAL RESOURCES
WATER CONSUMPTION
FISHERIES

EMISSIONS AND WASTE
EMISSIONS OF CARBON DIOXIDE (CO_2)
MUNICIPAL WASTE

WATER CONSUMPTION

Freshwater resources are of major environmental and economic importance. Their distribution varies widely among and within countries. In arid regions, freshwater resources may at times be limited to the extent that demand for water can be met only by going beyond sustainable use in terms of quantity.

Freshwater abstractions, particularly for public water supplies, irrigation, industrial processes and cooling of electric power plants, exert a major pressure on water resources, with significant implications for the quantity and quality of water resources. Main concerns relate to the inefficient use of water and to its environmental and socio-economic consequences: low river flows, water shortages, salinisation of freshwater bodies in coastal areas, human health problems, loss of wetlands, desertification and reduced food production.

Definition

Water abstractions refer to freshwater taken from ground or surface water sources, either permanently or temporarily, and conveyed to the place of use. If the water is returned to a surface water source, abstraction of the same water by the downstream user is counted again in compiling total abstractions.

Mine water and drainage water are included. Water used for hydroelectricity generation is an *in situ* use and is excluded.

Comparability

It should be borne in mind that the definitions and estimation methods employed by member countries may vary considerably and may have changed over time. In general, data availability and quality is best for abstractions for public supply, representing about 15% of the total water abstracted in OECD countries.

Long-term trends

Most OECD countries increased their water abstractions over the 1960s and 1970s in response to demand by the agricultural and energy sectors. Since the 1980s, some countries have stabilised their abstractions through more efficient irrigation techniques, the decline of water-intensive industries (*e.g.* mining, steel), increased use of cleaner production technologies and reduced losses in pipe networks. However, the effects of population growth have led to increases in total abstractions, in particular for public supply.

At world level, it is estimated that water demand rose by more than double the rate of population growth in the last century, with agriculture being the largest user of water.

Water abstractions in OECD countries
Year 1980 = 100

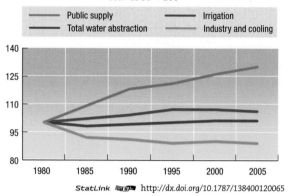

StatLink 🔢🔣 http://dx.doi.org/10.1787/138400120065

Sources

- OECD (2005), *OECD Environmental Data Compendium 2004*, updates from the 2004 OECD/Eurostat Questionnaire on the State of the Environment., OECD, Paris.

- OECD (2006), *Environment at a Glance: OECD Environmental Indicators*, OECD, Paris.

Further information
Analytical publications

- OECD, WHO (2003), *Assessing Microbial Safety of Drinking Water: Improving Approaches and Methods*, OECD, Paris.

- OECD (2006), *Environmental Performance Reviews – Water: the experience in OECD countries*, OECD, Paris.

- OECD (2006), *China in the Global Economy – Environment, Water Resources and Agricultural Policies: Lessons from China and OECD Countries*, OECD, Paris.

- OECD (2006), *Financing Water and Environment Infrastructure: The Case of Eastern Europe, the Caucasus and Central Asia*, OECD, Paris.

- OECD (2006), *OECD Trade Policy Studies – Liberalisation and Universal Access to Basic Services: Telecommunications, Water and Sanitation, Financial Services, and Electricity*, OECD, Paris.

- OECD (2006), *Water and Agriculture: Sustainability, Markets and Policies*, OECD, Paris.

- OECD (2003), *Social Issues in the Provision and Pricing of Water Services*, OECD, Paris.

Web sites

- OECD Environmental Indicators, *www.oecd.org/env/indicators*.

- OECD Water Supply and Sanitation Sector Reform, *www.oecd.org/env/water*.

OECD FACTBOOK 2007 – ISBN 978-92-64-02946-0 – © OECD 2007

Water abstractions

	Total gross abstractions Million m³					Per capita abstractions m³/capita
	1980	1985	1990	1995	2004 or latest available year	2004 or latest available year
Australia	10 900	14 600	..	24 071	18 767	930
Austria	3 342	3 580	3 807	3 449	3 816	470
Belgium	..	..		8 255	6 749	650
Canada	37 594	42 383	45 096	42 214	42 214	1 420
Czech Republic	3 622	3 679	3 623	2 743	2 028	200
Denmark	1 205	..	1 261	887	668	120
Finland	3 700	4 000	2 347	2 586	2 319	450
France	30 972	34 887	37 687	40 671		33 164	560
Germany	42 206	41 216		47 873	43 374	35 557	430
Greece	5 040	5 496	7 030	8 695	8 695	830
Hungary	4 805	6 267	6 293	5 976	5 591	550
Iceland	108	112	167	165	165	570
Ireland	1 070	..	..	1 176	1 176	330
Italy	..	..	..	..	41 982	730
Japan	86 000	87 198	88 889	89 078	86 210	680
Korea	17 510	18 580	20 570	23 670	26 193	550
Luxembourg	..	67	59	57	60	140
Mexico	56 003	..	..	73 672	75 431	730
Netherlands	9 198	9 349	7 984	6 507	8 937	560
New Zealand	..	..	..	..	5 410	1 410
Norway	..	2 025	..	2 420	3 391	750
Poland	15 131	16 409	15 164	12 924	11 548	300
Portugal	10 500	..	8 600	10 849	8 808	860
Slovak Republic	2 232	2 061	2 116	1 386	1 064	200
Spain	39 920	46 250	36 900	33 288	36 992	900
Sweden	4 106	2 970	2 968	2 725	2 676	300
Switzerland	2 589	2 646	2 665	2 571	2 518	350
Turkey	16 200	19 400	28 073	30 112	39 780	580
United Kingdom	13 514	11 533	12 052	12 117	13 649	250
United States	517 720	467 335	468 620	470 514	476 800	1 730
OECD total	993 300	974 200	987 700	995 200	1 002 400	890

StatLink http://dx.doi.org/10.1787/257012000030

Water abstractions
m³ per capita, 2004 or latest available year

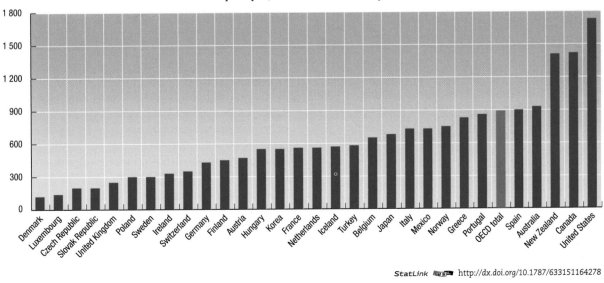

StatLink http://dx.doi.org/10.1787/633151164278

FISHERIES

Fisheries make an important contribution to sustainable income, employment opportunities and overall food protein intake. In certain countries, including at least two OECD countries – Iceland and Japan – fish is the main source of protein intake.

Definition

The figures refer to the tonnages of landed catches of marine fish, and cultivated fish and crustaceans taken from inland waters and sea tanks. Landed catches of marine fish for each country cover landings in both foreign and domestic ports. The table distinguishes between marine capture fisheries and aquaculture because of their different production systems and growth rates.

Long-term trends

The total production by OECD countries has decreased by more than 10% during the past decade. As the world fish production increased during the same period, the relative contribution of OECD countries dropped from 26% (in 1995) to 16% (in 2004). The decrease of the overall OECD production masks various tendencies. While aquaculture production increased by around 8% between 1995 and 2003, marine capture fisheries production dropped by 19%. This latter evolution mainly reflects both the worrying state of some major fish stocks, especially in the northern hemisphere, and changes in bilateral or international fishing arrangements regarding access to fish stocks in third countries' waters. Worldwide, the Food and Agriculture Organisation estimates that around 16% of the stocks are overexploited, 7% are collapsed, while around 50% of the stocks are fully exploited. The remaining is either not fully exploited (21%) or under-exploited (3%).

Marine fish capture fell particularly sharply in Denmark, Greece and Japan between 1995 and 2004; in these countries, the average annual decline exceeded 5%. A few countries did, however, increase captures – Canada, Australia and the Netherlands all raised their tonnages by an average of 1% or more per year between 1995 and 2004. Japan and the United States remained the largest producers despite their catches declining by approximately 5% and 1% a year, respectively.

Most countries increased their aquaculture production, with annual growth of over 10% in Turkey, Greece, Norway and Ireland. Aquaculture production fell rather sharply in Mexico, Finland and Sweden but, by 2004, aquaculture accounted for over 16% of total tonnages of fish production – up from 13% in 1995.

Comparability

The time series presented are relatively comprehensive and consistent across the years, but some of the variation over time may reflect changes in national reporting systems. In a few cases, the data shown are estimated by OECD.

Fish landings in domestic and foreign ports

As a percentage of OECD total, 2004

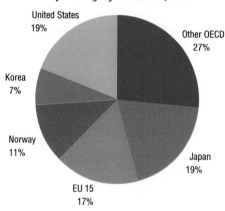

StatLink ⬛⬛⬛ http://dx.doi.org/10.1787/572823671785

Source

- OECD (2005), *Review of Fisheries in OECD Countries Vol. 2 – Country Statistics 2001-2003*, OECD, Paris.

Further information

Analytical publications

- OECD (2004), *Fish Piracy: Combating Illegal, Unreported and Unregulated Fishing*, OECD, Paris.
- OECD (2005), *Why Fish Piracy Persists: The Economics of Illegal, Unreported and Unregulated Fishing*, OECD, Paris.
- OECD (2006), *The Development Dimension – Fishing for Coherence: Proceedings of the Workshop on Policy Coherence for Development in Fisheries*, OECD, Paris.
- OECD (2006), *Financial Support to Fisheries: Implications for Sustainable Development*, OECD, Paris.
- OECD (2006), *Using Market Mechanisms to Manage Fisheries: Smoothing the Path*, OECD, Paris.
- OECD (2007), *The Human Side of Fisheries Adjustment*, OECD, Paris.

Statistical publications

- OECD (2005), *Review of Fisheries in OECD Countries: Volume 1: Policies and Summary Statistics, 2005 Edition*, OECD, Paris.

Websites

- OECD Fisheries, *www.oecd.org/agr/fish*.

Marine capture and aquaculture production
Thousand tonnes

	Fish landings in domestic and foreign ports							Aquaculture						
	1995	1999	2000	2001	2002	2003	2004	1995	1999	2000	2001	2002	2003	2004
Australia	201	210	185	187	187	201	228	24	34	37	40	44	44	48
Austria	..	..	..	..	..	..	..	4	..	..	..	..	..	..
Belgium	29	26	27	27	26	24	20	2	2	2	2	2	..	..
Canada	854	1 005	1 008	1 060	1 042	1 088	1 126	66	113	127	153	177	156	145
Czech Republic	..	..	..	..	..	..	..	19	19	19	20	19	20	19
Denmark	2 025	1 415	1 524	1 501	1 433	1 028	1 090	45	43	44	42	37	36	42
Finland	106	85	92	96	95	76	85	17	15	15	16	15	13	13
France	616	588	682	665	690	695	662	281	266	267	253	250	245	243
Germany	241	234	194	179	182	247	223	40	34	45	43	50	65	56
Greece	153	34	93	91	94	85	87	33	76	88	95	101	105	100
Hungary	..	..	..	..	..	..	..	9	..	..	..	..	..	..
Iceland	1 603	1 760	1 930	1 942	2 132	1 979	1 730	4	4	4	5	3	6	8
Ireland	379	269	291	305	281	259	..	27	44	41	54	53	63	..
Italy	301	265	387	339	304	312	288	225	217	228	264	260	192	232
Japan	7 450	5 311	5 092	4 814	4 495	4 743	4 515	1 390	1 315	1 292	1 311	1 385	1 301	1 260
Korea	2 322	2 306	2 090	2 142	1 867	1 831	1 601	1 017	777	667	668	794	844	938
Mexico	1 222	1 096	1 193	1 251	1 295	1 303	1 221	158	48	46	75	71	70	80
Netherlands	463	404	404	404	467	573	506	84	92	92	92	92	..	..
New Zealand	567	544	536	501	512	488	484	69	83	87	76	76	..	94
Norway	2 701	2 627	2 894	2 862	2 923	2 701	2 670	278	476	492	511	554	582	636
Poland	241	235	200	207	204	160	173	25	33	32	34	33	32	35
Portugal	242	190	172	173	181	184	..	5	6	8	8	8	..	6
Spain	1 075	1 102	1 002	941	747	774	701	224	321	312	313	328	313	362
Sweden	379	329	341	308	284	281	262	8	6	6	8	6	7	6
Switzerland	..	..	..	..	..	..	..	1	..	..	..	..	..	..
Turkey	577	524	461	484	523	463	505	22	63	79	67	61	80	94
United Kingdom	912	835	748	738	685	631	653	92	144	144	150	150	..	..
United States	4 783	4 428	4 245	4 434	4 407	4 402	4 449	413	382	373	371	393	420	..
EU 15 total	6 920	5 775	5 957	5 734	5 474	4 395	3 859	1 087	1 266	1 290	1 339	1 346	1 039	1 073
OECD total	29 442	25 820	25 791	25 587	24 612	23 754	23 279	4 567	4 612	4 544	4 671	4 922	4 594	4 417

StatLink http://dx.doi.org/10.1787/175045246555

Fish landings in domestic and foreign ports
Average annual growth in percentage, 1995-2004

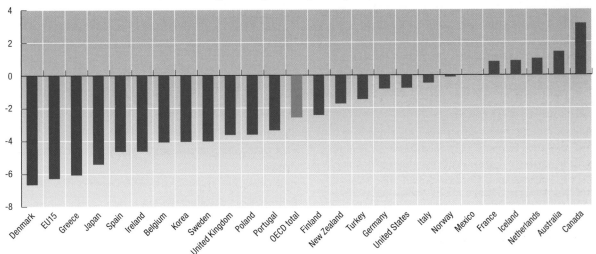

StatLink http://dx.doi.org/10.1787/326630500334

EMISSIONS OF CARBON DIOXIDE (CO₂)

Carbon dioxide (CO_2) makes up the largest share of "greenhouse gases". The addition of man-made greenhouse gases to the atmosphere disturbs the earth's radiative balance. This is leading to an increase in the earth's surface temperature and to related effects on climate, sea level rise and world agriculture.

Definition

The table refers to emissions of CO_2 from burning oil, coal and gas for energy use. Carbon dioxide also enters the atmosphere from burning wood and waste materials and from some industrial processes such as cement production. Emissions of CO_2 from these sources are a relatively small part of global emissions and are not included in these statistics. The *Revised 1996 IPCC Guidelines for National Greenhouse Gas Inventories* (see below) provide a fuller, technical definition of how CO_2 emissions have been estimated for this table. The forecasts provided in the table refer to the Reference Scenario of the *World Energy Outlook*.

Comparability

These emissions estimates are affected by the quality of the underlying energy data. For example, some countries, both OECD and non-OECD, have trouble reporting information on bunker fuels and incorrectly define bunkers as fuel used abroad by their own ships and planes. Since emissions from bunkers are excluded from the national totals, this affects the comparability across countries. On the other hand, since the estimates have been made using the same method and emission factors for all countries, in general, the comparability across countries is quite good.

Long-term trends

Global emissions of carbon dioxide have risen by 88% since 1971 and are projected to rise by another 52% by 2030. In 1971, the current OECD countries were responsible for 66% of the total. As a consequence of rapidly increasing emissions in the developing world, the OECD contributed 49% to the total in 2004, but this is expected to fall to 38% by 2030. By far, the largest increases in non-OECD countries occurred in Asia, where emissions in China have risen by 5.5% per annum between 1971 and 2004. The use of coal in China increased levels of CO_2 by 3.2 billion tonnes over the 33-year period.

Two significant downturns can be seen in OECD CO_2 emissions, following the oil shocks of the mid-1970s and early 1980s. Emissions from the economies in transition declined over the last decade, helping to offset the OECD increases between 1990 and the present. However, this decline did not stabilise global emissions as emissions in developing countries grew.

Disaggregating the emissions data shows substantial variations within individual sectors. Between 1971 and 2004, the combined share of electricity and heat generation and transport shifted from one-half to two-thirds of global emissions.

Fossil fuel shares in overall emissions changed slightly during the period. The relative weight of coal in global emissions has remained at approximately 40% since the early 1970s. The share of natural gas has increased from 15% in 1971 to 20% in 2004. Oil's share decreased from 49% to 40%. Fuel switching and the increasing use of non-fossil energy sources reduced the CO_2/total primary energy supply (TPES) ratio by 7% over the past 33 years.

Sources
- IEA (2006), *CO₂ Emissions from Fuel Combustion: 1971/2004*, IEA, Paris.
- IEA (2006), *World Energy Outlook 2006*, IEA, Paris.

Further information
Analytical publications
- IEA (2004), *Prospects for CO₂ Capture and Storage*, IEA, Paris.
- IEA (2005), *Act Locally, Trade Globally: Emissions trading for climate policy*, IEA, Paris.
- IEA (2006), *Energy Technology Perspectives: Scenarios and Strategies to 2050*, IEA, Paris.
- OECD (2004), *Can Cars Come Clean? Strategies for Low-Emission Vehicles*, OECD, Paris.

Statistical publications
- IEA (2006), *Energy Statistics of Non-OECD Countries*, IEA, Paris.
- IEA (2006), *Energy Statistics of OECD Countries*, IEA, Paris.

Methodological publications
- WMO, UNEP, OECD, IEA (1996), *Revised 1996 IPCC Guidelines for National Greenhouse Gas Inventories*, WMO, Geneva.

Online databases
- *CO₂ Emissions from Fuel Combustion.*

OECD FACTBOOK 2007 – ISBN 978-92-64-02946-0 – © OECD 2007

CO_2 emissions from energy use
Million tonnes

	1971	1990	1995	1996	1997	1998	1999	2000	2001	2002	2003	2004	2030
Australia	143	260	280	296	311	327	334	339	342	347	348	354	..
Austria	49	58	60	65	64	65	64	64	68	70	75	75	..
Belgium	118	109	114	122	119	121	117	118	120	112	120	116	..
Canada	340	429	461	476	493	498	508	530	523	531	556	551	..
Czech Republic	151	154	121	125	121	115	109	118	118	115	118	119	..
Denmark	56	51	58	71	61	57	54	50	52	51	56	51	..
Finland	40	55	56	64	61	57	57	55	60	64	73	69	..
France	435	355	357	371	364	387	380	379	388	379	388	387	..
Germany	984	966	878	901	872	864	833	827	846	833	845	849	..
Greece	25	71	73	76	79	84	83	88	90	90	94	94	..
Hungary	62	71	59	60	57	58	58	56	56	56	58	57	..
Iceland	1	2	2	2	2	2	2	2	2	2	2	2	..
Ireland	22	30	32	34	36	38	39	41	43	42	41	41	..
Italy	295	398	411	407	411	422	422	426	427	434	453	462	..
Japan	743	1 058	1 140	1 155	1 155	1 123	1 166	1 185	1 167	1 206	1 215	1 215	1 154
Korea	51	226	361	392	418	362	397	428	441	442	452	462	..
Luxembourg	15	11	8	8	8	7	8	8	8	9	10	11	..
Mexico	97	293	310	316	329	350	343	357	356	360	368	374	..
Netherlands	130	158	172	179	175	174	169	174	180	180	185	186	..
New Zealand	14	22	25	27	28	27	29	30	32	32	33	33	..
Norway	24	29	33	34	36	37	39	34	34	34	36	36	..
Poland	298	349	333	348	338	315	305	293	292	281	292	296	..
Portugal	15	40	49	47	49	54	61	60	59	63	59	60	..
Slovak Republic	39	57	41	41	42	40	39	37	39	38	39	38	..
Spain	121	207	236	225	243	251	271	286	288	304	312	330	..
Sweden	83	52	54	60	54	55	53	50	51	53	54	52	..
Switzerland	39	41	42	42	41	43	43	42	43	42	44	45	..
Turkey	42	129	155	172	181	182	181	203	184	194	204	209	..
United Kingdom	627	558	528	543	520	524	518	525	538	522	534	537	..
United States	4 297	4 842	5 109	5 290	5 436	5 485	5 530	5 701	5 623	5 654	5 713	5 800	7 138
EU 25 total	..	..	3 701	3 809	3 736	3 749	3 696	3 709	3 779	3 755	3 867	3 891	4 216
OECD total	9 357	11 078	11 561	11 948	12 104	12 124	12 209	12 506	12 469	12 541	12 777	12 911	15 495
Brazil	91	193	239	258	276	284	295	305	314	313	306	323	551
China	800	2 256	2 976	3 202	3 130	3 106	2 962	2 978	3 179	3 460	4 005	4 732	10 425
India	199	588	785	834	877	872	930	971	981	1 011	1 042	1 103	2 544
Russian Federation	..	..	1 589	1 562	1 451	1 433	1 473	1 513	1 516	1 503	1 538	1 529	1 883
South Africa	174	255	277	286	300	310	291	299	284	295	321	343	..
World	14 112	20 783	21 810	22 575	22 716	22 784	22 908	23 455	23 735	24 263	25 316	26 583	40 420

StatLink http://dx.doi.org/10.1787/843704411326

World CO_2 emissions from energy use, by region
Million tonnes

■ OECD total　■ Middle East　■ Former USSR　■ Non-OECD Europe　■ China　■ Other Asia　■ Latin America and Caribbean　■ Africa　■ Bunkers

StatLink http://dx.doi.org/10.1787/363278342610

MUNICIPAL WASTE

The amount of municipal waste generated in a country is related to the rate of urbanisation, the types and patterns of consumption, household revenue and lifestyles. While municipal waste is only one part of total waste generated, its management and treatment often absorbs more than one third of the public sector's financial efforts to abate and control pollution.

The main environmental concerns relate to the potential impact from inappropriate waste management on human health and the environment (soil and water contamination, air quality, land use and landscape).

Kilogrammes of municipal waste per capita – or "waste generation intensities" – are broad indicators of potential environmental pressure. They should be complemented with information on waste management practices and costs, and on consumption levels and patterns.

Definition

Municipal waste is waste collected and treated by or for municipalities. It covers waste from households, including bulky waste, similar waste from commerce and trade, office buildings, institutions and small businesses, yard and garden waste, street sweepings, the contents of litter containers, and market cleansing waste. The definition excludes waste from municipal sewage networks and treatment, as well as municipal construction and demolition waste.

Comparability

The definition of municipal waste and the surveying methods used vary from country to country.

The main problems relate to the coverage of household-like waste from commerce and trade, and of separate waste collections, carried out by private companies.

Data for Canada and New Zealand refer to household waste only.

OECD total does not include the Czech Republic, Hungary, Korea, Poland and the Slovak Republic.

Long-term trends

The quantity of municipal waste generated in the OECD area has been rising since 1980 and exceeded 590 million tonnes in recent years (570 kg per capita). Generation intensity – i.e. kilogrammes per capita – has risen mostly in line with private final consumption expenditure and GDP, but there has been a slowdown in the rate of growth in recent years.

The amount of municipal waste also depends on national waste management practices. Only a few countries have succeeded in reducing the quantity of solid waste to be disposed of. In most countries for which data are available, increased affluence, associated with economic growth and changes in consumption patterns, tends to generate higher rates of waste per capita.

Sources

- OECD (2005), *OECD Environmental Data Compendium 2004*, OECD, Paris.
- OECD (2006), *Environment at a Glance: OECD Environmental Indicators*, OECD, Paris.

Further information

Analytical publications

- OECD (2004), *Addressing the Economics of Waste*, OECD, Paris.
- OECD (2004), *Economic Aspects of Extended Producer Responsibility*, OECD, Paris.
- OECD (2004), *Toward Waste Prevention Performance Indicators*, OECD, Paris.

Websites

- OECD Environmental Indicators, *www.oecd.org/env/indicators*.
- OECD Waste Prevention and Management, *www.oecd.org/env/waste*.

Municipal waste generation

	Total amount generated Thousands tonnes					Generation intensities kg/capita
	1980	1985	1990	1995	2003 or latest available year	2003 or latest available year
Australia	10 000	..	12 000	..	13 200	690
Austria	..	..	3 204	3 476	4 502	560
Belgium	2 853	3 267	3 674	4 612	4 615	440
Canada	..	..	8 925 |	7 030	12 008	380
Czech Republic	..	2 600	..	3 200	2 857	280
Denmark	2 046	2 430	..	2 960	3 634	670
Finland	..	..	..	2 100	2 344	450
France	..	..	26 220	28 253	33 467	540
Germany	..	..	..	44 390 |	52 627	640
Greece	2 500	3 000	3 000	3 200	4 710	430
Hungary	..	..	5 500	4 752	4 696	460
Iceland	..	..	..	166	209	730
Ireland	640	1 100	..	1 848	3 001	760
Italy	14 041	15 000	20 000	25 780	30 038	520
Japan	43 995	43 450	50 441	50 694	52 097	410
Korea	..	20 994	30 646 |	17 438	18 519	390
Luxembourg	128	131	224 |	240	295	650
Mexico	..	..	21 062 |	30 510	33 758	320
Netherlands	7 050	6 933	7 430	8 469	9 656	600
New Zealand	880	..	1 140	1 431	1 541	400
Norway	1 700	1 968	2 000	2 722	3 170	700
Poland	10 055	11 087	11 098	10 985	9 925	260
Portugal	1 980	2 350	3 000	3 855	4 701	450
Slovak Republic	..	1 901	1 600	1 620 |	1 599	300
Spain	..	..	..	..	26 596	650
Sweden	2 510	2 650	3 200	3 555	4 211	470
Switzerland	2 790	3 398	4 101	4 200	4 838	660
Turkey	12 000	18 000	22 315	20 910	25 611	360
United Kingdom	..	..	27 100	28 900	36 841	610
United States	137 568	149 189	186 167	193 869	214 253	740
OECD total	369 000	399 000	481 000	522 000	594 000	570

StatLink 🔗 http://dx.doi.org/10.1787/602463565086

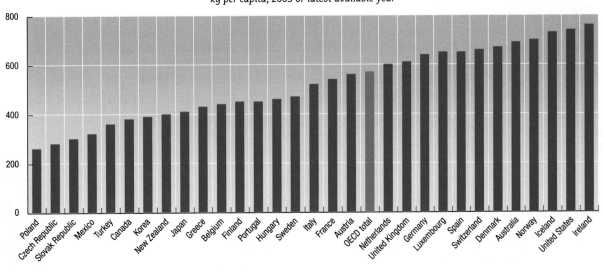

Municipal waste generation
kg per capita, 2003 or latest available year

StatLink 🔗 http://dx.doi.org/10.1787/800606761141

EDUCATION

OUTCOMES
INTERNATIONAL STUDENT ASSESSMENT
TERTIARY ATTAINMENT

EXPENDITURE ON EDUCATION
EXPENDITURE ON TERTIARY EDUCATION
PUBLIC AND PRIVATE EDUCATION EXPENDITURE

INTERNATIONAL STUDENT ASSESSMENT

How effective are school systems at providing young people with a solid foundation of knowledge and skills that will equip them for life and learning beyond school? OECD's Programme for International Student Assessment (PISA) assesses student knowledge and skills in mathematics, science, reading and cross-curricular competencies at age 15, i.e. towards the end of compulsory education.

PISA 2003 also asked students about their access to computers and how often they used them. These questions were asked in 25 OECD countries and the results are also reported on the following pages.

Definition

The PISA survey covers mathematics, reading, science and problem solving. For the 2003 round of PISA, three and a half hours of testing time was in mathematics, plus one hour each for reading, science and problem solving. Each student spent two hours on the assessment items.

Mathematical literacy is an individual's capacity to identify and understand the role that mathematics plays in the world, to make well-founded judgements and to use and engage with mathematics in ways that meet the needs of that individual's life as a constructive, concerned and reflective citizen.

Overview

PISA results for 2000 (the first round of PISA) and for 2003 are shown in the table for reading and science. Where no figures are shown for a country, either that country did not participate in the round or the response rates were too low to give reliable results. The graph shows the 2003 results for mathematics in terms of differences from the OECD average score (500). For Austria, Germany, Ireland and the Slovak Republic the mathematics scores are not significantly different from the OECD average.

There is large variation in the number of years that students reported having had access to computers. In seven countries, more than 50% of students reported that they had been using a computer for at least the last five years – i.e. since the age of about ten. Australia, Canada and the United States reported the highest percentages. At the other extreme, less than 25% of students in eight countries, including Italy and Japan, reported using computers for five or more years.

Use of computers is much more common at home than at school. In most participating countries, more than 70% of students frequently use computers at home, although in Japan, Mexico, Turkey and Russian Federation, less than 50% of students report frequent use.

Scientific literacy is the capacity to use scientific knowledge, to identify questions and to draw evidence-based conclusions in order to understand and help make decisions about the natural world and the changes made to it through human activity.

Reading literacy is understanding, using and reflecting on written texts, in order to achieve one's goals, to develop one's knowledge and potential and to participate in society.

Frequent users of computers are defined as all students who responded that they use computers either "Almost every day" or "A few times each week". Other possible answers for students were: "Between once a week and once a month", "Less than once a month" or "Never".

Comparability

Leading experts in participating countries advise on the scope and nature of the assessments and final decisions on this are taken by OECD governments. Substantial efforts and resources are devoted to achieving cultural and linguistic breadth and balance in the assessment materials and stringent quality assurance mechanisms are applied in translation, sampling and data collection.

Over a quarter of a million 15-year-old students in the 41 participating countries were assessed for PISA 2003. Because the results are based on probability samples, it is possible to calculate the standard errors of the estimates and these are shown in the tables.

Sources

- OECD (2001), *PISA Knowledge and Skills for Life – First Results from PISA 2000*, OECD, Paris.
- OECD (2004), *PISA Learning for Tomorrow's World: First Results from PISA 2003*, OECD, Paris.
- OECD (2006), *Are Students Ready for a Technology-Rich World? What PISA Studies Tell Us*, OECD, Paris.

Further information

Analytical publications

- OECD (2003), *PISA Literacy Skills for the World of Tomorrow – Further Results from PISA 2000*, OECD, Paris.
- OECD (2005), *PISA Problem Solving for Tomorrow's World First Measures of Cross-Curricular Competencies from PISA 2003*, OECD, Paris.
- OECD (2006), *Where Immigrant Students Succeed: A Comparative Review of Performance and Engagement in PISA 2003*, OECD, Paris.

Methodological publications

- OECD (2006), *Assessing Scientific, Reading and Mathematical Literacy: A Framework for PISA 2006*, OECD, Paris.

Online databases

- *OECD PISA Database.*

Websites

- PISA website, *www.pisa.oecd.org.*

Mean scores on the reading and science scale in PISA 2000 and PISA 2003

| | Reading scale | | | | Science scale | | | |
| | PISA 2000 | | PISA 2003 | | PISA 2000 | | PISA 2003 | |
	Mean score	S.E.	Mean score	S.E.	Mean score	S.E.	Mean score	S.E.
Australia	528	3.5	525	2.1	528	3.5	525	2.1
Austria	507	2.4	491	3.8	519	2.6	491	3.4
Belgium	507	3.6	507	2.6	496	4.3	509	2.5
Canada	534	1.6	528	1.7	529	1.6	519	2.0
Czech Republic	492	2.4	489	3.5	511	2.4	523	3.4
Denmark	497	2.4	492	2.8	481	2.8	475	3.0
Finland	546	2.6	543	1.6	538	2.5	548	1.9
France	505	2.7	496	2.7	500	3.2	511	3.0
Germany	484	2.5	491	3.4	487	2.4	502	3.6
Greece	474	5.0	472	4.1	461	4.9	481	3.8
Hungary	480	4.0	482	2.5	496	4.2	503	2.8
Iceland	507	1.5	492	1.6	496	2.2	495	1.5
Ireland	527	3.2	515	2.6	513	3.2	505	2.7
Italy	487	2.9	476	3.0	478	3.1	486	3.1
Japan	522	5.2	498	3.9	550	5.5	548	4.1
Korea	525	2.4	534	3.1	552	2.7	538	3.5
Luxembourg	441	1.6	479	1.5	443	2.3	483	1.5
Mexico	422	3.3	400	4.1	422	3.2	405	3.5
Netherlands	..	..	513	2.9	..	..	524	3.1
New Zealand	529	2.8	522	2.5	528	2.4	521	2.4
Norway	505	2.8	500	2.8	500	2.8	484	2.9
Poland	479	4.5	497	2.9	483	5.1	498	2.9
Portugal	470	4.5	478	3.7	459	4.0	468	3.5
Slovak Republic	..	..	469	3.1	..	..	495	3.7
Spain	493	2.7	481	2.6	491	3.0	487	2.6
Sweden	516	2.2	514	2.4	512	2.5	506	2.7
Switzerland	494	4.3	499	3.3	496	4.4	513	3.7
Turkey	..	..	441	5.8	..	..	434	5.9
United Kingdom	523	2.6	..	..	532	2.7	..	..
United States	504	7.1	495	3.2	499	7.3	491	3.1
OECD average	500	0.6	494	0.6	500	0.7	500	0.6
OECD total	499	2.0	488	1.2	502	2.0	496	1.1
Brazil	396	3.1	403	4.6	375	3.3	390	4.3
Russian Federation	462	4.2	442	3.9	460	4.7	489	4.1

StatLink ᵐˢᴸ http://dx.doi.org/10.1787/682102287864

Performance on the mathematics scale in PISA 2003

Standard errors are indicated on the graph by the figures in brackets

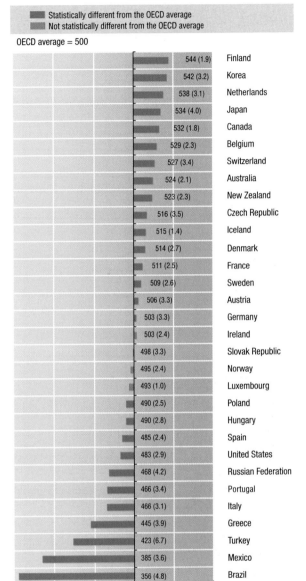

StatLink ᵐˢᴸ http://dx.doi.org/10.1787/361110188276

Computer usage by 15-year-old students

Percentage of 15-year-old students using computers frequently, 2003

	At school		At home	
	Percentage	Standard error	Percentage	Standard error
Australia	59	1.0	87	0.5
Austria	53	2.0	81	0.8
Belgium	27	0.9	84	0.5
Canada	40	0.9	90	0.3
Czech Republic	41	1.6	70	0.9
Denmark	68	1.6	84	0.7
Finland	36	1.5	78	0.6
Germany	23	1.2	82	0.6
Greece	45	2.4	57	1.2
Hungary	80	1.2	67	1.0
Iceland	41	0.8	89	0.6
Ireland	24	1.4	61	0.9
Italy	51	2.0	76	0.8
Japan	26	2.3	37	1.2
Korea	28	1.9	86	0.6
Mexico	54	1.9	48	1.8
New Zealand	43	1.2	79	0.7
Poland	44	1.8	59	1.1
Portugal	34	1.5	78	0.9
Slovak Republic	42	1.5	65	1.0
Sweden	48	1.5	89	0.5
Switzerland	30	1.4	81	0.6
Turkey	46	3.5	48	2.1
United States	43	1.4	83	0.7
OECD average	43	0.3	73	0.2
Russian Federation	43	2.1	43	2.0

StatLink ▩▦▤ http://dx.doi.org/10.1787/451761453535

Computer usage of 15-year-old students

Percentage of 15-year-old students using computers frequently, 2003

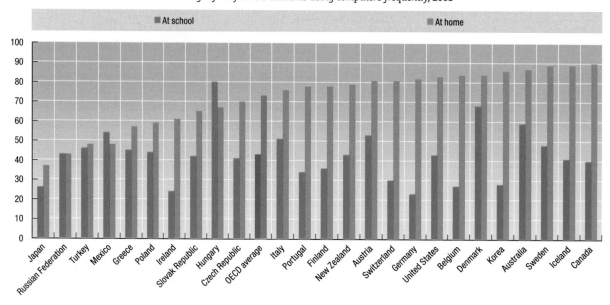

StatLink ▩▦▤ http://dx.doi.org/10.1787/327204574111

OECD FACTBOOK 2007 – ISBN 978-92-64-02946-0 – © OECD 2007

Percentage of 15-year-old students using computers
By number of years of usage, 2003

	Less than one year		One to Three years		Three to five years		More than five years	
	Percentage	Standard error	Percentage	Standard error	Percentage	Standard error	Percentage	Standard error
Australia	1.8	0.1	7.9	0.4	21.0	0.4	69.3	0.5
Austria	4.6	0.4	30.2	1.0	35.7	0.9	29.5	0.7
Belgium	7.7	0.4	30.2	0.7	28.2	0.6	33.9	0.7
Canada	1.6	0.1	10.0	0.3	22.2	0.4	66.2	0.5
Czech Republic	9.2	0.6	32.1	0.8	29.4	0.7	29.2	0.9
Denmark	2.0	0.2	17.5	0.6	28.2	0.8	52.3	0.9
Finland	2.2	0.2	17.3	0.6	30.0	0.7	50.5	0.9
Germany	4.7	0.4	30.3	0.9	31.7	0.8	33.3	0.9
Greece	21.5	1.0	40.8	1.0	23.7	0.9	14.0	1.0
Hungary	6.5	0.5	25.3	0.7	32.4	0.8	35.8	0.7
Iceland	1.9	0.3	18.7	0.7	29.9	0.7	49.5	0.9
Ireland	8.0	0.6	28.1	0.9	32.9	0.7	31.0	1.1
Italy	14.2	0.6	41.1	0.7	23.4	0.6	21.3	0.6
Japan	18.4	0.9	41.2	0.9	25.4	0.8	15.0	0.6
Korea	2.2	0.2	17.9	0.7	34.8	0.8	45.1	1.1
Mexico	38.8	1.8	33.2	1.0	13.6	0.8	14.4	1.8
New Zealand	4.4	0.4	16.1	0.7	24.1	0.7	55.4	0.9
Poland	10.7	0.7	44.1	1.0	24.5	0.9	20.7	1.0
Portugal	10.2	0.6	25.5	0.8	32.5	0.8	31.8	1.0
Slovak Republic	27.5	1.0	36.2	0.7	18.7	0.5	17.6	0.7
Sweden	1.4	0.2	11.7	0.6	29.7	0.9	57.1	1.0
Switzerland	5.4	0.4	28.8	0.7	31.5	0.7	34.3	0.7
Turkey	28.5	1.8	37.5	1.4	19.1	0.9	14.8	1.3
United States	3.3	0.3	12.6	0.5	22.0	0.6	62.1	1.0
OECD average	9.9	0.1	26.4	0.2	26.9	0.1	36.8	0.2
Russian Federation	46.6	2.0	33.5	1.2	11.2	0.8	8.7	..

StatLink http://dx.doi.org/10.1787/368178350154

Percentage of 15-year-old students using computers
By number of years of usage, 2003

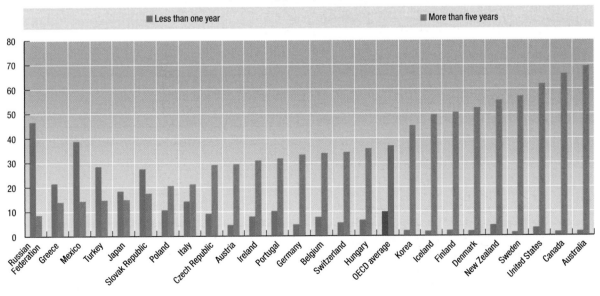

StatLink http://dx.doi.org/10.1787/656502523373

TERTIARY ATTAINMENT

The share of the population that has attained qualifications at the tertiary level is a key indicator of how well countries are placed to profit from technological and scientific progress. Differences between tertiary attainment of younger and older age groups is a measure of progress in the provision of higher education.

Definition

For each age group shown, those who have completed tertiary education are shown as a percentage of all persons in that age group. Tertiary education includes both tertiary-type "A programmes", which are largely theoretically-based and designed to provide qualifications for entry to advanced research programmes and professions with high skill requirements, as well as tertiary-type "B programmes" which are classified at the same level of competencies as tertiary-type A programmes but are more occupationally-oriented and lead to direct labour market access. The tertiary attainment profiles are based on the percentage of the population aged 25 to 64 that has completed that level of education.

Comparability

The International Standard Classification of Education (ISCED-97) is used to define the levels of education. See the *OECD Handbook for Internationally Comparative Education Statistics* for a description of ISCED-97 education programmes and attainment levels and their mappings for each country.

Long-term trends

OECD countries and the Russian Federation have seen significant increases in the proportion of the adult population attaining tertiary education over the last decades. In 2004, for the 25-64 year-old population, 15 countries out of 30 are grouped together within a range of 10 points between 23 and 33% of the population having attained the tertiary level. Three countries are performing remarkably high: Canada, the Russian Federation and the United States. Conversely, three countries are significantly below this average percentage in tertiary attainment where less than 12% of the population attain tertiary qualifications: Brazil, Italy and Turkey.

In the youngest age group, 25 to 34 years old, the OECD country mean for tertiary attainment increased from 20 to 31% between 1991 and 2004. In four countries – Canada, Japan, Korea and the Russian Federation – over 45% of this age group in 2004 obtained a tertiary qualification.

An indication of longer term trends can be obtained by comparing the current attainment levels of younger and older age cohorts. For instance, comparing the tertiary attainment levels of 25-34 year olds with those of 55-64 year olds indicates that in Korea, there has been an increase in tertiary attainment over the past 30 years of nearly 40 percentage points, some 26 percentage points higher than the OECD average increase over this period. In contrast, some OECD countries (the Czech Republic and Germany) have only seen increases of less than 3 percentage points over the same period.

Source
- OECD (2006), *Education at a Glance*, OECD, Paris.

Further information
Analytical publications
- Blöndal, S., S. Field and N. Girouard (2002), "Investment in Human Capital through Upper-Secondary and Tertiary Education", *OECD Economic Studies*, No. 34, 2002/I, OECD, Paris.
- OECD (2006), *Reviews of National Policies for Education*, OECD, Paris.

Methodological publications
- OECD (2004), *OECD Handbook for Internationally Comparative Education Statistics: Concepts, Standards, Definitions and Classifications*, OECD, Paris.

Websites
- OECD Centre for Educational Research and Innovation (CERI), *www.oecd.org/edu/ceri*.
- OECD Education at a Glance, *www.oecd.org/edu/eag2006*.

Tertiary attainment for age group 25-64
As a percentage of the population of that age group

	1991	1992	1993	1994	1995	1996	1997	1998	1999	2000	2001	2002	2003	2004
Australia	21.8	..	22.5	23.1	24.3	24.8	24.3	25.4	26.7	27.5	29.0	30.8	31.3	30.8
Austria	6.7	6.9	..	7.7	7.9	8.1	10.6	10.9	10.9	13.9	14.1	14.5	14.5	18.3
Belgium	19.6	20.2	..	22.3	24.6	23.9	25.1	25.3	26.7	27.1	27.6	28.1	29.0	29.8
Canada	29.9	30.8	..	34.2	34.9	35.6	37.3	38.1	39.2	40.0	41.6	42.6	44.0	44.6
Czech Republic	..	..	..	10.1	10.6	10.4	10.6	10.4	10.8	11.0	11.1	11.9	12.0	12.3
Denmark	18.3	19.2	..	19.6	20.4	20.9	..	25.4	26.5	25.8	26.5	27.4	31.9	32.4
Finland	25.0	25.9	..	26.8	27.7	28.4	29.4	30.2	31.3	32.0	32.3	32.6	33.3	34.0
France	15.2	16.0	17.1	17.8	18.6	19.2	20.0	20.6	21.5	22.0	23.0	24.0	23.4	23.9
Germany	20.5	20.1	..	20.4	22.2	21.8	22.6	23.0	22.9	23.5	23.2	23.4	24.0	24.9
Greece	..	..	..	17.9	17.4	18.9	15.5	16.8	17.5	17.6	17.8	18.3	18.3	20.6
Hungary	..	..	..	..	..	13.4	12.2	13.2	13.5	14.0	14.0	14.2	15.4	16.7
Iceland	..	..	..	..	..	20.8	20.9	21.0	22.4	23.2	24.6	26.3	26.3	27.8
Ireland	15.9	17.0	..	18.6	19.9	22.6	22.8	21.1	20.5	21.8	23.7	25.4	26.3	28.3
Italy	6.1	6.4	..	7.5	7.9	8.1	..	8.6	9.3	9.4	10.0	10.4	10.4	11.4
Japan	..	..	..	..	..	..	30.4	30.4	31.6	33.4	33.8	36.3	37.4	37.4
Korea	14.4	16.1	17.5	17.8	18.6	19.6	19.8	22.5	23.1	23.9	25.0	26.0	29.5	30.5
Luxembourg	..	..	..	..	18.1	19.0	..	..	18.3	18.3	18.1	18.6	14.9	22.9
Mexico	..	..	..	..	11.9	13.2	13.8	13.6	13.4	14.6	15.0	15.3	15.4	16.4
Netherlands	19.6	20.9	..	21.4	22.0	22.5	..	24.2	22.6	23.4	23.2	24.4	24.4	29.3
New Zealand	22.9	23.6	..	23.2	25.3	..	25.8	26.6	27.0	28.0	29.2	29.8	30.9	25.3
Norway	24.8	25.3	..	27.4	28.6	26.9	25.8	27.4	27.5	28.4	30.2	31.0	31.0	31.8
Poland	..	..	..	..	9.9	..	10.2	10.9	11.3	11.4	11.9	12.6	14.2	15.7
Portugal	6.7	..	..	10.7	11.0	10.9	..	8.3	8.7	8.9	9.1	9.3	10.8	12.5
Slovak Republic	..	..	..	11.3	11.1	11.5	10.5	10.3	10.1	10.4	10.9	11.0	11.8	12.4
Spain	9.9	13.1	..	15.0	16.1	17.5	18.6	19.7	21.0	22.6	23.6	24.4	25.2	26.4
Sweden	25.2	25.8	..	27.0	28.3	27.4	27.5	28.0	28.7	30.1	31.6	32.6	33.4	34.5
Switzerland	20.3	21.0	..	21.4	21.1	21.9	22.2	22.9	23.6	24.2	25.4	25.2	27.0	28.2
Turkey	6.3	4.8	..	7.0	8.4	..	7.6	7.5	8.1	8.3	8.4	9.1	9.7	9.1
United Kingdom	16.3	18.5	..	21.3	21.9	22.3	22.7	23.7	24.8	25.7	26.1	26.9	28.0	29.0
United States	30.1	30.2	..	32.2	33.3	33.9	34.1	34.9	35.8	36.5	37.3	38.1	38.4	39.1
OECD average	17.9	19.0	..	19.2	19.3	20.1	20.8	20.7	21.2	21.9	22.6	23.4	24.1	25.2
Brazil	..	..	..	..	..	..	..	..	..	..	..	..	..	7.8
Russian Federation	..	..	..	..	..	..	..	..	..	..	..	..	..	54.6

StatLink http://dx.doi.org/10.1787/621864704470

Tertiary attainment for age group 25-64
As a percentage of the population of that age group, 2004 or latest available year

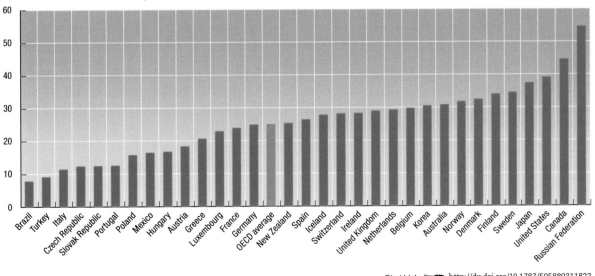

StatLink http://dx.doi.org/10.1787/505880311822

Tertiary attainment for age group 25-34
As a percentage of the population of that age group

	1991	1992	1993	1994	1995	1996	1997	1998	1999	2000	2001	2002	2003	2004
Australia	22.8	..	22.8	23.6	24.7	25.3	25.7	28.1	29.0	31.4	33.5	35.8	36.3	36.2
Austria	7.9	7.9	..	8.8	8.7	9.2	12.4	12.5	12.7	15.0	14.3	14.8	15.4	20.3
Belgium	26.8	27.2	..	30.0	32.9	32.2	33.1	33.8	34.4	36.0	37.5	37.6	38.9	40.7
Canada	32.9	34.2	..	37.8	39.3	40.6	44.1	45.5	46.8	48.3	50.5	51.2	52.8	53.3
Czech Republic	..	..	..	12.5	11.8	11.2	10.9	10.5	10.9	11.2	11.3	12.3	12.1	13.0
Denmark	18.7	19.5	..	19.7	20.3	20.7	..	26.8	28.6	29.3	29.1	30.6	35.1	34.9
Finland	33.3	33.5	..	34.1	35.0	35.2	36.4	36.0	37.4	37.6	38.2	39.2	39.8	38.0
France	20.1	21.6	23.1	24.3	25.4	26.0	27.8	29.6	30.9	32.4	34.2	36.1	37.4	38.1
Germany	19.6	18.8	..	18.7	20.8	20.3	21.0	21.5	21.5	22.3	21.8	21.7	21.8	22.9
Greece	..	..	..	25.0	26.0	28.2	22.3	24.3	24.6	24.3	24.0	24.1	23.7	24.6
Hungary	..	..	..	..	..	14.3	12.4	13.9	13.7	14.7	14.8	15.0	16.8	18.9
Iceland	..	..	..	..	..	23.7	23.0	24.2	27.6	27.8	26.5	29.1	29.1	31.3
Ireland	19.7	21.2	..	24.4	27.2	31.3	32.5	29.5	28.1	30.3	33.4	36.3	37.1	40.4
Italy	6.6	6.8	..	7.9	8.2	8.3	..	9.0	10.0	10.4	11.8	12.5	12.5	14.6
Japan	..	..	..	..	..	..	45.2	45.4	45.1	47.2	47.7	50.3	51.6	51.6
Korea	21.0	23.9	26.8	27.7	29.2	30.6	30.9	33.8	34.8	36.9	39.2	41.2	46.6	49.1
Luxembourg	..	..	..	..	..	..	..	..	21.2	22.9	23.4	22.6	18.7	30.9
Mexico	..	..	..	..	16.3	17.1	17.3	16.7	16.6	17.4	18.0	18.4	18.7	19.3
Netherlands	22.2	23.6	..	23.9	24.5	25.1	..	27.5	25.1	26.6	26.5	27.7	27.7	34.2
New Zealand	23.2	23.2	..	21.1	24.2	..	25.4	26.4	26.0	27.2	28.5	29.3	32.4	28.0
Norway	27.1	28.2	..	30.7	32.1	30.0	29.9	32.8	34.7	34.9	37.9	39.7	39.8	39.2
Poland	..	..	..	..	9.9	..	10.3	11.8	12.3	14.2	15.2	16.8	20.4	23.2
Portugal	8.5	..	..	13.2	13.5	14.4	..	11.5	12.2	13.0	14.0	15.0	16.3	18.6
Slovak Republic	..	..	..	12.5	11.6	12.4	10.4	11.3	11.1	11.2	11.9	11.9	13.2	14.3
Spain	16.3	22.5	..	25.2	26.6	28.6	30.3	32.0	33.5	34.1	35.5	36.7	37.5	38.1
Sweden	27.0	26.5	..	27.3	28.6	28.4	29.3	30.7	31.7	33.6	36.9	39.2	40.4	42.3
Switzerland	21.3	21.3	..	22.0	21.5	22.5	24.7	25.0	25.9	25.6	25.6	26.5	29.4	30.4
Turkey	6.1	5.6	..	6.6	7.5	..	7.3	7.8	8.7	8.9	9.1	10.5	11.4	10.8
United Kingdom	18.5	20.6	..	23.1	23.3	24.3	24.7	25.9	27.3	28.6	29.5	31.2	33.1	34.6
United States	30.2	30.2	..	32.0	33.6	35.2	35.7	36.2	37.4	38.1	39.1	39.3	38.7	39.0
OECD average	20.5	21.9	..	22.2	22.4	23.8	24.9	24.8	25.3	26.4	27.3	28.4	29.5	31.0
Brazil	..	..	..	..	..	..	..	..	..	..	..	..	..	7.9
Russian Federation	..	..	..	..	..	..	..	..	..	..	..	..	..	56.1

StatLink http://dx.doi.org/10.1787/043013130651

Tertiary attainment for age group 25-34
As a percentage of the population of that age group, 2004 or latest available year

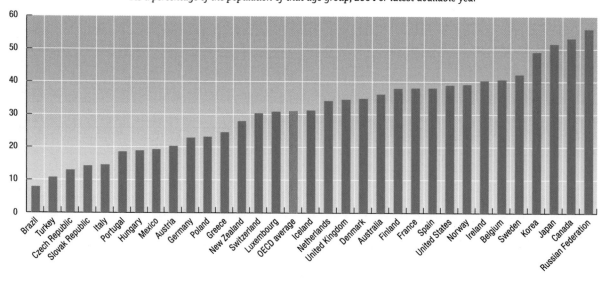

StatLink http://dx.doi.org/10.1787/454324685224

OECD FACTBOOK 2007 – ISBN 978-92-64-02946-0 – © OECD 2007

Tertiary attainment for age group 55-64

As a percentage of the population of that age group

	1991	1992	1993	1994	1995	1996	1997	1998	1999	2000	2001	2002	2003	2004
Australia	13.4	..	13.5	14.7	17.2	16.9	17.1	17.0	17.5	19.1	21.1	22.5	23.3	23.0
Austria	3.8	3.3	..	3.6	4.2	4.7	6.3	6.5	6.5	9.9	10.6	11.0	11.3	14.8
Belgium	8.6	9.2	..	11.1	13.1	12.7	13.7	13.8	15.7	16.8	17.1	18.2	18.9	20.0
Canada	18.8	19.2	..	23.0	23.6	25.1	24.3	25.7	27.4	28.3	30.1	32.1	33.8	34.5
Czech Republic	..	..	..	7.6	8.3	7.5	7.9	8.5	9.4	9.1	9.3	10.6	10.3	10.2
Denmark	11.9	12.6	..	13.2	13.8	14.3	..	19.3	19.0	18.2	20.2	24.2	25.9	27.3
Finland	12.2	12.8	..	13.9	15.5	17.0	17.9	19.3	20.7	22.7	23.4	23.4	24.2	25.4
France	6.6	7.3	7.9	8.4	8.9	9.6	10.5	11.2	12.4	13.3	14.1	15.2	13.9	14.4
Germany	16.0	15.7	..	16.5	17.5	17.5	18.4	19.3	19.4	20.2	20.2	20.6	21.6	22.8
Greece	..	..	..	9.1	7.8	8.4	7.5	7.8	8.4	8.5	9.0	9.7	10.6	11.6
Hungary	..	..	..	..	..	8.9	8.5	10.2	11.2	11.8	11.5	12.6	13.8	14.4
Iceland	..	..	..	..	..	9.5	11.6	10.8	11.3	13.5	14.8	16.7	..	17.4
Ireland	9.6	10.4	..	11.3	11.0	12.6	12.5	11.4	12.6	13.3	13.5	14.4	15.0	15.7
Italy	3.3	3.5	..	4.2	4.4	4.6	..	4.8	5.5	5.5	6.2	6.7	..	7.2
Japan	..	..	..	..	..	..	13.7	13.2	14.3	15.1	15.1	18.0	19.2	19.2
Korea	5.8	5.9	6.7	6.7	6.8	6.8	6.5	8.3	8.5	8.6	8.9	9.1	9.5	9.7
Luxembourg	..	..	..	..	..	..	..	..	12.0	13.0	13.5	14.4	10.6	15.9
Mexico	..	..	..	..	4.4	4.6	5.7	4.9	5.7	7.0	7.2	7.2	7.6	8.5
Netherlands	12.2	13.2	..	14.4	14.2	15.6	..	16.9	16.9	17.7	17.4	18.8	..	23.6
New Zealand	..	17.1	..	17.9	21.1	..	21.2	23.1	23.1	24.2	24.1	26.2	27.4	19.7
Norway	14.0	14.2	..	17.7	18.0	16.9	17.5	18.9	18.8	20.4	21.5	21.7	21.5	23.2
Poland	..	..	..	..	8.2	..	9.1	9.9	10.4	9.9	10.2	10.5	11.1	12.2
Portugal	3.4	..	..	5.6	5.9	6.2	..	4.7	4.5	4.7	4.9	4.6	5.6	6.7
Slovak Republic	..	..	..	7.0	7.5	7.2	6.1	6.7	6.9	7.8	8.6	8.6	8.9	9.3
Spain	4.2	5.2	..	5.6	6.0	7.1	7.6	8.1	8.7	9.7	10.3	10.5	11.0	12.4
Sweden	15.5	16.5	..	19.4	20.2	18.5	19.3	19.9	21.3	23.0	24.4	25.2	26.3	27.3
Switzerland	15.5	17.0	..	16.9	17.4	16.8	16.5	18.0	17.8	18.3	20.2	21.3	21.9	22.0
Turkey	4.6	1.7	..	4.3	5.9	..	4.6	4.5	5.3	5.9	5.9	6.3	7.3	6.6
United Kingdom	10.9	13.6	..	15.5	16.2	16.9	16.3	17.2	18.5	18.9	19.1	19.8	20.8	22.6
United States	21.9	21.9	..	23.6	24.3	25.6	26.2	27.2	28.0	29.7	30.6	33.2	34.7	36.2
OECD average	10.6	11.6	..	12.1	12.4	12.5	13.1	13.4	13.9	14.8	15.4	16.4	17.3	17.8
Brazil	..	..	..	..	..	..	..	..	..	..	..	..	..	3.7
Russian Federation	..	..	..	..	..	..	..	..	..	..	..	..	..	44.8

StatLink ᴹˢᴸ http://dx.doi.org/10.1787/256248743228

Tertiary attainment for age group 55-64

As a percentage of the population of that age group, 2004 or latest available year

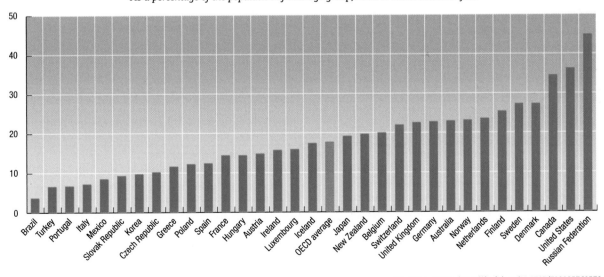

StatLink ᴹˢᴸ http://dx.doi.org/10.1787/703335763573

EXPENDITURE ON TERTIARY EDUCATION

Policy makers must balance the importance of improving the quality of educational services with the desirability of expanding access to educational opportunities, notably at the tertiary level. The comparative review of how trends in educational expenditure per student have evolved shows that in many OECD countries the expansion of enrolments, particularly in tertiary education, has not always been paralleled by changes in educational investment.

Definition

The indicator shows direct public and private expenditure on educational institutions in relation to the number of tertiary full-time equivalent students enrolled in these institutions. Public subsidies for students' living expenses have been excluded to ensure international comparability of the data.

Expenditure on education per student is obtained by dividing the total expenditure on educational institutions by the number of full-time equivalents students. Only those educational institutions and programmes are taken into account for which both enrolment and expenditure data are available.

Comparability

Expenditure in national currency for 2003 is converted to US dollars by PPP exchange rates. The PPP exchange rate is used because the market exchange rate is affected by many factors (interest rates, trade policies, expectations of economic growth, etc.) that have little to do with relative purchasing power of currencies in different countries.

The changes in expenditure on educational institutions per student are based on data from 1995 and 2003. The data on expenditure for 1995 were obtained by a special survey updated in 2003. OECD countries were asked to collect the 1995 data according to the definitions and the coverage of a joint UNESCO-OECD-Eurostat data collection programme. All expenditure data have been adjusted to 2003 prices using the GDP price deflator.

Long-term trends

In 2003, the level of expenditure per tertiary student on average in OECD countries was 11 254 US dollars converted using PPPs. This average masks a considerable variation of spending at tertiary level with three countries (Greece, Poland and the Slovak Republic) spending less than 5 000 US dollars per student rising up to a level of spending of more than 20 000 US dollars in Switzerland and the United States. OECD countries in which most R&D is performed by tertiary educational institutions tend to report higher expenditure per tertiary student than countries in which a large part of R&D is performed in other public institutions or by industry.

On average, for the countries where data are available, expenditure on tertiary education per student increased by 6% over the period 1995 to 2003. Despite this average increase however, there was a marked decrease in expenditure in five out of 24 OECD countries (Australia, the Czech Republic, Poland, Portugal and the Slovak Republic) and in the partner country Brazil which was largely due to a rapid increase in the number of tertiary students enrolled in the same period. On the other hand, expenditure per tertiary student rose significantly in Greece, Hungary, Ireland and Mexico despite a growth in enrolment of 93, 70, 34 and 48%, respectively.

Source

• OECD (2006), *Education at a Glance*, OECD, Paris.

Further information

Analytical publications

• OECD (2004), *Quality and Recognition in Higher Education: The Cross-border Challenge*, OECD, Paris.

• OECD (2004), *Internationalisation and Trade in Higher Education: Opportunities and Challenges*, OECD, Paris.

• OECD (2006), *Education Policy Analysis: Focus on Higher Education* , OECD, Paris.

• OECD (2006), *Reviews of National Policies for Education*, OECD, Paris.

• OECD (2006), *Higher Education Management and Policy*, OECD, Paris.

Methodological publications

• UIS, OECD and Eurostat (2002), *UOE Data Collection – 2002 Data Collection on Education Systems: Definitions, Explanations and Instructions*, OECD, Paris.

• OECD (2004), *OECD Handbook for Internationally Comparative Education Statistics: Concepts, Standards, Definitions and Classifications*, OECD, Paris.

Websites

• OECD, *Education at a Glance*, www.oecd.org/edu/eag2006.

Expenditure per student in tertiary education
Year 2003

	Index of change, year 1995 = 100			Expenditure per student in tertiary education: 2003 constant prices (US dollars)
	Expenditure	Number of students	Expenditure per student	
Australia	125	133	94	12 406
Austria	115	101	115	12 344
Belgium	..	..	..	11 824
Canada	138	107	128	19 992
Czech Republic	139	186	74	6 774
Denmark	126	107	118	14 014
Finland	122	114	107	12 047
France	..	..	..	10 704
Germany	114	105	108	11 594
Greece	244	193	126	4 924
Hungary	182	170	107	8 576
Iceland	..	..	..	8 023
Ireland	163	134	121	9 341
Italy	137	107	128	8 764
Japan	139	123	114	11 556
Korea	..	159	..	7 089
Mexico	167	148	113	5 774
Netherlands	112	109	103	13 444
New Zealand	111	..	..	8 832
Norway	112	111	100	13 772
Poland	170	269	63	4 589
Portugal	140	148	95	7 200
Slovak Republic	167	201	83	4 678
Spain	158	111	143	8 943
Sweden	141	141	100	16 073
Switzerland	174	119	146	25 900
Turkey	202	104	194	..
United Kingdom	120	120	100	11 866
United States	133	121	110	24 074
OECD average	146	138	106	11 254
Brazil	140	158	89	10 054
Russian Federation	..	..	..	2 451

StatLink 🔗 http://dx.doi.org/10.1787/146318247756

Changes in real expenditure on educational institutions in tertiary education
Percentage change 1995-2003

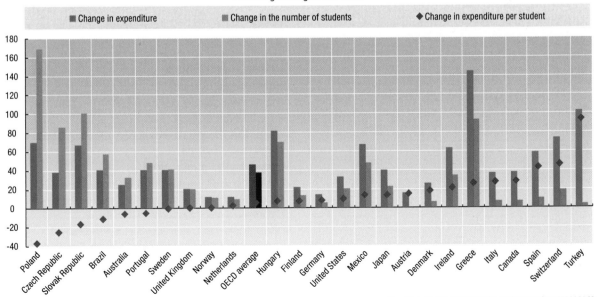

StatLink 🔗 http://dx.doi.org/10.1787/280675838368

PUBLIC AND PRIVATE EDUCATION EXPENDITURE

Expenditure on education is an investment that can help to foster economic growth, enhance productivity, contribute to personal and social development, and reduce social inequality. The proportion of total financial resources devoted to education is one of the key choices made in each country by governments, enterprises and individual students and their families.

Definition

This indicator covers expenditure on schools, universities and other public and private institutions involved in delivering or supporting educational services. Expenditure on institutions is not limited to expenditure on instructional services but also includes public and private expenditure on ancillary services for students and families, where these services are provided through educational institutions. At the tertiary level, spending on research and development can also be significant and is included in this indicator, to the extent that the research is performed by educational institutions.

In principle, public expenditure includes public subsidies to households attributable for educational institutions and direct expenditure on educational institutions from international sources. However, public subsidies for educational expenditure outside educational institutions (*e.g.* textbooks purchased by families, private tutoring sought for students, student living costs) are excluded. At the tertiary level, student living costs and forgone earnings can also account for a significant proportion of the costs of education.

Comparability

The broad definition of institutions outlined above ensures that expenditure on services, which are provided in some OECD countries by schools and universities and in others by agencies other than schools, are covered on a comparable basis. Additionally, to ensure comparability over time the data on expenditure for 1995 were obtained by a special survey updated in 2003; expenditure for 1995 was adjusted to the methods and definitions used in the 2003 data collection.

Long-term trends

In 2003, taking into account both public and private sources of funds, OECD countries as a whole spent 6.3% of their collective GDP on their educational institutions. The highest spending on educational institutions can be observed in Denmark, Iceland, Korea and the United States, with more than 7% of GDP. Seven out of 29 OECD countries for which data are available, however, spend less than 5% of GDP on educational institutions.

In all the countries, public and private expenditure on education increased by 5% or more between 1995 and 2003 in real terms. However, the increase in spending on education between 1995 and 2003 tended to fall behind the growth in national income in eight of the 21 OECD countries. Most notable differences are observed in Austria, Canada, Ireland, Norway and Spain where the proportion of GDP spent on education decreased by 0.4 or more in percentage points between 1995 and 2003.

It should be noted that growth in GDP masks the fact that there was a significant increase in real terms in spending on educational institutions in almost all of the OECD countries from 1995 to 2003. In addition, the size of the school age population shapes the demand for education and training, and national levels of teachers' salaries also affect the share of expenditure on education.

Source

• OECD (2006), *Education at a Glance*, OECD, Paris.

Further information

Analytical publications

• OECD (2006), *Schooling for Tomorrow – Think Scenarios, Rethink Education*, OECD, Paris.

• OECD (2006), *Starting Strong II: Early Childhood Education and Care*, OECD, Paris.

Methodological publications

• UIS, OECD and Eurostat (2002), *UOE Data Collection – 2002 Data Collection on Education Systems: Definitions, Explanations and Instructions*, OECD, Paris.

• OECD (2004), *OECD Handbook for Internationally Comparative Education Statistics: Concepts, Standards, Definitions and Classifications*, OECD, Paris.

Websites

• OECD, *Education at a Glance*, www.oecd.org/edu/eag2006.

Expenditure on educational institutions for all levels of education

As a percentage of GDP

	1995			2003		
	Public	Private	Total	Public	Private	Total
Australia	4.5	1.0	5.5	4.3	1.5	5.8
Austria	5.8	0.3	6.1	5.2	0.3	5.5
Belgium	..	..	..	5.9	0.2	6.1
Canada	6.2	0.8	7.0	4.6	1.3	5.9
Czech Republic	4.8	0.3	5.1	4.3	0.4	4.7
Denmark	6.0	0.2	6.2	6.7	0.3	7.0
Finland	6.2	..	6.3	6.0	0.1	6.1
France	..	..	..	5.8	0.5	6.3
Germany	4.4	0.9	5.4	4.4	0.9	5.3
Greece	2.9	..	3.0	4.0	0.2	4.2
Hungary	4.8	0.6	5.4	5.5	0.6	6.1
Iceland	..	..	..	7.5	0.5	8.0
Ireland	4.7	0.5	5.2	4.1	0.3	4.4
Italy	4.8	..	..	4.6	0.4	5.1
Japan	3.5	1.1	4.7	3.5	1.2	4.8
Korea	..	..	..	4.6	2.9	7.5
Mexico	4.6	1.0	5.6	5.6	1.2	6.8
Netherlands	4.4	0.2	4.7	4.6	0.4	5.0
New Zealand	4.8	..	..	5.7	1.2	6.8
Norway	6.8	0.4	7.1	6.5	0.1	6.6
Poland	5.3	..	..	5.8	0.7	6.4
Portugal	5.3	..	5.3	5.8	0.1	5.9
Slovak Republic	4.6	0.1	4.7	4.3	0.5	4.7
Spain	4.5	0.8	5.3	4.2	0.5	4.7
Sweden	6.1	0.1	6.2	6.5	0.2	6.7
Switzerland	5.3	..	..	6.0	0.6	6.5
Turkey	2.3	..	2.3	3.6	0.1	3.7
United Kingdom	4.8	0.7	5.5	5.1	1.0	6.1
United States	5.0	2.2	7.2	5.4	2.1	7.5
OECD average	..	..	..	5.2	0.7	5.9
OECD total	..	..	..	4.9	1.3	6.3
Brazil	3.7	..	..	4.4	..	..
Russian Federation	..	..	..	3.7	..	..

StatLink http://dx.doi.org/10.1787/336057344251

Total expenditure on educational institutions for all levels of education

As a percentage of GDP

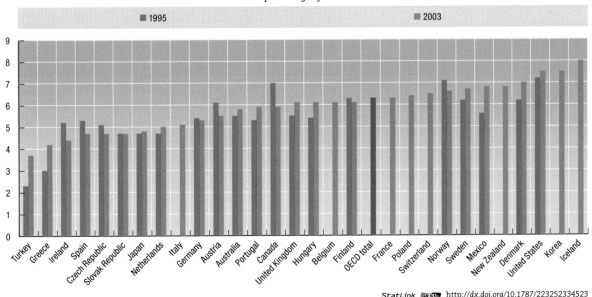

StatLink http://dx.doi.org/10.1787/223252334523

PUBLIC FINANCE

GOVERNMENT DEFICITS AND DEBT
GOVERNMENT DEFICITS
GOVERNMENT DEBT

PUBLIC EXPENDITURE AND AID
SOCIAL EXPENDITURE
LAW, ORDER AND DEFENCE EXPENDITURE
AGRICULTURAL SUPPORT ESTIMATES
GOVERNMENT SUPPORT FOR FISHING
OFFICIAL DEVELOPMENT ASSISTANCE

TAXES
TOTAL TAX REVENUE
TAXES ON THE AVERAGE WORKER

GOVERNMENT DEFICITS

Government deficits or surpluses are commonly assessed using the net borrowing (or net lending) figures of the general government sector in the national accounts. During the period since 1991, governments in most OECD countries have recorded deficits. Government deficits have to be met by borrowing from residents or foreigners.

Definition

The net borrowing/net lending of the general government is the balancing item of the non-financial accounts (according to the 1993 *System of National Accounts*). It is also equal to the difference between total revenue and total expenditure, including capital expenditure (in particular, gross fixed capital formation). The main revenue of general government consists of tax, social contributions, dividends and other property income. The main expenditure items consist of the compensation of civil servants, social benefits, interest on the public debt, subsidies and gross fixed capital formation. A negative figure indicates a deficit.

The data in the table are on a national accounts basis and may differ from the numbers reported to the European Commission under the excessive deficit procedure (EDP) for some EU countries and for some years.

Comparability

Data in this table are based on the 1993 *System of National Accounts* or on the 1995 *European System of Accounts* so that all countries are using a common set of definitions. In several OECD countries the accounts for 2000, 2001 or 2002 were affected by the sale of mobile telephone licences, recorded in national accounts as a negative expenditure (the sale of an asset) thereby reducing the deficit.

The averages shown for OECD are weighted averages.

Long-term trends

Government deficits are sensitive to the economic cycle as well as to government taxation and spending policies. For the OECD as a whole, deficits as a percentage of GDP reached a peak in 1993 but then fell steadily over the next six years and had turned into surpluses (net lending) at the peak of the economic cycle in 2000. Since then, deficits have been growing and the deficit to GDP ratio had become high in 2003 for most of the larger member countries including France, Germany, the United Kingdom, the United States and, especially, Japan. In 2004-2005 the deficit to GDP ratios were reduced in most countries with the exception of Hungary, Italy and Portugal.

In the run-up to monetary union, EU countries that expected to adopt the Euro followed fiscal policies aimed at reducing government deficits. Deficit reduction policies were successfully implemented in several other countries, including New Zealand (since 1994), Australia (since 1997), Denmark (since 1998) and Sweden (since 1998). Korea is the only country which has recorded surpluses throughout the period, although Norway has had surpluses in most years since 1990.

Source

- OECD (2007), *OECD Economic Outlook: December No. 80 – Volume 2006 Issue 2*, OECD, Paris.

Further information

Analytical publications

- OECD (2006), *OECD Economic Surveys*, OECD, Paris.

Statistical publications

- OECD (2006), *National Accounts of OECD Countries*, OECD, Paris.

Online databases

- *National Accounts*.
- *OECD Economic Outlook Statistics*.

Websites

- OECD Economic Outlook – Sources and Methods, *www.oecd.org/eco/sources-and-methods*.

Government net borrowing/net lending

As a percentage of GDP

	1992	1993	1994	1995	1996	1997	1998	1999	2000	2001	2002	2003	2004	2005
Australia	-6.0	-5.2	-4.5	-3.9	-2.2	-0.5	0.6	2.0	0.9	-0.8	0.8	1.6	1.6	1.6
Austria	-2.0	-4.4	-4.9	-5.7	-4.0	-1.8	-2.4	-2.3	-1.6	-0.1	-0.7	-1.8	-1.3	-1.6
Belgium	-8.0	-7.3	-5.0	-4.4	-3.8	-2.1	-0.8	-0.5	-	0.5	-	-	-0.1	-
Canada	-9.1	-8.7	-6.7	-5.3	-2.8	0.2	0.1	1.6	2.9	0.7	-0.1	-0.4	0.5	1.4
Czech Republic	..	..	..	-13.4	-3.3	-3.8	-5.0	-3.7	-3.7	-5.7	-6.8	-6.6	-2.9	-3.6
Denmark	-2.6	-3.8	-3.3	-2.9	-1.9	-0.5	-	1.4	2.3	1.2	0.2	-0.1	1.9	4.6
Finland	-5.5	-8.3	-6.7	-6.2	-3.5	-1.2	1.7	1.6	6.9	5.0	4.1	2.3	2.1	2.5
France	-4.4	-5.9	-5.5	-5.5	-4.1	-3.0	-2.6	-1.7	-1.5	-1.6	-3.2	-4.2	-3.7	-2.9
Germany	-2.5	-3.0	-2.3	-3.2	-3.3	-2.6	-2.2	-1.5	1.3	-2.8	-3.7	-4.0	-3.7	-3.2
Greece	-12.0	-13.1	-9.1	-9.9	-7.3	-6.5	-4.2	-3.4	-4.1	-4.9	-5.3	-6.2	-7.7	-5.1
Hungary	-7.3	-6.8	-11.4	-7.8	-6.1	-7.5	-8.5	-5.3	-3.0	-3.5	-8.2	-6.3	-5.3	-6.5
Iceland	-2.8	-4.5	-4.7	-2.9	-1.6	-	0.5	2.3	2.4	0.2	-0.8	-2.0	0.5	5.5
Ireland	-2.9	-2.7	-2.0	-2.0	-	1.6	2.2	2.6	4.6	0.8	-0.4	0.4	1.5	1.1
Italy	-10.4	-10.1	-9.1	-7.4	-7.0	-2.7	-3.1	-1.8	-0.9	-3.1	-3.0	-3.5	-3.5	-4.3
Japan	0.8	-2.4	-4.2	-5.1	-5.1	-4.1	-5.9	-7.5	-7.7	-6.4	-8.2	-8.0	-6.3	-5.3
Korea	1.4	2.2	2.9	3.8	3.4	3.3	1.6	2.7	5.4	4.6	5.4	0.4	2.5	2.5
Luxembourg	-0.2	1.5	2.5	2.4	1.2	3.7	3.4	3.4	6.0	6.1	2.1	0.3	-1.1	-1.0
Netherlands	-4.0	-2.7	-3.3	-4.3	-2.0	-1.3	-0.9	0.4	2.0	-0.3	-2.0	-3.1	-1.8	-0.3
New Zealand	-3.1	-0.4	3.1	2.9	2.8	1.6	0.1	-0.2	1.6	2.2	3.1	3.9	3.6	4.2
Norway	-1.9	-1.4	0.3	3.4	6.5	7.7	3.6	6.2	15.6	13.6	9.3	7.5	11.4	16.2
Poland	..	..	..	-4.4	-4.9	-4.6	-4.3	-1.8	-1.5	-3.7	-3.2	-4.7	-3.9	-2.4
Portugal	-4.5	-7.7	-7.4	-5.2	-4.5	-3.4	-3.0	-2.7	-3.0	-4.3	-2.9	-3.0	-3.2	-6.0
Slovak Republic	..	..	-6.8	-1.8	-8.6	-6.7	-4.8	-6.4	-11.8	-6.5	-7.7	-3.7	-3.0	-3.1
Spain	-3.7	-6.9	-6.5	-6.3	-4.7	-2.9	-3.0	-0.9	-0.9	-0.5	-0.3	-	-0.2	1.1
Sweden	-8.9	-11.3	-9.2	-6.9	-2.8	-1.0	1.9	2.3	5.0	2.6	-0.5	-0.2	1.6	2.8
Switzerland	-2.4	-2.7	-1.9	-1.2	-1.4	-2.4	-1.5	-	2.4	0.9	0.1	-1.3	-1.1	-0.5
United Kingdom	-6.4	-7.9	-6.8	-5.8	-4.1	-2.1	0.1	1.2	4.0	0.9	-1.7	-3.4	-3.3	-3.4
United States	-5.8	-4.9	-3.6	-3.1	-2.2	-0.8	0.4	0.9	1.6	-0.4	-3.8	-4.8	-4.6	-3.7
Euro area	-5.0	-5.7	-4.9	-5.0	-4.2	-2.6	-2.3	-1.3	-	-1.8	-2.6	-3.1	-2.8	-2.4
OECD total	-4.6	-4.9	-4.2	-4.0	-3.1	-1.7	-1.3	-0.8	0.3	-1.3	-3.2	-4.0	-3.4	-2.7

StatLink ᫸ http://dx.doi.org/10.1787/666354282323

Government net borrowing/net lending

As a percentage of GDP, average 2003-2005

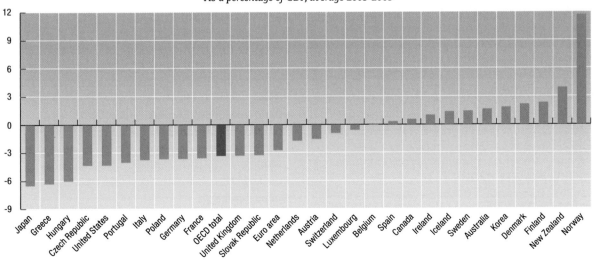

StatLink ᫸ http://dx.doi.org/10.1787/247172280434

GOVERNMENT DEBT

There are two standard ways to measure the extent of government debt – by reference to gross financial liabilities or by reference to net financial liabilities – the latter being measured as gross financial liabilities minus financial assets. Gross financial liabilities as a percentage of GDP is the most commonly used government debt ratio and is shown here.

Definition

For most countries, gross financial liabilities refer to the liabilities (short and long-term) of all the institutions in the general government sector, as defined in the 1993 *System of National Accounts* (SNA) or in the 1995 *European System of Accounts* (ESA). However, for Luxembourg the definition of debt applied under the Maastricht Treaty has been used. The Maastricht definition of debt essentially differs from the SNA definition in two respects. First, gross debt according to the Maastricht definition excludes trade credits and advances, as well as shares and insurance technical reserves. Second, government bonds are valued at nominal values instead of at market value or issue price plus accrued interest as required by the SNA rules. The United States and Canada also value government bonds at nominal value.

In principle, debts within and between different levels of government are consolidated; a loan from one level of government to another represents both an asset and an equal liability for the government as a whole and so it cancels out (is "consolidated") for the general government sector.

Comparability

The comparability of data can be affected in two ways. First, national differences in implementing SNA/ESA definitions can affect the comparability of government debt across countries. Second, changes in implementing SNA/ESA definitions can affect the comparability of data within a country over time.

Long-term trends

From 1990 to 1996, government gross financial liabilities were rising in most countries. Since then, government debt has been decreasing as a percentage of GDP in many of the 28 countries in the table. There are, however, exceptions: government debt ratios continued to increase particularly fast in Japan and Korea and significantly in France, Germany, Greece and Portugal. Korea's government debt ratio rose by over 8% per year from 1990 to 2005 but this is measured from a very low initial rate and by 2005, Korea's government debt ratio was still among the lowest in the OECD.

In 2005, government debt ratios exceeded 100% in Greece, Italy and Japan and was close to 100% in Belgium. Most countries were in a band between 40% and 70%, with two countries reporting debt ratios of under 20% – Australia and Luxembourg.

Source

• OECD (2007), *OECD Economic Outlook: December No. 80 – Volume 2006 Issue 2*, OECD, Paris.

Further information

Analytical publications

• OECD (2002), *Debt Management and Government Securities Markets in the 21st Century*, OECD, Paris.

• OECD (2006), *Credit Risk and Credit Access in Asia*, OECD, Paris.

• OECD (2006), *OECD Economic Surveys*, OECD, Paris.

Statistical publications

• OECD (2006), *National Accounts of OECD Countries*, OECD, Paris.

• OECD (2006), *Central Government Debt*, OECD, Paris.

Online databases

• National Accounts.

• OECD Economic Outlook Statistics.

Websites

• OECD Economic Outlook – Sources and Methods, *www.oecd.org/eco/sources-and-methods*.

General government gross financial liabilities
As a percentage of GDP

	1992	1993	1994	1995	1996	1997	1998	1999	2000	2001	2002	2003	2004	2005
Australia	27.4	30.7	40.1	41.9	39.1	37.4	32.3	28.0	25.0	22.1	20.1	18.8	17.2	16.9
Austria	57.0	61.7	64.9	69.2	69.6	66.0	67.4	70.0	69.6	70.5	71.8	69.8	69.4	69.6
Belgium	136.7	140.8	137.9	135.4	133.2	128.1	122.9	119.6	113.4	111.6	108.1	103.4	98.5	95.0
Canada	90.2	96.3	98.0	101.6	101.7	96.3	95.2	91.4	82.1	82.1	80.6	76.5	72.1	70.8
Czech Republic	..	..	..	..	..	..	..	..	..	..	33.1	40.6	39.8	37.5
Denmark	71.1	85.0	78.9	80.0	77.2	72.7	69.0	63.2	56.3	53.8	54.5	53.4	49.9	41.4
Finland	44.6	57.8	60.8	65.3	66.2	64.5	60.9	54.7	52.3	49.7	49.3	51.2	51.6	48.3
France	43.9	51.0	60.2	62.6	66.3	68.4	69.9	66.5	65.2	63.8	66.8	71.0	73.3	76.1
Germany	40.9	46.2	46.6	55.7	58.9	60.4	62.2	61.5	60.4	59.7	62.1	65.4	68.8	71.1
Greece	..	..	..	111.9	114.0	110.0	107.4	111.2	127.2	131.2	129.5	126.1	127.3	124.2
Hungary	80.2	90.9	90.6	88.2	76.0	66.5	64.5	65.3	59.0	58.1	58.9	59.0	62.1	64.5
Iceland	46.2	53.1	55.6	58.9	56.3	53.1	47.9	43.2	40.9	46.4	42.3	40.5	35.0	26.6
Ireland	..	..	..	..	..	..	61.4	50.7	40.7	37.9	35.9	34.7	33.5	32.5
Italy	..	..	..	121.8	128.1	129.7	132.0	125.7	121.0	120.1	119.0	116.9	117.5	120.4
Japan	68.6	74.7	80.2	87.7	95.3	102.3	114.9	128.9	137.1	145.2	154.0	160.2	168.1	173.1
Korea	6.4	5.6	5.2	5.5	5.9	7.5	13.1	15.6	16.3	17.4	16.6	18.4	22.6	24.9
Luxembourg	4.8	6.0	5.5	5.8	6.3	6.4	6.2	5.6	5.3	6.5	6.5	6.3	6.6	6.0
Netherlands	89.0	93.7	83.8	86.8	85.7	80.9	79.3	70.9	63.7	59.4	60.3	61.4	61.4	61.4
New Zealand	..	..	57.4	51.3	44.9	42.3	42.2	39.6	37.4	35.4	33.6	31.7	29.1	28.2
Norway	32.3	40.6	37.0	40.6	36.6	32.1	31.1	31.3	34.3	33.2	40.5	49.9	53.6	50.6
Poland	..	..	..	51.6	51.4	48.3	43.8	46.6	42.4	37.4	50.3	50.8	49.8	50.6
Portugal	..	..	..	68.8	68.4	64.6	64.9	60.9	60.2	61.6	65.0	66.4	68.4	72.8
Slovak Republic	..	..	..	38.5	37.0	38.6	40.7	51.5	58.7	58.8	51.5	49.8	47.5	41.9
Spain	51.9	65.5	64.1	68.8	75.6	74.5	74.3	68.4	66.2	61.6	59.8	54.7	52.7	50.1
Sweden	73.9	79.0	83.3	82.0	84.4	82.5	81.3	71.3	63.9	62.9	59.8	59.3	58.9	59.5
United Kingdom	39.5	49.3	47.5	52.4	52.2	53.0	53.6	48.5	45.7	41.0	41.3	41.8	43.7	46.7
United States	70.2	71.9	71.1	70.7	70.0	67.6	64.5	61.0	55.2	55.2	57.5	60.8	61.6	61.8
Euro area	49.2	55.4	58.5		72.1	77.3	79.4	79.9	78.2	75.1	73.8	74.1	75.1	76.0	77.3
OECD total	59.3	63.7	65.2		70.1	72.2	72.5	73.0	72.4	69.6	69.8	71.9	74.2	75.8	76.9

StatLink 🔗 http://dx.doi.org/10.1787/227413588602

General government gross financial liabilities
As a percentage of GDP

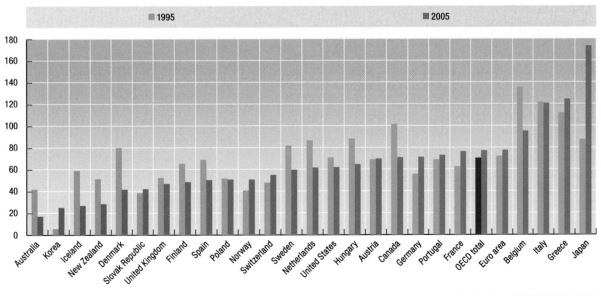

StatLink 🔗 http://dx.doi.org/10.1787/740680754054

SOCIAL EXPENDITURE

Social expenditures as a percentage of GDP are a measure of the extent to which governments assume responsibility for supporting the standard of living of disadvantaged or vulnerable groups.

Long-term trends

In 2003, on average, public social expenditure amounted to 21% of GDP, although there are significant cross-country variations. In Sweden, public social spending is about 31% while it is 5-6% in Mexico and Korea.

Changes in gross public social expenditures over time are also significant. Since 1980, gross public social expenditure has increased from about 16% to 21% of GDP in 2003 on average across 28 OECD countries. Experiences differ across OECD countries, but on average public social spending-to-GDP ratios increased most significantly in the early 1980s, early 1990s and, again in the beginning of this millennium, when the average public spending-to-GDP increased by 1% of GDP from 2000 to 2003. In between these decennial turning points spending-to-GDP ratios changed little; during the 1980s the average OECD public social spending to GDP ratio oscillated just below 20% of GDP while during the 1990s it trended downwards after the economic downturn in the early 1990s, but nevertheless remained above 20% of GDP.

It is convenient to divide expenditures according to their social purposes to better analyse policy focus and trends. Broadly speaking, the three biggest groups of social transfers are pensions (on average 8% of GDP), health (6%) and income transfers to the working-age population (5%). Public spending on other social services only exceeds 5% of GDP in the Nordic countries, where the public role in providing services to the elderly, the disabled and families is the most extensive.

Public support for families with children is nearly 2% of GDP on average, but this has increased in most countries since 1980. Family support exceeds 3% of GDP in the Nordic countries and Austria, as they have the most comprehensive public system of child allowances, paid leave arrangements and childcare. Moreover, governments also help families through the tax system; examples include the "quotient familial" in France and "income splitting" in Germany.

Social insurance spending related to work incapacity (disability, sickness and occupational injury benefits) has declined in as many countries as it has increased since 1980. Particularly large declines were found in Belgium and in the Netherlands.

Definition

Public social expenditure comprises cash benefits, direct "in-kind" provision of goods and services, and tax breaks with social purposes. To be considered "social", benefits have to address one or more social goals. Benefits may be targeted at low-income households, but they may also be for the elderly, disabled, sick, unemployed, or young persons. Programmes regulating the provision of social benefits have to involve: a) redistribution of resources across households, or b) compulsory participation. Social benefits are regarded as public when general government (that is central, state, and local governments, including social security funds) controls relevant financial flows. The expenditures shown here refer only to public social benefits and exclude similar benefits provided by private charities.

Comparability

For cross-country comparisons, the most commonly used indicator of social support is gross (before tax) public social expenditure related to GDP. Measurement problems do exist, particularly with regard to spending by lower tiers of government, which may be underestimated in some countries. As noted above, similar social benefits provided by private charities are excluded.

Source
- Social Expenditure Database.

Further information
Analytical publications
- Adema, W. and M. Ladaique (2005), Net Social Expenditure, 2005 Edition: More Comprehensive Measures of Social Support, OECD Social Employment and Migration Working Papers, No. 29, OECD, Paris.
- OECD (2002-2004), Babies and Bosses – Reconciling Work and Family Life, OECD, Paris.
- OECD (2003), Transforming Disability into Ability: Policies to Promote Work and Income Security for Disabled People, OECD, Paris.
- OECD (2007), Society at a Glance: OECD Social Indicators – 2006 Edition, OECD, Paris.
- OECD (2006), Starting Strong II: Early Childhood Education and Care, OECD, Paris.

Websites
- OECD Social and Welfare Statistics, www.oecd.org/ statistics/social.

Public social expenditure

As a percentage of GDP

	1990	1991	1992	1993	1994	1995	1996	1997	1998	1999	2000	2001	2002	2003
Australia	14.1	15.2	16.2	16.5	16.2	17.1	17.2	17.0	17.0	16.9	17.9	17.4	17.5	17.9
Austria	23.7	23.9	24.5	26.0	26.6	26.6	26.6	25.5	25.4	25.6	25.3	25.4	25.8	26.1
Belgium	25.0	25.8	25.9	27.0	26.5	26.4	26.9	25.8	26.1	25.9	25.3	25.7	26.1	26.5
Canada	18.4	20.6	21.3	21.2	20.2	19.2	18.4	17.7	18.0	17.0	16.7	17.3	17.3	17.3
Czech Republic	16.0	17.3	17.6	18.1	18.1	18.2	18.3	19.1	19.5	20.0	20.3	20.4	21.0	21.1
Denmark	25.5	26.3	26.8	28.6	29.4	28.9	28.2	27.2	27.0	26.8	25.8	26.4	26.9	27.6
Finland	24.5	29.6	33.6	29.9	29.2	27.4	27.1	25.2	23.2	22.8	21.3	21.4	21.9	22.5
France	25.3	26.0	26.6	28.1	28.1	28.3	28.6	28.5	28.7	28.8	27.6	27.5	27.9	28.7
Germany	22.5	23.7	25.7	26.1	26.1	26.6	27.1	26.4	26.7	26.7	26.6	26.7	27.4	27.6
Greece	18.6	18.0	18.1	19.1	19.1	19.3	20.0	20.0	20.6	21.4	21.3	22.3	21.3	21.3
Hungary	..	..	..	..	..	..	..	..	..	21.6	20.6	20.7	21.9	22.7
Iceland	14.0	14.5	15.0	15.3	15.2	15.5	15.2	14.9	14.9	15.4	15.3	15.6	17.3	18.7
Ireland	15.5	16.3	17.1	17.1	16.8	16.3	15.4	14.3	13.4	14.2	13.6	14.4	15.5	15.9
Italy	19.9	20.1	20.7	20.9	20.7	19.8	22.0	22.7	23.0	23.3	23.2	23.3	23.8	24.2
Japan	11.2	11.4	11.9	12.5	13.1	13.9	14.1	14.2	14.9	15.4	16.1	16.8	17.5	17.7
Korea	3.0	2.8	3.1	3.2	3.2	3.5	3.6	3.9	5.5	6.3	5.1	5.4	5.4	5.7
Luxembourg	21.9	22.3	22.7	23.1	22.9	23.8	23.8	22.5	21.6	21.7	20.4	19.8	21.6	22.2
Mexico	3.6	4.0	4.4	4.7	5.2	4.7	4.5	4.5	5.0	5.8	5.8	5.9	6.3	6.8
Netherlands	24.4	24.4	24.9	25.1	23.6	22.8	21.8	21.2	20.6	19.9	19.3	19.5	19.9	20.7
New Zealand	21.8	22.2	22.0	20.3	19.5	19.0	18.9	19.9	20.0	19.3	19.1	18.4	18.4	18.0
Norway	22.6	23.5	24.4	24.3	24.0	23.5	22.7	22.2	24.5	24.6	22.2	23.2	24.6	25.1
Poland	15.1	21.5	25.5	24.9	23.8	23.1	23.3	22.7	21.5	22.2	21.2	22.4	23.0	22.9
Portugal	13.7	14.7	15.5	17.0	17.2	18.1	18.7	18.6	19.0	19.5	20.2	20.9	22.2	23.5
Slovak Republic	..	..	..	..	..	18.9	18.7	18.2	18.2	18.8	18.1	17.8	17.9	17.3
Spain	20.0	20.7	21.8	23.2	22.1	21.5	21.4	20.8	20.7	20.4	20.4	20.2	20.2	20.3
Sweden	30.5	32.1	35.0	36.2	34.9	32.5	32.1	30.7	30.5	30.1	28.8	29.3	30.4	31.3
Switzerland	13.5	14.5	16.0	17.4	17.3	17.5	18.1	18.8	19.0	18.8	18.0	18.7	19.4	20.5
Turkey	7.6	8.2	8.5	8.3	7.9	7.5	9.7	10.8	11.1	13.2	..	..	..	..
United Kingdom	17.2	18.6	20.3	21.0	20.5	20.4	20.1	19.2	19.3	19.0	19.1	20.1	20.1	20.1
United States	13.4	14.4	15.1	15.3	15.3	15.4	15.2	14.9	14.8	14.6	14.6	15.2	16.0	16.2
EU15 average	21.9	22.8	24.0	24.6	24.2	23.9	24.0	23.2	23.0	23.1	22.5	22.9	23.4	23.9
OECD average	17.9	19.0	20.0	20.4	20.1	19.9	20.0	19.6	19.7	19.8	19.4	19.7	20.3	20.7

StatLink ⬛🖳 http://dx.doi.org/10.1787/581207043027

Public social expenditure

As a percentage of GDP, 2003

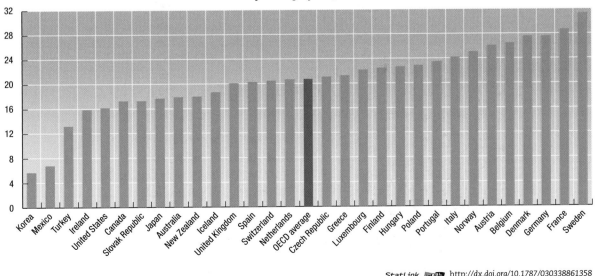

StatLink ⬛🖳 http://dx.doi.org/10.1787/030338861358

LAW, ORDER AND DEFENCE EXPENDITURE

Two essential tasks of a government are to protect the state from external aggression and maintain law and public order within its frontiers. Over the period considered here, the collapse of the Soviet Union led to a reduction in defence expenditures in many OECD countries, while the terror attacks in the United States led to increases in government expenditures on internal security. The figures shown here reflect these opposing influences.

Definition

The table is taken from national accounts sources, and the data conform to the definitions of the 1993 *System of National Accounts*. The expenditures cover all expenditures whether current or capital.

Law and order covers the police forces, intelligence services, prisons and other correctional facilities, the judicial system, and ministries of internal affairs. Note that the figures shown here do not include the costs of government-mandated security arrangements at airports, seaports and other border crossings. Nor, of course, do they include the provision of security in shopping-malls, football matches, concerts and other public gatherings, all of which have certainly increased in recent years.

Comparability

Data are taken from national accounts sources and have been compiled according to the *Classification of the Functions of Government* (COFOG). The distinction between current and capital expenditures in the case of defence expenditures has not proved easy to apply in some countries, but, in general, the data are broadly comparable.

Long-term trends

Within the total, the shares of the two components – law and order and defence – vary considerably between countries with high shares for defence expenditures in the United States, Korea, Norway, Denmark, France and Sweden and high shares for *law and order* in Iceland, Luxembourg, Ireland, Spain and Belgium. On average, the share of expenditures on law and order has generally been growing faster than *defence* and now accounts for more than half of the total for the countries shown in the table.

In 2004 – the latest year for which most countries can supply data – expenditure was highest in the United States and the United Kingdom, and lowest in Luxembourg, Iceland and Ireland. In the majority of countries the shares of expenditures on defence, law and order in GDP have been falling since 1995 with particularly large falls in Ireland, Norway, Sweden and France.

Source

• OECD (2006), *National Accounts of OECD Countries*, OECD, Paris.

Further information

Analytical publications

• OECD (2004), *The Security Economy*, OECD, Paris.

Methodological publications

• UN, OECD, IMF, Eurostat (eds.) (1993), *System of National Accounts 1993*, United Nations, Geneva, Paragraph XVIII.9, *http://unstats.un.org/unsd/sna1993*.

Online databases

• National Accounts.

OECD FACTBOOK 2007 – ISBN 978-92-64-02946-0 – © OECD 2007

Law, order and defence expenditure
As a percentage of GDP

	1992	1993	1994	1995	1996	1997	1998	1999	2000	2001	2002	2003	2004	2005
Austria	..	..	..	2.8	2.8	2.8	2.7	2.7	2.6	2.5	2.5	2.6	2.5	..
Belgium	3.4	3.4	3.3	3.2	3.2	3.2	3.1	3.1	3.1	3.1	3.3	3.3	..	..
Czech Republic	..	..	..	..	..	..	..	..	..	..	4.2	4.5	3.9	..
Denmark	3.4	3.4	3.4	3.2	3.2	3.1	3.2	3.1	2.9	3.0	3.0	3.0	3.1	..
Finland	4.3	4.0	4.2	4.0	4.1	3.9	3.7	3.5	3.3	3.2	3.2	3.4	3.6	..
France	..	..	..	4.3	4.3	4.1	3.9	3.8	3.6	3.7	3.8	3.7	3.7	3.7
Germany	3.6	3.6	3.4	3.3	3.3	3.2	3.2	3.2	3.2	3.2	3.2	3.1	3.0	..
Iceland	..	..	..	..	..	1.9	2.0	1.8	1.8	1.8	1.8	1.9	1.9	..
Ireland	3.5	3.4	3.4	3.1	2.9	2.8	2.7	2.5	2.4	2.4	2.2	2.1	2.2	..
Italy	3.8	3.8	3.8	3.5	3.6	3.5	3.5	3.5		3.4	3.4	3.5	3.8	3.4	..
Japan	..	..	..	..	2.2	2.2	2.2	2.3	2.3	2.3	2.3	2.3	2.3	..
Korea	..	..	..	4.5	4.7	4.6	4.7	4.5	4.4	4.3	4.3	4.3	4.3	..
Luxembourg	1.5	1.6	1.4	1.4	1.5	1.5	1.5	1.3	1.3	1.4	1.4	1.5	1.5	1.5
Netherlands	..	..	..	..	..	..	..	..	..	3.5	3.6	3.6	3.6	..
Norway	4.6	4.3	4.4	4.0	3.9	3.8	3.9	3.8	3.2	3.2	3.6	3.4	3.2	..
Portugal	..	..	..	..	..	..	..	3.7	3.8	3.7	3.8	3.8	3.8	..
Slovak Republic	..	..	..	..	..	..	..	..	..	..	..	4.1	2.5	..
Spain	..	..	..	..	..	..	..	..	3.2	3.3	3.3	3.2	3.3	..
Sweden	..	..	..	4.5	4.6	4.3	4.3	4.4	4.2	4.1	4.1	4.0	3.8	..
United Kingdom	6.8	6.5	6.2		5.8	5.4	5.4	5.2	5.0	5.4	5.4	5.4	5.6	5.5	..
United States	7.6	7.1	6.7	6.3	6.2	5.9	5.6	5.6	5.5	5.7	6.2	6.6	6.7	..

StatLink ᴍᴩ http://dx.doi.org/10.1787/142365340206

Law, order and defence expenditure
As a percentage of GDP

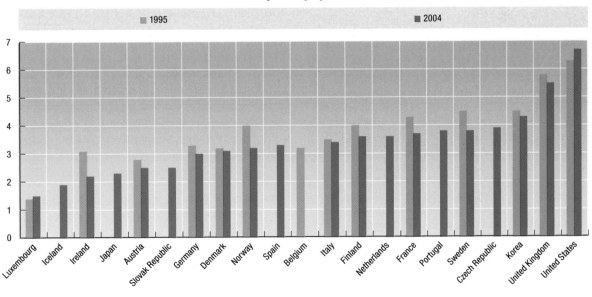

StatLink ᴍᴩ http://dx.doi.org/10.1787/284436170805

AGRICULTURAL SUPPORT ESTIMATES

During the mid-1980s, when the Uruguay Round of agricultural trade negotiations was getting underway, the OECD undertook to measure and codify support to the farm sector arising from agricultural policies. This led to the development of the producer support estimate (PSE), an indicator that is available on a timely and comprehensive basis for all 30 of the OECD's member countries (the European Union is treated as a single entity) and selected non-members. The measure includes budgetary transfers financed by taxpayers but also includes the implicit tax on consumers that arises from agricultural policies – border protection, and administered pricing – that raise farm prices above the levels that would otherwise prevail. The measure is agreed by OECD member countries and is widely recognised as the only available internationally comparable indicator.

Definition

The OECD PSE is an indicator of the annual monetary value of gross transfers from consumers and taxpayers to agricultural producers, measured at the farmgate level, arising from policy measures that support agriculture, regardless of their nature, objectives or impacts on farm production or income. It can be expressed as a total monetary amount, but is more usually quoted as a percentage of gross farm receipts (%PSE). This is the measure used here.

Comparability

Continuous efforts are made to ensure consistency in the treatment and completeness of coverage of policies in all OECD countries through the annual preparation of the Monitoring and Evaluation report. Each year, the provisional estimates are subject to review and approval by representatives of OECD's member countries, as are all methodological developments. The %PSE is the most appropriate and widely used measure to compare support across countries, commodities and time.

Long-term trends

There are large and increasing differences in the levels of support among OECD countries. Producer support estimates as a percentage of gross farm receipts (%PSE) currently range from almost zero to 68%. These differences reflect among other things, variations in policy objectives, different historical uses of policy instruments, and the varying pace and degrees of progress in agricultural policy reform. Over the longer term, the level of producer support has fallen in most OECD countries. The average %PSE in 2003-05 at 30% is lower than the 1986-88 average of 37% and has fallen in most countries. There has also been some change in the way support is delivered to the sector. Support known to be the most distorting in terms of production and trade is less dominant than in the past – 71% of total support during the 2003-2005 period compared to over 91% in 1986-1988.

In the table, data for Austria, Finland and Sweden are available separately until 1994 and data for the Czech Republic, Hungary, Poland and the Slovak Republic are available until 2003. Austria, Finland and Sweden are included in the EU15 from 1995. The Czech Republic, Hungary, Poland and the Slovak Republic, together with the 6 EU members which are not members of the OECD, are included in the EU25 from 2004. The OCDE total includes the Czech Republic, Hungary, Poland and the Slovak Republic for the entire period but excludes the 6 EU members not members of the OECD from 2004.

Producer support estimate for selected countries
As a percentage of value of gross farm receipts

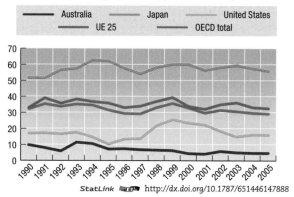

StatLink 📊🔢 http://dx.doi.org/10.1787/651446147888

Source
- OECD (2006), *Agricultural Policies in OECD Countries: At a Glance*, OECD, Paris.

Further information
Analytical publications
- OECD (2004), *Analysis of the 2003 CAP Reform*, OECD, Paris.
- OECD (2005), *Agricultural Policies in OECD Countries: Monitoring and Evaluation*, OECD, Paris.
- OECD (2005), *Environmentally Harmful Subsidies: Challenges for Reform*, OECD, Paris.
- OECD (2006), *OECD Review of Agricultural Policies*, OECD, Paris.
- OECD (2006), *OECD Sustainable Development Studies – Subsidy Reform and Sustainable Development: Economic, Environmental and Social Aspects*, OECD, Paris.
- OECD (2006), *OECD-FAO Agricultural Outlook: 2006-2015*, OECD, Paris.

Methodological publications
- OECD (2002), *Methodology for the Measurement of Support and Use in Policy Evaluation*, OECD, Paris.

Producer support estimate by country
As a percentage of value of gross farm receipts

	1992	1993	1994	1995	1996	1997	1998	1999	2000	2001	2002	2003	2004	2005
Australia	6.0	11.4	10.6	7.3	7.5	6.9	6.6	6.4	4.5	4.2	5.9	5.1	4.8	4.8
Austria	57.4	58.5	60.6	..	..	..	..	..	..	..	..	..	..	..
Canada	28.7	24.7	20.6	19.6	15.5	14.4	16.8	18.0	19.9	15.9	21.2	24.5	20.7	20.5
Czech Republic	20.2	24.5	16.4	10.9	11.5	6.4	26.2	23.2	16.6	23.2	25.0	28.6	..	..
Finland	66.2	64.1	69.0	..	..	..	..	..	..	..	..	..	..	..
Hungary	18.0	20.5	21.9	13.2	10.6	10.9	24.6	23.7	22.3	22.2	33.0	28.0	..	..
Iceland	67.0	60.2	55.7	53.7	56.7	58.7	66.3	67.5	61.2	57.0	67.4	68.3	63.1	66.5
Japan	56.7	57.6	62.7	62.2	57.7	54.2	58.2	60.1	60.1	56.4	58.3	59.4	57.6	56.0
Korea	72.3	72.7	73.1	72.0	64.1	63.0	56.5	65.4	66.5	62.1	65.3	61.2	62.9	63.0
Mexico	28.6	29.9	22.7	-4.8	5.1	14.8	17.8	17.8	23.7	19.3	26.3	19.2	12.2	14.3
New Zealand	1.8	1.6	2.3	2.6	2.0	2.1	1.6	1.6	1.0	0.6	1.5	2.0	2.2	2.6
Norway	69.4	69.1	69.0	64.8	65.8	68.9	71.0	71.7	66.9	66.7	74.4	71.5	66.6	64.3
Poland	9.1	16.7	22.1	16.0	20.9	18.6	28.9	26.6	11.9	15.1	18.7	8.1	..	..
Slovak Republic	21.8	30.1	25.2	11.8	0.1	13.9	32.3	25.7	25.3	15.7	21.4	25.4	..	..
Sweden	58.5	53.7	51.0	..	..	..	..	..	..	..	..	..	..	..
Switzerland	67.6	72.8	73.8	65.5	68.5	69.5	70.4	74.5	72.0	70.4	73.1	70.9	68.2	68.2
Turkey	26.9	23.4	14.3	13.0	15.6	24.8	26.3	22.3	20.7	3.1	20.4	28.2	25.5	24.9
United States	16.7	17.8	14.8	10.4	13.5	13.8	21.9	25.7	23.6	22.4	18.4	15.0	16.2	16.0
EU 25 total	35.6	38.1	36.6	35.7	32.9	33.8	36.7	39.2	33.7	31.9	34.8	35.9	33.0	32.4
OECD total	33.5	34.9	34.3	31.2	29.1	28.9	32.8	35.4	32.6	29.5	31.2	30.4	29.4	28.9
Brazil	..	..	..	-7.7	-3.4	-4.4	4.0	-0.8	4.4	3.4	3.8	4.7	3.6	5.9
China	..	-13.1	0.9	6.3	1.9	1.9	1.4	-2.1	4.0	6.5	7.2	9.9	6.8	8.4
Russian Federation	-110.2	-28.7	-4.1	13.7	18.5	27.0	19.0	0.8	4.6	14.3	18.0	15.9	19.3	15.5
South Africa	..	..	12.3	16.8	8.7	11.9	8.6	8.4	5.6	1.8	8.0	7.0	8.0	9.0

StatLink ⟪≋⟫ http://dx.doi.org/10.1787/331718685706

Producer support estimate by country
As a percentage of value of gross farm receipts

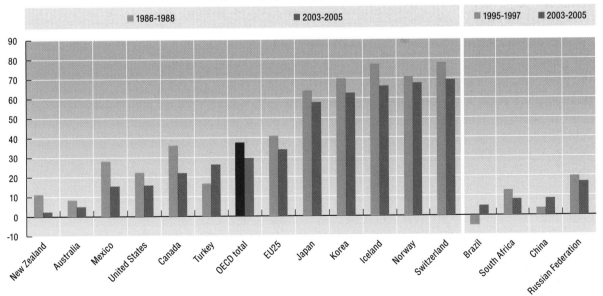

StatLink ⟪≋⟫ http://dx.doi.org/10.1787/341520676748

GOVERNMENT SUPPORT FOR FISHING

Catches from sea fishing have been declining both because of falling stocks due to over-fishing and because of national and international measures to preserve the remaining fish resources. This has been particularly marked in the Northern Hemisphere and has lead governments in many OECD countries to provide financial support to the fishing industry.

Definition

The time series "Government financial transfers (GFT)" provides an indicator of the financial support received by the fishery sector. GFTs consist of direct revenue enhancing transfers (direct payments), transfers that reduce the operating costs, and the costs of general services provided to the fishing industry. These general services consist mainly of fishery protection services but also include the costs of local area weather forecasting and the costs of navigation and satellite surveillance systems designed to assist fishing fleets.

Comparability

The data are relatively comprehensive and consistent across the years, but some year-to-year variations must be interpreted with caution, as they may reflect changes in national statistical systems. Note too that the general services provided by government may contain large and irregular capital investments. For example, the GFTs for Greece in 2001 and in particular for 2002 include the implementation cost of a satellite control system.

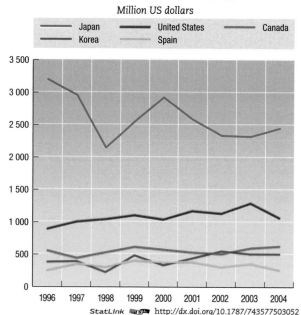

GFT for selected countries
Million US dollars

Japan — United States — Canada — Korea — Spain

StatLink http://dx.doi.org/10.1787/743577503052

Source

- OECD (2005), *Review of Fisheries in OECD Countries Vol. 2 – Country Statistics 2001-2003*, OECD, Paris.

Further information

Analytical publications

- Cox, A. (2003), *OECD Work on Defining and Measuring Subsidies in Fisheries*, OECD, Paris.
- Cox, A. (2004), *Subsidies and Deep-Sea Fisheries Management: Policy Issues and Challenges*, OECD, Paris.
- Cox, A. and C. Schmidt (2003), *Subsidies in the OECD Fisheries Sector: A Review of Recent Analysis and Future Directions*, background paper for the FAO Expert Consultation on Identifying, Assessing and Reporting on Subsidies in the Fishing Industry, Rome, 3-6 December 2002.
- OECD (2005), *Environmentally Harmful Subsidies: Challenges for Reform*, OECD, Paris.
- OECD (2006), *OECD Sustainable Development Studies – Subsidy Reform and Sustainable Development: Economic, Environmental and Social Aspects*, OECD, Paris.
- OECD (2007), *The Human Side of Fisheries Adjustment*, OECD, Paris.
- Schmidt, C. (2004), *Globalisation, Industry Structure, Market Power and Impact on Fish Trade Opportunities and Challenges for Developed (OECD) Countries*, paper prepared for the FAO Industry and Expert Consultation on International Trade, Rio de Janeiro, Brazil, 3-5 December 2003.

Websites

- OECD Fisheries, *www.oecd.org/agr/fish*.

Long-term trends

Overall transfers to the fishing industry have been fluctuating at around USD 6 billion during the last decade. This represents around 15% of the value of the total catch from maritime capture. Most of the GFTs cover general services, which represent approximately 78% of the total GFTs. The remaining spending consists of direct payments (around 13% of total GFTs) and cost reducing transfers (around 9% of total GFTs).

Government financial transfers for fishing

Thousand US dollars

	1996	1997	1998	1999	2000	2001	2002	2003	2004
Australia	37 391	41 230	..	..	82 272	75 902	78 038	95 558	95 560
Belgium	4 970	4 949	..	4 473	6 849	2 830	1 607	1 668	6 327
Canada	545 301	433 309	..	606 443	564 497	521 355	497 771	589 975	618 786
Czech Republic	..	..	..	269	241	223	235	..	..
Denmark	85 771	82 030	90 507	27 765	16 316	..	68 769	37 659	28 504
Finland	28 978	26 198	26 888	19 236	13 908	16 510	16 025	20 231	19 397
France	158 203	140 807	..	71 665	166 147	141 786	155 283	179 740	236 810
Germany	81 567	63 215	16 488	31 276	29 834	28 988	28 208	7 343	6 087
Greece	52 308	46 958	26 908	43 030	87 315	86 957	88 334	119 045	97 609
Iceland	43 770	38 678	36 954	39 763	41 978	28 310	28 955	48 348	55 704
Ireland	112 673	98 880	..	143 184	..	..	63 632	64 960	64 960
Italy	162 625	91 811	..	200 470	217 679	231 680	159 630	149 270	170 055
Japan	3 186 363	2 945 785	2 135 946	2 537 536	2 913 149	2 574 086	2 323 601	2 310 744	2 437 933
Korea	367 793	378 994	211 927	471 556	320 449	428 313	538 695	495 280	495 280
Mexico	14 201	16 808	..	..	..	..	..	177 000	114 000
Netherlands	39 927	35 849	..	..	1 389	12 779	12 443	6 569	5 218
New Zealand	37 241	40 397	29 412	29 630	27 273	15 126	18 981	38 325	50 134
Norway	172 694	163 437	153 046	180 962	104 564	99 465	156 340	139 200	142 315
Poland	8 148	7 927	..	..	..	..	..	..	..
Portugal	71 847	65 077	..	28 674	25 578	25 066	24 899	26 930	26 930
Spain	246 473	344 581	296 642	399 604	364 096	376 614	301 926	353 290	256 569
Sweden	62 320	53 452	26 960	31 053	25 186	22 505	24 753	30 650	34 421
Turkey	28 665	15 114	..	1 277	26 372	17 721	16 167	16 300	16 300
United Kingdom	115 359	128 066	90 833	75 968	81 394	73 738	..	82 691	87 487
United States	891 160	1 002 580	1 041 000	1 103 100	1 037 710	1 169 590	1 130 810	1 290 440	1 064 400

StatLink ⟨⟩ http://dx.doi.org/10.1787/355637441617

Government financial transfers

Average annual growth in percentage, 1996-2004

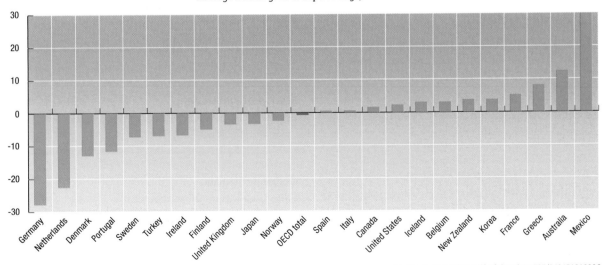

StatLink ⟨⟩ http://dx.doi.org/10.1787/248451313306

OFFICIAL DEVELOPMENT ASSISTANCE

The promotion of economic and social development in non-member countries has been a principal objective of the OECD since its foundation. The share of national income devoted to official development assistance (ODA) is widely regarded as a test of a country's commitment to international development, and there is a long-standing United Nations target for developed countries to devote 0.7% of their gross national income (GNI) to ODA. The tables in this section show total ODA as shares of GNI as well as the geographical distribution of bilateral ODA.

Definition

Official development assistance is defined as government aid to developing countries designed to promote the economic development and welfare of recipient countries. Loans and credits for military purposes are excluded. The aid may be provided bilaterally, from donor to recipient, or it may be channelled through a multilateral development agency such as the United Nations or the World Bank.

Aid includes grants, "soft" loans, and the provision of technical assistance. Soft loans are those where the grant element is at least 25%. ODA is usually measured on a net basis, i.e. after subtracting loan repayments from the gross aid flows. Data on the geographical distribution of aid are presented on a gross basis to show the level of new aid provided during the period.

The OECD maintains a list of developing countries and territories, and only aid to these countries counts as ODA. The list is periodically updated and currently contains over 150 countries or territories which had per capita incomes of less than USD 10 066 in 2004 (by comparison, per capita income in OECD countries averaged over USD 35 000 in that year). Note that of the 30 member countries of the OECD, only the 22 shown in the table are members of the Development Assistance Committee (DAC), along with the European Commission.

Comparability

Statistics on ODA are compiled according to a set of directives drawn up by the DAC and each country's statistics are subject to regular peer reviews by other DAC members. Data for Greece are available only since 1996 as Greece joined the DAC in 1999. From 1990 to 1992 inclusive, forgiveness of non-ODA debt was reportable as a part of a country's ODA but was excluded from the DAC total.

Sources

• *Development Assistance Committee Aid Statistics.*

Further information

Analytical publications

• OECD (2006), The Development Dimension, *The Development Effectiveness of Food Aid: Does Tying Matter?*, OECD, Paris.

• OECD (2006), *Creditor Reporting System: Aid Activities for Basic Social Services in 2004*, OECD, Paris.

• OECD (2006), The Development Dimension, *The Development Dimension – Aid for Trade: Making it Effective*, OECD, Paris.

• OECD (2007), *OECD Journal on Development: Development Co-operation – 2006 Report*, OECD, Paris.

Statistical publications

• OECD (2005), *International Development Statistics on CD-Rom*, OECD, Paris.

• OECD (2006), *Geographical Distribution of Financial Flows to Aid Recipients 2000/2004: 2006 Edition*, OECD, Paris.

Online databases

• *International Development Statistics.*

Websites

• DAC Aid Statistics home page, *www.oecd.org/dac/stats.*

• OECD, Calculation of the Grant Element of Loans, *www.oecd.org/dataoecd/15/0/31738575.pdf.*

• International Development Statistics, *www.oecd.org/dac/ stats/idsonline.*

Long-term trends

The weighted average shown in the graph is the total ODA provided by DAC members as a percentage of their total GNI; it amounted to 0.33% in 2005. The unweighted average, measuring "average country effort", was 0.47% in 2005. The decline since 1990 in both the weighted and unweighted averages has been halted and reversed in the last five years, as DAC members increase their aid following the commitments they made at the Monterrey 2002 Financing for Development Conference.

ODA shares of GNI declined to their lowest point in 1997 but, since 2002, have been increasing again. If DAC members meet the commitments they made at the G8 Summit in Gleneagles to double aid to Africa, ODA/GNI ratios are expected to rise further. Sixteen of the 22 DAC members have committed to remain at or to attain the 0.7% target.

Net official development assistance
As a percentage of gross national income

	1992	1993	1994	1995	1996	1997	1998	1999	2000	2001	2002	2003	2004	2005
Australia	0.37	0.35	0.34	0.34	0.27	0.27	0.27	0.26	0.27	0.25	0.26	0.25	0.25	0.25
Austria	0.11	0.11	0.17	0.27	0.23	0.24	0.22	0.24	0.23	0.34	0.26	0.20	0.23	0.52
Belgium	0.39	0.39	0.32	0.38	0.34	0.31	0.35	0.30	0.36	0.37	0.43	0.60	0.41	0.53
Canada	0.46	0.45	0.43	0.38	0.32	0.34	0.30	0.28	0.25	0.22	0.28	0.24	0.27	0.34
Denmark	1.02	1.03	1.03	0.96	1.04	0.97	0.99	1.01	1.06	1.03	0.96	0.84	0.85	0.81
Finland	0.64	0.45	0.31	0.31	0.33	0.32	0.31	0.33	0.31	0.32	0.35	0.35	0.37	0.46
France	0.63	0.63	0.62	0.55	0.48	0.44	0.38	0.38	0.30	0.31	0.37	0.40	0.41	0.47
Germany	0.37	0.35	0.33	0.31	0.32	0.28	0.26	0.26	0.27	0.27	0.27	0.28	0.28	0.36
Greece	..	..	..	..	0.15	0.14	0.15	0.15	0.20	0.17	0.21	0.21	0.16	0.17
Ireland	0.16	0.20	0.25	0.29	0.31	0.31	0.30	0.31	0.30	0.33	0.40	0.39	0.39	0.42
Italy	0.34	0.31	0.27	0.15	0.20	0.11	0.20	0.15	0.13	0.15	0.20	0.17	0.15	0.29
Japan	0.30	0.27	0.29	0.27	0.20	0.21	0.27	0.27	0.28	0.23	0.23	0.20	0.19	0.28
Luxembourg	0.26	0.35	0.40	0.36	0.44	0.55	0.65	0.66	0.71	0.76	0.77	0.81	0.83	0.82
Netherlands	0.86	0.82	0.76	0.81	0.81	0.81	0.80	0.79	0.84	0.82	0.81	0.80	0.73	0.82
New Zealand	0.26	0.25	0.24	0.23	0.21	0.26	0.27	0.27	0.25	0.25	0.22	0.23	0.23	0.27
Norway	1.16	1.01	1.05	0.86	0.83	0.84	0.89	0.88	0.76	0.80	0.89	0.92	0.87	0.94
Portugal	0.35	0.28	0.34	0.25	0.21	0.25	0.24	0.26	0.26	0.25	0.27	0.22	0.63	0.21
Spain	0.27	0.28	0.28	0.24	0.22	0.24	0.24	0.23	0.22	0.30	0.26	0.23	0.24	0.27
Sweden	1.03	0.99	0.96	0.77	0.84	0.79	0.72	0.70	0.80	0.77	0.84	0.79	0.78	0.94
Switzerland	0.45	0.33	0.36	0.34	0.34	0.34	0.32	0.35	0.34	0.34	0.32	0.39	0.41	0.44
United Kingdom	0.31	0.31	0.31	0.29	0.27	0.26	0.27	0.24	0.32	0.32	0.31	0.34	0.36	0.47
United States	0.20	0.15	0.14	0.10	0.12	0.09	0.10	0.10	0.10	0.11	0.13	0.15	0.17	0.22
DAC total	0.33	0.30	0.29	0.26	0.25	0.22	0.23	0.22	0.22	0.22	0.23	0.25	0.26	0.33
of which: EU members	0.43	0.43	0.41	0.37	0.37	0.33	0.33	0.31	0.32	0.33	0.35	0.35	0.35	0.44

StatLink ⟨≣⟩ http://dx.doi.org/10.1787/487148670474

Net official development assistance
As a percentage of gross national income, 2005

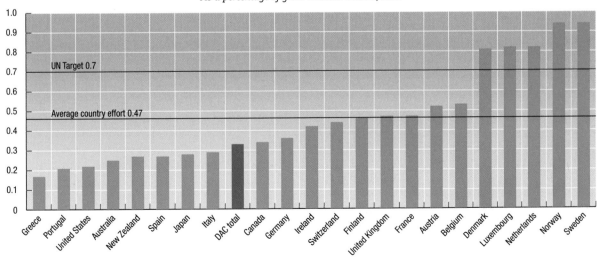

StatLink ⟨≣⟩ http://dx.doi.org/10.1787/600024803482

Major recipients by region of total gross bilateral ODA from DAC countries

Million US dollars, 3-year averages

	1991-1993		1994-1996		1997-1999
Sub-Saharan Africa	12 139	**Sub-Saharan Africa**	11 372	**Sub-Saharan Africa**	9 310
Mozambique	959	Côte d'Ivoire	822	Mozambique	698
Tanzania	887	Mozambique	748	Tanzania	666
Zambia	709	Tanzania	595	Côte d'Ivoire	495
Côte d'Ivoire	608	Ethiopia	529	Cameroon	413
Kenya	591	Senegal	494	Uganda	408
Cameroon	551	Kenya	451	South Africa	408
Ethiopia	475	Zambia	443	Madagascar	395
Senegal	456	Cameroon	436	Senegal	387
Ghana	438	Uganda	383	Ghana	375
Somalia	436	Ghana	372	Ethiopia	357
Middle East and North of Africa	10 064	**Middle East and North of Africa**	6 410	**Middle East and North of Africa**	3 938
Egypt	5 459	Egypt	2 152	Egypt	1 570
Israel	1 841	Israel	1 458	Morocco	459
Morocco	710	Morocco	527	Jordan	350
Jordan	411	Jordan	423	Palestinian Administered Areas	329
Algeria	367	Algeria	325	Tunisia	242
South and Central Asia	4 604	**South and Central Asia**	5 009	**South and Central Asia**	4 356
India	1 773	India	1 803	India	1 554
Bangladesh	982	Bangladesh	903	Bangladesh	773
Pakistan	775	Pakistan	775	Pakistan	560
Sri Lanka	416	Sri Lanka	432	Sri Lanka	358
Nepal	275	Nepal	265	Nepal	230
Far East Asia and Oceania	9 460	**Far East Asia and Oceania**	10 365	**Far East Asia and Oceania**	9 600
Indonesia	2 460	China	2 439	Indonesia	2 096
China	2 002	Indonesia	2 116	China	2 025
Philippines	1 511	Philippines	1 204	Thailand	1 004
Thailand	780	Thailand	957	Philippines	956
New Caledonia	365	Viet Nam	583	Viet Nam	823
Malaysia	352	French Polynesia	434	French Polynesia	389
French Polynesia	340	New Caledonia	430	New Caledonia	365
Europe	1 914	**Europe**	1 599	**Europe**	1 915
States Ex-Yugoslavia Unspecified	834	Bosnia	542	Bosnia	606
Turkey	762	Turkey	430	Serbia and Montenegro	281
Albania	206	States Ex-Yugoslavia Unspecified	231	Turkey	265
Latin America and Caribbean	6 098	**Latin America and Caribbean**	5 192	**Latin America and Caribbean**	4 472
Bolivia	591	Nicaragua	575	Peru	494
Nicaragua	579	Bolivia	555	Bolivia	437
Peru	554	Haiti	433	Nicaragua	365
El Salvador	492	Mexico	404	Brazil	341
Jamaica	387	Peru	390	Honduras	258
Honduras	361	Brazil	332	Colombia	250

StatLink http://dx.doi.org/10.1787/601364383142

Major ODA recipients by region

Sub-Saharan Africa, South and Central Asia, Far East Asia and Oceania, million US dollars

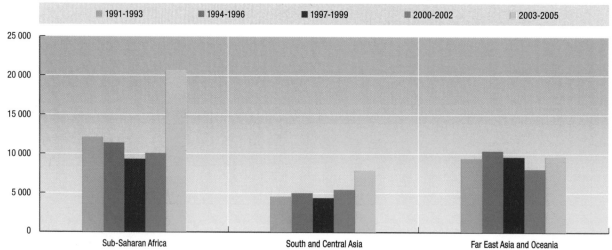

StatLink http://dx.doi.org/10.1787/251182200770

Major recipients by region of total gross bilateral ODA from DAC countries (cont.)

Million US dollars, 3-year averages

	2000-2002		2003-2005
Sub-Saharan Africa	10 047	Sub-Saharan Africa	20 619
Mozambique	1 094	Congo, Democratic Republic.	2 478
Tanzania	891	Nigeria	2 180
Côte d'Ivoire	516	Ethiopia	1 123
Uganda	493	Ghana	1 092
Cameroon	426	Tanzania	1 010
Ghana	422	Zambia	938
Ethiopia	415	Sudan	887
Zambia	398	Mozambique	745
South Africa	371	Cameroon	709
Kenya	349	Uganda	686
Middle East and North of Africa	3 713	Middle East and North of Africa	13 837
Egypt	1 398	Iraq	9 314
Morocco	455	Egypt	1 246
Jordan	427	Jordan	748
Palestinian Administered Areas	332	Morocco	631
Tunisia	304	Palestinian Administered Areas	555
South and Central Asia	5 436	South and Central Asia	7 958
India	1 538	India	1 734
Pakistan	823	Afghanistan	1 697
Bangladesh	792	Pakistan	1 140
Afghanistan	477	Bangladesh	858
Sri Lanka	375	Sri Lanka	616
Far East Asia and Oceania	8 043	Far East Asia and Oceania	9 721
China	1 836	China	2 481
Indonesia	1 578	Indonesia	1 864
Viet Nam	962	Viet Nam	1 213
Thailand	942	Philippines	1 081
Philippines	934	Thailand	836
Cambodia	264	Cambodia	323
Papua New Guinea	240	Malaysia	299
Europe	2 736	Europe	2 617
Serbia and Montenegro	1 049	Serbia and Montenegro	754
Bosnia	377	Turkey	393
Turkey	372	Bosnia	308
Latin America and Caribbean	4 820	Latin America and Caribbean	6 025
Bolivia	586	Nicaragua	757
Peru	536	Bolivia	713
Nicaragua	459	Colombia	641
Colombia	398	Peru	584
Brazil	355	Honduras	534
Honduras	348	Brazil	377

StatLink http://dx.doi.org/10.1787/013414628323

Major ODA recipients by region

Middle East and North Africa, Europe, Latin America and Caribbean, million US dollars

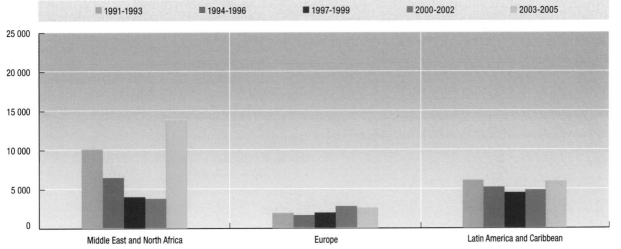

StatLink http://dx.doi.org/10.1787/144660320442

TOTAL TAX REVENUE

Total tax revenue as a percentage of GDP indicates the share of a country's output that is collected by the government through taxes. It can thus be regarded as one measure of the degree to which the government controls the economy's resources. Taxes on incomes and profits as a percentage of GDP represents the amount of resources collected by government directly from the incomes of people and companies. Taxes on goods and services as a percentage of GDP represents the amount of resources the government collects from people as they spend their income on goods and services.

Definition

Taxes are defined as compulsory, unrequited payments to general government. They are unrequited in the sense that benefits provided by government to taxpayers are not normally in proportion to their payments.

Taxes on incomes and profits cover taxes levied on the net income or profits (gross income minus allowable tax reliefs) of individuals and enterprises. They also cover taxes levied on the capital gains of individuals and enterprises, and gains from gambling.

Taxes on goods and services covers all taxes levied on the production, extraction, sale, transfer, leasing or delivery of goods, and the rendering of services, or on the use of goods or permission to use goods or to perform activities. They consist mainly of value added and sales taxes.

Note that the sum of taxes on goods and services and taxes on income and profits do not equal total tax revenues, which also includes payments by employers and employees made under compulsory social security schemes as well as payroll taxes, taxes related to the ownership and transfer of property, and other taxes.

Comparability

The data are collected in a way that makes them as internationally comparable as possible. Country representatives have agreed on the definition of each type of tax and how they should be measured in all OECD countries, and they are then responsible for submitting data that conform to these rules. The rules are set out in "The OECD Interpretative Guide" at the end of each edition of *Revenue Statistics*.

Source
- OECD (2005), *Revenue Statistics 1965-2004 – 2005 Edition*, OECD, Paris.

Further information
Analytical publications
- OECD (2004), *Recent Tax Policy Trends and Reforms in OECD Countries*, OECD Tax Policy Studies, No. 9, OECD, Paris.
- OECD (2005), *Consumption Tax Trends: VAT/GST and Excise rates, Trends and Administration Issues, 2005 Edition*, OECD, Paris.
- OECD (2006), *The Political Economy of Environmentally Related Taxes*, OECD, Paris.
- OECD (2006), *OECD Tax Policy Studies – N.15 Encouraging Savings through Tax-Preferred Accounts*, OECD, Paris.

Statistical publications
- OECD (2006), *Taxing Wages: 2004/2005 – 2005 Edition*, OECD, Paris.

Methodological publications
- *Electronic Model Tax Convention (eMTC)*, www.sourceoecd. org/reference/modeltax.
- OECD (1992-2005), *Model Tax Convention on Income and on Capital*, yearly updates, OECD, Paris.
- OECD (2005), *Model Tax Convention on Income and on Capital Model Tax Convention on Income and on Capital*, condensed version, OECD, Paris.

Online databases
- *Taxing Wages Statistics.*
- *Revenue Statistics of OECD Member Countries.*

Websites
- Tax Administration in OECD Countries: Comparative Information Series (2004), www.oecd.org/ctp/ta.
- OECD Centre for Tax Policy and Administration, www.oecd.org/ctp.

Long-term trends

Total tax revenue as a percentage of GDP followed a slow upward trend in almost all OECD countries during the 1990s. However, in 2000, the upward trend stopped, and, since 2001, the average tax revenues as a percentage of GDP for OECD countries have declined slightly.

Taxes on income and profit as a percentage of GDP showed no overall trend in the first half of the 1990s. However, from 1996, there was an upward trend in most countries until 2000, after which it has fallen back.

Taxes on goods and services as a percentage of GDP have been remarkably stable since 1992. There was a slight upward trend in the first half of the 1990s, followed by a stabilisation.

Total tax revenue

As a percentage of GDP

	1991	1992	1993	1994	1995	1996	1997	1998	1999	2000	2001	2002	2003	2004
Australia	27.0	26.5	26.9	28.0	28.8	29.4	29.2	30.0	30.5	31.1	29.6	30.5	30.7	31.2
Austria	40.0	41.4	41.9	41.7	41.1	42.4	43.9	43.9	43.5	42.6	44.6	43.7	42.9	42.6
Belgium	42.2	41.8	43.3	43.6	43.6	44.0	44.5	45.2	45.2	44.9	44.9	45.0	44.7	45.0
Canada	36.4	36.0	35.4	35.2	35.6	35.9	36.7	36.7	36.4	35.6	34.8	33.7	33.6	33.5
Czech Republic	..	..	40.4	38.9	37.5	36.5	36.9	35.5	36.5	36.0	36.2	37.0	37.6	38.4
Denmark	45.9	46.3	47.7	48.7	48.8	49.2	49.0	49.3	50.1	49.4	48.4	47.8	47.7	48.8
Finland	45.6	45.1	44.5	46.6	45.6	46.9	46.1	46.0	46.4	47.7	45.7	45.6	44.6	44.2
France	42.6	42.0	42.3	42.8	42.9	44.1	44.3	44.2	45.2	44.4	44.0	43.4	43.1	43.4
Germany	36.0	37.0	37.0	37.2	37.2	36.5	36.2	36.4	37.1	37.2	36.1	35.4	35.5	34.7
Greece	28.8	29.8	30.3	30.6	31.7	39.3	33.2	35.1	36.1	37.3	36.2	37.2	36.3	35.0
Hungary	45.6	45.3	46.2	43.7	42.1	40.4	38.7	38.5	38.8	38.7	38.7	38.4	38.1	38.1
Iceland	31.3	32.1	31.1	30.6	31.2	32.3	32.2	35.7	38.2	38.3	36.5	36.4	37.8	38.7
Ireland	33.7	34.0	34.0	35.1	32.5	32.4	31.7	31.3	31.5	31.7	29.5	28.1	28.7	30.1
Italy	38.2	40.6	42.2	40.2	40.1	41.8	43.2	41.7	42.5	42.3	42.0	41.4	41.8	41.1
Japan	28.7	27.0	27.1	26.3	26.9	26.9	27.3	26.9	26.5	27.1	27.3	26.2	25.7	26.4
Korea	18.5	18.5	19.0	19.4	19.4	20.0	21.0	21.1	21.5	23.6	24.1	24.4	25.3	24.6
Luxembourg	33.4	34.1	36.5	36.7	37.0	37.5	39.3	39.4	38.3	39.1	39.6	39.0	38.2	37.8
Mexico	17.3	17.6	17.7	17.2	16.7	16.7	17.5	16.6	17.3	18.5	18.8	18.1	19.0	19.0
Netherlands	43.4	43.2	43.6	41.6	40.2	39.8	40.2	38.4	39.7	39.5	38.2	37.5	37.0	37.5
New Zealand	35.6	35.9	36.0	36.6	36.6	34.8	35.0	33.4	33.4	33.6	33.0	34.6	34.4	35.6
Norway	41.4	40.7	39.8	41.0	41.1	41.1	41.8	42.7	43.0	43.0	43.2	43.6	42.9	44.0
Poland	34.8	35.7	39.7	37.8	37.0	36.8	36.0	35.3	33.0	32.5	34.4	35.5	34.9	34.4
Portugal	28.8	30.8	29.3	30.1	31.7	32.6	32.7	32.9	33.9	34.1	33.8	34.5	35.0	34.5
Slovak Republic	..	..	..	..	..	..	..	37.0	34.6	33.2	32.1	32.4	31.2	30.3
Spain	32.8	33.8	32.8	32.9	32.1	31.9	32.9	33.2	34.1	34.2	33.8	34.2	34.3	34.8
Sweden	50.3	47.7	46.6	46.8	48.1	50.0	51.2	51.7	52.1	53.4	51.3	49.7	50.1	50.4
Switzerland	25.7	26.2	26.7	27.2	27.8	28.3	27.9	28.9	29.1	30.5	30.1	30.1	29.4	29.2
Turkey	21.0	22.4	22.7	22.2	22.6	25.4	27.9	28.4	31.3	32.3	35.1	31.1	32.8	31.3
United Kingdom	35.3	34.3	33.2	33.7	35.0	34.6	35.2	36.3	36.7	37.2	37.0	35.5	35.4	36.0
United States	27.1	26.9	27.1	27.5	27.9	28.3	28.7	29.3	29.4	29.9	28.8	26.5	25.7	25.5
EU15 average	38.5	38.8	39.0	39.2	39.2	40.2	40.2	40.3	40.8	41.0	40.3	39.9	39.7	39.7
OECD average	34.5	34.7	35.2	35.2	35.1	35.7	35.9	36.0	36.4	36.6	36.3	35.9	35.8	35.9

StatLink http://dx.doi.org/10.1787/754034371003

Total tax revenue

As a percentage of GDP, 2004

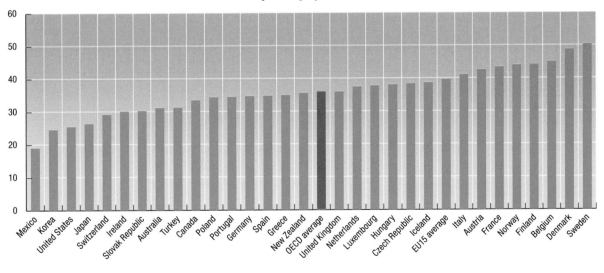

StatLink http://dx.doi.org/10.1787/607150481852

Taxes on income and profits
As a percentage of GDP

	1991	1992	1993	1994	1995	1996	1997	1998	1999	2000	2001	2002	2003	2004
Australia	15.1	14.7	14.6	15.2	15.9	16.6	16.5	17.7	18.3	18.1	16.7	17.2	17.4	18.2
Austria	10.6	11.1	11.3	10.3	10.9	11.9	12.7	12.9	12.5	12.2	14.0	13.0	12.7	12.5
Belgium	15.6	15.0	16.0	16.4	16.9	17.0	17.4	17.9	17.5	17.6	17.9	17.7	17.4	17.4
Canada	17.1	16.1	15.7	15.8	16.5	16.9	17.9	17.7	18.1	17.8	16.7	15.4	15.2	15.6
Czech Republic	..	..	10.3	9.7	9.4	8.2	8.8	8.2	8.4	8.2	8.7	9.1	9.5	9.7
Denmark	27.7	28.2	29.1	30.0	30.1	30.2	29.8	29.4	29.6	29.8	28.7	28.5	28.6	29.5
Finland	17.3	16.3	15.0	16.3	16.5	18.2	17.7	18.1	18.0	20.6	18.7	18.5	17.3	17.1
France	7.2	6.7	6.9	7.0	7.0	7.4	8.1	10.2	10.8	11.1	11.2	10.4	10.0	10.1
Germany	11.5	11.9	11.4	11.0	11.3	10.5	10.2	10.7	11.1	11.2	10.4	9.9	9.7	9.5
Greece	5.8	5.6	5.7	6.6	7.0	7.0	7.5	8.9	9.2	10.2	8.8	8.8	8.2	8.2
Hungary	12.6	9.9	9.6	9.2	8.8	8.9	8.4	8.6	9.1	9.4	9.9	10.1	9.4	9.0
Iceland	9.1	9.5	10.1	10.2	10.7	11.3	11.6	13.5	14.9	15.5	16.0	16.1	17.0	17.0
Ireland	12.9	13.2	13.6	14.1	12.7	13.1	13.1	12.9	13.1	13.2	12.2	11.0	11.3	11.8
Italy	13.8	15.2	15.6	14.0	14.2	14.5	15.3	13.6	14.4	14.0	14.3	13.4	12.9	12.9
Japan	14.0	12.0	11.5	10.3	10.3	10.3	10.1	9.0	8.5	9.4	9.1	8.0	7.9	8.5
Korea	5.8	5.8	5.7	5.9	6.2	6.0	5.5	6.4	5.3	6.8	6.4	6.2	7.1	6.9
Luxembourg	12.6	11.8	13.5	13.9	14.6	14.9	15.6	15.1	13.9	14.1	14.3	14.4	13.9	12.6
Mexico	4.7	5.2	5.5	5.2	4.1	4.0	4.6	4.7	5.0	5.0	5.2	5.2	5.0	4.7
Netherlands	14.5	13.6	14.2	11.6	10.6	10.8	10.5	10.1	10.1	10.0	10.1	10.2	9.4	9.2
New Zealand	20.7	21.0	21.1	22.3	22.4	20.7	20.9	19.4	19.4	20.1	19.5	20.7	20.5	21.7
Norway	14.9	13.3	13.4	14.3	14.4	14.9	15.8	15.8	16.0	19.2	19.3	18.9	18.6	20.3
Poland	7.8	11.5	12.6	11.6	11.3	10.9	10.6	10.4	10.1	9.9	9.7	10.0	6.2	6.1
Portugal	8.0	8.9	8.1	7.9	8.1	8.7	8.8	8.6	9.1	9.6	9.1	8.9	8.5	8.3
Slovak Republic	..	..	..	..	..	..	..	9.5	8.5	7.1	7.0	6.9	6.8	5.7
Spain	10.2	10.1	9.8	9.3	9.4	9.2	9.8	9.4	9.6	9.7	9.6	10.0	9.7	9.8
Sweden	18.6	18.2	19.1	19.9	18.9	19.6	20.2	20.1	21.1	21.5	19.2	17.5	18.2	19.0
Switzerland	11.9	12.4	12.0	12.5	12.0	12.4	12.0	12.6	12.2	13.4	12.7	13.0	12.6	12.7
Turkey	7.3	7.3	7.3	6.6	6.4	6.7	7.6	9.4	9.8	9.5	10.1	7.7	7.8	6.9
United Kingdom	13.1	12.3	11.6	12.0	12.8	12.7	13.0	14.1	14.1	14.6	14.7	13.5	13.0	13.2
United States	11.9	11.8	12.1	12.3	12.8	13.5	14.0	14.4	14.6	15.1	14.1	11.7	11.1	11.1
EU15 average	13.3	13.2	13.4	13.3	13.4	13.7	14.0	14.1	14.3	14.6	14.2	13.7	13.4	13.4
OECD average	12.6	12.4	12.5	12.5	12.5	12.6	12.9	13.0	13.1	13.5	13.2	12.7	12.4	12.5

StatLink 🔒 http://dx.doi.org/10.1787/753167751313

Taxes on income and profits
As a percentage of GDP, 2004

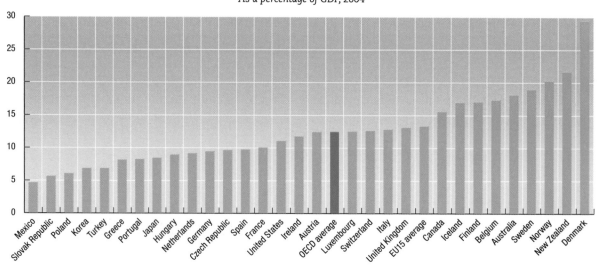

StatLink 🔒 http://dx.doi.org/10.1787/523850762346

OECD FACTBOOK 2007 – ISBN 978-92-64-02946-0 – © OECD 2007

Taxes on goods and services
As a percentage of GDP

	1991	1992	1993	1994	1995	1996	1997	1998	1999	2000	2001	2002	2003	2004
Australia	7.5	7.5	7.9	8.2	8.4	8.2	8.0	8.2	8.0	8.9	8.9	9.2	9.1	8.9
Austria	12.3	12.5	12.3	12.9	11.5	11.9	12.3	12.3	12.4	12.0	12.1	12.3	12.1	12.0
Belgium	11.1	11.1	11.2	11.4	11.2	11.5	11.7	11.1	11.5	11.4	11.0	11.1	11.0	11.3
Canada	9.4	9.5	9.4	9.2	9.0	9.0	9.0	9.1	8.8	8.6	8.8	8.9	8.8	8.7
Czech Republic	..	..	13.5	13.0	12.1	12.0	11.4	11.0	11.7	11.4	11.0	11.0	11.2	12.0
Denmark	15.2	14.9	15.0	15.5	15.7	16.1	16.1	16.4	16.5	15.9	15.9	16.0	15.7	16.0
Finland	14.5	14.3	14.0	14.3	13.8	13.9	14.4	14.1	14.4	13.8	13.5	13.8	14.3	14.0
France	11.6	11.1	11.2	11.6	11.7	12.2	12.0	11.9	12.0	11.4	11.1	11.1	11.0	11.1
Germany	9.7	10.0	10.3	10.7	10.4	10.3	10.1	10.0	10.4	10.5	10.4	10.3	10.4	10.1
Greece	13.3	14.2	13.8	13.2	13.1	13.3	13.5	13.1	13.4	13.2	13.7	14.0	13.4	13.0
Hungary	15.1	16.3	17.1	16.2	17.1	16.4	15.2	15.0	15.6	15.7	15.0	14.4	15.0	15.5
Iceland	16.0	15.9	15.5	15.0	15.2	15.6	15.3	16.9	17.9	17.2	15.0	14.6	15.2	15.9
Ireland	13.7	13.7	13.0	13.7	13.2	13.0	12.6	12.2	12.2	12.2	11.0	11.1	11.0	11.4
Italy	10.7	11.0	10.9	11.4	10.9	10.8	11.2	11.5	11.7	11.8	11.2	11.2	10.7	10.8
Japan	4.0	4.0	4.1	4.2	4.3	4.3	4.7	5.3	5.4	5.2	5.3	5.3	5.2	5.3
Korea	8.2	8.4	8.3	8.4	8.4	8.8	9.0	8.0	8.6	9.0	9.5	9.5	9.4	8.9
Luxembourg	8.4	9.2	10.0	10.2	9.9	9.8	10.4	10.5	10.4	10.6	10.4	10.4	10.5	11.5
Mexico	9.3	8.9	8.3	8.1	9.0	9.3	9.4	8.3	8.6	9.8	9.7	8.9	10.0	10.5
Netherlands	11.0	11.1	10.7	10.9	10.9	11.3	11.2	11.1	11.6	11.5	11.8	11.6	11.7	12.0
New Zealand	12.6	12.8	12.9	12.3	12.2	12.2	12.2	12.1	12.1	11.6	11.8	12.1	12.1	12.0
Norway	14.5	15.2	15.3	15.8	15.9	15.6	15.5	16.0	15.7	13.8	13.6	13.7	13.3	13.1
Poland	9.1	10.8	13.6	13.5	13.0	13.2	12.3	12.1	12.4	11.8	11.5	12.4	12.6	12.4
Portugal	12.1	13.2	12.5	13.4	12.5	12.8	12.4	12.7	12.8	12.3	12.3	12.9	13.5	13.3
Slovak Republic	..	..	..	..	..	..	..	12.5	12.2	12.0	11.2	11.6	11.1	12.1
Spain	9.3	9.6	8.8	9.3	9.2	9.3	9.5	9.8	10.2	10.1	9.7	9.6	9.7	9.8
Sweden	13.3	12.4	12.7	12.1	13.3	12.9	13.0	12.9	12.8	12.9	12.9	13.1	13.2	13.0
Switzerland	5.4	5.2	5.3	5.3	6.1	6.0	6.0	6.2	6.7	6.8	7.0	6.8	6.9	6.9
Turkey	6.1	6.7	7.2	8.3	8.5	9.7	10.3	10.2	11.2	13.6	14.1	14.6	16.2	14.9
United Kingdom	11.7	11.9	11.7	11.8	12.3	12.2	12.2	11.9	12.1	11.9	11.6	11.5	11.6	11.5
United States	4.9	4.9	5.0	5.1	5.0	4.9	4.9	4.9	4.8	4.8	4.7	4.7	4.7	4.7
EU15 average	11.9	12.0	11.9	12.2	12.0	12.1	12.2	12.1	12.3	12.1	11.9	12.0	12.0	12.1
OECD average	10.7	10.9	11.1	11.2	11.2	11.3	11.2	11.2	11.5	11.4	11.2	11.3	11.4	11.4

StatLink ᴍᶳᴸ http://dx.doi.org/10.1787/685168025808

Taxes on goods and services
As a percentage of GDP, 2004

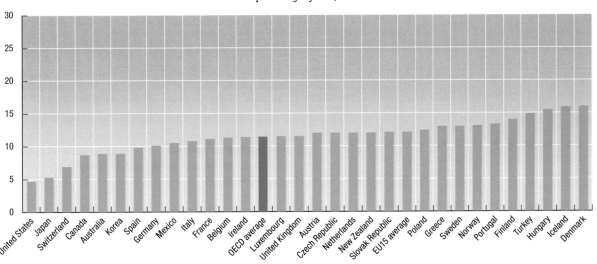

StatLink ᴍᶳᴸ http://dx.doi.org/10.1787/381628036017

TAXES ON THE AVERAGE WORKER

This series, taxes on a single average worker, measures the difference between the salary cost of a single average worker to their employer and the amount of disposable income (net wage) that they receive. This "tax wedge" represents the extent to which the tax system discourages employment.

Definition

The taxes included in the measure are personal income taxes, employees' social security contributions and employers' social security contributions. For the few countries that have them, it also includes payroll taxes. The amount of these taxes paid in relation to employing one average worker is expressed as a percentage of their labour cost (gross wage plus employers' social security contributions and payroll tax).

An average worker (AW) is defined as somebody who earns the average income of full-time workers of the country concerned in sectors C-K of the International Standard Industrial Classification (ISIC). The average worker is single, meaning that he or she does not receive any tax relief in respect of a spouse, unmarried partner or child.

Comparability

The types of taxes included in the measure are fully comparable across countries, as they are based on common definitions agreed by all OECD countries and published in *Revenue Statistics*.

The income levels of the workers are different in each country, but they are each equal to the average income of full-time workers in ISIC sectors C-K. Thus, they can be regarded as income levels that correspond to comparable types of work in each country. Before 2000, the wage measure only covered full-time manual workers in manufacturing.

The information on the AW income level is supplied by the ministries of finance in all OECD countries and is based on national statistical surveys. The amount of taxes paid by the single worker is calculated by applying the tax laws of the country concerned. Thus, the tax rates are the result of a modeling exercise rather than direct observation of taxes actually paid.

Data for Australia from 1996 include payroll taxes. Data for earlier years are not available on the same basis.

Source
- OECD (2006), *Taxing Wages: 2004/2005 – 2005 Edition*, OECD, Paris.

Further information
Analytical publications
- Immervoll, H. (2004), *Average and Marginal Effective Tax Rates Facing Workers in the EU: A Micro-Level Analysis of Levels, Distributions and Driving Factors*, OECD Social Employment and Migration Working Papers, No. 19, OECD, Paris.
- OECD (2006), *OECD Tax Policy Studies: No. 11: The Taxation of Employee Stock Options*, OECD, Paris.
- OECD (2006), *OECD Tax Policy Studies – N.15 Encouraging Savings through Tax-Preferred Accounts*, OECD, Paris.
- OECD (2007), *Benefits and Wages: OECD Indicators*, OECD, Paris.

Statistical publications
- OECD (2005), *Revenue Statistics 1965-2004 – 2005 Edition*, OECD, Paris.

Websites
- OECD Tax Policy Analysis, *www.oecd.org/ctp/tpa*.
- OECD Centre for Tax Policy and Administration, *www.oecd.org/ctp*.
- OECD Benefits and Wages, *www.oecd.org/els/social/workingincentives*.

Long-term trends

On average, the taxes on an average worker increased until 1997 and have since declined, in both the European Union and the OECD as a whole. However, there are important differences between countries. Those that have experienced an overall increase in the taxes on an average worker since 2000 include Iceland, Japan and Turkey. Countries that have experienced an overall decline include Denmark, Finland, Ireland, Luxembourg and the Slovak Republic.

Taxes on the average worker
As a percentage of labour cost

	1991	1993	1994	1995	1996	1997	1998	1999	2000	2001	2002	2003	2004	2005
Australia	..	..	..	..	29.3	29.6	30.2	30.4	30.6	27.3	27.7	28.0	28.0	28.3
Austria	39.1	40.0	39.7	41.2	41.5	45.6	45.8	45.9	47.3	46.9	47.1	47.4	47.5	47.4
Belgium	53.7	54.6	54.6	56.3	56.4	56.6	56.8	56.9	57.1	56.7	56.3	55.7	55.4	55.4
Canada	29.0	30.8	31.4	31.5	32.1	32.3	31.7	31.1	33.2	32.0	32.1	32.0	32.0	31.6
Czech Republic	..	42.6	42.8	43.2	42.6	42.9	42.8	42.7	42.7	42.6	42.9	43.2	43.5	43.8
Denmark	46.7	47.0	45.2	45.2	44.8	45.2	43.7	44.5	44.3	43.6	42.6	42.6	41.3	41.4
Finland	44.5	49.3	50.5	51.2	50.3	48.9	48.8	47.4	47.8	46.4	45.9	45.0	44.5	44.6
France	..	..	51.6	49.1	49.7	48.7	47.6	48.1	49.6	49.8	49.8	49.8	49.8	50.1
Germany	46.4	46.4	48.3	50.2	51.2	52.3	52.2	51.9	53.9	53.0	53.6	51.5	53.3	51.8
Greece	33.0	35.3	35.1	35.6	35.8	35.8	36.1	35.7	38.4	38.1	37.7	37.7	38.3	38.8
Hungary	..	..	..	51.4	52.0	52.0	51.6	50.7	52.7	54.0	53.7	50.8	51.8	50.5
Iceland	20.1	22.0	22.9	23.1	24.5	24.4	25.9	26.0	26.1	26.9	28.4	29.2	29.4	29.0
Ireland	39.8	40.0	38.4	36.9	36.1	33.9	33.0	32.4	28.9	25.8	24.5	24.2	26.2	25.7
Italy	48.8	49.2	49.9	50.3	50.8	51.5	47.5	47.2	46.4	46.0	46.0	45.0	45.4	45.4
Japan	21.5	21.2	21.6	19.5	19.4	20.7	19.6	24.0	24.8	24.9	30.5	27.4	27.4	27.7
Korea	..	..	..	6.9	6.3	12.4	14.7	16.1	16.4	16.4	16.1	16.3	17.2	17.3
Luxembourg	33.9	34.9	35.1	34.3	34.5	35.2	33.8	34.6	38.2	36.2	33.6	34.1	34.6	35.3
Mexico	24.4	26.6	26.5	27.2	25.4	20.8	21.9	14.1	16.8	15.9	17.5	18.1	16.2	18.2
Netherlands	46.5	45.7	45.6	44.8	43.8	43.6	43.5	44.3	39.7	37.2	37.4	37.1	38.6	38.6
New Zealand	23.8	24.0	24.3	24.5	22.3	21.6	20.0	19.4	19.4	19.4	19.5	19.7	20.0	20.5
Norway	41.2	36.8	36.9	37.5	37.6	37.4	37.5	37.3	38.6	39.2	38.6	38.1	38.1	37.3
Poland	..	44.1	..	44.7	44.7	43.9	43.2	43.0	43.2	42.9	42.9	43.1	43.3	43.6
Portugal	33.2	33.3	34.1	33.7	33.8	33.9	33.8	33.4	37.3	36.4	36.6	36.8	36.8	36.2
Slovak Republic	..	..	..	..	..	..	..	..	41.8	42.8	42.5	42.9	42.5	38.3
Spain	36.5	38.0	38.8	38.5	38.8	39.0	39.0	37.5	38.6	38.8	39.1	38.5	38.7	39.0
Sweden	46.0	45.6	46.8	49.3	50.2	50.7	50.7	50.5	50.1	49.1	47.8	48.2	48.4	47.9
Switzerland	27.3	28.7	28.7	30.6	30.4	30.0	30.0	29.8	30.0	30.1	30.1	29.7	29.4	29.5
Turkey	41.2	40.0	36.1	35.3	38.3	40.7	39.8	30.3	40.4	43.6	42.5	42.2	42.8	42.7
United Kingdom	33.2	32.6	33.3	33.4	32.6	32.0	32.0	30.8	32.1	31.8	31.9	33.3	33.4	33.5
United States	31.3	31.2	31.2	31.0	31.1	31.1	31.0	31.1	29.7	29.6	29.4	29.2	29.1	29.1
EU15 average	41.5	42.3	43.1	43.3	43.4	43.5	43.0	42.7	43.3	42.4	42.0	41.8	42.1	42.1
OECD average	36.0	37.0	37.4	37.3	37.3	37.5	37.2	36.6	37.9	37.5	37.5	37.2	37.4	37.3

StatLink ᠍ http://dx.doi.org/10.1787/081222228772

Income tax plus employee and employer contributions
As a percentage of labour cost

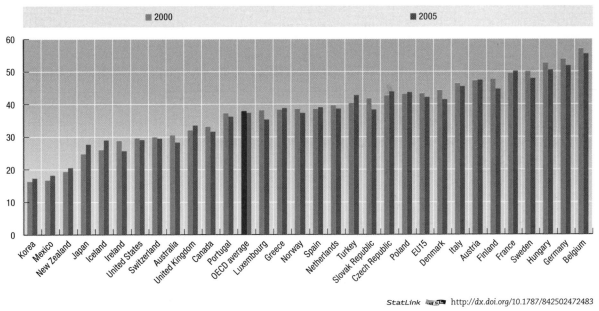

StatLink ᠍ http://dx.doi.org/10.1787/842502472483

QUALITY OF LIFE

HEALTH
LIFE EXPECTANCY
INFANT MORTALITY
OBESITY
PUBLIC AND PRIVATE HEALTH EXPENDITURE

LEISURE
TOURISM: HOTEL NIGHTS
RECREATION AND CULTURE

SOCIETY
YOUTH INACTIVITY
INCOME INEQUALITY
PRISON POPULATION

TRANSPORT
ROAD NETWORK
ROAD MOTOR VEHICLES AND ROAD FATALITIES

LIFE EXPECTANCY

Life expectancy at birth remains one of the most frequently quoted indicators of health status.

Gains in life expectancy in OECD countries in recent decades have been due to a number of important factors affecting mortality rates, including rising living standards, improved lifestyle and better education, as well as advances in access to care and the efficacy of medicine. Other factors, such as better nutrition, sanitation and housing also played a role, particularly in countries with developing economies.

Long-term trends

In 2004, the country with the highest life expectancy was Japan, with 82.1 years for the entire population, followed by Switzerland, Iceland, Sweden, Australia, Spain and France, where life expectancy also reached 80 years or more. On average, across OECD countries, life expectancy at birth for the entire population reached 78.3 years in 2004, up from 68.5 in 1960.

Gains in life expectancy were steady over the past four decades in most countries, averaging 1.8 years in the 1960s, and 2.3 years in the 1970s, 1980s and 1990s. Increases in life expectancy have been particularly pronounced in countries that started with relatively low levels. In Turkey, life expectancy at birth increased by over 20 years between 1960 and 2004, rapidly catching up with the OECD average. Similarly, in Mexico, life expectancy increased by more than 17 years since 1960. A significant reduction in infant mortality rates has contributed to these gains.

The gender gap in life expectancy stood at 5.7 years on average across OECD countries in 2004, with life expectancy reaching 75.4 years for men and 81.1 years for women. This gender gap increased by less than one year on average across countries over the entire period from 1960 to 2004. But this result hides different trends between earlier and later decades. While the gender gap in life expectancy increased substantially in many countries during the 1960s and the 1970s, it narrowed during the past two decades, as gains in life expectancy for men exceeded those for women in several OECD countries. The narrowing of the gender gap in life expectancy in many countries over the past two decades has been attributed partly to the narrowing in risk factor behaviours, especially smoking, between men and women, accompanied by falls in mortality rates from cardiovascular disease among men.

It is difficult to estimate the relative contribution of the numerous non-medical and medical factors that might affect variations in life expectancy over time and across countries. Higher national income (as measured by GDP per capita) is generally associated with higher life expectancy at birth across OECD countries, although the relationship is less pronounced at higher levels of income.

Definition

Life expectancy measures how long on average people would live based on a given set of age-specific death rates. However, the actual age-specific death rates of any particular birth cohort cannot be known in advance. If age-specific death rates are falling (as has been the case over the past decades in OECD countries), actual life spans will be higher than life expectancy calculated with current death rates.

Comparability

Each country calculates its life expectancy according to methodologies that can vary somewhat. These differences in methodology can affect the comparability of reported life expectancy estimates as different methods can change a country's estimates by a fraction of a year. For Korea, data shown for 2000 relate to 1999.

Source
- OECD (2006), *OECD Health Data 2006*, OECD, Paris.

Further information

Analytical publications
- OECD (2002), *Measuring Up: Improving Health System Performance in OECD Countries*, OECD, Paris.
- OECD (2003), *A Disease-based Comparison of Health Systems: What is Best and at what Cost?*, OECD, Paris.
- OECD (2004), *The OECD Health Project: Towards High-Performing Health Systems*, OECD, Paris.

Statistical publications
- OECD (2005), *Health at a Glance: OECD Indicators*, OECD, Paris.
- OECD (2006), *Society at a Glance: OECD Social Indicators – 2006 Edition*, OECD, Paris.

Online databases
- *OECD Health Data*.

Websites
- OECD Health Data, *www.oecd.org/health/healthdata*.

Life expectancy at birth: total
Number of years

	1960	1970	1980	1990	1995	2000	2001	2002	2003	2004
Australia	70.9	70.8	74.6	77.0	77.9	79.3	79.7	80.0	80.3	80.6
Austria	68.7	70.0	72.6	75.5	76.6	78.1	78.6	78.8	78.8	79.3
Belgium	70.6	71.0	73.4	76.1	77.3	78.3	78.5	78.6	78.8	..
Canada	71.3	72.9	75.3	77.6	78.1	79.3	79.6	79.7	79.9	..
Czech Republic	70.7	69.6	70.3	71.5	73.2	75.0	75.3	75.4	75.4	75.8
Denmark	72.4	73.3	74.3	74.9	75.3	76.9	77.0	77.2	77.5	77.6
Finland	69.0	70.8	73.4	74.9	76.5	77.6	78.1	78.2	78.5	78.8
France	70.3	72.2	74.3	76.9	77.9	79.0	79.2	79.4	79.4	80.3
Germany	69.6	70.4	72.9	75.2	76.5	78.0	78.4	78.3	78.6	78.6
Greece	69.9	72.0	74.5	77.1	77.7	78.1	78.5	78.8	78.9	79.0
Hungary	68.0	69.2	69.1	69.4	69.9	71.7	72.3	72.6	72.6	72.8
Iceland	72.9	74.3	76.7	78.0	78.0	80.1	80.2	80.6	81.2	81.0
Ireland	70.0	71.2	72.9	74.9	75.7	76.5	77.1	77.8	78.3	..
Italy	69.8	72.0	74.0	76.9	78.1	79.6	79.8	79.9	79.7	..
Japan	67.8	72.0	76.1	78.9	79.6	81.2	81.5	81.8	81.8	82.1
Korea	52.4	62.6	66.4	71.8	73.5	75.5	76.4	76.9	77.4	..
Luxembourg	69.4	70.3	72.5	75.4	76.6	78.0	78.0	78.2	78.0	..
Mexico	57.5	60.9	67.2	71.2	72.7	74.1	74.4	74.6	74.9	75.2
Netherlands	73.5	73.7	75.9	77.0	77.5	78.0	78.3	78.4	78.6	79.2
New Zealand	71.3	71.5	73.2	75.4	77.1	78.7	78.7	78.7	79.2	79.2
Norway	73.6	74.2	75.8	76.6	77.8	78.7	78.9	79.0	79.6	79.9
Poland	67.8	70.0	70.2	71.5	72.0	73.8	74.3	74.6	74.7	75.0
Portugal	64.0	67.5	71.5	73.9	75.2	76.6	76.9	77.2	77.4	..
Slovak Republic	70.6	69.8	70.6	71.0	72.4	73.3	73.6	73.8	73.9	74.1
Spain	69.8	72.0	75.6	76.8	77.9	79.2	79.5	79.6	80.3	80.5
Sweden	73.1	74.7	75.8	77.6	78.8	79.7	79.9	79.9	80.2	80.6
Switzerland	71.6	73.8	76.2	77.4	78.5	79.8	80.2	80.4	80.6	81.2
Turkey	48.3	54.2	58.1	66.1	67.9	70.5	70.6	70.8	71.0	71.2
United Kingdom	70.8	71.9	73.2	75.7	76.6	77.8	78.1	78.2	78.5	..
United States	69.9	70.9	73.7	75.3	75.7	76.8	77.1	77.2	77.5	..
OECD average	68.5	70.3	72.7	74.9	76.0	77.3	77.6	77.8	78.1	78.3

StatLink http://dx.doi.org/10.1787/164358567703

Life expectancy at birth: total
Number of years, 2004 or latest available year

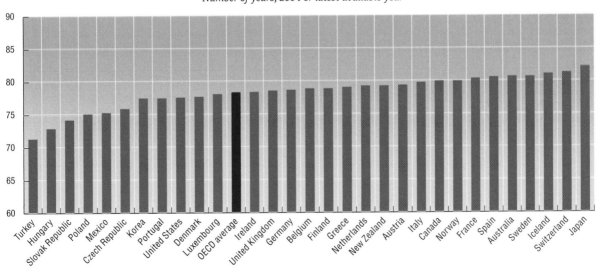

StatLink http://dx.doi.org/10.1787/536256868442

Life expectancy at birth: men
Number of years

	1960	1970	1980	1990	1995	2000	2001	2002	2003	2004
Australia	67.9	67.4	71.0	73.9	75.0	76.6	77.0	77.4	77.8	78.1
Austria	65.4	66.5	69.0	72.2	73.3	75.1	75.6	75.8	75.9	76.4
Belgium	67.7	67.8	70.0	72.7	73.9	75.1	75.4	75.6	75.9	..
Canada	68.4	69.3	71.7	74.4	75.1	76.7	77.0	77.2	77.4	..
Czech Republic	67.9	66.1	66.8	67.6	69.7	71.6	72.1	72.1	72.1	72.6
Denmark	70.4	70.7	71.2	72.0	72.7	74.5	74.7	74.8	75.1	75.2
Finland	65.5	66.5	69.2	70.9	72.8	74.2	74.6	74.9	75.1	75.3
France	67.0	68.4	70.2	72.8	73.9	75.3	75.5	75.8	75.9	76.7
Germany	66.9	67.2	69.6	72.0	73.3	75.0	75.5	75.4	75.7	75.7
Greece	67.3	70.1	72.2	74.6	75.0	75.6	76.1	76.4	76.5	76.6
Hungary	65.9	66.3	65.5	65.1	65.3	67.4	68.1	68.4	68.4	68.6
Iceland	70.7	71.2	73.7	75.4	75.9	78.4	78.1	78.7	79.7	79.2
Ireland	68.1	68.8	70.1	72.1	72.9	73.9	74.5	75.2	75.8	..
Italy	67.2	69.0	70.6	73.6	74.9	76.6	76.7	76.8	76.8	..
Japan	65.3	69.3	73.4	75.9	76.4	77.7	78.1	78.3	78.4	78.6
Korea	51.1	59.0	62.3	67.7	69.6	71.7	72.8	73.4	73.9	..
Luxembourg	66.5	67.1	69.1	72.3	73.0	74.8	75.2	74.9	75.0	..
Mexico	55.8	58.5	64.1	68.3	70.0	71.6	71.9	72.1	72.4	72.7
Netherlands	71.5	70.8	72.5	73.8	74.6	75.5	75.8	76.0	76.2	76.9
New Zealand	68.7	68.3	70.0	72.4	74.4	76.3	76.3	76.3	77.0	77.0
Norway	71.3	71.0	72.3	73.4	74.8	76.0	76.2	76.4	77.1	77.5
Poland	64.9	66.6	66.0	66.7	67.6	69.7	70.2	70.4	70.5	70.7
Portugal	61.2	64.2	67.7	70.4	71.6	73.2	73.5	73.8	74.2	..
Slovak Republic	68.4	66.7	66.8	66.6	68.4	69.1	69.5	69.8	69.9	70.3
Spain	67.4	69.2	72.5	73.3	74.3	75.8	76.1	76.2	76.9	77.2
Sweden	71.2	72.2	72.8	74.8	76.2	77.4	77.6	77.7	77.9	78.4
Switzerland	68.7	70.7	72.8	74.0	75.3	76.9	77.4	77.8	78.0	78.6
Turkey	46.3	52.0	55.8	63.8	65.6	68.1	68.2	68.4	68.6	68.8
United Kingdom	67.9	68.7	70.2	72.9	74.0	75.4	75.7	75.9	76.2	..
United States	66.6	67.1	70.0	71.8	72.5	74.1	74.4	74.5	74.8	..
OECD average	66.0	67.2	69.3	71.6	72.7	74.3	74.7	74.9	75.2	75.4

StatLink http://dx.doi.org/10.1787/676013520168

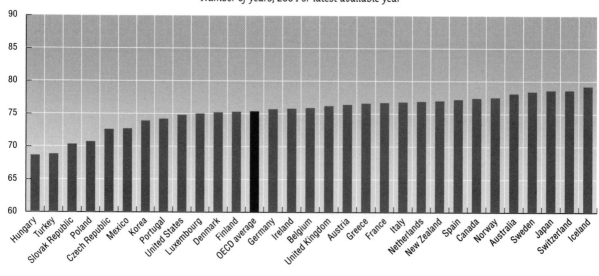

Life expectancy at birth: men
Number of years, 2004 or latest available year

StatLink http://dx.doi.org/10.1787/252656274546

OECD FACTBOOK 2007 – ISBN 978-92-64-02946-0 – © OECD 2007

Life expectancy at birth: women

Number of years

	1960	1970	1980	1990	1995	2000	2001	2002	2003	2004
Australia	73.9	74.2	78.1	80.1	80.8	82.0	82.4	82.6	82.8	83.0
Austria	71.9	73.4	76.1	78.8	79.9	81.1	81.5	81.7	81.6	82.1
Belgium	73.5	74.2	76.8	79.4	80.7	81.4	81.7	81.7	81.7	..
Canada	74.2	76.4	78.9	80.8	81.1	81.9	82.1	82.1	82.4	..
Czech Republic	73.4	73.0	73.9	75.4	76.6	78.4	78.5	78.7	78.7	79.0
Denmark	74.4	75.9	77.3	77.7	77.8	79.3	79.3	79.5	79.9	79.9
Finland	72.5	75.0	77.6	78.9	80.2	81.0	81.5	81.5	81.8	82.3
France	73.6	75.9	78.4	80.9	81.8	82.7	82.9	83.0	82.9	83.8
Germany	72.4	73.6	76.1	78.4	79.7	81.0	81.3	81.2	81.4	81.4
Greece	72.4	73.8	76.8	79.5	80.3	80.5	80.9	81.1	81.3	81.4
Hungary	70.1	72.1	72.7	73.7	74.5	75.9	76.4	76.7	76.7	76.9
Iceland	75.0	77.3	79.7	80.5	80.0	81.8	82.2	82.5	82.7	82.7
Ireland	71.9	73.5	75.6	77.6	78.4	79.1	79.6	80.3	80.7	..
Italy	72.3	74.9	77.4	80.1	81.3	82.5	82.8	82.9	82.5	..
Japan	70.2	74.7	78.8	81.9	82.9	84.6	84.9	85.2	85.3	85.6
Korea	53.7	66.1	70.5	75.9	77.4	79.2	80.0	80.4	80.8	..
Luxembourg	72.2	73.4	75.9	78.5	80.2	81.1	80.7	81.5	81.0	..
Mexico	59.2	63.2	70.2	74.1	75.3	76.5	76.8	77.1	77.4	77.6
Netherlands	75.4	76.5	79.2	80.1	80.4	80.5	80.7	80.7	80.9	81.4
New Zealand	73.9	74.6	76.3	78.3	79.7	81.1	81.1	81.1	81.3	81.3
Norway	75.8	77.3	79.2	79.8	80.8	81.4	81.5	81.5	82.0	82.3
Poland	70.6	73.3	74.4	76.3	76.4	77.9	78.3	78.7	78.8	79.2
Portugal	66.8	70.8	75.2	77.4	78.7	80.0	80.3	80.5	80.5	..
Slovak Republic	72.7	72.9	74.3	75.4	76.3	77.4	77.7	77.7	77.8	77.8
Spain	72.2	74.8	78.6	80.3	81.5	82.5	82.8	82.9	83.6	83.8
Sweden	74.9	77.1	78.8	80.4	81.4	82.0	82.1	82.1	82.5	82.7
Switzerland	74.5	76.9	79.6	80.7	81.7	82.6	83.0	83.0	83.1	83.7
Turkey	50.3	56.3	60.3	68.3	70.2	72.8	73.0	73.2	73.4	73.6
United Kingdom	73.7	75.0	76.2	78.5	79.2	80.2	80.4	80.5	80.7	..
United States	73.1	74.7	77.4	78.8	78.9	79.5	79.8	79.9	80.1	..
OECD average	71.0	73.4	76.0	78.2	79.1	80.3	80.5	80.7	80.9	81.1

StatLink 🔗 http://dx.doi.org/10.1787/146480833866

Life expectancy at birth: women

Number of years, 2004 or latest available year

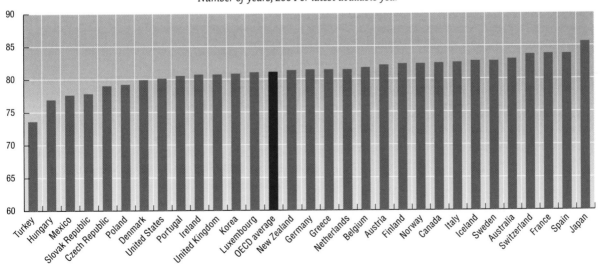

StatLink 🔗 http://dx.doi.org/10.1787/565028475058

INFANT MORTALITY

Numerous studies have focused on infant mortality rates as an indicator of the importance of medical and non-medical determinants of health. Infant mortality rates, the rate at which babies of less than one year of age die, reflect the effect of economic and social conditions on the health of mothers and newborns as well as the effectiveness of health systems. The fact that some countries with a high level of health expenditure, such as the United States, do not necessarily exhibit low levels of infant mortality has led to the conclusion that more health spending is not necessarily required to obtain better results. A whole body of research suggests that many factors outside of the quality and efficiency of the health system, such as income inequality, the social environment, and the individual lifestyles and attitudes are all factors influencing infant mortality rates.

Definition

Infant mortality is the number of deaths of children under one year of age expressed per 1 000 live births.

Comparability

Some of the international variation in infant and neonatal mortality rates may be due to variations among countries in registering practices of premature infants (whether they are reported as live births or fetal deaths). In several countries, such as in the United States, Canada and the Nordic countries, very premature babies with relatively low odds of survival are registered as live births, which increases mortality rates compared with other countries that do not register them as live births.

Long-term trends

All OECD countries have seen remarkable progress in reducing infant mortality rates from the levels of 1970, when the average was approaching 30 deaths per 1 000 live births. The average in 2004 stood at less than 6 deaths per 1 000 live births, which equates to an average reduction of over 75%. Portugal has seen its infant mortality rate reduced by over 90% since 1970, going from the country with the highest rate in Europe to one with an infant mortality rate among the lowest in the OECD in 2004. Large reductions in infant mortality rates are also seen in some of the other southern European countries, such as Italy, Spain and Greece.

Around two-thirds of the deaths that occur during the first year of life are neonatal deaths (i.e. during the first four weeks). Congenital malformations, low birth weight of pre-term infants and other conditions arising during pregnancy are the principal factors contributing to neonatal mortality in OECD countries. With an increasing number of women deferring childbearing and the rise in multiple births linked with fertility treatments, the number of pre-term births has tended to increase. For some countries with historically low infant mortality rates, such as the Nordic countries and Western Europe, this has contributed to a leveling-off or reversal of the downward trend in infant mortality rates over the past few years. For deaths beyond a month (post neonatal mortality), there tends to be a greater range of causes – the most common being birth defects, SIDS (sudden infant death syndrome), infections and accidents.

Source

• OECD (2006), *OECD Health Data 2006*, OECD, Paris.

Further information

Analytical publications

• OECD (2002), *Measuring Up: Improving Health System Performance in OECD Countries*, OECD, Paris.

• OECD (2004), *The OECD Health Project: Towards High-Performing Health Systems*, OECD, Paris.

• OECD (2004), *The OECD Health Project: Towards High-Performing Health Systems – Policy Studies*, OECD, Paris.

Statistical publications

• OECD (2007), *Health at a Glance: OECD Indicators*, OECD, Paris.

• OECD (2006), *Economic Valuation of Environmental Health Risks to Children*, OECD, Paris.

Online databases

• *OECD Health Data*.

Infant mortality
Deaths per 1 000 live births

	1970	1980	1990	1995	2000	2001	2002	2003	2004
Australia	17.9	10.7	8.2	5.7	5.2	5.3	5.0	4.8	4.7
Austria	25.9	14.3	7.8	5.4	4.8	4.8	4.1	4.5	4.5
Belgium	21.1	12.1	6.5	5.9	4.8	4.5	4.4	4.3	4.3
Canada	18.8	10.4	6.8	6.0	5.3	5.2	5.4	5.3	..
Czech Republic	20.2	16.9	10.8	7.7	4.1	4.0	4.1	3.9	3.7
Denmark	14.2	8.4	7.5	5.1	5.3	4.9	4.4	4.4	4.4
Finland	13.2	7.6	5.6	3.9	3.8	3.2	3.0	3.1	3.3
France	18.2	10.0	7.3	4.9	4.4	4.5	4.1	4.0	3.9
Germany	22.5	12.4	7.0	5.3	4.4	4.3	4.2	4.2	4.1
Greece	29.6	17.9	9.7	8.1	5.4	5.1	5.1	4.0	4.1
Hungary	35.9	23.2	14.8	10.7	9.2	8.1	7.2	7.3	6.6
Iceland	13.3	7.8	5.8	6.0	3.0	2.7	2.3	2.4	2.8
Ireland	19.5	11.1	8.2	6.4	6.2	5.7	5.1	5.1	4.9
Italy	29.0	14.6	8.2	6.2	4.5	4.7	4.5	4.2	4.1
Japan	13.1	7.5	4.6	4.3	3.2	3.1	3.0	3.0	2.8
Korea	45.0	..	..	..	..	..	5.3	..	..
Luxembourg	25.0	11.4	7.3	5.6	5.1	5.8	5.1	4.9	3.9
Mexico	79.4	51.0	36.2	27.6	23.3	22.4	21.4	20.5	19.7
Netherlands	12.7	8.6	7.1	5.5	5.1	5.4	5.0	4.8	4.1
New Zealand	16.7	13.0	8.4	6.7	6.3	5.6	6.2	..	..
Norway	12.7	8.1	6.9	4.0	3.8	3.9	3.5	3.4	3.2
Poland	36.7	25.5	19.3	13.6	8.1	7.7	7.5	7.0	6.8
Portugal	55.5	24.2	11.0	7.5	5.5	5.0	5.0	4.1	4.0
Slovak Republic	25.7	20.9	12.0	11.0	8.6	6.2	7.6	7.9	6.8
Spain	28.1	12.3	7.6	5.5	3.9	3.4	4.1	3.6	3.5
Sweden	11.0	6.9	6.0	4.1	3.4	3.7	3.3	3.1	3.1
Switzerland	15.1	9.1	6.8	5.0	4.9	5.0	5.0	4.3	4.2
Turkey	145.0	117.5	55.4	43.0	28.9	27.8	26.7	28.7		24.6
United Kingdom	18.5	12.1	7.9	6.2	5.6	5.5	5.2	5.3	5.1
United States	20.0	12.6	9.2	7.6	6.9	6.8	7.0	6.9	6.8
OECD average	28.1	17.9	11.0	8.4	6.7	6.4	6.2	6.0	5.7

StatLink http://dx.doi.org/10.1787/077481206452

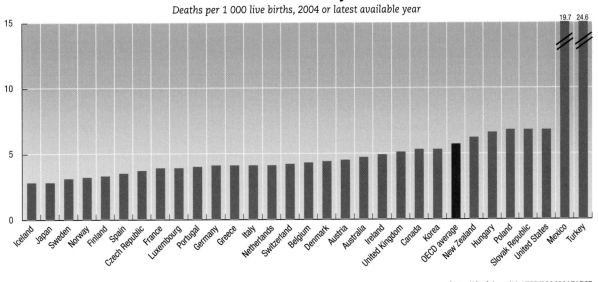

Infant mortality
Deaths per 1 000 live births, 2004 or latest available year

StatLink http://dx.doi.org/10.1787/083632171767

OBESITY

Obesity is a known risk factor for several diseases such as diabetes, hypertension, cardiovascular disease, respiratory problems (asthma) and musculoskeletal diseases (arthritis). At an individual level, several factors can lead to obesity, including excessive calorie consumption, lack of physical activity, genetic predisposition and disorders of the endocrine system.

Because obesity is associated with higher risks of chronic illnesses, it is linked to significant additional health care costs.

Definition

The most frequently used measure of overweight and obesity is based on the body mass index (BMI), which is a single number that evaluates an individual's weight status in relation to height (weight/height^2, with weight in kilograms and height in meters). Based on the WHO current classification, individuals with a BMI between 25 and 30 are defined as overweight, and those with a BMI over 30 as obese.

Comparability

The BMI classification may not be suitable for all ethnic groups, who may have equivalent levels of risk at lower BMI (for example, Asians) or higher BMI. It is also not suitable to measure overweight and obesity among children.

For most countries, data on obesity are self-reported through population-based health interview surveys. The exceptions are Australia, Canada (2004), New Zealand, the United Kingdom and the United States, where the data are derived from health examinations whereby actual measures are taken of people's height and weight. These differences in data collection methodologies seriously limit data comparability. Estimates from health examinations are generally higher and more reliable than those coming from health interviews.

Long-term trends

More than 50% of adults are now defined as either being overweight or obese in no less than 10 OECD countries: the United States, the United Kingdom, Mexico, Australia, Canada, Greece, New Zealand, Luxembourg, Hungary and the Czech Republic. By comparison, overweight and obesity rates are much lower in the OECD's two Asian countries (Japan and Korea) and in some European countries (France and Switzerland), although overweight and obesity rates are also increasing in these countries. Focusing only on obesity, the prevalence of obesity among adults varies from a low of 3% in Japan and Korea to a high of 32% in the United States.

Based on consistent measures of obesity over time, the rate of obesity has more than doubled over the past twenty years in the United States, while it has almost tripled in Australia and more than tripled in the United Kingdom. The obesity rate in many Western European countries has also increased substantially over the past decade.

Gender differences are striking. In all countries, more men are overweight than women, but in just over half of OECD countries, more women are obese than men. Taking overweight and obesity together, the rate for women exceeds that for men in only two countries – Mexico and Turkey.

Source

• OECD (2006), *OECD Health Data 2006*, OECD, Paris.

Further information

Analytical publications

• OECD (2004), *The OECD Health Project: Towards High-Performing Health Systems*, OECD, Paris.

Statistical publications

• OECD (2007), *Health at a Glance: OECD Indicators*, OECD, Paris.

Websites

• OECD Health Data, *www.oecd.org/health/healthdata*.

• Session on Obesity and Health at the OECD Forum 2004, *www.oecd.org/forum2004*.

Overweight and obese population aged 15 or more by gender
2004 or latest available year

	Females			Males			Total		
	Overweight	Obese	Overweight and obese	Overweight	Obese	Overweight and obese	Overweight	Obese	Overweight and obese
Australia	28.2	21.4	49.6	45.3	21.9	67.2	36.7	21.7	58.4
Austria	21.3	9.1	30.4	54.3	9.1	63.4	37.0	9.1	46.1
Belgium	24.4	13.4	37.8	38.7	11.9	50.6	31.4	12.7	44.1
Canada	29.5	22.5	52.1	40.8	22.3	63.0	35.1	22.4	57.5
Czech Republic	30.7	16.1	46.7	42.5	13.4	55.9	36.2	14.8	51.1
Denmark	24.9	9.1	34.0	39.8	9.8	49.6	32.3	9.5	41.7
Finland	26.6	13.5	40.1	44.8	14.9	59.7	35.0	14.1	49.2
France	19.6	9.3	29.0	31.1	9.8	40.5	25.1	9.5	34.6
Germany	28.9	12.3	41.2	44.1	13.6	57.7	36.3	12.9	49.2
Greece	29.9	18.2	48.1	41.1	26.0	67.1	35.2	21.9	57.1
Hungary	29.8	18.0	47.8	38.7	19.6	58.3	34.0	18.8	52.8
Iceland	28.0	12.4	40.4	44.7	12.4	57.1	35.9	12.4	48.8
Ireland	25.0	12.0	37.0	41.0	14.0	55.0	34.0	13.0	47.0
Italy	25.8	8.7	34.5	42.1	9.3	51.3	33.6	9.0	42.6
Japan	18.7	3.7	22.4	25.2	2.6	27.8	21.6	3.2	24.9
Korea	25.9	3.5	29.4	29.6	2.8	32.4	27.4	3.2	30.6
Luxembourg	25.4	18.5	43.9	41.1	18.8	59.9	34.6	18.6	53.3
Mexico	35.8	28.6	64.4	40.6	19.2	59.8	38.1	24.2	62.3
Netherlands	29.8	12.1	41.9	41.7	9.6	51.3	35.6	10.9	46.5
New Zealand	28.4	21.7	50.2	42.1	20.1	62.2	35.2	20.9	56.2
Norway	27.0	8.2	35.2	41.7	8.4	50.1	34.4	8.3	42.7
Poland	26.6	12.5	39.1	39.5	12.6	52.1	32.8	12.5	45.3
Portugal	31.8	14.0	45.8	42.3	11.4	53.7	36.8	12.8	49.6
Slovak Republic	24.9	15.6	40.5	42.0	15.2	57.2	32.2	15.4	47.6
Spain	27.6	13.4	40.9	43.5	12.9	56.3	35.3	13.1	48.4
Sweden	25.4	9.9	35.3	40.1	9.8	49.9	32.8	9.8	42.6
Switzerland	21.8	7.5	29.3	37.5	7.9	45.4	29.4	7.7	37.1
Turkey	28.9	14.5	43.4	33.6	9.7	43.3	31.6	12.0	43.4
United Kingdom	34.7	23.8	58.5	43.9	22.7	66.5	39.0	23.0	63.0
United States	28.6	33.2	61.8	39.7	31.1	70.8	34.1	32.2	66.3

StatLink http://dx.doi.org/10.1787/110802436338

Obesity
Percentage of population aged 15 and above with a BMI greater than 30, 2004 or latest available year

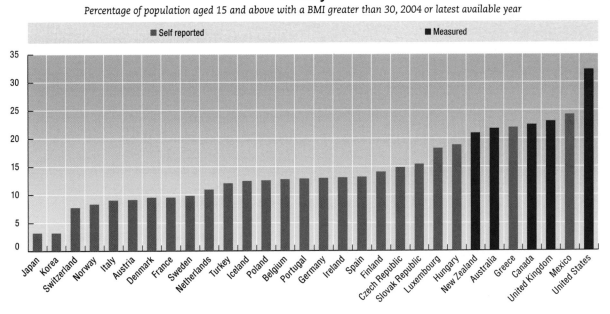

StatLink http://dx.doi.org/10.1787/513567226333

PUBLIC AND PRIVATE HEALTH EXPENDITURE

In most OECD countries, expenditures on health are a large and growing share of both public and private expenditure. The level of health spending varies widely across countries, reflecting different market and social factors as well as the different financing and organisational structures of the health system in each country.

Long-term trends

In terms of total health spending per capita, the United States is way ahead of the next highest spending countries – Luxembourg, Switzerland and Norway, and well over double the unweighted average of all OECD countries. At the other end of the scale, Poland, the Slovak Republic, Mexico and Turkey spend well below half the OECD average.

Since 1990, health spending has grown faster than GDP in every OECD country except Finland, although this growth has not been constant. For example, between 1997 and 2004, health expenditure increased by 4.3% per year on average, twice the overall economic growth rate. This compares with the previous period (1992-1997), when the growth rate of health expenditure was 2.6% – only slightly above that of overall economic growth.

In most OECD countries, the bulk of healthcare costs is financed through taxes, with 73% of health spending on average publicly funded in 2004. Ensuring sustainable financing of health systems is critical for governments, as health spending as a share of GDP is projected to increase further due to costly new medical technologies and population ageing.

Although the public share of health spending has fallen in countries such as Poland, Hungary and the Czech Republic which had a relatively high public share of health spending in 1990, it has risen in countries where it was low, such as Korea, Mexico, Switzerland and the United States. In Korea, for example, the public share of health spending rose from 39% in 1990 to just over 50% in 2004. In the United States, it increased from 40% to 45% between 1990 and 2004. Although the private sector in the United States continues to play the dominant role in financing, public spending on health per capita is still greater than that in most other OECD countries, because overall spending on health is much higher than in other countries.

Definition

Total expenditure on health measures the final consumption of health care goods and services (i.e. current health expenditure) plus capital investment in health care infrastructure. This includes spending by both public and private sources (including households) on medical services and goods, public health and prevention programmes and administration. Excluded are health-related expenditure such as medical training and research and development. The two major components of total current health expenditure are expenditure on personal health care and expenditure by governments on collective services.

Comparability

The definition of total health expenditure can vary among countries: particular areas affecting the comparability are the treatment of long-term care, the degree of inclusion of expenditure of non-profit institutions and corporations, and the coverage of capital formation. For Belgium, Japan and the Slovak Republic, data shown for 2004 actually refer to 2003. The 1990 data for Germany refer to 1992 and to 1991 for Hungary. For Denmark, the chart shows current expenditure rather than total.

Health expenditure per capita, converted to US dollars using purchasing power parities (PPP), can be used to compare the overall level of consumption of health goods and services across countries. The economy-wide PPPs for GDP are used as these are the most available and reliable conversion rates.

Source
- OECD (2006), *OECD Health Data 2006*, OECD, Paris.

Further information
Analytical publications
- OECD (2004), *The OECD Health Project: Towards High-Performing Health Systems*, OECD, Paris.
- OECD (2004), *The OECD Health Project: Private Health Insurance in OECD Countries*, OECD, Paris.

Statistical publications
- OECD (2007), *Health at a Glance: OECD Indicators*, OECD, Paris.

Methodological publications
- OECD (2000), *A System of Health Accounts*, OECD, Paris.

Online databases
- *OECD Health Data*.

Total and public expenditure on health

	US dollars calculated using PPPs						As a percentage of the OECD average					
	Public expenditure on health per capita			Total expenditure on health per capita			Public expenditure on health per capita			Total expenditure on health per capita		
	1990	2000	2004	1990	2000	2004	1990	2000	2004	1990	2000	2004
Australia	876	1 653	2 107	1 306	2 398	3 120	101	117	114	110	122	122
Austria	976	1 863	2 207	1 328	2 667	3 124	113	132	120	112	136	122
Belgium	..	1 726	2 165	1 341	2 277	3 044	..	122	117	113	116	119
Canada	1 295	1 760	2 210	1 737	2 503	3 165	149	125	120	146	128	124
Czech Republic	547	887	1 214	561	980	1 361	63	63	66	47	50	53
Denmark	1 259	1 962	..	1 522	2 380	2 881	145	139	..	128	121	113
Finland	1 148	1 289	1 712	1 419	1 716	2 235	132	91	93	120	87	87
France	1 174	1 858	2 475	1 532	2 450	3 159	135	132	134	129	125	123
Germany	1 576	2 097	2 341	1 934	2 632	3 043	182	149	127	163	134	119
Greece	453	849	1 141	844	1 616	2 162	52	60	62	71	82	84
Hungary	530	606	917	594	856	1 276	61	43	50	50	44	50
Iceland	1 380	2 166	2 777	1 593	2 623	3 331	159	154	151	134	134	130
Ireland	571	1 326	2 063	794	1 809	2 596	66	94	112	67	92	101
Italy	1 097	1 499	1 852	1 387	2 083	2 467	126	106	100	117	106	96
Japan	866	1 599	1 832	1 116	1 967	2 249	100	113	99	94	100	88
Korea	139	359	591	361	778	1 149	16	25	32	30	40	45
Luxembourg	1 427	2 663	4 603	1 533	2 982	5 089	165	189	250	129	152	199
Mexico	124	235	307	306	506	662	14	17	17	26	26	26
Netherlands	962	1 424	1 894	1 435	2 257	3 041	111	101	103	121	115	119
New Zealand	820	1 252	1 611	995	1 605	2 083	95	89	87	84	82	81
Norway	1 153	2 541	3 311	1 393	3 080	3 966	133	180	180	117	157	155
Poland	275	413	552	300	590	805	32	29	30	25	30	31
Portugal	441	1 178	1 334	674	1 624	1 824	51	83	72	57	83	71
Slovak Republic	..	532	687	..	595	777	-	38	37	-	30	30
Spain	687	1 088	1 484	873	1 520	2 094	79	77	80	74	77	82
Sweden	1 428	1 928	2 399	1 589	2 271	2 825	165	137	130	134	116	110
Switzerland	1 063	1 768	2 382	2 029	3 179	4 077	123	125	129	171	162	159
Turkey	103	284	418	168	451	580	12	20	23	14	23	23
United Kingdom	825	1 502	2 164	987	1 858	2 508	95	106	117	83	95	98
United States	1 093	2 017	2 727	2 752	4 588	6 102	126	143	148	232	234	238
OECD average	867	1 411	1 844	1 186	1 961	2 560	100	100	100	100	100	100

StatLink http://dx.doi.org/10.1787/553146018005

Public and private expenditure on health
US dollars per capita, calculated using PPPs, 2004 or latest available year

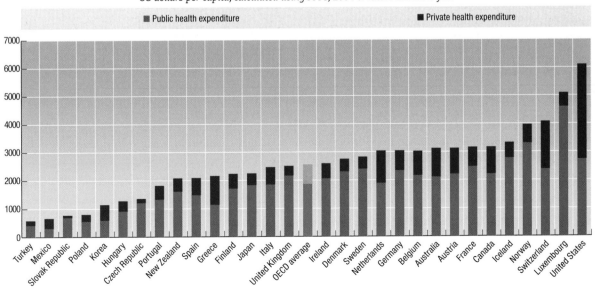

StatLink http://dx.doi.org/10.1787/741434626747

TOURISM: HOTEL NIGHTS

Arrivals of non-resident tourists in accommodation is one of the standard measures of international tourism activity. It excludes tourists who take their holidays in their own country.

Definition

This statistic refers to the number of non-residents who arrive at the frontier and intend to stay at least one night in a hotel or similar establishment such as apartment-hotels, motels, roadside inns, beach hotels, residential clubs, boarding houses, and similar accommodation providing limited hotel services. Note that arrivals of non-resident tourists does not show the number of travellers. When a person visits the same country several times a year, each visit is counted as a separate arrival and if a person visits several countries during the course of a single trip, his/her arrival in each country is recorded as a separate arrival. Same day visitors are excluded as are tourists who stay with friends or relatives.

Comparability

Several OECD countries cannot provide statistics according to the standard definition given above. Australia, Canada, Japan, China, India, South Africa and the United States report the number of non-residents arriving at their borders who intend to stay for at least one night, whether or not in a hotel or similar establishment. The figures for Korea and New Zealand are similar except that they also include same day visitors (very few in both countries).

Long-term trends

Over the period as a whole, the United States recorded the largest number of arrivals in hotels and similar establishments followed by China, France, Italy and Spain.

The 9/11 terrorist attacks resulted in sharp falls in arrivals in the United Kingdom, Mexico and the United States but did not noticeably affect arrivals in most other countries. Countries in central and eastern Europe have recorded strong increases in arrivals since 1990. The graph shows annual growth in arrivals of non-residents averaged over the period since 1998. Arrivals declined in Brazil, the United Kingdom, Switzerland, Norway and Greece but grew at 6% per year or more in New Zealand, Iceland, Japan, India, Slovak Republic, Turkey and China.

Tourism 2020 Vision is the World Tourism Organization's (UNWTO) long-term forecast and assessment of the development of tourism up to the first 20 years of the new millennium. Although the evolution of tourism in the last few years has been irregular, UNWTO maintains its long-term forecast for the moment. The underlying structural trends of the forecast are believed not to have significantly changed. Experience shows that in the short term, periods of faster growth (1995, 1996, 2000) alternate with periods of slower growth (2001 and 2002).

UNWTO's *Tourism 2020 Vision* forecasts that international arrivals will reach over 1.56 billion by the year 2020. East Asia and the Pacific, South Asia, the Middle East and Africa are forecasted to record growth at rates of over 5% per year, compared with the world average of 4.1%. The more mature tourism regions, Europe and the Americas, are expected to show lower than average growth rates. Europe will maintain the highest share of world arrivals, although there will be a decline from 60% in 1995 to 46% in 2020.

Sources
- *The Statistical Office of the European Communities (Eurostat).*
- *World Tourism Organization (UNWTO).*

Further information

Analytical publications
- OECD (2006), *Climate Change in the European Alps: Adapting Winter Tourism and Natural Hazards Management*, OECD, Paris.

Statistical publications
- Eurostat (2002), *Yearbook on Tourism Statistics*, Eurostat, Luxembourg.
- UNWTO (2005), *Yearbook of Tourism Statistics*, Madrid.

Methodological publications
- UN, Eurostat, OECD, UNWTO (2001), *Tourism Satellite Account: Recommended Methodological Framework*, OECD, Paris.

Websites
- Eurostat, *http://europa.eu.int/comm/eurostat/.*
- UNWTO, *www.world-tourism.org.*
- OECD work on tourism, *www.oecd.org/cfe/tourism.*

OECD FACTBOOK 2007 – ISBN 978-92-64-02946-0 – © OECD 2007

Arrivals of non-resident tourists in hotels and similar establishments and at borders
Thousands

	1992	1993	1994	1995	1996	1997	1998	1999	2000	2001	2002	2003	2004	2005
Australia	2 603	2 996	3 362	3 726	4 165	4 318	3 825	4 109	4 530	4 435	4 420	4 354	4 774	5 020
Austria	13 664	13 032	12 878	12 464	12 533	12 329	12 803	12 755	13 240	13 279	13 487	13 748	14 075	14 542
Belgium	3 861	3 719	3 947	4 138	4 469	4 710	4 859	4 983	5 163	5 117	5 323	5 261	5 385	5 409
Canada	14 741	15 105	15 972	16 932	17 286	17 669	18 870	19 411	19 627	19 679	20 057	17 534	19 095	..
Czech Republic	..	..	2 448	2 891	3 696	4 013	4 067	4 141	3 863	4 439	4 314	4 485	5 346	5 686
Denmark	..	..	..	..	1 307	1 317	1 305	1 268	1 347	1 310	1 284	1 294	1 363	1 350
Finland	..	1 447	1 633	1 587	1 537	1 618	1 655	1 613	1 751	1 774	1 796	1 800	1 825	1 828
France	28 402	26 270	27 121	27 018	27 096	29 625	32 339	34 267	36 474	35 097	36 093	32 520	33 988	35 033
Germany	13 292	12 071	12 269	12 683	13 042	13 745	14 457	14 965	16 719	15 754	15 672	15 979	17 620	18 761
Greece	6 208	6 209	6 659	6 250	5 973	6 785	7 276	7 229	7 767	6 946	6 654	6 574	6 313	7 143
Hungary	..	..	2 122	2 116	2 202	2 188	2 472	2 401	2 604	2 669	2 659	2 599	2 951	3 140
Iceland	..	..	..	..	311	354	400	431	451	465	513	569	615	643
Ireland	1 598	1 643	1 901	..	..	..	3 077	3 343	5 491	3 577	..	..	..	..
Italy	17 366	17 919	21 074	23 467	24 929	25 133	25 927	26 530	28 797	29 138	29 340	28 174	29 916	30 870
Japan	3 582	3 410	3 468	3 345	3 837	4 218	4 106	4 438	4 757	4 772	5 239	5 212	6 138	6 728
Korea	3 231	3 331	3 580	3 753	3 684	3 908	4 250	4 660	5 322	5 147	5 347	4 754	5 818	6 022
Luxembourg	492	507	492	496	461	508	525	580	589	577	599	581	613	667
Mexico	4 805	5 174	5 159	6 718	7 491	8 155	8 157	9 501	9 867	9 410	7 869	8 556	9 972	10 691
Netherlands	3 900	3 778	4 456	4 797	4 999	6 163	7 432	7 550	7 738	7 445	7 433	6 931	7 602	8 081
New Zealand	1 056	1 157	1 323	1 409	1 529	1 497	1 485	1 607	1 787	1 909	2 045	2 104	2 334	2 366
Norway	2 375	2 556	2 830	2 880	2 746	2 702	2 829	2 857	2 787	2 686	2 561	2 439	2 556	2 656
Poland	2 210	2 315	2 540	2 792	3 020	2 919	2 695	1 982	2 505	2 488	2 536	2 701	3 385	3 723
Portugal	3 672	3 372	3 809	4 000	4 069	4 314	4 974	4 911	5 119	4 934	5 060	4 906	5 152	5 378
Slovak Republic	371	536	680	735	758	660	701	767	836	927	1 041	1 043	1 094	1 203
Spain	12 483	12 914	15 310	16 286	17 008	18 250	20 199	26 799	27 150	27 012	26 611	27 249	27 620	29 029
Sweden	1 572	1 629	1 830	1 995	2 091	2 143	2 304	2 320	2 465	2 586	2 577	2 552	2 610	2 736
Switzerland	7 528	7 225	7 358	6 946	6 730	7 039	7 185	7 154	7 821	7 455	6 868	6 530	..	..
Turkey	3 700	4 072	3 716	4 617	6 440	9 382	7 539	4 805	6 789	8 769	9 859	8 983	10 962	12 937
United Kingdom	13 306	14 259	14 927	17 118	16 890	17 110	16 304	17 019	17 019	17 019	14 176	14 397	13 172	..
United States	47 262	45 779	44 753	43 490	46 636	47 875	46 377	48 510	51 237	46 927	43 582	41 218	46 085	49 408
Brazil	1 428	1 402	1 529	1 709	2 266	2 419	3 854	3 754	3 868	3 331	3 536	2 633	3 068	3 215
China	16 512	18 982	21 070	20 034	22 765	23 770	25 073	27 047	31 229	33 167	36 803	32 970	41 761	46 809
India	1 868	1 765	1 886	2 124	2 288	2 374	2 359	2 482	2 649	2 537	2 384	2 726	3 457	3 915
Russian Federation	3 009	5 896	4 643	..	..	..	..	..	7 030	7 400	7 943	8 521	9 164	..
South Africa	2 703	3 358	3 897	4 488	4 915	4 976	5 732	5 890	5 872	5 787	6 430	6 505	6 678	7 369

StatLink ⟐ http://dx.doi.org/10.1787/446724128667

Arrivals of non-resident tourists staying in hotels and similar establishments
Average annual growth in percentage, 1998-2005 or latest available period

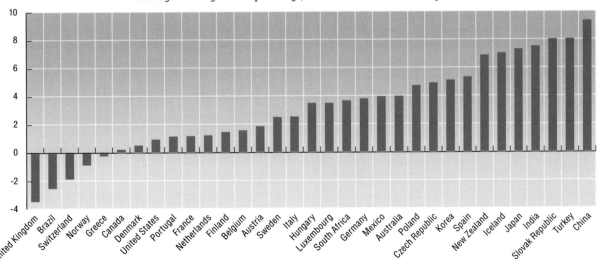

StatLink ⟐ http://dx.doi.org/10.1787/360470761314

RECREATION AND CULTURE

In general, percentages of GDP spent on recreation and culture are positively correlated with per capita income – the richer the country, the higher the percentage expenditure on culture and recreation – but there are some striking exceptions. Ireland (rich) spends relatively little on recreation and culture while the Czech Republic (poor) spends a rather high share.

Definition

Household expenditure on recreation and culture includes purchases of audio-visual, photographic and computer equipment; CDs and DVDs; musical instruments; camper vans; caravans; sports equipment; toys; domestic pets and related products; gardening tools and plants; newspapers; tickets to sporting matches, cinemas and theatres; and spending on gambling (including lottery tickets) less any winnings. It excludes expenditures on restaurants, hotels, and travel and holiday homes but includes package holidays.

Government expenditures include administration of sporting, recreational and cultural affairs as well as the maintenance of zoos, botanical gardens, public beaches and parks; support for broadcasting services and, where present, support for religious, fraternal, civic, youth and other social organizations (including the operation and repair of facilities and payment to clergy and other officers.) Also included are grants to artists and arts companies. Capital outlays such as the construction of sports stadiums, public swimming pools, national theatres, opera houses and museums are included.

Comparability

The data in these tables are all taken from the OECD's national accounts database and are compiled according to a common set of definitions.

Long-term trends

In most countries, household expenditures on recreation and culture have remained fairly stable at around 5% of GDP over the last decade. Notable exceptions were the Slovak Republic, Japan and Mexico where household expenditures grew much faster than average. In some countries, notably Ireland, Poland and Korea, expenditures declined considerably as shares of GDP. By the end of the period, household expenditures were well above the OECD average in the United Kingdom, Australia and Austria and much below it in Mexico and Ireland.

Data on government expenditures on recreation, culture and religion are available for fewer countries. In most of these countries, government expenditure amounts to between 1 and 2% of GDP. By the end of the period, government expenditures were much higher than average in Luxembourg, Denmark and (particularly) Iceland and below 0.5% of GDP in Japan, the United States and Greece. Over the period covered, they have grown quite rapidly in Korea, Greece, France and Iceland but have fallen in Sweden, United Kingdom, Finland, Germany and Austria.

The third table shows the combination of private and public expenditures on recreation and culture. As shares of GDP they are between 5 and 7% in most countries but somewhat higher in Iceland, the United Kingdom, Austria and the Czech Republic, and substantially lower in Ireland and Korea.

Source

• OECD (2006), *National Accounts of OECD Countries*, OECD, Paris.

Further information

Analytical publications

• OECD (2005), *Culture and Local Development*, OECD, Paris.

Household expenditure on recreation and culture

As a percentage of GDP

	1992	1993	1994	1995	1996	1997	1998	1999	2000	2001	2002	2003	2004	2005
Australia	6.4	6.7	6.9	7.2	7.2	7.3	7.3	7.2	7.3	7.1	7.2	7.2	7.1	6.9
Austria	6.7	6.7	6.6	6.4	6.5	6.5	6.7	6.9	6.9	6.9	6.9	6.8	6.8	6.7
Belgium	..	..	..	4.8	4.9	5.0	5.0	5.1	5.2	5.2	4.8	4.8	4.7	..
Canada	5.2	5.3	5.5	5.5	5.6	5.6	5.7	5.7	5.7	5.7	5.8	5.7	5.6	5.5
Czech Republic	..	..	..	5.5	5.8	6.4	6.3	6.2	6.1	6.2	6.0	6.2	6.0	6.0
Denmark	5.1	5.1	5.1	5.1	5.3	5.3	5.3	5.2	5.2	5.1	5.1	5.2	5.2	5.1
Finland	5.5	5.4	5.3	5.3	5.6	5.4	5.4	5.4	5.4	5.3	5.3	5.5	5.5	5.6
France	4.8	4.8	4.8	4.8	4.8	4.8	4.9	5.0	5.1	5.1	5.2	5.2	5.2	5.2
Germany	5.2	5.2	5.1	5.1	5.2	5.3	5.4	5.5	5.6	5.6	5.4	5.3	5.3	5.3
Greece	..	..	..	..	..	..	..	..	4.8	4.8	4.8	4.8	5.1	5.4
Hungary	..	..	..	..	..	..	..	..	4.1	4.2	4.1	4.2	4.2	4.3
Iceland	6.6	6.3	7.1	7.2	7.1	6.6	6.7	7.0	7.2	6.9	6.9	6.7	6.6	6.5
Ireland	..	..	..	4.0	4.1	3.7	3.4	3.1	3.4	3.4	3.0	3.0	3.2	3.1
Italy	4.3	4.3	4.3	4.2	4.3	4.3	4.4	4.5	4.5	4.4	4.3	4.2	4.3	4.2
Japan	..	..	..	..	5.6	5.7	5.7	5.8	6.3	6.3	6.3	6.3	6.3	..
Korea	4.0	4.0	4.2	4.3	4.2	4.0	3.4	3.6	4.1	4.2	4.4	4.0	3.6	3.7
Luxembourg	..	..	..	3.9	3.9	3.9	4.0	3.7	3.6	3.8	3.8	3.7	3.7	3.5
Mexico	2.3	2.3	2.2	1.9	1.8	1.9	2.0	2.0	2.0	2.0	1.9	1.9	2.0	
Netherlands	..	..	..	5.2	5.3	5.3	5.5	5.6	5.5	5.4	5.3	5.1	4.9	4.8
New Zealand	5.5	5.7	6.1	6.3	6.5	6.7	6.9	7.0	7.2	7.1	..	..	..	..
Norway	5.1	5.2	5.3	5.4	5.5	5.5	5.8	5.8	5.2	5.3	5.6	5.7	..	..
Poland	..	..	..	4.8	5.3	5.1	5.3	5.1	5.2	4.6	4.5	4.6	4.6	..
Portugal	..	..	..	4.1	4.1	4.2	4.1	4.1	4.2	4.1	4.1	4.2	..	..
Slovak Republic	..	..	..	4.0	4.2	4.2	4.3	4.6	4.7	5.4	5.2	4.8	4.7	5.0
Spain	..	..	..	5.2	5.3	5.3	5.6	5.7	5.7	5.7	5.6	5.6	5.6	..
Sweden	..	5.3	5.2	5.0	5.0	5.2	5.4	5.6	5.6	5.7	5.6	5.6	5.5	..
Switzerland	5.3	5.3	5.3	5.3	5.2	5.2	5.2	5.2	5.1	5.0	5.0	5.0	4.9	4.9
United Kingdom	6.3	6.4	6.4	6.8	7.0	7.2	7.3	7.4	7.4	7.4	7.5	7.6	7.7	7.7
United States	5.5	5.7	5.9	6.1	6.2	6.2	6.2	6.3	6.4	6.4	6.4	6.4	6.4	6.4

StatLink 🔗 http://dx.doi.org/10.1787/404132480732

Household expenditure on recreation and culture

2004 or latest available year

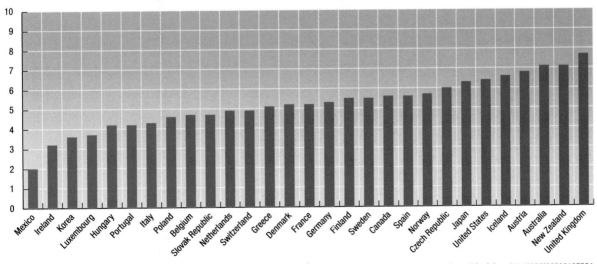

StatLink 🔗 http://dx.doi.org/10.1787/682528107584

Government expenditure on recreation and culture
As a percentage of GDP

	1992	1993	1994	1995	1996	1997	1998	1999	2000	2001	2002	2003	2004	2005
Australia	..	..	..	..	..	..	0.5	0.5	0.5	0.5	0.5	..	..	..
Austria	..	..	..	1.2	1.1	1.1	1.1	1.1	1.0	1.1	1.0	1.0	1.0	..
Belgium	0.8	0.9	0.9	0.9	0.9	0.9	0.9	0.9	1.0	0.9	1.3	1.3	..	..
Czech Republic	..	..	..	..	..	..	..	..	..	..	1.2	1.2	1.3	..
Denmark	1.5	1.6	1.7	1.6	1.7	1.6	1.6	1.6	1.6	1.6	1.6	1.6	1.8	..
Finland	1.5	1.3	1.2	1.3	1.4	1.4	1.3	1.2	1.2	1.2	1.2	1.2	1.2	..
France	..	..	..	1.1	1.1	1.1	1.1	1.2	1.1	1.2	1.3	1.4	1.4	1.5
Germany	0.9	0.8	0.8	0.8	0.8	0.7	0.7	0.7	0.7	0.7	0.7	0.7	0.7	..
Greece	0.1	0.1	0.1	0.2	0.2	0.2	0.2	0.3	0.3	0.3	0.3	0.3	0.3	..
Iceland	2.3	2.7	2.6	2.3	2.2	2.4	2.5	2.6	2.7	2.6	2.7	2.8	2.8	..
Ireland	0.4	0.4	0.5	0.4	0.5	0.4	0.5	0.5	0.5	0.6	0.6	0.5	0.5	..
Italy	0.8	0.8	0.8	0.8	0.9	0.9	0.9	1.0	0.9	0.9	0.9	0.9	1.0	..
Japan	..	..	..	..	0.2	0.2	0.2	0.2	0.2	0.2	0.2	0.2	0.2	..
Korea	..	..	..	0.4	0.4	0.5	0.6	0.6	0.7	0.7	0.6	0.8	0.8	..
Luxembourg	1.4	1.5	1.5	1.5	1.6	1.7	1.7	1.8	1.6	1.7	1.8	2.0	2.0	1.9
Netherlands	..	..	..	..	..	..	..	..	..	1.4	1.5	1.4	1.4	..
Norway	1.6	1.6	1.4	1.3	1.2	1.2	1.2	1.2	1.1	1.1	1.2	1.2	1.2	..
Portugal	..	..	..	..	..	..	..	1.2	1.1	1.1	1.1	1.2	1.2	..
Slovak Republic	..	..	..	..	..	..	..	..	..	..	..	1.1	1.2	..
Spain	..	..	..	..	..	..	..	..	1.4	1.4	1.4	1.4	1.4	..
Sweden	..	..	..	1.9	1.9	1.8	1.8	1.8	1.1	1.1	1.1	1.1	1.0	..
United Kingdom	0.8	0.8	0.8	0.7	0.7	0.6	0.6	0.7	0.7	0.6	0.6	0.6	0.5	..
United States	0.3	0.3	0.3	0.3	0.3	0.3	0.3	0.3	0.3	0.3	0.3	0.3	0.3	0.3

StatLink http://dx.doi.org/10.1787/483078010148

Government expenditure on recreation and culture
2004 or latest available year

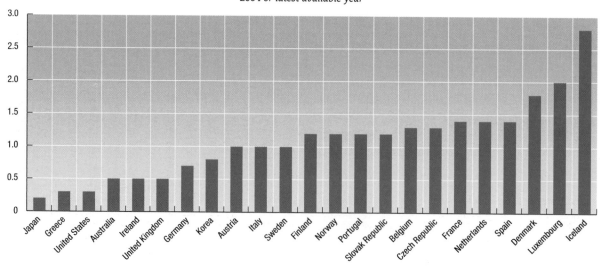

StatLink http://dx.doi.org/10.1787/423335510267

OECD FACTBOOK 2007 – ISBN 978-92-64-02946-0 – © OECD 2007

Household and government expenditure on recreation and culture

As a percentage of GDP

	1992	1993	1994	1995	1996	1997	1998	1999	2000	2001	2002	2003	2004	2005
Australia	..	..	..	..	..	..	7.8	7.7	7.8	7.6	7.8	..	..	..
Austria	..	..	..	7.6	7.7	7.7	7.8	8.1	7.9	8.0	7.9	7.8	7.8	..
Belgium	..	..	..	5.6	5.7	5.9	5.9	6.1	6.2	6.1	6.1	6.1	..	..
Czech Republic	..	..	..	..	..	..	..	..	..	..	7.2	7.4	7.3	..
Denmark	6.6	6.7	6.8	6.8	6.9	6.9	6.8	6.8	6.7	6.7	6.7	6.8	7.0	..
Finland	7.0	6.6	6.5	6.6	7.0	6.8	6.7	6.6	6.6	6.5	6.5	6.7	6.7	..
France	..	..	..	5.9	5.9	5.9	6.1	6.1	6.2	6.3	6.5	6.6	6.6	6.7
Germany	6.0	6.0	5.9	5.9	5.9	6.0	6.1	6.2	6.3	6.3	6.1	6.0	6.0	..
Greece	..	..	..	..	..	..	..	..	5.1	5.1	5.1	5.1	5.4	..
Iceland	8.9	9.0	9.7	9.5	9.3	9.0	9.2	9.5	9.9	9.6	9.6	9.6	9.4	..
Ireland	..	..	..	4.5	4.6	4.1	3.9	3.6	3.9	3.9	3.6	3.5	3.7	..
Italy	5.1	5.1	5.1	5.0	5.2	5.3	5.3	5.4	5.4	5.3	5.2	5.1	5.2	..
Japan	..	..	..	..	5.8	5.9	5.9	6.0	6.4	6.5	6.5	6.5	6.5	..
Korea	..	..	..	4.7	4.6	4.5	4.0	4.3	4.8	4.9	5.0	4.8	4.4	..
Luxembourg	..	..	..	5.4	5.5	5.6	5.7	5.5	5.2	5.4	5.6	5.7	5.7	5.5
Netherlands	..	..	..	..	..	..	..	..	..	6.8	6.8	6.6	6.4	..
Norway	6.7	6.7	6.7	6.7	6.7	6.7	7.1	7.1	6.3	6.4	6.8	6.9	..	..
Portugal	..	..	..	..	..	..	..	5.3	5.2	5.2	5.3	5.5	..	..
Slovak Republic	..	..	..	..	..	..	..	..	..	..	..	5.9	5.8	..
Spain	..	..	..	..	..	..	..	..	7.1	7.1	7.0	7.0	6.9	..
Sweden	..	..	..	6.9	6.9	7.0	7.2	7.3	6.7	6.8	6.7	6.7	6.6	..
United Kingdom	7.1	7.2	7.2	7.6	7.7	7.8	7.9	8.1	8.0	8.0	8.2	8.2	8.3	..
United States	5.8	6.0	6.2	6.4	6.5	6.5	6.5	6.6	6.7	6.7	6.7	6.7	6.7	6.7

StatLink ᴍᴤ⅊ http://dx.doi.org/10.1787/713805571188

Household and government expenditure on recreation and culture

2004 or latest available year

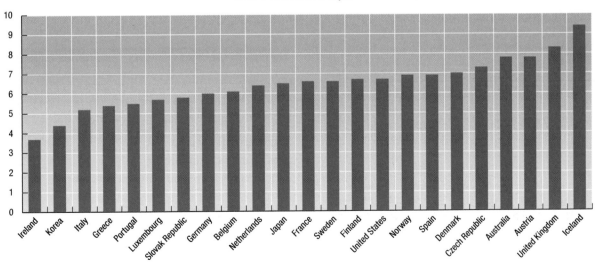

StatLink ᴍᴤ⅊ http://dx.doi.org/10.1787/027341700823

YOUTH INACTIVITY

If young people are not in employment and not at school, there are good reasons to be concerned about their current well-being and their future prospects. Low educational attainments and the growing importance of educational attainment for successful integration into the workforce make it difficult for those leaving school without adequate qualifications to move into jobs with good career prospects. The shares of young persons who are neither in employment nor in education is an indicator of those who are candidates to later become the "socially excluded" – persons with incomes below or at the poverty-line and who lack the skills to improve their economic situation.

Definition

The indicator presents the proportion of youths aged 15 to 19 who are not in education, training or employment as a percentage of the total number of all in that age group. Youths in education include those attending part-time as well as full-time education, but exclude those in non-formal education and educational activities of very short duration. Employment is defined according to the ILO Guidelines and covers all those who have worked for monetary gain for at least one hour in the week previous to the enquiry date.

Comparability

Standard definitions are specified for both "being in education" and "being in employment" and countries try to apply these criteria correctly. The main problem of comparability is that in some countries, youths performing compulsory military service are neither recorded as being in employment nor in education; they are therefore included in the numerator of the ratio although they could reasonably be considered to be both in training and in employment. However, in countries where there is still conscription, the duration of military services is quite short and reallocation of military conscripts to the employment/education category would not much change the figures given here.

Long-term trends

On average, across the countries for which data are available, around 7.7% of teenagers were neither in school nor at work in 2004. Differences across countries are large: in Denmark, Germany, Iceland, Luxembourg, Netherlands, Norway and Poland less than 4% were in this situation while the shares exceeded 10% in Portugal, Spain, the United Kingdom, Mexico and Turkey.

For the OECD as a whole, there has been a decline in the percentages of all teenagers who are neither in employment nor education, but the decline has been most marked for females. The fact that young people, and particularly females, spend more time in education than they did a decade ago has contributed to this.

Several features of the labour markets and training systems affect the ease of transition from school to work. OECD reviews of youths' transition from school to work have identified Nordic and English-speaking countries as those where this process is smoother than in countries in Continental and Southern Europe countries. Beyond waste of human capital and risks of marginalisation in the labour markets, delays in settling into jobs will lead many youths to live longer with their parents and defer the formation of independent families, further compounding fertility declines.

Source

• OECD (2006), *Society at a Glance: OECD Social Indicators – 2006 Edition*, OECD, Paris.

Further information
Analytical publications

• OECD (2000), *From Initial Education to Working Life: Making Transitions Work*, OECD, Paris.

• OECD (2006), *Society at a Glance: OECD Social Indicators – 2006 Edition*, OECD, Paris.

• OECD (2006), *OECD Employment Outlook*, OECD, Paris.

• OECD (2007), *Jobs for Youth*, OECD, Paris.

Websites

• Youth Employment Summit, *www.yesweb.org*.

Youths aged between 15 and 19 who are not in education nor in employment

As percentage of persons in that age group

	Males							Females						
	1998	1999	2000	2001	2002	2003	2004	1998	1999	2000	2001	2002	2003	2004
Australia	9.0	7.3	6.4	7.9	6.9	6.4	7.6	8.7	7.5	7.3	7.2	7.2	7.2	7.4
Austria	..	..	..	..	8.1	5.8	7.2	..	..	..	..	4.4	5.4	7.5
Belgium	10.8	6.3	6.7	6.0	7.3	6.9	5.8	10.8	7.3	6.3	6.4	6.4	7.4	3.9
Canada	8.0	7.9	7.8	6.9	7.3	7.5	8.4	6.9	6.6	6.6	5.6	5.9	6.2	6.6
Czech Republic	6.7	10.2	7.3	6.4	5.8	5.4	5.0	7.7	9.1	8.5	7.3	6.3	6.2	6.4
Denmark	1.5	4.2	1.9	4.7	2.4	2.9	0.7	2.1	2.6	3.6	2.7	2.4	3.1	2.3
Finland	..	..	..	..	..	..	5.1	5.5	5.2	4.6	6.1	5.3	6.4	5.5
France	3.5	3.5	3.4	3.4	3.7	..	6.2	2.6	3.0	3.2	3.5	3.2	..	4.5
Germany	3.1	4.2	5.2	4.9	4.3	4.7	3.5	3.7	4.9	6.3	5.3	5.1	4.8	3.7
Greece	7.0	8.1	6.9	5.7	5.2	8.6	7.6	12.7	12.6	11.1	9.8	7.5	10.1	10.7
Hungary	12.4	11.8	8.6	8.8	8.3	6.6	6.6	11.1	11.3	8.6	7.8	7.8	6.9	5.8
Iceland	2.8	0.4	1.0	2.0	..	..	..	2.5	2.5	3.3	1.0	..	..	..
Ireland	..	5.0	4.5	4.3	5.2	5.3	8.3	..	5.5	4.3	3.9	4.5	5.0	8.7
Italy	14.5	14.0	12.2	12.1	10.8	..	9.1	15.9	15.6	14.1	13.0	10.3	..	10.3
Luxembourg	6.4	3.6	1.6	1.6	1.7	2.4	2.1	5.8	6.3	1.7	2.0	4.3	2.0	3.1
Mexico	7.5	6.3	7.6	7.2	7.4	8.1	7.6	30.8	28.9	29.0	28.2	27.4	27.8	26.3
Netherlands	2.6	2.8	3.8	3.8	4.7	..	2.5	2.9	3.1	3.6	4.5	4.4	..	2.2
Norway	1.5	1.5	2.3	3.3	3.7	3.1	4.2	2.3	1.9	1.2	2.7	2.8	2.2	2.8
Poland	4.7	5.2	5.0	6.2	3.5	3.8	3.0	4.9	3.9	4.0	5.4	2.6	2.7	2.1
Portugal	6.9	6.7	6.2	5.4	7.7	8.2	9.7	9.7	9.6	9.2	9.5	6.8	9.4	11.0
Slovak Republic	21.7	22.5	27.8	27.9	17.7	15.2	8.6	14.9	18.1	24.7	24.9	13.5	9.9	7.1
Spain	10.1	9.4	7.7	6.6	6.9	7.3	10.0	9.6	9.3	8.2	7.3	7.5	7.4	10.8
Sweden	6.4	4.8	4.7	5.4	5.9	5.1	7.8	2.9	2.5	2.4	3.1	3.3	3.4	4.0
Switzerland	4.0	8.0	7.3	6.4	5.8	7.1	7.6	5.7	7.1	8.5	7.2	5.8	8.8	6.8
Turkey	14.2	14.5	17.8	19.2	21.7	22.6	24.7	42.7	41.5	46.5	47.0	45.6	44.3	47.1
United Kingdom	..	..	8.2	8.3	8.2	9.7	10.2	..	..	7.9	8.0	8.9	9.2	10.5
United States	6.5	6.1	6.8	6.9	6.4	..	6.5	8.2	8.7	7.3	8.0	7.5	..	7.3
OECD average	7.7	7.5	7.4	7.5	7.3	7.5	6.9	9.6	9.4	9.3	9.1	8.1	8.9	8.5

StatLink ⌗🔢 http://dx.doi.org/10.1787/506660867147

Percentage of youths aged between 15 and 19 who are not in education nor in employment

Year 2005

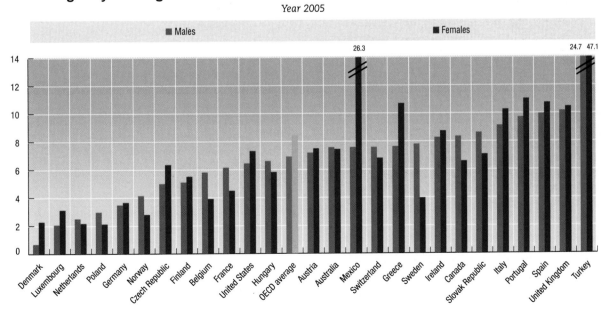

StatLink ⌗🔢 http://dx.doi.org/10.1787/042124157080

INCOME INEQUALITY

The distribution of incomes within a country is important for at least two reasons. Inequalities may create incentives for people to improve their situation through work, innovation or acquiring new skills. On the other hand, crime, poverty and social exclusion are often seen as linked to inequalities of income distribution.

Definition

Income is here defined as *household disposable income*, broadly following the definitions of the 1993 *System of National Accounts*. It consists of earnings from work, property income such as interest and dividends, and pensions and other social security benefits; income taxes and social security contributions paid by households are deducted.

The equality of disposable incomes among individuals is measured here by the *Gini Coefficient*. This is a common measure of equality and ranges from 0 in the case of "perfect equality" (each share of the population gets the same share of income) to 100 in the case of "perfect inequality" (all income goes to the share of the population with the highest income). Household income is adjusted to take account of household size. See Sources, below, for a detailed definition of the Gini Coefficient and of the adjustment for household size.

Comparability

"2000" data refer to the year 2000 in all countries except for Australia, Austria and Greece (1999); for Germany, Luxembourg, New Zealand and Switzerland (2001); and for the Czech Republic, Mexico and Turkey (2002). "Mid-1990s" data refer to the year 1995 in all countries except for Austria (1993); for Australia, Denmark, France, Germany, Greece, Ireland, Japan, Mexico and Turkey (1994); and for the Czech Republic and New Zealand (1996). "Mid-1980s" data refer to the year 1983 in Austria, Belgium, Denmark and Sweden; 1984 in Australia, France, Italy and Mexico; 1985 in Canada, Japan, the Netherlands, Spain and the United Kingdom; 1986 in Finland, Luxembourg, New Zealand and Norway; 1987 in Ireland and Turkey; 1988 in Greece; and 1989 in the United States.

Data were provided by national experts using common definitions. In many cases, however, countries have had to make several adjustments to their source data. Small changes between periods and small differences across countries are usually not significant.

Long-term trends

There is considerable variation in levels of income inequality across OECD countries. For years around 2000, the Gini coefficient of income inequality is lowest in Denmark and Sweden, and highest in Mexico and Turkey – the two OECD countries with lowest per capita income. On average, across the 20 countries for which data are available since the mid-1980s, the Gini coefficient of income inequality increased from 29 to 31 but this increase may be within the margin of error for statistics on income distribution. The safest conclusion is that, for these 20 countries as a whole, there was little or no change.

There were, however, some striking changes for several countries when years around 2000 are compared with the mid-1980s. Household income distribution became markedly more equal in Spain and Ireland, and there were smaller reductions in inequality in Australia, Denmark and France.

At the other end of the scale, the Gini coefficients increased (greater inequality) by 10-20% in Norway, Japan, Italy and the United Kingdom and by over 20% in Sweden, New Zealand and Finland. Note, however, that despite the large increase in Sweden, the Gini coefficient is still one of the lowest in the OECD area.

Source

• Förster, M. and M. Mira d'Ercole (2005), *Income Distribution and Poverty in OECD Countries in the Second Half of the 1990s*, OECD Social Employment and Migration Working Papers, No. 22, OECD, Paris.

Further information
Analytical publications

• Jomo, K. S. (2001), *Globalisation, Liberalisation, Poverty and Income Inequality in Southeast Asia*, OECD Development Centre Working Papers, No. 185, OECD, Paris.

• Kayizzi-Mugerwa, S. (2001), *Globalisation, Growth and Income Inequality: The African Experience*, OECD Development Centre Working Papers, No. 186, OECD, Paris.

• OECD (2004), *Income Disparities in China: An OECD Perspective*, OECD, Paris.

• OECD (2005), *Extending Opportunities: How Active Social Policy Can Benefit Us All*, OECD, Paris.

• OECD (2007), *Society at a Glance: OECD Social Indicators – 2006 Edition*, OECD, Paris.

• Uchimura, H. (2005), *Impact of Changes in Social Institutions on Income Inequality in China*, OECD Development Centre Working Papers, No. 243, OECD, Paris.

Websites

• OECD Social and Welfare Statistics, *www.oecd.org/statistics/social*.

Distribution of household disposable income among individuals

Gini coefficients, mid-1980s to years around 2000

	Mid-1980s	Mid-1990s	2000
Australia	31.2	30.5	30.5
Austria	23.6	23.8	25.2
Canada	28.7	28.3	30.1
Czech Republic	..	25.7	26.0
Denmark	22.8	21.3	22.5
Finland	20.7	22.8	26.1
France	27.6	27.8	27.3
Germany	..	28.3	27.7
Greece	33.6	33.6	34.5
Hungary	..	29.4	29.3
Ireland	33.1	32.4	30.4
Italy	30.6	34.8	34.7
Japan	27.8	29.5	31.4
Luxembourg	24.7	25.9	26.1
Mexico	45.1	52.0	48.0
Netherlands	23.4	25.5	25.1
New Zealand	27.0	33.1	33.7
Norway	23.4	25.6	26.1
Poland	..	38.9	36.7
Portugal	..	35.9	35.6
Spain	36.7	33.9	32.9
Sweden	19.9	21.1	24.3
Switzerland	..	..	26.7
Turkey	43.5	49.1	43.9
United Kingdom	28.6	31.2	32.6
United States	33.8	36.1	35.7
OECD average	29.3	30.9	31.0

StatLink http://dx.doi.org/10.1787/148737274436

Distribution of household disposable income among individuals

Measured by Gini coefficients

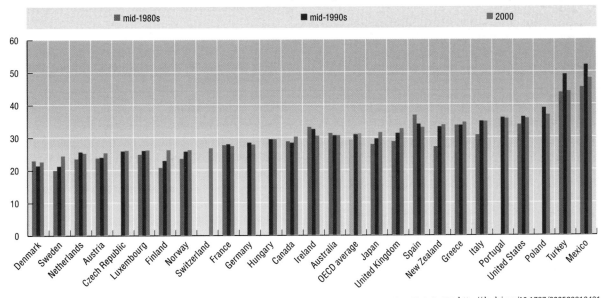

StatLink http://dx.doi.org/10.1787/833580312431

PRISON POPULATION

Crime causes great suffering to victims and their families, but the costs associated with imprisonment can also be considerable. These costs are normally justified by reference to a combination of three societal "needs": to inflict retribution; to deter others from behaving in a similar way; and to prevent re-offending.

Definition

Not everyone in prison has been found guilty of a crime, especially those awaiting trial or adjudication. The indicator here considers the total prison population, including pre-trial detainees and remand prisoners.

Comparability

The indicator here considers the total prison population, including pre-trial detainees and remand prisoners, per 100 000 of national population. This information has been collected by the International Centre for Prison Studies, every 3 years or so since 1992.

Additional comparative information is available from the above source, such as shares in total prison population of pre-trial detainees / remand prisoners, female prisoners , young prisoners, foreign prisoners, and occupancy levels in percentage (based on official prison capacity).

Long-term trends

Over the last fifteen years, most OECD countries have experienced a continuous rise in their prison population rates. On average, across the 30 OECD countries, this rate has increased from a level of 100 persons per 100 000 unit of the total population in the early 1990s to around 130 persons in 2004. The prison population rate is highest in the United States, where more than 700 per 100 000 population were in prison in 2004: such level is three to four times higher than second highest country (Poland), and has increased rapidly. This increase extends to most other OECD countries. Since 1992, the prison population rate has more than doubled in the Netherlands, Mexico, Japan, the Czech Republic, Luxembourg, Spain and the United Kingdom, while it appears to have declined only in Canada, Iceland and Korea.

There are large differences across countries in the make-up of the prison population. On average, one in four prisoners is a pre-trial detainee or a remand prisoner, but these two categories account for a much higher share of the prison population in Turkey, Mexico and Luxembourg. Women and youths (aged below 18) account, on average, for 5% and 2% of the prison population respectively. A much larger share of prisoners is accounted for by foreigners (close to 20% of all prisoners, on average), with this share exceeding 40% of the total in Luxembourg, Switzerland, as well as Australia, Austria, Belgium and Greece. In several countries, the rapid rise in the prison population has stretched beyond the receptive capacity of existing institutions; occupancy levels are above 100% in more than half of OECD countries, and above 125% in Greece, Hungary, Italy, Spain and Mexico.

Source
• Walmsley, R. (2005), *World Prison Population List (sixth edition)*, International Center for Prison Studies, London. *www.prisonstudies.org.*

Further information
Analytical publications
• OECD (2007), *Society at a Glance: OECD Social Indicators – 2006 Edition*, OECD, Paris.
• UN Office on Drugs and Crime (2004), *United Nations Surveys on Crime Trends and the Operations of Criminal Justice Systems (ninth survey)*, UNODC, Vienna, *www.unodc. org/unodc/crime_cicp_surveys.html.*

Websites
• OECD Social and Welfare Statistics, *www.oecd.org/ statistics/social.*
• United Nations Office on Drugs and Crime, *www.unodc.org.*

Prison population rate

Number per 100 000 population

	1992	1995	1998	2001	2004
Australia	89.0	96.0	107.0	116.0	120.0
Austria	87.0	77.0	86.0	85.0	96.5
Belgium	71.0	75.0	81.0	85.0	88.0
Canada	123.0	131.0	126.0	116.0	107.0
Czech Republic	123.0	181.0	209.0	210.0	169.0
Denmark	66.0	66.0	64.0	59.0	70.0
Finland	65.0	59.0	50.0	59.0	66.0
France	84.0	89.0	86.0	78.0	91.0
Germany	71.0	81.0	96.0	96.0	96.0
Greece	61.0	56.0	68.0	79.0	82.0
Hungary	143.0	124.0	132.0	152.0	163.0
Iceland	101.0	119.0	103.0	110.0	39.0
Ireland	61.0	57.0	71.0	78.0	85.0
Italy	81.0	87.0	85.0	95.0	97.0
Japan	37.0	37.0	40.0	48.0	58.0
Korea	130.0	136.0	152.0	133.0	121.0
Luxembourg	89.0	114.0	92.0	80.0	121.0
Mexico	98.0	102.0	133.0	164.0	177.5
Netherlands	49.0	66.0	85.0	95.0	123.0
New Zealand	129.0	128.0	146.0	157.0	168.0
Norway	58.0	55.0	57.0	59.0	65.0
Poland	153.0	163.0	148.0	183.0	210.0
Portugal	93.0	124.0	146.0	131.0	129.0
Slovak Republic	119.0	138.0	138.0	129.0	165.0
Spain	90.0	102.0	114.0	117.0	138.0
Sweden	63.0	65.0	60.0	68.0	81.0
Switzerland	79.0	80.0	85.0	71.0	81.0
Turkey	54.0	82.0	102.0	89.0	100.0
United Kingdom	90.1	100.2	124.5	124.4	138.7
United States	505.0	600.0	669.0	685.0	725.0
OECD average	102.1	113.0	121.8	125.0	132.4

StatLink http://dx.doi.org/10.1787/462100374737

Prison population rate

Number per 100 000 population, 2004

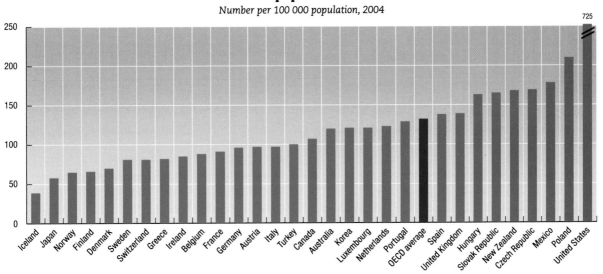

StatLink http://dx.doi.org/10.1787/353316863471

ROAD NETWORK

Motorways impact on the quality of life in several ways. Primarily, they make journeys by passenger cars both safer and easier. On the other hand, motorways may detract from the quality of life of those who live near them, and their construction may have harmful effects on the environment.

Definition

A motorway is defined as a road, specially designed and built for motor traffic, which does not serve properties bordering on it, and which:

- is provided, except at special points or temporarily, with separate carriageways for the two directions of traffic, separated from each other, either by a dividing strip not intended for traffic, or exceptionally by other means ;
- does not cross at level with any road, railway or tramway track, or footpath ;
- is specially sign-posted as a motorway and is reserved for specific categories of road motor vehicles.

In calculating the length of motorways, entry and exit lanes are included irrespectively of the location of the sign-posts. Urban motorways are also included.

Comparability

The data on motorways are regarded as broadly comparable for most countries. However, the figures for Canada are expressed in two-lane equivalent kilometres, the figures for Mexico refer to toll roads only, and Spain classifies some express roads as motorways although they do not exactly meet the definition given above. For some countries, the data are reported for financial rather than calendar years.

Long-term trends

Motorway networks have been growing in all OECD countries for which data are available.

OECD countries fall into three groups when the annual growth rates are considered. There are six countries where motorway networks have been growing at 6% or more each year: Finland, Korea, Portugal, Turkey, Ireland and Greece. These countries had relatively small networks at the beginning of the 1990s so that rapid growth was easy to achieve. There is a middle group of ten countries which recorded growth rates of 3 to 6% each year; this group includes Japan, France and the Scandinavian countries. At the lower end, there are ten OECD countries plus Russian Federation with growth rates of less than 2% per year; this group includes Canada, Germany, the Netherlands and the United States, where the motorway network was already mature at the beginning of the period, having been built up over several decades.

The size of a country's motorway network is generally correlated with a country's size, but the United Kingdom and Turkey are exceptions in having relatively small motorway networks, while in Germany, France and Spain the motorway networks are extensive relative to their size, whether size is defined by population or by surface area.

Source

- ECMT (2005), *Trends in the Transport Sector*, ECMT, Paris.

Further information

Analytical publications

- ECMT (2006), *ECMT Annual Report 2005*, ECMT, Paris.
- OECD (2006), *Decoupling the Environmental Impacts of Transport from Economic Growth*, OECD, Paris.

Methodological publications

- UNECE, ECMT, Eurostat (2003), *Glossary for Transport Statistics*, ECMT, Paris.

Websites

- European Conference of Ministers of Transport, *www.cemt.org*.

Length of the motorway network
Kilometers

	1992	1993	1994	1995	1996	1997	1998	1999	2000	2001	2002	2003	2004	2005
Austria	1 554	1 567	1 589	1 596	1 607	1 613	1 613	1 634	1 633	1 644	1 644	1 670	1 677	1 677
Belgium	1 658	1 665	1 666	1 666	1 674	1 679	1 682	1 691	1 702	1 727	1 729	1 729	1 747	1 747
Canada	15 983	15 983	15 983	15 983	15 983	15 983	15 983	15 983	15 983	16 600	16 900	16 900	16 900	16 900
Czech Republic	356	356	390	425	487	487	499	499	499	518	518	518	546	564
Denmark	696	737	786	796	825	900	902	922	953	971	1 009	1 270	1 278	1 278
Finland	318	337	388	394	431	444	473	512	549	591	603	653	653	653
France	7 440	7 645	8 030	8 247	8 596	8 864	9 303	9 626	9 766	10 068	10 223	10 379	10 486	10 486
Germany	11 013	11 080	11 143	11 190	11 190	11 246	11 309	11 427	11 515	11 712	11 786	12 037	12 044	12 044
Greece	..	..	..	..	..	..	357	444	636	742	742	880	880	880
Hungary	269	269	293	335	365	382	448	448	448	448	533	542	569	569
Ireland	32	51	68	70	70	70	94	94	103	125	125	176	192	192
Italy	6 289	6 352	6 401	6 473	6 473	6 473	6 473	6 478	6 478	6 478	6 478	6 478	6 478	6 478
Japan	..	5 054	5 410	5 410	5 932	6 114	6 402	6 455	6 617	6 851	6 915	7 196	7 196	7 196
Korea	..	..	..	..	..	..	2 107	2 425	2 477	2 567	3 060	3 486	3 489	3 489
Luxembourg	95	100	121	123	115	118	118	114	114	115	126	135	146	146
Netherlands	2 134	2 167	2 178	2 208	2 222	2 236	2 250	2 268	2 265	2 281	2 281	2 308	2 342	2 342
New Zealand	156	156	156	156	156	156	156	184	226	167	169	169	171	171
Norway	437	512	524	527	560	570	570	589	606	636	629	664	664	664
Poland	257	231	245	246	258	264	268	317	358	398	405	405	552	552
Portugal	520	579	587	687	710	797	1 252	1 441	1 482	1 659	1 835	1 835	1 835	1 835
Slovak Republic	200	198	198	198	215	219	292	295	296	296	302	313	316	316
Spain	6 209	6 577	6 485	6 962	7 295	7 750	8 569	8 893	9 049	9 571	9 739	10 286	10 286	10 286
Sweden	991	1 044	1 145	1 262	1 350	1 428	1 437	1 484	1 501	1 507	1 544	1 591	1 591	1 700
Switzerland	..	..	..	..	..	1 258	1 262	1 267	1 270	1 305	1 342	1 351	1 341	1 357
Turkey	757	1 070	1 167	1 246	1 493	1 500	1 528	1 726	1 749	1 851	1 851	1 851	1 851	1 851
United Kingdom	2 785	2 756	2 839	3 200	3 200	3 300	3 300	3 400	3 500	3 610	3 611	3 611	3 657	3 657
United States	73 198	73 274	73 274	73 274	73 274	73 274	88 915	89 232	89 426	89 996	89 848	91 287	91 287	91 287
Russian Federation	..	..	..	..	..	..	29 000	29 000	29 000	29 000	29 260	29 260	29 260	29 260

StatLink http://dx.doi.org/10.1787/238546764367

Growth of the motorway network
Average annual growth in percentage, 1992-2005

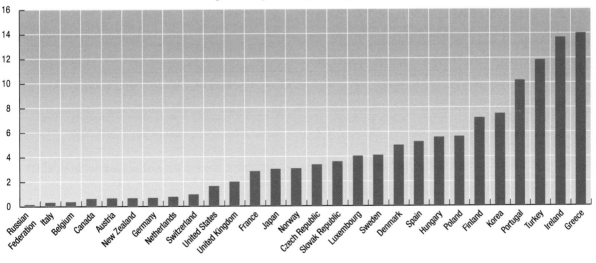

StatLink http://dx.doi.org/10.1787/153281416115

ROAD MOTOR VEHICLES AND ROAD FATALITIES

The number of road motor vehicles is high and rising among OECD countries, and reducing road accidents is a concern in all countries. The tables in this section show the numbers of road motor vehicles per thousand inhabitants and two indicators of road safety – the number of road fatalities per million inhabitants and the number of road fatalities per million vehicles.

Definition

A road motor vehicle is a vehicle running on wheels and intended for use on roads with an engine providing its sole means of propulsion and which is normally used for carrying persons or goods or for drawing, on the road, vehicles used for the carriage of persons or goods. Thus buses, coaches, freight vehicles and motor cycles are included as well as passenger motor cars. Motor vehicles running on rails are excluded.

Road fatality means any person killed immediately or dying within 30 days as a result of a road accident.

Comparability

Road motor vehicles are attributed to the countries where they are registered while deaths are attributed to the countries in which they occur. As a result, ratios of fatalities to million inhabitants and of fatalities to million vehicles cannot strictly be interpreted as indicating the proportion of a country's population that is at risk of suffering a fatal road accident or the likelihood of a vehicle registered in a given country being involved in a fatal accident. In practice, however, this is not considered to be a serious problem because discrepancies between the numerators and denominators tend to cancel out.

The numbers of vehicles entering the existing stock is usually accurate but information on the numbers of vehicles withdrawn from use is less certain.

Long-term trends

In 2005, ratios of motor vehicles to population range from 780 per thousand inhabitants in Portugal to 86 in Turkey. Over the periods shown in the table, ratios of vehicles to population increased in all countries except in the United States. Sharp increases of this ratio occurred in Greece, Poland, Iceland and Russian Federation.

In 2005, road fatalities per million inhabitants ranged from over 237 per million inhabitants in Russian Federation to 46 in the Netherlands. Over the periods shown in the table, rates have decreased in all countries except in the Russian Federation with particularly sharp falls in Portugal, Slovenia, New Zealand, Luxembourg, Finland and Spain.

Road fatality rates per million inhabitants are an ambiguous indicator of road safety since the number of accidents depends to a great extent on the number of vehicles in each country. The last chart shows the number of fatalities per million vehicles together with fatalities per million inhabitants. Both ratios refer to 2005. Rates per million vehicles are affected by driving habits, traffic legislation and the effectiveness of its enforcement, road design and other factors over which governments may exercise control. In 2005, fatality rates per million vehicles were less than 100 in the Netherlands, Iceland, Norway, Sweden and Switzerland, but exceeded 400 in Slovak Republic, Korea, Turkey and 1 200 in Russian Federation. Note that low fatality rates per million inhabitants may be associated with very high fatality rates per million vehicles. For example, a country with a small vehicle population may show a low fatality rate per million inhabitants but a high fatality rate per vehicle.

Source
• ECMT (2005), *Trends in the Transport Sector*, ECMT, Paris.

Further information

Analytical publications
• ECMT (2004), *Road Safety Performance: National Peer Review: Lithuania*, ECMT, Paris.
• ECMT (2006), *ECMT Annual Report 2005*, ECMT, Paris.
• ECMT (2006), *Speed Management*, ECMT, Paris.

Statistical publications
• ECMT (2003), *Statistical Report on Road Accidents*, ECMT, Paris.

Methodological publications
• UNECE, ECMT, Eurostat (2003), *Glossary for Transport Statistics*, ECMT, Paris.

Websites
• European Conference of Ministers of Transport, *www.cemt.org*.

Road motor vehicles
Per thousand population

	1992	1993	1994	1995	1996	1997	1998	1999	2000	2001	2002	2003	2004	2005
Australia	..	..	..	603	599	591	626	629	623	625	634	643	653	665
Austria	503	515	528	543	495	509	529	544	555	563	535	542	553	554
Belgium	441	454	464	487	494	482	490	500	511	517	520	525	531	528
Canada	627	595	569	565	565	564	583	568	574	573	582	585	586	580
Czech Republic	..	434	455	333	383	383	369	373	373	383	394	409	417	431
Denmark	370	373	374	386	398	406	411	420	421	425	428	432	434	441
Finland	445	425	422	427	434	436	451	465	476	481	488	503	523	541
France	505	509	518	520	526	532	548	559	573	583	587	598	604	604
Germany	427	478	523	540	547	551	556	564	570	582	589	593	597	603
Greece	257	271	283	298	313	328	351	378	406	428	450	454	478	503
Hungary	216	232	239	253	257	262	255	261	270	283	300	317	334	341
Iceland	465	457	433	453	467	554	574	609	636	688	694	709	745	732
Ireland	286	295	305	318	348	367	387	409	425	442	445	458	458	439
Italy	556	562	562	573	581	586	603	622	632	656	660	678	677	678
Japan	493	507	520	537	566	575	580	586	592	596	600	604	605	604
Korea	..	..	..	..	..	..	254	236	237	243	243	256	263	269
Luxembourg	542	580	580	625	669	675	671	666	693	719	728	736	751	740
Netherlands	414	419	426	430	443	450	464	461	478	496	504	516	523	528
New Zealand	..	645	649	658	654	636	643	659	679	684	688	699	719	737
Norway	458	461	465	474	467	491	498	503	511	516	521	527	538	545
Poland	203	210	222	232	246	261	272	286	309	325	347	357	375	378
Portugal	407	439	438	501	533	569	610	654	698	711	756	748	773	780
Slovak Republic	222	248	247	213	217	232	245	253	259	265	272	280	250	250
Spain	412	422	419	447	464	481	502	526	541	557	567	561	602	573
Sweden	452	444	442	447	450	456	468	481	494	497	500	504	502	513
Switzerland	494	487	492	498	504	511	518	528	536	545	551	558	565	568
Turkey	53	61	64	68	97	105	111	116	124	92	94	88	87	86
United Kingdom	453	441	439	428	448	458	474	486	493	516	533	526	543	536
United States	779	725	719	771	783	784	792	765	754	759	766	776	769	761
Russian Federation	..	98	111	124	139	145	154	161	174	182	191	194	194	194

StatLink http://dx.doi.org/10.1787/881614071656

Road motor vehicles
Per thousand population

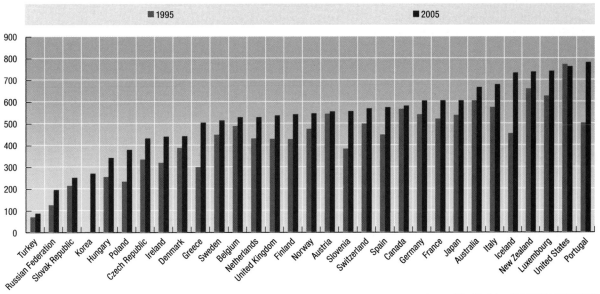

StatLink http://dx.doi.org/10.1787/111412027276

Road fatalities
Per million population

	1992	1993	1994	1995	1996	1997	1998	1999	2000	2001	2002	2003	2004	2005
Australia	113	111	109	111	108	95	94	93	95	90	87	82	79	81
Austria	177	161	167	150	127	137	121	135	122	119	118	114	108	94
Belgium	166	165	167	148	134	134	147	136	143	144	131	117	112	104
Canada	128	125	111	113	103	101	97	98	95	90	93	87	85	85
Czech Republic	150	147	158	154	152	155	132	141	145	130	140	142	136	126
Denmark	111	108	105	111	98	93	94	97	93	80	86	80	68	61
Finland	119	96	94	86	79	85	78	83	77	83	80	73	72	72
France	173	166	156	154	147	145	153	145	137	138	128	101	93	88
Germany	131	123	121	116	107	104	95	95	91	85	83	80	71	65
Greece	177	176	183	195	206	201	207	201	193	178	159	145	151	145
Hungary	193	163	152	155	135	137	136	130	118	122	141	131	129	127
Iceland	92	91	44	90	37	55	98	75	113	84	101	80	79	64
Ireland	118	122	113	122	125	129	124	110	110	107	96	84	94	83
Italy	138	124	123	122	115	116	118	116	115	117	117	105	98	90
Japan	92	106	102	100	93	89	85	82	82	79	75	70	66	62
Korea	..	..	..	..	..	..	226	232	218	171	152	151	136	132
Luxembourg	177	196	166	169	170	142	134	133	172	159	140	118	109	101
Netherlands	84	82	84	86	76	74	68	69	68	62	61	63	49	46
New Zealand	188	172	164	162	141	144	132	134	121	118	103	115	107	99
Norway	76	65	65	70	58	69	79	68	76	61	68	61	56	49
Poland	181	165	175	179	165	189	183	174	163	143	152	148	150	143
Portugal	274	240	222	242	241	222	213	200	186	161	165	148	124	118
Slovak Republic	131	120	127	130	119	154	160	125	120	116	116	121	113	111
Spain	154	163	143	147	139	142	150	144	143	135	129	128	115	89
Sweden	88	72	67	65	61	61	60	65	67	65	63	59	53	49
Switzerland	121	104	97	98	87	83	84	81	82	75	70	74	69	55
Turkey	106	108	97	97	86	81	76	69	58	45	62	56	62	62
United Kingdom	78	70	67	66	65	65	62	62	62	63	63	62	57	55
United States	154	156	156	159	158	158	154	153	149	148	149	147	145	145
Russian Federation	245	250	239	221	199	188	198	203	203	213	228	248	241	237

StatLink 🔗 http://dx.doi.org/10.1787/648463235317

Road fatalities
Per million population

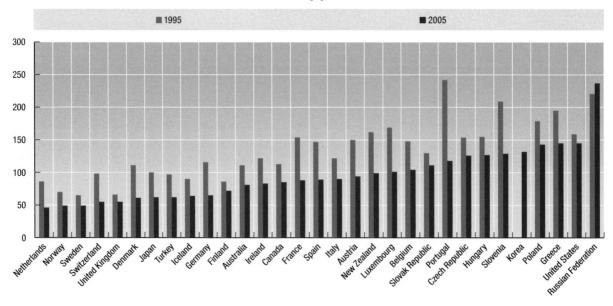

StatLink 🔗 http://dx.doi.org/10.1787/884266314335

OECD FACTBOOK 2007 – ISBN 978-92-64-02946-0 – © OECD 2007

Road fatalities
Per million vehicles

	1992	1993	1994	1995	1996	1997	1998	1999	2000	2001	2002	2003	2004	2005
Australia	..	..	..	183.9	179.9	161.5	149.5	147.7	152.8	143.2	138.4	134.8	134.8	121.1
Austria	352.8	311.9	315.5	277.0	257.1	269.0	228.1	247.7	219.3	210.9	220.5	211.2	199.1	168.8
Belgium	376.5	362.2	359.8	293.6	270.2	278.0	299.9	272.7	280.5	279.0	251.0	225.6	208.5	197.1
Canada	205.0	209.5	195.8	200.1	182.1	178.9	166.9	172.9	166.1	156.3	160.5	149.6	149.6	145.7
Czech Republic	..	339.6	348.2	461.4	404.4	404.4	358.5	379.5	388.4	338.9	356.2	346.8	331.2	292.7
Denmark	300.7	288.6	280.6	287.1	245.6	228.2	228.0	230.5	221.0	189.1	201.1	187.4	173.1	138.6
Finland	267.0	224.5	223.2	202.2	181.2	195.4	171.7	179.4	160.6	173.2	163.4	144.3	142.7	133.5
France	340.8	324.9	300.2	293.5	277.7	270.1	276.0	256.5	238.9	235.9	217.8	169.6	154.4	145.0
Germany	307.3	257.1	230.6	214.1	195.5	188.9	170.9	167.7	159.9	145.5	140.8	135.3	119.5	107.8
Greece	753.1	715.1	704.4	656.3	630.7	622.4	591.3	531.7	476.0	414.4	341.7	337.7	312.2	287.9
Hungary	895.2	702.7	635.7	613.5	523.9	523.3	532.8	498.9	436.5	430.1	469.6	414.1	404.7	372.1
Iceland	198.3	198.3	205.1	198.3	79.4	100.0	170.9	123.5	177.8	131.9	155.9	121.1	121.1	88.0
Ireland	411.7	414.8	371.0	384.3	359.5	350.9	319.7	269.5	258.0	242.3	215.8	183.7	207.8	188.8
Italy	231.7	207.2	205.1	198.5	185.5	184.7	182.6	186.5	181.9	178.8	177.0	165.7	153.1	132.8
Japan	186.2	209.7	196.4	186.3	163.9	155.0	147.2	139.6	138.4	132.5	125.2	124.9	124.9	102.6
Korea	..	..	..	..	..	..	891.8	983.4	919.5	702.9	612.7	509.9	509.9	491.2
Luxembourg	346.0	329.0	320.3	263.6	257.1	195.8	199.3	200.0	248.4	221.5	192.0	160.6	148.5	136.1
Netherlands	203.9	194.6	197.5	200.8	171.3	165.1	145.7	148.9	141.6	124.5	120.8	122.6	95.9	86.9
New Zealand	..	267.4	253.4	246.7	216.0	225.7	205.7	202.6	177.6	172.8	149.1	144.2	144.2	133.7
Norway	165.7	141.5	140.1	147.6	124.2	139.6	159.1	134.9	148.1	117.7	132.0	117.3	106.9	88.9
Poland	890.3	783.6	789.0	770.4	668.7	723.6	672.0	609.3	526.6	440.5	438.9	413.5	418.7	377.3
Portugal	590.9	479.1	444.3	419.5	452.1	390.7	349.7	305.3	265.7	226.9	217.6	198.0	165.7	151.4
Slovak Republic	588.7	441.4	477.7	577.9	527.8	629.9	620.0	481.3	463.2	396.8	396.8	372.1	346.4	445.8
Spain	373.7	385.8	347.8	327.8	300.7	295.6	298.7	273.1	264.5	242.3	227.1	228.2	200.4	155.3
Sweden	194.3	162.8	151.7	144.7	134.9	134.0	128.2	136.2	134.7	131.6	125.3	117.3	106.4	95.0
Switzerland	244.5	213.1	196.7	196.1	172.6	161.9	161.8	154.2	153.2	137.5	127.2	133.5	124.7	96.7
Turkey	..	..	..	..	886.6	770.8	680.5	596.4	469.4	391.0	391.0	574.5	641.5	725.6
United Kingdom	172.3	153.5	147.0	148.5	140.6	137.1	125.5	121.9	119.2	117.1	113.4	118.4	109.0	103.4
United States	197.5	214.7	217.3	206.1	202.2	201.0	196.1	200.0	197.2	195.1	194.9	189.2	189.2	188.9
Russian Federation	..	2 555.6	2 166.2	1 785.3	1 427.9	1 294.2	1 285.9	1 261.4	1 165.4	1 172.1	1 195.9	1 280.8	1 241.4	1 221.6

StatLink ᠁᠍ᡅ᠊ http://dx.doi.org/10.1787/143488425063

Road fatalities
Per million vehicles and per million population, 2005

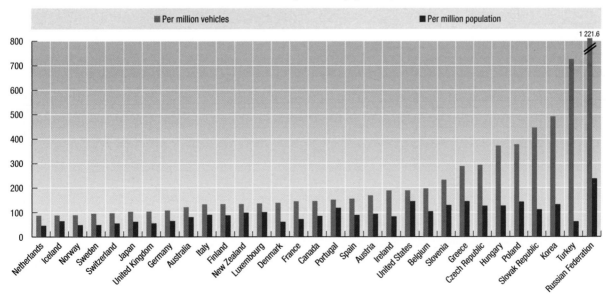

StatLink ᠁᠍ᡅ᠊ http://dx.doi.org/10.1787/653035568006

SPECIAL FOCUS

MIGRATION

INTRODUCTION

The statistics in this section present a broad overview of international migration movements and of immigrant educational and labour market outcomes. As recently as five years ago, international statistical comparisons of immigrant flows and stocks would not have been possible, because the data required to present such an overview on a reasonably comparable basis either did not exist or existed only in a very partial way. In part this was due to the complexity of the national laws and regulations governing international migration movements. In recent years OECD has been working to be able to provide comparable data on migration related phenomena. The brief description which follows may be useful in understanding the nature of international migration.

International migration movements are almost always subject to restrictions. All OECD countries regulate the movements of non-nationals (non-citizens), to a greater or lesser extent. Only nationals (citizens) generally enjoy the right of free movement, both with respect to entry into or departure from their home country. In almost all countries, certain non-nationals are accorded the right of free entry and of stay for short periods, for example for tourism, as part of reciprocal agreements between countries. Most other non-nationals require an entry visa before they can enter the territory of a receiving state. The visa generally only accords the right to stay in the country for a short period of time, often three months. The right of free entry and stay may be extended, both in time and in scope, to include the right of residence and the exercise of an economic activity, either as part of regional agreements (Australia/New Zealand) or broader supra-national political or economic unions (the European Union).

The right of a non-national to stay or reside in a country for a more extended period manifests itself through the granting of a residence permit. The criteria considered in assessing whether or not to grant a permit generally includes the candidate's reasons for wishing to stay in the country, which can include study, family reunification or formation, an extended visit, protection from persecution, employment or settlement. Persons granted a permit for reasons other than employment or settlement may or may not be authorised to exercise an economic activity in the country or may be authorised to do so on a limited basis. Certain types of movements (reunification with spouse and children or protection from persecution) are generally recognised human rights and are therefore generally not subject to interdiction, although some constraints may be placed on movements of this kind as well.

The duration of a residence permit will vary depending on the circumstances and/or reason for migration and the permit itself may or may not be renewable. Permit durations can vary from as little as three months for seasonal workers in some countries, one year for students or unskilled workers, more extended stays for the highly qualified or immigrants admitted for humanitarian reasons and indefinite duration in the case of settlement migration.

Countries differ significantly with respect to how longer term movements are treated. So-called "settlement countries", namely Australia, Canada, New Zealand and the United States, grant the right of permanent residence upon entry to certain categories of immigrants, sometimes selected on the basis of their characteristics. In most other countries, the permit granted at entry is almost always a temporary one, even for immigrants whose stay in the country is likely to be indefinite. Over time, permits of longer duration are granted and eventually, the right to indefinite stay. Thus a temporary permit in these countries does not necessarily mean a temporary migration. In some cases, persons in the country on a restricted or temporary status, such as international students, may be allowed to change status and to enter the labour market or even to remain in the country indefinitely.

Certain migration movements can be unauthorised, either because persons enter a country illegally or enter legally but overstay beyond the period allowed them at the time of entry. Such entries are almost never covered in the immigration statistics. Unauthorised immigrants, however, may appear in data sources on the immigrant population (such as surveys or censuses), especially if there is no legal obstacle to, or penalty for, declaring oneself or following a legalisation process.

The type of regulations and constraints described here vary from country to country and affect the nature of the statistics produced and available. They make the production of comparable statistics on international migration a challenging undertaking.

See *www.oecd.org/std/statisticsbrief: No. 9, July 2005: The Comparability of International Migration Statistics: Problems and Prospects.*

TRENDS IN INFLOWS OF FOREIGN NATIONALS

Despite differing national views concerning who is an immigrant, it is possible to give, on a more or less comparative basis, some idea of trends in immigration on the basis of official data through the use of indices. Although the levels may not be comparable, the year-to-year changes are less subject to comparability problems.

Definition

An immigrant is variously defined as a person who obtains the right of permanent residence (settlement countries: Australia, Canada, New Zealand and the United States), who obtains a residence permit of a minimum limited duration (generally one year or more), or who registers in a population register and intends to stay in the host country for longer than a specified number of months.

Long-term trends

After some signs of stabilisation in 2002-2003, migration flows into OECD countries increased again in 2004. However, the situation is far from uniform across countries. The Scandinavian countries as well as Germany, Ireland, Japan, Luxembourg and Turkey show little to any increase relative to 2003, while inflows have increased strongly in Australia, Austria, Finland, Spain, the United Kingdom and the United States. On the other hand, in all countries for which information is available, outflows of foreigners increased as well over the same period, except in the United Kingdom.

Moreover, recent changes in immigration vary a lot from one country to another. In the United States, grants of green cards rose by about 240 000 after a decline of similar magnitude in 2003 as a result of constraints introduced in the aftermath of the events of September 11th 2001. The increase may reflect more the processing of previous backlogs than a real upward trend. Spain experienced an increase in municipal registrations of foreigners of almost 50 per cent compared to 2003. The increase includes some irregular migrants and an undetermined proportion of temporary migrants.

Except for Germany, Hungary, Sweden, Switzerland and the United States levels in immigration registered in 2004 tend to be significantly larger than those registered at the beginning of the nineties. North America has registered a recent increase but levels of immigration in 2004 are still below those registered in 2001. This is not the case in either Europe or in Australia. While Spain and the United Kingdom (and to a lesser extent Austria, France and Poland) reported a continuous increase in immigration over this period, Denmark, Germany, Hungary, the Netherlands and New Zealand experienced a slight and continuous downturn.

Comparability

Official data on immigration are from different sources: data on settlement or long-term permits for Australia, Canada, France, Mexico, New Zealand, Poland, Portugal and the United States; a border-crossing survey for the United Kingdom, the Labour Force Survey for Ireland. Data for Italy and Turkey are from residence permits but include many temporary entries. Data for all other countries are from population registers or registers of foreigners. From 2001 on, data for the Czech Republic are not comparable with data for previous years. The last column of the table gives a figure for "permanent-type" authorised immigration in 2004 for 17 countries on a roughly comparable basis (see "Immigration by category of entry").

In countries where an immigrant is defined as a settler or someone who obtains a residence permit of a minimum limited duration (generally one year or more), a significant number of persons entering with temporary permits are excluded by definition. In the case of Germany, for example, more than half of the recorded inflows of foreigners concern short-term movements that are not counted as immigration in many other OECD countries.

Source
• OECD (2006), *International Migration Outlook: SOPEMI – 2006 Edition*, OECD, Paris.

Further information
Analytical publications
• OECD (2001), *Migration Policies and EU Enlargement: The Case of Central and Eastern Europe*, OECD, Paris.
• OECD (2003), *Migration and the Labour Market in Asia: Recent Trends and Policies – 2002 Edition*, OECD, Paris.
• OECD (2004), *Migration for Employment: Bilateral Agreements at a Crossroads*, OECD, Paris.
• OECD (2004), *Trade and Migration: Building Bridges for Global Labour Mobility*, OECD, Paris.
• OECD (2005), *OECD Employment Outlook – 2005 Edition*, OECD, Paris.
• OECD (2006), *Local Economic and Employment Development (LEED) – From Immigration to Integration: Local Solutions to a Global Challenge* , OECD, Paris.
• OECD (2006), *OECD Employment Outlook* , OECD, Paris.

Statistical publications
• OECD (2006), *Labour Force Statistics 1985-2005: 2006 Edition*, OECD, Paris.

Methodological publications
• Lemaître, G. (2005), "The Comparability of International Migration Statistics, Problems and Prospects", *OECD Statistics Brief*, No 9, July, OECD, Paris.

Online databases
• *International Migration Statistics.*

OECD FACTBOOK 2007 – ISBN 978-92-64-02946-0 – © OECD 2007

Inflows of foreign nationals in OECD countries

Year 2000 = 100

Standardised data,
Thousands

	1985	1990	1995	1996	1997	1998	1999	2000	2001	2002	2003	2004	2004
Australia	68.2	105.8	76.3	101.0	88.2	80.6	88.7	100.0	120.7	104.6	113.7	131.6	167 300
Austria	..	..	..	..	..	89.8	109.7	100.0	113.4	140.4	147.3	165.2	59 600
Belgium	65.5	88.1	92.7	90.6	85.9	88.5	100.9	100.0	115.1	122.6	120.1	126.4	..
Canada	37.1	95.1	93.6	99.4	95.0	76.6	83.5	100.0	110.2	100.7	97.3	103.7	235 800
Czech Republic	..	..	139.6	175.3	235.4	187.9	161.1	100.0		267.9	1 032.6	1 358.8	1 201.9	..
Denmark	67.9	65.7	144.0	108.1	89.2	92.9	88.5	100.0	110.0	96.2	81.8	82.1	15 900
Finland	..	71.3	80.6	82.8	89.4	91.6	87.1	100.0	121.2	109.5	103.6	126.4	11 500
France	..	..	54.3	53.9	82.9	123.2	89.8	100.0	115.3	133.5	145.5	149.1	175 200
Germany	61.4	129.8	121.5	109.1	94.8	93.3	103.9	100.0	105.6	101.5	92.7	92.8	202 300
Hungary	..	184.5	69.4	68.0	65.8	79.5	99.8	100.0	100.6	89.0	95.9	89.7	..
Ireland	..	..	48.9	77.3	85.3	78.1	79.9	100.0	117.6	143.5	118.7	119.4	..
Italy	..	..	..	..	..	40.9	98.7	100.0	85.7	142.9	..	117.6	156 400
Japan	45.3	64.7	60.7	65.2	79.5	76.8	81.5	100.0	101.6	99.4	108.1	107.6	88 300
Korea	..	..	..	..	..	..	..	100.0	93.1	92.2	96.1	..	..
Luxembourg	61.0	86.3	88.9	85.6	86.9	98.3	109.1	100.0	102.4	101.8	106.7	104.8	..
Mexico	..	116.0	97.7	105.0	112.3	118.3	102.6	100.0	86.9	78.7	..	..	..
Netherlands	..	88.9	73.3	84.5	84.0	89.4	85.8	100.0	103.4	94.8	80.5	71.3	57 000
New Zealand	..	..	148.5	113.5	87.4	72.7	82.4	100.0	144.6	126.2	114.1	96.2	41 600
Norway	54.1	56.5	59.3	61.9	79.3	96.3	116.0	100.0	91.5	110.8	96.4	100.3	25 400
Poland	..	..	..	..	..	32.5	109.2	100.0	135.1	190.3	190.9	231.9	..
Portugal	..	..	31.5	22.9	20.7	40.7	66.2	100.0	885.8	386.0	131.8	88.8	13 100
Spain	..	..	..	..	..	17.3	30.0	100.0	119.1	133.9	129.8	195.2	..
Sweden	65.4	124.8	84.6	68.8	78.5	83.7	81.1	100.0	103.5	111.7	112.6	111.6	49 100
Switzerland	..	118.5	102.7	86.8	82.0	84.6	97.5	100.0	116.3	114.0	105.9	112.5	82 600
Turkey	..	..	..	..	..	..	..	100.0	95.9	93.8	90.5	92.5	..
United Kingdom	47.2	61.8	57.6	63.0	69.9	82.2	91.0	100.0	102.2	111.7	124.8	166.2	302 800
United States	67.1	180.8	84.8	107.8	93.9	77.0	76.1	100.0	125.2	125.2	83.1	111.3	946 100
OECD average	58.2	102.4	86.2	87.1	89.8	83.7	92.8	100.0		109.4	114.8	111.1	122.0	..

StatLink ᴍ⁵ᴸ http://dx.doi.org/10.1787/877713554780

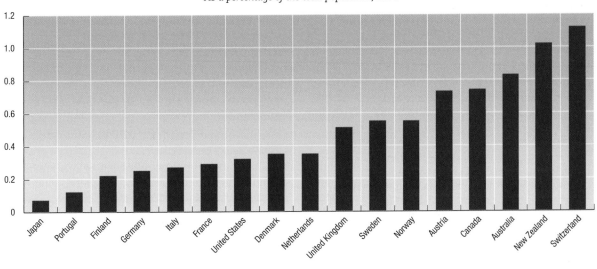

Inflows of foreign nationals, standardised data
As a percentage of the total population, 2004

StatLink ᴍ⁵ᴸ http://dx.doi.org/10.1787/348727878383

IMMIGRATION BY CATEGORY OF ENTRY

Using new data recently compiled on permanent-type immigration according to the mode of entry, it is now possible to have a clearer idea of the nature of international immigration flows for a large number of OECD countries.

Definition

Immigrants here are defined as persons entering the resident population with a permit that is permanent or more or less indefinitely renewable. Also included are persons arriving on a long-term basis under a free-movement regime. Note that not all persons joining the resident population have actually entered the country during the data year shown. Some of them may have entered in a previous year on a temporary basis, such as international students, working holidaymakers, trainees, etc. and been subsequently granted the right to stay in the country on a long-term basis. These are known as "status changers".

Overview

On average across the countries shown in the table, over twenty-five percent of total immigration consists of persons arriving for labour-related reasons. Most immigration, however, remains family related and consists of family reunification and formation as well as of family members accompanying workers. In all countries a certain proportion of inflows consist of movements over which governments have limited discretionary control, essentially because they involve movements subject to international treaties or conventions (free movement within the European Union, the Geneva Convention on Refugees, etc.) or that are considered as generally recognised human rights (the right of residents or citizens to live with their families or to marry or adopt whom they wish). In some countries (France, Norway, Sweden), long-term immigration consists almost entirely of such non-discretionary movements, whereas other countries (Australia, Canada, Switzerland, the United Kingdom) admit significant number of additional immigrants, who are generally workers and their families.

In countries such as Australia, Canada and New Zealand, the national administration plays a significant role in selecting labour immigrants, assigning points to candidates based on characteristics such as age, education and occupation that are deemed to contribution to integration, and selecting those candidates that have more than a threshold level of points. In most other countries, it is employers who select immigrant workers based on their labour needs and subject to constraints (for example, minimum qualifications or salary levels) imposed by national governments.

Comparability

The series shown are the first attempt to apply a standardised definition to statistics of international immigration. They are not, however, based on the definition specified in the United Nations Recommendations on International Migration Statistics (1998), which defines a long-term international migrant as a person who moves to a country other than that of his or her usual residence for a period of at least a year. This definition was not used because it is not possible to produce comparable statistics on this basis for very many countries.

The statistics presented here are based on permit data, which may have a certain number of limitations. Not every international immigrant requires a permit. A permit may be granted in one year but used in another, it may never actually be used and in some cases, a person may receive more than one permit. However, the quality problems associated with these are likely to be small compared to the serious comparability problems associated with using published national statistics, whose coverage varies by as much as a factor of one to three.

For certain countries in the accompanying table, the number of persons in the accompanying-family-of-worker category cannot be estimated separately and is included in the family-reunification column. For the OECD average, the two categories have been combined and the total appears in the family reunification column.

Source
- OECD (2006), *International Migration Outlook: SOPEMI – 2006 Edition*, OECD, Paris.

Further information

Analytical publications
- OECD (2006), "Managing migration – Are quotas and numerical limits the solution?", *International Migration Outlook: SOPEMI – 2006 Edition*, OECD, Paris.

Statistical publications
- OECD (2005), *OECD Employment Outlook – 2005 Edition*, OECD, Paris.
- OECD (2006), *Labour Force Statistics 1985-2005: 2006 Edition*, OECD, Paris.
- OECD (2006), *OECD Employment Outlook*, OECD, Paris.

Methodological publications
- Lemaître, G. (2005), "The Comparability of International Migration Statistics, Problems and Prospects", *OECD Statistics Brief*, No. 9, July, OECD, Paris.
- Lemaître, G., T. Liebig and C. Thoreau (2006), *Harmonised statistics on immigrant inflows – preliminary results, sources and methods*.

Online databases
- *International Migration Statistics*.

Immigration by category of entry

As a percentage of total entries, 2004

	Work	Accompanying family of workers	Family reunification or formation	Humanitarian and accompanying family	Other (ancestry-based, pensioners, etc.)	Number of persons
Australia	32	30	26	10	1	167 300
Austria	24	15	47	12	2	59 600
Canada	25	32	26	17	0	235 800
Denmark	44	14	26	9	7	16 900
France	12	..	68	7	13	175 200
Germany	19	12	33	7	29	202 300
Italy	32	6	55	2	4	156 400
Japan	22	..	42	0	35	88 300
Netherlands	27	..	50	23	0	57 000
New Zealand	26	33	32	9	0	41 600
Norway	26	..	46	28	..	25 400
Portugal	57		36	0	7	13 100
Sweden	24	..	61	13	2	49 100
Switzerland	40	..	47	5	7	82 600
United Kingdom	42	19	15	17	6	302 800
United States	8	9	66	8	10	946 100
OECD average	29	..	52	11	8	..

StatLink ⬛️🔢 http://dx.doi.org/10.1787/454671242453

Immigration by category of entry, standardised definition

Year 2004

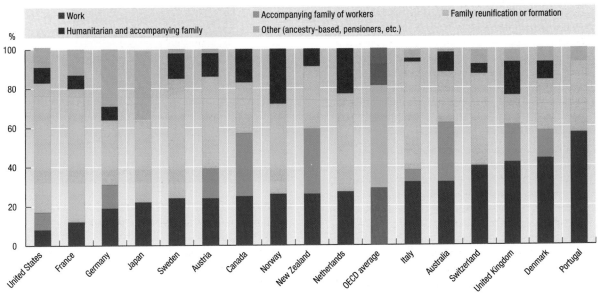

StatLink ⬛️🔢 http://dx.doi.org/10.1787/528465175686

INFLOWS OF ASYLUM SEEKERS

An important component of international migration flows are asylum seekers, *i.e.* persons seeking protection in the country of arrival, under the Geneva Convention on Refugees. This has been a highly controversial channel of entry during the 1990s, because of the perception that it was being used by economic migrants as a way of entering OECD countries.

Long-term trends

Asylum seeking increased substantially with the fall of the Iron Curtain and reached a peak in 1992, as a result of the crisis in the former Yugoslavia. The main host countries reacted by speeding up procedures for deciding asylum applications, introducing restrictive measures such as extending the number of countries subject to visa requirements or by limiting the legal appeal channels. Two general rules also began to be applied to requests for asylum: the safe-country-of-origin rule by which requests for asylum from identified "safe" countries were automatically refused; and the safe-country-of-transit rule, which stipulated that an asylum seeker had to make his/her application in the first "safe" country through which he/she passed. In 2000 and 2001, the increase in regional conflicts increased the number of asylum seekers throughout the OECD area. Since then, the number of asylum seekers arriving in OECD countries has again shown a marked downward trend, with a fall of about 50% since 2001.

Since 2003, France has replaced the United States as the most important destination country for asylum seeking. In absolute numbers, flows also remain high in the United Kingdom and Germany – despite a strong decline in these two countries since 2001/2002. In relative terms, requests remain high in Austria, Sweden, Luxembourg, Belgium and Switzerland – although there were declines in these countries (with the exception of Belgium) from 2004 to 2005.

In all OECD countries, recognition rates are low. Generally significantly less than one in five asylum requests is accepted by the host country. Some asylum seekers are allowed to stay on humanitarian grounds, although they are not formally recognised as refugees. Currently, refugees, other persons admitted for humanitarian reasons and accompanying family account for less than 10% of long-term migration to OECD countries. With the continuing fall in asylum seeking, this proportion is likely to fall as well.

Definition

Asylum-seekers are persons who have applied for asylum or refugee status, but who have not yet received a final decision on their application. In principle, each country subsequently decides to whom to grant refugee status among asylum applicants. This status can be granted, among others, under the 1951 Convention relating to the Status of Refugees (the so-called Geneva Convention) – of which all OECD countries are signatories. In other cases a special "protection status" may be granted to asylum claimants who are unable to return to their origin countries because of conflict conditions. Those refused refugee or protection status are in principle supposed to return to their country of origin.

Comparability

The data are taken from the United Nations High Commissioner for Refugees (UNHCR) database. In most OECD countries, there are separate administrative registers for asylum seekers, and the numbers are reported to the UNHCR. Due to the registering and the administrative procedures involved in treating asylum requests, they are generally accurate and thus of good comparability.

Inflows of asylum seekers
Number of persons, 2005

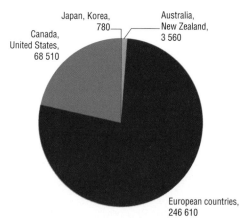

StatLink http://dx.doi.org/10.1787/781251431013

Source

• United Nations High Commissioner for Refugees (UNHCR) database.

Further information
Analytical publications

• OECD (2006), *International Migration Outlook: SOPEMI – 2006 Edition*, OECD, Paris.

Inflows of asylum seekers into OECD countries

Year 2000=100   *Persons*

	1985	1990	1995	1996	1997	1998	1999	2000	2001	2002	2003	2004	2005	2005
Australia	..	93	58	75	71	62	72	100	95	45	33	24	25	3 210
Austria	37	125	32	38	37	76	110	100	165	215	177	135	123	22 470
Belgium	12	30	27	29	28	51	84	100	58	44	40	36	37	15 960
Canada	38	107	76	76	66	70	86	100	129	115	93	75	58	19 740
Czech Republic	..	18	16	25	24	46	82	100	206	97	130	62	46	4 020
Denmark	71	43	42	48	42	77	101	100	103	50	38	27	19	2 260
Finland	1	87	27	22	31	40	98	100	52	109	102	122	112	3 560
France	75	141	53	45	55	58	80	100	140	152	154	151	129	50 050
Germany	94	246	163	148	133	126	121	100	112	91	64	45	37	28 910
Greece	45	200	43	53	142	96	50	100	178	184	265	145	294	9 050
Hungary	...	45	2	2	3	91	147	100	122	82	31	21	21	1 610
Iceland	4	29	21	17	25	79	71	100	217	488	333	313	389	90
Ireland	..	..	4	11	36	42	71	100	94	106	72	44	39	4 320
Italy	26	31	11	4	12	71	214	100	62	103	86	62	61	9 500
Japan	13	15	24	68	112	62	103	100	163	116	156	197	171	370
Korea	..	..	..	2	102	40	9	100	91	86	200	349	953	410
Luxemburg	..	18	63	42	69	275	470	100	111	168	249	254	129	800
Netherlands	13	48	67	51	78	103	97	100	74	43	31	22	28	12 350
New Zealand	..	43	44	85	96	127	99	100	103	64	54	37	23	350
Norway	8	37	13	16	21	77	94	100	136	161	147	73	50	5 400
Poland	..	..	18	70	77	74	64	100	99	113	151	176	119	5 440
Portugal	31	33	204	121	133	163	137	100	104	109	39	48	49	110
Slovak Republic	..	..	23	27	41	33	85	100	524	623	666	732	224	3 490
Spain	30	109	72	60	63	84	106	100	120	80	75	70	66	5 260
Sweden	89	180	55	35	59	79	69	100	144	203	192	142	108	17 530
Switzerland	55	203	97	102	136	235	262	100	117	148	118	81	57	10 060
Turkey	..	44	68	74	89	120	116	100	89	67	70	69	69	3 910
United Kingdom	6	39	56	37	42	59	92	100	93	104	61	41	31	30 460
United States	21	91	184	132	65	44	40	100	129	124	91	65	60	48 770
OECD Total	34	99	84	71	65	78	96	100	110	107	85	65	55	319 050

StatLink http://dx.doi.org/10.1787/347368352135

Inflows of asylum seekers into the main destination countries

Number of persons

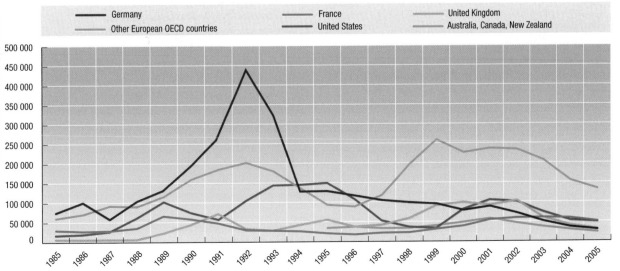

StatLink http://dx.doi.org/10.1787/385812465226

TRENDS IN MIGRATION

Migration movements include not only entries of persons of foreign nationality, on which public attention tends to be focused; they also include movements of nationals and emigrants. Net migration summarises the overall effect of these movements. It is in more and more OECD countries the main source of increases in population.

Definition

Net migration is defined as the total number of immigrant nationals and foreigners minus the total of emigrant foreigners and nationals. Arrivals and departures for purposes such as tourism and business travel are not included in the statistics.

Comparability

The main sources of information on migration vary across countries, which poses problems for the comparability of available data on inflows and outflows. However, since the comparability problems generally relate to the extent to which short-term movements are covered, taking the difference between arrivals and departures tends to eliminate the movements that are the main source of

non-comparability. The net migration data, however, are subject to caution, because unauthorised movements are not taken into account in the inflows and these are significant in some countries. In addition, the data on outflows are of uneven quality, with departures being only partially recorded in many countries or having to be estimated in others.

Net migration rate is used in demographic accounting to describe the contribution of international migration to population increase, the other component being natural increase, the difference between births and deaths in a given year.

Long-term trends

Since 1995 Poland is the only OECD country among the countries shown in the table that has shown negative net migration on a systematic basis. Among countries showing significant increases in population (> 0.5%) over the 1995-1999 period as a result of international migration are Australia, Canada, Spain, Ireland and Luxembourg. Since then Italy, Portugal and Switzerland have joined the list. Former emigration countries (Ireland, Italy, Portugal and Spain) thus figure prominently among high net migration countries, a trend which is likely to continue.

There are nonetheless a number of countries where net migration is currently contributing less to population increase than was the case five to ten years ago. These include Luxembourg, Greece, Denmark, the Netherlands and Germany. Those where it is contributing more are the same four former emigration countries as well as Austria and Switzerland. Indeed, all but eight OECD countries are showing a larger contribution to population growth from net migration in recent years. With the retirement of baby-boomers in the near future, to be replaced by smaller entering labour force cohorts, labour supply needs may well increase and OECD countries see a continuing rise in net migration.

Source
- OECD (2006), *Labour Force Statistics 1985-2005: 2006 Edition*, OECD, Paris.

Further information
Analytical publications
- OECD (2001), *Migration Policies and EU Enlargement: The Case of Central and Eastern Europe*, OECD, Paris.
- OECD (2003), *Migration and the Labour Market in Asia: Recent Trends and Policies – 2002 Edition*, OECD, Paris.
- OECD (2004), *Migration for Employment: Bilateral Agreements at a Crossroads*, OECD, Paris.
- OECD (2004), *Trade and Migration: Building Bridges for Global Labour Mobility*, OECD, Paris.
- OECD (2006), *International Migration Outlook: SOPEMI – 2006 Edition*, OECD, Paris.
- OECD (2006), *Local Economic and Employment Development (LEED) – From Immigration to Integration: Local Solutions to a Global Challenge*, OECD, Paris.

Statistical publications
- OECD (2006), *OECD Employment Outlook* , OECD, Paris.

Methodological publications
- Dumont, J.-C. and G. Lemaître (2005), *Counting Immigrants and Expatriates in OECD Countries: A New Perspective*, OECD Social Employment and Migration Working Papers, No. 25, OECD, Paris.

Online databases
- *International Migration Statistics*.

OECD FACTBOOK 2007 – ISBN 978-92-64-02946-0 – © OECD 2007

Net migration rate
Per 1 000 population

	1985	1990	1995	1996	1997	1998	1999	2000	2001	2002	2003	2004	2005
Australia	5.6	7.3	5.9	5.3	3.9	4.8	5.5	5.8	7.0	5.6	5.5	5.2	..
Austria	0.7	7.6	0.3	0.5	0.2	1.1	2.5	2.2	2.2	4.2	4.4	6.2	5.9
Belgium	0.0	2.0	1.3	1.3	0.6	0.7	1.7	1.4	..	..	..	..	..
Canada	2.6	6.5	5.5	5.6	5.2	3.9	5.2	6.5	7.9	6.8	6.2	6.2	..
Czech Republic	0.2	0.1	1.0	1.0	1.2	0.9	0.9	0.6	−0.8	1.2	2.5	1.8	3.5
Denmark	1.8	1.6	5.5	3.2	2.3	2.1	1.7	1.7	2.2	1.7	1.1	0.9	1.2
Finland	0.6	1.4	0.6	0.6	0.8	0.6	0.6	0.4	1.2	1.0	1.0	1.1	1.5
France	0.7	1.4	0.7	0.6	0.7	0.8	1.0	1.2	1.4	1.6	1.7	1.7	1.6
Germany	1.5	16.3	4.9	3.4	1.1	0.6	2.5	2.0	3.3	2.7	1.7	1.0	..
Greece	0.6	6.3	7.3	6.6	5.7	5.1	4.1	2.7	3.5	3.5	3.4	..	..
Hungary	−2.1	1.7	1.7	1.7	1.7	1.7	1.7	1.7	1.0	0.4	1.6	1.8	1.7
Ireland	−9.3	−2.2	1.6	4.6	5.1	4.5	6.4	8.4	10	8.4	7.8	11.6	..
Italy	−0.5	0.2	1.6	2.6	2.2	1.6	1.8	3.1	2.2	6.1	10.6	9.6	..
Japan	0.0	0.0	−0.4	−0.1	0.1	0.3	−0.1	0.3	1.1	−0.4	0.5	..	..
Luxembourg	2.5	10.2	11.2	8.9	9.0	9.5	10.9	8.3	2.5	5.9	4.6	3.5	5.8
Netherlands	1.7	4.0	2.1	2.8	3.1	3.9	3.8	3.4	4.3	3.3	0.0	1.2	0.6
New Zealand	−5.8	2.7	7.7	6.6	2.0	−1.7	−2.3	−2.9	2.5	9.7	8.7	3.7	1.7
Norway	1.4	0.5	1.4	1.4	2.5	3.2	4.3	2.0	1.8	3.7	2.4	2.8	3.9
Poland	−0.5	−0.4	−0.5	−0.3	−0.3	−0.3	−0.4	−0.5	−0.4	−0.5	−0.4	−0.2	−0.3
Portugal	−1.9	−3.9	2.2	2.6	2.9	3.2	3.7	4.6	6.3	6.8	6.1	4.5	..
Slovak Republic	−0.6	−0.4	0.5	0.4	0.3	0.2	0.3	0.3	0.2	0.2	0.2	0.5	0.6
Spain	0.4	0.9	0.9	1.3	1.6	3.1	4.9	8.9	10.1	15.7	14.5	..	..
Sweden	1.3	4.1	1.2	0.7	0.7	1.2	1.6	2.8	3.3	3.5	3.2	2.8	3.0
Switzerland	2.1	8.4	2.1	−0.8	−1.0	0.2	2.3	2.8	5.8	6.7	5.9	5.4	4.6
Turkey	2.1	1.8	1.6	1.6	1.6	1.5	1.5	..	..	..	..	..	..
United Kingdom	1.6	1.2	1.0	0.9	0.9	1.7	2.3	2.5	2.5	2.5	..	..	..
United States	2.7	3.1	4.4	4.6	4.8	4.2	4.4	4.6	4.5	4.4	4.1	3.7	3.5
OECD average	0.3	3.1	2.7	2.5	2.2	2.2	2.7	2.8	3.4	4.2	4.0	3.4	2.4

StatLink ‹‹‹‹‹ http://dx.doi.org/10.1787/822014164567

Net migration rate
Per 1 000 population, annual average 2000-2005 or latest available period

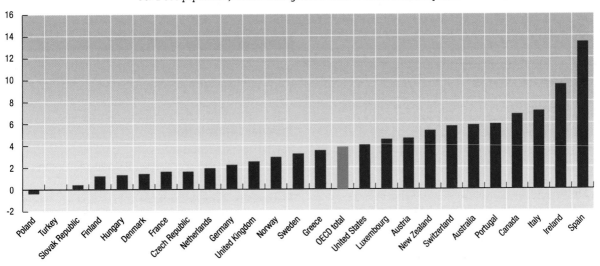

StatLink ‹‹‹‹‹ http://dx.doi.org/10.1787/228225504034

IMMIGRANT POPULATION

National views on the appropriate definition of the immigrant population vary from country to country. Despite this, it is now possible to provide an internationally comparable picture of the size of the immigrant population, based either on nationality or on country-of-birth criteria. Strictly speaking, the immigrant population consists of persons residing in a country but born in another country. The definition based on nationality is commonly used in a certain number of countries and reflects a legal view of immigration.

Definition

Nationality and place of birth are the two criteria most commonly used to define the "immigrant" population. The foreign-born population covers all persons who have ever migrated from their country of birth to their current country of residence. The foreign population consists of persons who still have the nationality of their home country. It may include persons born in the host country.

Comparability

The difference across countries between the size of the foreign-born population and that of the foreign population depends on the rules governing the acquisition of citizenship in each country. In some countries, children born in the country automatically acquire the citizenship of their country of birth (jus solis, the right of soil) while in other countries, they retain the nationality of their parents (jus sanguinis, the right of blood). In others, they retain the nationality of their parents at birth but receive that of the host country at their majority. Differences in the ease with which immigrants may acquire the citizenship of the host country explain part of the gap between the two series. For example, residency requirements vary from as little as two years in Australia to as much as ten years in some countries. The naturalisation rate is high in settlement countries such as Australia, Canada, New Zealand and in some European countries including Belgium, Sweden and the Netherlands. In general, the foreign-born criterion gives substantially higher percentages for the immigrant population than the definition based on nationality. This is because many foreign-born persons acquire the nationality of the host country and no longer appear as foreign nationals. The place of birth, however, does not change, except when there are changes in country borders.

The data shown for the year 2000 come from a special census data collection covering almost all OECD countries. See the next statistic on the following pages for details on this data source. Note that the foreign-born here include persons born abroad as nationals of their current country of residence. The prevalence of such persons among the foreign-born can be significant in some countries, in particular France and Portugal (repatriations from former colonies).

For a number of countries, reliable data on the foreign-born population are available only at time of census. To make up for this deficiency, the OECD Secretariat has developed data series for a certain number of countries, applying two estimation methods, which depend on the auxiliary information available for estimation. These methods are described and evaluated at *www.oecd.org/els/migration/foreignborn*.

For the foreign-born population the data year shown under the 2000 column is 1999 for France; 2001 for Greece, Italy, the Slovak, Republic, Spain; 2002 for Poland; and 2003 for Belgium and Germany. For the foreign population it is 1999 for France; 2001 for Australia, Canada, Greece; 2002 for Poland; and 2003 for Italy.

Long-term trends

Not surprisingly, the foreign-born population has increased in the past decade in all countries for which data are available. It is especially high in Australia, Canada, Luxembourg, New Zealand and Switzerland. This increase is likely to continue into the future, with further immigration needs. By contrast, the foreign population tends to increase more slowly, because inflows of foreign nationals tend to be counterbalanced by persons acquiring the nationality of the host country. It thus gives a partial view of the evolution of immigration trends.

Source

- OECD (2006), *International Migration Outlook: SOPEMI – 2006 Edition*, OECD, Paris.

Further information

Analytical publications

- OECD (2006), *International Migration Outlook: SOPEMI – 2006 Edition*, OECD, Paris.

Methodological publications

- Lemaître, G. and C. Thoreau (2006), *Estimating the foreign-born population on a current basis*, OECD, Paris.
- OECD (2005), "Counting immigrants and expatriates in OECD countries – a new perspective", *Trends in International Migration: SOPEMI – 2004 Edition*, OECD, Paris.

OECD FACTBOOK 2007 – ISBN 978-92-64-02946-0 – © OECD 2007

Foreign-born and foreign populations

As a percentage of the total population   *As a percentage of all foreign-born*

	Foreign-born population			Foreign population			Foreign-born nationals
	1995	2000	2004	1995	2000	2004	2000
Australia	23.0	23.0	23.6	..	7.4	..	68.4
Austria	..	10.5	13.0	8.5	8.8	9.5	40.9
Belgium	9.7	10.3	11.4	9.0	8.4	8.4	40.8
Canada	16.6	17.4	18.0	..	5.3	..	72.6
Czech Republic	..	4.2	4.9	1.5	1.9	2.5	79.8
Denmark	4.8	5.8	6.3	4.2	4.8	4.9	40.3
Finland	2.0	2.6	3.2	1.3	1.8	2.1	41.6
France	..	10.0	..	..	5.6	..	53.1
Germany	11.5	12.5	12.9	8.8	8.9	8.9	..
Greece	..	10.3	..	..	7.0	..	41.5
Hungary	2.8	2.9	3.2	1.4	1.1	1.4	71.1
Ireland	..	8.7	11.0	2.7	3.3	5.5	45.2
Italy	..	2.5	..	1.7	2.4	3.9	47.5
Japan	..	..	..	1.1	1.3	1.5	..
Korea	..	..	..	0.2	0.4	0.9	..
Luxembourg	..	..	..	33.4	37.3	39.0	13.0
Mexico	0.4	0.5	..	..	..	..	..
Netherlands	9.1	10.1	10.6	4.7	4.2	4.3	65.0
New Zealand	..	17.2	18.8	..	..	..	..
Norway	5.5	6.8	7.8	3.8	4.0	4.6	47.6
Poland	..	1.6	..	..	0.1	..	96.1
Portugal	5.4	5.1	6.7	1.7	2.1	4.3	66.3
Slovak Republic	..	2.5	3.9	0.4	0.5	0.4	84.2
Spain	..	5.3	..	1.3	2.2	4.6	30.9
Sweden	10.5	11.3	12.2	5.2	5.4	5.1	62.5
Switzerland	21.4	21.9	23.5	18.9	19.3	20.2	29.3
Turkey	..	1.9	..	..	..	..	79.2
United Kingdom	6.9	7.9	9.3	3.4	4.0	4.9	..
United States	9.3	11.0	12.8	..	6.6	..	46.4
OECD average	9.3	8.6	11.2	5.7	5.9	6.8	54.9

StatLink http://dx.doi.org/10.1787/615583184240

Foreign-born population by nationality status

As a percentage of total population, circa 2000

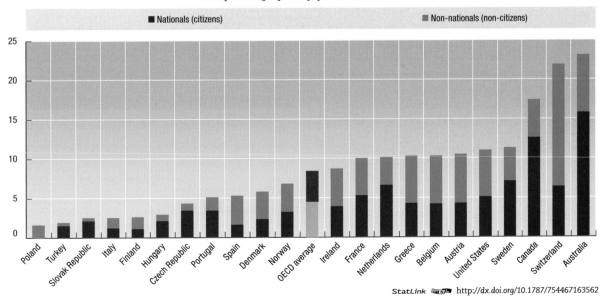

StatLink http://dx.doi.org/10.1787/754467163562

IMMIGRANT POPULATION BY REGION OF ORIGIN AND GENDER

At the time of the 2000 censuses, about 80 million residents in OECD countries were immigrants. With the OECD database on the foreign-born, some basic information on the origin, characteristics and distribution of immigrants is now available for the first time for almost all OECD countries.

Definition

Immigrants, or foreign-born persons, are persons who are born in a different country from the one in which they currently reside.

Comparability

The data are mainly based on the year 2000 round of censuses. Due to their comprehensive coverage, censuses are particularly well-adapted to identifying and studying small population groups. In several countries, however, there has been no population census and it has been necessary to turn to data from population registers or from large-sample surveys.

Data for Japan and Korea were not available by country of birth. For these countries, it has been assumed that the country of nationality is the country of birth. This seems a reasonable assumption for the foreign-born, given the very low rate and number of naturalisations in Japan and Korea. However, it will tend to overestimate the number of foreign-born relative to other countries, because persons born in Japan and Korea to foreigners will tend also to be recorded as foreign and thus be classified as foreign-born.

Figures for Germany and the Netherlands are estimates based on labour force survey data. Because the data on immigrants from certain countries of origin appear in larger geographic groupings for these countries, it is not always possible to distinguish between immigrants from OECD and those from non-OECD countries. For Germany and Turkey, the data do not permit the identification of immigrants from Latin America, who appear in the statistics for other regions. In addition, the German labour force survey only identifies whether or not a person was born abroad, but not the country of birth. For foreigners born abroad, it was assumed that the country of nationality was the country of birth. For nationals born abroad (naturalised foreign-born persons and "ethnic" German immigrants who obtained German nationality upon entry into Germany), the German Socio-Economic Panel was used to adjust the data for Germany for those countries of birth for which the samples were of sufficient size.

Overview

The origins of the immigrant population vary widely across OECD countries. About half of all immigrants to OECD countries originate in another OECD country. The proportions range from as low as 6 per cent of immigrants in Japan aged 15 and above being born in another OECD country to around 80 per cent in Luxembourg, the Slovak Republic, Ireland and the Czech Republic.

The data also show that the geographical origin of the immigrant population strongly reflects historical links and geographical proximity. France and Portugal, for example, have many immigrants who have been born in Africa, which is to a considerable degree attributable to their colonial past. Cultural and linguistic or geographical proximity is also mirrored in the large share of Latin Americans among immigrants to Mexico and Spain, and of Asian immigrants to Japan.

In most OECD countries, women account for a larger proportion of the immigrant stock than men. The share of women is particularly pronounced among immigrants from Latin America. The only country with sizeable immigration from Latin America where men are more numerous is Japan. Many of these are descendants of former Japanese emigrants to Latin America.

In contrast, men are more numerous among the immigrants from Africa in almost all OECD countries where immigration from Africa has been important, with the notable exceptions of Portugal and the United Kingdom.

Source

• OECD (2006), *International Migration Outlook: SOPEMI – 2006 Edition*, OECD, Paris.

Further information
Methodological publications

• OECD (2005), "Counting immigrants and expatriates in OECD countries – a new perspective", *Trends in International Migration: SOPEMI – 2004 Edition*, OECD, Paris.

Online databases

• *International Migration Statistics*.

OECD FACTBOOK 2007 – ISBN 978-92-64-02946-0 – © OECD 2007

Foreign-born population, aged 15 and above by region of origin and gender

Circa 2000

	As a percentage from each region among total foreign-born					As a percentage of women among the foreign-born by region					As a percentage of women among all foreign-born
	OECD	Asia and Oceania (non-OECD)	Africa	Latin America (non-OECD)	Europe (non-OECD)	OECD	Asia and Oceania (non-OECD)	Africa	Latin America (non-OECD)	Europe (non-OECD)	All continents
Australia	58.2	27.9	4.3	1.9	7.7	49.8	52.7	49.8	52.3	49.5	50.6
Austria	50.5	5.6	2.4	0.5	40.9	54.2	48.9	32.2	62.4	51.0	52.1
Belgium	66.1	5.4	22.8	1.9	3.7	53.3	56.8	46.8	59.8	55.3	51.9
Canada	44.3	33.8	5.2	10.3	6.4	51.9	51.8	47.8	54.8	51.0	51.9
Czech Republic	78.1	4.8	0.4	0.3	16.4	55.1	39.2	23.5	37.5	56.5	54.5
Denmark	50.1	27.8	8.2	2.2	11.7	52.5	49.6	46.0	57.1	53.9	51.4
Finland	40.6	12.8	7.2	1.3	38.1	43.4	49.4	33.3	52.5	61.5	50.4
France	39.7	7.3	49.0	1.4	2.6	53.3	49.9	48.0	57.3	53.5	50.5
Germany	79.8	1.3	4.1	..	14.8	46.1	48.1	27.9	..	52.8	50.8
Greece	28.2	8.3	5.1	0.6	57.7	57.8	37.0	48.9	68.5	47.7	49.9
Hungary	23.6	3.6	0.6	0.4	71.8	58.7	40.1	19.2	48.2	56.1	55.9
Ireland	80.4	7.3	6.5	0.8	5.1	51.7	44.1	46.4	47.2	44.8	50.4
Italy	39.1	9.0	20.2	10.7	21.0	60.2	49.3	41.2	64.5	53.5	54.4
Japan	5.9	76.5	0.4	16.9	0.3	37.0	56.3	20.8	44.7	72.2	53.2
Luxemburg	85.6	2.5	4.1	1.0	6.7	50.3	55.9	51.4	61.8	50.6	50.6
Mexico	65.8	2.6	0.3	30.3	0.9	48.6	43.3	39.7	52.2	56.3	49.5
Netherlands	35.5	18.7	18.5	25.0	2.2	53.7	48.8	44.4	53.7	47.4	51.4
New Zealand	54.7	38.1	4.8	0.6	1.7	51.2	53.0	51.0	53.9	50.8	51.9
Norway	45.9	28.7	9.5	4.4	11.5	51.5	49.9	43.1	52.3	56.4	51.1
Poland	20.5	1.3	0.3	0.1	77.7	57.8	42.0	26.1	41.5	61.1	59.9
Portugal	25.8	2.6	56.7	11.4	3.5	53.6	46.7	51.3	51.9	23.2	50.9
Slovak Republic	85.0	1.3	0.2	0.2	13.3	56.6	32.2	25.2	36.5	57.3	56.3
Spain	33.5	4.0	19.4	36.8	6.3	51.9	41.9	36.9	56.1	45.3	49.7
Sweden	47.8	23.0	6.0	5.9	17.3	52.7	50.0	44.7	50.3	52.4	51.4
Switzerland	66.7	6.5	4.5	3.5	18.8	53.0	52.5	48.4	66.5	49.9	52.2
Turkey	34.8	6.2	0.4	..	58.6	52.0	44.8	39.2	..	53.4	52.2
United Kingdom	39.0	32.3	17.1	7.0	4.6	56.5	50.7	50.9	55.6	50.2	53.3
United States	47.0	21.4	2.7	25.2	3.6	49.3	51.0	44.9	52.4	52.8	50.4
OECD Total	46.5	20.2	9.5	15.0	8.8	51.0	51.3	46.8	53.1	52.6	51.2

StatLink http://dx.doi.org/10.1787/804145430641

Foreign-born population by region of origin

As a percentage of total foreign-born population, aged 15 and above, circa 2000

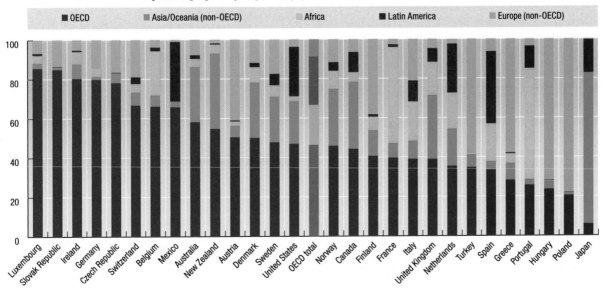

StatLink http://dx.doi.org/10.1787/516224313186

EDUCATIONAL OUTCOMES FOR CHILDREN OF IMMIGRANTS

The OECD's Programme for International Student Assessment (PISA) assesses student knowledge and skills in mathematics, science, reading and cross-curricular competencies at age 15, *i.e.* towards the end of compulsory education.

PISA also asked students about their country of birth and the country of birth of their parents, which makes it possible to identify children with a migration background and to compare their educational outcomes with those of native students.

Definition

On the PISA Survey, see the Factbook section on Education Outcomes.

Second generation refers to native-born students both of whose parents are foreign-born. Immigrant students are students who are foreign-born. Natives are native-born students who have at least one parent who is native-born.

The figures show the points differences in the PISA (2003) scores for mathematical and reading literacy between native-born, on the one hand, and immigrant and second generation students, on the other. A positive difference means that children of immigrants are trailing behind children of the native-born.

"Unadjusted" refers to the observed points differences in the raw scores, "adjusted" to the differences after adjusting for the effect of differences in socio-economic background of students. The socio-economic background is a composite indicator, based on the following variables: the Highest International Socio-Economic Index of Occupational Status (HISEI), the highest level of education of the student's parents, the index of home educational resources and the index of possessions. For each test, the mean score across all OECD countries was standardised to 500 points, with a standard deviation of 100 points.

The unadjusted differences for mathematics are not significantly different from zero for Australia, Canada and only for immigrant students in New Zealand. After adjustment, the point differences are not significant in Australia and the United States. On the reading scale, the unadjusted differences are not significant for second generation students in Australia. The adjusted differences are not significantly different from zero for the second generation in Australia, Denmark, France, New Zealand, Sweden and the United States.

Comparability

More than 220 000 students were assessed in OECD countries for PISA 2003. Immigrants and second generation represented about five and four per cent, respectively, of the total 15-year-old student population in the OECD. Only for countries where the share of students with a migration background was sufficiently large could the differences *vis-à-vis* natives be calculated. Values that are not statistically significantly different from zero are not shown in the graph. OECD countries that are not shown in the table are those for which the sample sizes were insufficient to ensure reliable estimates.

The outcomes for the second generation are of particular interest, since these students have been born in the respective countries and thus, in principle, were educated in the same educational system as natives. This is not necessarily the case for students who are immigrants themselves, since some of them may have immigrated after some years of schooling abroad. It is thus more difficult to interpret gaps between natives and immigrants than between natives and the second generation.

Overview

The second generation now constitutes a significant and growing share of students in many OECD countries and their integration is of increasing policy concern, particularly in Europe. In the OECD area as a whole, they tend to perform better than immigrant students, as one would expect since the former have been born in the country of assessment and were entirely educated in the host country. In most countries for which data are available, there are nevertheless significant gaps between natives and the second generation. This is particularly the case for Germany and Belgium, where the gaps in the raw scores for the second generation amount to the equivalent of about two years of schooling. Gaps are also large in Denmark, Switzerland, the Netherlands, Austria and France, but tend to be small or even insignificant in the traditional immigration countries. Adjusting for socio-economic background generally reduces the gaps by about half, but even then, second generation students often remain at a substantial disadvantage, particularly in Germany, Belgium, Switzerland, Denmark, the Netherlands and Austria.

Source

• *OECD PISA Database.*

Further information

Analytical publications

• OECD (2006), *Where Immigrant Students Succeed: A Comparative Review of Performance and Engagement in PISA 2003*, OECD, Paris.

PISA results for children of immigrants

Year 2003

	Share of all 15-year-old students		Points differences compared with natives							
			Mathematics				Reading			
	Second generation	Immigrant students	Unadjusted		Adjusted		Unadjusted		Adjusted	
			2nd. gen.	Immig. students	2nd. gen.	Immig. students	2nd. gen.	Immig. students	2nd. gen.	Immig. students
Australia	12	11	5	2	−4	1	4	12	5	11
Austria	4	9	56	63	26	40	73	77	31	46
Belgium	6	5	92	109	47	73	84	117	40	81
Canada	9	11	−6	7	−8	10	10	19	12	22
Denmark	3	3	70	65	36	40	57	42	26	19
France	11	3	48	72	14	40	48	79	12	45
Germany	7	9	93	71	45	22	96	86	48	37
Greece	1	7	..	47	..	29	..	48	..	31
Luxembourg	16	17	31	45	11	16	47	69	27	39
Netherlands	7	4	59	79	26	54	50	61	22	40
New Zealand	7	13	32	5	16	9	22	25	5	29
Norway	2	3	..	61	..	40	..	68	..	46
Sweden	6	6	34	92	15	66	20	89	0	63
Switzerland	9	11	59	89	36	60	53	93	32	64
United States	8	6	22	36	−1	10	22	50	1	23

StatLink 🔍 http://dx.doi.org/10.1787/025232010244

Reading performance of the second generation

Gaps in the PISA reading score between native students and second generation students, 2003

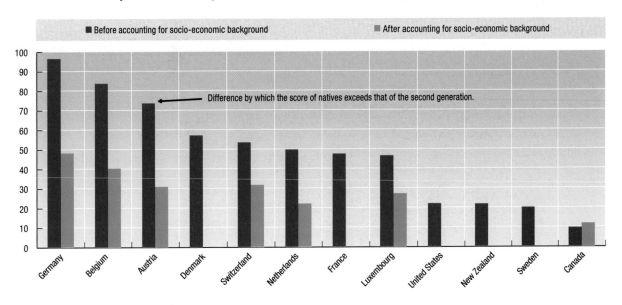

StatLink 🔍 http://dx.doi.org/10.1787/300683848242

EDUCATION ATTAINMENT OF IMMIGRANTS

The educational attainment of immigrants tends to vary considerably across countries. In some countries, low-educated persons are more prevalent among the foreign-born than the native-born; in other countries, it is the reverse. This reflects historical migration patterns as well as the effect of migration policies that favour, whether deliberately or by default, one kind of migration relative to another.

Definition

Immigrants are defined here as the foreign-born population, that is, persons who have actually changed countries since birth. Education levels are given by the International Standard Classification of Education (ISCED), which classifies attainment levels on the basis of completed educational programmes of a certain length and orientation.

Comparability

The foreign-born population consists of the usual residents of a country who were born in another country, irrespective of what their nationality at birth was. What constitutes a "usual resident" tends to differ from country to country, but the differences bear on a small proportion

of the immigrant stock and so can generally be ignored without risk of distorting the general picture. The lower age limit used in the table is not ideal, because it tends to include many young persons who have not yet completed their education.

Countries that are long-standing immigration countries tend to have immigrant population with an age structure similar to that of the native-born populations, or perhaps even skewed toward older ages, especially if immigration levels have declined in recent decades. In more recent immigration countries, the immigrant population tends to be younger and to show higher attainment levels, simply because educational levels have been increasing in all countries over time.

The education of immigrants has in most if perhaps not all cases been obtained in the country of origin. The education level is generally reported by the immigrant and the coding of the qualification according to national categories may sometimes be approximate. It is clear from looking at the chart, for example, that the proportion of immigrants with high education levels in many countries tends to be similar to that of the native-born, with some notable outliers (Ireland, Mexico, Portugal, Turkey and the United Kingdom). Some of this may be due to the fact that entry policies (at least for labour migrants) tend to reflect employer skill requirements, which in turn are mirrored by the educational attainment of native-born workers. However, it may also be the case that the structure of the national education system and the distribution of national attainment levels tend to influence how foreign qualifications are classified.

The data shown here come from a special Census data collection described in the section dealing with the foreign-born population by region and sex.

Long-term trends

The educational distribution of the foreign population in OECD describes the result of some forty plus years of international immigration. As such it reflects labour needs in OECD countries, both in the past and more recently, as well as the evolution of attainment levels in the principal origin countries over the past decades. Because international migration is strongly affected by networks, the educational attainment of past migrants tends to influence that of current and even future migrants, because spouses tend to have similar educational levels and because networks tend to operate within socio-economic groups. However, in all countries, attainment levels are increasing, as generally are the formal educational qualifications for many jobs.

One can thus expect that the educational attainment of immigrants will continue to increase, the more so as destination countries implement policies to favour more highly educated immigrants. However, many labour needs are beginning to appear in less qualified occupations such those in construction, hotels and restaurants, cleaning services and care for children and the elderly. If these needs are filled by immigration, the educational credentials of new immigrants may not always keep pace with the average qualifications of new entrants to the labour force.

Source
• International Migration Statistics.

Further information
Analytical publications
• OECD (2002), International Mobility of the Highly Skilled, OECD, Paris.
• OECD (2006), Education at a Glance: OECD Indicators – 2006 Edition, OECD, Paris.
Methodological publications
• OECD (1999), Classifying Educational Programmes: Manual for ISCED-97 Implementation in OECD Countries – 1999 Edition, OECD, Paris.
• OECD (2005), "Counting immigrants and expatriates in OECD countries – a new perspective", Trends in International Migration: SOPEMI – 2004 Edition, OECD, Paris.

The educational attainment of the native- and foreign-born populations

As a percentage of the population aged 15 and above within each group, circa 2000

	Native-born				Foreign-born			
	Less than upper secondary	Upper secondary and post-secondary non-tertiary	Tertiary	All persons	Less than upper secondary	Upper secondary and post-secondary non-tertiary	Tertiary	All persons
Australia	46	16	39	100	38	19	43	100
Austria	33	56	11	100	49	39	11	100
Belgium	47	30	23	100	54	24	22	100
Canada	32	37	31	100	30	32	38	100
Czech Republic	23	67	10	100	38	49	13	100
Denmark	41	40	19	100	49	32	19	100
Finland	40	36	23	100	53	28	19	100
France	46	37	17	100	55	27	18	100
Germany	24	57	19	100	44	41	15	100
Greece	54	32	13	100	45	40	15	100
Hungary	45	44	11	100	41	39	20	100
Ireland	48	29	23	100	30	29	41	100
Italy	64	28	8	100	54	33	12	100
Japan	25	47	27	100	26	44	30	100
Korea	36	37	27	100	24	44	32	100
Luxembourg	29	59	13	100	37	42	22	100
Mexico	72	17	11	100	37	26	38	100
Netherlands	41	40	19	100	53	29	18	100
New Zealand	30	43	27	100	19	50	31	100
Norway	21	56	23	100	18	51	31	100
Poland	31	58	10	100	48	40	12	100
Portugal	80	12	8	100	55	26	19	100
Slovak Republic	28	62	10	100	29	56	15	100
Spain	64	17	19	100	55	23	22	100
Sweden	25	52	23	100	30	46	24	100
Switzerland	26	56	18	100	42	35	24	100
Turkey	79	15	5	100	49	34	17	100
United Kingdom	51	29	20	100	41	25	35	100
United States	22	51	27	100	40	34	26	100
OECD average	41	40	18	100	41	36	23	100

StatLink ＊＊＊ http://dx.doi.org/10.1787/767175437254

Tertiary attainment of the native- and foreign-born populations

As a percentage of the population aged 15 and above within each group, circa 2000

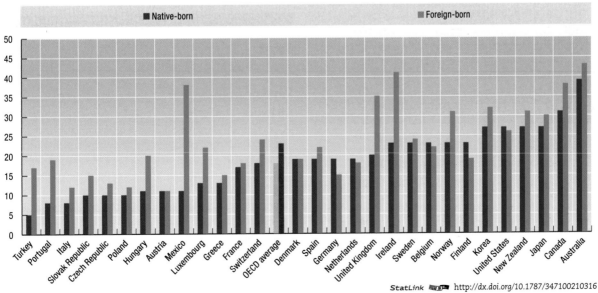

StatLink ＊＊＊ http://dx.doi.org/10.1787/347100210316

MIGRATION OF THE HIGHLY EDUCATED

Concern with brain drain is not limited to developing countries. It arose during the dot com period in a number of European countries in the late 1990s when it was feared that many high technology graduates were leaving their home countries for high-paying jobs elsewhere, especially in the United States. It arises periodically when statistics are published on international students abroad or on the emigration of highly educated persons. Rarely evoked are the gains from immigration of the highly educated.

Definition

The figures in the table show, as a percentage of the total number of residents with tertiary education, the number of foreign-born persons living in each country, and the number of persons with tertiary education born in the country but living in another OECD country.

Tertiary education programmes include those that terminate with standard university degrees but also cover shorter university programmes and high-level practical/technical/occupationally specific education programmes that are geared to direct entry into the labour market. Tertiary attainment means completion of a tertiary education programme with a recognised qualification; persons partially completing a level are classified in the previous level attained.

Comparability

The tertiary qualifications of the foreign-born referred to in the statistics presented here may not necessarily have been obtained abroad. They may include degrees obtained by persons who arrived in the host country quite young and who obtained some or all of their education there. They also cover the qualifications obtained by international students who thereafter emigrate to the country where they obtained their qualifications or elsewhere. Likewise, the qualifications of native-born persons may have been obtained in another country as a result of study abroad.

The data also do not include emigration to non-OECD countries, which would tend to result in smaller net "gains" for some countries and larger "losses" for others.

In addition, although all tertiary programmes are treated equivalently in the table and chart, there are significant differences among tertiary qualifications. Some programmes may be two-year vocational programmes, some 5-year first-degree programmes and others professional qualifications obtained after long years of tertiary study. The nature of the programmes and the distribution of the qualifications obtained can differ considerably across countries, as can the quality of the programmes themselves, which may come from institutions in countries at widely varying levels of development. Notwithstanding these data comparability problems, the picture of gains from international migration conveyed by the available statistics is more than likely a fairly accurate one.

The data shown here are from a special Census data collection described in "The immigrant population by region of origin and gender".

Overview

The issue of the extent of gains (or losses) from international migration is one that periodically comes to the forefront of policy agendas. Countries are afraid of losing their "best and brightest" to movements abroad, whether for study or for longer term expatriation, if not always permanent settlement. On the other hand, countries that recruit significant numbers of highly educated persons from developing countries are accused of contributing to brain drain from these countries and of hampering their economic development.

Until recently there was little information on the actual extent of movement and on the net balance between immigration and emigration of persons with university qualifications. The results show that only a few countries gain from intra-OECD migration of the highly educated. These are Australia, Canada Luxembourg, Norway, Spain, Sweden, Switzerland and the United States. If immigration of persons with university qualifications from outside the OECD is factored in, however, the balance becomes significantly positive for another set of countries, including Belgium, Germany, Greece and Portugal. For most other countries, the negative net balance is considerably reduced. In short, although many OECD countries lose from migration of the highly educated, immigration from developing countries tends to considerably offset the loss.

Source
• *International Migration Statistics.*

Further information
Analytical publications
• OECD (1999), *Classifying Educational Programmes: Manual for ISCED-97 Implemention in OECD Countries – 1999 Edition,* OECD, Paris.
• OECD (2002), *International Mobility of the Highly Skilled,* OECD, Paris.
• OECD (2006), *Education at a Glance: OECD Indicators – 2006 Edition,* OECD, Paris.
Methodological publications
• OECD (2005), "Counting immigrants and expatriates in OECD countries – a new perspective", *Trends in International Migration: SOPEMI – 2004 Edition,* OECD, Paris.

OECD FACTBOOK 2007 – ISBN 978-92-64-02946-0 – © OECD 2007

Foreign-born persons with tertiary attainment

As a percentage of all residents with tertiary attainment, circa 2000

	Immigrants from other OECD countries, (A)	Emigrants to other OECD countries (B)	Immigrants less emigrants within the OECD zone (A – B)	Immigrants from the rest of the world (C)	Total "net" foreign-born persons with tertiary attainment(A – B + C)
Australia	16.8	2.4	14.4	12.1	26.5
Austria	9.1	13.8	−4.7	5.2	0.5
Belgium	5.9	6.4	−0.5	4.2	3.7
Canada	10.3	5.4	4.9	15.5	20.4
Czech Republic	4.1	8.7	−4.5	2.2	−2.3
Denmark	4.4	7.3	−2.9	3.2	0.3
Finland	0.9	6.8	−5.9	1.3	−4.6
France	4.2	4.4	−0.2	8.2	8.0
Germany	2.8	7.3	−4.5	8.6	4.1
Greece	4.8	9.4	−4.6	7.3	2.7
Hungary	1.4	9.7	−8.3	4.5	−3.8
Ireland	14.0	26.1	−12.1	4.0	−8.1
Italy	2.8	7.3	−4.5	3.3	−1.2
Japan	0.2	1.1	−0.9	0.5	−0.4
Korea	0.2	1.4	−1.2	0.2	−1.0
Luxembourg	43.1	15.4	27.7	5.8	33.5
Mexico	0.8	6.9	−6.1	0.5	−5.6
Netherlands	3.3	8.9	−5.6	4.4	−1.2
New Zealand	14.6	24.4	−9.8	10.0	0.2
Norway	5.2	4.9	0.3	3.0	3.2
Poland	0.4	10.2	−9.8	2.3	−7.6
Portugal	4.1	11.2	−7.0	11.2	4.1
Slovak Republic	3.3	16.0	−12.8	0.9	−11.9
Spain	2.7	2.3	0.5	3.8	4.2
Sweden	6.9	5.4	1.5	7.3	8.8
Switzerland	20.0	10.8	9.1	7.3	16.4
Turkey	3.4	4.9	−1.5	2.7	1.2
United Kingdom	6.5	14.9	−8.4	9.4	1.0
United States	4.2	0.7	3.5	9.2	12.7
OECD average	6.9	8.8	−1.9	5.4	3.6

StatLink ⟪⟫ http://dx.doi.org/10.1787/536834682825

Foreign-born persons with tertiary attainment

As a percentage of all residents with tertiary attainment, circa 2000

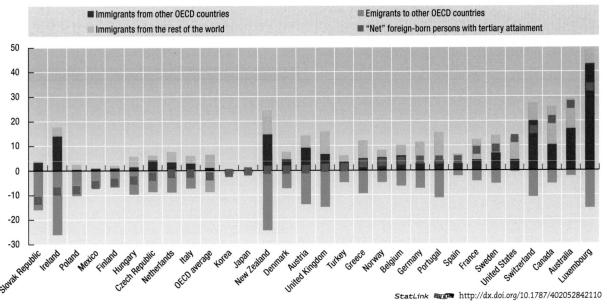

StatLink ⟪⟫ http://dx.doi.org/10.1787/402052842110

EMPLOYMENT RATES OF THE FOREIGN- AND THE NATIVE-BORN

Foreign-born workers account for a significant and growing share of the labour force in most OECD countries, a phenomenon that continued even in the face of the recent economic downswing. However the integration of immigrants into the labour market is not always a simple matter, particularly for women and young people.

Long-term trends

Notwithstanding a recent slowdown, the past decade has been notable for a relatively sharp increase in employment in several member countries. The employment of both immigrants and natives has increased in many OECD countries (especially in the United States, Spain, France, Italy, the United Kingdom, Australia and the Netherlands), with the exception of Austria and Sweden. In the United Kingdom, immigrants contributed to and benefited from over 30% of net job creation, while in Spain, the Netherlands, Portugal, Italy and Sweden, the percentage was equal to or in excess of 20%.

The overall picture regarding progress in immigrant access to employment is relatively positive. The employment rate of the foreign-born ranged from around 50% (Belgium, Denmark, Finland and Germany) to more than 70% (Portugal, Switzerland, Australia, Canada and the United States). With the exception of South Europe, Hungary and Luxembourg, the employment rate of the foreign-born was generally below the rate for the native-born.

In all countries under consideration, except in South Europe, Hungary and Luxembourg, foreign-born women have lower employment rates than their native-born counterparts. In 2004, less than 60% of immigrant women aged 15 to 64 had a job, except in Norway, Portugal and Switzerland. To a certain extent this indicator overestimates their participation to the labour market as they are more often in part-time employment. Immigrants from non-OECD member countries have proportionally even lower employment rates. In addition, the differences between native and immigrant women increase with the level of education.

Over the last decade, the employment rate of foreign-born women increased more rapidly than that of immigrant men in all countries under review. Spain, Italy, the Netherlands and Portugal have seen the largest increase in the employment rate of immigrant women since 1995.

Definition

The employment-to-population ratio is calculated as the share of the employed in the total population of working age. The denominator includes the labour force (employed and unemployed) and the inactive population. The working age population is generally defined as 15-64.

Comparability

All data for the European countries are from the European Union Labour Force Survey (second quarter). The national labour force survey, the Survey of Labour and Income Dynamics and the Current Population Survey (CPS, March supplement) are used respectively for Australia, Canada and the United States. A person is considered as being in employment if he or she did any work for pay or profit during the reference week. This includes all part-time and temporary work.

Source

- OECD (2006), *International Migration Outlook: SOPEMI – 2006 Edition*, OECD, Paris.

Further information

Analytical publications

- OECD (2004), *Migration for Employment: Bilateral Agreements at a Crossroads*, OECD, Paris.
- OECD (2006), *Local Economic and Employment Development (LEED) – From Immigration to Integration: Local Solutions to a Global Challenge* , OECD, Paris.

Online databases

- *International Migration Statistics.*

Employment rate of foreign- and native-born populations

As a percentage of the working age population

| | Men | | | | | | Women | | | | | |
| | Native | | | Foreign-born | | | Native | | | Foreign-born | | |
	1995	2000	2004	1995	2000	2004	1995	2000	2004	1995	2000	2004
Australia	78.2	78.7	80.6	71.6	72.7	76.2	69.8	71.4	65.9	61.8	63.5	57.6
Austria	77.5	76.2	73.4	78.5	76.1	70.2	59.4	59.9	61.4	57.5	58.3	53.7
Belgium	67.8	70.8	68.9	58.9	62.2	60.3	46.9	53.8	54.9	31.9	37.3	40.1
Canada	75.9	77.4	..	75.6	77.0	..	62.0	66.0	..	55.0	59.6	..
Czech Republic	..	..	72.3	..	..	64.5	..	..	56.2	..	..	49.9
Denmark	78.9	80.9	79.1	51.2	59.0	55.8	69.5	73.9	73.5	41.5	48.3	44.8
Finland	61.8	71.2	70.5	..	50.4	65.7	58.4	65.3	66.8	..	..	47.1
France	68.2	69.8	69.1	65.7	66.7	66.6	53.6	56.6	58.1	44.1	45.6	47.9
Germany	..	73.8	70.4	..	66.3	63.5	..	59.6	60.5	..	46.6	46.5
Greece	72.3	70.9	73.3	70.4	78.1	81.4	37.8	41.1	45.3	42.5	44.9	47.2
Hungary	..	62.6	62.9	..	69.4	74.6	..	49.4	50.4	..	49.8	50.8
Ireland	66.9	75.6	75.3	63.9	74.9	74.3	41.3	53.1	56.0	41.9	55.2	54.0
Italy	65.6	67.4	69.8	78.9	82.4	80.7	35.6	39.3	45.0	37.5	40.5	49.1
Luxembourg	70.7	73.2	68.8	81.3	78.1	77.6	38.8	46.5	47.6	48.8	55.3	54.8
Netherlands	77.0	84.0	81.9	56.2	69.9	68.4	54.9	65.6	68.1	38.4	48.8	50.1
Norway	..	82.3	78.6	..	74.6	70.6	..	74.6	73.4	..	63.5	62.2
Portugal	71.5	75.5	74.2	65.4	80.5	77.1	54.5	60.3	61.5	49.9	62.9	64.1
Slovak Republic	..	..	62.9	..	..	66.7	..	..	50.7	..	..	43.3
Spain	60.8	70.8	73.2	59.7	75.2	78.8	31.1	41.0	47.3	35.8	45.9	54.1
Sweden	76.2	75.9	75.7	55.1	61.3	63.6	74.2	73.4	72.9	52.2	56.6	59.1
Switzerland	..	..	85.6	..	..	81.2	..	..	72.7	..	..	63.8
United Kingdom	75.4	78.6	78.1	67.4	71.1	72.8	62.3	65.7	66.9	51.4	53.0	55.0
United States	76.5	77.2	73.0	77.2	82.0	80.2	65.8	68.4	65.4	53.6	57.7	56.2

StatLink http://dx.doi.org/10.1787/285670233063

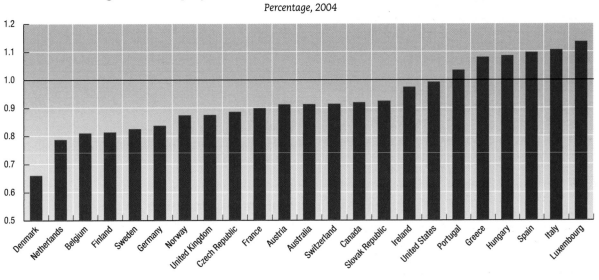

Foreign-born employment rate relative to native-born employment rate

Percentage, 2004

StatLink http://dx.doi.org/10.1787/086178132674

UNEMPLOYMENT RATES OF THE FOREIGN- AND THE NATIVE-BORN

Immigrant workers are more affected by unemployment in older European immigration countries while in North America, in Australia and to a lesser extent in Southern Europe, the unemployment rate tends to depend less on the place of birth. Some groups, such as young immigrants, women or older immigrants have particular difficulties finding jobs.

Long-term trends

In 2004, immigrants in the majority of European OECD countries were relatively harder hit by unemployment than was the native population. In the Slovak Republic, in Finland, Germany, France and Belgium, the unemployment rate of immigrants is higher than 15%. The rate is more than twice the level observed for the native-born in Finland and Belgium. This is also the case for Sweden, Denmark, Austria and the Netherlands. In Switzerland, the unemployment rate is below 9% but the difference between the foreign- and native-born rates is also significant. In other countries, however, especially the main settlement countries (Australia, Canada, the United States) and recent immigration countries (Italy, Spain, Greece), the unemployment rate does not vary much by birth status.

The period since 1995 has seen some sizable declines in the unemployment rates of the foreign-born, both men and women, in a number of countries, among them Australia, Denmark and Sweden, Greece (men only) Ireland, the Netherlands, Spain and the United Kingdom. At the same time, labour market conditions have stagnated in a number of other countries and have had adverse consequences for immigrants in Germany and Portugal.

More than 15% of the immigrant women in the labour force are seeking employment in Belgium, Germany, Finland, France, Greece, Spain, and the Slovak Republic. In relative terms, the unemployment rate of immigrant women is at least twice as high as that of natives in Austria, Denmark, Finland, Luxembourg, the Netherlands, Sweden and Switzerland. The difference in absolute values vis-à-vis the native-born is systematically positive, but does not generally increase with the level of qualifications.

Definition

The unemployment rate is calculated as the share of the unemployed to the total labour force (employed and unemployed persons). In accordance with the ILO standards, unemployed persons consist of those persons who report that they are without work during the reference week, that they are available for work and that they have taken active steps to find work during the four preceding weeks.

Comparability

All data for the European countries are issued from the European Union Labour Force Survey (second quarter). The national labour force survey, the Survey of Labour and Income Dynamics and the CPS, Current Population Survey (March supplement) are used respectively for Australia, Canada and the United States. Even if unemployment levels can at times be affected by changes in the survey design (this is the case for France since 2004) and by survey implementation problems (e.g. non-response), the unemployment rates are generally consistent over time.

Source

• OECD (2006), *International Migration Outlook: SOPEMI – 2006 Edition*, OECD, Paris.

Further information

Analytical publications

• OECD (2006), *Local Economic and Employment Development (LEED) – From Immigration to Integration: Local Solutions to a Global Challenge* , OECD, Paris.

Online databases

• *International Migration Statistics*.

OECD FACTBOOK 2007 – ISBN 978-92-64-02946-0 – © OECD 2007

Unemployment rates of foreign- and native-born populations

As a percentage of total labour force

	Men						Women					
	Native			Foreign-born			Native			Foreign-born		
	1995	2000	2004	1995	2000	2004	1995	2000	2004	1995	2000	2004
Australia	8.4	6.6	5.6	10.6	6.5	5.5	7.7	5.8	5.7	9.6	7.0	5.6
Austria	3.6	4.3	4.3	6.6	8.7	11.2	4.6	4.2	4.3	7.3	7.2	10.7
Belgium	6.3	4.2	5.6	16.9	14.7	14.9	11.2	7.4	7.5	23.8	17.5	15.0
Canada	8.6	5.7	..	10.4	6.1	..	9.8	6.2	..	13.3	8.7	..
Czech Republic	..	..	7.0	..	..	12.4	..	..	9.6	..	..	13.5
Denmark	6.4	3.4	4.6	20.5	9.5	11.8	8.4	4.3	5.2	20.7	9.6	12.7
Finland	17.7	10.3	9.9	..	..	21.3	16.1	12.0	10.2	..	..	25.3
France	9.1	7.7	8.0	16.6	14.5	13.8	13.6	11.3	9.9	19.0	19.7	17.4
Germany	..	6.9	10.3	..	12.9	18.3	..	8.0	9.6	..	12.1	15.2
Greece	6.1	7.4	6.5	14.0	9.5	6.5	13.7	16.6	15.7	20.8	21.1	19.1
Hungary	..	7.3	5.9	..	..	2.0	..	5.8	5.9	..	..	6.4
Ireland	12.0	4.4	4.9	16.8	..	6.7	11.9	4.2	3.7	15.4	..	5.3
Italy	9.3	8.4	6.4	..	6.5	6.2	16.3	14.9	10.1	23.5	21.2	13.2
Luxembourg	..	..	2.4	..	..	4.4	..	..	4.5	..	..	9.6
Netherlands	4.9	1.8	3.6	19.5	5.4	10.3	7.7	3.0	4.3	19.8	7.6	10.6
Norway	..	3.4	4.3	..	6.8	8.9	..	3.2	3.7	..	..	7.3
Portugal	6.6	3.1	5.7	..	3.9	9.8	7.8	4.9	7.4	..	5.4	9.6
Slovak Republic	..	..	17.8	..	..	17.9	..	..	19.5	..	..	30.5
Spain	18.0	9.5	7.8	24.4	12.4	11.4	30.5	20.5	15.1	30.5	20.7	17.1
Sweden	7.9	5.1	6.2	24.8	12.3	14.2	6.6	4.2	5.2	18.5	10.8	12.6
Switzerland	..	..	2.9	..	..	7.5	..	..	3.4	..	..	9.2
United Kingdom	9.9	5.9	4.7	14.2	9.6	7.3	6.7	4.6	3.9	10.9	7.8	7.3
United States	6.2	4.5	6.9	7.9	4.5	5.8	5.3	4.2	5.5	8.2	5.5	6.8

StatLink http://dx.doi.org/10.1787/054448388734

Foreign- and native-born unemployment rates

As a percentage of total labour force, 2004

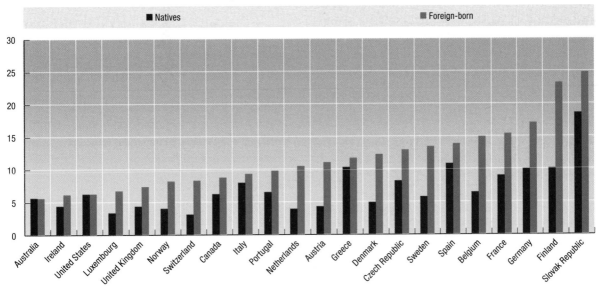

StatLink http://dx.doi.org/10.1787/250863576180

REMITTANCES

Remittances in recent years have exceeded official development aid by factor of more than two to one. This has brought to the fore the importance of transfers by immigrants to their families in origin countries for improving their welfare and living conditions. As a consequence, more and more attention is being paid to remittances as a possible boost to development in origin countries.

Definition

The data presented use a broad definition of remittances that is believed to better capture the extent of remittances than what appears under the heading of workers' remittances. They include i) workers' remittances recorded under the heading "current transfers" in the current account of the balance of payments; ii) compensation of employees, which includes wages, salaries and other benefits of non-resident workers, such as border or seasonal workers; iii) migrants' transfers, which are recorded under capital transfers in the capital account and can include, for example, assets brought back to the country of origin.

The figures for remittances comprise transfers of money not only from immigrants in OECD countries, but from all foreign countries.

Comparability

The data shown here are compiled from receiving countries and generally only include officially recorded remittances. These may exclude amounts transferred that are less than a particular threshold value. Remittances transferred by informal methods or brought back by migrants in their pockets and not reported are not counted, nor are in-kind transfers of jewelry, consumer goods, etc. Informal transfers are believed to be significant and can amount to as much as fifty percent of total remittances in some countries. The differences between countries in the coverage of incoming remittances are unknown.

The table covers the top 30 countries of origin based on remittances-as-a-percentage-of-GDP, among those with over 250 000 immigrants residing in OECD countries.

Overview

The issue of immigrant remittances is not a new one but it has acquired a certain prominence in recent years, because of the realisation that immigrants are transferring to their home countries amounts that significantly exceed the development aid given to the same countries by host-country governments of the countries where they are working. In certain countries, in particular Honduras, Lebanon, Bosnia-Herzegovina and Haiti, the amounts transferred are equivalent to close to twenty percent of the national gross domestic product.

As migration continues to increase (by over 3 million persons per year among long-term migrants as well as significantly many short-term migrants), the amounts transferred will continue to increase. Immigrants tend to transfer more in the early years after arrival but less as time goes on and the settlement decision becomes more definitive.

The presence of many Caribbean and Latin American countries in the table reflects the importance of the United States as a major destination country for persons from these countries.

A certain number of OECD countries appear towards the bottom of the table, not all of them for migration-related reasons, however. The remittances for Belgium in particular reflect essentially the large number of residents of that country working cross-border in the Netherlands and especially Luxembourg.

Sources
- United Nations Statistics Division (Population).
- World Development Indicators, World Bank (GDP).
- International Monetary Fund (Remittances).
- *International Migration Statistics*.

Further information
Analytical publications
- OECD (2005), *The Development Dimension – Migration, Remittances and Development*, OECD, Paris.
Methodological publications
- OECD (2005), "Counting immigrants and expatriates in OECD countries – a new perspective", *Trends in International Migration: SOPEMI – 2004 Edition*, OECD, Paris.

Remittances to major remittance receiving countries
Year 2005

Remittances				Immigrant population in OECD countries
	Million US dollars	As a percentage of GDP	Amount per person in the population, US$	Thousands of persons
Honduras	1 796	22.5	249	304
Lebanon	4 924	22.2	1 377	354
Bosnia and Herzegovina	1 843	19.7	472	614
Haiti	811	19.1	95	506
Jamaica	1 623	16.7	612	841
Albania	1 290	15.4	412	626
El Salvador	2 564	15.1	373	892
Philippines	13 566	13.8	163	2 084
Guyana	100	12.8	133	323
Dominican Republic	2 700	9.5	304	781
Guatemala	2 591	8.2	206	536
Morocco	4 221	8.2	134	1 613
Bangladesh	4 252	7.1	30	325
Sri Lanka	1 590	6.8	77	353
Tunisia	1 432	5.0	142	444
Romania	4 467	4.5	206	1 226
Ecuador	1 610	4.4	122	563
Bulgaria	1 121	4.2	145	648
Pakistan	4 280	3.9	27	755
Egypt	3 341	3.7	45	337
Croatia	1 222	3.3	269	524
Mexico	21 772	2.8	203	9 430
India	21 727	2.8	20	2 095
Colombia	3 345	2.7	73	802
Nigeria	2 273	2.3	17	294
Belgium	7 158	2.0	687	408
Peru	1 440	1.8	51	462
Portugal	3 017	1.7	287	1 336
Poland	3 547	1.2	92	2 313
New Zealand	1 281	1.2	318	465

StatLink http://dx.doi.org/10.1787/715625278530

Remittances to major remittance receiving countries
As a percentage of GDP, 2005

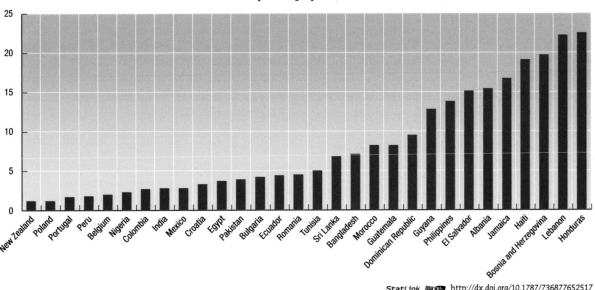

StatLink http://dx.doi.org/10.1787/736877652517

Analytical index

OECD FACTBOOK 2007 – ISBN 978-92-64-02946-0 – © OECD 2007

OECD FACTBOOK 2007 – ISBN 978-92-64-02946-0 – © OECD 2007

M

Machinery investment, *see*: Investment rates 36

Major ODA recipients by region 202

Major recipients by region of total bilateral gross ODA from DAC countries 202

Manufacturing, *see*: Employment and number of enterprises in manufacturing 57

Manufacturing, *see*: Relative unit labour costs in manufacturing 99

Marine capture and aquaculture production 167

Mean scores on the reading and science scales in PISA 175

Migration, *see*: Trends in migration 250

Migration of the highly educated 260

Mobile cellular subscribers 160

Mortality, *see*: Infant mortality 216

Multi-factor productivity 46

Multinationals, *see*: Activities of multinationals 80

Municipal waste 170

Municipal waste generation 171

N

National GDP per capita 31

National income per capita 28

Net migration rate 251

Net official development assistance 201

NNI, *see*: Gross and net national income per capita 29

NNI, *see*: National income per capita 28

Nominal effective exchange rates 97

Number of triadic patent families 151

O

Obesity 218

Official development assistance 200

Oil, *see*: Production of crude oil by region 115

Oil prices 116

Oil production 114

Outflows of foreign direct investment 79

Outward and inward FDI stocks 77

Overweight, *see*: Overweight and obese population aged 15 or more by gender 219

Overweight and obese population aged 15 or more by gender 219

P

Partner countries and regions of OECD merchandise exports 73

Partner countries and regions of OECD merchandise imports 72

Partner countries and regions of OECD merchandise trade 71

Part-time employment 128

Patents 150

Percentage of 15-year-old students using computers 177

Percentage of elderly population by country 21

Percentage of the total labour force living in regions with an unemployment rate above the national average 143

Percentage of youths aged between 15 and 19 who are not in education nor in employment 229

Performance on the mahematics scale in PISA 179

PISA, *see*: International student assessment 174

PISA, *see*: Performance on the mahematics scale in PISA 175

PISA, *see*: PISA results for children of immigrants 257

PISA, *see*: Reading performance of the second generation 257

PISA results for children of immigrants 257

Population, *see*: Index of geographic concentration of elderly population 17

Population aged 65 and over 19

Population density, *see*: Range of variation in regional population density 17

Population growth rates 14

PPI, *see*: Producer Price Indices (PPI) 88

PPI: manufacturing 89

PPP, *see*: Rates of conversion 92

Price indices, *see*: Producer Price Indices (PPI) 88

OECD FACTBOOK 2007 – ISBN 978-92-64-02946-0 – © OECD 2007

R

S

OECD FACTBOOK 2007 – ISBN 978-92-64-02946-0 – © OECD 2007

W

Y

This book has...

StatLinks

A service that delivers Excel® files from the printed page!

Look for the *StatLinks* at the bottom right-hand corner of the tables or graphs in this book. To download the matching Excel® spreadsheet, just type the link into your Internet browser, starting with the *http://dx.doi.org* prefix.
If you're reading the PDF e-book edition, and your PC is connected to the Internet, simply click on the link.
You'll find *StatLinks* appearing in more OECD books.

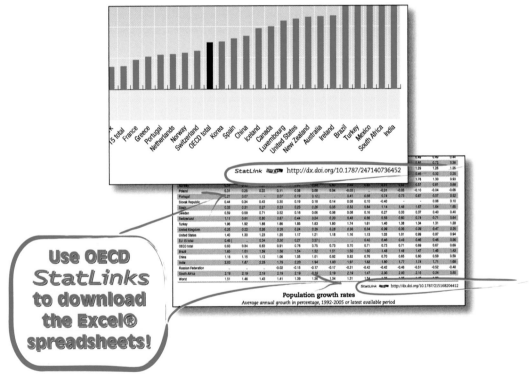

StatLink : another innovation from OECD Publishing.

Learn more at *www.oecd.org/statistics/statlink*

We'd like to hear what you think about our publications and
services like *StatLinks*: e-mail us at oecdpublishing@oecd.org